# TRADE COOPER

## The Purpose, Design an(
## Preferential Trade Agr

Preferential trade agreements (PTAs) have been proliferating for more than two decades, with the negotiations for a Transatlantic Trade and Investment Partnership and a Trans-Pacific Partnership being just the tip of the iceberg. This volume addresses some of the most pressing issues related to the surge in these agreements. It includes chapters written by leading political scientists, economists and lawyers who theoretically and empirically advance our understanding of trade agreements. The key theme is that PTAs vary widely in terms of design. The authors provide explanations of why we see these differences in design and whether and how these differences matter in practice. The tools for understanding the purposes and effects of PTAs that are offered will guide future research and inform practitioners and trade policy experts about progress in the scientific inquiry into PTAs.

ANDREAS DÜR is professor of international politics at the University of Salzburg, Austria. His research interests include trade policy, international institutions and interest group politics.

MANFRED ELSIG is associate professor of international relations and deputy managing director of the World Trade Institute, University of Bern, Switzerland. He is also the director of the National Centre of Competence in Research (NCCR) on Trade Regulation.

# TRADE COOPERATION

The Purpose, Design and Effects of
Preferential Trade Agreements
World Trade Forum

Edited by
ANDREAS DÜR
MANFRED ELSIG

CAMBRIDGE
UNIVERSITY PRESS

# CAMBRIDGE
## UNIVERSITY PRESS

University Printing House, Cambridge CB2 8BS, United Kingdom

One Liberty Plaza, 20th Floor, New York, NY 10006, USA

477 Williamstown Road, Port Melbourne, VIC 3207, Australia

314-321, 3rd Floor, Plot 3, Splendor Forum, Jasola District Centre, New Delhi - 110025, India

79 Anson Road, #06-04/06, Singapore 079906

Cambridge University Press is part of the University of Cambridge.

It furthers the University's mission by disseminating knowledge in the pursuit of education, learning and research at the highest international levels of excellence.

www.cambridge.org
Information on this title: www.cambridge.org/9781107444676

© Cambridge University Press 2015

First published 2015
First paperback edition 2018

*A catalogue record for this publication is available from the British Library*

ISBN 978-1-107-08387-5 Hardback
ISBN 978-1-107-44467-6 Paperback

# CONTENTS

*List of figures*     *page* viii
*List of tables*     x
*List of contributors*     xii
*Preface*     xxii
*List of abbreviations*     xxiv

1   Introduction: the purpose, design and effects of preferential trade agreements     1
ANDREAS DÜR AND MANFRED ELSIG

PART I   Why do countries sign PTAs?

2   Technology, politics and economic exchanges: historical patterns in international economic agreements     25
MOONHAWK KIM

3   The political economy of preferential trade agreements     56
EDWARD D. MANSFIELD AND HELEN V. MILNER

4   Weak governments and preferential trade agreements     82
JEAN-LOUIS ARCAND, MARCELO OLARREAGA AND LAURA ZORATTO

5   Natural trading partners? A public opinion perspective on preferential trade agreements     113
VÍCTOR UMAÑA, THOMAS BERNAUER AND GABRIELE SPILKER

6   Regionalisation in search of regionalism: production networks and deep integration commitments in Asia's PTAs     134
SOO YEON KIM

PART II   The design of PTAs

7   Imitation and innovation in international governance: the diffusion of trade agreement design     167
LEONARDO BACCINI, ANDREAS DÜR AND YORAM Z. HAFTEL

8 PTA design, tariffs and intra-industry trade 195
MARK MANGER

9 Audiovisual goods and services in preferential trade agreements 218
KERRY A. CHASE

10 Competition policy and free trade: antitrust provisions in PTAs 246
ANU BRADFORD AND TIM BÜTHE

11 PTAs and public procurement 275
STEPHANIE J. RICKARD

12 Trade agreements, violent conflict and security 295
YORAM Z. HAFTEL

13 Dispute settlement provisions in PTAs: new data and new concepts 319
TODD ALLEE AND MANFRED ELSIG

PART III The effects of PTAs

14 Preliminary examination of heterogeneous effects on international trade of economic integration agreements 355
SCOTT L. BAIER, JEFFREY H. BERGSTRAND AND MATTHEW W. CLANCE

15 Effects of deep versus shallow trade agreements in general equilibrium 374
PETER EGGER AND SERGEY NIGAI

16 Revisiting the trade effects of services agreements 392
ANIRUDH SHINGAL

17 Trade agreements as protection from risk 408
JEFFREY KUCIK

18 What do we know about preferential trade agreements and temporary trade barriers? 433
CHAD P. BOWN, BAYBARS KARACAOVALI AND PATRICIA TOVAR

PART IV   PTAs and the multilateral trading system

19   The dialectical relationship of preferential and multilateral trade
     agreements    465
     THOMAS COTTIER, CHARLOTTE SIEBER-GASSER AND
     GABRIELA WERMELINGER

20   Forget about the WTO: the network of relations between PTAs
     and double PTAs      497
     JOOST PAUWELYN AND WOLFGANG ALSCHNER

21   Plurilateral agreements, variable geometry and the
     WTO       533
     BERNARD HOEKMAN

22   Referring PTA disputes to the WTO dispute settlement
     system      555
     JAMES FLETT

     Index      580

# FIGURES

1.1 Number of PTAs over time, 1945–2013        *page* 5
1.2 PTAs 1992 and 2013        6
1.3 Change in type and membership over time        7
1.4 Change in the contents of PTAs        8
3.1 Relative risks of ratifying a PTA, derived from the base model in
      Table 3.1        73
4.1 The need for credibility-driven trade agreements        87
4.2 Which governments sign credibility-driven PTAs?        89
5.1 Example of a choice task        125
5.2 Marginal effects        126
6.1 Regional trade agreements in Asia, 1975–2013        135
6.2 Depth of integration scores by country        141
6.3 Depth of integration in PTAs over time, 1971–2013        143
7.1 The data on the PTA design        173
7.2 EU model (subset of agreements)        174
7.3 US model        175
8.1 Adjustment and product differentiation        202
8.2 Vertical intra-industry trade, 1998–2006        205
8.3 Contribution to relative risk of exclusion (model 2)        213
10.1 How competition policy is addressed        254
10.2 Percentage of PTAs with a competition article or chapter, five-year
       moving average        257
10.3 PTA-established working groups for the discussion of competition
       policy        265
10.4 Provisions indicating concerns about selective enforcement        266
10.5 Provisions indicating desire to enhance enforcement        268
11.1 Depth of PTAs        281
12.1 A two-way graph of conflict and security        310
12.2 A two-way graph of hegemony and security        311
12.3 A two-way graph of nonrivalry and security        311
14.1 Treatment effect for all agreements        363
14.2 Treatment effect for all free trade agreements        364

14.3 Treatment effect for all customs union agreements 365
14.4 Treatment effect for all common market agreements 365
14.5 Treatment effect for all economic union agreements 366
15.1 Correlation between average exports and the number of provisions
     adopted 381
15.2 Counterfactual experiments 389
16.1 Top services export flows (US$ billion, average 1999–2010) 396
17.1 Distribution of design scores 421
17.2 Substantive effects for model 5 425
18.1 Turkey's imports subject to imposed temporary trade barriers by PTA
     partner status 444
18.2 Argentina's average tariffs on imports of footwear in categories subject
     to the 1997 safeguard 449
18.3 Argentina's imports of footwear in categories subject to the
     1997 safeguard 450
18.4 Turkey's imports of footwear from selected source countries 454
18.5 Turkey's imports of footwear from selected EU source countries 454
18.6 Turkey's import prices of footwear from selected source countries 455
18.7 Dominican Republic's imports of polypropylene bags and tubular
     fabrics 457
18.8 Dominican Republic's imports of polypropylene bags and tubular
     fabrics from selected CAFTA source countries 458
19.1 Bilateral conventions in force in 1886 470
19.2 PTAs with commitments to liberalise, or an intention to liberalise, trade
     in services (1956–2010) 478
20.1 Few countries have many PTAs, many countries have few PTAs 505
20.2 The global PTA network 507
20.3 Who signs the deepest agreements on average? 509
20.4 The depth of PTAs 511
20.5 The network of deep PTAs 512
20.6 An Asia–America cluster emerges through mega-regionals 513
20.7 Mega-regionals are likely to transform the PTA network to resemble the
     appearance of the bilateral investment treaty (BIT) network 514
20.8 Double PTAs in the PTA network 515
20.9 The double PTA network 516
20.10 The double PTA network after the conclusion of mega-regionals
     (extract) 517

# TABLES

3.1 The political and economic influences on PTA ratification,
1952–2011 *page* 70

4.1 Government's welfare mindedness $a_{it}$ 95

4.2 Government's bargaining weight $\sigma$ 97

4.3 Summary statistics of $P^c$ by type of agreement 98

4.4 The effect of credibility on PTA formation, 1988–2000 100

4.5 The effect of credibility on PTA formation, 1988–2000 (OLS estimates) 102

4.6 The impact of credibility-driven PTAs on imports 103

5.1 Attributes and their values 124

5.2 Description of the attributes 125

6.1 Production network trade and investment commitments in PTAs 147

7.1 Explaining similarity to the EU 184

7.2 Explaining similarity to NAFTA 186

7.3 Substantive effects 187

8.1 Regression results 212

8.2 Conditional marginal effects (Tobit model) 212

9.1 Partial commitments for audiovisual services in PTAs 229

9.2 Improvements over GATS for audiovisual services in PTAs 232

9.3 Correlates of audiovisual services commitments in PTAs 233

9.4 Trade flows and leverage in audiovisual services commitments 237

9.5 Cultural distance and audiovisual services commitments 241

10.1 All good things go together? Format of competition provisions as a
function of PTA depth 258

11.1 PTAs with procurement rules 278

11.2 Tender criteria 284

12.1 Fuzzy-set membership scores on four variables 304

12.2 Main instruments and activities of REOs with a high level of security
cooperation 306

12.3 Levels of consistency and coverage for conflict, hegemony and
nonrivalry 310

13.1 PTAs with a dispute settlement provision 324

13.2 PTAs with a consultation provision 325

13.3 PTAs with various types of dispute settlement 326
13.4 Overlap between types of dispute settlement 329
13.5 Forum choice in PTA dispute settlement 331
13.6 Features of dispute settlement proceedings 332
13.7 Number of references to mutually agreeable solutions (MAS)
(by number of agreements) 335
13.8 Sanctions in PTA dispute settlement 337
13.9 Exceptions in PTA dispute settlement 340
13.10 Conceptualising degree of *delegation* in PTA dispute settlement
provisions 342
13.11 Conceptualising amount of *information provision* in PTA dispute
settlement provisions 343
13.12 Conceptualising level of *enforcement* in PTA dispute settlement
provisions 345
13.13 Conceptualising *settlement promotion* in PTA dispute settlement
provisions 346
13.14 Conceptualising *flexibility* in PTA dispute settlement provisions 348
14.1 Determinants of EIA partial effects 369
15.1 Average exports and the average number of adopted provisions in trade
agreements 380
15.2 Types of trade agreements 382
15.3 Trade cost variables 384
15.4 Estimation results 385
15.5 Results of the counterfactual experiment 387
16.1 Decile distribution of bilateral services exports (avg. 1999–2010) 397
16.2 Results (2WFE) from estimating Eq. (16.1) on positive exports 399
16.3 Results (2WFE) from estimating Eq. (16.1) on all exports 400
16.4 Lagged effects of STAs for positive exports 401
17.1 Components of design measures 420
17.2 Baseline results 424
17.3 Heckman selection estimation 428
18.1 TTB policy-imposing economies and affected imports in 2011 442
18.2 The discriminatory nature of safeguards in the four case studies 448
20.1 Centrality of countries in the PTA network 508

# CONTRIBUTORS

TODD ALLEE is assistant professor of government and politics at the University of Maryland. He holds a PhD in political science from the University of Michigan and previously served on the faculty at the University of Illinois. His research focuses on international organisations, international trade, the World Trade Organization, foreign direct investment, dispute settlement and territorial conflict resolution. His work has been published in journals such as *American Political Science Review, International Organization, World Politics, International Studies Quarterly* and *Journal of Conflict Resolution.*

WOLFGANG ALSCHNER is a PhD candidate in international law and a teaching assistant at the Graduate Institute of International and Development Studies in Geneva, Switzerland. Prior to taking up his studies, he worked for several years as a consultant in the International Investment Agreements Section of the United Nations Conference on Trade and Development. In his PhD thesis, he explores the design and evolution of international investment agreements from an interdisciplinary angle. Other research interests include World Trade Organization law, law and economics and the empirical analysis of law.

JEAN-LOUIS ARCAND is director of the Centre for Finance and Development and professor of international economics at the Graduate Institute of International and Development Studies in Geneva. He is a founding fellow of the European Union Development Network and senior fellow at the Fondation pour les études et recherches sur le développement international. He was assistant and then associate professor at the University of Montréal, and professor at the Centre d'études et de recherches en développement international. He holds a PhD in economics from Massachusetts Institute of Technology. His research focuses on the microeconomics of development.

LEONARDO BACCINI is assistant professor of international political economy at the London School of Economics and Political Science. His research interests are in the area of international political economy and comparative political economy. He is the author of *Cutting the Gordian Knot of Economic Reform: How International Institutions Promote Liberalization* and of several articles published or forthcoming in leading journals. Information on his publications and working papers can be found at https://sites.google.com/site/leonardobaccini/.

SCOTT L. BAIER is associate professor in the John E. Walker Department of Economics at Clemson University, South Carolina. He is also a BB&T scholar and director of the BB&T Center for Education and Economic Policy Studies. His main areas of research are in international trade and economic growth.

JEFFREY H. BERGSTRAND is associate dean for graduate programs and professor of finance in the Mendoza College of Business, concurrent professor of economics in the College of Arts and Letters and faculty fellow in the Helen Kellogg Institute for International Studies at the University of Notre Dame in Notre Dame, Indiana. He is also a research network fellow of CESifo in Munich, Germany. His current research focuses on determinants of bilateral trade flows, of bilateral foreign direct investment flows and of international economic trade and foreign direct investment agreements.

THOMAS BERNAUER is a professor of political science at ETH Zurich. He and his research group are based at the Center for Comparative and International Studies, a joint institution of ETH Zurich and the University of Zurich, and at ETH Zurich's Institute for Environmental Decisions. In his research and teaching, he focuses on international environmental and economic issues. He is the author or coauthor of 10 books, more than 80 journal articles and book chapters and many other types of publication. His publications have appeared in political science, economics and natural sciences journals.

CHAD P. BOWN is a lead economist at the World Bank and a research fellow at the Centre for Economic Policy Research. He is a member of the Council on Foreign Relations, and he serves on the editorial boards of a number of journals that cover the law, politics and economics of international trade policy. He was formerly a tenured professor of economics at Brandeis

University, and his government service included time as senior economist in the White House on the President's Council of Economic Advisers. Bown has also been a fellow at the Brookings Institution and the visiting scholar at the World Trade Organization Secretariat in Geneva.

ANU BRADFORD is professor of law at Columbia Law School. Before joining Columbia Law School in 2012, she was an assistant professor at the University of Chicago Law School. Her research focuses on international economic law, especially international trade law, and European Union law. A prominent contributor to legal and policy debates over the need for, and limits of, an antitrust regime in the World Trade Organization, she also practised antitrust law at Clearly Gottlieb Steen & Hamilton in Brussels for two years. Her work has been published in *University of Chicago Law Review, Harvard International Law Journal, Virginia Journal of International Law* and other law reviews and journals.

TIM BÜTHE is an associate professor of political science and public policy at Duke University, North Carolina, and a senior fellow for the Rethinking Regulation project at the Kenan Institute for Ethics. His research focuses on the politics of international economic relations and how institutions empower and constrain political actors, especially in antitrust/competition policy, foreign aid, foreign direct investment and the transnational regulation of product and financial markets. His publications include *The New Global Rulers: The Privatization of Regulation in the World Economy* (2011) as well as articles in *American Political Science Review, American Journal of Political Science, International Organization, World Politics* and other journals and edited volumes.

KERRY A. CHASE is an associate professor in the Department of Politics at Brandeis University in Waltham, Massachusetts. He is the author of *Trading Blocs: States, Firms, and Regions in the World Economy* (2005) and articles in *International Organization, World Trade Review* and other journals. His recent research investigates the political economy of trade in audiovisual material, and he has completed a book manuscript on this subject titled *Trading Cultural Goods: The Contentious Politics of Filmed Entertainment.*

MATTHEW W. CLANCE is currently a senior lecturer at the University of Pretoria in South Africa. He received his PhD from the John E. Walker Department of Economics at Clemson University, South Carolina, in

2012. His current research focus is international trade and applied econometrics. In 2011, he worked for the Federal Reserve Bank of Atlanta as a research associate on projects related to macroeconomic variables, financial crises and economic freedom.

THOMAS COTTIER was educated at the University of Bern and the University of Michigan Law School. He was a visiting fellow at Cambridge University, United Kingdom. Since 1992, he has been a full professor of European and international economic law and the managing director of the World Trade Institute of the University of Bern. He directed the National Centre of Competence in Research Trade Regulation from 2005 to 2013. Formerly, he was the deputy-director general of the Swiss Intellectual Property Office. He served on the Swiss negotiating team of the Uruguay Round from 1986 to 1993 and as a member or chair of several General Agreement on Tariffs and Trade and World Trade Organization dispute settlement panels.

ANDREAS DÜR is professor of international politics at the University of Salzburg. His research interests are trade policy, international institutions and interest group politics. He is the author of a large number of publications in journals such as *British Journal of Political Science, European Journal of Political Research, International Studies Quarterly* and *Journal of Conflict Resolution.* Among his publications is also *Protection for Exporters: Discrimination and Power in Transatlantic Trade Relations, 1930–2010* (2010).

PETER EGGER is professor of economics at ETH Zurich and head of a department at the KOF Swiss Economic Institute, also at ETH Zurich. He held positions as associate professor of economics at the University of Innsbruck and as full professor of economics at the University of Munich prior to his appointment at ETH. He is also a research fellow of the Centre for Economic and Policy Research based in London and a research director of the Global Economy Area of the CESifo research network based in Munich. In addition, he is a research affiliate at the Centre of Business Taxation at Oxford University, the Norwegian Centre for Taxation and the Federal Reserve Bank of Dallas. He is editor-in-chief of the *Review of International Economics.* His research agenda covers topics in international economics, public economics and econometrics. He has published more than 100 articles in peer-reviewed international journals in economics.

MANFRED ELSIG is associate professor of international relations and deputy managing director of the World Trade Institute, University of Bern. He is the director of the National Centre of Competence in Research Trade Regulation (http://www.nccr-trade.org). He holds a PhD from the University of Zurich in political science (2002). His research focuses on international political economy, international organisations, international courts, preferential trade agreements and European trade policy. His work has been published in journals such as *European Union Politics*, *European Journal of International Relations*, *International Studies Quarterly*, *Review of International Organizations*, *Review of International Political Economy* and *World Trade Review*. He is the co-editor of *Governing the WTO: Past, Present and Beyond Doha* (Cambridge University Press, 2011).

JAMES FLETT works in the World Trade Organization (WTO) Team of the European Commission Legal Service. He has 25 years of experience in the field of international trade law. He frequently represents the European Commission before the Court of Justice of the European Union and the European Union in proceedings before the WTO. He regularly advises the Commission on WTO law. He graduated from the London School of Economics and Political Science and has a master's degree in European law from the College of Europe, Bruges. He is a qualified solicitor. Before joining the Commission Legal Service, he spent several years working for international law firms in London and Brussels, with a particular emphasis on international trade law. He speaks frequently at conferences and universities and has published widely on WTO law.

YORAM Z. HAFTEL is an associate professor in the Department of International Relations at the Hebrew University of Jerusalem. His research agenda touches on the sources, design and effects of international organisations and agreements. His book, *Regional Economic Institutions and Conflict Mitigation: Design, Implementation, and the Promise of Peace* (2012), explores the relationships between variation in regional economic organisations and regional security. In other projects he explores the politics of investment treaty ratification and renegotiation. He has published peer-reviewed articles on these and other topics in such journals as *International Organization*, *International Studies Quarterly* and *Review of International Organizations*.

BERNARD HOEKMAN is a professor and director of global economics at the Robert Schuman Centre for Advanced Studies, European University Institute in Florence, Italy. His previous positions include director of the International Trade Department and research manager in the Development Research Group of the World Bank, and economist in the General Agreement on Tariffs and Trade Secretariat. He is a graduate of Erasmus University Rotterdam and holds a PhD in economics from the University of Michigan. He is a Centre for Economic and Policy Research research fellow and a senior associate of the Economic Research Forum for the Arab countries Turkey and Iran.

BAYBARS KARACAOVALI is an assistant professor of economics at the University of Hawaii at Manoa. He was an assistant professor of economics at Fordham University, New York, and a consultant in the Development Economics Research Group of the World Bank prior to joining the University of Hawaii. He received his PhD in economics from the University of Maryland at College Park, and BA and MA degrees from Bogazici University in Istanbul, Turkey. His main research interests are in international trade, political economy of trade policy and development economics. His publications include articles in *International Economic Review* and *Journal of International Economics.*

MOONHAWK KIM is an assistant professor in the Department of Political Science at the University of Colorado, Boulder. His research addresses the causes and consequences of evolution in international governance of trade. He focuses on the evolution of dispute settlement procedures and the increasing linkages to nontrade issues in both the multilateral and preferential trade institutions. In his current project, he examines the causes and consequences of changes over time in the membership scope and the design features of preferential trade agreements. His work on these and other topics appears in *World Politics, International Studies Quarterly* and *International Theory.*

SOO YEON KIM is associate professor of political science at the National University of Singapore. She holds a PhD in political science from Yale University and a BA in political science and international studies from Yonsei University. She is the author of *Power and the Governance of Global Trade: From the GATT to the WTO* (2010). Her main research areas are free trade agreements (FTAs), World Trade Organization disputes and emerging markets. Her current project focuses on FTAs in Asia, in particular, the effect of multinational firms and production networks on states' commitments in behind-the-border trade rules.

JEFFREY KUCIK is an assistant professor of political science and director of the MA in International Relations program at City College of New York. He was previously a research scholar at the Niehaus Center for Globalization and Governance at Princeton University. Prior to that, he spent three years at University College London as director of the MSc in International Public Policy. He holds a PhD in political science from Emory University. His work focuses on trade and international economic cooperation. He has a particular interest in trade institutions and politics of market risk.

MARK MANGER is associate professor at the Munk School of Global Affairs, University of Toronto, specialising in political economy, following appointments at McGill University and the London School of Economics. He is the author of *Investing in Protection: The Politics of Preferential Trade Agreements between North and South* (Cambridge University Press, 2009) and articles published in *International Studies Quarterly, Journal of Conflict Resolution, Review of International Political Economy, World Development* and *World Politics*. His research focuses on the comparative and international political economy of Japan and the Asia-Pacific region.

EDWARD D. MANSFIELD is the Hum Rosen Professor of Political Science, chair of the Political Science Department and director of the Christopher H. Browne Center for International Politics at the University of Pennsylvania, Philadelphia. His research focuses on international security and international political economy. He is the author of *Power, Trade, and War* (1994), *Electing to Fight: Why Emerging Democracies Go to War* (with Jack Snyder) (2005) and *Votes, Vetoes, and the Political Economy of International Trade Agreements* (with Helen V. Milner) (2012).

HELEN V. MILNER is the B. C. Forbes Professor of Politics and International Affairs at Princeton University and the director of the Niehaus Center for Globalization and Governance at Princeton's Woodrow Wilson School. She was the chair of the Department of Politics from 2005 to 2011. She has written extensively on issues related to international political economy, the connections between domestic politics and foreign policy, globalisation and regionalism and the relationship between democracy and trade policy.

SERGEY NIGAI is a postdoctoral researcher at the Chair of Applied Economics: Innovation and Internationalisation at ETH Zurich and a CESifo research affiliate. He received his PhD from ETH Zurich in 2012. His research interests mainly lie in the areas of international trade with a focus on structural estimation and general equilibrium modelling of multicountry models. His research has focused on quantifying the effects of different trade policies on economic outcomes in a global economy.

MARCELO OLARREAGA is professor of economics at the University of Geneva and research fellow at the Centre for Economic Policy Research in London. Before joining the University of Geneva, he worked in the Research Department of the World Bank and in the Economics Research Division of the World Trade Organization. He holds a PhD in economics from the University of Geneva. He is currently doing research on the political economy of trade policy and trade agreements, barriers to developing countries' exports and distributional and poverty impacts of trade reforms.

JOOST PAUWELYN is professor of international law at the Graduate Institute of International and Development Studies (IHEID) in Geneva, Switzerland, and codirector of the Institute's Centre for Trade and Economic Integration. He is also senior advisor with the law firm of King & Spalding LLC, practising both World Trade Organization (WTO) law and investor–state arbitration. Before joining the IHEID, he was a tenured professor at Duke Law School, North Carolina, and worked as legal officer for the WTO Secretariat.

STEPHANIE J. RICKARD is an associate professor at the London School of Economics. She earned her PhD at the University of California, San Diego, and her BA at the University of Rochester, New York. Her research examines how political institutions influence economic policies, and it appears in journals such as *International Organization, Journal of Politics, British Journal of Political Science* and *Comparative Political Studies*. Her current research includes a study of 'buy national' procurement policies and an investigation into how domestic politics affect International Monetary Fund loan negotiations.

ANIRUDH SHINGAL is a senior research fellow at the World Trade Institute (WTI) and coleader of the National Centre of Competence in Research work package on the impact assessment of trade. Holder of a PhD in economics from the University of Sussex, he specialises in international economics, applied econometrics and development. His research on trade in services, government procurement and preferential trade agreements has been published in peer-reviewed journals as well as by the World Bank, the European Commission and the Commonwealth Secretariat. He is also affiliated with the Centre for the Analysis of Regional Integration at Sussex and has also worked with the World Bank, World Trade Organization and the private sector. He graduated summa cum laude from the MILE Programme of the WTI and also holds a master's degree in economics from the Delhi School of Economics. His undergraduate degree was in economics (honours) from St. Stephen's College, Delhi University.

CHARLOTTE SIEBER-GASSER is a doctoral research fellow at the World Trade Institute, University of Bern, and is about to finish her PhD thesis on South–South preferential trade in services. She holds an MLaw degree from the universities of Bern and Fribourg and an MA degree in development studies from the University of Manchester, United Kingdom. Her research interests include trade law and development, and labour migration and investment. These have translated into articles on the General Agreement on Trade in Services, tied aid and labour migration. Her work has been published in *Swiss Review of International and European Law*, in *Jusletter* and in an edited volume.

GABRIELE SPILKER is a postdoctoral researcher in the International Political Economy group of Thomas Bernauer at the Center for Comparative and International Studies and the Institute for Environmental Decisions. She was a Fritz Thyssen Fellow at the Weatherhead Center for International Affairs at Harvard University for the academic year 2011–12. Her main research interests are in the area of international political economy, international cooperation, globalisation and environmental politics. Her work has been published in *British Journal of Political Science, European Journal of Political Research, Journal of Peace Research* and *Rationality and Society* and in several edited volumes.

PATRICIA TOVAR is a professor of economics at the Pontificia Universidad Católica del Perú. From 2005 to 2012, she was an assistant professor of economics at Brandeis University, with a joint appointment in the Department of Economics and the International Business School. Prior to that, she worked as an economist at the Central Bank of Peru. She has also been a consultant for the World Bank. She received her PhD in economics from the University of Maryland at College Park and her BS from the Pontificia Universidad Católica del Perú. Her research interests are in international trade, trade policy and political economy.

VÍCTOR UMAÑA is a PhD student in the International Political Economy group of Thomas Bernauer at the Center for Comparative and International Studies. He is a doctoral research fellow at the World Trade Institute and a researcher in the Latin American Center for Competitiveness and Sustainable Development at INCAE Business School. His main research interests are the political economy of international trade agreements, agricultural trade and the nexus of trade and sustainability.

GABRIELA WERMELINGER was educated at the University of Bern, the University of Lucerne and the Autonomous University of Madrid. She is a doctoral student and research fellow at the World Trade Institute and the Institute of European and International Economic Law, University of Bern. Her doctoral dissertation topic is marine genetic resources. She holds an MLaw degree from the University of Bern. Her research interests include trade law and sustainability, intellectual property law, law of the sea, investment law and environmental law, European law, Switzerland–EU relations and financial service regulation.

LAURA ZORATTO is an economist at the World Bank (WB) Group currently focusing on the analysis of behaviourally informed public policy interventions to improve service delivery. Prior to joining the WB, she worked as a consultant at the WB Research Group and as a research assistant at the University of Geneva while concluding her PhD in international economics. In Brazil, she has worked for several years on trade, competitiveness and energy-related projects with DAI Inc., USAID, Inter-American Development Bank, the Brazilian Development Bank and others.

# PREFACE

Preferential trade agreements (PTAs) are currently the major venue for regulating international trade. Over the past 30 years, PTAs have mushroomed, with nearly all countries now having signed at least one. Many of these agreements not only reduce tariffs but also regulate issues as diverse as foreign direct investments, intellectual property rights and public procurement. Many PTAs even include provisions regarding nontrade issues such as democracy, environmental protection and human rights.

Much research has been devoted to the study of PTAs. So far, however, this research has mainly followed disciplinary borders, with political scientists, lawyers and economists working in relative isolation from each other. Moreover, existing research has failed to fully capture variation in the design of PTAs. With some PTAs as short as one or two pages and other PTAs as long as a thousand pages, the variation in design is likely to be key to understanding both the causes and consequences of PTAs.

With the aim of advancing the state of the art, we invited leading scholars on PTAs from political science, law and economics to the World Trade Forum – an annual event taking place at the World Trade Institute (WTI) in Bern – in October 2013. Participants in the conference took stock of what we know about the purpose, design and effects of PTAs, but they also looked beyond their specific research agendas to combine insights from different disciplines. Knowledge creation is a collective endeavour and is characterised by contestation and thinking outside the box. This is what we attempted to do. We have benefited greatly from this exchange, and we wish to thank all participants for their inputs that form the basis of this volume.

This volume does not pretend to be the definitive account of trade cooperation through bilateral and plurilateral venues. Rather, we hope that it will inspire new research that will further improve our understanding of PTAs. Ongoing trade cooperation initiatives such as the Transatlantic Trade and Investment Partnership and the Trans-Pacific Partnership make such research particularly important. The tools for understanding the purposes and effects of PTAs that this volume offers should be helpful in guiding this research agenda.

In the course of editing this volume, we have incurred numerous debts. We are grateful to the WTI for financial support and for hosting the World Trade Forum conference that allowed us to put together this volume. Susan Kaplan from the WTI provided editorial support. At Cambridge University Press, we would like to thank Kim Hughes for her excellent guidance throughout the entire process and her continued support for the World Trade Forum series.

# ABBREVIATIONS

| | |
|---|---|
| AANZFTA | ASEAN–Australia–New Zealand FTA |
| ACTA | Anti-Counterfeiting Trade Agreement |
| ADB | Asian Development Bank |
| ADR | alternative dispute resolution |
| AFT | Aid for Trade |
| AFTA | ASEAN Free Trade Area |
| ANES | American National Election Study |
| APEC | Asia-Pacific Economic Cooperation |
| APTA | Asia-Pacific Trade Agreement |
| ARIC | Asian Regional Integration Center |
| ASEAN | Association of Southeast Asian Nations |
| ATE | average treatment effect |
| ATOP | Alliance Treaty Obligations and Provisions |
| BEC | UN Registry of Broad Economic Categories |
| BIT | bilateral investment treaty |
| BRIC countries | Brazil, Russia, India and China |
| CACM | Central American Common Market |
| CAFTA-DR | Dominican Republic–Central America FTA |
| CBD | Convention on Biological Diversity |
| CBM | confidence-building measure |
| CEMAC | Economic and Monetary Community of Central Africa |
| CES | constant elasticity of substitution |
| CIS | Commonwealth of Independent States |
| CM | common market |
| CMA | critical mass agreement |
| COMESA | Common Market for Eastern and Southern Africa |
| CPC | Central Product Classification |
| CRTA | Committee on Regional Trade Agreements |
| CU | customs union |
| CUSFTA | Canada–US Free Trade Agreement |
| CVD | countervailing duty |
| DFQF | duty-free, quota-free |
| DSB | Dispute Settlement Body |

| | |
|---|---|
| DSM | dispute settlement mechanism |
| DSP | dispute settlement provision |
| DSU | Dispute Settlement Understanding |
| EAC | East African Community |
| ECJ | European Court of Justice |
| ECOWAS | Economic Community Of West African States |
| ECU | European Currency Unit |
| EEA | European Economic Area |
| EEC | European Economic Community |
| EFTA | European Free Trade Association |
| EIA | economic integration agreement |
| EPA | economic partnership agreement |
| EU | European Union |
| FAO | The Food and Agriculture Organization of the United Nations |
| fsQCA | fuzzy-set qualitative comparative analysis |
| FTA | free trade agreement |
| GATS | General Agreement on Trade in Services |
| GATT | General Agreement on Tariffs and Trade |
| GCC | Gulf Cooperation Council |
| GDP | gross domestic product |
| GPA | Agreement on Government Procurement |
| GPTAD | Global Preferential Trade Agreements Database (World Bank) |
| GSP | Generalized System of Preferences |
| HIIT | horizontal intra-industry trade |
| ICC | International Chamber of Commerce |
| ICJ | International Court of Justice |
| ICSID | International Centre for Settlement of Investment Disputes |
| IEC | International Electrotechnical Commission |
| IGO | international governmental organisation |
| ILC | International Law Commission |
| IMF | International Monetary Fund |
| IPPC | International Plant Protection Convention |
| IPS | Imperial Preference System |
| ISIC | International Standard Industrial Classification |
| ISO | International Organization for Standardization |
| ITA | Ministerial Declaration on Trade in Information Technology Products (Information Technology Agreement) |
| ITC | International Trade Commission |
| LAIA | Latin American Integration Association |
| MEAT | Most Economically Advantageous Tender |
| MFN | most favoured nation |
| NAFTA | North American Free Trade Agreement |

| | |
|---|---|
| NT | national treatment |
| NTB | nontariff barrier |
| OECD | Organisation for Economic Co-operation and Development |
| OIE | World Organisation for Animal Health (formerly International Office of Epizootics) |
| PA | plurilateral agreement |
| PAFTA | Pan-Arab Free Trade Area |
| PBEC | Pacific Basin Economic Council |
| PECC | Pacific Economic Cooperation Council |
| PPMs | processes and production methods |
| PRIO | Peace Research Institute Oslo |
| PTA | preferential trade agreement |
| RCEP | Regional Comprehensive Economic Partnership |
| REO | regional economic organisation |
| RM | Reichsmark |
| RTAA | Reciprocal Trade Agreements Act |
| RTA-IS | (WTO) Regional Trade Agreements Information System |
| SADC | Southern African Development Community |
| SCM Agreement | Agreement on Subsidies and Countervailing Measures |
| SDT | special and differential treatment |
| SPARTECA | South Pacific Regional Trade and Economic Cooperation Agreement |
| SPS Agreement | Agreement on the Application of Sanitary and Phytosanitary Measures |
| TBT Agreement | Agreement on Technical Barriers to Trade |
| TiSA | Trade in Services Agreement |
| TPP | Trans-Pacific Partnership |
| TRIMs Agreement | Agreement on Trade-Related Investment Measures |
| TRIPS Agreement | Agreement on Trade-Related Aspects of Intellectual Property Rights |
| TRQ | tariff-rate quota |
| TTB | temporary trade barrier |
| TTIP | Transatlantic Trade and Investment Partnership |
| UEMOA | West African Economic and Monetary Union (Union économique et monétaire ouest-africaine) |
| UNCTAD | United Nations Conference on Trade and Development |
| UNEP | United Nations Environment Programme |
| UNIDO | United Nations Industrial Development Organization |
| VCLT | Vienna Convention on the Law of Treaties |
| VIIT | vertical intra-industry trade |
| WAEMU | West African Economic and Monetary Union |
| WCT | WIPO Copyright Treaty |

| | |
|---|---|
| WDI | World Development Indicators |
| WHO | World Health Organization |
| WIPO | World Intellectual Property Organization |
| WITS | World Integrated Trade Solution |
| WPPT | WIPO Performances and Phonograms Treaty |
| WTO | World Trade Organization |

1

# Introduction

## The purpose, design and effects of preferential trade agreements

ANDREAS DÜR AND MANFRED ELSIG

## A. Introduction

Preferential trade agreements (PTAs), defined as agreements that liberalise trade between two or more countries but that do not extend this liberalisation to all countries (or at least to a majority of countries), are mushrooming around the globe.[1] The European Union (EU) is currently negotiating trade agreements with countries such as India, Japan, Malaysia, Thailand, the United States and Vietnam. The Transatlantic Trade and Investment Partnership (TTIP) envisaged by the EU and the United States might eventually cover one-third of world trade. This mega project is mirrored by the negotiations for a Trans-Pacific Partnership (TPP), with participating countries such as Australia, Brunei Darussalam, Chile, Japan, Malaysia, New Zealand, Peru, Singapore, the United States and Vietnam. The TTIP and the TPP are currently the most high-profile PTA negotiations under way, but a large number of smaller PTAs are being negotiated in parallel.

Together, the many smaller and larger agreements that have already been signed, or that are currently under negotiation, make PTAs the most prominent and important governance instrument of our times for regulating trade and investment flows. They have become the main tool for

We are grateful to Marcelo Olarreaga for helpful comments on an earlier version of this chapter. We also acknowledge financial support from NCCR Trade (www.nccr-trade.org).
[1] Many terms have been used for these agreements, including *regional trade agreements, free trade agreements* and *economic integration agreements*. We use the term *preferential trade agreements* to stress the preference given to partners in the same agreement. Our definition excludes nonreciprocal agreements, where one side makes unilateral concessions (e.g. the General System of Preferences), and the 'open regionalism', where a group of countries unconditionally extend trade-liberalizing measures on a most-favoured-nation basis.

achieving market opening and for providing regulatory innovation as multilateral negotiations within the ambit of the World Trade Organization (WTO) have produced only modest results for the last two decades. Moreover, negotiations on plurilateral agreements in the areas of investment (for the Multilateral Agreement on Investment) and intellectual property rights (for the Anti-Counterfeiting Trade Agreement) have failed to produce results that would have been acceptable to a larger number of countries and important segments of civil society. Countries have thus relied on PTAs to regulate issues ranging from trade in goods and services to investment, intellectual property rights, competition, standards and government procurement rules.

Although PTAs have attracted considerable scholarly attention, the jury is still out on several key questions. Why do countries sign PTAs? What explains variation in the design of PTAs? How effective are PTAs in promoting trade and changing domestic law and institutions? And what are the consequences of the spread of PTAs for the world trading system? This volume attempts to give answers to these questions and in doing so breaks new ground in several respects. First, the book brings together innovative research by economists, lawyers and political scientists. A multidisciplinary approach seems highly promising for a topic such as PTAs, which involves economic, legal and political aspects. Nevertheless, the various disciplines studying PTAs have produced literatures that hardly talk to each other. The purpose of this volume is to take stock of the empirical and theoretical advances that have been made in the study of trade agreements in the three disciplines. It also aims to stimulate cross-fertilisation across these literatures, by showing how researchers from different disciplines tackle the same substantive questions.

Second, so far much of the literature on PTAs has failed to recognise that PTAs are very heterogeneous. Some PTAs include many member countries, others few; some PTAs cover a large number of different issues, from trade in services to government procurement, whereas others are very narrow; and some PTAs include very far-reaching provisions, whereas others are relatively shallow. A substantial proportion of the existing literature on PTAs consists of either case studies that fail to put the key features of a specific PTA into a broader context or quantitative studies that operationalise PTAs in the form of a dichotomous variable, that is, a variable that only captures the presence or absence of a PTA. This state of the art is problematic as both the causes and consequences of PTAs should vary across agreements of different scope, depth and flexibility. In this volume, we take stock of and contribute to a recent literature that zeroes in on design differences across PTAs.

Finally, compared to the 1990s, when research on PTAs first started to pick up, the phenomenon under study has changed considerably. As discussed previously, not only have many new agreements been signed over the past 10 years but also these agreements differ in key respects from the agreements signed even a decade before. By taking into account agreements signed in the 2000s, this volume allows for an assessment of which of the findings of the early studies remain valid, based on a much richer empirical foundation.

In the remainder of this introduction, we first put current PTAs into their historical context, illustrating how they have changed over time, before introducing four major questions that provide the structure for this volume. We discuss the literature related to these guiding questions and highlight the contribution of the various chapters to advancing our knowledge related to PTAs.

## B. PTAs, past and present

Countries have been signing trade agreements for a long time. The nineteenth century, in particular, saw the spread of trade agreements in Europe (Pahre 2008). The Anglo-French commercial treaty of 1860 was of great significance, as it ushered in a period of relatively free trade in Europe that lasted until the 1880s. In the period between the two world wars, countries also resorted to PTAs. In the Ottawa agreements (1932), for example, the United Kingdom exchanged preferential tariff concessions with its dominions and colonies. In parallel, the United States used the Reciprocal Trade Agreements Act (1934) to conclude trade agreements with Latin American countries, as well as with Canada and the United Kingdom. The effects of these agreements, however, have been seen as far less benign than the agreements signed in the nineteenth century; many observers have blamed them for accentuating the negative effects of the Great Depression (Kindleberger 1973).

After World War II, with a few prominent exceptions, multilateral trade agreements within the framework of the General Agreement on Tariffs and Trade (GATT, 1947) trumped the formation of PTAs. The GATT itself, of course, was originally only a plurilateral agreement signed by 23 countries. But since most countries that engaged in significant amounts of international trade at that time were covered by the GATT's provisions, its discriminatory aspect was limited. Internally, the GATT was built on the principle of nondiscrimination, meaning that any concessions towards one member had to be extended to all members of the GATT.[2] Under Article XXIV of the GATT, however, states were allowed to enter into PTAs, but only if these agreements removed 'substantially all' barriers to trade and if the agreements did not increase trade barriers against third countries (Jackson 1997). Only a few countries made use of this exemption in the first four decades of the GATT, the European Economic Community being the main exception.

In 1979, GATT contracting parties agreed upon the so-called enabling clause, which allowed less-developed countries to grant each other preferences that do not meet the criteria specified in Article XXIV.[3] Under this cover, Latin American countries exchanged preferences in the framework of the Latin American Integration Association and south-east Asian countries in the context of the South Asian Free Trade Agreement. Moreover, developed countries could grant developing countries one-sided preferences. Nevertheless, the number of agreements notified to the WTO under this clause remained limited; before 1990, only nine such enabling-clause agreements were notified to the WTO.[4]

Not until the early 1990s, therefore, did PTAs become a prominent tool for economic cooperation. The rediscovery of PTAs started with the deepening of European integration as a result of the Single Market Programme and the signing of the North American Free Trade Agreement (NAFTA) in 1992. In Europe, the end of the Cold War and the dissolution of the Soviet Union created demand for PTAs in the form of association agreements to manage economic relations with former members of the Warsaw Pact. In the Americas, countries started to sign PTAs in the wake of the creation of NAFTA. What followed was a spread of PTAs known in the 1990s as 'new regionalism' (De Melo and Panagariya 1992). Although initially Asian countries hardly participated in this new wave of PTAs, this situation changed radically around the year 2000. Currently, the majority of the agreements under negotiation involve Asian countries.

More than 700 PTAs were signed between the end of World War II and 2013, the large majority since 1990 (see Figure 1.1).[5] More recently, the

---

[2] Dür (2010) shows how the principle of nondiscrimination was a response to the proliferation of PTAs in the interwar period.
[3] www.wto.org/English/docs_e/legal_e/enabling1979_e.htm [last accessed 10 February 2014].
[4] http://rtais.wto.org/ui/PublicMaintainRTAHome.aspx [last accessed 10 February 2014].
[5] We draw on data from Dür, Baccini and Elsig (2014). The data can be downloaded from the Design of Trade Agreements (DESTA) Database at www.designoftradeagreements.org [last accessed 10 February 2014].

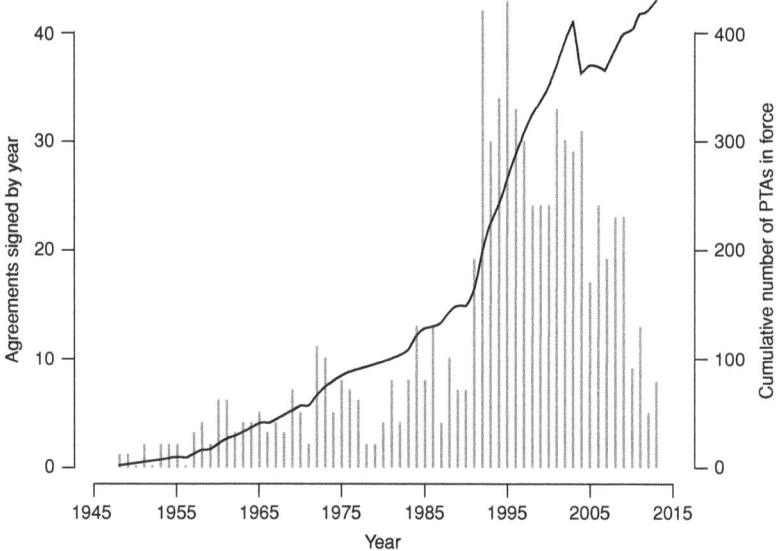

**Figure 1.1** Number of PTAs over time, 1945–2013
*Source:* authors' illustration based on data from Dür *et al.* 2014.

number of agreements concluded per year has again been falling, indicating that many of the country pairs that can benefit from a preferential trade link already have a PTA. Up to the early 1990s, European countries were by far the most avid signers of PTAs (see Figure 1.2). In fact, by 1992, major countries such as China and Japan had not yet signed a PTA.[6] By 2013, countries in the Americas had nearly caught up with their European counterparts with respect to the number of agreements signed. Moreover, as noted previously, Asian countries, such as Singapore, have become prominent actors in the spread of PTAs. Most recently, China has shown increasing interest in negotiating PTAs. Illustratively, Switzerland signed a PTA with China in 2013, and Australia and Norway are currently engaged in negotiations with that country.

Even more striking than the shift from Europe to the Americas and Asia as the hot spots of PTA negotiations is the fact that many of the new agreements are signed by countries from different continents. No fewer than 26 of 39 PTAs currently (as of November 2013) listed by the WTO

---

[6] We compare here to the situation in 1992, because this is the first year after the dissolution of the Soviet Union, meaning that most countries that are in existence in 2013 also existed in 1992.

**1992**

**2013**

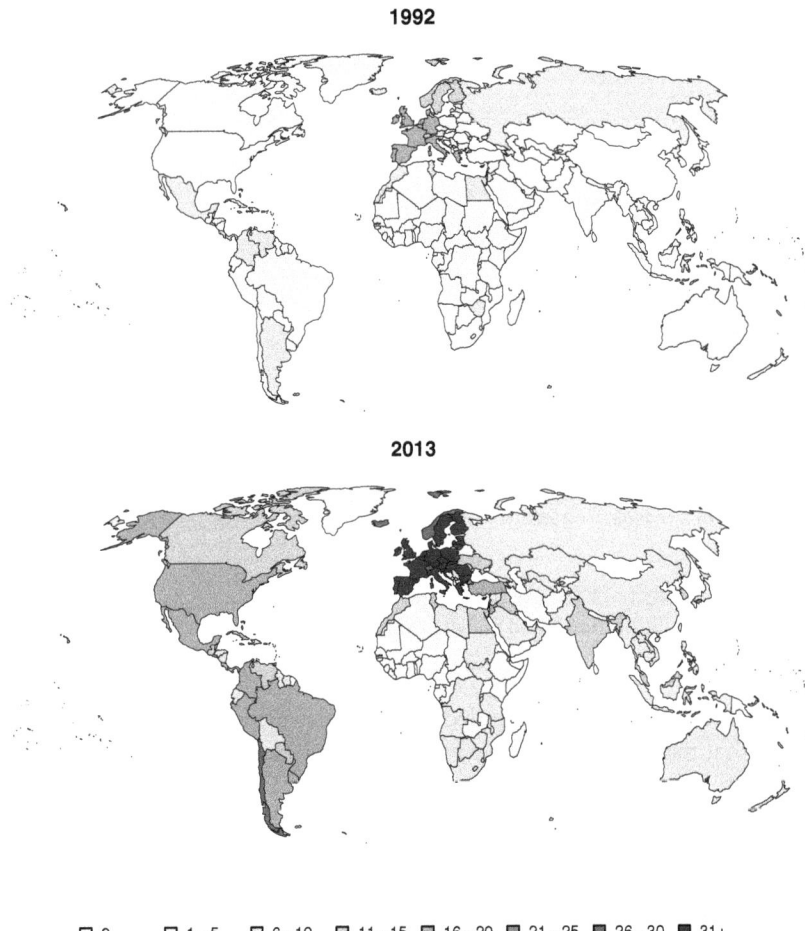

☐ 0      ☐ 1–5    ☐ 6–10   ☐ 11–15   ■ 16–20   ■ 21–25   ■ 26–30   ■ 31+

**Figure 1.2**   PTAs 1992 and 2013
*Source:* authors' illustration based on data from Dür *et al.* 2014.

under the label of 'early announcement' go beyond a continent.[7] This includes the TTIP and the TPP but also less obvious pairings, such as Canada–Ukraine. 'Regionalism' thus is no longer an appropriate label for this development.

PTAs also vary in terms of type and number of members (see Figure 1.3). The term *PTA* encompasses partial free trade agreements, full free trade agreements and customs unions. Partial agreements cut

---

[7]   See http://rtais.wto.org/UI/PublicEARTAList.aspx [last accessed 10 February 2014].

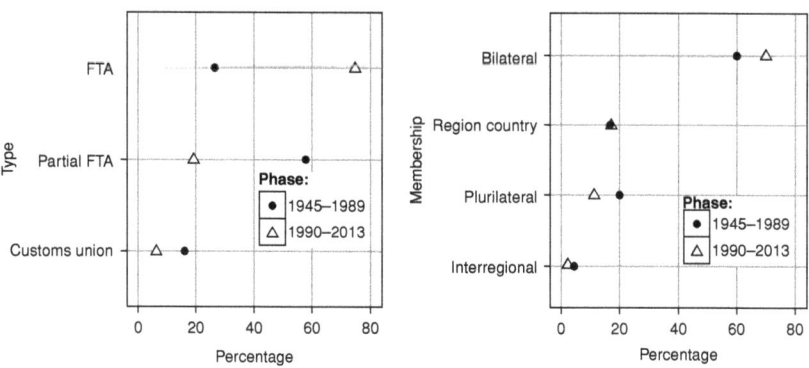

**Figure 1.3** Change in type and membership over time
*Source:* authors' illustration based on data from Dür *et al.* 2014.

tariffs for only a select number of products, and often these cuts do not reduce tariffs to zero. Full free trade agreements, by contrast, liberalise all or substantially all trade among member countries after a negotiated transition period. Customs unions add a common external tariff to a free trade area. Whereas early agreements were mainly of the partial free trade agreement type (with a few customs unions), most recent agreements establish full free trade areas, with customs unions particularly having become very rare.

Moreover, a substantial number of the early agreements were of a pluri-lateral type; that is, they had more than two member countries (see the right-hand pane of Figure 1.3). Many of these agreements are open to new members. The Rome Treaty that established the European Economic Community (1957), for example, was originally signed by 6 countries, and then expanded to include 28 member countries by 2013. Similarly, the agreement creating the Central American Common Market (1960) was signed by 4 countries and then expanded to also include Costa Rica in 1962. More recent agreements, by contrast, are slightly more likely to be of a bilateral nature. The membership of bilateral agreements does not tend to expand; rather, we see that existing members of bilateral agreements sign new agreements with third countries. Not yet captured by the data shown in Figure 1.3, the ongoing negotiations for 'mega-regionals', namely, the TTIP and the TPP, may suggest a return to plurilateral agreements in the near future.

But arguably the largest shift in the negotiation of PTAs has been with respect to the contents of these agreements (see Figure 1.4). With a few notable exceptions, most agreements prior to NAFTA covered only trade

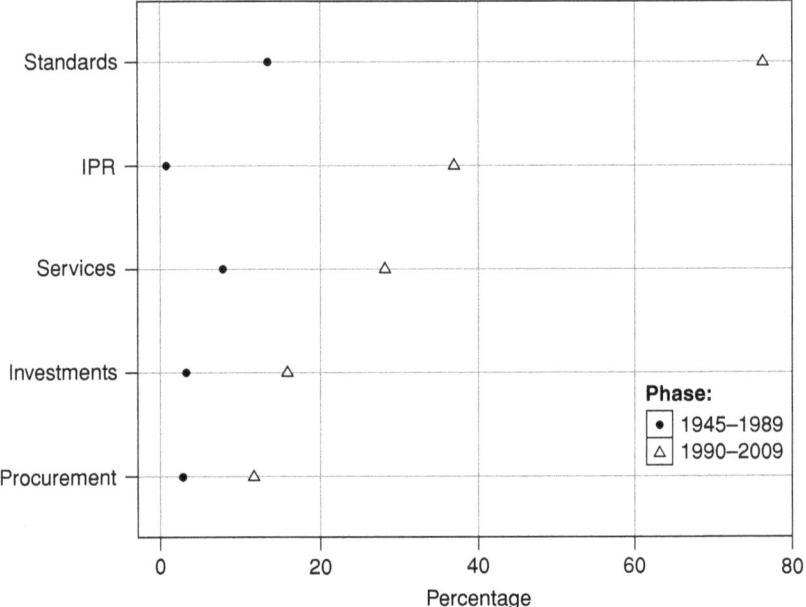

**Figure 1.4**   Change in the contents of PTAs
*Source:* authors' illustration based on data from Dür *et al.* 2014.

in goods. NAFTA heralded a much more encompassing type of PTA that contains not only provisions on trade in goods but also on behind-the-border issues such as technical barriers to trade, government procurement, investment, services, competition law and intellectual property rights (IPRs). As shown in Figure 1.4, many PTAs now have a similar breadth to NAFTA.

Increasingly, the scope of PTAs even goes beyond the regulation of economic issues: nontrade issues have become more prominent, ranging from environmental concerns and the promotion of human and labour rights to addressing new and old security threats (e.g. Hafner-Burton 2005; Spilker and Böhmelt 2013). It is this increasing scope and variation in actual commitment levels that makes PTAs such a fascinating object of study. Building on this discussion, we now move on to present the four key questions that inform this volume and then briefly outline the contributions by the authors.

## C. Why do countries sign PTAs?

The question why countries sign PTAs started to attract scholarly attention at the time of the formation of the first PTAs in the decades following

World War II. A prominent early explanation for the creation of the EU (originally the European Economic Community, which in turn followed the European Coal and Steel Community) focused on the key actors' pursuit of geopolitical goals such as peace and security. As summarised by Andrew Moravcsik (1998: 6), these arguments suggest that 'postwar European leaders who constructed and extended the EC [European Community] sought to tie down the Germans, balance the Russians, establish a third force against the Americans, overcome right-wing and Communist extremism at home, or suppress nationalism to realise a distinctive vision of European federalism'. Similar arguments have been made for other PTAs. A government may value a PTA for geopolitical reasons if it can use the PTA to increase another country's dependence, allowing it to extract concessions from that country (Hirschman 1945). Alternatively, the aim of a PTA can be to increase a country's military capacity by creating more trade and thus increasing national income (Gowa 1994). A final geopolitical motivation for trade agreements may be to tackle new security threats, including terrorism and organised crime.

PTAs may also be created to generate welfare gains for the participating countries. In fact, Scott Baier and Jeffrey Bergstrand (2004) found that variables that capture the net aggregate economic gains of the participating countries alone can successfully explain the overwhelming majority of PTA ties.[8] A specific welfare-related objective for PTAs may be to allow governments to reduce tariffs without incurring negative terms of trade effects (Bagwell and Staiger 1998). Countries may also benefit in welfare terms if PTAs give firms the opportunity to exploit economies of scale. PTAs offer firms a larger market for their products. A larger market, in turn, allows firms to increase their production and thus to reap gains from lower unit costs. Even if a government is indifferent to its country's welfare, lobbying by firms that expect gains from economies of scale may motivate it to sign PTAs (Chase 2005). Pressure in favour of a PTA may also come from exporters that expect gains from a PTA (Grossman and Helpman 1995). Such exporter lobbying may be particularly strong in countries that are excluded from existing PTAs. Discrimination may impose costs on exporters in these third countries, creating an incentive for them to become politically active and to push their governments to also pursue PTAs (Baccini and Dür 2012; Baldwin 1993; Dür 2010).

Moreover, governments may sign PTAs to tie their hands or lock in specific policies. In the words of John Whalley (1998: 71), 'by binding

[8] Some of these variables, such as geographic distance, may also capture other factors, such as geopolitics.

the country to the masthead of an international trade treaty, any future reversal of domestic policy reform becomes more difficult to implement'. Finally, democratic governments may use PTAs as a signal to domestic audiences (Mansfield and Milner 2012). The argument is that voters have limited information about government preferences and policies. When the country experiences economic difficulties, the median voter may then punish the incumbent, not knowing whether government policies or an exogenous shock is responsible for the economic downturn. Voters do not oust governments that signed PTAs, however, because signing PTAs is a credible signal that the government is pursuing economically sound policies.

In the first part of this volume, five chapters contribute to this literature. In Chapter 2, Moonhawk Kim argues that changes in what he calls the technological and political infrastructure can explain the broad patterns of the historical development of PTAs. The available technology determines the ease with which goods and services can be traded across borders, and thus the demand for PTAs; and the number of states in the international system, the distribution of power among states and the presence of war shape the supply of PTAs. Based on an analysis of five periods (1840–1914, 1920s and 1930s, 1947–90, 1991–2000 and 2001–13), he finds support for this argument. Edward Mansfield and Helen Milner (Chapter 3) then test a series of explanations for the creation of PTAs, including the role of economic factors, international politics and domestic politics. Based on a data set that covers PTAs signed up to 2011, they find support for all three explanations. Most importantly, they reconfirm their previous finding that domestic institutions matter: democratic countries are more likely, and countries with many veto players are less likely, to sign PTAs.

In Chapter 4, Jean-Louis Arcand, Marcelo Olarreaga and Laura Zoratto take up the idea that governments may use PTAs to lock in specific policies. They not only find empirical support for this argument but also estimate the welfare benefits that accruc to a country from applying this lock-in strategy. Among their more specific findings is the notion that credibility reasons are particularly important for weak governments and for small countries that sign PTAs with large ones. Importantly, PTAs signed for credibility reasons lead to an increase in imports that is substantially larger than that from comparable agreements. Víctor Umaña, Thomas Bernauer and Gabriele Spilker (Chapter 5) then use a survey experiment to investigate to what extent public opinion may explain different aspects of the new regionalism. Among other things, they find that voters in democracies favour PTAs with other democracies and with culturally and geographically close countries. These findings may contribute to an explanation of key aspects of the recent spread of PTAs: democratic countries are indeed more likely to sign PTAs with other democracies, and cultural proximity also tends to explain the formation of PTAs. Recent PTAs, however, often include geographically distant countries, which begs the question of which factors trump public opinion.

In Chapter 6 Soo Yeon Kim asks why, after some delay, Asian governments have jumped on to the bandwagon of signing PTAs. Her explanation focuses on the role of production networks that create demand for greater cross-border integration. She shows empirically that production networks can also explain the design of PTAs. The greater the share of trade in parts and components in the overall trade of two countries, the deeper the agreement these two countries will sign.

Overall, these five chapters suggest that there is no single cause that drives the spread of PTAs. Domestic factors are clearly important (Chapters 3–5), but international factors cannot be neglected, either (Chapters 2 and 3). However, what also becomes clear is that considering variation in the design of PTAs may help answer the question of the causes of PTAs. Explanations for the design and a discussion of design differences of PTAs make up the second part of the volume.

## D. The design of PTAs

The second part of the book looks in more detail at the design features of PTAs. This focus is important because countries' reasons for signing trade agreements can be fully understood only by focusing on the content of PTAs; states are *ex ante* willing to enter an agreement only if they anticipate some gains from liberalising specific areas. Gaining insights into variation in PTA design will also benefit research on the impact of these agreements on a wide array of issue areas (discussed later). Multiple attempts have thus been made in the past 10 years to collect data on issue-specific areas (Estevadeordal, Suominen and Teh 2009; Kucik 2012), the PTAs of key trading powers (Horn, Mayroidis and Sapir 2010) and PTAs in particular regions (Hicks and Kim 2012). In this context, the Design of Trade Agreements (DESTA) Database has been the most ambitious project to collect design data over time and across areas (see Dür, Baccini and Elsig 2014).

This research has been used to measure the extent of concessions in relation to liberalisation (the depth of an agreement), the degree of opt-outs both short and long term (flexibility) and how PTA provisions can be enforced through dispute settlement mechanisms (enforceability). Using these measures, the literature has shown that some design features are a function of PTA-inherent characteristics. For instance, the flexibility and depth of an agreement are related (Baccini, Dür and Elsig, forthcoming), and there is also a relationship between depth and enforceability (Downs, Rock and Barsoom 1996).

Building on this literature, the contributions to this volume offer a series of novel explanations for the design of PTAs. In Chapter 7, Leonardo Baccini, Andreas Dür and Yoram Haftel argue that in designing PTAs, countries select from a series of 'model PTAs'. Concretely, countries can decide whether they want to sign an EU-type, a NAFTA-type, or a Southern-type PTA. Using data from DESTA, the authors explain which countries opt for which model. They find that over time, countries are increasingly signing NAFTA-type agreements; by contrast, the appeal of the EU model seems to be declining. Bilateral and North–South agreements are particularly likely to follow the NAFTA model. The level of development, however, does not seem to influence the choice of PTA design.

Chapter 8 by Mark Manger focuses on the depth of agreements. His analysis shows how the type of trade structure affects market access related to tariff elimination negotiated in PTAs. Focusing on a sample of PTAs including Asian economies, he finds that if PTA partners' trade relations are characterised by intra-industry trade, this is more likely to lead to liberalisation than is a trade structure that is endowment based. In Chapter 9, Kerry Chase then analyses provisions regarding audiovisual services in PTAs. Using a data set of 116 services PTAs, he presents an index of audiovisual services commitments. He finds that countries make greater commitments when they have made concessions on audiovisual services liberalisation in the WTO, when PTAs are deep, when they opt for a negative-list approach and when the United States is a member of the PTA. Fewer commitments are observed when PTA parties use a positive-list approach, when PTAs are concluded between developing and developed countries and when PTAs include Canada or the EU.

The contribution by Anu Bradford and Tim Büthe (Chapter 10) focuses on competition-related content in PTAs. It is one of the first studies to address, in a systematic way, whether and how competition policy has been taken up in these agreements. Using a random sample from the list of agreements in the DESTA data set, they first show a trend towards the inclusion of competition chapters and competition articles in trade agreements. They then present two theoretical perspectives on what states might achieve in regulating competition in PTAs. Their findings, although mixed, suggest that states are not concerned about the use of competition policy as a protectionist device, but they have a genuine desire to combat anticompetitive practices. Countries include competition provisions in PTAs in response to the opportunities for cross-border collusion created by market integration.

Stephanie Rickard's chapter (Chapter 11) focuses on the public procurement rules in PTAs. She describes the commitments contained in PTAs and then provides potential explanations as to why they are included in PTAs. Her argument rests on the finding that the procurement rules contained in PTAs are rather shallow (and flexible) and do not seem to be effective; that is, they do not increase foreign buying by governments. This suggests that governments use procurement chapters in PTAs as political cover when they have to buy foreign goods or services.

An interesting and overlooked nexus exists between trade and security. Contributing to the study of this relationship, Chapter 12, by Yoram Haftel, focuses on the landscape of security institutions within a subset of PTAs: regional economic organisations. He shows how security substructures have become an important feature of formerly predominantly economic cooperation projects. He offers three explanations for the nesting of security institutions, namely, intraregional violent conflict, the existence of a regional hegemon and the absence of regional rivalries within a region. He shows using a fuzzy-set qualitative comparative analysis (fsQCA) which of the explanations presents a necessary condition for the presence of security cooperation institutions. The evidence lends support to the absence of rivalry explanation, but not to the other two.

Finally, in Chapter 13 Todd Allee and Manfred Elsig focus on the design and role of dispute settlement mechanisms in PTAs. They show that dispute settlement in PTAs exhibits more variation than has been acknowledged so far. After presenting various specificities of processes and obligations in the dispute settlement provisions, they present new ideas on how to think about dispute settlement in the context of PTAs. These concepts go beyond the usual narrow focus on how legalised litigation is. They portray more nuanced roles of dispute settlement systems, such as providing information, enforcing commitments, promoting settlement or allowing for targeted flexibility, and suggest variables to measure these concepts and make them fruitful for empirical investigation.

## E. The effects of PTAs

Analyses of the effects of PTAs, especially on trade flows, have a long tradition. In his seminal contribution, Jacob Viner (1950) distinguished between the trade-creating and trade-diverting effects of PTAs. He showed that intra-PTA liberalisation of trade can create new trade between partners in the PTA; it can also lead to a diversion of trade from more efficient producers outside the PTA towards less-efficient producers inside the PTA. In the decades following Viner's discovery, a steady flow of publications reported on studies of the trade effects of particular PTAs (e.g. Aitken 1973). Only in the late 1980s, however, did research on the trade effects of PTAs really take off. When the United States first concluded the US–Canada agreement, and later NAFTA, economists tried to find out what consequences these agreements would have. Early on, Paul Wonnacott and Mark Lutz (1989) suggested that PTAs among 'natural trading partners' could be expected to be trade creating; for other PTAs, trade diversion would dominate. In his influential book, Jeffrey Frankel (1997) then found that most regional trade blocs have a substantial effect on trade flows and that trade creation often trumps trade diversion.

Much of this early literature, however, suffered from several shortcomings. First, PTAs are not exogenous to trade flows; larger trade flows may make countries sign PTAs. Interestingly, once this endogeneity is accounted for, the estimated trade effects of PTAs become even more pronounced (Baier and Bergstrand 2007). Second, the effects of PTAs on trade flows may differ depending on whether two countries already trade a specific product or whether no trade has so far taken place. Research into this issue showed that PTAs do not create trade where none existed before, but they are related to an increase in positive trade flows (Egger et al. 2011). Finally, the early literature largely failed to account for the significant differences in the design of PTAs. Remedying this shortcoming shows that most trade is created by deep PTAs; shallow PTAs only have a small effect on trade flows (Dür, Baccini and Elsig 2014).

The literature on the effects of PTAs is not limited to analyses of trade flows. Much research has also tackled the question of whether PTAs attract foreign direct investment (for example, Büthe and Milner 2008; Peinhardt and Allee 2012). In addition, some recent studies have looked at the consequences of PTAs for human rights in member countries (Hafner Burton 2009). Finally, PTAs have been linked to the presence and absence of international conflict and war (Haftel 2012; Mansfield and Pevehouse

2000). Remarkably, for most of these areas, research has found that PTAs make a difference. Evidently, the relevance of PTAs goes far beyond trade.

The contributions included in the third part of this volume nicely complement and build on this literature. In Chapter 14, Scott Baier, Jeffrey Bergstrand and Matthew Clance argue that since PTAs are signed for different reasons, they are likely to vary in terms of their effects on trade. In fact, the authors' empirical analysis shows that the effects of PTAs on trade flows vary strongly across PTAs. Although nearly all agreements increase trade flows, for some PTAs these effects are negligible, and for others they are large. They find that variation in the depth of agreements only partly explains variation in the size of the agreements' trade effects. Other factors, such as distance between member countries, common language, religion or legal origins, explain a large amount of the variation in trade effects.

The chapter by Peter Egger and Sergey Nigai (Chapter 15) addresses the same question of heterogeneous effects of PTAs but comes to a quite different conclusion. Using a measure of scope based on the presence or absence of 48 cooperation areas in an agreement, they find that differences in design matter a great deal for the trade effects of PTAs. These gains in trade that result from deep PTAs also translate into welfare gains for member countries: thus deep PTAs on average are welfare improving, with gains of up to 10 per cent for most countries.

Anirudh Shingal's chapter (Chapter 16) offers still another extension of this literature: not only can the effects of PTAs on trade be expected to vary across PTAs but also PTAs may have different effects for different types of 'products'. Concretely, Shingal analyses the impact of PTAs on trade in services. His study takes account of the endogeneity of membership in services PTAs and also considers that services trade agreements are not implemented in one go. Moreover, the chapter advances the state of the art in drawing on a data set that covers more countries for a longer time period. The findings show that PTAs increase trade in services, but that much of this effect is driven by the EU.

In Chapter 17, Jeffrey Kucik shows that PTAs may affect not only levels of trade but also volatility in trade flows. Volatility in trade flows leads to costs, for example, by accentuating business cycles and reducing job security. Governments thus have an incentive to reduce volatility, and PTAs offer one instrument to achieve this objective. But, Kucik argues, PTAs will be effective in achieving this aim only if they both tie the hands of their members and offer members some flexibility to react to shocks.

The empirical evidence does indeed show that flexible agreements have a greater impact on the reduction of volatility than rigid agreements do.

Finally, Chapter 18 by Chad Bown, Baybars Karacaovali and Patricia Tovar investigates the effect of PTAs on the use of temporary trade barriers. Relying on four case studies, they show that governments can react in very different ways to the creation of a PTA. In some cases, they use temporary trade barriers to reinforce discrimination in favour of PTA members; in other cases, they use the same barriers to reduce discrimination. The contribution suggests that the relationship between PTA obligations and the use of temporary trade barriers needs further examination and that a more in-depth focus on the design could be one way forward.

These chapters thus offer support for this volume's main argument that it is important to study the design of PTAs. Clearly, the effects of PTAs vary depending on whether they are shallow or deep and whether they are flexible or rigid. This may also prove an important insight for the debate on the relationship between PTAs and the multilateral trading system, which we take up in the fourth part of this volume.

## F. PTAs and the multilateral trading system

The final part of the book focuses on the relationship between preferentialism and multilateralism. PTAs have dominated the international trade regulation landscape for the past 15 years. By contrast, progress in the WTO negotiations has been limited since the conclusion of a series of post-Uruguay agreements, including the Information Technology Agreement (ITA), in the late 1990s. The deal on food security and trade facilitation reached at the 2013 Bali Ministerial conference of the WTO has also not provided momentum to swiftly conclude the Doha Round of multilateral trade negotiations that has been ongoing since 2001. Nevertheless, with WTO rules having been integrated in PTAs, the multilateral trading system remains important. This point is reinforced by the fact that the WTO now has 159 members, meaning that the fate of the WTO is crucial for global economic governance. The study of the relationship between preferentialism and the multilateral trading system thus remains pertinent.

The main question that has been debated in this context is whether PTAs are stumbling blocks or stepping stones for multilateral trade liberalisation (for an overview of the debate, see Panagariya 1999). On the one hand, PTAs have been pictured as a stumbling block for further liberalisation and rule making in the WTO (Bhagwati 1991). By investing in bilateral and regional trade deals, so the argument goes, the pressure on states to liberalise multilaterally decreases. This also deprives the multilateral system, characterised by package deals, of the opportunity to offer sufficient benefits to all participating actors, because PTAs reduce potential multilateral gains. On the other hand, PTAs are characterised as stepping stones towards multilateral liberalisation (Lawrence 1996). They serve as venues where innovation and further liberalisation takes place, not only creating incentives to engage in 'open regionalism' but also offering possibilities for 'multilateralising' PTA-specific rules (see Baldwin and Low 2009). This latter view sees PTAs and the multilateral system as complementary. As stated in the declaration of the Ministerial Meeting of the WTO in Doha (2001), 'regional trade agreements can play an important role in promoting the liberalisation and expansion of trade' (World Trade Organization 2001: 1).

Despite much research into this question, particularly informed by a legal perspective that has focused on the compatibility of PTA commitments with WTO obligations (Bartels and Ortino 2006), on the empirical side, the jury is still out. The four contributions to this volume that address this topic bring out new and innovative aspects related to the PTA–multilateralism debate to advance on this state of the art. Thomas Cottier, Charlotte Sieber-Gasser and Gabriela Wermelinger propose in Chapter 19 a legal-historical analysis of what they view as a dialectical relationship between multilateralism and preferentialism. That multilateralism and preferentialism can stimulate each other has so far been largely overlooked in this debate. Moreover, whereas most work zooms in on tariff liberalisation, their contribution addresses regulatory progress. They show that, for instance, the intellectual property rights part of the multilateral system (Agreement on Trade-Related Aspects of Intellectual Property Rights (TRIPS agreement)) was inspired by bilateral agreements between European states in the early nineteenth century. By contrast, they trace how innovation in services regulation was strongly shaped both by progress in the 1980s in the General Agreement on Tariffs and Trade (GATT) and the Uruguay Round negotiations leading to the General Agreement on Trade in Services (GATS) and some innovation in US and EU trade deals. The GATS commitments and regulatory philosophy today influence the services chapters of the new-generation PTAs. Drawing from various examples, the authors are optimistic that innovation in today's PTAs can be brought back to the multilateral table.

Whereas much of the debate has focused on the relationship between the WTO and PTAs, Chapter 20 by Joost Pauwelyn and Wolfgang Alschner suggests that the concerns of legal scholars about fragmentation of international trade law have not sufficiently addressed challenges stemming from the relations among PTAs themselves. In their contribution, they carry out an analysis of the contemporary PTA network that shows the existence of several regional PTA clusters (which confirms the results presented in Chapter 7), with the EU at the centre of the network. Pauwelyn and Alschner also show that the signing of the mega-regionals that are currently being negotiated would transform this network and lead to a 'ball of wool'-like PTA network. Building on this network analysis, they then focus on double-PTAs, that is, agreements where the same countries find themselves parties to at least two different PTAs, usually with distinct compositions of PTA members. They focus on not only the reasons why states engage in double-PTAs but also how these interrelate. This issue of overlapping membership in PTAs could have great implications for the WTO that have so far not been analysed.

Whereas the contribution by Pauwelyn and Alschner focuses on inter-PTA relations, Bernard Hoekman (Chapter 21) argues that PTAs might have led to a renaissance of sectoral or plurilateral approaches within (or in parallel to) the WTO. These mechanisms have received more attention in recent years as countries excluded from the mega-regional arrangements, such as the TPP and the TTIP, have started to explore ways in which to gradually multilateralise the best features of regulatory cooperation established in PTAs into the WTO. He encourages an active use of variable geometry with leadership provided by a number of middle powers, that is, countries with a moderate influence on world affairs.

Finally, the contribution by James Flett brings the reader back to what is currently the most successful feature of the WTO, its so-called jewel in the crown, the dispute settlement mechanism established with the creation of the WTO in 1995. Flett suggests ways in which this system could be made available for PTA parties in the interpretation of PTA law. He reminds the reader of the need to have a strong and binding dispute settlement system. One question that arises from this analysis is whether special terms of reference could be drawn upon to allow PTA disputes to be litigated in the WTO. According to him, such an approach would have advantages for both PTA and WTO Members. Finally, he addresses practical concerns related to financing, scheduling, third parties, adjudicative responsibility and WTO consistency. He shows how, if WTO and PTA members are willing, the WTO flagship institution could be 'regionalised'.

These contributions show that the relationship between the multilateral system and PTAs is multifaceted, that legal questions of coherence start to become more prevalent in PTAs with increasing numbers of double-PTAs and that innovation in plurilateral and sectoral agreements could prove important for multilateralising PTAs.

## G. Conclusion

PTAs have become the dominant form of trade cooperation at the beginning of the twenty-first century. The chapters in this volume provide an overview of advances in the study of PTAs, offer new insights, suggest novel answers to long-standing research questions and sketch new avenues for future research. The volume shows that research on PTAs in law, political science and economics may profit from cross-fertilisation between disciplines in order to push the research frontier forward. Law scholarship has so far mainly focused on the question of compatibility between WTO and PTA obligations. Future scholarship following in the footsteps of the legal contributions in this volume could develop a more diverse research agenda. Combining forces with other disciplines might help in particular to answer questions related to enforcement (see Horn, Mayroidis and Sapir 2010) and implementation of PTA commitments and on how PTAs affect domestic law. Economics research has mainly focused on both the economic rationale for signing PTAs and the estimation of PTAs' effects on trade flows. Contributions to this volume show that paying greater attention to variation in the design of PTAs – a point that has been pushed mainly by political scientists and lawyers – can help advance economists' research agendas. Finally, political science approaches have sharpened our understanding of the politics surrounding the negotiations of trade agreements and have highlighted the multiple purposes these agreements might serve while taking the rule of law seriously and engaging with the economics literature on the design and effects.

What future avenues exist for PTA research? Certainly, the continued political attention devoted to PTAs and the ongoing work to provide more accurate data on PTAs will provide further momentum in the study of PTAs. In this future work, researchers should pay increased attention to the effects of PTAs not only on economic indicators but also on domestic institutions, politics and law. Moreover, research should increasingly focus on the diffusion of best practices in PTA regulation and theorise the conditions under which, and what type of, regulatory innovation may be multilateralised through the WTO or unilaterally applied by non-PTA members. In addition, the new mega-deals that are on the horizon will pose interesting research questions. Which templates will be agreed upon and to what degree are these suitable for other PTAs? To what extent will countries be able to deviate from the EU–US model? Finally, what will China's trade cooperation strategy look like? This is not only a question of distributional consequences or the need to minimise transaction costs but also it suggests that PTAs may be used more and more as a prominent vehicle for pursuing strategic foreign policy objectives in a multipolar trade world. This volume might help prepare the basis for tackling these and other research questions as it calls for the study of PTAs using advanced methods that draw on a multidisciplinary setting and collect systematic information on various PTA dimensions, such as scope, depth, flexibility, enforcement and implementation of these agreements.

## References

Aitken, Norman D. 1973. 'The Effect of the EEC and EFTA on European Trade: A Temporal Cross-Section Analysis.' *American Economic Review* 63 (5): 881–92.

Baccini, Leonardo, and Dür, Andreas. 2012. 'The New Regionalism and Policy Interdependence.' *British Journal of Political Science* 42 (1): 57–79.

Baccini, Leonardo, Dür, Andreas, and Elsig, Manfred. Forthcoming. 'The Politics of Trade Agreement Design: Revisiting the Depth-Flexibility Nexus.' *International Studies Quarterly*.

Bagwell, Kyle, and Staiger, Robert. 1998. 'Will Preferential Agreements Undermine the Multilateral Trading System?' *Economic Journal* 108 (449): 1162–82.

Baier, Scott L., and Bergstrand, Jeffrey H. 2004. 'Economic Determinants of Free Trade Agreements.' *Journal of International Economics* 64 (1): 29–63.

2007. 'Do Free Trade Agreements Actually Increase Members' International Trade?' *Journal of International Economics* 71 (1): 72–95.

Baldwin, Richard. 1993. 'A Domino Theory of Regionalism.' NBER Working Papers No. 4465, National Bureau of Economic Research, Cambridge MA.

Baldwin, Richard, and Low, Patrick, eds. 2009. *Multilateralizing Regionalism: Challenges for the Global Trading System.* Cambridge: Cambridge University Press.

Bartels, Lorand, and Ortino, Federico, eds. 2006. *Regional Trade Agreements and the WTO Legal System.* Oxford, England: Oxford University Press.

Bhagwati, Jagdish N. 1991. *The World Trading System at Risk.* Princeton, NJ: Princeton University Press.

Büthe, Tim, and Milner, Helen V. 2008. 'The Politics of Foreign Direct Investment into Developing Countries: Increasing FDI through International Trade Agreements?' *American Journal of Political Science* 52 (4): 741–62.

Chase, Kerry A. 2005. *Trading Blocs: States, Firms, and Regions in the World Economy.* Ann Arbor: University of Michigan Press.

De Melo, Jaime, and Panagariya, Arvind. 1992. *The New Regionalism in Trade Policy: An Interpretive Summary of a Conference.* Washington, DC: World Bank eLibrary.

Downs, George W., Rocke, David M., and Barsoom, Peter N. 1996. 'Is the Good News about Compliance Good News about Cooperation?' *International Organization* 50 (3): 379–406.

Dür, Andreas. 2010. *Protection for Exporters: Power and Discrimination in Transatlantic Trade Relations, 1930–2010.* Ithaca, NY: Cornell University Press.

Dür, Andreas, Baccini, Leonardo, and Elsig, Manfred. 2014. 'The Design of International Trade Agreements: Introducing a New Dataset.' *Review of International Organizations* 9 (3): 353–75.

Egger, Peter, Larch, Mario, Staub, Kevin E., and Winkelmann, Rainer. 2011. 'The Trade Effects of Endogenous Preferential Trade Agreements.' *American Economic Journal: Economic Policy* 3 (3): 113–43.

Estevadeordal, Antoni, Suominen, Kati, and Teh, Robert, eds. 2009. *Regional Rules in the Global Trading System.* Cambridge: Cambridge University Press.

Frankel, Jeffrey. 1997. *Regional Trading Blocs in the World Economic System.* Washington, DC: Institute for International Economics.

Gowa, Joanne. 1994. *Allies, Adversaries, International Trade.* Princeton, NJ: Princeton University Press.

Grossman, Gene M., and Helpman, Elhanan. 1995. 'The Politics of Free Trade Agreements.' *American Economic Review* 85 (4): 667–90.

Hafner-Burton, Emilie M. 2005. 'Trading Human Rights: How Preferential Trade Agreements Influence Government Repression.' *International Organization* 59 (3): 593–629.

2009. *Forced to Be Good: Why Trade Agreements Boost Human Rights.* Ithaca, NY: Cornell University Press.

Haftel, Yoram Z. 2012. *Regional Economic Institutions and Conflict Mitigation: Design, Implementation and the Promise of Peace.* Ann Arbor: University of Michigan Press.

Hicks, Raymond, and Kim, Soo Yeon. 2012. 'Reciprocal Trade Agreements in Asia: Credible Commitment to Trade Liberalization or Paper Tigers?' *Journal of East Asian Studies* 12 (1): 1–29.

Hirschman, Albert O. 1945. *National Power and the Structure of Foreign Trade.* Berkeley: University of California Press.

Horn, Henrik, Mavroidis, Petros, and Sapir, André. 2010. 'Beyond the WTO? An Anatomy of EU and US Preferential Trade Agreements.' *World Economy* 33 (11): 1565–88.

Jackson, John H., ed. 1997. *The World Trading System: Law and Policy of International Economic Relations,* 2nd edn. Cambridge: Cambridge University Press.

Kindleberger, Charles P. 1973. *The World in Depression, 1929–1939.* London: Penguin Press.

Kucik, Jeffrey. 2012. 'The Domestic Politics of Institutional Design: Producer Preferences over Trade Agreement Rules.' *Economics and Politics* 24 (2): 95–118.

Lawrence, Robert. 1996. *Regionalism, Multilateralism, and Deeper Integration.* Washington, DC: Brookings Institution.

Mansfield, Edward D., and Milner, Helen V. 2012. *Votes, Vetoes, and the Political Economy of International Trade Agreements.* Princeton, NJ: Princeton University Press.

Mansfield, Edward D., and Pevehouse, John C. 2000. 'Trade Blocs, Trade Flows, and International Conflict.' *International Organization* 54 (4): 775–808.

Moravcsik, Andrew. 1998. *The Choice for Europe: Social Purpose and State Power from Messina to Maastricht.* Ithaca, NY: Cornell University Press.

Pahre, Robert. 2008. *Politics and Trade Cooperation in the Nineteenth Century: The 'Agreeable Customs' of 1815–1914.* Cambridge: Cambridge University Press.

Panagariya, Arvind. 1999. 'The Regionalism Debate: An Overview.' *World Economy* 22 (4): 455–76.

Peinhardt, Clint, and Allee, Todd. 2012. 'Failure to Deliver: The Investment Effects of U.S. Preferential Economic Agreements.' *World Economy* 35 (6): 757–83.

Spilker, Gabriele, and Böhmelt, Tobias. 2013. 'The Impact of Preferential Trade Agreements on Governmental Repression Revisited.' *Review of International Organizations* 8 (3): 343–61.

Viner, Jacob. 1950. *The Customs Union Issue.* New York: Carnegie Endowment for International Peace.

Whalley, John. 1998. 'Why Do Countries Seek Regional Trade Agreements?' In *The Regionalization of the World Economy*, edited by Jeffrey A. Frankel, 63–89. Chicago: University of Chicago Press.

Wonnacott, Paul, and Lutz, Mark. 1989. 'Is There a Case for Free Trade Areas?' In *Free Trade Areas and U.S. Trade Policy*, edited by Jeffrey J. Schott, 59–84. Washington, DC: Institute for International Economics.

World Trade Organization. 2001. 'Ministerial Declaration.' Ministerial Conference, 4th Session, Doha, 9–14 November. www.wto.org/english/thewto_e/minist_e/min01_e/mindecl_e.htm.

# PART I

## Why do countries sign PTAs?

# 2

# Technology, politics and economic exchanges

## Historical patterns in international economic agreements

MOONHAWK KIM

## A. Introduction

In recent decades, preferential trade agreements (PTAs) have proliferated (Mansfield 1998; Mansfield and Milner 1999, 2012). Unlike the numerous regional agreements formed by groups of three or more closely neighbouring states during the 1960s and 1970s, the latest resurgence has been characterised by bilateral agreements between nonneighbouring states, sometimes between two geographically very remote economies. The proliferation of these agreements has garnered attention from scholars and analysts alike, interested in the causes of their formation and in their effects on trade flows. On the political science side, scholars have focused on domestic institutional factors (e.g. Mansfield, Milner and Pevehouse 2007, 2008), while on the economics side, scholars have focused on 'gravity' factors, namely, economic size and distance (e.g. Baier and Bergstrand 2004; Baier et al. 2008).

Although many of these recent analyses reach back to the beginning of the post–Second World War period, the focus has primarily been on the post–Cold War period when the proliferation began. Such analyses, however, fail to take into account the variation in historical contexts that is likely to have shaped economic actors' and states' behaviour with respect to international economic cooperation. The proliferation of PTAs in the 1990s and 2000s occurred in a specific political and economic context. In this chapter, I seek to address this myopia by examining the historical patterns of economic agreements over the past two centuries.

Whereas Irwin (1993) and Estevadeordal and Suominen (2009) have engaged in a similar endeavour, the novel contribution of this chapter is to propose a single framework within which we can situate the historical evolution of commercial agreements. In particular, I seek to account for the broad patterns in the membership scope of agreements and the types of provisions in the agreements.

I argue that the broader context in which international economic exchanges take place helps account for the variation in these dimensions. In particular, I identify two *infrastructures* that shape such contexts – one is technological and the other is political. Technological infrastructure captures the speed and costs of carrying out cross-border exchanges, more specifically, the costs of transportation. This infrastructure in turn shapes the demand for economic agreements by private actors, as they lobby for interstate governance institutions that can reduce frictions in carrying out economic exchanges. Political infrastructure captures the scope of countries across which private actors can carry out exchanges and the stability with which they can do so. An overall political bargain that exists or not among states at a given time shapes the scope. This infrastructure in turn influences the supply of economic agreements by states. For example, when the political bargains are narrow or unstable, states do not form agreements that are extensive and highly facilitative of economic exchanges. I examine the broad historical patterns of economic agreements since the middle of the nineteenth century.

In the next section, I develop the argument about the role of infrastructures for international economic exchanges. In the discussion, I focus more on the technological infrastructure, which has implications for how economic activities are organised. I also discuss the factors that shape the political infrastructure before generating some broad expectations about the patterns of economic agreements. In the subsequent sections, I trace the changes in the two infrastructures and the characteristics of economic agreements in five historical periods, starting with the post–Industrial Revolution era and ending with the current post–information revolution era. The last section concludes the chapter by summarising the main ideas and offering some speculations about the future.

## B. Infrastructure for exchanges

Economic actors have been engaging in economic exchanges across the borders of political entities for millennia. These exchanges, however, are always embedded in a broader social, economic and political context (Granovetter 1985; Polanyi 2001; Ruggie 1982). In particular, the context in which international economic exchanges take place influences the demand for and the supply of economic agreements. I argue two types of infrastructure are critical – one technological and the other political.

## I. Technological infrastructure

Historically, the three economic activities – production, consumption and exchanges – were usually highly localized. Technological changes lower the costs of transporting factors, goods and information *within* and *across* countries, thereby enabling these activities to take place on a larger scale (Irwin 1993; Waltz 1970). I use the term *technology* broadly here – not only does it include innovations in tangible tools and equipment but also social, economic and organisational innovations that facilitate trans-portation and movement (North 1958). As the movement of "stuff" – both tangibles and intangibles – becomes easier and less costly, actors organise economic activities differently. The transformative effects materialise first within local and domestic economies. The effects then extend to economic activities at the international level.

In this context, *technological infrastructure* influences the costs of making exchanges. The totality of means available at any particular time for transporting stuff from one place to another also structures economic activities that actors carry out at the international level. Enterprising merchants carried out long-distance trade long before steamboats and jet aeroplanes. What limited global trade was the technological constraint of transporting things, especially heavy ones. Merchants engaged in trade of things only when the value-to-weight ratios were high. These were things that were light and easy to transport but also highly valuable, such as spices (Greif 2006). Technological innovations ease these constraints on the value-to-weight ratios and expand international economic activities.

More generally, the technological infrastructure affects three aspects of economic exchanges at the international level. First, as the costs of transportation decrease, the distances across which exchanges take place increase. When transportation is cheaper, economic actors in countries that are farther apart can engage in more trade than before. This increase in geographical distance probably also increases the social and cultural distance between the actors engaging in an exchange.

Second, as discussed previously, the value-to-weight ratio necessary to make a cross-border exchange cost-effective falls. Trade in items with lower values or in heavier items becomes more likely. Accordingly, the composition of items that states trade becomes more diverse (Hummels 2007). Similarly, when transportation is cheaper, the time it takes to carry out an exchange decreases. When goods and factors of production move around the globe faster, economic activities overall, not simply exchanges, happen faster as well.

Third, lower trade costs resulting from technological innovations also alter the structure of trade; that is, whether states carry out trade based on factor endowments or based on economies of scale. Bergstrand and Egger (2006) demonstrate that the share of intra-industry trade – based on economies of scale – increases as transportation costs fall. As Manger (Chapter 8 in this volume) argues, states' trade structure in turn affects whether and how they liberalise trade through trade agreements.

By facilitating exchanges, technological innovations alter two other economic activities as well – consumption and production. In addition to lower costs of consumption, innovations also depersonalise consumption. Whereas the material effects of exchanges taking place over longer distances might be beneficial for the consumer, the psychological effects of consuming products from far-flung places produced by unknown people may offset those benefits. Umaña, Bernauer and Spilker (Chapter 5 in this volume) show that individuals in fact prefer their countries' trade partners to be countries that are geographically and culturally closer.

More prominently, lower costs of transportation around the world lead to significant reorganisation of production. First, firms become able to source their inputs from and sell their outputs to other countries, whereas previously they sourced their inputs and sold their outputs only locally or nationally. Second, as transportation costs decline even further, firms become able to "unbundle" their production (Baldwin 2011). They can separate out their production processes into discrete parts and carry out each component in whichever part of the world is most efficient for that process.

More generally, beyond these two organisational changes, the pace of economic activities and the resulting economic changes quickens as well. When things move faster around the world, economic actors need to respond to changes quickly too. The heightened pace of change also increases the uncertainty that economic actors face. Kucik (Chapter 17 in this volume) maintains that when states design trade agreements with sufficient flexibility, the agreements can shield them from volatility in global markets.

The political implications of these changes occurring over time are significant. First, they alter the politically relevant set of actors. When international trade is based on factor endowments, the cleavages are along factoral lines if factor mobility is high or along sectoral lines if factor mobility is low (Hiscox 2002). As production becomes unbundled, factor endowments become less important and economies of scale become more so. This in turn shifts the political cleavages away from the factoral and sectoral lines. Firms' productivity and competitiveness distinguish them even within the same industry (Melitz and Trefler 2012). The cleavages are along the competitiveness lines, with efficient and exporting firms on the one side and inefficient import-competing ones on the other.

Second, the nature of economic competition changes along with the changes in the organisation of production. Initial competition in the international economy was related to market *access*. States controlled their borders and competed over gaining and granting access to other states' markets. Conflicts and cooperation related to 'at-the-border' measures. Unbundling of production – in part facilitated by the reduction of the at-the-border measures – shifts the focus of competition to within markets. Rather than market access, *market structure* becomes the new focus. Conflicts and cooperation relate to 'behind-the-border' measures, to how competitive an industry is and to how regulatory measures affect the concentration of market power in national economies. Kim (Chapter 6 in this volume) and Bradford and Büthe (Chapter 10 in this volume) offer a closer examination of such deep integration efforts in trade agreements with regard to investment and competition, respectively.

## II. Political infrastructure

Whereas technological infrastructure reflects the technical costs of economic exchanges, political infrastructure indicates the political possibilities and constraints for economic exchanges. Political infrastructure summarises the scope and stability of the beneficial exchanges economic actors can carry out in the world. *Scope* refers to the number of political entities – states – across which economic actors can engage in exchanges, and *stability* refers to whether the exchanges can be interrupted or prevented through political intervention of one or more states.

Numerous factors shape the political infrastructure for economic exchanges during a given period. Mansfield and Milner (Chapter 3 in this volume) examine some of these factors in greater detail. Here, I briefly discuss four factors. First, political economic ideologies affect political infrastructure. For example, mercantilism, the ideology that reigned prior to the nineteenth century, greatly limited the scope and stability of beneficial economic exchanges. Economic activities were to serve the state and exchanges were deemed to be zero-sum (Gilpin 1987).

Second, the international distribution of power affects political infrastructure. The presence of a hegemon can ensure wide scope and high stability of economic exchanges, even if the hegemon's reach is not fully global

(Keohane 1997; Krasner 1976; Lake 1984, 1993). This facilitates formation of commercial agreements. Correspondingly, absence of a hegemon
can create uncertainty and instability in the global economy, reducing
the combination of partners with whom states can form economic agreements. This argument is in contrast to Mansfield and Milner's argument
that hegemonic decline leads to increases in trade agreements.

Third, war and violent conflicts shape political infrastructure (Findlay
and O'Rourke 2009). Such conflicts reduce the scope of exchanges by creating or reestablishing enmity among states. They also reduce the stability
of exchanges by creating the expectation that one or both states would
intervene to interrupt the economic exchanges between the hostile states.
Although I do not address the reverse causality, commercial agreements
can affect the likelihood of violent conflicts as well (Haftel, Chapter 12 in
this volume).

Fourth, international institutions for governing economic relations
can provide political infrastructure. In conjunction with the incumbent
hegemon, or in its stead, institutions can promote cooperation among a
sizeable and growing membership of countries and safeguard the stability
of those exchanges (Keohane 1984), thereby maintaining a large scope for
exchanges among countries.

### III. Demand for and supply of international commercial agreements

Combining the two infrastructures for economic exchanges, I argue the
following. Whereas the technological infrastructure shapes economic
actors' demand for commercial agreements, the political infrastructure
shapes states' supply of them.

A key premise in this argument is that the extent of the market is mis-
matched with the extent of governance. The former always exceeds the latter. Given the mismatch, private actors will demand additional governance
to reduce frictions and inefficiencies in their organisation of production.
In this context, the technological infrastructure determines the features
of economic agreements that economic actors demand. These actors will
demand governance features that will enable full exploitation of the technological possibilities to increase or maintain their competitiveness with
respect to others. As production and transportation technologies change,
the actors' demands will evolve accordingly.

Whether states can and do form economic agreements with features that private actors demand is determined by the extant political infrastructure. Some conditions – mercantilism, wars, absence of a

hegemon – inhibit or constrain the formation of agreements, whereas others – liberalism and presence of a hegemon and of a multilateral institution – foster formation of agreements. Accordingly, attributes of political infrastructure help to account for how prevalent economic agreements are during a given period. Moreover, the partnerships in economic agreements are likely to be explained by the scope of political infrastructure, whether it is global, regional or more limited.

In this manner, examining both the technological and the political infrastructures for economic exchanges can help explain the overall patterns of economic agreements. In particular, in the following section, I examine the partnerships (bilateral or regional) and the provisions (e.g. tariffs, investments, regulations).

## C. Evolution of infrastructures and agreements

I examine five sequential periods. These are the post–Industrial Revolution (1840–1914), post–World War I (1920s and 1930s), post–World War II (1947–90), post–Cold War (1991–2000) and post–information revolution (2001–13) periods.

These periods match up with the types of trade that states and economic actors engaged in. During the first period, most exchanges were based on the factor endowments of countries (Heckscher–Ohlin trade). After the interlude of the interwar years, economic actors quickly moved towards intra-industry trade (Krugman 1979) and 'new' trade. In the post–Cold War years, firms began to emerge as the key actors of interest in the international economy (Bernard *et al.* 2007), and this can be termed 'new new' trade.

### I. Post–Industrial Revolution period (1840–1914)

This was the first era of globalisation, facilitated by both the Industrial Revolution and the transport revolution. Both innovations increased the pace of economic activities and changes. Economic activities became more complex, with manufacturing increasingly involving imported inputs. Although Great Britain provided political stability as the undisputed leader of this era, it did not guarantee stability that would have allowed economic actors to anticipate engaging in long-term exchanges. A consequence of this highly competitive yet politically stable environment was the spread of generally weak bilateral trade agreements.

## 1. Technological infrastructure

Until the end of the eighteenth century, the world economy was largely characterised by the mercantilist policies of the powerful states. As Findlay and O'Rourke argue, by the year 1000 CE, most of the interregional trade routes were in place. Between the years 1500 and 1800, trade increased on the extensive margins with new trade routes developing among regions that previously had not been trading. During the nineteenth century, however, the international economy changed drastically. 'As a result of the Industrial Revolution, the *intensity* of these interactions [in interregional trade] would increase at a historically unprecedented rate' (Findlay and O'Rourke 2009: 365–6).

The principal technological innovation during this period was in transportation. O'Rourke and Williamson document the 'transport revolution' in detail (1999: Chap. 3), and they highlight three major transformations – steamships, railroads and refrigeration. All three enabled movement of a greater variety of goods, over longer distances, for lower costs. As the economic data broadly show, Findlay and O'Rourke maintain that 'the new transport technologies were so cost-reducing that their effects swamped those of rising European and American protectionism' (Findlay and O'Rourke 2009: 402).[1]

These and other innovations resulting from the Industrial Revolution had more specific and far-reaching consequences for the organisation of production. One of the most visible consequences was the development of large-scale factories and the corresponding urbanisation of countries. In addition to transportation, a series of innovations in spinning, weaving and bleaching also led to an increase in the production of cotton textiles, the industry leading the revolution at the time (Findlay and O'Rourke 2009: 319–20). The innovations spread to other parts of Europe – a spread which Great Britain initially attempted to thwart because 'the growth of the cotton textile industry in Europe was based on replacing imports of British cotton fabric with imports of British cotton yarn' (325).

The sequencing of industrialisation and technological changes across Europe had consequences for the organisation of production as well. Because Britain mechanised first and other European countries did so later, 'a "vertical" division of labor appeared with these countries importing industrial raw materials and semifinished goods such as cotton and

---

[1]  Harley (1988) collects and analyses the sources of changes in ocean freight costs during this period and argues against North (1958).

worsted yarn, iron billets, bars, and girders as intermediate inputs from Britain' (Findlay and O'Rourke 2009: 326–7).

## 2. Political infrastructure

This was the era of British hegemony. The multifaceted nature of British leadership was apparent. As the birthplace of the Industrial Revolution, Britain was the industrial leader. It also led in finances and in its military supremacy. Along with the end of the Napoleonic Wars and the settlements reached at the Congress of Vienna in 1815, British leadership created a world in which actors could engage in economic exchanges worldwide.

Whatever openness that Britain pursued, however, was probably the result of its domestic interests rather than to some deep and newfound ideological commitment to liberalism (Findlay and O'Rourke 2009: 101). Morrison (2012) argues that Britain opened up its trade long before the repeal of the Corn Laws in 1846. More critically, Nye (2007) argues that characterisation of Britain as a free-trader is misplaced – Britain in fact had higher tariffs than France did in nonmanufactured goods.

More generally, a comparison to the second half of the twentieth century is useful. In addition to the uncertain strength of Britain's commitment to openness, the era lacked a multilateral institution for governing and managing interstate trade relations. Irwin (1993: 101) maintains that 'there was no primary sponsor with the economic standing or diplomatic ability or willingness to cajole or manage the arrangement, to punish defectors or free-riders, or to consolidate the abundance of bilateral treaties'.

In short, the political infrastructure facilitated broad scope of exchange worldwide, but the actors did not have an expectation of long-term stability in those exchanges. The pace of the technological changes rapidly altered trade patterns, periodically bringing new, efficient and large-scale producers to the international market. No guarantee existed as to whether an economy that was open one day would remain open the next day. In other words, although economic actors were free to engage in international trade with others, the relationships were precarious.

## 3. Patterns of economic agreements: competition for weak bilateralism

The rapidly changing technological context compelled states to adapt quickly, but the resulting cooperation would be fragile because of the absence of an institution to pursue and manage further liberalisation.

The pattern of economic agreements anticipated by these technological and political infrastructures is the following: states would pursue rapid but fragile bilateral cooperation to maintain their competitiveness. The infrastructures argument also expects the cooperation to be bilateral to enable states to retain the flexibility to alter their trade policies on a partner-by-partner basis.

Economic agreements during this time – usually incorporating the most-favoured-nation (MFN) principle (Pahre 2001) – spread quickly throughout a network (Lazer 1999) but did not succeed in maintaining liberal trade through economically hard times (Irwin 1993) and in fact probably did not generate systematic effects on trade flows (Accominotti and Flandreau 2008).

When the pace of change in economic activities is fast, states are expected to respond rapidly to any marginal changes that affect the competitiveness of their domestic firms. One state forming a trade agreement with another immediately creates discriminatory treatment against all its other trade partners. The excluded states have an incentive to reduce or eliminate the discrimination through an agreement of their own. This dynamic is heightened when the agreements incorporate the MFN provision, allowing others with MFN status to receive the tariff treatments negotiated between two parties. Lazer (1999) advances this argument, and similar arguments have been advanced for the twentieth-century trade agreements as well (Baldwin and Jaimovich 2010; e.g. Bergsten 1996; Egger and Larch 2008). The cascading effect of this dynamic leads to a rapid spread of agreements and formation of a dense network.

Irwin (1993) points out the deficiencies of these agreements, highlighting that international economic cooperation was in fact quite fragile. He identifies a host of characteristics: the lack of further liberalisation after the initial agreements, the absence of any limits on tariff rates or hikes in those rates and the frequent inclusion of expiration or renegotiation clauses.

Koremenos (2001) argues that expiration and renegotiation clauses facilitate interstate cooperation by offering the parties flexibility when the future state of the world is uncertain. The frequent use of these provisions in the nineteenth-century agreements is consistent with the expectations of the infrastructures argument. The rapidly changing economic context led states to be hesitant about committing to a long-term agreement. Data from Pahre (2008) show that many agreements had provisions for expiration after 6, 10 or 12 years. States designed some treaties to last only 3 or 4 years. Moreover, as the practice of international law has always allowed, states were permitted to withdraw from or denounce most treaties if they gave a 12-month, or sometimes shorter, period of notice to the other party.

## II. Post–World War I period (1920s and 1930s)

Wars can destroy physical implementations of technologies, but not the technologies themselves. States could repair damaged transportation systems (Hynes, Jacks and O'Rourke 2009) but could not easily restore the domestic and the international political dynamics that had been transformed during and because of the war. The absence of political infrastructure – the lack of economic actors' ability to carry out broad and stable economic exchanges – shaped the economic agreements states concluded during this period.

### 1. Technological infrastructure

The technological innovations and progress that came about during the nineteenth century did not disappear during the First World War. All the benefits of the transportation revolution remained, and the technological infrastructure for international economic exchanges survived. The critical difference during this period was the absence of political infrastructure among states at the global level.

### 2. Political infrastructure

World War I's longer-term impact on international trade was disastrous. In particular, Findlay and O'Rourke (2009: 435) argue that the war 'changed the nature of domestic and international politics, as well as the structures of individual economies, in such a way to make it much more difficult, if not impossible, to return to the "normalcy" of the late nineteenth century'. Thus, although there was no reversal of the innovations in the technological infrastructures that expanded exchanges during the nineteenth century, the destruction of the political infrastructure set the context for international exchanges during this period. Findlay and O'Rourke outline a series of changes that occurred as a result of the war, but the most important consequence was that the political and economic changes made a return to the pre-1914 gold standard difficult (436–41).

States' inability to restore the gold standard of the nineteenth century led to the absence of stable exchange rates. This in turn reduced the scope and stability of the exchanges economic actors could carry out. As James (2002: 116) argues, 'Worldwide currency and financial instability in the early 1920s made for very rapidly changing cost calculations.' Moreover, although trade recovered somewhat in the 1920s, growth in exchanges required movement of capital. 'In the 1930s, when such capital was no longer available because of changes in the world's financial markets, the growth rates of trade collapsed' (103–4).

The shift in focus to domestic political economy after the war resulted from two sets of sources, one political and the other economic. The political reasons were twofold. One was the wartime legacy of self-sufficiency, the need for which countries realised after having engaged in a war that lasted much longer than they initially anticipated (James 2002: 110). The other was the democratisation of domestic politics and the concomitant rise of trade unions (Findlay and O'Rourke 2009: 439–40). The economic reason is closely tied to the *attempted* monetary arrangement at the time. Irwin (2012) argues – drawing on his earlier work with Eichengreen (2009) – that states' attempts to maintain the gold standard led to protectionist policies.

In short, an overarching political infrastructure at the international level was lacking during the 1920s and the 1930s. States' endeavour to create such an infrastructure also failed. James (2002: 109) points out that international conferences in 1927 and 1933 and the efforts of the League of Nations Economic and Financial Committee to counter the movement to restrict international trade failed. In the aftermath of the Smoot–Hawley tariffs in the United States, some states desired to liberalise trade. However, the issue was intertwined with other economic issues, such as debt and reparations, which limited the success of states' negotiations. Moreover, the continuing belief among political leaders that trade liberalisation necessitated unconditional MFN 'militated against the success' of states bargaining to lower their trade barriers (James 2002: 120). No one was willing to multilateralise their trade liberalisation through the application of the MFN norm.

## 3. Patterns of economic agreements: political and economic blocs

Given that the political infrastructure was utterly lacking at the global level during this period despite the presence of the technological infrastructure for extensive exchanges, the argument in this chapter anticipates very limited economic agreements, especially in terms of the partnerships that could form. At best, states would conclude agreements with others with whom they anticipated engaging in stable exchanges over time.

The economic agreements during this period took on a particular form, reflecting the limited political infrastructure. Irwin (2012) points out that 'most of the "trade blocs" of the period were rooted not so much in discriminatory tariff treatment as in quota allocations, clearing arrangements, payments deals, and currency linkages' (138–9). These ended up being de facto discrimination with respect to current account activities.

In addition to the extensive discussion by Eichengreen (1996), Gowa and Hicks (2013: 464) provide a table of trade blocs and their membership. The currency blocs – gold bloc, sterling bloc – and the exchange control bloc came about as a function of states' relationship with the gold standard or their relationship with the dominant trade partner. Two other arrangements were more intentional and explicitly political. Britain formed the Imperial Preference System (IPS), and Germany formed the Reichsmark (RM) bloc.

The United States was not part of any of the trade and currency blocs. In 1934, the US Congress passed the Reciprocal Trade Agreements Act (RTAA). Bailey, Goldstein and Weingast (1997) advance an institutional account of how the RTAA solved a domestic political problem and locked in a balance in favour of liberalisation. Schnietz (2003) supports this explanation, whereas Hiscox (1999) argues against the 'magic bullet' institutionalist argument.

The passage of the RTAA – which on its own only reconfigured trade policymaking procedures in the United States – is more fully understood in the context of the lack of political infrastructure for international exchanges and other states' responses to it. The RTAA created the platform on which the United States could create a stable infrastructure for exchanges at the international level, if only for states that were willing to engage in negotiations with it. Before the start of the Second World War, the United States negotiated 21 reciprocal agreements under the RTAA (Brown 1950: 20). Despite the initial negotiating successes, the United States had trouble finding partners outside the Americas, except for a few European ones. This hurdle further demonstrated the lack of a broader political infrastructure. Given the origins of the trade and currency arrangements during this period, the fact that they had no systematic impact on trade flows is understandable (Gowa and Hicks 2013).

## III. Post–World War II period (1947–1990)

This is the period that heralded the second era of globalisation. Just as the benefits of the first era were mainly confined to the two sides of the Atlantic, the benefits of this era were limited mainly to the Western economies. The contest between the Soviet Union and the United States effectively divided the world economy. The United States and the new multilateral institution governing trade – General Agreement on Tariffs and Trade (GATT) – provided expectations of wide and stable international exchange around the world. Key technological innovations amplified the importance of economies of scale and diminished the role of factor-endowment-based comparative advantage.

### 1. Technological infrastructure

The era after the Second World War did not experience a dramatic revolution in transportation as the nineteenth century had done. This, however, does not diminish the significance of the innovations that occurred during this period, namely, jet aircraft engines and containerisation of shipping goods (Hummels 2007: 132). Hummels best summarises the consequences of these changes for organisation of production: 'Improvements in the quality of transportation services – like greater speed and reliability – allow corresponding reorganizations of global networks of production and new ways of coping with uncertainty in foreign markets.'

Air transportation experienced rapid changes, 'including improvements in avionics, wing design, materials, and most importantly the adoption of jet engines' (Hummels 2007: 137). Citing Gordon (1990), Hummels argues that much of the price decline in air transport resulting from these changes took place during the early part of the period (1955–72), coinciding with the introduction of jet engines.

Ocean shipping experienced significant changes as well. Hummels catalogues three factors (Hummels 2007: 140–1). First, open registry allowing ships to register under 'flags of convenience' – that is, countries with lower regulatory costs – lowered operating costs by 12 to 27 per cent. Second, the increasing amount of trade created a scale effect in which each ocean liner could fill its capacity without making multiple stops in different countries. Last, 'containerized shipping is thought by many specialists to be one of the most important transportation revolutions in the twentieth century' (141). It lowered overall transportation costs, as goods could travel long distances by diverse modes of transportation without requiring repacking. By reducing the time that ships spent docked at ports, containerisation also enabled bigger and faster ships to be cost-effective.

These changes restructured production in significant ways. As Hummels *et al.* (2001) argue, one of the key effects was the vertical specialisation of production, which enabled firms to carry out each stage of manufacturing in a different country. The lowering of transportation costs facilitated this reorganisation. Hummels *et al.* (2001) show that for 10 developed and 4 developing countries, vertical specialisation accounted for 21 per cent of their exports, and such specialization increased 30 per cent between 1970 and 1990. In the authors' framework, the production chain need not be long: a country using an input imported from another to produce a good for export to a third country constitutes vertical specialisation. Although such production networks later became more sophisticated and complex, the foundation for decentralised systems of organising production was created during this period.

This reorganisation in conjunction with the decline in transportation costs reduced the importance of comparative advantage in factor endowments and intensified the importance of economies of scale. On the one hand, firms could locate each component of the production process in those places that possessed the comparative advantage in that component. On the other hand, firms placed greater emphasis on reducing the average cost of production by increasing the output. Consequently, the size of markets to which firms could sell became increasingly important.

## 2. Political infrastructure

The political infrastructure of international exchanges is characterised by two related components – the hegemony of the United States, at least in the Western Hemisphere, and the presence of a multilateral institution for governing international trade. As Goldstein and Gowa (2002) argue, the United States in the years immediately after the end of the Second World War faced a commitment problem with respect to its overwhelming power in the world economy. Other states were uncertain as to whether the United States would abuse its market power over smaller economies and behave opportunistically. The United States initially sought to make a credible commitment to keeping its markets open by advocating and creating institutional constraints against itself through the proposed International Trade Organization (ITO). This need for an external commitment mechanism receded when the onset of the Cold War required the United States to maintain openness to its allies.

Throughout much of this period, the United States' security-driven commitment to a liberal international economy in part provided the political infrastructure for international economic exchanges. Firms based in various states in the Western world could engage in extensive economic exchanges with the assurance that such exchanges would continue to take place. Indeed, cross-border economic flows grew steadily throughout this period.

Multilateral governance of trade, through the GATT, supplemented the US commitment to liberalism by providing the political infrastructure for economic exchanges. Keohane (1984) argues that the institution in fact maintained the commitment to openness even in the face of the decline in US hegemony and the corresponding weakening of the state's commitment to an open economy. Bargaining among member states through multiple negotiating rounds successfully lowered trade barriers over the postwar decades (Barton *et al.* 2006).

The provision of political infrastructure under both the US commitment and multilateral governance, however, waned towards the end of this period, most notably during the last decade before the end of the Cold War. Perhaps because of the détente between the United States and the Soviet Union beginning at the end of the 1960s or because of the erosion of US hegemony with the rapid recovery of the European and Japanese states, US commitment to a liberal international economy diminished over time. During the 1980s, the United States continuously relied on unilateral trade policies and trade remedies rather than on seeking to resolve trade conflicts at the GATT (Goldstein and Gowa 2002: 159).

Correspondingly, the GATT also suffered from increasing noncompliance among members (Lipson 1982) and from the difficulty in successfully concluding negotiations among an expanding membership (Kahler 1992). The declining strength of the GATT is also confirmed in a quantitative analysis of institutional effects. Goldstein, Rivers and Tomz (2007) show that the GATT had the greatest impact on trade flows during its early years and that the effect then steadily declined.[2]

In short, for much of the period, the political infrastructure for international economic exchanges was strong and stable. In its contest against the Soviet Union, the United States guaranteed an open economy in the Western world. The GATT channelled and supplemented that guarantee

---

[2] Goldstein, Rivers and Tomz (2007) are part of a wider ongoing debate on whether and how the GATT/WTO affects trade flows. See, e.g., Gowa and Kim (2005), Liu (2009), Rose (2004), and Tomz, Goldstein and Rivers (2007).

and maintained the expectations of stability under which economic actors could engage in exchanges. This infrastructure did weaken towards the end of the period, but states sought to bolster it by negotiating stronger rules and procedures in the multilateral institution, some of the results of which states had reaped by the end of the period (Croome 1999).

## 3. Patterns of economic agreements: emulating the European Community

The political infrastructure of the period guaranteed stable international exchanges among numerous countries in the world. The technological infrastructure strengthened the importance of economies of scale, which in turn focused attention on the size of the internal markets that firms had access to. The expectation for economic agreements based on these characteristics of the infrastructure is that states would seek to increase their internal market size by forming agreements with their neighbours. This is the logic that Chase (2003) advances in the context of US firms' support of the North American Free Trade Agreement (NAFTA) and Milner (1997) advances more generally.[3] Some firms prefer to increase their competitiveness by moderately increasing the size of the market to the regional level before confronting stronger competition at the global level. This allows them to increase production and reduce the average cost, thereby exploiting economies of scale. Regional economic integration is the means to pursue this strategy, balancing negotiations costs and market size.

Consistent with this expectation, the dominant form of economic agreements in this era was regional economic organisations (REOs). These are agreements among three or more economies in geographical proximity seeking to cooperate on economic policies, including and transcending trade policies. Many of these organisations may have mimicked the European Community in an effort to replicate this entity's success. The argument in this chapter provides an alternative logic for why groups of states pursued regional integration.

Among the 47 agreements signed between 1957 and 1990, 40 per cent (19 of them) created a form of REO.[4] Examples include the Arab Maghreb Union, Economic Community of Great Lakes Countries (CEPGL, in

---

[3] See also Milner (1988) and Estevadeordal and Suominen (2009).
[4] The data on agreements are from three combined sources – the World Trade Organization (WTO) Regional Trade Agreements Information System (RTA-IS), the World Bank's Global Preferential Trade Agreements Database (GPTAD) and McGill University's Preferential and Regional Trade Agreements Database.

French), European Free Trade Association (EFTA) and South Pacific Regional Trade and Economic Cooperation Agreement (SPARTECA). The next highest category was the 13 bilateral agreements that the European Community signed with various countries around the world such as Andorra (1990), Iceland (1972) and Syria (1977), constituting 28 per cent of the agreements. By contrast, only 9 agreements were purely bilateral.

The argument in this chapter differs from the extensive literature on whether regional/preferential agreements are 'stumbling blocks' or 'building blocks' (Baldwin 2008; Bhagwati 2008; Viner 1950; Winters 1996). The infrastructures argument identifies the multilateral institution as fostering and encouraging regionalism by creating an increasingly competitive global economy, within which firms, states and regions compete, compelling states to pursue economic integration. In this manner, the argument is consistent with what Cottier, Sieber-Gasser and Wermelinger (Chapter 19 in this volume) argue. The argument also points out that the domino theory of trade agreements (Baldwin 1995; Baldwin and Jaimovich 2010; Bergsten 1996; Lazer 1999) is spurious in that the source of competitive pressure is not other regional and preferential agreements but the multilateral trading system.

## IV. Post–Cold War period (1991–2000)

This was a period of major political and economic changes. The Cold War rivalry between the United States and the Soviet Union ended without a major conflict. The third wave of democracy swept around the world. Technological changes ushered in the era of the information revolution. This was also the main period of proliferation of bilateral trade agreements.

### 1. Technological infrastructure

Along with the end of the Cold War, which brought optimism about the state of the world, rapidly evolving technological innovations contributed to hopefulness about peaceful interdependence of the countries of the world. Although perhaps too much of a cheerleader for technology, Friedman (2005: Chap. 2) identifies the 10 relevant innovations.Some of the changes he highlights relate to flow of information, while others focus on how the new information flows in turn enabled commerce and businesses to restructure. The fundamental changes in information flows he identifies are the following: the Internet and search engines, interoperability among software packages and the democratisation of information technology through personal and mobile devices.

These 'flatteners', as Friedman calls them, facilitated other flatteners, namely, new ways of organising production. The information flows empowered sophisticated organisation of logistics – moving goods and services from one place to another – as demonstrated by the prominent rise of the United Parcel Service (UPS). More generally, during the 1990s, firms began to accelerate outsourcing and offshoring parts of their businesses.

Combining these strategies, supply chains increase the efficiency of production and lower the costs by producing components in different parts of the world and linking them together through advanced systems of shipping and delivery. Actors reorganised production in response to falling costs of transportation. Initially, production increasingly relied on imported inputs (i.e., offshoring and outsourcing) after which the entire production process became dispersed to various parts of the world economy (i.e., supply chains).

In this context, the reach of multinational corporations grew further and the pace of economic changes grew faster. Firms' competitiveness in this context required that they adapt to the rapidly changing conditions and reduce as much friction in their transactions as possible.

## 2. Political infrastructure

The fall of the Soviet Union did initially create some expectation that a liberal order would reign in the global economy (Fukuyama 2006). The end of the Cold War, however, also saw the end of the exogenous commitment mechanism, which ensured that the United States would maintain open markets and facilitate international economic exchanges. At the beginning of this period, the negotiations to strengthen the multilateral governance of trade were mired in difficulties. The instability in the political infrastructure from the previous period carried over to the start of this period.

Given the asymmetrically dominant power of the United States and the corresponding commitment problem over maintaining an open economy that reemerged for the state, Goldstein and Gowa (2002) argue that the United States sought a commitment device in creating the World Trade Organization (WTO). As it had with the original design of the ITO after the Second World War, the United States vested greater authority in the institution, strengthened the dispute settlement procedures and continued to allow the questionable exemption of PTAs.

Although in many ways the WTO did not ultimately reduce the asymmetry of power among its members, the redesigned multilateral institution governing trade created stable expectations about continued economic exchanges at the international level. The political infrastructure that the institution provided, however, was narrower than what the economic conditions demanded. As described previously, the dramatic changes in information technology led to significant reorganisation of production. This reorganisation in turn involved and impinged on international economic activities beyond those states governed initially through the GATT and subsequently through the WTO.

### 3. Patterns of economic agreements: bilateral regulatory competition

The expectation about the pattern of economic agreements based on the technological and political infrastructures during this period is that states would engage in bilateral regulatory competition. Economic actors' competitiveness depended on reducing friction in all of their relevant economic activities. For two complementary reasons, the behind-the-border measures – that is, domestic regulatory policies – gained in importance during this period. Successful liberalisation of at-the-border measures led states to impose greater regulatory barriers as well as reveal their underlying differences in domestic regulations.

The increased importance of regulatory differences created a constituency of economic actors that sought to reduce them. Although, with the creation of the WTO, states incorporated more regulatory policies into the institution, further cooperation at the WTO was hampered by differences between the North and the South. This created an opportunity for economic agreements outside the WTO to coordinate on regulatory measures.

This chapter's argument anticipates that regulatory competition would be bilateral in nature. The heightened regulatory competition among states required them to react quickly and flexibly in forming commercial agreements. As the experiences of the Uruguay Round of trade negotiations demonstrated, multilateral agreements through the GATT/WTO could provide neither the speed nor the adaptability needed to enable states to compete in forming trade agreements.

This logic on the part of a few key states, however, had the potential of igniting a spread of bilateral agreements like the one during the nineteenth century. A state coordinating on regulatory measures with another would create de facto discrimination with respect to all its other trade partners.

The breakdown in the categories of agreements signed during this period is consistent with these expectations about the dominance of bilateralism. Among the 188 agreements signed during this period, nearly 60 per cent were bilateral agreements – agreements between two states. The mean year of signing bilateral agreements during this period was 1996. That was also the year when states signed the largest number of bilateral agreements. Bilateral agreements that the European Union (EU) signed with a state or another REO constitute another 11 per cent. Similarly, other REOs signed bilateral agreements with a state or another REO, accounting for approximately 14 per cent of all the agreements. Formation or expansion of REOs constitute the remaining 15 per cent.

Horn, Mayroidis and Sapir (2010) highlight the increased emphasis of bilateral economic agreements on regulatory measures in their comparison of trade agreements concluded by the EU and the United States. They distinguish provisions in agreements that build on those contained in the WTO (WTO+) versus provisions in agreements that the WTO agreements currently do not cover (WTO-X). Among WTO+ rules, those concerning sanitary and phytosanitary (SPS) policies and technical barriers to trade (TBT) relate closely to domestic regulatory policies. Among the 14 agreements signed by the EU, 8 contain SPS rules and all of them contain TBT rules. Among the 14 agreements signed by the United States, 13 contain SPS rules, TBT rules or both.

The pattern is more interesting among the WTO-X provisions. Horn *et al.* identify 38 policy areas and code the number of provisions in trade agreements that fall into each of these areas. The policy areas range from anticorruption and labour market regulations to terrorism and visa and asylum. Each EU agreement has WTO-X provisions that cover an average of 22 of these 38 areas. By contrast, each US agreement has WTO-X provisions that cover an average of only 6 of these 38 areas. Analysis of a broader sample by Kohl (2012) provides consistent characterisation of trade agreements in terms of the focus on regulatory measures. These systematic differences in the design of PTAs are consistent with what Baccini, Dür and Haftel (Chapter 7 in this volume) find.

The gap between the technological infrastructure and the political infrastructure also helps account for the increasing blending of trade and investment in how states govern their economic activities. However, a more direct political economic relationship exists between the two forms of economic exchanges. With pure outsourcing, in which firms from different countries engage in contractual relationships, trade agreements can facilitate the economic exchanges. When firms in one country seek to carry out production in a different country via foreign direct investment (FDI), these firms have an interest in protecting and promoting their investment abroad. Bilateral investment treaties (BITs) provide such protection and increase capital flows (e.g. Elkins, Guzman and Simmons 2006).

The importance of investments is reflected in the dramatic rise of BITs during this time period. In the data combined from the records of the International Centre for Settlement of Investment Disputes (ICSID) and the United Nations Conference on Trade and Development (UNCTAD), states signed a total of 3079 BITs between 1959 and 2012. States signed more than 51 per cent of these agreements during the decade after the end of the Cold War. States signed 426 additional agreements in the three years after the end of this period (2001–3), accounting for an additional 14 per cent.

When firms engage in vertical FDI and trade, their interests straddle promotion of both trade and investment. This is the argument that Hicks and Johnson (2013) advance for the rise of 'investment-inclusive PTAs' (IIPTAs), or trade agreements that include extensive investment provisions (Manger 2012). They provide the relative frequency of three types of trade agreements – conventional ones, ones that mention investment and IIPTAs. During the 1990s, states created 124 conventional agreements, 22 of which included mention of investment, and 8 IIPTAs. During the 2000s, states created 70 conventional agreements, 18 of which mentioned investment, and 48 IIPTAs.

### V. Post–information revolution period (2001–2013)

The years since 2000 have been complex. On the technological side, the information revolution of the 1990s culminated and spread. This led to widespread formation of production networks and reliance on global value chains. On the political side, the terrorist attacks of 11 September 2001 shaped much of the international political climate for the subsequent decade. The period has also been characterised by the long-drawn-out process of the Doha Round of multilateral trade negotiations and the countless attempts to resuscitate it. Increases in conventional trade agreements were slower during this period, but new forms of economic integration are emerging.

## 1. Technological infrastructure

One of the world flatteners that Friedman (2005) discussed was the supply chain and sophisticated logistics of companies such as UPS and FedEx. Although these firms emerged in the 1990s, in the years since the bursting of the 'dot-com bubble' in 2000 they came of age. Even companies such as Apple – now synonymous with fully globalised production of electronic gadgets – manufactured computers domestically until the late 1990s. The company shut down its last US manufacturing facility in Elk Grove, California, only in 2004, at which point most of its manufacturing took place in Chinese factories.[5]

As discussed earlier, Baldwin (2011) characterises this as 'unbundling' of production. This has resulted in complex forms of supply chains, which some refer to as 'production networks'. These are 'group[s] of interconnected firms that are dispersed across different countries, in which each firm contributes to a different stage of the manufacturing process depending on the relative cost advantage of their locations' (Kim, Chapter 6 in this volume). Others refer to 'global value chains' (GVCs), which consist of firms 'producing items with components sourced from around the globe' (Elms and Low 2013: 1). Although firms have been engaging in such activities for centuries, what Elms and Low argue is that these activities are different now in terms of 'speed, scale, depth and breadth of global interactions' (1).

Elms (2013) argues that rules governing international economic flows among states have fallen way behind the economic activities on the ground. In addition to the insufficient incorporation of services and investments or coordination of standards in extant agreements, even the rules about traditional trade policies – that is, those about tariffs – conflict with GVCs. Extending this logic, Kim (Chapter 6 in this volume) argues that the spread of production networks has led to trade agreements with deeper integration.

## 2. Political infrastructure

The optimism of the 1990s had fully subsided by this point. The Internet-driven economy did not prove to be the panacea that economic actors once expected it to be. The main turning point came in 2001 with the terrorist attacks on the World Trade Center towers in New York and on

---

[5] 'A Short History of Apple's Manufacturing in the U.S.,' *Wall Street Journal*, 6 December 2012.

the Pentagon. International conflicts were no longer among two or more states but between states on the one hand and terrorist organisations such as Al-Qaeda on the other. This increased the importance of cooperation among states over security-related issues for the remainder of the period.

The prominence of security issues did not undermine or detract from states' attempt to strengthen the multilateral governance of international trade. In November 2001 in Doha, Qatar, the governments of the WTO Members agreed to launch a new multilateral negotiating round. This was in stark contrast to the Ministerial Conference in Seattle two years before, where widespread protests accompanied member governments' disagreement over the terms under which a new negotiation round was to be launched.

In the 13 years since the launch of the Doha Round, members have failed to make substantial progress that would allow them to complete the deal. What has become clear is that in the foreseeable future, states will not be able to advance international trade governance through 'legislative' means; that is, by creating new rules through bargaining. The remaining means of liberalisation, Goldstein and Steinberg (2009) argue, is through the judicial approach, where states maintain and perhaps advance liberalisation by litigating over the existing set of rules.

Thus, although actors maintain expectations about the broad scope of international economic exchanges, these expectations are precarious. Especially with the global financial crisis that damaged the world economy in 2007–8, and whose repercussions continue to affect many economies, the general consensus on the benefits of unqualified open economy has diminished.

### 3. Patterns of economic agreements: resurgence of regionalism

The technological and political infrastructures lead states to pursue a particular form of interstate economic agreements. At the beginning of the period – characterised by continued importance of and linkages between trade and investment – economic agreements dealing with both activities flourished. In the 2000s, investment-inclusive PTAs were the only type of PTA whose absolute counts of new agreements increased. An overwhelming majority of the IIPTAs signed during this period are bilateral (Hicks and Johnson 2013: 48). Some involve existing REOs, such as the EU, EFTA and the Caribbean Community (CARICOM). Among the 34 IIPTAs signed between 2001 and 2007, 29 are purely bilateral agreements between two states.

Another aspect of trade agreements, at least those by the United States, during this period is the linkage between trade and security. Aggarwal (2013: 104) asserts that a set of US PTAs involved security linkages as the main element. More strongly, Ludema (2007) argues that security concerns dominated US PTA strategy. This is consistent with the preeminence of interest in security and terrorism issues during this period.

Whereas the dominant form of international economic integration during the 1990s and early 2000s was bilateral PTAs, the emerging form of integration is regionalism. Capling and Ravenhill (2011) identify the problem succinctly. Although trade agreements in the Asia–Pacific region have proliferated, neither the extant regional institution – the Asia Pacific Economic Cooperation (APEC) – nor the global institution – the WTO – is able to address the increasing distortion in investment and trade in the world of complex supply chains. Gordon (2012) identifies domestic political problems that have hampered US trade policies. For both sets of analysts, these explain the launching of the Trans-Pacific Partnership (TPP) agreement by the United States. Elms (2013) maintains that the ongoing TPP negotiations, if completed, have the potential to facilitate and foster economic activities based on global value chains. Elms points to another burgeoning institution – the Regional Comprehensive Economic Partnership (RCEP) developed by the 10 member states of the Association of Southeast Asian Nations (ASEAN) and their 6 trade agreement partners – as a potential agreement to facilitate value chains.

The increasing focus by states on their regions is a natural consequence of the current infrastructures. Economic actors operating in extensive value chains are likely to find the world economy, which is compartmentalised by bilateral agreements – either PTAs or IIPTAs – to be inefficient and inadequate. The uncertain longevity of the current political infrastructure at the global level also leads states to seek stability in stronger regional institutions.

## D. Conclusion

In this chapter I have argued that the availability of technological tools and the nature of the political bargain at the international level – what I refer to as the technological infrastructure and the political infrastructure, respectively – shape the patterns of economic agreements that states sign in various historical periods. The argument accounted for the following patterns: the widespread bilateral agreements entailing weak commitment and generating weak effects in the nineteenth century; the regional and preferential blocs with little systematic effect on trade flows during the interwar years; the numerous regional economic organisations emulating the European Community during the Cold War; the proliferation of bilateral agreements going above and beyond traditional trade measures covered by the GATT/WTO at the end of the twentieth and the beginning of the twenty-first centuries and the resurgence of agreements involving many countries in a region in the current period.

The technological infrastructure has evolved over time as a result of research, developments and innovations in science and technology. These changes have continuously altered the way economic actors structure consumption and production around the world. The political infrastructure has exogenously varied, depending on the rise and fall of great powers and the ability of states around the world to create and sustain a political bargain through and outside multilateral economic institutions.

Given this argument in the chapter, two factors can help anticipate, albeit very imperfectly, what economic agreements in the coming years and decades may look like. First, it is not clear what kinds of innovations will emerge in the future and what the third unbundling of production might look like. Regardless, firms are likely to seek to exploit those changes to further enhance their competitiveness. The trend in technological changes in the entire period under analysis has been facilitation of *decentralisation* and dispersion in production. This will further quicken the pace of economic activities, and only the efficient and productive firms will thrive. In this environment, even regional agreements with broad membership will be insufficient. Should the demands for further governance from private actors increase, states may need to return to the multilateral venue to provide it.

Second, the nature of political infrastructure in the future is difficult to foresee. No clear pattern or trend exists for how the distribution of power and the political bargain among states at the global level have evolved. The linchpin in the future political infrastructure may be the results of the negotiations between the United States and the EU on the Transatlantic Trade and Investment Partnership (TTIP). As the two main status quo economic powers in the world economy, the United States and the EU have the ability to structure the bargain that will influence economic flows not only between themselves but throughout the international economy. The political leaders involved in the negotiations are likely to realise their significance, especially given the failure of the WTO Members to shape a new bargain in the multilateral venue.

## References

Accominotti, Olivier, and Flandreau, Marc. 2008. 'Bilateral Treaties and the Most-Favored-Nation Clause: The Myth of Trade Liberalization in the Nineteenth Century.' *World Politics* 60 (2): 147–88.

Aggarwal, Vinod K. 2013. 'U.S. Free Trade Agreements and Linkages.' *International Negotiation* 18 (1): 89–110.

Baier, Scott L., and Bergstrand, Jeffrey H. 2004. 'Economic Determinants of Free Trade Agreements.' *Journal of International Economics* 64 (1): 29–63.

Baier, Scott L., Bergstrand, Jeffrey H., Egger, Peter, and McLaughlin, Patrick A. 2008. 'Do Economic Integration Agreements Actually Work? Issues in Understanding the Causes and Consequences of the Growth of Regionalism.' *World Economy* 31 (4): 461–97.

Bailey, Michael, Goldstein, Judith, and Weingast, Barry R. 1997. 'The Institutional Roots of American Trade Policy.' *World Politics* 49 (3): 309–38.

Baldwin, Richard. 1995. 'The Domino Theory of Regionalism.' In *Expanding Membership of the European Union*, edited by Pertti Haaparanta and Jaakko Kiander, 25–53. Cambridge: Cambridge University Press.

   2008. 'Big-Think Regionalism: A Critical Survey.' NBER Working Paper No. 14056. National Bureau of Economic Research, Cambridge, MA.

   2011. *21st Century Regionalism: Filling the Gap Between 21st Century Trade and 20th Century Trade Rules*. London: Centre for Economic Policy Research.

Baldwin, Richard, and Jaimovich, Dany. 2010. *Are Free Trade Agreements Contagious?* London: Centre for Economic Policy Research.

Barton, John, Goldstein, Judith L., Josling, Timothy E., and Steinberg, Richard. 2006. *The Evolution of the Trade Regime: Politics, Law and Economics of the GATT and WTO*. Princeton, NJ: Princeton University Press.

Bergsten, C. Fred. 1996. *Competitive Liberalization and Global Free Trade: A Vision for the Early 21st Century*. Washington, DC: Institute for International Economics.

Bergstrand, Jeffrey H., and Egger, Peter. 2006. 'Trade Costs and Intra-Industry Trade.' *Review of World Economics* 142 (3): 433–58.

Bernard, Andrew B., Jensen, J. Bradford, Redding, Stephen J., and Schott, Peter K. 2007. 'Firms in International Trade.' *Journal of Economic Perspectives* 21 (3): 105–30.

Bhagwati, Jagdish N. 2008. *Termites in the Trading System: How Preferential Agreements Undermine Free Trade*. New York: Oxford University Press.

Brown, William Adams, Jr. 1950. *The United States and the Restoration of World Trade: An Analysis and Appraisal of the ITO Charter and the General Agreement on Tariffs and Trade*. Washington, DC: Brookings Institution.

Capling, Ann, and Ravenhill, John. 2011. 'Multilateralising Regionalism: What Role for the Trans-Pacific Partnership Agreement?' *Pacific Review* 24 (5): 553–75.

Chase, Kerry A. 2003. 'Economic Interests and Regional Trading Arrangements: The Case of NAFTA.' *International Organization* 57 (1): 137–74.

Croome, John. 1999. *Reshaping the World Trading System: A History of the Uruguay Round*. 2nd and Rev. edn. Geneva: Kluwer Law International.

Egger, Peter, and Larch, Mario. 2008. 'Interdependent Preferential Trade Agreement Memberships: An Empirical Analysis.' *Journal of International Economics* 76 (2): 384–99.

Eichengreen, Barry J. 1996. *Globalizing Capital: A History of the International Monetary System*. Princeton, NJ: Princeton University Press.

Eichengreen, Barry, and Irwin, Douglas A. 2009. *The Slide to Protectionism in the Great Depression: Who Succumbed and Why?* Cambridge, MA: National Bureau of Economic Research.

Elkins, Zachary, Guzman, Andrew T., and Simmons, Beth A. 2006. 'Competing for Capital: The Diffusion of Bilateral Investment Treaties, 1960–2000.' *International Organization* 60 (4): 811–46.

Elms, Deborah K. 2013. 'Fostering Global Value Chains (GVCs) in Asia-Pacific Preferential Trade Agreements (PTAs).' Paper presented at the Annual Meeting of the American Political Science Association, Chicago, IL.

Elms, Deborah K., and Low, Patrick. 2013. 'Introduction.' In *Global Value Chains in a Changing World*, edited by Deborah K. Elms and Patrick Low, 1–9. Geneva: World Trade Organization.

Estevadeordal, Antoni, and Suominen, Kati. 2009. *The Sovereign Remedy? Trade Agreements in a Globalizing World*. Oxford, England: Oxford University Press.

Findlay, Ronald, and O'Rourke, Kevin H. 2009. *Power and Plenty*. Princeton, NJ: Princeton University Press.

Friedman, Thomas L. 2005. *The World Is Flat: A Brief History of the Twenty-First Century*. New York: Farrar, Straus and Giroux.

Fukuyama, Francis. 2006. *End of History and the Last Man*. New York: Simon and Schuster.

Gilpin, Robert. 1987. *The Political Economy of International Relations*. Princeton, NJ: Princeton University Press.

Goldstein, Judith, and Gowa, Joanne. 2002. 'US National Power and the Post-War Trading Regime.' *World Trade Review* 1 (2): 153–70.

Goldstein, Judith, Rivers, Doug, and Tomz, Michael. 2007. 'Institutions in International Relations: Understanding the Effects of GATT and the WTO on World Trade.' *International Organization* 61 (1): 37–67.

Goldstein, Judith L., and Steinberg, Richard H. 2009. 'Regulatory Shift: The Rise of Judicial Liberalization at the WTO.' In *The Politics of Global Regulation*, edited by Walter Mattli and Ngaire Woods, 211–41. Princeton, NJ: Princeton University Press.

Gordon, Bernard K. 2012. 'Trading Up in Asia.' *Foreign Affairs* 91 (4): 17–22.

Gordon, Robert. 1990. *The Measurement of Durable Goods Prices*. Chicago: University of Chicago Press.

Gowa, Joanne, and Hicks, Raymond. 2013. 'Politics, Institutions, and Trade.' *International Organization* 67 (3): 439–67.

Gowa, Joanne, and Kim, Soo Yeon. 2005. 'An Exclusive Country Club: The Effects of GATT on Trade, 1950–94.' *World Politics* 57 (4): 453–78.

Granovetter, Mark. 1985. 'Economic Action and Social Structure.' *American Sociological Review* 91 (3): 481–510.

Greif, Avner. 2006. *Institutions and the Path to the Modern Economy: Lessons from Medieval Trade.* Cambridge: Cambridge University Press.

Hicks, Raymond, and Johnson, Kristina. 2013. 'The Politics of Globalizing Production.' Unpublished manuscript, Princeton, NJ.

Hiscox, Michael J. 1999. 'The Magic Bullet? The RTAA, Institutional Reform, and Trade Liberalization.' *International Organization* 53 (4): 669–98.

2002. *International Trade and Political Conflict: Commerce, Coalitions, and Mobility.* Princeton, NJ: Princeton University Press.

Horn, Henrik, Mavroidis, Petros C., and Sapir, André. 2010. 'Beyond the WTO? An Anatomy of EU and US Preferential Trade Agreements.' *World Economy* 33 (11): 1565–88.

Hummels, David. 2007. 'Transportation Costs and International Trade in the Second Era of Globalization.' *Journal of Economic Perspectives* 21 (3): 131–54.

Hummels, David, Ishii, Jun, and Yi, Kei-Mu. 2001. 'The Nature and Growth of Vertical Specialization in World Trade.' *Journal of International Economics* 54 (1): 75–96.

Hynes, William, Jacks, David S., and O'Rourke, Kevin H. 2009. *Commodity Market Disintegration in the Interwar Period.* Cambridge, MA: National Bureau of Economic Research.

Irwin, Douglas A. 1993. 'Multilateral and Bilateral Trade Policies in the World Trading System.' In *New Dimensions in Regional Integration: An Historical Perspective,* edited by Jaime De Melo and Arvind Panagariya, 90–119. Cambridge: Cambridge University Press.

2012. *Trade Policy Disaster.* Cambridge, MA: MIT Press.

James, Harold. 2002. *The End of Globalization: Lessons from the Great Depression.* Cambridge, MA: Harvard University Press.

Kahler, Miles. 1992. 'Multilateralism with Small and Large Numbers.' *International Organization* 46 (3): 681–708.

Keohane, Robert O. 1984. *After Hegemony: Cooperation and Discord in the World Political Economy.* Princeton, NJ: Princeton University Press.

1997. 'Problematic Lucidity.' *World Politics* 50 (1): 150–70.

Kohl, Tristan. 2012. 'I Just Read 296 Trade Agreements.' Paper presented at the 6th Annual Conference on the Political Economy of International Organizations, Mannheim, Germany. http://www.cris.unu.edu/fileadmin/workingpapers/W-2013-9.pdf.

Koremenos, Barbara. 2001. 'Loosening the Ties That Bind: A Learning Model of Agreement Flexibility.' *International Organization* 55 (2): 289–325.

Krasner, Stephen D. 1976. 'State Power and the Structure of International Trade.' *World Politics* 28 (3): 317–47.

Krugman, Paul R. 1979. 'Increasing Returns, Monopolistic Competition, and International Trade.' *Journal of International Economics* 9 (4): 469–79.

Lake, David A. 1984. 'Beneath the Commerce of Nations.' *International Studies Quarterly* 28 (2): 143–70.

——— 1993. 'Leadership, Hegemony, and the International Economy: Naked Emperor or Tattered Monarch with Potential.' *International Studies Quarterly* 37 (4): 459–89.

Lazer, David. 1999. 'The Free Trade Epidemic of the 1860s.' *World Politics* 51 (4): 447–83.

Lipson, Charles. 1982. 'The Transformation of Trade: The Sources and Effects of Regime Change.' *International Organization* 36 (2): 417–55.

Liu, Xuepeng. 2009. 'GATT/WTO Promotes Trade Strongly: Sample Selection and Model Specification.' *Review of International Economics* 17 (3): 428–46.

Ludema, Rodney D. 2007. 'Allies and Friends: the Trade Policy Review of the United States, 2006.' *World Economy* 30 (8): 1209–21.

Manger, Mark S. 2012. 'Vertical Trade Specialization and the Formation of North-South PTAs.' *World Politics* 64 (4): 622–58.

Mansfield, Edward D. 1998. 'The Proliferation of Preferential Trading Arrangements.' *Journal of Conflict Resolution* 42 (5): 523–43.

Mansfield, Edward D., and Milner, Helen V. 1999. 'The New Wave of Regionalism.' *International Organization* 53 (3): 589–627.

——— 2012. *Votes, Vetoes, and the Political Economy of International Trade Agreements.* Princeton, NJ: Princeton University Press.

Mansfield, Edward D., Milner, Helen V., and Pevehouse, Jon C. 2007. 'Vetoing Cooperation: The Impact of Veto Players on International Trade Agreements.' *British Journal of Political Science* 37 (3): 403–32.

——— 2008. 'Democracy, Veto Players and the Depth of Regional Integration.' *World Economy* 31 (1): 67–96.

Melitz, Marc J., and Trefler, Daniel. 2012. 'Gains from Trade When Firms Matter.' *Journal of Economic Perspectives* 26 (2): 91–118.

Milner, Helen V. 1988. *Resisting Protectionism: Global Industries and the Politics of International Trade.* Princeton, NJ: Princeton University Press.

——— 1997. 'Industries, Governments, and Regional Trade Blocs.' In *The Political Economy of Regionalism,* edited by Edward D. Mansfield and Helen V. Milner, 77–106. New York: Columbia University Press.

Morrison, James Ashley. 2012. 'Before Hegemony.' *International Organization* 66 (3): 395–428.

North, Douglass C. 1958. 'Ocean Freight Rates and Economic Development 1750–1913.' *Journal of Economic History* 18 (4): 537–55.

Nye, John V. C. 2007. *War, Wine and Taxes.* Princeton, NJ: Princeton University Press.

O'Rourke, Kevin H., and Williamson, Jeffrey G. 1999. *Globalization and History: The Evolution of a Nineteenth-Century Atlantic Economy*. Cambridge, MA: MIT Press.

Pahre, Robert. 2001. 'Most-Favored-Nation Clauses and Clustered Negotiations.' *International Organization* 55 (4): 859–90.

     2008. *Politics and Trade Cooperation in the Nineteenth Century: The 'Agreeable Customs' of 1815–1914*. New York: Cambridge University Press.

Polanyi, Karl. 2001. *The Great Transformation: The Political and Economic Origins of Our Time*, 2nd edn. Boston: Beacon Press.

Rose, Andrew K. 2004. 'Do We Really Know That the WTO Increases Trade?' *American Economic Review* 94 (1): 98–114.

Ruggie, John Gerard. 1982. 'International Regimes, Transactions, and Change: Embedded Liberalism in the Postwar Economic Order.' *International Organization* 36 (2): 379–415.

Schnietz, Karen E. 2003. 'The Reaction of Private Interests to the 1934 Reciprocal Trade Agreements Act.' *International Organization* 57 (1): 213–33.

Tomz, Michael, Goldstein, Judith L., and Rivers, Douglas. 2007. 'Do We Really Know That the WTO Increases Trade? Comment.' *American Economic Review* 97 (5): 2005–18.

Viner, Jacob. 1950. *The Customs Union Issue*. New York: Carnegie Endowment for International Peace.

Waltz, Kenneth N. 1970. 'The Myth of National Interdependence.' In *The International Corporation*, edited by Charles P. Kindleberger, 205–23. Cambridge, MA: MIT Press.

Winters, L. Alan. 1996. 'Regionalism versus Multilateralism.' Policy Research Working Paper No. 1687. World Bank, Washington, DC.

# 3

# The political economy of preferential trade agreements

## EDWARD D. MANSFIELD AND HELEN V. MILNER

## A. Introduction

Over the past 20 years, the global trading system has experienced a set of pronounced and profound changes. The so-called BRIC countries (Brazil, Russia, India and China) have risen in importance, with China now conducting almost as much overseas commerce as the United States does. At the same time, the system has experienced a number of jarring disruptions, most notably the 2008 financial crisis and the accompanying Great Recession, which prompted what one study characterized as 'the steepest fall of world trade in recorded world history' (Gawande, Hoekman and Cui 2011: 5). All of this occurred against an institutional backdrop that has changed in important ways as well. In 1995, the World Trade Organization (WTO) replaced the General Agreement on Tariffs and Trade (GATT), a development that was greeted with much fanfare and anticipation. However, the WTO has experienced a series of setbacks, particularly the failure of the Doha Round of multilateral negotiations, which commenced in 2001 and has yet to yield an agreement.

But perhaps the most important development in the world trading system has been the rapid proliferation of preferential trade agreements (PTAs), a set of institutions that include free trade agreements, customs unions, common markets and economic unions. Such agreements have dotted the international landscape for centuries, but they have become especially pervasive over the past few decades (Mansfield and Milner 1999; Pahre 2008). In fact, a recent study by the WTO (2011) concludes that, during this time, the number of PTAs increased more than fourfold, and more than 300 agreements of this sort currently exist. This development has stimulated intense interest on the part of social scientists.

Portions of this chapter draw on Mansfield and Milner (2012: Chaps. 3 and 4).

For more than half a century, researchers have debated the economic and political implications of PTAs, placing particular emphasis on how these agreements affect the welfare of countries and the stability of the multilateral trading system.

More recently, social scientists have expressed growing interest in the factors that give rise to PTAs. In this chapter, we analyse the political economy of PTA formation. Using the most-up-to-date data covering the period from 1952 until 2011, we examine the international sources of trade agreements, including political–military relations, strategic interaction and the GATT/WTO system. We also analyse the domestic sources of PTAs, placing primary emphasis on a country's regime type and number of veto players – that is, independent groups in the country with the ability to block policy change. Consistent with our previous work, we argue that democratic countries are particularly likely to join PTAs and that the odds of a country acceding to such an agreement rise if the number of veto players is relatively small (Mansfield and Milner 2012). In line with our earlier studies, we find considerable evidence to support these claims. We also find that international politics and various economic factors play a large role in PTA formation.

## B. The domestic politics of PTA formation

Although it is frequently acknowledged that political factors shape PTAs, surprisingly few systematic attempts have been made to address exactly which ones most strongly influence the formation of these agreements. Some of the research that has been conducted on this topic focuses on domestic interest groups. PTAs discriminate against third parties, yielding rents for certain domestic actors who may constitute a potent source of support for a PTA (Gunter 1989: 9). Industries that could ward off competitors located in third parties or expand their share of international markets if they were covered by a PTA have obvious reasons to press for its establishment (Haggard 1997). So do export-oriented industries that stand to benefit from the preferential access to foreign markets afforded by a PTA. Gilligan (1997) maintains that firms in such sectors have a preference for PTAs because they are reciprocal agreements; these firms will realize substantial gains from reciprocal trade liberalization, but not from unilateral liberalization. Similarly, Milner (1997), Mattli (1999) and Chase (2005) argue that exporters in industries marked by economies of scale have particular reason to press for PTAs. Membership will furnish them with access to a larger market, thereby helping them reduce production costs and increase profitability. Multinational corporations also have reason to press for PTAs that protect their trading and production networks (Manger 2009).

PTAs therefore hold some appeal for public officials who need to attract the support of both import-competing and export-oriented sectors. The domestic political viability of a prospective PTA, the extent to which it will create or divert trade and the range of products that it will cover hinge partly on the preferences of and the influence wielded by key sectors in each country. Public officials must strike a balance between promoting a country's aggregate economic welfare and accommodating interest groups whose support is needed to retain office. Grossman and Helpman (1995: 668) argue that the political viability of a PTA often depends on the amount of discrimination it yields. Agreements that divert trade will benefit certain interest groups, while creating costs borne by the populace at large. If these groups have more political clout than other segments of society, then a PTA that is trade diverting stands a better chance of being established than one that is trade creating (Grossman and Helpman 1995: 681; Pomfret 1988: 190). Grossman and Helpman also find that by excluding some sectors from a PTA, governments can increase the domestic support for it, thus helping to explain why many PTAs do not cover politically sensitive industries.

## I. Democracy

In addition to the role played by key sectors of the economy and other interest groups, we have argued that domestic institutions affect the formation of PTAs (Mansfield and Milner 2012; Mansfield, Milner and Pevehouse 2007; Mansfield, Milner and Rosendorf 2002). All political leaders depend on the support of constituents to stay in power. However, the means by which leaders retain office depends on the type of political regime. In democracies, leaders must stand for office in regular and competitive elections. In autocracies, by contrast, they must maintain the allegiance of small, select groups within the country. Greater political competition for office spurs democratic leaders to sign international trade agreements.

Leaders are frequently ensnared between pressures exerted by interest groups and the preferences of voters. Special interests often press for policies – such as protectionist trade policies – that adversely affect the economy. Leaders may want to satisfy some interest groups in order to generate benefits such as campaign contributions. But capitulating in the face of interest-group demands would have very harmful economic consequences and could imperil their hold on office. Leaders face a credibility problem. They have a hard time convincing the public that they will not accede to special interest demands. When elections take place in combination with poor economic circumstances, voters may blame incumbents for economic problems and vote them out of office. Leaders prefer not to comply with interest group demands if they can credibly convince voters that any economic downturn was due to circumstances beyond their control rather than an outgrowth of complying with such demands.

Trade agreements provide a mechanism to achieve this end. They allow leaders to commit to a lower level of protectionism than they might otherwise desire, but to signal to voters that they will not allow trade policy to be guided by special interests. Once voters are convinced that leaders are generally abiding by the terms of the agreement, they are likely to believe leaders who claim that their policies were not the cause of hard economic times. In turn, leaders are more likely to retain office because voters will not blame them for any downturn in the country's economic performance. The more electoral competition there is, the more leaders have to worry about being ejected from office and the greater the problems stemming from their inability to make credible commitments about trade policy.

Of course, voters do not display much interest in many policy issues, but economic policy and performance are typically matters of substantial concern (Kiewiet 1983; Lewis-Beck 1988). Voters may not know much about trade policy, but we expect them to keep abreast of a country's economic condition. When the economy sours, voters will be more likely to reject incumbents, unless leaders can furnish information that the downturn was due to circumstances beyond their control rather than rent-seeking or incompetence. PTAs can help to provide such information, either by directly monitoring and reporting on members' behaviour or because the participating countries have reason to publicize any deviation from the arrangement by a member. Hence, we argue that democracies – where the voting public determines whether the incumbent retains office – should be more likely than other regime types to sign such agreements.

For autocracies, the calculations differ. Interest group pressures for protectionism in autocracies vest leaders of these countries with an incentive to resist entering PTAs that reduce the rents they can provide to supporters. Equally, electoral competition is less likely to determine their fate. Consequently, autocrats have less incentive than their democratic counterparts to enter into agreements.

## II. Veto players

Like most international agreements, PTAs do not have direct effect in signatory countries. In order for the terms of the arrangement to take hold, it has to be ratified by some set of domestic veto players (Yarbrough and Yarbrough 1992: 35). We argue that the number of such players affects the transaction costs that governments bear when ratifying a PTA. More veto players increase these costs, thereby reducing the incentives of leaders to try to negotiate and ratify PTAs.

We view the state as an aggregation of institutions populated by actors with varying preferences who share decision-making authority. The distribution of decision-making power among these actors, and the extent to which their preferences diverge, define the number of veto players. These players have the ability to block policy change, and their assent is necessary to alter existing policies (Tsebelis 2002). Conceptually, regime type and veto players are distinct, and we treat them as such. Veto players exist in all types of regimes. Even in nondemocratic countries, domestic politics is rarely a pure hierarchy with a unitary decision-maker and no constraints on the leaders. Domestic groups with varying preferences who have veto power often compete for influence over policy and dictators depend on them in making policy and retaining office. Democratic regimes are even more likely to have veto players than are nondemocratic regimes, although the number of such players varies considerably among democracies. Generally, the legislature and the executive vie for control over decision-making in democracies. Sometimes two or more political parties or coalitions compete. Domestic political institutions determine how such control is distributed among the relevant actors.

In most countries, the executive branch sets the agenda in foreign affairs and has the power to initiate foreign economic policy. However, veto players must ratify policy choices made by the executive, such as the choice to join a trade agreement. Formally, the head of state in a democracy – the prime minister, president, chancellor, or premier – is often required by the national constitution to obtain the approval of the legislature for international agreements, including PTAs. He or she will therefore need to anticipate the legislature's (or any other veto player's) reaction to the proposed arrangement and ensure it is domestically acceptable.

Ratification can also be less formal. In dictatorships, shifts in foreign economic policy frequently require the support of groups such as the military or local leaders. Implicitly, these groups have ratified a trade agreement if they had the ability to veto it and chose not to. Informal ratification also occurs in democracies. If a leader needs to change a domestic law, norm, or practice to implement a PTA, even if no formal vote on the trade agreement itself is required, a legislative vote on any necessary domestic change becomes a vote on the agreement.

Because of this ratification constraint, veto players affect the formation of PTAs. As the number of veto players increases, so does the likelihood that at least one such player will have a constituency that is adversely affected by the PTA and therefore will block its ratification. To ratify an agreement when many veto players exist is costly for political leaders. They either have to modify the agreement to fit the preferences of the veto groups or they have to bribe the veto groups into accepting the agreement. These means of securing ratification generate transaction costs for leaders. The greater these transaction costs, the less likely leaders are to enter into trade agreements and the more difficult it will be to secure ratification. In our model, then, ratification domestically is the critically important step at the end of the process.

## C. The international politics of PTAs

Whereas relatively little research has focused on the domestic politics of PTA formation, considerable effort has been made to address the international political sources of such agreements. One strand of research has centred on whether PTA formation is influenced by hegemony, that is, by whether there is a single country that is powerful enough and willing to manage the international system. Some scholars have suggested that hegemony is largely unrelated to PTAs (e.g. McKeown 1991); others maintain that it has some modest effect on these arrangements (e.g. Oye 1992; Yarbrough and Yarbrough 1992); and still others place considerable emphasis on hegemony's influence but disagree about the nature of its effect.

That the lack of a stable hegemon fosters the formation of PTAs is a longstanding argument among the last of these groups of scholars (Gilpin 1987; Kindleberger 1973; Krasner 1976). Central to this argument is the claim that these blocs are discriminatory and thus antithetical to the maintenance of a multilateral trading system. Equally, establishing and maintaining this type of system form a collective good that will be underprovided absent a stable hegemon (Gilpin 1987; Kindleberger 1973). By virtue of its size, a hegemon, like a privileged group, has incentives to provide collective goods regardless of the contributions to them made by other states.[1] Although researchers advancing this argument disagree about the nature of these incentives, they agree that hegemonic decline reduces this state's contribution to the stability of the multilateral economic system and promotes the formation of preferential commercial arrangements.

However, this is not the only reason why the erosion of hegemony might stimulate the proliferation of PTAs. Waning US hegemony may have prompted the creation and expansion of PTAs by a small group of powers that felt these arrangements would assist them in managing the global economy (Yarbrough and Yarbrough 1992). Drawing smaller states into preferential arrangements with a relatively liberal cast towards third parties might reduce the capacity of these states to establish a series of more protectionist blocs, bind them to decisions about the system made by the leading powers and contribute to the maintenance of an open global trading system.

Whereas these arguments suggest that stable hegemony inhibits the formation of PTAs, the opposite view has also been advanced. Underlying the latter position is the assumption that states have an incentive to maximize their income. Countries with sufficient market power therefore have reason to impose an optimal tariff. Since a hegemon is likely to be vested with such power (Gowa 1994), other states may band together in PTAs to offset it. PTAs have more market power than their constituent members, states prefer to limit their susceptibility to the imposition of an optimal tariff (since the tariff reduces their gains from trade) and states (or groups of states) can more easily deter and respond to the imposition of optimal protection as their market power rises (Krugman 1993).

In addition to hegemony, which is a feature of the global distribution of power, there may be a more general tendency for power relations to guide PTA formation. More powerful countries, for example, may pressure weaker countries to join PTAs in order to exploit them and reinforce the asymmetric power relationship (Gruber 2000; Hirschman (1945) 1980; McLaren 1997). This pressure may take the form of strong-arm tactics, but it may also stem from potential economic benefits that are sufficiently large to make rejecting PTA membership with a powerful country very difficult. The relationship may also serve to entrap the weaker country. By changing patterns of trade, the agreement may make the weaker party increasingly dependent on the stronger one, as the weaker party restructures its economy to serve the larger country's market, thereby enhancing

---

[1]    On privileged groups, see Olson (1965).

the asymmetric power relationship (McLaren 1997). Alternatively, weaker countries may eschew PTAs with much larger counterparts if they seek to reduce their dependence on more sizable states and the associated harm to their power. Instead, they may band together with states of a similar size in an effort to counterbalance the more powerful countries.

Patterns of political–military cooperation and conflict are also likely to influence the formation of PTAs. Trade agreements promote the free flow of goods and services among member states, yielding efficiency gains that enhance the national incomes of the participating countries. These gains in income can be used to enhance the trade partners' political–military capacity (Hirschmann (1945) 1980). But because the gains from trade do not accrue uniformly to countries, increased overseas commerce stemming from a trade agreement is likely to affect their political–military capacity and hence power relations among them. Because of this security externality stemming from open trade, political–military allies have a greater incentive to establish PTAs than other states (Gowa 1994; Mansfield 1993). In PTAs composed of allies, the economic gains from liberalization bolster the alliance's overall political–military capacity, and the common security aims of members attenuate the political–military risks that states benefiting less from the arrangement might otherwise face from those benefiting more. Adversaries, by contrast, have few political reasons to form a PTA since some participants are likely to derive greater economic benefits than are others, and those that gain less may suffer a reduction in their relative political–military power as a result.

International analyses of PTA formation have also emphasized strategic interdependence. Particularly important in this regard is whether PTA formation and expansion are characterized by positive contagion; that is, whether the creation of a PTA begets the development of additional PTAs and a country joining a PTA encourages other countries to do likewise. Many studies have concluded that this is the case (e.g. Fernández and Portes 1998; Oye 1992; Pomfret 1988; Yarbrough and Yarbrough 1992). A PTA's creation, for example, may prompt fears by countries located outside the commercial union that the agreement will degrade their competitiveness, thereby leading them to form a rival bloc. So, too, a state joining a PTA may raise the concern by its economic rivals (outside the bloc) that this state's preferential access to an expanded market will furnish it with a competitive advantage, thus inducing them to join other PTAs to obtain similar benefits.

In the same vein, positive contagion in the rates of PTA formation or states' involvement in PTAs may be due to a demonstration effect:

the appearance that a PTA is benefiting members can foster the creation of additional commercial unions by countries eager to realize similar gains (Pomfret 1988; Yarbrough and Yarbrough 1992). Further, as noted previously, PTAs heighten members' market power and hence their bargaining power (Fernández and Portes 1998; Oye 1992). PTAs are likely to be formed in reaction to one another, and states are likely to join PTAs in response to one another, because the proliferation of preferential arrangements erodes the bargaining power of states that remain outside them.

Substantial evidence suggests that strategic interaction has indeed guided the establishment of PTAs (Baccini and Dür 2012; Baldwin and Jaimovich 2012). It is often argued, for example, that deepening European integration contributed to the formation of the North American Free Trade Agreement (NAFTA) (Bhagwati 1991: 72; Fernández and Portes 1998) and that NAFTA spurred the development of, and agreements to establish future, bilateral economic arrangements within both the Western Hemisphere and the Asia-Pacific region (Serra *et al.* 1997: 8–9). Strategic interaction lies at the heart of Baldwin's (1995) 'domino theory' of PTAs. Baldwin argues that remaining outside a large PTA is especially costly for exporters because they have restricted access to the grouping's sizable market, and firms located in member states experience efficiency gains as the result of competing in this market. As the PTA grows larger, so do the costs stemming from being a third party. This has prompted various PTAs to form in reaction to NAFTA and the European Union (EU).

Finally, the GATT/WTO and its global reach may affect the prevalence of PTAs. International regimes have long been thought to affect states' behaviour (Keohane 1984; Krasner 1982; Ruggie 1982), and the multilateral trade regime is usually seen as one of the most robust. The original purposes of the GATT were to ensure an open multilateral trading system and to combat the discriminatory trade agreements that marked the interwar period and contributed to both economic and political–military friction. One possibility is that states accede to the GATT/WTO because they want access to an open trading system. They have less reason to form PTAs than do states that do not participate in the GATT/WTO since the multilateral regime already furnishes the openness that they desire. Another possibility, however, is that GATT/WTO Members are especially likely to form PTAs because doing so: (1) allows them to bargain as a block in GATT/WTO negotiations, thereby increasing their bargaining power; (2) allows them to achieve greater openness than is achievable in GATT/WTO negotiations, which are conducted by a large number of states with heterogeneous interests; (3) is a GATT/WTO-permissible means of discriminating against certain members of the multilateral regime or (4) creates a measure of insurance for states interested in promoting openness that are concerned that the GATT/WTO system might falter (Mansfield and Reinhardt 2003). We therefore expect the multilateral trade regime to affect the formation of PTAs, but the nature of its influence is unclear.

### D. A statistical model of PTA ratification

To test the arguments described earlier, we estimate the following baseline model:

$$
\begin{aligned}
PTA\ Ratification_{ij} \\
= \beta_0 + \beta_1\ Regime\ Type_i + \beta_2\ Veto\ Players_i \\
+ \beta_3\ Existing\ PTA_{ij} + \beta_4\ Trade_{ij} + \beta_5\ GDP_i + \beta_6\ \Delta GDP_i \\
+ \beta_7\ Dispute_{ij} + \beta_8\ Alliance_{ij} + \beta_9\ Former\ Colony_{ij} \\
+ \beta_{10}\ Contiguity_{ij} + \beta_{11}\ Distance_{ij} + \beta_{12}\ Hegemony \\
+ \beta_{13}\ Post-Cold\ War + \beta_{14}\ GDP\ Ratio_{ij} \\
+ \beta_{15}\%\ Dyads\ Ratifying\ PTA + \beta_{16}\ GATT/WTO_{ij} \\
+ \beta_{17} - \beta_{24}\ Regional\ Fixed\ Effects_i + \varepsilon_{ij}
\end{aligned}
\tag{3.1}
$$

Our dependent variable, *PTA Ratification*$_{ij}$, is the log of the odds that state $i$ ratifies a PTA with state $j$ in year $t$, where we observe 1 if this occurs and 0 otherwise. As in our earlier work, we focus on reciprocal agreements and exclude agreements where one state unilaterally grants another country preferential access to its market (Mansfield and Milner 2012). Ratification of a PTA is central for our analysis since it represents the culmination of the agreement's passage through the domestic political process. Signing an agreement with other countries initiates this process; but domestic politics can change over time, and it is only when domestic ratification is achieved that all domestic constraints have been accommodated. Hence, for our argument – especially about veto players – ratification is the crucial hurdle. If the exact year of ratification could not be determined, we rely on the date that state $i$ signed the PTA with state $j$. Because most agreements are ratified relatively soon after they are formed and because ratification dates are missing less than 30 per cent of the time, this is a reasonable approach.

Since states *i* and *j* need not – and, indeed, often do not – ratify a preferential arrangement in the same year, our unit of analysis is the annual 'directed dyad'. Thus, for each dyad in each year, there is one observation corresponding to state *i* and a second observation corresponding to state *j*. Each monadic variable, as we explain later, is included in this model only once, for the country listed as *i* in each particular observation. Of course, analysing directed dyads doubles the number of observations in the sample, thereby producing standard errors that are too small. To correct this problem, we cluster the standard errors over the undirected dyad.

The independent variables in our model can be divided into three groups. One set taps the domestic political factors that we discussed earlier. A second group of variables taps international political factors. A third set taps geographical and economic factors that are not the primary focus of our analysis but that might nonetheless affect PTA formation.

## I. Domestic politics

Our primary domestic political focus is on a state's regime type and veto players. First, *Regime Type$_i$* is country *i*'s regime type in year *t*. We code this variable using data drawn from the Polity IV Project and an index developed by Gurr *et al.* (1989).[2] This index combines data on five factors that help to capture the institutional differences between democracies and autocracies that we emphasized earlier: the competitiveness of the process for selecting a country's chief executive, the openness of this process, the extent to which institutional constraints limit a chief executive's decision-making authority, the competitiveness of political participation within a country and the degree to which binding rules govern political participation within it. Following Gurr *et al.* (1989) and Jaggers and Gurr (1995), these data are used to create a measure ranging from 1 for a highly autocratic state to 21 for a highly democratic country.

Second, *Veto Players$_i$* measures the constraints on policy change in country *i* in year *t*, based on the number of independent, constitutionally mandated institutions that have different political preferences and can exercise veto powers over policy decisions. We rely on Henisz's (2000 and 2002) index of veto players, which ranges from 0 to 1 and considers the presence of effective branches of government outside the executive's control, the extent to which these branches are controlled by the same

---

[2] These data were obtained from www.systemicpeace.org/polity/polity4.htm.

political party as the executive and the homogeneity of preferences within these branches.[3]

## II. International politics

As we discussed earlier, political relations between states may influence whether they join the same PTA. Military hostilities between states are likely to discourage economic cooperation and thus reduce states' propensity to sign PTAs, whereas political–military cooperation is likely to promote economic cooperation. As such, we include two variables in the model. First, $Dispute_{ij}$ equals 1 if countries $i$ and $j$ are involved in an armed interstate conflict in year $t - 1$, 0 otherwise, using data compiled by the Peace Research Institute Oslo (PRIO).[4] Second, $Alliance_{ij}$ equals 1 if countries $i$ and $j$ are members of a political–military alliance in year $t - 1$, 0 otherwise. We code this variable using the Alliance Treaty Obligations and Provisions (ATOP) data (Leeds et al. 2002), which we have updated to 2011.[5]

Power politics may also affect PTA formation. To determine whether power disparities influence the establishment of preferential arrangements, we include $GDP\ Ratio_{ij}$, which is the natural logarithm of the ratio of the country gross domestic products (GDPs) for each dyad. In computing this variable, the larger GDP is always in the numerator; hence,

---

[3] Henisz has developed two measures of veto players, one that includes the judiciary and one that does not. We use the latter measure because there is little reason to believe that the judiciary would influence the decision to enter a PTA. However, our results are similar when we use the alternative measure.

[4] We use v.4–2012 of the data set, accessed at www.pcr.uu.se/research/ucdp/datasets/ucdp_prio_armed_conflict_dataset/. The data include four types of conflict: (1) extrasystemic armed conflict occurs between a state and a nonstate group outside its own territory; (2) interstate armed conflict occurs between two or more states; (3) internal armed conflict occurs between the government of a state and one or more internal opposition group(s) without intervention from other states; and (4) internationalized internal armed conflict occurs between the government of a state and one or more internal opposition group(s) with intervention from other states (secondary parties) on one or both sides. Type 3 conflicts were dropped. We kept the other three types and expanded the data so that all possible dyads between the countries on side A and those on side B were created. Data that did not have an independent country as one of the sides were then dropped. See Gleditsch et al. (2002) and UCDP/PRIO Armed Conflict Dataset Codebook, v.4–2008.

[5] We use version 3.0 of the ATOP data, specifically the atop3'0ddyr.dta file, which is the directed dyad data set available at http://atop.rice.edu/. These data end in 2003. There were 258 alliances in the ATOP data without an end date. We checked whether any of these had terminated since 2003. We also identified 45 alliances that formed after 2003 (a few of which ended before 2011).

a negative sign on the coefficient of this variable would indicate that a greater disparity between the countries decreases the likelihood of ratification. In addition, *Hegemony* is the proportion of global GDP produced by the state with the largest GDP (in our sample, the United States for each year). This variable therefore takes on the same value for each country in a given year $t - 1$.

As we mentioned earlier, various studies have concluded that the formation of PTAs is marked by contagion or diffusion. We therefore include the percentage of all dyads in the system that ratified a PTA in the previous year, *% Dyads Ratifying*. Finally, because membership in the GATT/WTO may influence the establishment of PTAs, we introduce *GATT/WTO$_{ij}$* to the model. It equals 1 if countries $i$ and $j$ are both members of the GATT in each year prior to 1995 or if they are both members of the WTO from 1995 on, and 0 otherwise.[6]

## III. Additional independent variables

In addition to domestic and international politics, a variety of factors are likely to affect PTA formation and should therefore be included in Eq. (3.1). First, it is widely recognized that geography shapes trade relations and trade agreements. We introduce two variables to capture distance. *Contiguity$_{ij}$* is a dummy variable that is coded 1 if countries $i$ and $j$ share a common border. *Distance$_{ij}$* is the logarithm of the capital-to-capital distance between $i$ and $j$. It is useful to include both variables since some states have distant capitals (e.g. Russia and China) yet share borders, whereas other states do not share borders but are in relatively close proximity (e.g. Benin and Ghana).[7] We also include regional fixed effects, using the eight regional categories identified by the World Bank, since the prevalence of PTAs varies across regions.

Second, we account for various economic factors that are likely to shape trade agreements. *Trade$_{ij}$* is the logarithm of the total value of trade (in constant 2000 US dollars) between countries $i$ and $j$.[8] Various observers

---

[6]  For data on GATT/WTO membership, see www.wto.org/english/thewto_e/whatis_e/tif_e/org6_e.htm.

[7]  Data on distance and contiguity are taken from CEPII's gravity data set, available at www.cepii.fr/CEPII/en/bdd_modele/presentation.asp?id=8.

[8]  The International Monetary Fund's *Direction of Trade Statistics* is our primary source of trade data. We deflate these data using the US GDP deflator. Note that we add 0.001 to all values of trade because some dyads conduct no trade in particular years and the logarithm of zero is undefined.

argue that increasing economic exchange creates incentives for domestic groups that benefit as a result to press governments to enter PTAs, since these arrangements help to avert the possibility that trade relations will break down in the future (e.g. Nye 1988). Moreover, heightened overseas commerce can increase the susceptibility of firms to predatory behaviour by foreign governments, prompting them to press for the establishment of PTAs that limit the ability of governments to behave opportunistically (Yarbrough and Yarbrough 1992).

In addition to economic relations between countries, economic conditions within countries are likely to influence PTA formation. Particularly important in this regard is a state's economic size. Large states (in economic terms) may have less incentive to seek the expanded market access afforded by PTA membership than their smaller counterparts. We therefore analyse $GDP_i$, the logarithm of country $i$'s GDP (in constant 2005 international dollars). Moreover, fluctuations in economic growth may also affect whether states enter preferential arrangements. On the one hand, some research indicates that downturns in the business cycle lead states to seek membership in such arrangements (Mattli 1999). On the other hand, increased growth is likely to increase a country's demand for imports and its supply of exports, creating an incentive to gain preferential access to overseas markets. To address this issue, we introduce $\Delta GDP_i$, the change in $GDP_i$ from $t-1$ to $t$.[9]

Third, because previous research has found that a former colonial relationship between $i$ and $j$ increases the likelihood that they will enter the same PTA, we include *Former Colony_{ij}*, which equals 1 if countries $i$ and $j$ had a colonial relationship that ended after World War II, 0 otherwise.[10] Fourth, we include *Existing PTA_{ij}*, which indicates whether countries $i$ and $j$ are already members of the same PTA(s). There is reason to expect that participating in one arrangement is likely to affect a state's proclivity to create or join another with the same partner. Finally, it is widely argued that the end of the Cold War precipitated a rush to enter PTAs. We therefore include *Post–Cold War*, which equals 0 until 1988 and 1 thereafter.

Whereas our earlier research covered the period from 1951 (for variables measured in year $t-1$ and 1952 for variables measured in year $t$) to 2004, in this chapter we extend the analysis to 2011 (Mansfield and Milner 2012). Because the observed value of the dependent variable is

---

[9]  GDP data are also obtained from the Penn World Table 7.1.
[10]  Data on former colonial relations are taken from Kurian (1992).

Table 3.1 *The political and economic influences on PTA ratification,*
*1952–2011*

| | Base model | Dyadic fixed effects | Dyad and year fixed effects | 5-year PTA diffusion |
|---|---|---|---|---|
| Veto Players | −0.555** | −0.932** | −0.758** | −0.579** |
| | (0.089) | (0.100) | (0.104) | (0.090) |
| Regime Type | 0.0174** | 0.0284** | 0.0182** | 0.0186** |
| | (0.003) | (0.004) | (0.004) | (0.003) |
| Trade (logged) | 0.0330** | 0.0494** | 0.0222** | 0.0462** |
| | (0.003) | (0.004) | (0.005) | (0.003) |
| GDP (logged) | 0.00138 | 0.0724 | 0.380** | −0.0142 |
| | (0.011) | (0.046) | (0.053) | (0.011) |
| ΔGDP | −0.595** | −0.308* | −0.129 | −1.067** |
| | (0.123) | (0.154) | (0.164) | (0.136) |
| Dispute | 0.329 | −0.0936 | −0.184 | 0.283 |
| | (0.259) | (0.295) | (0.302) | (0.254) |
| Alliance | 0.320** | −0.644** | −0.478** | 0.321** |
| | (0.053) | (0.050) | (0.052) | (0.053) |
| Former Colony | −1.469** | | | −1.512** |
| | (0.339) | | | (0.340) |
| Contiguity | −0.580** | | | −0.586** |
| | (0.060) | | | (0.060) |
| Distance (logged) | −1.051** | | | −1.041** |
| | (0.049) | | | (0.049) |
| Hegemony | 4.829** | −6.891** | | 4.756** |
| | (0.428) | (0.730) | | (0.420) |
| GDP Ratio | −0.177** | −0.238** | −0.215** | −0.179** |
| | (0.009) | (0.039) | (0.040) | (0.009) |
| Existing PTA | 0.101* | −2.321** | −2.180** | −0.0268 |
| | (0.053) | (0.038) | (0.041) | (0.053) |
| Dyads Ratify PTA | 41.28** | 21.78** | | |
| | (1.118) | (1.070) | | |
| Dyads Ratify PTA (5-year average) | | | | 5.970** |
| | | | | (2.003) |
| Post–Cold War | 0.811** | 1.454** | | 1.193** |
| | (0.040) | (0.045) | | (0.037) |
| GATT/WTO | 0.177** | 0.492** | 0.589** | 0.126** |
| | (0.029) | (0.040) | (0.042) | (0.028) |
| South Asia | −0.323** | | | −0.322** |
| | (0.125) | | | (0.125) |

Table 3.1 (cont.)

| | Base model | Dyadic fixed effects | Dyad and year fixed effects | 5-year PTA diffusion |
|---|---|---|---|---|
| M. East & N. Africa | 0.132+ | | | 0.116 |
| | (0.080) | | | (0.079) |
| Sub-Saharan Africa | 0.933** | | | 0.942** |
| | (0.062) | | | (0.061) |
| Europe & C. Asia | 0.112 | | | 0.0286 |
| | (0.072) | | | (0.071) |
| S. America & Carib. | 0.447** | | | 0.457** |
| | (0.083) | | | (0.082) |
| N. & C. America | 0.0352 | | | 0.0255 |
| | (0.071) | | | (0.070) |
| Western Europe | −0.197** | | | −0.195** |
| | (0.073) | | | (0.073) |
| Intercept | 1.893** | | | 2.684** |
| | (0.446) | | | (0.445) |
| N | 1 069 452 | 228 586 | 228 586 | 1 069 452 |
| Clusters | 29 394.00 | | | 29 394.00 |
| Log-likelihood | −43 930.38 | −26 857.12 | −24 198.74 | −44 570.93 |

Note: Entries are logistic regression estimates with robust standard errors (clustered on dyads) in parentheses. All tests of statistical significance are two-tailed.
** $p < 0.01$
* $p < 0.05$
+ $p < 0.10$.

dichotomous, we use logistic regression to estimate the model. Tests of statistical significance are based on robust standard errors clustered on the dyad to address any potential problems with heteroscedasticity or the directed dyad research design. To account for temporal dependence in the formation of PTAs, we include a spline function of the number of years that has elapsed (as of $t$) since each dyad last formed a PTA with knots at years 1, 4 and 7, as suggested by Beck, Katz and Tucker (1998). In Table 3.1, however, the estimates of this function are omitted to conserve space. Finally, $\varepsilon_{ij}$ is a stochastic error term.

## E. The results

The results of our analysis are presented in Table 3.1. The first column shows the parameter estimates of Eq. (3.1). The second column reports the estimates after including dyad-specific fixed effects to account for any unobserved heterogeneity in the data. The results in the third column are generated after including both dyad-specific and year-specific fixed effects. The fourth column shows the parameter estimates with an alternative diffusion measure, suggested by Baccini and Dür (2012). Rather than focusing on the percentage of dyads ratifying a PTA, the measure of diffusion used in the fourth column averages this percentage over the previous five years because it might take more than a year for a diffusive process to work its way through the system.

We find substantial evidence that, as expected, the likelihood of PTA ratification grows if countries are more democratic and if they are marked by fewer veto players. As in our previous studies, the coefficient estimates of $Regime\ Type_i$ are positive, the coefficients of $Veto\ Players_i$ are negative and all of them are statistically significant (Mansfield and Milner 2012; Mansfield, Milner and Pevehouse 2007; Mansfield, Milner and Rosendorff 2002). The magnitude of their effects is greatest when we include dyad-specific fixed effects, indicating that within dyad variation in regime type and veto players has an especially potent impact on PTA ratification. The size of these effects is smallest in the base model.

To illustrate the size of the effects of these variables, we initially calculated the 'relative risk' of state $i$ ratifying a PTA with state $j$ if the former state is democratic or if it is autocratic. More specifically, this risk is the predicted probability of state $i$ entering a PTA with state $j$ if state $i$ is democratic (which we define here as $Regime\ Type_i = 19$) divided by the predicted probability of state i entering a PTA if it is autocratic (which we define here as $Regime\ Type_i = 3$), holding constant the remaining variables in the model.[11] As shown in Figure 3.1, a democracy is about 32 per cent more likely to enter a PTA than an autocracy, based on the results presented in the first column of Table 3.1. Turning to the effects of veto players, we compare the predicted probability of state $i$ forming a PTA when it has few players – which we define as the 10th percentile in the data – with the predicted probability when it has many of them – which we define as the 90th percentile in the data, holding constant the remaining variables in the model. Based on the results in the first column of Table 3.1, a state with few $Veto\ Players_i$ is about 33 per cent more likely to ratify a PTA than one with more $Veto\ Players_i$. These results clearly indicate that domestic politics plays an important role in shaping the decision

---

[11]   The continuous variables are held constant at their median values, and the dichotomous variables are held constant at their modal values.

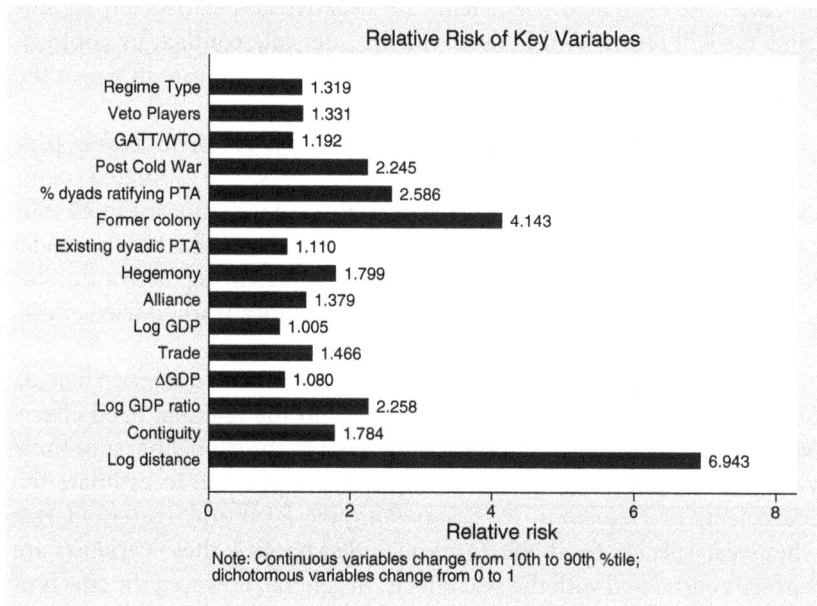

**Relative Risk of Key Variables**

Note: Continuous variables change from 10th to 90th %tile; dichotomous variables change from 0 to 1

**Figure 3.1**  Relative risks of ratifying a PTA, derived from the base model in Table 3.1

to enter preferential arrangements. Furthermore, the magnitude of these effects is comparable to what we reported in earlier work that covered a somewhat shorter period (Mansfield and Milner 2012: Chap. 4).

Various economic and international factors also bear heavily on PTA formation. States that conduct large amounts of trade tend to establish these agreements. The estimated coefficients of $Trade_{ij}$ are positive and statistically significant. There is also some evidence that recessions prompt states to ratify PTAs. The coefficient estimate of $\Delta GDP_i$ is negative in each case, and it is statistically significant in three out of four instances.

Our results also indicate that power politics helps to shape the formation of trade agreements. First, the coefficient estimates of $GDP\ Ratio_{ij}$ are negative and statistically significant, indicating that asymmetries in national income inhibit the ratification of PTAs and that states tend to form PTAs with counterparts that are similarly sized. Second, when fixed effects are not included in the model, there is ample evidence that allies tend to form PTAs. The estimated coefficients of $Alliance_{ij}$ in the first and fourth columns of Table 3.1 are positive and statistically significant. When fixed effects are included (in the second and third columns of this table), however, the estimated coefficients are negative and statistically significant. We will return to this issue shortly. Interstate conflict, by contrast, has little influence on PTA formation since there is no case in which the effect of $Dispute_{ij}$ is statistically significant.

In addition, the results indicate that GATT/WTO membership promotes the ratification of preferential arrangements. The estimated coefficients of $GATT/WTO_{ij}$ are positive and statistically significant in all four cases. Equally, the impact of $Existing\ PTA_{ij}$ depends on whether the model is estimated with fixed effects: its estimated coefficient is positive and significant in the base model, but negative and significant when fixed effects are introduced.

It is important to recognize that we cannot estimate the coefficients of $Former\ Colony_{ij}$, $Contiguity_{ij}$, $Distance_{ij}$ and the regional fixed effects when dyad-specific fixed effects are included in the model because these variables are time invariant. Equally, it is not possible to estimate the coefficients of $Hegemony$, % $Dyads\ Ratifying\ PTAs$ and $Post–Cold\ War$ when year-specific fixed effects are included because these variables are perfectly correlated with the year effects. In general, however, the effects of these variables are consistent across the other model specifications. States tend to eschew entering PTAs with their former colonies. Furthermore, they tend to join preferential agreements with states that are located nearby (since the coefficient of $Distance_{ij}$ is negative and significant), but not contiguous (since the coefficient of $Contiguity_{ij}$ is negative and significant).

Turning to the systemic variables, there is evidence of PTA diffusion and that the odds of ratifying such an agreement rose in the aftermath of the Cold War. The estimated coefficient of $Post–Cold\ War$ is positive and statistically significant in each instance, at least partly because of efforts by countries that were part of the Soviet orbit to become more tightly integrated into the global (especially the western European) economy after the Berlin Wall fell and the Soviet Union collapsed. The coefficient of % $Dyads\ Ratifying\ PTAs$ is positive as well, which indicates that PTA formation tends to cluster over time. In the fourth column, we replace this variable with a measure of diffusion that is calculated as the average percentage of dyads ratifying PTAs over the previous five years. The coefficient estimate of this variable is smaller than that of % $Dyads\ Ratifying$ $PTAs$ but is nonetheless positive and statistically significant. The estimated coefficients of $Hegemony$, however, are less consistent. The coefficient is positive and significant without dyad-specific fixed effects, but negative and significant with fixed effects.

The effects of alliances, existing PTA membership and hegemony change in key ways when we introduce fixed effects in the model. This undoubtedly reflects the fact that the vast bulk of dyads (almost 83.5 per cent of the country pairs in our sample) never form a PTA. These dyads are not used to generate the parameter estimates because introducing fixed effects leads us to assume that none of the independent variables in our model, except for the fixed effects, influences the probability of these dyads ratifying a PTA. It is for this reason that Beck and Katz (2001: 487–8) warn that using fixed-effects models to analyse time-series cross-section data with a binary dependent variable is 'pernicious' and yields 'estimates that are so far off as to be completely useless'. This problem is exacerbated in our case because some independent variables display little or no change over time, even among the dyads that do form PTAs. These dyads are also excluded when estimating the coefficients of such variables. The upshot is that, given the sparseness of our data, very few dyads are used to estimate the model's parameters when including fixed effects, and fewer still are used to estimate some coefficients. There is no reason to believe that these few pairs are a representative sample of the population of all dyads. Consequently, although we have included results based on a fixed-effects specification because certain studies advocate this modelling strategy (Green, Kim and Yoon 2001), we think it is prudent to view the results in columns 2 and 3 with the greatest caution and to place primary emphasis on the remaining results in Table 3.1.

Our analysis shows that a wide variety of factors influence PTA formation. Yet, even after accounting for domestic economic conditions, regional factors and international influences, we find strong evidence that regime type and veto players shape the political calculus of governments contemplating PTAs. Our argument is not that the effect of domestic politics is larger than that of all these other influences. In fact, some international factors have a more sizable impact than either regime type or veto players. Countries were almost three times as likely to enter a PTA after the Cold War, for example, as during this era. Equally, if the geographical distance between a pair of states is at the 90th percentile found in our data set, then they are about seven times less likely to form a preferential agreement than a pair whose distance is at the 10th percentile in the data. On the whole, however, the effects of GATT/WTO membership, alliances, trade, GDP, the change in GDP and existing PTA membership are roughly the same or smaller than those of regime type and veto players.

## F. Conclusion

Using a new data set covering the period from 1952 until 2011, we find that PTAs have important domestic and international political roots. From a domestic political standpoint, democracy promotes PTA formation, and a greater number of veto players inhibit this process. Underlying the effects of democracy is the difficulty that leaders have in convincing constituents that they will ignore special interest pleading for trade protection. This creates a major problem for heads of state because voters may hold them responsible for hard economic times, based on the assumption that the economic conditions were caused by giving in to interest groups' demands when this was not the case. Leaders can help to address this problem by entering a PTA. Since this problem is more severe in more competitive electoral systems, democratic chief executives are especially likely to join PTAs.

Furthermore, leaders face transaction costs when making a trade agreement. The domestic ratification process contributes considerably to the magnitude of these costs. As the number of veto players rises, ratification of a PTA becomes more difficult. Our results confirm that these two different domestic political factors – the nature of the regime and the number of veto players – play a significant role in determining whether countries are willing and able to establish a PTA.

International politics also shapes the establishment of PTAs. Member states in the GATT/WTO are more likely to form PTAs than are other states. Rather than inhibiting their formation as originally intended, the multilateral trade regime has permitted them to flourish and perhaps even encouraged countries to seek them out. It is notable that two large PTAs are currently being negotiated by long-standing and key members of the WTO. The Transatlantic Trade and Investment Partnership (TTIP), which is being negotiated between the EU and the United States, would be the largest preferential trade agreement in history. The Trans-Pacific Partnership (TPP) would include the United States, Australia, Brunei, Canada, Chile, Malaysia, Mexico, New Zealand, Peru, Singapore, Japan and Vietnam. Earlier research indicates that particular features of the GATT/WTO – most notably multilateral negotiating rounds and membership size – also affect PTA formation, an issue that merits additional attention in future research (Mansfield and Milner 2012; Mansfield and Reinhardt 2003).

In addition, power relations play an important role in shaping PTAs. States tend to form trade agreements with similarly sized counterparts rather than with states that are much larger or smaller, perhaps because weaker states recognize the potential of being exploited if they band together with a much stronger country. Hegemony seems to promote the formation of trade agreements, a finding that is at odds with hegemonic stability theory. As expected, allies are more likely to conclude trade agreements than are other states, PTAs were formed more rapidly after than during the Cold War and contagion has contributed to the proliferation of PTAs.

There are a wide variety of important issues involving the political economy of PTAs that we have not addressed in this chapter and that merit attention in future research. One issue that we have not addressed is whether governments comply with PTAs once they become members. Another involves the longevity of PTAs. Of the roughly 400 agreements in the current WTO Regional Trade Agreement database, nearly 46 per cent are inactive. Does this imply that many PTAs are ineffective? Some PTAs have been renounced or suspended, suggesting that they failed. A much larger number of agreements, however, were renegotiated or replaced by agreements that aimed to achieve deeper integration among member states. Consequently, the death of PTAs does not unequivocally signal a lack of compliance or of effectiveness; it may signal greater cooperation among the participating countries. Compliance is an important issue in international relations, and future research on trade agreements should attempt to address this complex issue.

For decades, social scientists have debated whether PTAs hurt or help the international system. Some observers have expressed concern about discriminatory trading blocs that might foster political animosity, as occurred during the 1930s, and splinter the world economy (Bhagwati 2008; Gilpin 1987). Others, however, believe that current trade agreements are designed differently from those that marked the period prior to World War II. More open and less discriminatory, current PTAs are viewed as less of a threat to global economic and political stability. In addition, various trade agreements are forming across geographical regions. Agreements such as the TPP and the TTIP could help to limit any division of the world trading system into exclusive regional blocs. Furthermore, contemporary trade agreements tend to reduce trade barriers. Compared to trade agreements formed in some earlier eras, recently formed PTAs generally have been a force for spreading liberalization and promoting integration rather than for carving out exclusive, discriminatory regional blocs.

A related concern is whether PTAs will undermine the WTO. Most contemporary PTAs have been approved by the WTO, and provisions for

PTAs were made by the GATT when it was initially established. Although the GATT did a poor job of monitoring PTAs, the WTO has developed a more robust monitoring system. This new discipline is intended to make the WTO's multilateralism more consistent with these preferential agreements and to give the WTO a greater say in the development of such agreements. Indeed, if the Doha Round of multilateral trade negotiations fails, the WTO may turn to PTAs as its main mechanism for lowering trade barriers and coordinating economic policies. Our results so far do not provide evidence to support the concerns that discriminatory regional blocs will arise and undermine the global multilateral trading system (Bhagwati 2008). Instead, there seems to have been a good deal of compatibility between the two so far, suggesting that contemporary PTAs are unlikely to threaten either the WTO or international peace and prosperity.

### References

Baccini, Leonardo, and Dür, Andreas. 2012. 'The New Regionalism and Policy Interdependence.' *British Journal of Political Science* 42 (1): 57–79.

Baldwin, Richard. 1995. 'A Domino Theory of Regionalism.' In *Expanding Membership of the European Union*, edited by Richard Baldwin, Pertti Haaparanta and Jaakko Kiander, 25–53. New York: Cambridge University Press.

Baldwin, Richard, and Jaimovich, Dany. 2012. 'Are Free Trade Agreements Contagious?' *Journal of International Economics* 88 (1): 1–16.

Beck, Nathaniel, and Katz, Jonathan N. 2001. 'Throwing Out the Baby with the Bath Water: A Comment on Green, Kim, and Yoon.' *International Organization* 55 (2): 487–95.

Beck, Nathaniel, Katz, Jonathan N., and Tucker, Richard. 1998. 'Taking Time Seriously: Time-Series-Cross-Section Analysis with a Binary Dependent Variable.' *American Journal of Political Science* 42 (4): 1260–88.

Bhagwati, Jagdish. 1991. *The World Trading System at Risk.* Princeton, NJ: Princeton University Press.

2008. *Termites in the Trading System: How Preferential Agreements Undermine Free Trade.* New York: Oxford University Press.

Chase, Kerry A. 2005. *Trading Blocs: States, Firms, and Regions in the World Economy.* Ann Arbor: University of Michigan Press.

Fernández, Raquel, and Portes, Jonathan. 1998. 'Returns to Regionalism: An Analysis of Nontraditional Gains from Regional Trade Agreements.' *World Bank Economic Review* 12 (2): 197–220.

Gawande, Kishore, Hoekman, Bernard, and Cui, Yue. 2011. 'Determinants of Trade Policy Responses to the 2008 Financial Crisis.' Policy Research Working Paper No. 5862. World Bank, Washington, DC.

Gilligan, Michael J. 1997. *Empowering Exporters: Reciprocity, Delegation, and Collective Action in American Trade Policy.* Ann Arbor: University of Michigan Press.

Gilpin, Robert 1987. *The Political Economy of International Relations.* Princeton, NJ: Princeton University Press.

Gleditsch, Nils Petter, Wallensteen, Peter, Eriksson, Mikael, Sollenberg, Margareta, and Strand, Håvard. 2002. 'Armed Conflict 1946–2001: A New Dataset.' *Journal of Peace Research* 39 (5): 615–37.

Gowa, Joanne 1994. *Allies, Adversaries, and International Trade.* Princeton, NJ: Princeton University Press.

Green, Donald P., Kim, Soo Yeon, and Yoon, David H. 2001. 'Dirty Pool.' *International Organization* 55 (2): 441–68.

Grossman, Gene M., and Helpman, Elhanan. 1995. 'The Politics of Free Trade Agreements.' *American Economic Review* 85 (4): 667–90.

Gruber, Lloyd. 2000. *Ruling the World: Power Politics and the Rise of Supranational Institutions.* Princeton, NJ: Princeton University Press.

Gunter, Frank R. 1989. 'Customs Union Theory: Retrospect and Prospect.' In *Economic Aspects of Regional Trading Agreements*, edited by David Greenaway, Thomas Hyclak and Robert J. Thornton, 1–30. New York: Harvester Wheatsheaf.

Gurr, Ted R., Jaggers, Keith, and Moore, Will H. 1989. *Polity II: Political Structures and Regime Change, 1800–1986.* Ann Arbor, MI: Inter-University Consortium for Political and Social Research.

Haggard, Stephan. 1997. 'Regionalism in Asia and the Americas.' In *The Political Economy of Regionalism*, edited by Edward D. Mansfield and Helen V. Milner, 20–49. New York: Columbia University Press.

Henisz, Witold J. 2000. 'The Institutional Environment for Multinational Investment.' *Journal of Law, Economics and Organization* 16 (2): 334–64.

2002. 'The Institutional Environment for Infrastructure Investment.' *Industrial and Corporate Change* 11 (2): 355–89.

Hirschman, Albert O. (1945) 1980. *National Power and the Structure of Foreign Trade.* Berkeley: University of California Press.

Jaggers, Keith, and Gurr, Ted Robert. 1995. 'Tracking Democracy's Third Wave with the Polity III Data.' *Journal of Peace Research* 32 (4): 469–82.

Keohane, Robert O. 1984. *After Hegemony: Cooperation and Discord in the World Political Economy.* Princeton, NJ: Princeton University Press.

Kiewiet, D. Roderick. 1983. *Macroeconomics and Micropolitics: The Electoral Effects of Economic Issues.* Chicago: University of Chicago Press.

Kindleberger, Charles P. 1973. *The World in Depression.* Berkeley: University of California Press.

Krasner, Stephen D. 1976. 'State Power and the Structure of International Trade.' *World Politics* 28 (3): 317–47.

1982. 'Structural Causes and Regime Consequences: Regimes as Intervening Variables.' *International Organization* 36 (2): 185–205.

Krugman, Paul R. 1993. 'Regionalism versus Multilateralism: Analytical Notes.' In *New Dimensions in Regional Integration*, edited by Jaime de Melo and Arvind Panagariya, 58–79. New York: Cambridge University Press.

Kurian, George T. 1992. *Encyclopedia of the Third World*. New York: Facts on File.

Leeds, Brett A., Ritter, Jeffrey, Mitchell, Sara, and Long, Andrew. 2002. 'Alliance Treaty Obligations and Provisions, 1815–1944.' *International Interactions* 28 (3): 237–60.

Lewis-Beck, Michael S. 1988. *Economics and Elections: The Major Western Democracies*. Ann Arbor: University of Michigan Press.

Manger, Mark. 2009. *Investing in Protection: The Politics of Preferential Trade Agreements between North and South*. New York: Cambridge University Press.

Mansfield, Edward D. 1993. 'Effects of International Politics on Regionalism in International Trade.' In *Regional Integration and the Global Trading System*, edited by Kym Anderson and Richard Blackhurst, 199–217. New York: Harvester Wheatsheaf.

Mansfield, Edward D., and Milner, Helen V. 1999. 'The New Wave of Regionalism.' *International Organization* 53 (3): 589–627.

2012. *Votes, Vetoes, and the Political Economy of International Trade Agreements*. Princeton, NJ: Princeton University Press.

Mansfield, Edward D., Milner, Helen V., and Pevehouse, Jon C. 2007. 'Vetoing Cooperation: The Impact of Veto Players on Preferential Trading Arrangements.' *British Journal of Political Science* 37 (3): 403–32.

Mansfield, Edward D., Milner, Helen V., and Rosendorff, B. Peter. 2002. 'Why Democracies Cooperate More: Electoral Control and International Trade Agreements.' *International Organization* 56 (3): 477–513.

Mansfield, Edward D., and Reinhardt, Eric. 2003. 'Multilateral Determinants of Regionalism: The Effects of GATT/WTO on the Formation of Preferential Trading Arrangements.' *International Organization* 57 (4): 829–62.

Mattli, Walter. 1999. *The Logic of Regional Integration: Europe and Beyond*. New York: Cambridge University Press.

McLaren, John. 1997. 'Size, Sunk Costs, and Judge Bowker's Objection to Free Trade.' *American Economic Review* 87 (3): 400–20.

McKeown, Timothy J. 1991. 'A Liberal Trading Order? The Long-Run Pattern of Imports to the Advanced Capitalist States.' *International Studies Quarterly* 35 (2): 151–72.

Milner, Helen V. 1997. 'Industries, Governments, and the Creation of Regional Trade Blocs.' In *The Political Economy of Regionalism*, edited by Edward D. Mansfield and Helen V. Milner, 77–106. New York: Columbia University Press.

Nye, Joseph S. 1988. 'Neorealism and Neoliberalism.' *World Politics* 40 (2): 235–51.

Olson, Mancur. 1965. *The Logic of Collective Action.* Cambridge, MA: Harvard University Press.

Oye, Kenneth A. 1992. *Economic Discrimination and Political Exchange: World Political Economy in the 1930s and 1980s.* Princeton, NJ: Princeton University Press.

Pahre, Robert. 2008. *Politics and Trade Cooperation in the Nineteenth Century: the "Agreeable Customs" of 1815–1914.* New York: Cambridge University Press.

Pomfret, Richard. 1988. *Unequal Trade: The Economics of Discriminatory International Trade Policies.* Oxford, England: Basil Blackwell.

Ruggie, John G. 1982. 'International Regimes, Transactions, and Change: Embedded Liberalism in the Postwar Economic Order.' *International Organization* 36 (2): 379–415.

Serra, Jaime, Aguilar, Guillermo, Cardoba, Jose, Grossman, Gene, Hills, Carla, Jackson, John, Katz, Julius, Noyola, Pedro, and Wilson, Michale. 1997. *Reflections on Regionalism.* Washington, DC: Brookings Institution.

Tsebelis, George. 2002. *Veto Players: How Political Institutions Work.* Princeton, NJ: Princeton University Press.

World Trade Organization. 2011. *World Trade Report 2011.* Geneva: WTO.

Yarbrough, Beth V., and Yarbrough, Robert M. 1992. *Cooperation and Governance in International Trade: The Strategic Organizational Approach.* Princeton, NJ: Princeton University Press.

# 4

# Weak governments and preferential trade agreements

JEAN-LOUIS ARCAND, MARCELO OLARREAGA
AND LAURA ZORATTO

> Economists have always been aware that the determinants of trade policy are
> deep down political.
>
> – Dani Rodrik, *Handbook of International Economics*, Vol. 3

## A. Introduction

The standard theory of trade agreements explains their existence as a way of solving terms-of-trade externalities among large countries (Bagwell and Staiger 1999). By giving each other reciprocal concessions, countries can internalise terms-of-trade externalities and achieve a more efficient outcome. Thus, even if economists recognise that trade policy at the national level is mainly explained by politics as the preceding quotation from Rodrik (1995) suggests, standard trade theory has mainly focused on the internalisation of terms-of-trade externalities.

This gap has started to be filled recently as the literature has provided new rationales for trade agreements where internal politics play an important role and lead to political gains associated with trade agreements. An important contribution to this literature is by Maggi and Rodriguez-Clare

We are grateful to Todd Allee, Leonardo Baccini, Richard Baldwin, John Brown, Tim Büthe, Olivier Cadot, Celine Carrère, Andreas Dür, Peter Egger, Manfred Elsig, Delfim Gomes-Neto, Chris Grigoriou, Sylviane Guillaumont, Keith Head, Bernard Hoekman, Simon Hug, Beata Joavorcik, Hiau Looi Kee, Soo Yeon Kim, Pravin Krishna, Thierry Mayer, Monika Mrázová, Doug Nelson, Emanuel Ornelas, Caglar Ozden, Pascalis Raimondos-Moller, Cristian Ugarte, Anthony Venables, Adrian Wood and participants at seminars at CESifo Global Economy meeting, CERDI, Geneva Trade and Development Workshop, LACEA's Medellin annual meetings, London School of Economics, Oxford University, PEIO conference in Zurich, Universidade do Minho, Sorbonne, Warwick's Trade Cost Conference in Venice, World Bank and World Trade Institute in Bern. We are also grateful to the Swiss Network of International Studies, the Swiss National Research Fund and the World Bank for funding.

(1998), who explain how governments that face time-inconsistency problems in their interactions with domestic lobbies could use the external enforcement provided by trade agreements to achieve a better outcome. Their idea is simple. In a world where capital is immobile across sectors in the short run, but mobile in the long run, the government gets compensated by lobbies in the domestic political game for the static short-run distortions induced by trade protection (the consumption and the mobile factor-induced production inefficiencies). However, it does not get compensated for the long-run capital allocation inefficiencies associated with overinvestment in the sector where domestic lobbying is expected to lead to higher levels of protection. If these long-run capital allocation inefficiencies are large relative to the potential static gains derived from the political game by the government, trade agreements can be used as an external enforcement to credibly commit to trade reform and avoid the long-run misallocation of resources.

There is anecdotal evidence that governments sign preferential trade agreements (PTAs) to lock in domestic reforms. John Whalley (1998) argued that Mexican negotiators of the North American Free Trade Agreement (NAFTA) were less concerned about securing an exchange of concessions between themselves and their negotiating partners than they were about making unilateral concessions to larger negotiating partners with whom they had little negotiating leverage. The idea was clearly to help lock in domestic policy reform. Salas and Zabludovksy (2004), two Mexican negotiators, go one step further, arguing that NAFTA went beyond lock-in policy reforms by helping create and consolidate institutions that reduced judicial uncertainty and anchored Mexico's trade regime, such as the investor-state dispute settlement mechanism.[1] There is also evidence that the signing of international agreements increases a government's credibility, as measured by country-risk ratings. Indeed, Dreher and Voigt (2008) correlate country-risk ratings with a measure of membership in international organisations and find a positive and statistically significant correlation, especially in countries with weak governments and institutions.[2]

---

[1] In a similar vein, during the failed bilateral trade negotiations between Uruguay and the United States in the mid 2000s, if Uruguay's Foreign Affairs Ministry was reluctant to concede on government procurement, the Ministry of Finance was keen on taking the opportunity offered by the bilateral trade agreement to reform its government procurement policies, using the external enforcement as a policy constraint.

[2] More recently, Liu and Ornelas (2011) show that a larger share of trade coming from PTA partners makes it less likely that an end to a democratic regime will be observed. This is

Our objective in this chapter is twofold. First, to provide systematic evidence on whether governments sign PTAs to solve time-inconsistency problems and boost credibility in governments' policies. Second, if this is the case, we wish to provide a dollar estimate of the value given by governments to PTAs that help solve time-inconsistency problems.[3] To answer the first question one could envisage a survey of government officials on their rationale for signing PTAs. But the answers are likely to postrationalise outcomes. More importantly, it would leave us without a set-up to assess the value that governments may give to solving time-inconsistency issues. Thus, to answer both questions we adopt a model-based approach that is based on the predictions in Maggi and Rodriguez-Clare's seminal paper.

There are two main predictions in Maggi and Rodriguez-Clare (1998): first, that incentives to precommit through trade agreements will be stronger in weak governments, defined as those for which the government's weight when bargaining with domestic lobbies over political rents is small. Indeed, if governments can extract most of the lobbying rent from the bargaining game, then there will be little overinvestment by producers as they get a small share of the lobbying rent. Second, Maggi and Rodriguez-Clare predict that precommitment through trade agreements will be used by governments that are neither too sensitive to nor too unaffected by domestic lobbying. In the former case, the governments would rather extract the lobbying rents, whereas in the second they do not really need external enforcement.

Importantly, Mitra (2002) shows that Maggi and Rodriguez-Clare's (1998) predictions do not depend on the assumption of lack of capital mobility in the long run but that they apply in a much more general context. Any model in which there is a resource cost incurred prior to lobbying through actions taken in the expectation of successful lobbying at the next stage will lead to this result. Mitra (2002) obtains similar results to the ones in Maggi and Rodriguez-Clare (1998) in a model with perfect capital mobility but where fixed costs are associated with lobby formation.

---

because, as in Ornelas (2005), the creation of a PTA reduces political rents, and this makes politicians motivated by office rents in less democratic regimes less attracted by staying in office.

[3]  This is crucial in understanding why some countries may sign agreements that hurt them from a strictly market access or terms of trade point of view.

Two more recent papers explain why governments may prefer not to commit to full free trade but rather to tariff bounds (or preferential tariffs). Limão and Tovar (2009) explain why commitment to a tariff bound in trade agreements[4] can be justified if contributions have a diminishing marginal utility for the government.[5] The reason is again simple. A higher tariff may yield a higher joint surplus in the bargaining game between the government and domestic lobbies. But in the presence of diminishing marginal utility from contributions for the government, this higher tariff that results in higher contributions may actually reduce the share of the government in the total pie. A tariff bound can credibly improve the government's bargaining position and compensate for the fall in the joint surplus. The diminishing marginal utility of lobby contributions to the government could be justified, for example, by the long-run misallocation of capital in the set-up of Maggi and Rodriguez-Clare (1998). Similarly, Maggi and Rodriguez-Clare (2007) found that tariff ceilings will actually be preferred to exact tariff commitments because the former allow for the lobbying game to continue, and therefore for the government to collect contributions after the trade agreement is signed. This in turn reduces the net return on capital in the 'wrong' sector, which mitigates the overinvestment problem.[6]

In this chapter we first build on Maggi and Rodriguez-Clare's (1998) set-up to show that if PTAs need to be self-enforcing, then governments that want to overcome their time-inconsistency problems will sign PTAs with larger trading partners. Indeed, agreements with larger partners are more likely to be self-enforceable, as they tend to offer larger market access gains and therefore reduce the incentives to deviate from what was originally agreed. We then provide empirical evidence regarding the importance of credibility considerations when signing PTAs. Finally, we explore the potential heterogeneity of the impact of credibility-motivated PTAs on trade flows; that is, are agreements signed for credibility reasons more or less trade creating? Theoretically, one could expect both results. On the one hand, credibility may increase (and the long-run misallocation be reduced) only in the presence

---

[4]  This is linked to WTO's multilateral negotiations, but as we will argue later, it also encompasses PTAs even when what is negotiated involves internal free trade.

[5]  See also Drazen and Limão (2008) for a similar result in a more general context.

[6]  This is done in a model that allows for both commitment-motivated trade agreements and terms of trade externalities and, more importantly, that allows for *ex ante* lobbying on the government decision to precommit.

of sufficiently trade-creating PTAs, and therefore this will be the type of agreement that governments wishing to increase their credibility will sign. On the other hand, too much trade creation may limit the extent to which governments can extract rents from lobbies in the lobbying game as in Limão and Tovar (2009) or Maggi and Rodriguez-Clare (2007), where tariff bounds are preferred by governments to exact tariff commitments.

Results suggest that credibility considerations are an important determinant of preferential PTAs. Credibility-driven PTAs tend to be signed by governments with low bargaining power vis-à-vis domestic lobbies, and there is a U-shaped relationship between a government's sensitivity to domestic lobbies and the probability of signing a PTA, as predicted by Maggi and Rodriguez-Clare (1998). This U-shaped relationship in weak governments is particularly noticeable when governments sign PTAs with larger countries. We also find that credibility-motivated PTAs tend to lead to more trade creation. Back-of-the-envelope calculations based on the estimates described previously suggest that the value of solving time inconsistency through PTAs is estimated at an average of 1.8 per cent of gross domestic product (GDP), which is as large as the traditionally estimated static economic gains from PTAs.

The rest of this chapter is organised as follows. Section B provides a theoretical framework to examine credibility motives for PTAs and their impact on trade flows. Section C describes the econometric strategy, and Section D discusses the empirical results. Section E provides some concluding remarks.

## B. Credibility-driven PTAs

In this section we draw on the very elegant model of Maggi and Rodriguez-Clare (1998) to explain the main determinants of credibility-driven trade agreements. We then relax the assumption that trade agreements are enforceable and look into determinants of self-enforcement in PTAs. Finally, we explore differences in the impact on trade flows between credibility-driven PTAs and other PTAs.

Assume a 2-sector, 2-factor, small, open economy that cannot influence world prices. Capital is sector-specific in the short run, but not in the long run. We assume that only owners of capital in the import-competing sector (let us assume it is manufacturing) get politically organised to lobby the government for trade protection. They offer the government political contributions in exchange for higher levels of protection. The

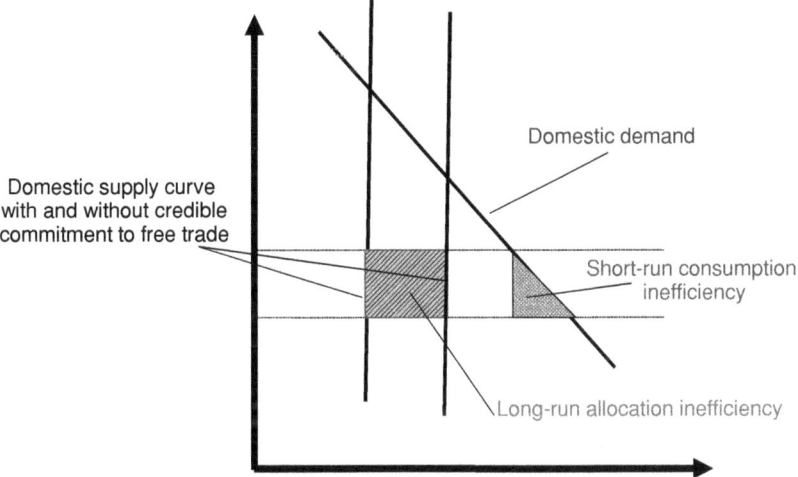

**Figure 4.1**   The need for credibility-driven trade agreements

government's objective function is a weighted sum of social welfare and lobby contributions where social welfare enters with a weight equal to $a$, that is, $V = (1 - a) C + aW$. Thus, the larger is $a$, the less sensitive is the government to lobbies' contributions and the more it cares about social welfare when making trade policy decisions.

The timing of the game is as follows. In the first stage, depending on expected returns on capital in the two sectors, owners of capital decide in which sector to invest. In the second stage, the government and the manufacturing lobby engage in Nash bargaining over trade policy, in which government bargaining power is given by $\sigma$ and lobby bargaining power by $1 - \sigma$.

In such a set-up there will be overinvestment in the manufacturing sector in the first stage if capital owners expect the government to be sensitive to lobby contributions ($a < 1$) in the second stage and their share of the lobbying game to be sufficiently large ($\sigma$ not too large). Indeed, in such a case they will allocate a larger share of capital to the manufacturing sector than under free trade, and this will create a production distortion for which the government will not be compensated in the second stage. The only compensation the government will get in the second stage is that associated with the protection-induced consumption distortion. This is illustrated in Figure 4.1, where the expectation of protection in the second stage induces more investment in the manufacturing sector, shifting the supply curve outwards. This creates a long-run inefficiency that can potentially be much larger than the short-run inefficiencies.[7] This uncompensated long-run distortion creates incentives for the government to precommit to free trade in the first stage even if this implies forgoing the lobby's contributions in the second stage. This will certainly be the case if the bargaining weight of the government is zero ($\sigma = 0$), which implies that the lobby's contributions will only just compensate for the consumption distortion and leave the government worse off than if it had precommitted to free trade in the first stage.

On the other hand, if the government enjoys a sufficiently large share of the joint surplus, then this may compensate for the long-run production distortion, and the government will prefer not to commit to free trade and benefit from the large lobby contributions. Actually, if $\sigma = 1$, then there is no overinvestment as all of the joint surplus will be captured by the government, and owners of capital in the manufacturing sector will be left indifferent between their lobbying game and the free trade returns. Thus, there are no incentives for owners of capital to invest in the manufacturing sector beyond the level observed at free trade prices, and therefore no need to precommit. In other words, if the government grabs all the rents from the political game, it can credibly precommit *ex ante* to any policy without any need to tie its hands. But if the government grabs only a small share of the political game, that is, $\sigma$ is low, this means the government is weak and it cannot credibly precommit *ex ante*. A trade agreement can then be useful.[8]

The first empirical prediction in Maggi and Rodriguez-Clare (1998) has to do with the relationship between the weight the government assigns to social welfare in its objective function and the value for the government of using a trade agreement as a commitment device, that is, $G = V^* - V = aW^* - (1 - a)C - aW = a(W^* - W) - (1 - a)C$. To describe $G(a)$ we proceed in two steps. First, we evaluate the slope of $G(a)$ at $a = 1$ and then the slope of $G(a)$ at $a = 0$. $G(a)$ at $a = 1$ is negative. Indeed, at $a = 1$ there are no political contributions given so that the government

---

[7] In Figure 4.1 we illustrate short-run inefficiencies only on the consumption side because the short-run supply curve is supposed to be perfectly inelastic. In a more general model, where short-run production is not completely inelastic, the government could also be compensated for the short-run production distortion.

[8] There is an important literature in political sciences that started with Katzenstein (1978) that uses a very similar definition of weak and strong states. In that literature weak governments are those that allow interest groups to determine their policies. In our framework, this is more directly connected to $a$ than $\sigma$, but as we will see later $\sigma$ is partly determined by $a$. Governments with a high $a$, that is, less sensitive to the requests of interest groups, tend to have higher $\sigma$'s.

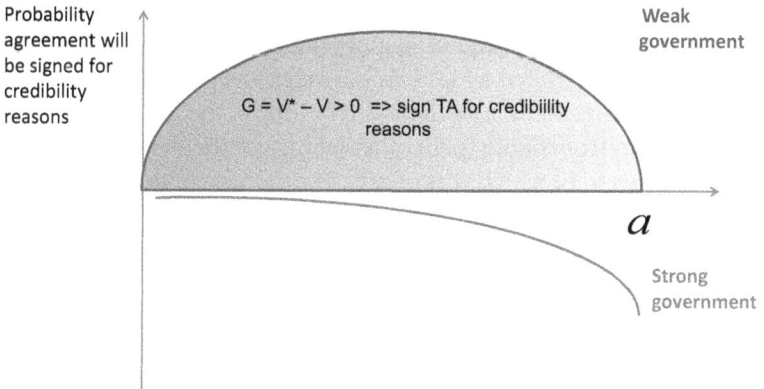

**Figure 4.2**  Which governments sign credibility-driven PTAs?

does not value them in its objective function. This means that there are no long-run distortions and therefore no need for a commitment device. This implies that when the government already puts a very high value on social welfare, an increase in $a$ will make commitment through a trade agreement less valuable and therefore less likely. The intuition is simple: if the government already cares a lot (exclusively) about social welfare, then there is no need to use trade agreements as a commitment device. Thus, the $G(a) = 0$ at $a = 1$, and the slope is negative (i.e. as $a$ is reduced from $a = 1$, the value of $G(a)$ increases). Similarly, if $a = 0$, the government cares only about lobbying contributions, and therefore it does not care about the long-run distortions, which implies that the value of the trade agreement is also null ($G(a) = 0$ at $a = 0$). Now as $a$ increases, and the government starts caring about social welfare, and therefore about the long-run distortions, the value of $G(a)$ increases as long as the drop in lobbying contributions $G$ is not too large. This will be more likely in the case of weak governments (low $\sigma$), as they tend to get a small share of the lobbying rents (and therefore a drop in something that is small will be dominated by the increase in social welfare as $a$ increases). This implies that at $a = 0$ the slope of $G(a)$ is positive for weak governments and negative for strong governments. All this is illustrated in Figure 4.2, which leads to the first prediction:

> *First prediction: PTAs are more likely to be used as a commitment device in countries with intermediate values of a when governments are weak.*

We have assumed so far that PTAs are perfectly enforceable, but it is unclear what the external mechanism is that would enforce these agreements at the international level.[9] Governments may be tempted to deviate from their commitments in a previously signed PTA if the short-run political gains offered by lobbies outweigh the gains associated with respecting the agreement. And there is very little at the international level to prevent them from doing so. In other words, for the PTA to be enforceable there needs to be a high cost of exit. The damage to the international reputation of the country is one example. Other countries will be reluctant to sign agreements with governments that have not respected their PTA obligations in the past. Another example is the potential response of the trading partner, which will punish the deviation by its partner by withdrawing market access concessions. In this case, lobby contributions may compensate for the short-run inefficiencies associated with higher levels of protection but may not be sufficiently large to compensate for the losses suffered by the partner's trade policy response. Indeed, the withdrawal of preferences by the partner will be more costly the larger the partner's market. This leads to our second prediction:[10]

> Second prediction: PTAs are more likely to be used as commitment devices when countries sign agreements with relatively large partners.

Finally, we turn to the impact of credibility-driven PTAs on trade flows: are they likely to lead to more or less trade creation? Or, in other words, are countries seeking to use PTAs as a commitment device more likely to sign agreements with partners that will lead to more trade creation? To address this question, assume that there are two potential partners with which the domestic government could sign a PTA: if signed with partner A, then the agreement is fully trade creating and will lead to the same level of investment in the manufacturing sector as under free trade. If the agreement is signed with partner B, there will be some trade diversion in the Lipsey (1957) sense, which will generate overinvestment in the domestic manufacturing sector, as prices will be above free trade prices.

The trade-off for the domestic government is then quite simple. The PTA with partner A will result in the socially optimal level of investment in the manufacturing sector, but there will be no contributions from lobbies left, as there will be nothing to bargain over. The PTA with partner B, on the other hand, will allow for overinvestment in the manufacturing sector, although the overinvestment will not be as large as under no commitment.

---

[9]   For a thorough discussion of the enforcement of trade agreements, see Bown and Hoekman (2008).

[10]   A formal proof is available from the authors upon request.

Thus, the long-run misallocation of resources for which the government is not compensated will be smaller than under no commitment but larger than if the PTA is signed with country A. On the other hand, the agreement with B will allow the government to receive contributions in the second stage, making it more attractive than the agreement with A. In other words, a less-trade-creating agreement will reduce the size of the pie but may increase the government's share of this pie and therefore may be more attractive than a pure trade-creating agreement in which a government's lobbying rents are forgone. Thus, it seems that whether credibility-driven PTAs are more or less trade creating is an empirical question.

Interestingly, it can be shown that PTAs likely to be more trade creating are those where governments are really weak and with more intermediate values of $a$. Indeed, as argued earlier, $V^A = aW^a > V = (1 - a)C + aW^{11}$ when $\sigma$ is sufficiently small and $a$ neither too small nor too large. The same reasoning applies when comparing $V^B$ to $V$. The trade agreement with country B will be signed only if $\sigma$ is sufficiently small, so that not too much weight is given to the forgone contribution, and when $a$ is neither too large nor to small, so that there is an economic rationale for the agreement.

To determine whether the government will prefer an agreement with partner A to one with B, let us apply the same type of logic as in Maggi and Rodriguez-Clare (1998). An agreement with A will be preferable if:

$$V^A > V^B \Leftrightarrow a(W^A - W^B) - (1 - a)C^B \equiv G^{A-B} > 0 \quad (4.1)$$

It is then straightforward to apply the same reasoning we used earlier to show that an agreement with A will be preferred in countries with weaker governments and more intermediate values of $a$. Thus, the more important the time-inconsistency problem faced by the government, the more likely the government will be to sign a more trade-creating agreement.

## C. Empirical framework

We proceed in two steps. We first estimate the two predictions of the previous section regarding the determinants of credibility-driven PTAs and build a measure of credibility motives behind the signing of each agreement. In the second step we test whether the impact of PTAs on

---

[11] Where $V$ is here the value of the government's objective function in the absence of a trade agreement, and $V^A$ the value of the trade agreement with A.

imports varies depending on whether credibility was an important force behind the signing of the agreement.

## I. Testing the credibility motivation

We investigate whether, controlling for market access reasons and the political affinity between two countries, credibility motivations influence the probability of those countries signing an agreement.

Building on the specification used by Baier and Bergstrand (2004 and 2007) or Egger *et al.* (2009) to explain PTAs, we add the credibility determinants suggested by the two predictions made previously. The basic reduced-form equation to be estimated is then:

$$
\begin{aligned}
PTA_{ijt} = {} & \beta_0 + \beta_1 \, a_{it} + \beta_2 \, a_{it}^2 + \beta_3 \, (1 - \sigma_{it})^* \, a_{it} + \beta_4 \, (1 - \sigma_{it})^* \, a_{it}^2 \\
& + \beta_5 \, (1 - \sigma_{it}) + \beta_6 \, RS_{ijt} + \beta_7 \, RS_{ijt}^* \, (1 - \sigma_{it})^* \, a_{it} \\
& + \beta_8 \, RS_{ijt}^* \, (1 - \sigma_{it})^* \, a_{it}^2 + \beta_9 \, MS_{jt} + \beta_{10} \, DMS_{ijt} \\
& + \beta_{11} \, AI_{ijt} + \beta_{ij} + e_{ijt}
\end{aligned}
\tag{4.2}
$$

where $PTA_{ijt}$ is a binary variable indicating whether countries $i$ and $j$ have a trade agreement at time $t$; $\beta$ represents parameters to be estimated and $\beta_{ij}$ represents country-pair fixed effects to control for anything that is country-pair-specific such as distance, colonial links, a common border, differences in capital-labour ratios and in real GDPs in the initial year as in Baier and Bergstrand (2004); $a_{it}$ is the weight the government of country $i$ grants to domestic aggregate welfare at time $t$ and $1 - \sigma$ is a measure of this government's relative weakness in the bargaining game with lobbies at time $t$. Subsequently we describe how these two determinants of credibility-driven PTAs are measured. Note that $a$ enters in a quadratic form and is interacted with $1 - \sigma$ as suggested by the first prediction; moreover, $a$ $(a^2)$ and $1 - \sigma$ are interacted with RS, which captures the relative size of $j$'s market with respect to $i$'s market (following the second prediction). MS is the market size of country $j$ at time $t$ as in Head and Mayer (2011),[12] DMS is the absolute value of the difference in market size between countries $i$ and $j$ at time $t$ and AI is the affinity index between the two countries at time $t$, as in Baier and Bergstrand (2007); $e$ is the error term. The appendix to this chapter and Table A4.3 with summary statistics provide more information on those variables.

---

[12] We also use GDP as a robustness check.

Because our dependent variable is binary, we use a conditional ML estimation appropriate for the panel logit model with country-pair fixed effects.[13]

The first prediction implies $\beta_3 > 0$ and $\beta_4 < 0$, and the second prediction implies $\beta_7 > 0$ and $\beta_8 < 0$. In the next section we describe how we measure a government's welfare mindedness ($a$) and bargaining strength/weakness ($\sigma$).

## 1. Measuring governments' welfare mindedness

Governments' welfare mindedness ($a$) is estimated using the methodology presented in Gawande, Krishna and Olarreaga (2009) based on the Grossman–Helpman 'Protection for Sale' (1994) setting. In this model, the existing level of tariffs in a country is the result of government – which values both its population's welfare and the contribution it receives from import-competing domestic producers – and lobbies maximising their own objective functions. The first-order condition associated with the government's maximisation in the second stage of the Nash game can be written as follows:[14]

$$\frac{t_{its}}{1 + t_{its}} = \frac{1 - \alpha_{it}}{\alpha_{it}} \frac{y_{its}}{m_{its}\varepsilon_{its}} \quad (4.3)$$

where $t_{its}$ is the MFN tariff in country $i$ at time $t$ in sector $s$, $y$ is domestic production, $m$ are imports and $\varepsilon$ is the absolute value of the import demand elasticity. The country- and time-varying parameter $a_{it}$ can be estimated using the cross-sector variation of Eq. (4.3). Note that some of the right-hand-side variables suffer from endogeneity bias of measurement error (e.g. elasticities are estimates provided in Kee, Nicita and Olarreaga (2009)). One solution is to rewrite (4.3) as

$$\frac{t_{its}}{1 + t_{its}} \frac{\varepsilon_{is}m_{its}}{y_{its}} = \frac{1 - \alpha_{it}}{\alpha_{it}} = \theta_{it}. \quad (4.4)$$

We use a stochastic version of this equation to estimate $\theta_{it} = (1 - a_{it})/a_{it}$: we calculate the left-hand side of Eq. (4.4) and regress it on

---

[13] Fixed-effects estimation is possible for the panel logit model, but not for other binary panel models such as probit because of the incidental parameters problem (Cameron and Trivedi 2005). The bias if we were to use a probit estimation will be relatively important when $t$ is small relative to $ij$, which is the case here where $t$ is approximately 10 and $ij$ approximately 10 000. This is not the case in other set-ups such as Egger *et al.* (2009).

[14] We assume that all $s$ ectors that are import competing are politically organised.

country-pair dummies. Using this estimate, we then retrieve $a$, which varies by country and year; it is given by $a_{it} = 1/(1 + \theta_{it})$. Our estimates of $a$ vary between 0 and 1 and reflect the importance a government attributes to aggregate welfare relative to the contributions it receives from domestic groups (in a trade set-up). The higher $a$, the higher the government's welfare mindedness.

The estimates of $a$ are displayed in Table A4.1 of the appendix to this chapter. The lowest $a$'s belong to Ethiopia and Bangladesh. In general, richer countries and large middle-income countries, such as Singapore and Japan, have higher $a$. Countries with lower $a$ are also among the most corrupt: the Spearman rank correlation between our estimates of $a$ and the 2005 Corruption Perception Index from Transparency International is 0.52.

Equation (4.8) shows that the estimates of $a$ depend not only on the level of tariffs but also on the import-penetration ratio $(m/y)$ and import demand elasticities, their covariance with tariffs and their covariance with each other. As Gawande, Krishna and Olarreaga (2009) note, the incidence of tariffs in industries with high import demand elasticities reveals the willingness of governments to trade aggregate welfare for contributions (low $a$). The incidence of tariffs in industries with high import-penetration ratios reveals the same, since distorting prices in those sectors creates large deadweight losses. As such, it is not surprising that the correlation between the estimates of $a$ and average tariff is relatively low (−0.32).

Table 4.1 indicates how our estimates of $a_{it}$ correlate with different measures of corruption such as the Corruption Perception Index, the number of parking violations by diplomats (from Fisman and Miguel 2007), the corruption index from the World Bank Governance Indicators database (Kaufman, Kraay and Mastruzzi 2009) and average tariffs and GDP per capita. All coefficients have the expected signs: corrupt countries are associated with lower $a$'s as are countries with higher average tariffs. Richer countries have higher $a$'s.

## 2. Measuring governments' bargaining weight

To estimate the government's bargaining weight $\sigma$, we define the contribution that the lobby offers the government in the second stage of the game to obtain a certain level of protection. Under Nash bargaining, the contribution is a weighted sum of the welfare loss incurred by the

Table 4.1 *Government's welfare mindedness* $a_{it}$

|  | (I) | (II) | (III) | (IV) | (V) | (VI) |
|---|---|---|---|---|---|---|
| CPI 2005 | 0.008 94*** |  |  |  |  | 0.042 2*** |
|  | (0.000 879) |  |  |  |  | (0.007 28) |
| Diplomatic |  | −0.000 644** |  |  |  | 0.001 71*** |
| violations |  | (0.000 307) |  |  |  | (0.000 324) |
| Corruption |  |  | 0.155*** |  |  | −0.584*** |
| WB |  |  | (0.015 3) |  |  | (0.076 0) |
| Average tariff |  |  |  | −0.001 82*** |  | −0.001 80*** |
|  |  |  |  | (0.000 371) |  | (0.000 389) |
| Log of GDP |  |  |  |  | 0.087 5** | 0.062 3* |
| per capita |  |  |  |  | (0.034 3) | (0.033 7) |
| Constant | 0.467*** | 0.896*** | 0.644*** | 0.993*** | 0.017 3 | −0.768*** |
|  | (0.040 0) | (0.039 8) | (0.031 4) | (0.034 3) | (0.341) | (0.111) |
| Observations | 290 | 279 | 290 | 290 | 287 | 279 |
| R-squared | 0.939 | 0.938 | 0.939 | 0.945 | 0.940 | 0.945 |

*Note:* All regressions are estimated using OLS with country and year fixed effects. Standard errors in parentheses.
CPI, Corruption Perception Index of Transparency International; WB, World Bank's Governance Indicators' corruption index.
* $p < 0.1$
** $p < 0.05$
*** $p < 0.01$

government and the lobby's willingness to pay for protection:

$$C = (1 - \sigma) \left[ \frac{a}{1 - a} \left( W^* - W \right) \right] + \sigma \left[ \left( p - p^* \right) y \right]. \quad (4.5)$$

The first term in square brackets is the value of the welfare loss for the government associated with a given level of protection relative to a dollar of contribution, and the second term is the value for the lobby of obtaining a given level of protection assuming that the short-run supply is perfectly inelastic as in Figure 4.1. If the government's bargaining weight is close to 1, then the government will get all the rents away from the lobbies. If the government is weak ($\sigma = 0$), then it will only be left indifferent with respect to its level of welfare under free trade.

Taking the derivative of ([Contribution]) with respect to tariffs, recalling that the level of production is fixed in this second stage by assumption, and then, using the first order condition of the government's maximisation problem,[15] we obtain:[16]

$$\frac{\Omega_{its}}{2 - \Omega_{its}} = \sigma_{it} \quad \text{where } \Omega_{its} = \frac{a_{it}}{1 - a_{it}} \frac{t_{its}}{1 + t_{its}} \frac{m_{its}}{y_{its}} \varepsilon_{its}. \quad (4.6)$$

We then estimate $\sigma_{it}$ using a stochastic version of Eq. (4.6) for each country and year. Table A4.2 of the appendix to this chapter presents the average estimates of $1 - \sigma$ (government's weakness/lobby's strength) by country, with an overall mean of 0.86. This relatively large bargaining weight for lobbies vis-à-vis governments is in accordance with the assumption of the Grossman and Helpman (1994) model, in which lobbies are assumed to capture all the rents from the lobbying game.[17]

The five countries with the strongest governments (in terms of share of lobbying rents captured by the government) are Bangladesh, Trinidad and Tobago, Venezuela, India and Thailand. The five countries with weakest governments are Sweden, Ethiopia, Singapore, Australia and France. We examine how our estimates correlate with a number of political variables from the World Bank's Political Institutions Database (Beck *et al.* 2001) and present results in Table 4.2. The only statistically significant result we obtained is for the Government Herfindhal index (the sum of squares of the share of seats in the government by each political party), which correlates positively with the bargaining weight of the government, suggesting that governments that are more concentrated tend to be stronger when bargaining over lobbying rents.[18]

## 3. How important are credibility motivations?

Using the estimates from the conditional ML of Eq. (4.1), we can then predict the likelihood of observing a trade agreement between two partners

---

[15]   If the government's FOC is satisfied, then $\partial C / \partial t = -a/(1 - a) * dW/dt$, where $dW/dt = -\varepsilon mt/(1 + t)$.

[16]   The welfare loss is linearly approximated by the Harberger triangle; that is, $W^* - W = 1/2 * \Delta m * t = 1/2 * m * \varepsilon * t/(1 + t)$.

[17]   As mentioned earlier, Eq. (4.6) suggests that a larger $a$ implies a larger $\sigma$ and therefore a stronger government.

[18]   Note that there is no correlation between the estimates of $a$ in the previous subsection and the estimates of $\sigma$. The correlation coefficient is 0.04.

Table 4.2 *Government's bargaining weight σ*

|  | (I) | (II) | (III) | (IV) | (V) |
|---|---|---|---|---|---|
| Finite term | 0.123 | | | | 0.109 |
| | (0.198) | | | | (0.209) |
| Herfindahl government | | 0.261** | | | 0.271** |
| | | (0.105) | | | (0.113) |
| Margin of opposition | | | 0.0309 | | −0.0986 |
| | | | (0.154) | | (0.168) |
| Log of GDP per capita | | | | 0.196 | 0.284 |
| | | | | (0.217) | (0.279) |
| Constant | 0.0262 | −0.277 | 0.103 | −1.956 | −1.575 |
| | (0.255) | (0.283) | (0.260) | (2.162) | (1.440) |
| Observations | 260 | 260 | 281 | 287 | 251 |
| $R^2$ | 0.296 | 0.317 | 0.292 | 0.296 | 0.319 |

*Note:* OLS regressions include country and year fixed effects. Standard errors in parentheses.
* $p < 0.1$
** $p < 0.05$
*** $p < 0.01$

at time $t$:

$$P_{ijt} = \frac{\exp^{x'\beta}}{\sum_l \exp^{x'\beta}} \tag{4.7}$$

where $l$ represents a country pair and the denominator is therefore a constant within a country pair. The probability model used in the conditional logit is not the unconditional probability $P(Y = 1 \mid X)$, but the probability of a positive outcome conditional on one positive outcome in the country-pair group. As such, the underlying model has a different intercept for each group.

To differentiate between credibility- and market-access-driven PTAs, we calculate the predicted probability of a positive outcome considering only explanatory variables associated with the credibility argument (the triple interactions of $(1 - \sigma)$ and the relative size of country $j$ with respect to $i$), which we call $P^c$ henceforth:

$$P_{ijt}^c = \frac{\exp^{xc'\beta}}{\sum_l \exp^{xc'\beta}}. \tag{4.8}$$

Table 4.3 *Summary statistics of $P^c$ by type of agreement*

| North–North PTAs | | | | | | | |
|---|---|---|---|---|---|---|---|
| obs | mean | sd | max | min | p25 | p50 | p75 |
| 2 264 | 0.14 | 0.34 | 1 | 0 | 0 | 0 | 2e-14 |
| South–South PTAs | | | | | | | |
| obs | mean | sd | max | min | p25 | p50 | p75 |
| 9 592 | 0.23 | 0.42 | 1 | 0 | 0 | 0 | 0.01 |
| North–South PTAs | | | | | | | |
| obs | mean | sd | max | min | p25 | p50 | p75 |
| 6 236 | 0.16 | 0.36 | 0.98 | .0 | 0 | 0 | 3e-32 |
| South–North PTAs | | | | | | | |
| obs | mean | sd | max | min | p25 | p50 | p75 |
| 1 905 | 0.23 | 0.41 | 1 | 0 | 0 | 0 | 0.02 |
| All agreements | | | | | | | |
| Obs | mean | sd | max | min | p25 | p50 | p75 |
| 19 997 | 0.20 | 0.39 | 1 | 0 | 0 | 0 | 1e-10 |

How does the probability that an agreement will be signed for credibility reasons vary by region? Using Eq. (4.8), we estimated $P_{ijt}^c$ for different types of agreements. Results are reported in Table 4.3. South–North agreements have a higher $P^c$ on average than all other types of agreements (24 per cent), followed by South–South (23 per cent), North–South (16 per cent) and North–North agreements (14 per cent). Developing countries are more likely to sign PTAs for credibility reasons.

## II. Do credibility-driven PTAs affect trade differently?

We are now able to analyse the impact of credibility-driven PTAs on bilateral flows using $P^c$. To disentangle whether there is heterogeneity in the way credibility-motivated PTAs affect imports, we turn to the workhorse of the trade literature: the gravity equation. To control for the same variables as in the most recent work on the impact of PTAs on bilateral trade flows, we introduce country-pair-specific fixed effects. This controls for bilateral distance, colonial linkages, a common border or any other geographical or time-invariant institutional determinant of bilateral flows (see Carrère 2006 or Baier and Bergstrand 2007 or 2009).

We also use alternative gravity specifications. In a second specification we introduce time∗exporter dummies to control for general equilibrium effects such as those affecting trade flows through exporter-country price indices (see Baier and Bergstrand 2007 or Egger *et al.* 2009).[19] We also estimate a more traditional gravity specification controlling for distance, common language and remoteness as in Carrère (2006). We estimate those specifications using ordinary least squares (OLS) and negative binomial (NB), where the latter controls for the presence of zeros in bilateral trade data.[20]

## D. Results

Table 4.4 presents the results of the effect of credibility motivations on the formation of PTAs between two countries. More specifically, we test the two predictions from the extended Maggi and Rodriguez-Clare model of Section B.

The first prediction – PTAs are more likely to be used as a commitment device in countries with intermediate values of $a$ when governments are weak – is confirmed by our estimates of $\beta_3$ and $\beta_4$, which are both statistically significant. The second prediction is also confirmed: the signs of the coefficients for the interactions $RS_{ijt}^*(1 - \sigma_{it})^*a_{it}$ and $RS_{ijt}^*(1 - \sigma_{it})^*a_{it}^2$ confirm that a PTA is more likely to be used as a commitment device when countries sign agreements with relatively larger partners.

In column 3 of Table 4.4, we correct our estimates of $a_{it}$ and $\sigma_{it}$ for the fact that they have been estimated ($a_{it}$ and $\sigma_{it}$ are generated regressors). To minimise the measurement error bias in the estimation of Eq. (4.6), we apply the error correction suggested by Fuller (1987) and Gawande (1997).[21] Results of the estimation of Eq. (4.6) using the corrected $\tilde{a}_{it}$ and $\tilde{\sigma}_{it}$ do not change significantly, as shown in column 3 of Table 4.4.

---

[19] Note that time*importer effects are not included because our variable of interest ($P_{i,jt}^c$, interacted with the RTA dummy) depends on importer's characteristics.

[20] Because the assumption of equidispersion does not hold, the Poisson PML does not take full account of the heteroscedasticity in the model, and therefore we use the NB estimator, which is more general than the Poisson model (Cameron and Trivedi 2005).

[21] Given that $a_{it}$ is estimated with a measurement error equal to $u_{it}$ and standard error $\sigma_{uit}$, the corrected $a_{it}$ (or $\tilde{a}_{it}$) is then (a similar correction is undertaken for $\sigma_{it}$):

$$\tilde{a}_{it} = \overline{a} + \frac{\sigma_a^2 - \overline{\sigma_u^2}}{\sigma_{uit}^2}(a_{it} - \overline{a}).$$

Table 4.4 *The effect of credibility on PTA formation, 1988–2000*

| PTA $= 1$ or $0$ | (I) | (II) | (III) Gawande/Fuller correction |
|---|---|---|---|
| Welfare mindedness $(a)$ | 85.12*** | −426.7** | −716.62 |
| | (25.24) | (200.4) | (460.54) |
| Welfare mindedness squared $(a^2)$ | −56.30*** | 228.5** | 377.75 |
| | (15.37) | (115.7) | (257.74) |
| Government's weakness $(1 - \sigma)$ | | −331.5*** | −396.49* |
| | | (111.9) | (224.36) |
| $a^*(1 - \sigma)$ | | 734.8*** | 820.83 |
| | | (254.8) | (500.9) |
| $a^{2*}(1 - \sigma)$ | | −406.8*** | −426.12 |
| | | (144.7) | (279.18) |
| Relative size $(j/i)$(RS) | | 263.4*** | 688.16** |
| | | (97.88) | (648.20) |
| $a^{2*}(1 - \sigma)^*$RS | | 773.4*** | 1 720.11** |
| | | (243.0) | (316.2) |
| $a^{2*}(1 - \sigma)^*$RS | | −433.7*** | −964.86** |
| | | (135.7) | (357.16) |
| $a^*$RS | | −600.5*** | −1 550.18** |
| | | (218.8) | (608.06) |
| $a^{2*}$RS | | 340.0*** | 869.99** |
| | | (122.3) | (335.96) |
| $(1 - \sigma)^*$RS | | −343.9*** | −764.92** |
| | | (108.7) | (293.93) |
| Market size of partner $(MS_j)$ | 3.41e-05*** | 4.55e-05** | 0.000 036** |
| | (1.24e-05) | (1.83e-05) | (0.000 016) |
| Abs. value of size difference (DMS) | 286.2** | 325.3** | 386.87*** |
| | (139.0) | (152.7) | (154.29) |
| UN Affinity Index (AI) | 1.902* | 2.510** | 3.966*** |
| | (1.083) | (1.121) | (1.076) |
| Observations | 936 | 936 | 936 |

*Note:* All regressions are estimated using a maximum likelihood conditional logit, which controls for time-invariant country-pair-specific unobservables. Standard errors in parentheses.

\* $p < 0.1$
\*\* $p < 0.05$
\*\*\* $p < 0.01$

Table 4.5 provides OLS estimates showing that the inverted U-shaped relationship is obtained using a linear probability model as well. The turning point using the conditional logit estimates occurs for values of $a = 0.8$, that is, when the weight given to social welfare in the government's objective function is four times larger than the weight given to political contributions.

We revert to Table 4.6 to examine the impact of credibility-driven PTAs on the trade flows between pairs of countries. In both gravity specifications (with country-pair and time fixed effects, and exporter-year and country-pair fixed effects), the coefficient on the interaction PTA*$P^c$ is insignificant, suggesting no particular effect of credibility-driven PTAs on trade flows between the pair of countries. Nevertheless, once we account for the presence of zeros in the trade matrix and estimate the gravity equation with NB as in column 5 of Table 4.6, we find that credibility-driven PTAs are trade creating. The likelihood-ratio test of $H_0 : \alpha = 0$ rejects the null hypothesis that the variance function parameter of the NB model is 0; that is, there is overdispersion in the data and therefore the NB model is preferred to the Poisson (Cameron and Trivedi 2005).

### I. The value of PTAs

Using these estimates, we can provide an estimate of the value that governments grant to PTAs that are signed for credibility reasons. Indeed, our estimates suggest that an agreement that is signed for credibility reasons leads to an increase in imports that is 7 per cent larger than if the agreement is signed for other reasons. This implies that the government is willing to give up a certain amount of lobbying contributions for credibility reasons.[22] Using the expression in Eq. (4.6) and our estimates of $a$ and $\sigma$, we can estimate the loss in contributions that the government is willing to incur to sign for credibility reasons. To do so, first note that we can translate the additional change in imports into a price effect using import

where $\bar{a}$ and $\sigma_a^2$ are the sample mean and variance of $a$, respectively. It can readily be seen from the formula that $a_{it}$ is measured without error ($\tilde{a}_{it} = a_{it}$) whenever the variance of the measurement error of one observation is equal to the difference between the sample variance of $a_{it}$ and the mean variance of $u_{it}$ (i.e. when the fraction above $= 1$). If the denominator is large, $\tilde{a}_{it}$ is approximated by the sample mean of $a$ ($\bar{a}$); and if the sample variance of $a_{it}$ is large relative to the measurement error (the numerator), $\tilde{a}_{it}$ is approximated by the estimated $a_{it}$.

[22] Ideally, what we would like to measure is the production inefficiency associated with the absence of commitment, but this is something for which we have no data.

Table 4.5 *The effect of credibility on PTA formation, 1988–2000 (OLS estimates)*

| | (I) | (II) |
|---|---|---|
| Welfare mindedness ($a$) | 15.91*** | −10.49 |
| | (5.133) | (23.88) |
| Welfare mindedness squared ($a^2$) | −10.30*** | 3.761 |
| | (3.092) | (14.09) |
| Government's weakness ($1 - \sigma$) | | −18.94* |
| | | (11.36) |
| $a^*(1 - \sigma)$ | | 41.37 |
| | | (26.98) |
| $a^{2*}(1 - \sigma)$ | | −22.67 |
| | | (15.87) |
| Relative size ($j/i$)(RS) | | 19.90** |
| | | (7.907) |
| $a^*(1 - \sigma)^*$RS | | 52.95*** |
| | | (20.07) |
| $a^{2*}(1 - \sigma)^*$RS | | −30.43** |
| | | (11.81) |
| $a^*$RS | | −47.46** |
| | | (18.73) |
| $a^{2*}$RS | | 27.72** |
| | | (11.02) |
| $(1 - \sigma)^*$RS | | −22.92*** |
| | | (8.459) |
| Market size of partner (MS$_j$) | 2.70e-09** | 1.69e-09 |
| | (1.23e-09) | (1.22e-09) |
| Abs. value of size difference (DMS) | 0.076 0*** | 0.072 1*** |
| | (0.027 1) | (0.026 3) |
| UN Affinity Index (AI) | 0.217 | 0.521*** |
| | (0.184) | (0.192) |
| Constant | −6.789*** | 5.587 |
| Observations | 936 | 936 |
| $R^2$ | 0.057 | 0.133 |
| Number of country pairs | 138 | 138 |

*Note:* All regressions include country-pair fixed effects. Standard errors in parentheses.

* $p < 0.1$
** $p < 0.05$
*** $p < 0.01$

Table 4.6 *The impact of credibility-driven PTAs on imports*

| Log of imports | (I) | (II) | (III) | (IV) | (V) Imports |
|---|---|---|---|---|---|
| Log of GDP ($i$) | 1.247*** | 1.245*** | 1.279*** | 0.861*** | 0.134*** |
| | (0.125) | (0.125) | (0.125) | (0.021 9) | (0.007 61) |
| Log of GDP ($j$) | 1.199 9*** | 1.201 8*** | | 1.217 3*** | 0.458*** |
| | (0.191) | (0.118) | | (0.016) | (0.006 13) |
| PTA | 0.309*** | 0.307*** | 0.284*** | 0.303*** | 0.600*** |
| | (0.082 2) | (0.082 6) | (0.088 0) | (0.070 5) | (0.028 1) |
| $P^c$ | | −0.006 38 | −0.027 0 | −0.039 1 | −0.080 9*** |
| | | (0.025 1) | (0.027 0) | (0.025 5) | (0.015 8) |
| PTA*$P^c$ | | 0.012 4 | 0.028 1 | 0.064 4 | 0.073 9** |
| | | (0.064 2) | (0.065 8) | (0.062 0) | (0.030 3) |
| Common language | | | | 0.670*** | |
| | | | | (0.091 3) | |
| Log inverse of distance | | | | 1.194*** | |
| | | | | (0.055 7) | |
| Remoteness | | | | −0.007 16 | |
| | | | | (0.013 3) | |
| Constant | −51.88*** | −51.89*** | −24.01*** | −32.88*** | −14.78*** |
| | (4.233) | (4.235) | (3.168) | (0.828) | (0.236) |
| Observations | 17 920 | 17 920 | 17 920 | 15 049 | 18 716 |
| $R^2$ | 0.089 | 0.089 | 0.941 | 0.721 1 | |
| Number of country pairs | 3 724 | 3 724 | | 2 936 | 3 256 |

*Note:* OLS regressions in columns I and II have country-pair and year fixed effects. OLS regression in column III has exporter-year and country-pair fixed effects, and column IV has year fixed effects. Conditional FE NB regression in column V has country-pair and year fixed effects. Bootstrapped standard errors in parentheses for columns I to IV.
* $p < 0.1$
** $p < 0.05$
*** $p < 0.01$

demand elasticities; that is, $\Delta p = (p/\varepsilon) \cdot \Delta m/m$. Then, differentiating Eq. (4.5) with respect to prices, we obtain:

$$\Delta C = -(1-\sigma)\frac{a}{1-a} \cdot \Delta W + \sigma \Delta p \cdot y \qquad (4.9)$$

where $\Delta W$ can be linearly approximated by the Harberger triangle as $1/2 \cdot \Delta m |\Delta p|$. Substituting the change in prices above into the change in welfare expression and into Eq. (4.9), it can be rearranged as:

$$\frac{\Delta C}{py} = -\frac{1}{|\varepsilon|}\frac{\Delta m}{m}\left(\sigma + \frac{1}{2}(1-\sigma)\frac{a}{1-a}\frac{\Delta m}{m}\frac{m}{y}\right). \qquad (4.10)$$

Equation (4.10) suggests that the more elastic import demand, the smaller the loss in contributions as a share of total production for a given percentage change in imports. The reason is simple. A more elastic import demand implies that domestic demand is very elastic, and therefore the change in domestic prices following the change in imports should not be too large so that it will not lead to a large decline in producer surplus and therefore contributions. On the other hand, the larger $a$, the larger the loss in contributions that the government is willing to endure to solve its time-inconsistency problems. Finally, an increase in the bargaining weight that the government has increases the value for the government of signing a trade agreement unless $a$ is very large: with an increase in imports of 7 per cent and assuming an imports-to-output ratio of 50 per cent, $a$ needs to be larger than 0.987 for the loss in contributions to decline with $\sigma$. It is important to note at this point that the fact that the probability of the agreement being signed is low does not affect the potential value of the agreement. For example, if $a$ is large, the agreement is valuable for the government because it increases welfare. Similarly, if $\sigma$ is 0, the government has strong incentives to sign for credibility reasons because it does not get anything from the lobbying game, but the value of the trade agreement is also likely to be small because there is not much to lose in terms of political contributions.

Expression (4.10) can then be computed for every country at the sample mean, and the results are reported in Table A4.4 of the appendix to this chapter. Our estimates suggest that to sign for credibility reasons governments may be willing to forgo on average around 1.8 per cent of the value of production (or GDP given the model's assumptions) in lobbies' contributions.[23] Countries for which the value of PTAs signed for credibility reasons is higher are Bangladesh and Trinidad and Tobago, where the value of the trade agreement signed for credibility reasons could represent approximately 4 per cent of GDP. Countries for which the value for the government of PTAs signed for credibility reasons is likely

---

[23] To calculate the value of PTAs per credibility reason in each country, we used the import-to-output ratios per country.

to be small are Ethiopia and Bolivia, where the gains represent less than 0.1 per cent of GDP (for Ethiopia). The heterogeneity across countries is explained by differences in import demand elasticities, import-to-output ratios, $\sigma$'s and $a$'s.

## E. Concluding remarks

We provided empirical evidence regarding the importance of credibility considerations when signing PTAs based on the theoretical predictions of Maggi and Rodriguez-Clare (1998). Results suggest that credibility-driven PTAs tend to be signed by governments with low bargaining power vis-à-vis domestic lobbies and that there is a U-shaped relationship between a government's sensitivity to domestic lobbying and the probability of the government signing a PTA, in particular when the partner is relatively large. Interestingly, credibility considerations tend to be a stronger cause of PTAs when these are signed by developing countries regardless of whether the partner is a developed or a developing country (as long as the partner is relatively larger). We also found that credibility-motivated PTAs tend to lead to more trade creation. The value of PTAs signed for credibility reasons varies depending on the weight governments give to social welfare in their objective function and their bargaining power when sharing political rents with lobbies. On average they represent 1.8 per cent of GDP.

One avenue for future research may be to move away from the view of trade agreements being homogeneous and to try to understand the determinants of deeper forms of trade agreements. For example, do credibility issues play a relatively more important role in explaining the adoption of deeper forms of trade agreements? Could this explain the larger impact that credibility-driven PTAs have on trade flows? These new predictions could be tested using the measures of depth in trade agreements in Dür, Baccini and Elsig (2014).

## Appendix to Chapter 4

We use the Design of Trade Agreements Database provided in Dür, Baccini and Elsig (2014) to construct our PTA variable based on the date the agreements entered into force (see www.designoftradeagreements.org/). The database contains more than 500 agreements during our sample period, which spans from 1948 to 2007; 329 of these agreements were still in force in 2007. A total of 1319 country-pair trade deals are registered up

Table A4.1 *Estimates of government's welfare mindedness a*

| Country | a | SD | Dev. from overall mean |
|---|---|---|---|
| Japan | 0.9878 | 0.0017 | 0.1265 |
| Italy | 0.9819 | 0.0051 | 0.1206 |
| Brazil | 0.9799 | 0.0044 | 0.1186 |
| Romania | 0.9785 | 0 | 0.1173 |
| Spain | 0.9750 | 0.0028 | 0.1138 |
| South Korea | 0.9741 | 0.0051 | 0.1128 |
| USA | 0.9737 | 0.0021 | 0.1125 |
| Turkey | 0.9721 | 0.0032 | 0.1108 |
| Taiwan | 0.97 | 0.0049 | 0.1087 |
| Germany | 0.9676 | 0.0072 | 0.1063 |
| France | 0.9674 | 0.0048 | 0.1061 |
| United Kingdom | 0.9664 | 0.0026 | 0.1052 |
| Argentina | 0.9634 | 0.0049 | 0.1022 |
| China | 0.9617 | 0.0132 | 0.1004 |
| Finland | 0.9581 | 0.0011 | 0.0969 |
| Australia | 0.953 | 0.0056 | 0.0917 |
| Poland | 0.9503 | 0.0087 | 0.0891 |
| Colombia | 0.9454 | 0.016 | 0.0841 |
| Denmark | 0.9415 | 0.0057 | 0.0803 |
| South Africa | 0.9307 | 0.0443 | 0.0695 |
| Latvia | 0.9304 | 0.0094 | 0.0692 |
| Hungary | 0.9284 | 0.0288 | 0.0672 |
| Greece | 0.9184 | 0.0125 | 0.0572 |
| Nepal | 0.9146 | 0 | 0.0534 |
| Malaysia | 0.9087 | 0.0231 | 0.0474 |
| Chile | 0.9047 | 0.0047 | 0.0435 |
| India | 0.9010 | 0.0302 | 0.0398 |
| Sweden | 0.9008 | 0 | 0.0396 |
| Venezuela | 0.8994 | 0.0627 | 0.0381 |
| Ireland | 0.8949 | 0.0043 | 0.0337 |
| Peru | 0.8845 | 0 | 0.0232 |
| Uruguay | 0.8833 | 0.0507 | 0.0220 |
| Guatemala | 0.8817 | 0.0173 | 0.0204 |
| Philippines | 0.8755 | 0.0105 | 0.0142 |
| Norway | 0.8750 | 0.0198 | 0.0137 |
| Indonesia | 0.8750 | 0.0430 | 0.0137 |
| Netherlands | 0.8733 | 0.0107 | 0.0121 |

Table A4.1 (cont.)

| Country | a | SD | Dev. from overall mean |
|---|---|---|---|
| Costa Rica | 0.8423 | 0.0428 | −0.0189 |
| Egypt | 0.8077 | 0.0267 | −0.0536 |
| Kenya | 0.7875 | 0.0477 | −0.0737 |
| Ecuador | 0.7640 | 0.044 | −0.0972 |
| Mexico | 0.7572 | 0.0588 | −0.1041 |
| Malawi | 0.7437 | 0.0092 | −0.1176 |
| Morocco | 0.723 | 0.0897 | −0.1383 |
| Thailand | 0.723 | 0.0950 | −0.1383 |
| Trinidad and Tobago | 0.7056 | 0.0120 | −0.1557 |
| Cameroon | 0.6985 | 0.09 | −0.1627 |
| Sri Lanka | 0.6200 | 0.0332 | −0.2413 |
| Bangladesh | 0.4731 | 0 | −0.3882 |
| Bolivia | 0.3863 | 0.1053 | −0.4749 |
| Ethiopia | 0.2137 | 0 | −0.6476 |

to 2000, but just 1134 are still in force or signed for later implementation. That means that approximately 11 per cent of the pairs of countries were covered by some sort of trade agreement in the year 2000. Among these agreements, 65 per cent are classified as pure free trade agreements (FTAs), and the others are partial scope agreements, currency unions and others. For our analysis, we use all types of registered agreements. We limit the period of investigation to 1988–2000 because of the availability of data on trade, production and protection by sector (Nicita and Olarreaga 2006) used to construct $a$ and $\sigma$ (government's welfare mindedness and bargaining weight vis-à-vis lobbies, respectively). We have 6026 country pairs in the final sample (where $a$ and $\sigma$ are not missing values for at least one year).

Data on the Real Market Potential of countries, which we use to proxy for market size, are from Head and Mayer (2009). The Affinity of Nations Index (1946–2002) that measures the interest similarity between pairs of countries based on the votes in the United Nations General Assembly is from Gartzke (2006). All politically related data (the margin of majority of the government in Congress, the Herfindhal measure of concentration of government parties in Congress, whether a country has a finite term for its government, etc.) come from the World Bank database of Political

Table A4.2 *Estimates of government's bargaining weakness* $(1 - \sigma)$

| Country | $(1 - \sigma)$ | SD | Dev. from overall mean |
|---|---|---|---|
| Bangladesh | 0 | 0 | −0.8621 |
| Trinidad and Tobago | 0.4785 | 0.6768 | −0.3835 |
| Venezuela | 0.562 | 0.59 | −0.3 |
| India | 0.5804 | 1.195 | −0.2816 |
| Thailand | 0.6686 | 0.1784 | −0.1934 |
| Denmark | 0.7119 | 0.6498 | −0.1502 |
| Malawi | 0.7166 | 0.5559 | −0.1455 |
| South Korea | 0.7404 | 0.4157 | −0.1217 |
| Morocco | 0.7453 | 0.1593 | −0.1168 |
| Poland | 0.749 | 0.5957 | −0.1131 |
| Nepal | 0.764 | 0 | −0.0981 |
| Brazil | 0.7877 | 0.2353 | −0.0744 |
| Philippines | 0.8238 | 0.5618 | −0.0383 |
| Hungary | 0.8320 | 0.1762 | −0.03 |
| Malaysia | 0.8333 | 0.5964 | −0.0287 |
| Ecuador | 0.8333 | 0.3844 | −0.0287 |
| Uruguay | 0.8408 | 0.3234 | −0.0213 |
| Romania | 0.8522 | 0 | −0.0099 |
| Indonesia | 0.8581 | 0.4336 | −0.004 |
| Mexico | 0.8647 | 0.2658 | 0.0026 |
| Ireland | 0.8732 | 0.0575 | 0.0111 |
| Colombia | 0.8841 | 0.2032 | 0.022 |
| Latvia | 0.8865 | 0.1186 | 0.0244 |
| Sri Lanka | 0.9007 | 1.018 | 0.0386 |
| Egypt | 0.9077 | 1.926 | 0.0456 |
| Argentina | 0.9164 | 0.1792 | 0.0543 |
| Spain | 0.9167 | 0.1686 | 0.0546 |
| Greece | 0.9188 | 1.047 | 0.0567 |
| Finland | 0.9349 | 0.0694 | 0.0729 |
| South Africa | 0.9376 | 2.272 | 0.0755 |
| China | 0.9509 | 10.422 | 0.0888 |
| United Kingdom | 0.9579 | 0.3656 | 0.0958 |
| Cameroon | 0.9597 | 0.2665 | 0.0976 |
| Costa Rica | 0.961 | 0.1545 | 0.0989 |
| Peru | 0.963 | 0 | 0.1009 |
| Turkey | 0.9634 | 0.1714 | 0.1014 |
| Norway | 0.9673 | 0.1052 | 0.1052 |
| Japan | 0.9691 | 0.0345 | 0.1071 |

Table A4.2 (cont.)

| Country | $(1 - \sigma)$ | SD | Dev. from overall mean |
|---|---|---|---|
| Taiwan | 0.97 | 0.1283 | 0.108 |
| USA | 0.9726 | 0.0447 | 0.1106 |
| Kenya | 0.9783 | 0.1151 | 0.1162 |
| Guatemala | 0.9789 | 0.0756 | 0.1168 |
| Chile | 0.9806 | 10.276 | 0.1186 |
| Netherlands | 0.9809 | 0.0134 | 0.1188 |
| Germany | 0.9814 | 0.1113 | 0.1193 |
| Italy | 0.9867 | 0.2520 | 0.1246 |
| Bolivia | 0.9871 | 0.0418 | 0.125 |
| France | 1 | 0.0157 | 0.1379 |
| Australia | 1 | 0.2288 | 0.1379 |
| Ethiopia | 1 | 0 | 0.1379 |
| Sweden | 1 | 0 | 0.1379 |

Table A4.3 *Summary statistics*

| Variable | Mean | SD | Min. | Max. | $N$ |
|---|---|---|---|---|---|
| RTA | 0.121 | 0.326 | 0 | 1 | 69 161 |
| FTA | 0.065 | 0.247 | 0 | 1 | 69 161 |
| Government's welfare mindedness $a$ | 0.89 | 0.128 | 0.214 | 0.994 | 290 |
| $a$ after correction | 0.95 | 0.642 | −0.342 | 12.44 | 290 |
| Government's bargaining weakness $(1 - \sigma)$ | 0.878 | 0.237 | 0 | 1 | 290 |
| $(1 - \sigma)$ after ME correction | 0.881 | 0.233 | 0 | 1 | 290 |
| Market size of partner $(MS_j)$, in thousand USD | 29 127 | 159 366 | 263 | 2 262 526 | 68 961 |
| Relative size $(j/i)(RS)$ | −0.701 | 2.288 | −8.517 | 8.227 | 68 961 |
| Abs. value of size difference (DMS) | 9.011 | 2.066 | −1.527 | 14.631 | 68 961 |
| UN Affinity Index (AI) | 0.693 | 0.229 | −0.468 | 1 | 46 343 |
| Imports | 294 982 | 2 792 603 | 0 | 231 032 976 | 177 786 |
| Log of imports | 8.271 | 3.864 | −6.908 | 19.258 | 106 300 |
| Log of GDP($i$) | 25.505 | 1.701 | 20.855 | 29.915 | 69 161 |
| Log of GDP($j$) | 23.855 | 2.192 | 18.921 | 29.915 | 69 161 |

Table A4.4 *Estimates of the credibility value of PTAs for the government*

| Country | Credibility value as % of production | Country | Credibility value as % of production |
|---------|-----------------------|---------|-----------------------|
| Ethiopia | 0.052 | Colombia | 1.78 |
| Bolivia | 0.142 | Morocco | 1.8 |
| Germany | 1.84 | Kenya | 0.351 |
| Cameroon | 0.537 | Finland | 1.86 |
| Peru | 0.584 | Philippines | 1.91 |
| India | 0.648 | Hungary | 1.96 |
| Sweden | 0.752 | Greece | 1.96 |
| Egypt | 0.785 | France | 2.09 |
| Chile | 0.824 | Thailand | 2.19 |
| Sri Lanka | 0.933 | Malawi | 2.2 |
| Mexico | 0.945 | Romania | 2.3 |
| Norway | 0.977 | Venezuela | 2.34 |
| Costa Rica | 1.02 | Poland | 2.42 |
| Indonesia | 1.06 | Nepal | 2.42 |
| Netherlands | 1.17 | United Kingdom | 2.5 |
| Japan | 1.18 | Malaysia | 2.61 |
| USA | 1.23 | Taiwan | 2.68 |
| China | 1.25 | Turkey | 2.74 |
| Ecuador | 1.29 | Spain | 2.78 |
| Argentina | 1.45 | South Korea | 3.15 |
| Guatemala | 1.48 | Denmark | 3.23 |
| Uruguay | 1.48 | Italy | 3.46 |
| Ireland | 1.68 | Latvia | 3.64 |
| South Africa | 1.68 | Trinidad and Tobago | 3.67 |
| Australia | 1.69 | Bangladesh | 4.33 |
| Brazil | 1.7 | | |

Institutions (Beck *et al.* 2001). The Corruption Perception Index is from Transparency International, the Corruption Index from the Worldwide Governance Indicators Database (Kaufman, Kraay and Mastruzzi 2009) and the parking violations by diplomats from Fisman and Miguel (2007). Bilateral import data are from the United Nations Commodity Trade Statistics Database – COMTRADE (SITC classification revision 1), and data on GDP and GDP per capita are from the World Development Indicators (WDI). Table A4.3 contains summary statistics for all variables used.

## References

Bagwell, Kyle, and Staiger, Robert. 1999. 'An Economic Theory of GATT.' *American Economic Review* 89 (1): 215–48.

Baier, Scott, and Bergstrand, Jeffrey. 2004. 'Economic Determinants of Free Trade Agreements.' *Journal of International Economics* 64 (1): 29–63.

2007. 'Do Free Trade Agreements Actually Increase Members' International Trade?' *Journal of International Economics* 71 (1): 72–95.

2009. 'Estimating the Effects of Free Trade Agreements on International Trade Flows Using Matching Econometrics.' *Journal of International Economics* 77 (1): 63–76.

Beck, Thorsten, Clarke, George, Groff, Alberto, Keefer, Philip, and Walsh, Patrick. 2001. 'New Tools in Comparative Political Economy: The Database of Political Institutions.' *World Bank Economic Review* 15 (1): 165–76.

Bown, Chad, and Hoekman, Bernard. 2008. 'Developing Countries and Enforcement of Trade Agreements: Why Dispute Settlement Is Not Enough.' *Journal of World Trade* 42 (3): 177–203.

Cameron, Colin, and Trivedi, Pradin. 2005. *Microeconometrics – Methods and Applications.* Cambridge: Cambridge University Press.

Carrère, Céline. 2006. 'Revisiting the Effects of Regional Trading Agreements on Trade Flows with Proper Specification of the Gravity Model.' *European Economic Review* 50 (2): 223–47.

Drazen, Allan, and Limão, Nuno. 2008. 'A Bargaining Theory of Inefficient Redistribution.' *International Economic Review* 49 (2): 621–57.

Dreher, Axel, and Voigt, Stefan. 2008. 'Does Membership in International Organizations Increase Government's Credibility? Testing the Effects of Delegating Power.' KOF Working Paper No. 109. KOF Swiss Economic Institute, Zurich.

Dür, Andreas, Baccini, Leonardo, and Elsig, Manfred. 2014. 'The Design of International Trade Agreements: Introducing a New Dataset.' *Review of International Organizations* 9 (3): 353–75.

Egger, Peter, Larch, Mario, Staub, Kevin, and Winkelmann, Rainer. 2009. 'The Trade Effects of Endogenous Preferential Trade Agreements.' CESifo Working Paper Series No. 3253. CESifo Group, Munich.

Fisman, Raymond, and Miguel, Edward. 2007. 'Corruption, Norms, and Legal Enforcement: Evidence from Diplomatic Parking Tickets.' *Journal of Political Economy* 115 (6): 1020–48.

Fuller, Wayne. 1987. *Measurement Error Models.* New York: Wiley.

Gartzke, Erik. 2006. 'The Affinity of Nations Index, 1946–2002.' http://pages.ucsd.edu/~egartzke/datasets.htm.

Gawande, Kishore. 1997. 'Generated Regressors in Linear and Nonlinear Models.' *Economic Letters* 54 (2): 119–26.

Gawande, Kishore, Krishna, Pravin, and Olarreaga, Marcelo. 2009. 'What Governments Maximize and Why: The View from Trade.' *International Organization* 63 (3): 491–532.

Grossman, Gene, and Helpman, Elhanan. 1994. 'Protection for Sale.' *American Economic Review* 84 (4): 833–50.

Head, Keith, and Mayer, Thierry. 2011. 'Gravity, Market Potential and Development.' *Journal of Economic Geography* 11 (2): 281–94.

Kaufmann, Daniel, Kraay, Aart, and Mastruzzi, Massimo. 2009. 'Worldwide Governance Indicators (WGI) Project.' http://info.worldbank.org/governance/wgi/index.asp.

Katzsenstein, Peter. 1978. *Between Power and Plenty: Foreign Economic Policies in Advanced Industrial States.* Madison: University of Wisconsin Press.

Kee, Hiau Looi, Nicita, Alessandro, and Olarreaga, Marcelo. 2009. 'Estimating Trade Restrictiveness Indices.' *Economic Journal* 119 (534): 172–99.

Limão, Nuno, and Tovar, Patricia. 2009. 'Policy Choice: Theory and Evidence from Commitment via International Trade Agreements.' NBER Working Paper No. 14655. National Bureau of Economic Research, Cambridge, MA.

Lipsey, Richard. 1957. 'The Theory of Customs Unions: Trade Diversion and Welfare.' *Economica* 24 (93): 40–6.

Liu, Xuepeng, and Ornelas, Emanuel. 2011. 'Free Trade Agreements and the Consolidation of Democracy.' Mimeo, London School of Economics, London.

Maggi, Giovanni, and Rodríguez-Clare, Andrés. 1998. 'The Value of Trade Agreements in the Presence of Political Pressures.' *Journal of Political Economy* 106 (3): 574–601.

2007. 'A Political Economy Theory of Trade Agreements.' *American Economic Review* 97 (4): 1374–1405.

Mitra, Devashish. 2002. 'Endogenous Political Organizations and the Value of Trade Agreements.' *Journal of International Economics* 57 (2): 473–85.

Nicita, Alessandro, and Olarreaga, Marcelo. 2006. 'Trade, Production and Protection 1976–2004.' *World Bank Economic Review* 21 (1): 165–75.

Ornelas, Emanuel. 2005. 'Rent Destruction and the Political Viability of Free Trade Agreements.' *Quarterly Journal of Economics* 120 (4): 1475–1506.

Rodrik, Dani. 1995. 'Political Economy of Trade Policy.' In *Handbook of International Economics*, Vol. 3, edited by Gene M. Grossman and Kenneth S. Rogoff, 1457–94. Amsterdam: North Holland.

Salas, Fernando, and Zabludovski, Jaime. 2004. 'NAFTA as a Tool to Precommit Market Openness.' Mimeo, Stanford University, CA.

Whalley, John. 1998. 'Why Do Countries Seek Regional Trade Agreements?' In *The Regionalization of the World Economy*, edited by Jeffrey A. Frankel, 63–90. Chicago: University of Chicago Press.

# 5

# Natural trading partners?

## A public opinion perspective on preferential trade agreements

VÍCTOR UMAÑA, THOMAS BERNAUER
AND GABRIELE SPILKER

## A. Introduction

The rapid proliferation of preferential trade agreements (PTAs), both in numbers and scope, is one of the most noteworthy developments in the world economy in recent decades. Since 1990 the number of PTAs in force has quadrupled to more than 300 (World Trade Organization 2011). Even those countries that used to take an explicit anti-PTA stance, such as the United States, Member States of the European Union (EU), China and Japan, seem to have abandoned their strong focus on multilateral trade liberalisation and have been negotiating PTAs, motivated by what observers regard as a 'competitive liberalization' strategy (Evenett and Meier 2008).

The United States, for example, has thus far concluded 14 PTAs, including the North American Free Trade Agreement (NAFTA) as well as PTAs with several countries from three different continents. The EU has negotiated trade agreements with most of its Member States' former colonies in Africa and the Caribbean, as well as other countries in Latin America and Asia. Japan and China have concluded agreements with countries in Asia, Europe and the Americas. The most recent, and arguably the most far-reaching, development in this 'new regionalism' trend (Mansfield and Milner 1999) concerns the negotiations on two very large-scale PTAs: the Trans-Pacific Partnership (TPP) agreement and the Transatlantic Trade and Investment Partnership (TTIP).

The existing literature identifies various macrolevel factors that tend to motivate countries to form PTAs instead of or in addition to engaging in multilateral trade liberalisation. These include the possibility to discriminate among potential trade partner countries (Krugman 1994), which is not possible within the WTO context; the search for economies of scale (Chase 2003; Milner 1997); the stagnation of multilateral negotiations at the WTO (Mansfield and Reinhardt 2003) and competition among countries to obtain or maintain access to foreign markets (Baccini and Dür 2012; Baldwin 1993, 1997). The literature has also identified several country-level characteristics that may increase the propensity of any given pair of countries to establish a PTA. These characteristics include economic size, economic similarity, geographical proximity (Baier and Bergstrand 2004), political system characteristics (Mansfield and Milner 2012; Mansfield, Milner and Pevehouse 2008; Milner and Kubota 2005) and psychic distance (Dow and Karunaratna 2006; Frankel, Stein and Wei 1998; Guiso, Sapienza and Zingales 2009).

In this chapter we examine the role of public opinion in explaining some of the key features of the new regionalism. In particular, we are interested in what characteristics make countries more (or less) attractive as a preferential trading partner from the viewpoint of citizens (voters). Such research is valuable for both analytical and normative reasons. Analytically, to the extent the median voter model is of relevance to understanding government decisions, which a large body of literature in political economy accepts, we should assume that public opinion on trade, and on PTAs specifically, has at least some influence on choices of partners for and contents of PTAs (Beaulieu 2002; Blonigen 2011; Facchini and Mayda 2008; Hicks, Milner and Tingley 2013; Hiscox 2006; Mansfield and Mutz 2009; O'Rourke and Sinnot 2001; Scheve and Slaughter 2001). Normatively, such research can inform us about the extent to which policy choices by democratic governments line up with voters' preferences.

PTAs have in fact become a source of political contestation in many instances (Mansfield and Milner 2012). For example, in the European Union, the Single European Act and the Treaty on the European Union, which fully liberalised internal trade and capital markets, required ratification in some member countries, forcing political and economic elites to convince citizens of the benefits of trade openness (Kaltenthaler, Gelleny and Ceccoli 2004). In Canada, the national election of 1988 was widely regarded also as a referendum on the Canada–US Free Trade Agreement (CUSFTA) (Balistreri 1997). In Switzerland, several referenda and initiatives have dealt with EU–Swiss relations (Anson and Cadot 2004). Similarly, in Costa Rica, the fate of the Dominican Republic–Central America FTA (CAFTA-DR) was the key issue in the general election of 2006 and was finally decided in a referendum in 2007 (Hicks, Milner and Tingley 2013; Urbatsch 2013). Interestingly, in Costa Rica, as the campaign developed, it became apparent that voters were not necessarily 'for' or 'against' trade liberalisation per se. Rather, the debate evolved around some key characteristics of the PTA, such as the partner country (the United States) and some specific provisions of the agreement (Hicks, Milner and Tingley 2014; Urbatsch 2013).

The preceding example points to an important limitation of existing research on trade policy preferences. Many of the most influential studies rely on a single survey item for the dependent variable (see, for example, Blonigen 2011; Mayda and Rodrik 2005; O'Rourke and Sinnot 2001; Scheve and Slaughter 2001). One of the most popular survey items in this regard is from the American National Election Study (ANES): 'Some people have suggested placing new limits on foreign imports in order to protect American jobs. Others say that such limits would raise consumer prices and hurt American exports. Do you favor or oppose placing new limits on imports, or haven't you thought much about this?'

This approach is problematic not only for methodological (measurement error) reasons but also for substantive ones. Notably, individuals may have different preferences with respect to different forms and degrees of trade liberalisation, and they may evaluate trade based on differing criteria, for instance, with respect to their own personal well-being, their country's well-being or affective or rationalistic frames (Nguyen and Bernauer 2013). For these reasons, the research reported in this chapter concentrates on a particular form of trade liberalisation, namely, PTAs, with an emphasis on trade partner country characteristics; and we rely on conjoint analysis to capture the multidimensionality of trade policy preferences.

Drawing on macrolevel theories that identify various characteristics of natural trading partners, we develop a set of hypotheses concerning factors that are likely to make other countries more (or less) attractive as preferential trading partners. We then use a conjoint analysis to test these arguments. This approach is equivalent to a choice experiment in which respondents are asked to consider PTAs with countries that vary on a specific set of attributes (e.g. geographical location, economic size, environmental standards) and to express their preferences for particular types of partner countries. This setup allows us to identify whether and to what extent particular partner country characteristics matter when citizens are evaluating the pros and cons of PTAs.

The next section explains what PTAs are. Then, we develop our theoretical arguments. We then outline the empirical study design before presenting and discussing the results.

## B. Preferential trade agreements

To begin with, we discuss the policy measures with regard to which we examine individuals' preferences. PTAs are instruments of policy cooperation and coordination that allow countries to grant reciprocal and preferential access to members' markets without extending these preferences to third parties. This means that PTAs allow for discrimination against nonmember countries. Modern PTAs cover more sectors and regulate more economic policies than the WTO agreements do. These features are the highlights of what is called 'new regionalism' (Mansfield and Milner 1999). By addressing behind-the-border regulations, such as those concerning the environment, social and labour market issues, migration, investment, government procurement, technical barriers to trade (TBT) or anticompetitive practices, modern PTAs facilitate global production networks and affect a larger set of actors than do traditional multilateral forms of trade liberalisation (Mansfield and Milner 2012).

The inherent discrimination of PTAs, which contradicts the cornerstone of the multilateral trading system – the nondiscrimination principle – is tolerated by the World Trade Organization (WTO) agreements under Article XXIV of the General Agreement on Tariffs and Trade (GATT) of 1994, which governs trade in goods, and Article V of the General Agreement on Trade in Services (GATS). These provisions state that customs unions and free trade areas are permitted if tariffs or trade regulations instituted by these agreements are not higher or more restrictive than those applicable in the constituent territories prior to the formation of those agreements.

PTAs can be classified according to various criteria, including the following (World Trade Organization 2011):

- level of development of the countries involved (participation of developed or developing countries only, or of both developed and developing countries);
- geographical coverage (intra- or cross-regional PTAs) within/across regions, for example, Asia (East, West, Oceania), the Americas (North, South, Central, Caribbean), Europe, Middle East, Africa and the Commonwealth of Independent States (CIS);
- type (bilateral, plurilateral, or PTAs between regional blocs);
- degree of market integration (e.g. free trade agreement, customs union) and issue coverage (e.g. goods, services, regulatory issues).

The last of these categories is especially interesting as it pertains to key characteristics of modern PTAs. PTAs that deal exclusively with border measures are often defined as 'shallow' agreements. In contrast, PTAs that include rules on other domestic policies are often referred to as 'deep' agreements (Lawrence 1996). By regulating policies related to investment, competition, technical barriers, government procurement and migration, among others, the most recent wave of PTAs includes 'deep' agreements. These policies are in fact vital to firms involved in intra-industry trade, offshoring and outsourcing. Analysts thus highlight the complementarity between trade and governance, which is at the core of successful trade agreements (Yi 2003). In other words, modern PTAs could be depicted as an institutional response to the increasing complexity of trade and the growth in global production networks, a salient phenomenon in the contemporary international economy (Baldwin 2011). Moreover, PTAs have proven to be flexible and pragmatic instruments that allow trade and investment issues to be linked with postmaterialist values, such as environmental and social concerns.

## C. Theoretical arguments

Our unit of analysis is the individual. In democracies, public opinion is a critical factor in the trade liberalization process and as such voters' preferences are important in influencing the government stance on trade policy (Facchini and Mayda 2008; Kaltenthaler, Gelleny and Ceccoli 2004; Mansfield and Mutz 2009). Moreover, as Mayda and Rodrik (2005) points out, individual attitudes should be an integral part of a political economy model of trade. Several macrolevel arguments have been advanced to explain the determinants of the new regionalism as well as the associated choices made by governments. However, this literature makes important but largely untested assumptions about the preferences and beliefs of individuals.

In this chapter, we concentrate on trading partner choices rather than preferences concerning the content of PTAs, which we will address in further research. We prioritise partner country choices in this chapter because, arguably, the most salient feature of PTAs is that, in contrast to multilateral trade liberalisation, they are discriminatory. This means that they involve explicit choices by governments to form a PTA with a specific country or countries. In the following we briefly outline a set of macrolevel arguments and derive the microlevel implications from them.

## I. Geographical proximity and economic size

The natural trading partner hypothesis claims that trade agreements among countries that already trade intensively are more likely to be trade creating. However, a more recent take on this hypothesis flips the argument around and suggests that PTAs are endogenous, which means that they are the response to, rather than the source of, large trade flows (Lawrence 1998).

Building on the gravity model of trade, several authors (Baier and Bergstrand 2004; Bergstrand, Egger and Larch 2010; Frankel, Stein and Wei 1998; Rauch 1999) have identified geographical proximity and similar economic size as key factors that enhance the probability of two countries establishing a PTA. The gravity model is the standard empirical framework used to predict how country dyads match up in international trade. It takes its name from the prediction that the volume of trade between two countries will be directly proportional to the product of their economic masses (as measured by gross domestic product (GDP)) and inversely proportional to the distance between them (Rauch 1999). Empirical results in fact show that bilateral trade falls sharply as distance increases, after correcting for country size (Linders, Burger and van Oort 2008).

Specifically, Bergstrand, Egger and Larch (2010) observe that countries closer to each other in terms of physical distance, pairs of countries with larger gross domestic products (GDPs) and pairs of countries whose economic size is similar have a higher probability of forming a PTA – or enlarging an existing PTA – sooner than countries that do not share these three characteristics.

We should also expect these factors to play a role at the micro level, where individual citizens (voters) form their preferences with respect to PTAs. Physical proximity contributes to familiarity, which could in turn increase trust and reduce uncertainty. Thus, countries that are closer in terms of distance should be preferred over more remote ones. From a rationalistic viewpoint, voters are likely to prefer welfare-enhancing agreements with similar or larger economies, implying that countries of a substantial economic size should be the preferred trading partners.

## II. Psychic distance

It is widely accepted that trade costs resulting from trade policy or geographical distance (transport and logistics) do not fully explain bilateral trade flows and that trade may also be hampered by intangible barriers arising from cultural and institutional differences between countries (Linders, Burger and van Oort 2008).

Besides the simple gravity model, augmented gravity equations show that certain political and cultural variables, such as level of democracy, political affinity, shared colonial history, language and religion, help explain trade flows and the formation of PTAs (Frankel, Stein and Wei 1998; Liu 2010; Rauch 1999). Such factors may be regarded as proxies for psychic distance, a construct mainly used in the international business literature. This concept refers to a set of intangible factors that may explain resistance to (or support for) trade. The reasoning is that psychic distance tends to hamper the flow of information between economic actors and markets, thus inhibiting firms' ability to learn about partners and creating more uncertainty about those markets in the minds of managers (Dow and Karunaratna 2006). More generally, these factors are presumed to increase transaction costs, both real and perceived, and influence firms' perceptions of the attractiveness of doing business with another country. Dow and Karunaratna (2006), for instance, examine seven of these elements in the bilateral trade flows of 38 countries, namely, differences in culture, major languages, major religions, political ideology, education systems, levels of democracy and time zones. They find that differences in language, education and political systems have a statistically significant trade-inhibiting effect.

Recent studies also contend that generalised social trust and trust in other countries and their people are likely to influence trade preferences (Kaltenthaler and Miller 2013; Nguyen and Bernauer 2013; Spilker, Schaffer and Bernauer 2012). Guiso, Sapienza and Zingales (2009), for instance, find that geographical distance between two countries, their proximity and commonality between their languages and religions have significant effects on bilateral trust (i.e. how much individuals in one country trust people from the other country). It turns out that trust levels are affected not only by the characteristics of the other country but also by cultural commonalities concerning religion, history of conflicts and genetic and somatic factors. More importantly, the authors also find that lower levels of bilateral trust are associated with less trade between two countries, less portfolio investment and less foreign direct investment. These results suggest that perceptions rooted in culture are important determinants of economic exchange (Guiso Sapienza and Zingales 2009).

In this chapter we consider two specific factors that proxy for psychic distance: religion and language. Religion is closely associated with culture, and it is considered a major component of conflict between groups (Boyacigiller 1990; Triandis 2000). Differences in religion are widely regarded as a source of miscommunication between groups and have the potential to disrupt the flow of information, and thus to influence patterns of trade. Countries that share a common religion have been shown to trade more (Linders *et al.* 2005). For example, Lewer and Van den Berg (2007) find that a shared Buddhist, Confucian, Hindu, Eastern Orthodox Catholic or Protestant religion has a significant positive influence on bilateral trade.

Language is widely considered to be a key facet of psychic distance and is thus likely to influence patterns of international trade. Differences in language may increase both the costs and the risks associated with economic transactions, whereas similarities may produce efficiency gains (Dow and Karunaratna 2006). Many expanded gravity models include a dummy variable for language and find that commonalities in this regard help explain bilateral trade between pairs of countries (Bergstrand, Egger and Larch 2010; Frankel, Stein and Wei 1998; Lewer and Van den Berg 2007; Linders, Burger and van Oort 2008; Liu 2010; Rauch 1999).

Again, we should expect these factors to also play a role at the micro level, where individual citizens (voters) form their preferences with respect to PTAs. Specifically, we expect individuals to prefer PTAs with countries that are more similar in terms of language and religion.

## III. Political system

Existing research shows that democracies are more likely to form PTAs with each other (Mansfield and Milner 2012). Moreover, from a more rationalistic viewpoint, democratic institutions are likely to constrain the ability of governments to use trade barriers as a strategy for generating political support. Following this argument, Milner and Kubota (2005) find that regime change towards democracy is associated with trade liberalisation. They argue that democratisation tends to empower new groups of voters who prefer less protectionism (Milner and Kubota 2005). Accordingly, political leaders use trade agreements as signalling devices for demonstrating to domestic constituencies that they are implementing sensible policies. At the individual level, shared democracy should matter for voters. Individuals are likely to expect democracies to abide by and respect the rules of trade agreements and to use for peaceful purposes the increased wealth derived from commercial exchange.

Therefore, we should expect shared democracy to increase the probability of voters choosing a particular partner with which to form a trade agreement.

## IV. Military or security alliance

International trade has not only economic implications. It can also affect military and security relations between countries. Mercantilists and their intellectual heirs, namely, proponents of realism and strategic trade theory, have emphasised geostrategic effects of trade imbalances and asymmetric gains from trade. They advocate caution when 'trading with the enemy'. Liberal institutionalists, on the other hand, have pointed to peace-promoting effects of international trade because countries that trade more face higher opportunity costs in the event of hostilities (Bussmann and Schneider 2007). Empirically, the peace-promoting effect of trade remains somewhat contested, whereas the evidence for more trade among countries with closer military or security ties is quite robust (Mansfield and Milner, Chapter 3 in this volume).

The latter finding – closer military or security ties – can also inform theorising on PTA formation. With respect to PTA partner country choices, we expect individuals to be more likely to view trade through a realist lens (see, e.g., Morrow, Siverson and Tabares 1998), in the sense that they prefer PTAs with countries with which they already have security or military ties.

## V. Postmaterialism

As noted at the beginning of this chapter, modern PTAs not only deal with measures at the border (i.e. tariffs and quotas) but often include other provisions that reach quite a long way into the domestic realm, for instance, in areas such as environmental protection, labour rights and competition policy. One of the most noteworthy features of modern PTAs is that they increasingly deal with environmental and social issues. These issues are covered by the multilateral trading rules marginally (e.g. by Article XX of the GATT), and they are not on the table in the Doha Round negotiations. In contrast, recent PTAs, such as those involving the United States, Canada or the European Union, include important binding clauses on labour and environmental issues. This means that noncompliance with environmental or labour standards could lead to trade sanctions under these PTAs.

The existing literature has examined linkages between postmaterialist values, such as environmental and social concerns, and trade, at both the macro and micro levels (Bechtel, Bernauer and Meyer 2012). Intense debates about the implications of trade liberalisation for environmental and labour standards, as well as the aforementioned trend towards including environmental and labour protection clauses in modern PTAs, suggest that, at least in advanced democracies, such postmaterial concerns play an important role in the trade policy choices of governments (Cottier 2002; Hafner-Burton 2005; Spilker and Böhmelt 2012).

We should thus expect individuals with strong environmental and social concerns to express less support for free trade in general (see Bechtel, Bernauer and Meyer 2012). However, it tends to be easier to address such concerns and set environmental and social standards in PTAs than it is in the global setting of the WTO. One implication of this is that we should expect individuals in advanced industrialised democracies (where postmaterialist values are more prevalent) to prefer PTAs with countries that have similar or higher environmental and labour standards.

## D. Empirical study design

We use a choice-based conjoint analysis to examine the hypotheses outlined previously. The advantage of this approach is that, very much like in the real world, respondents (voters) are confronted with proposals for PTAs that vary with respect to various characteristics of the partner countries, such as those set out in the preceding hypotheses. The essence of the conjoint approach is that respondents are asked to consider a set of different partner country characteristics simultaneously and then to express their preferences. In the set-up we use, this allows us to identify how important particular trade partner characteristics are within a given set of different characteristics.

Up to now, this methodology has been used mainly in marketing research to analyse consumer trade-offs and to forecast demand, define pricing strategies, measure willingness to pay and develop products (Green, Krieger and Wind 2001). In a choice-based conjoint analysis, respondents rank or rate two or more hypothetical profiles (in our case, proposals for PTAs) that combine multiple attributes. This enables the researcher to estimate the relative influence of each attribute value on the resulting choice or rating (Hainmueller, Hopkins and Yamamoto 2014). Typically, respondents are asked to complete several choice tasks, each of which usually consists of two profiles (e.g. products, candidates, policy proposals) with a fixed set of attributes (e.g. product price, income of candidate, whether a potential PTA partner country is large or small) whose values vary between and across the choice tasks. Recent research in political science has used this approach to test several hypotheses simultaneously, for example, with regard to the choice of political candidates, immigrants or bailout packages (Hainmueller, Hopkins and Yamamoto 2014).

Hainmueller, Hopkins and Yamamoto (2014) point out four advantages of conjoint analysis. First, it offers enhanced realism by confronting respondents with various pieces of information at one time (e.g. multiple attributes of a policy proposal) and then asking them to make choices. Second, it can be used to evaluate the relative explanatory power of different hypotheses that relate to these treatment components. This takes research beyond unidimensional tests that simply reject or fail to reject one specific causal hypothesis. Third, conjoint experiments may help in addressing problems of social desirability in survey research, as they provide respondents with multiple means to internally justify any particular choice or rating. Fourth, they can also provide insights into politically relevant issues of policy design.

In line with the hypotheses outlined previously, we focus on eight attributes of PTAs: economic size, location, language, religion, political system and military or security alliances as well as the environmental standards and labour standards of potential partner countries. Table 5.1 offers an overview of attributes and their possible expressions (often referred to also as values or traits). The latter are worded for the United States because our empirical testing concentrates on that country.

Our survey, whose key component is the conjoint analysis of trade partner characteristics outlined in Table 5.1, was conducted in September and October 2013. The sample includes 1000 respondents from the United States recruited via Amazon Mechanical Turk (MTurk). MTurk is an online labour market. Our sample is, therefore, a convenience sample rather than a national (proportional) random sample. For our present purposes, this sampling approach is acceptable for two reasons. First, as shown by Berinsky, Huber and Lenz (2012), the sociodemographics of the MTurk population is fairly congruent with the sociodemographic distributions of large national surveys in the United States, such as the ANES. Second, in an experimental set-up, instead of a standard survey, average treatment effects can be reliably identified if the sample is not heavily biased on some variables that moderate the effect of the treatment condition on the outcome variable of interest.

Table 5.1 *Attributes and their values*

| Attribute | Value |
|---|---|
| Location | Africa, Asia-Pacific, Central America and the Caribbean, South America, Europe |
| Economic size compared to the USA | Same size, a bit smaller, considerably smaller |
| Religion | Predominantly Christian, predominantly Islam, Diverse |
| Political system | Democratic, partly democratic, not democratic |
| Worker rights, compared to the USA | Weaker, stronger, similar |
| Environmental protection, compared to the USA | Weaker, stronger, similar |
| Language | Widely spoken, not widely spoken |
| Military or security alliance with the USA | Yes, no |

We started the conjoint part of the survey by giving respondents a set of instructions, with the following introductory text:

> The United States is currently negotiating international trade agreements with other countries. The purpose of such trade agreements is to make it easier for producers from other countries to sell their goods and services in the United States (imports), and to make it easier for producers based in the United States to sell their goods and services in other countries (exports). The United States is considering different partner countries for such trade agreements. These partner countries may differ with respect to their characteristics.

We then presented a table describing each of the attributes before proceeding to the actual choice tasks (Table 5.2).

The profiles of each partner country were presented side by side, with each pair of profiles on a separate screen. Figure 5.1 offers an illustration. It shows a particular choice task received by a participant. Each participant was asked to complete six such choice tasks.

We used a completely independent randomisation of the values of each attribute presented to the respondent. To facilitate the tasks for respondents while also minimising primacy and recency effects, we followed Hainmueller, Hopkins and Yamamoto (2014) and presented attributes in a randomised order that was fixed across the pairings for each

Table 5.2 *Description of the attributes*

| Characteristic | Description |
| --- | --- |
| Economic size | Partner countries may be of different economic size. They may have the same economic size as the United States, or they may be smaller. |
| Language | The main language spoken in the partner country may be English or some other language. |
| Location | Partner countries may be located on the American continent or on some other continent. |
| Religion | Partner countries may practice one main religion such as Christianity or Islam or may be religiously diverse with several religions practiced. |
| Political system | Partner countries may be democratic, partly democratic or not democratic. |
| Environmental protection | The environmental protection standards in partner countries may be stronger, similar or weaker compared to the standards in the United States. |
| Labour rights | The worker rights protection standards in partner countries may be stronger, similar or weaker compared to the standards in the United States. |
| Military or security alliance | Partner countries may have or may not have a military/ security alliance with the United States. |

**Please compare these two countries carefully. They may appear similar but differ in some important characteristics.**

| Characteristics | Country 1 | Country 2 |
| --- | --- | --- |
| Worker rights protection standards, compared to the U.S. | Weaker | Stronger |
| Political system | Democratic | Democratic |
| Military / security alliance with the U.S. | No | Yes |
| Size of the economy, compared with the U.S. | Considerably smaller | A bit smaller |
| English | Not widely spoken | Widely spoken |
| Location | Asia Pacific | South America |
| Religion | Predominantly Christian | Diverse |
| Environmental protection standards, compared to the U.S. | Similar | Weaker |
| Which country would you prefer? | O | O |

Figure 5.1   Example of a choice task

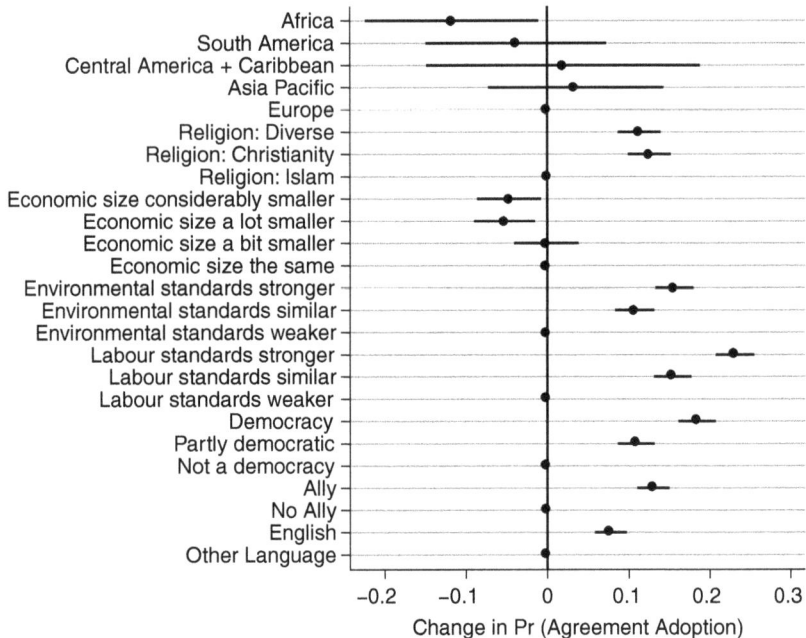

**Figure 5.2**   Marginal effects

respondent. This implied that both the row in which a specific dimension was presented (e.g. Location) and the content of each cell (e.g. Central America and the Caribbean) were determined randomly. Respondents were asked to choose between the two possible trading partners. This choice-based design enables us to evaluate the role of each attribute value in the assessment, by the respondent, of one partner country relative to another.

## E. Results

Figure 5.2 shows the effects of all attributes relative to the respective baseline category. Specifically, it displays estimates of the average marginal component-specific effect of a given value for each characteristic of a partner country on the probability of supporting the proposed trade agreement. The point indicates the regression estimate, and the line indicates the 95 per cent confidence interval. The respective baseline category is displayed as a point on the zero line. These estimates are based on the attributes and values shown in Table 5.1.

As shown in Figure 5.2, the results, of which we discuss the implications in more detail in the next section, correspond largely to our theoretical predictions. For example, respondents are less likely to prefer partner countries with a different language than those whose language is English. The same holds for countries with an Islamic religious tradition. Partner countries with higher labour or environmental standards are more popular than are countries with weaker ones. Moreover, democratic countries are preferred over nondemocratic ones. Finally, economic size of the partner country matters, but only if it is considerably smaller than the size of the United States.

With respect to location, African countries are clearly not preferred as trading partners. However, the results for the other locations, although they have the expected sign, are not statistically significant.

As described previously, the analysis is based on a convenience sample, which is not representative of the US population. In particular, our sample obtained through MTurk is skewed with respect to education, income, gender and political ideology. To ensure that these factors did not influence the results presented earlier, we ran the analysis for each of the dimensions of these variables separately (e.g. for well-educated versus less-well-educated respondents). Because none of these results differ significantly from those presented previously, we are confident that our findings really show a more general pattern of voters' preferences with regard to PTA partner country characteristics.

## F. Discussion

One of the most important features of PTAs, which is at least partly responsible for the rapid proliferation of this particular form of trade liberalisation, is that they allow for discrimination between trade partner countries. This implies that governments are making important trade policy choices when they decide to establish a PTA with another country or a group of other countries. On the assumption that public opinion is an important determinant of government choices in this respect, and that it is also interesting to understand from a normative perspective on democracy, we have examined the microlevel implications of theoretical macroarguments on choices of partner countries for preferential trade. Specifically, we have studied a set of characteristics that are likely to make other countries more (or less) attractive PTA partners.

We hypothesised that voters in democratic countries tend to favour PTAs with countries that are closer in terms of geographical and psychic distance, are of similar economic size, are democratic and have high environmental and labour rights standards. Using a conjoint experiment with a sample of US respondents, we found robust empirical support for most of these arguments.

As expected, commonalities in language, religion, security alliance and concerns regarding labour and environmental standards increase the attractiveness of a particular trading partner. These results fit well with macrolevel findings showing that religion, shared interests and language are important moderators of trade flows between country dyads. At the individual level, they connect well with more general arguments about physical and psychic distance being related to ethnocentricity, international animosity and attitudes towards out-group, which have been identified as robust predictors of individual trade policy preferences (Mansfield and Mutz 2009; Mayda and Rodrik 2005). Moreover, the inclination towards preferring agreements with countries with higher environmental and labour standards supports other findings in the trade policy literature that trade preferences are at least partly driven by sociotropic concerns (Mansfield and Mutz 2009).

The mixed results for geographical location might arise because, whereas the gravity model of trade focuses on geographical distance as such, our attributes denote world regions or continents. According to studies in consumer and market psychology, consumers tend to rely on heuristics from national images when making purchasing decisions. Such national images might thus affect support for bilateral trade (Klein, Ettenson and Morris 1998). In other words, locations such as South America and Central America and the Caribbean might be specific enough to convey national images rather than simply capturing pure geographical distance considerations. This issue should be looked into in further research.

With respect to economic size, respondents from the United States tend to prefer PTA partner countries that are either of the same economic size or smaller to partner countries that are a lot smaller. This result supports our theoretical predictions that PTAs with partner countries that differ greatly in economic size are less attractive. The reasoning on the macro level is that PTAs between countries with similar economic size should be welfare enhancing (Baier and Bergstrand 2004). The connection to the individual level is explained by Grossman and Helpman (1995). In their seminal article about the political economy of PTAs, they show that a PTA will emerge when there is balance in the potential trade between partner countries. The average voter should thus support trade policies, that is, PTAs that are welfare enhancing, because they further trade between two countries with similar economic size (Grossman and Helpman 1995).

As regards the policy implications of our findings, it appears that many countries have already formed PTAs with countries that correspond to the 'ideal type' as proposed by our conjoint results. Hence, the pool of potential trading partners that are closer in geographical terms and that have a similar language and religion as well as similar environmental and social standards is almost exhausted (Dür and Elsig, Chapter 1 in this volume). In fact, as noted by Bergstrand, Egger and Larch (2010), there is a trend for PTAs to be formed or enlarged sooner among closer and economically larger countries. As time passes, the distance among PTA members increases, and the economic size of partners decreases. In other words, the next crop of trade agreements – the mega-agreements – involves a very heterogeneous group of countries with major differences in economic size, political system, location, language, religion, standards and levels of development. For example, the negotiations on the TPP, originally established by Brunei, New Zealand, Chile and Singapore, now also involve the United States, Vietnam, Peru, Australia, Malaysia, Mexico and Canada. Other countries that have requested to join these negotiations include Colombia, Costa Rica, Laos, the Philippines, Indonesia, Bangladesh and India. In light of our findings, negotiating and implementing such agreements constitute enormous challenges for policymakers depending on domestic public support. Political campaigns to this end will have to overcome the overall tendency of citizens to prefer trade partners that are similar. One interesting question for policymakers as well as researchers in this regard is whether there are trade-offs between acceptable PTA partners and acceptable PTA content, and whether PTAs among more diverse countries are likely to be 'shallower' and less trade creating.

## References

Anson, Jose, and Cadot, Olivier. 2004. 'Beyond the "Röstigraben": The Swiss Electorate Divided About the EU.' *Swiss Journal of Economics and Statistics* 2 (1): 171–206.

Baccini, Leonardo, and Dür, Andreas. 2012. 'The New Regionalism and Policy Interdependence.' *British Journal of Political Science* 42 (1): 57–79.

Baier, Scott L., and Bergstrand, Jeffrey H. 2004. 'Economic Determinants of Free Trade Agreements.' *Journal of International Economics* 64 (1): 29–63.

Baldwin, Richard E. 1993. 'A Domino Theory of Regionalism.' NBER Working Paper No. 4465. National Bureau of Economic Research, Cambridge, MA.

2011. '21st Century Regionalism: Filling the Gap Between 21st Century Trade and 20th Century Trade Rules.' WTO Staff Working Paper ERSD-2011-08. World Trade Organization Economic Research and Statistics Division, Geneva.

Balistreri, Edward J. 1997. 'The Performance of the Heckscher-Ohlin-Vanek Model in Predicting Endogenous Policy Forces at the Individual Level.' *Canadian Journal of Economics* 30 (1): 1–17.

Beaulieu, Eugene. 2002. 'Factor or Industry Cleavages in Trade Policy? An Empirical Analysis of the Stolper–Samuelson Theorem.' *Economics & Politics* 14 (2): 99–131.

Bechtel, Michael M., Bernauer, Thomas, and Meyer, Reto. 2012. 'The Green Side of Protectionism: Environmental Concerns and Three Facets of Trade Policy Preferences.' *Review of International Political Economy* 19 (5): 837–66.

Bergstrand, Jeffrey H., Egger, Peter, and Larch, Mario. 2010. 'Economic Determinants of the Timing of Preferential Trade Agreement Formations and Enlargements.' Paper presented at the IX Annual Conference of The Euro-Latin Study Network on Integration and Trade (ELSNIT): Revisiting Regionalism, Appenzell, Switzerland.

Berinsky, Adam J., Huber, Gregory A., and Lenz. Gabriel S. 2012. 'Evaluating Online Labor Markets for Experimental Research: Amazon. Com's Mechanical Turk.' *Political Analysis* 20 (3): 351–68.

Blonigen, Bruce A. 2011. 'Revisiting the Evidence on Trade Policy Preferences.' *Journal of International Economics* 85 (1): 129–35.

Boyacigiller, Nakiye. 1990. 'The Role of Expatriates in the Management of Interdependence, Complexity and Risk in Multinational Corporations.' *Journal of International Business Studies* 21 (3): 357–81.

Bussmann, Margit, and Schneider, Gerald. 2007. 'When Globalization Discontent Turns Violent: Foreign Economic Liberalization and Internal War.' *International Studies Quarterly* 51 (1): 79–97.

Chase, Kerry A. 2003. 'Economic Interests and Regional Trading Arrangements: The Case of NAFTA.' *International Organization* 57 (1): 137–74.

Cottier, Thomas. 2002. 'Trade and Human Rights: A Relationship to Discover.' *Journal of International Economic Law* 5 (1): 111–32.

Dow, Douglas, and Karunaratna, Amal. 2006. 'Developing a Multidimensional Instrument to Measure Psychic Distance Stimuli.' *Journal of International Business Studies* 37 (5): 578–602.

Evenett, Simon J., and Meier, Michael. 2008. 'An Interim Assessment of the US Trade Policy of "Competitive Liberalization".' *World Economy* 31 (1): 31–66.

Facchini, Giovanni, and Mayda, Anna Maria. 2008. 'From Individual Attitudes Towards Migrants to Migration Policy Outcomes: Theory and Evidence.' *Economic Policy* 23 (56): 651–713.

Frankel, Jeffrey A., Stein, Ernesto, and Wei, Shang-Jin. 1998. 'Continental Trading Blocs: Are They Natural or Supernatural?' In *The Regionalization of the World Economy*, edited by Jeffrey A. Frankel, 91–120. Chicago: University of Chicago Press.

Green, Paul E., Krieger, Abba M., and Wind, Yoram. 2001. 'Thirty Years of Conjoint Analysis: Reflections and Prospects.' *Interfaces* 31 (3 supplement): S56–S73.

Grossman, Gene M., and Helpman, Elhanan. 1995. 'The Politics of Free-Trade Agreements.' *American Economic Review* 85 (4): 667–90.

Guiso, Luigi, Sapienza, Paola, and Zingales, Luigi. 2009. 'Cultural Biases in Economic Exchange?' *Quarterly Journal of Economics* 124 (3): 1095–1131.

Hafner-Burton, Emilie M. 2005. 'Trading Human Rights: How Preferential Trade Agreements Influence Government Repression.' *International Organization* 59 (3): 593–629.

Hainmueller, Jens, Hopkins, Daniel J., and Yamamoto, Teppei. 2014. 'Causal Inference in Conjoint Analysis: Understanding Multi-Dimensional Choices via Stated Preference Experiments.' *Political Analysis* 22 (1): 1–30.

Hicks, Raymond, Milner, Helen V., and Tingley, Dustin H. 2014. 'Trade Policy, Economic Interests, and Party Politics in a Developing Country: The Political Economy of CAFTA-DR.' *International Studies Quarterly* 58:106–17. doi:10.1111/isqu.12057.

Hiscox, Michael J. 2006. 'Through a Glass and Darkly: Attitudes Toward International Trade and the Curious Effects of Issue Framing.' *International Organization* 60 (3): 755–80.

Kaltenthaler, Karl C., Gelleny, Ronald D., and Ceccoli, Stephen J. 2004. 'Explaining Citizen Support for Trade Liberalization.' *International Studies Quarterly* 48 (4): 829–52.

Kaltenthaler, Karl C., and Miller, William J. 2013. 'Social Psychology and Public Support for Trade Liberalization.' *International Studies Quarterly* 57 (4): 784–90.

Klein, Gabrielle, Ettenson, Richard, and Morris, Marlene. 1998. 'The Animosity Model of Foreign Product Purchase: An Empirical Test in the People's Republic of China.' *Journal of Marketing* 62 (1): 89–100.

Krugman, Paul R. 1994. *Rethinking International Trade*. Cambridge, MA: MIT Press.

Lawrence, Robert Z. 1996. *Regionalism, Multilateralism, and Deeper Integration*. Washington, DC: Brookings Institution Press.

———. 1998. 'Comment on Barry Eichengreen, Douglas A. Irwin: The Role of History in Bilateral Trade Flows.' In *The Regionalization of the World Economy*, edited by Jeffrey A. Frankel, Shang-Jin Wei and Ernesto Stein, 57–9. Chicago: University of Chicago Press.

Lewer, Joshua J., and Van den Berg, Hendrik. 2007. 'Religion and International Trade: Does the Sharing of a Religious Culture Facilitate the Formation of

Trade Networks?' *American Journal of Economics and Sociology* 66 (4): 765–94.

Linders, Gert-Jan M., Beugelsdijk, Sjoerd, de Groot, Henri L. F., and Slangen, Arjen. 2005. 'Cultural and Institutional Determinants of Bilateral Trade Flows.' Tinbergen Institute Discussion Paper TI 2005–074/3:1–31. Tinbergen Institute, Amsterdam, the Netherlands.

Linders, Gert-Jan M., Burger, Martijn J., and van Oort, Frank G. 2008. 'A Rather Empty World: The Many Faces of Distance and the Persistent Resistance to International Trade.' *Cambridge Journal of Regions, Economy and Society* 1 (3): 439–58.

Liu, Xuepeng. 2010. 'Testing Conflicting Political Economy Theories: Full-Fledged versus Partial-Scope Regional Trade Agreements.' *Southern Economic Journal* 77 (1): 78–103.

Mansfield, Edward D., and Milner, Helen V. 1999. 'The New Wave of Regionalism.' *International Organization* 53 (3): 589–627.

Mansfield, Edward D., and Milner, Helen V. 2012. *Votes, Vetoes, and the Political Economy of International Trade Agreements*. Princeton, NJ: Princeton University Press.

Mansfield, Edward D., Milner, Helen V., and Pevehouse, Jon C. 2008. 'Democracy, Veto Players and the Depth of Regional Integration.' *World Economy* 31 (1): 67–96.

Mansfield, Edward D., and Mutz, Diana C. 2009. 'Support for Free Trade: Self-Interest, Sociotropic Politics, and Out-Group Anxiety.' *International Organization* 63 (3): 1–34.

Mansfield, Edward D., and Reinhardt, Eric. 2003. 'Multilateral Determinants of Regionalism: The Effects of GATT/WTO on the Formation of Preferential Trading Arrangements.' *International Organization* 57 (4): 1–35.

Mayda, Anna Maria. 2006. 'Why Are People More Pro-Trade Than Pro-Migration?' CReAM Discussion Paper No. 11. Centre for Research and Analysis of Migration, London.

Mayda, Anna Maria, and Rodrik, Dani. 2005. 'Why Are Some People (and Countries) More Protectionist Than Others?' *European Economic Review* 49 (6): 1393–1430.

Milner, Helen V. 1997. 'Industries, Governments and the Creation of Regional Trade Blocs.' In *The Political Economy of Regionalism*, edited by Edward D. Mansfield and Helen V. Milner, 77–106. New York: Columbia University Press.

Milner, Helen V., and Kubota, Keiko. 2005. 'Why the Move to Free Trade? Democracy and Trade Policy in the Developing Countries.' *International Organization* 59 (1): 1–38.

Morrow, James D., Siverson, Randolph M., and Tabares, Tressa E. 1998. 'The Political Determinants of International Trade: The Major Powers, 1907–90.' *American Political Science Review* 92 (3): 649–61.

Nguyen, Quynh, and Bernauer, Thomas. 2013. 'Does Social Trust Increase Support for Free Trade? Evidence from a Field Survey Experiment in Vietnam.' http://ssrn.com/abstract=2359342.

O'Rourke, Kevin H., and Sinnot, Richard. 2001. 'The Determinants of Individual Trade Policy Preferences: International Survey Evidence.' *Brookings Trade Forum: 2001*, edited by Susan M. Collins and Dani Rodrik, 157–206. Washington, DC: Brookings Institution Press.

Rauch, James E. 1999. 'Networks versus Markets in International Trade.' *Journal of International Economics* 48 (1): 7–35.

Scheve, Kenneth F., and Slaughter, Matthew J. 2001. 'What Determines Individual Trade-Policy Preferences?' *Journal of International Economics* 54 (2): 267–92.

Spilker, Gabriele and Böhmelt, Tobias. 2012. 'The Impact of Preferential Trade Agreements on Governmental Repression Revisited.' *Review of International Organizations* 8 (3): 343–61.

Spilker, Gabriele, Schaffer, Lena Maria, and Bernauer, Thomas. 2012. 'Does Social Capital Increase Public Support for Economic Globalisation?' *European Journal of Political Research* 51 (6): 756–84.

Triandis, Harry C. 2000. 'Culture and Conflict.' *International Journal of Psychology* 35 (2): 145–52.

Urbatsch, Robert. 2013. 'A Referendum on Trade Theory: Voting on Free Trade in Costa Rica.' *International Organization* 67 (1): 197–214.

World Trade Organization. 2011. *World Trade Report 2011*. Geneva: WTO.

Yi, Kei Mu. 2003. 'Can Vertical Specialization Explain the Growth of World Trade?' *Journal of Political Economy* 111 (1): 52–102.

# 6

---

# Regionalisation in search of regionalism

Production networks and deep integration commitments
in Asia's Ptas

SOO YEON KIM

## A. Introduction

Asia is a latecomer to the preferential trade agreement (PTA) scene. While regionalism was on the rise and Ptas were proliferating in the 1990s, Asia was an anomalous region that experienced increasing trade flows but saw little progress in forming international institutions, such as trade agreements, to govern them (Mansfield and Milner 1999). Indeed, an established body of literature led by Amitav Acharya (2001) supports the 'ASEAN Way', which captures the tendency of Asian countries to eschew formal institutions and binding legal commitments. This phenomenon is supported by the characteristics of Asia's regionalisation, which has relied heavily on the private sector to drive and to manage economic integration. Societal organisations, especially business organisations, such as the Pacific Economic Cooperation Council (PECC) and the Pacific Basin Economic Council (PBEC), as well as the extensive and powerful network formed by the Chinese diaspora have been instrumental in producing a 'market-oriented, decentralized Asia-Pacific' (Funabashi 1995).

This pattern of private-sector-led regionalisation has changed dramatically in recent years, especially in the region's PTA landscape. Increasingly, governments have taken the lead in governing economic exchange across borders, by enthusiastically embracing the global trend in Ptas that commit states to legal obligation in the liberalisation and management of

The author is grateful to Li Xiang, Hanson Mah and Terence Tan for excellent and timely research assistance. This chapter employs *preferential trade agreement* (PTA) as a general term to refer to trade agreements outside the World Trade Organization (WTO). PTA here is interchangeable with free trade agreement (FTA) and regional trade agreement (RTA).

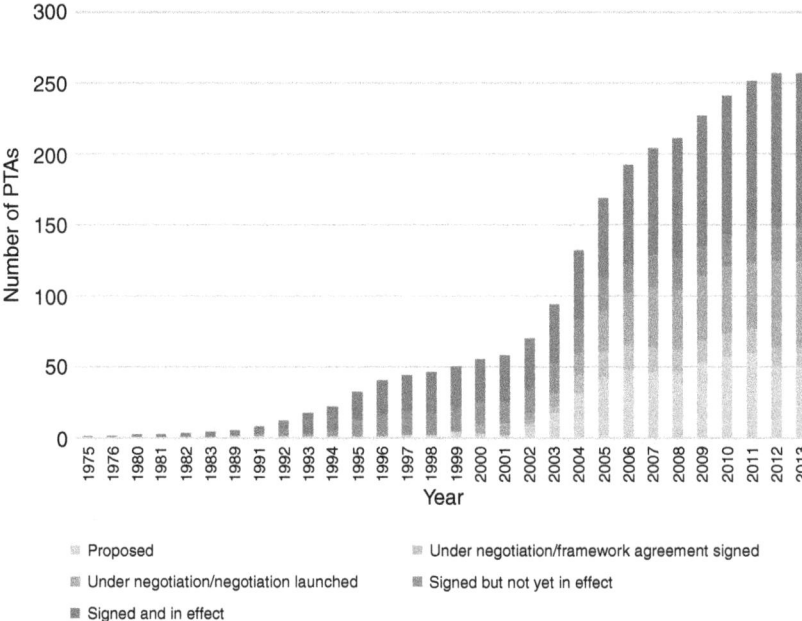

**Figure 6.1** Regional trade agreements in Asia, 1975–2013
*Source:* Asia Regional Integration Center (ARIC), Asian Development Bank (ADB). As of January 2013.

trade relations. Asia is now one of the most active sites of PTA projects (Crawford and Fiorentino 2004; Fiorentino, Verdeja and Toqueboeuf 2006), and the region has continued to consolidate the drive towards greater regionalism. As Figure 6.1 shows, according to the most recent report from the Asian Regional Integration Center (ARIC) of the Asian Development Bank (ADB), 109 agreements are in effect, with another 23 awaiting ratification, and approximately the same number has been proposed or agreements are under negotiation.[1] Even Mongolia, long the outlier in PTA participation as the only World Trade Organization (WTO) member with no trade agreements, has joined the PTA bandwagon, as it is currently negotiating accession to the Asia-Pacific Trade Agreement (APTA) and a PTA with Japan (UNESCAP 2013).[2]

Why has Asia become such an active region in the formation of PTAs, and why, in particular, have governments become more actively involved in forming international institutions? Given the dearth of institutional

---

[1] http://aric.adb.org/fta.    [2] www.unescap.org/tid/aptiad/agg_db.aspx.

history of the region, it is surprising that countries in the region have participated at all in forming international institutions, much less formed them with speed and strong commitments. The explosion of PTAs involving Asian countries may simply be a regional reaction to the global trend, in which trade agreements have proliferated, especially and increasingly as the Doha Round negotiations have not resulted in a successful multilateral trade round. Yet this explanation does not account for the wide variability in the quality of Asia's PTAs, which range from the very brief India–Bhutan FTA to the extensive Korea–US FTA, a highly legalised and complex agreement that runs the gamut of trade and trade-related liberalisation commitments. Alternatively, the PTA projects may reflect the consolidation of regionalism that began in the aftermath of the Asian Financial Crisis. However, this explanation does not account for the fact that the Association of Southeast Asian Nations (ASEAN) countries began negotiations on the creation of the ASEAN Free Trade Area in 1992, well before the outbreak of the financial crisis. As Ravenhill (2008) notes, the link between the crisis and the subsequent FTA wave may be little more than a coincidence.

This study offers an explanation that highlights the institutional demands of production networks and the role of multinational firms as political actors in their host countries in determining governments' willingness to enter into deep integration PTAs, both with regional and extraregional partners. In particular, the increasing prevalence and economic importance of production networks in Asia have driven governments to make deep integration commitments in their PTAs, in which states commit to harmonisation and greater compatibility in domestic trade-related regulations that are relevant to the operations of multinational firms. This explanation complements Manger's analysis of Japan and South Korea's PTAs, which finds that intra-industry trade, relative to endowment-based trade, promotes tariff liberalisation in PTAs (Manger, Chapter 8 in this volume). Overall, this study examines the extent to which regionalisation – the increasing flows of trade and investment – has contributed to the momentum of regionalism through PTAs, in which states seek active cooperation and coordination in trade-related economic policy (Fishlow and Haggard 1992; Mansfield and Milner 1999: 591).

This chapter considers three main features in Asian regionalism through PTAs:

- the institutional complexity encoded in PTAs, as seen through commitments regarding the depth of integration;

- the extent to which the deep integration commitments are shaped by participation in production networks, as measured by trade in parts and components and by foreign direct investment (FDI) inflows;
- commitments made in the protection and liberalisation of investment in PTA commitments. Investment and trade are integral to the operation of production networks, whether in Asia or beyond, and the analysis highlights the extent to which production network trade and investment affect states' commitments in regulating investments.

## B. Production networks and Asia's economic integration

Production networks have been a key driver of Asia's economic integration, linking the production facilities and offices of multinational firms that are dispersed across different countries. Production networks reflect the increasingly complex international supply chain in what Richard Baldwin has called the 'second unbundling' (Baldwin 2011: 3). Early examples of this phenomenon include the US–Canada or French–German trade in motor vehicles and parts in the 1970s, but the next leap involved production that was divided between developed and developing countries, facilitated by advancements in information and communications and technology (ICT) and significant wage differences (Ando and Kimura 2005; Feenstra 1998). International trade as a result of production unbundling is also known as outward processing trade, or vertical specialisation trade (Hummels, Ishii and Yi 2001; Manger 2009), in which imports of intermediate inputs are used for the production of goods that are subsequently exported. As vertical specialisation trade took off in Asia in the 1980s, the region came to earn the label 'Factory Asia' to reflect the extensive unbundling of production in the region (Ando and Kimura 2005; Athukorala 2005).

Multinational firms with production networks in Asia include the likes of Procter & Gamble and General Electric, as well as Toyota and the local agribusiness giant Wilmar. Within the ASEAN countries, for example, Procter & Gamble, whose presence dates back to 1935 when it opened its first affiliate in the Philippines, has manufacturing operations dispersed across Indonesia, Malaysia, Singapore, Thailand and Vietnam, as well as in the Philippines, that cover the full spectrum of its value chain. Toyota, whose first investments were made in the 1960s in Southeast Asia, now carries out production in motor vehicle parts and components in Malaysia, Indonesia, Thailand, the Philippines and Vietnam, with service operations based in Singapore. ASEAN, in particular, has been an important player in the international supply chain, and 10 of the world largest motor vehicle manufacturers have production facilities spread across several member countries (ASEAN 2013). The textiles and garments industry also figures prominently in ASEAN's participation in the international supply chain and in local production networks, with companies such as Nike, Adidas, H&M, Target and Marks and Spencer employing contract manufacturers from Cambodia, Indonesia and Vietnam as well as operating production facilities. Vietnam, in particular, is a major source for brands such as Gap, Columbia, LL Bean and Walmart (ASEAN 2013).

Production networks comprise a 'trade, investment, and services' nexus (Baldwin 2011), at the heart of which is a multinational firm seeking to reduce production costs and attain greater efficiency. A significant portion of trade within production networks consists of intermediate goods, whose production is driven by investment and supported by services that facilitate communications and movement of goods. The important supporting roles of investment and services call for strong commitments in behind-the-border trade rules as well as low tariffs, as the successful operation of production networks hinges on the infrastructure, institutional apparatus and regulations that facilitate cross-border production. Local rules figure strongly where offshoring by multinational firms separates geographically the suppliers of inputs from the final goods producers. PTAs can deliver commitments on such domestic trade-related rules that would lower the cost of doing business.

## C. Deep integration PTAs

This study investigates how participation in production network trade has shaped deep integration commitments in Asia's PTAs. *Deep integration*, consistent with the institutional demands of production networks, refers to a process of economic integration that erodes differences in national economic policies and regulations and increases their compatibility across different economies to facilitate economic exchange. As a concept, deep integration is often associated with Robert Z. Lawrence (1995), who published a study that examined the tensions between PTAs and national autonomy. Its main conceptual property is 'behind-the-border' integration, synonymous with 'positive integration' and the liberalisation approach of the WTO era. Positive integration involves the active promulgation of domestic rules and regulations that make a country's trade regime WTO-consistent. It stands in contrast to the 'negative integration' or 'shallow integration' approach taken during the General Agreement on Tariffs and Trade (GATT) years, during which member states only committed *not* to raise 'barriers at the border' such as tariffs, quantitative restrictions and indirect taxes that discriminated against foreign firms.

Deep integration commitments in PTAs are directed towards strengthening the contestability of national markets for foreign firms through reforms in the trade-related rules and regulations of partner economies. Provisions that promote deep integration are characterised by three core features (Kim forthcoming):

1. *protection* of foreign firms' economic interests;
2. *liberalisation* of trade, especially 'beyond-the-border' barriers that go beyond traditional border barriers and
3. *harmonisation* of trade rules across partner countries (Kim, forthcoming).

Deep integration commitments are perhaps the most notable innovation of the modern PTA, which began to flourish in the 1990s as the international supply chain became more complex. Examples of deep integration PTAs include the North American Free Trade Agreement (NAFTA), the European Union's PTAs, the more recent economic partnership agreements (EPAs) and the Trans-Pacific Partnership (TPP) agreement currently under negotiation. Such agreements are found not only in the PTAs of the developed North or between countries of the North and the South but increasingly between developing countries.

In terms of provisions in PTAs, deep integration commitments are directed towards harmonisation or at least mutual recognition of domestic trade-related regulations (Birdsall and Lawrence 1999), which goes as far back as Tinbergen's (1954) early work on the institutional features of economic integration. Deep integration PTAs are wide in the scope of trade-related issue areas that they cover (Koremenos, Lipson and Snidal 2001), with some commitments going beyond the purview of existing WTO agreements. The sectors and issue areas that are covered in deep integration PTAs include not only services, product and production standards, government procurement, investment, competition policy, labour and environmental policies but also the protection of intellectual property rights and even newly emerging governance areas such as e-commerce. Such regulatory commitments are found in tandem with low tariffs, which makes sense because the harmonisation of trade-related rules becomes a feasible enterprise only once barriers at the border, such as tariffs, have been lowered and provide the foundation for the reform of domestic institutions. In the case of ASEAN, for example, the move toward the ASEAN

Free Trade Area has been accompanied by the reduction of internal tariffs to zero for 98.6 per cent of 98176 tariff lines (ASEAN 2013).

## D. The Trans-Pacific Partnership agreement: a deep integration PTA for the twenty-first century

At the time of writing, one of the most important deep integration PTA projects for Asia is the Trans-Pacific Partnership (TPP) agreement, currently under negotiation and involving 12 countries, including the United States. The TPP is the cornerstone of the Obama administration's economic policy in Asia and the economic arm of the 'Asian Pivot'. As an institutional form, the TPP is a twenty-first-century deep integration agreement that advances 'regulatory coherence' as one of its key objectives.[3] It is touted as a 'fully regional agreement' designed to facilitate the development of production and supply chains among member countries.[4] The TPP is represented by negotiating parties as a high-standard agreement among 'like-minded' countries that covers core areas of deep integration, such as investment, services, competition, labour, the environment and e-commerce as well as the traditional areas of market access in goods and trade remedies. The objective of 'regulatory coherence' is especially relevant to this study of Asia's PTAs. The commitments of this agreement would be geared towards supporting the production networks of multinational firms across the 12 partner economies.

## E. Free trade agreements in Asia across space and time

The existing PTAs in Asia vary widely in their deep integration commitments. Utilising information on PTA provisions gathered by the United Nations Economic and Social Commission for Asia and the Pacific (UNESCAP), Figure 6.2 shows the level of deep integration in PTAs signed by countries in the region, including both agreements with other Asian countries and those outside the region. Figure 6.2 illustrates depth of integration commitments across agreements signed by countries of Northeast Asia, Southeast Asia, South Asia and the Pacific Island countries,

---

[3] The current members of the agreement are Australia, Brunei Darussalam, Canada, Chile, Malaysia, Mexico, New Zealand, Peru, Singapore, the United States and Vietnam. Most recently, the United States proposed the entry of Japan into the TPP negotiations. www.ustr.gov.

[4] www.ustr.gov/about-us/press-office/fact-sheets/2011/november/outlines-trans-pacific-partnership-agreement.

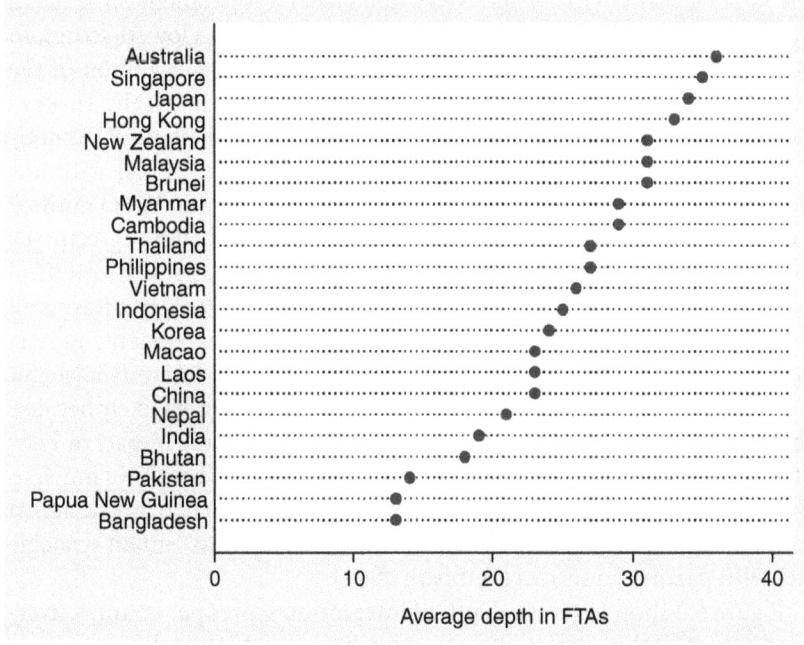

**Figure 6.2**   Depth of integration scores by country
*Source:* Author calculations.

including Australia, New Zealand and Papua Guinea. Deep integration commitments cover a comprehensive set of provisions, including market access for goods, investment, services, trade facilitation, rules of origin and an 'others' category that includes issue areas such as competition, intellectual property rights, labour and environmental standards, government procurement, dispute settlement and technical cooperation. Each agreement was given a depth of integration score that is essentially a count of all explicit provisions under items of each category included in the PTA. The UNESCAP categorisation covers 58 items across the six categories. A detailed list of the provisions included for the depth of integration score is provided in the appendix to this chapter.

Utilising the UNESCAP categorisation provides a cursory but illustrative view of the depth of PTAs in Asia. In terms of the agreements themselves, the 10 agreements with the greatest depth of integration scores are all free trade agreements (FTAs) and economic integration agreements (EIAs) that cover both goods and services. They are also recent agreements, as all of them were signed after 2000, and have been notified to the WTO under GATT Article XXIV and General Agreement on Trade in Services (GATS) Article V. The 10 agreements with the lowest scores, in contrast, have not been notified to the WTO, with the exception of the Japan–Peru FTA (GATT Article XXIV and GATS Article V), the Turkey–Korea FTA (GATT Article XXIV) and the Lao PDR–Thailand PTA, notified under the Enabling Clause. Even among the next 5 PTAs with low depth of integration scores, the agreements were either not WTO notified or were notified under the Enabling Clause.[5] These shallow agreements are consistent with the recent scholarship that emphasizes the political motivations of trade agreements in Asia (Ravenhill 2009, 2010). Ravenhill (2010), for example, argues that the spread of trade agreements in Asia is largely a 'political domino' effect. Private economic interests have not been active in the negotiations over these agreements, most likely because the agreements are unlikely to have much of an economic impact or benefit for businesses in the region. Rather, the political factors have much to do with strategic interests. The US agreements, in particular, are designed to reward political and economic reforms in as well as to cement strategic ties with partner countries (Feinberg 2006).

Figure 6.2 shows average depth of integration scores per country, averaged across all the agreements a country has signed. Australia, Japan and Singapore, on average, are signatories of PTAs with high depth of integration scores. Just below this tier are many of the ASEAN countries. Taiwan, Bangladesh and Papua New Guinea have the lowest depth of integration scores. Over time, as shown in Figure 6.3, the long-term pattern in depth of integration in PTAs is a positive one, as agreements appear generally to be increasing in their strength and quality. However, this pattern is inconsistent and varies widely in the short term.

Scores rose consistently during the years 2000–10, when the region was most active in forming PTAs, but that trend appears to be on the decline. The most recent agreements have lower depth of integration scores. This suggests that high-standard agreements are mostly attributable to the characteristics of signatories rather than a general and systematic evolution of agreement templates over time. Moreover, countries that tend to sign PTAs with higher depth of integration scores also improve upon their templates. This development may be driven by the United States and its

---

[5] They are the Asia-Pacific Trade Agreement (signed 1975, Enabling Clause), Group of 8 PTA (2006, not notified to the WTO), India–Sri Lanka FTA (1998, Enabling Clause), Pakistan–Iran FTA (2004, not notified to the WTO) and the India–Bhutan FTA (2006, Enabling Clause).

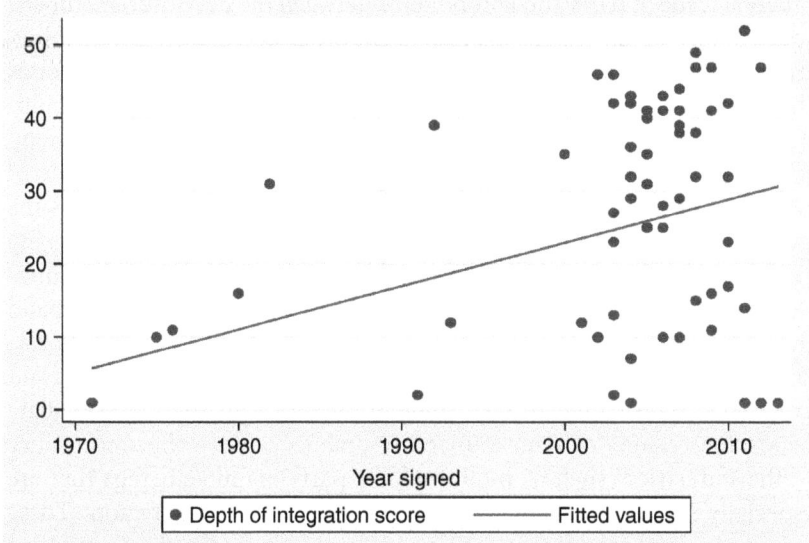

**Figure 6.3**   Depth of integration in PTAs over time, 1971–2013
*Source:* Author calculations.

generations of PTA templates, including the model of the US–Singapore FTA that was followed by the Korea–US FTA and, most recently, the TPP as its most developed 'next-generation' PTA.

## F. Production networks and depth of integration in PTAs

The next part of the analysis examines the role of production networks in Asia in determining the depth of integration in the region's PTAs. The unit of analysis is the PTA dyad, in which each member of the agreement is paired with all other members. Because of limitations on data availability, the time frame covered for this empirical analysis is 1988–2011, thus including a smaller set of agreements than the total number that were signed during this period. The dependent variable is the depth of integration score for a given PTA, and this score ranges between 0 and 49. The cumulative number of provisions covered by the UNESCAP data actually reaches a maximum of 58, but no agreement includes every provision, although all are found in at least some of the agreements.

The independent variable of interest is trade that is related to production networks, which is measured as the average annual dollar value of bilateral trade in parts and components between the PTA-dyad members, weighted by their respective gross domestic products (GDPs) and log-transformed. *Trade in parts and components* refers specifically to goods that are 'parts and accessories of capital goods (except transport equipment)' (code 42*) and 'parts and accessories of transport equipment' (code 53*) under the UN Registry of Broad Economic Categories (BEC).[6] Data were obtained from the UN Comtrade Database. It is perhaps the most commonly used measure for capturing global production sharing (Hoekman and Kostecki 2009; Ng and Yeats 1999) as a result of limitations on data availability, although other studies have sought to expand the range of intermediate goods covered under this label (Athukorala 2010) or have proposed measures such as trade in value added (Elms and Low 2013). This study employs trade in these categories of intermediate goods for reasons of data availability and to capture the importance of the industries (such as motor vehicle parts manufacturing) that are especially significant in the production networks of the region. These data were weighted by the GDP of each country in the dyad, averaged across the dyad to reflect the importance of production network trade to the domestic economy in both countries and log-transformed. This dyadic measure was then averaged once again across the 10-year period preceding the signing of the PTA, covering the years for which data were available.

The analysis also controls for several factors that may affect both production network trade and the depth of integration in PTAs. Perhaps the most important of the controls is foreign direct investment (FDI), which has been the engine of production networks, enabling multinational firms to establish and to operate manufacturing sites. FDI is measured as the dyadic average of annual FDI inflows as a proportion of GDP. Data were obtained from the World Development Indicators (WDI) (2013). The analysis controls for trade openness and economic growth, both also averaged across the dyad. Trade openness for each member is measured as the sum of the country's exports and imports weighted by its GDP. The two trade openness figures were then averaged across the two dyad members. Economic growth is the average annual growth in GDP (calculated on the basis of constant local currency) of the two dyad members. Data on individual countries' trade openness and economic growth figures were also obtained from WDI (2013).

---

[6] http://unstats.un.org/unsd/tradekb/Knowledgebase/Intermediate-Goods-in-Trade-Statistics.

The analysis also controls for economic asymmetry, indicated by the ratio of the larger to smaller GDP per capita of the two countries to capture the disparity in economic size and development. This measure is constructed along the lines of the capability ratio (Singer, Brenner and Stuckey 1972) to indicate disparities in power based on material capabilities. The data on GDP per capita were obtained from the WDI (2013). The analysis also takes account of two key political variables that reflect the domestic politics of trade, namely, regime type and veto players (Mansfield and Milner 2012; Mansfield, Milner and Pevehouse 2007). Regime type is operationalised as the average Polity score for the two dyad members, and veto players as the dyadic average of the Political Constraint Index provided in Henisz (2000).[7] Values of all control variables were also averaged across the 10-year period before the PTA was signed for those years when data were available.

## G. Selection and endogeneity issues

Before presenting the results of the analysis, it is important to address potential concerns regarding selection bias and endogeneity issues. First, one possible criticism of this research design may be that only certain countries sign on to PTAs in the first place, and this thus poses a selection problem with respect to the analysis of the depth of integration commitments in these PTAs. This issue hinges on the assumption that only some countries sign PTAs; however, this assumption is untenable given the increasingly upward trend in PTA formation, whether in Asia or elsewhere. Rather than only some countries signing on to PTAs, the trend is definitively in the direction of 'proliferation', as there is a general trend for all countries to seek out PTA partners to manage trade. Mongolia is an important case in point. Even this country that has a long-standing status as the only country without a PTA is currently in negotiations with Japan and has approached the United States and Canada.[8] The fact that virtually all countries in the global economy have joined a PTA and continue to seek additional agreements invalidates the criticism that only certain countries sign on to PTAs, thus mitigating concerns regarding a possible selection effect.

---

[7] The Polity data were obtained from http://www.systemicpeace.org/polity/polity4.htm, and the Political Constraint Index from http://www-management.wharton.upenn.edu/henisz/.

[8] http://www.bilaterals.org/?±-mongolia-±. Accessed 24 December 2013.

A second possible concern is the endogeneity of production network trade, levels of which may be responding to the dependent variable – the quality of the trade agreement. This concern relies on the assumption that firms that conduct trade respond to the trade agreement *before* it is signed or even comes into effect, or as it is being negotiated, perhaps increasing trade in anticipation of the benefits of the trade agreement. However, this assumption is also untenable. Firms are unlikely to increase their trade-related activities even before the legal measures of the trade agreement are implemented, much less signed. The tangible benefits of the trade agreement, such as lower tariffs, will not yet have come into effect, and thus firms that engage in trade have no incentive to increase trade when there is nothing to be gained from doing so insofar as the agreement is concerned. Rather, they have an incentive to wait until the agreement is in effect to benefit from lower tariffs and thus their increased competitiveness in the agreement partner's market. Firms may well adjust production plans to increase their exports in anticipation of the signing and implementation of the agreement, but the movement of their goods should be expected to increase only when the liberalisation measures have taken effect. Thus, there is a temporal dimension to the causal order: the depth of integration in PTAs is influenced by existing levels of production network trade; this trade, however, should be influenced by the trade agreement only *after* it has been put into effect.

## H. Results

Table 6.1 presents the results of the cross-sectional analysis of PTA dyads. The 10-year pre-PTA period was adopted to minimise the loss of observations due to missing data. Moreover, it also allows the analysis to take into account the lengthy pre-PTA period of initial investment by multinational firms, during which production networks were established and operating in the Asian region. In addition, the time frame incorporates the duration of the proposal and more lengthy negotiation stage of the PTA, which is often even preceded by the negotiation and signing of a framework agreement.

The results of the analysis show that trade in parts and components between countries in the dyad has a positive effect on the depth of integration in their PTA commitments. A one-percentage-point increase in the average level of production network trade between dyad members is associated with an increase of approximately 1.4 points in the depth of integration score of a PTA. Given that the baseline score is approximately 22.5 (indicated by the intercept where all independent variables are set to

Table 6.1 *Production network trade and investment commitments in PTAs*

|  | Depth of integration | Investment commitments |
|---|---|---|
| Trade in parts and components | 1.439** | 0.398** |
|  | (0.279) | (0.133) |
| FDI inflows | − 0.880* | 0.115 |
|  | (0.375) | (0.186) |
| Trade openness | 0.107** | 0.011 |
|  | (0.022) | (0.014) |
| Economic asymmetry | 2.524* | 1.020 |
|  | (1.026) | (0.528) |
| Economic growth | 0.749 | − 0.108 |
|  | (0.485) | (0.233) |
| Democracy | 0.537 | 0.364* |
|  | (0.337) | (0.172) |
| Veto players | − 23.560* | − 4.888 |
|  | (9.770) | (5.005) |
| Constant | 22.513** | 6.843* |
|  | (5.053) | (2.798) |
| $R^2$ | 0.31 | 0.15 |
| $N$ | 208 | 191 |

*Note:* Ordinary least squares with robust standard errors.
* $p < 0.10$
** $p < 0.05$

zero), this result indicates that an increase of 10 per cent in production network trade may well lead to high-quality PTAs that are close to the uppermost values in depth of integration commitments. Among the control variables, FDI inflows into each country appear not to have an impact on the depth of integration score of a PTA. This result underscores the weakness of this widely used measure. As a measure that is constructed from national-level FDI inflows rather than dyadic FDI flows, however, this operationalisation of FDI may not adequately capture the importance of investment activities between the dyad members. Nor does this analysis account for FDI stocks, which would indicate the level of existing economic interests of foreign firms that may drive the PTA process.

As for the remaining control variables, the general trade openness of the dyad members appears to have a small but positive impact on PTA commitments, reflecting the importance of participation in the global economy for a country's bilateral agreements. At the same time, economic conditions measured in terms of long-term economic growth do not seem to have an effect on the quality of bilateral agreements concluded by dyad members. The result for economic asymmetry, or the disparity in development measured in terms of the ratio of per capita incomes, suggests this variable may be an effective proxy for disparity in economic power. The analysis finds that the greater the developmental disparity, the higher the depth of integration score in a PTA, suggesting that the more developed country is the driver for strong commitments. Finally, for the political variables, democracy has no discernible impact on the institutional quality of PTAs even though democratic countries may be more likely to sign trade agreements (Umaña, Bernauer and Spilker, Chapter 5 in this volume). In contrast, political constraints figure strongly in PTA commitments. Notably, dyads in which members are constrained by numerous veto players tend towards PTAs without strong deep integration commitments. This result complements the analysis by Mansfield and Milner (Chapter 3 in this volume), which finds that countries with more veto players are less likely to sign a trade agreement. This study finds that if such countries do sign a PTA, they are also likely to avoid deep integration commitments.

## I. A case study in deep integration commitments: investment provisions

As a refinement to the preceding analysis that examines the depth of integration represented by the whole agreement, this part of the study provides a closer look at investment provisions in these PTAs. Commitments in investment comprise one of the pillars of a PTA that promotes the formation of production networks and also facilitates their operations where they exist. For Asian countries, in particular, attracting investment has been one of the major motivations behind government decisions to sign a PTA. In the case of the ASEAN Free Trade Area (AFTA) agreement, for example, officials were explicit about the need to attract investment to the region and to prevent the diversion of FDI as key arguments. In the early 1990s, and well before the Asian Financial Crisis, FDI was already on the decline (Nesadurai 2003: 82–7). AFTA negotiators, in their consultations with experts during the drafting of the agreement, took into account the general conclusion of numerous studies that the major impact of trade agreement projects such as NAFTA and the European Single Market would be further decline in FDI flows to the region. The need to address this FDI 'crisis' and to prevent further diversion of FDI, especially to China, spurred the cooperation that produced AFTA in 1992 (Khong and Nesadurai 2007: 51).

This analysis relies on a detailed coding of investment provisions in PTAs, which captures the dimensions of protection and liberalisation (Kotschwar 2009) that are explicitly stated as agreement provisions. The coding of investment provisions covers 33 components across the following 10 broad categories:

1. sectoral coverage to include portfolio investment as well as FDI, which reflects how broadly investment is defined;
2. investor–state dispute settlement and the ability of private economic actors to protect their economic interests in host countries;
3. positive- or negative-list bindings in most-favoured nation (MFN) and national treatment (NT);
4. scope of MFN and NT as they concern the stages of investment: establishment, acquisition, postestablishment and (re)sale;
5. investment protection, covering 'fair and equitable treatment', repatriation of profits and expropriation;
6. restrictions on transfers and payments;
7. performance requirements;
8. restrictions on senior management and board of directors, in terms of membership and temporary entry provisions;
9. denial of benefits for third-party investors; and
10. general transparency provisions regarding the publication of laws and regulations and the availability of a national enquiry point, which are applicable to all provisions in the trade agreements.

These categories encompass provisions emphasised in both Kotschwar (2009) and Miroudot (2011), in which the latter focuses on the PTA-formation strategies of developing countries. They comprise a comprehensive set of provisions on investment that are found in PTAs in general. The analysis relies on an additive index that was constructed by summing up the level of protection or liberalisation that is captured by each category. The appendix to this chapter provides the detailed 33-point coding scheme and the values assigned to each component.

The empirical analysis is similar to that carried out for the depth of integration scores covering the entire agreement. The dependent variable is now defined as the index for investment commitments, and the major independent variable of interest remains the same: trade in parts and components as a percentage of GDP, averaged across the two countries in the dyad for the 10 years preceding the signing of the PTA. The additional independent variable of interest in this particular analysis is FDI, again measured in terms of annual FDI inflows as a percentage of

GDP. As the outcome of interest is the set of investment commitments, the impact of FDI is expected to be positive. The analysis employs the same control variables as for the analysis of depth of integration: trade openness, economic asymmetry, economic growth, regime type and veto players. Also as earlier, values of all control variables are averaged across the 10-year period preceding the signing of the PTA. The results of the analysis are presented in the second column of Table 6.1. They provide a comparison of how parts and components trade affects both the broad depth of integration score and the investment provisions in particular.

Production network trade as measured by trade in parts and components is associated not only with deep PTAs more broadly but also with stronger commitments in individual provisions concerning the protection and liberalisation of investment. The estimates for the effect of production network trade are not comparable across the two different scales of the dependent variables – depth of integration and strength of investment commitments. Nevertheless, the results indicate that trade that is related to production networks may well have a specific positive impact on investment commitments in the direction of greater liberalisation and protection of investor interests. The effects of the control variables are generally weak: trade openness, economic asymmetry, economic growth and political constraints appear not to have an impact on the strength of investment commitments. However, democratic dyads are associated with stronger investment commitments in their PTAs, which offers an interesting parallel to the broader question of democracies and trade agreements (Mansfield, Milner and Rosendorff 2002). Democratic dyads not only are more likely to sign or enter into trade agreements but, as this study shows, are more likely to do so in agreements with strong commitments in areas such as investment.

The results of this analysis on investment provisions also draw on the scholarship that examines the trade–investment connections surrounding PTAs. One well-known study by Büthe and Milner (2008) shows that trade agreements increase investment because of the credible commitment that they signal to investors regarding the treatment of assets, even after controlling for the possible endogeneity of PTAs. Büthe and Milner (2008) and the present study both employed inflows of FDI in a given year as a percentage of FDI, and both show that 'new' investment drives neither the signing nor the strength of investment commitments in trade agreements. This raises the question of the role of 'old' investments, or FDI stocks, in shaping investment commitments. Old investment as reflected in FDI stocks highlights the role of incumbent economic interests, that is, the economic interests of multinational firms that already have existing investments and also have strong interests in protecting their regulatory advantage in host countries.

## J. Conclusion

This chapter has focused on the role of production networks in shaping commitments in Asia's PTAs. As the region continues its push towards greater regional integration, PTAs have emerged as an important institutional mechanism for managing trade relations. Deep integration commitments in PTAs are an integral part of protection, liberalisation and harmonisation of domestic trade-related regulations that are intended to facilitate the establishment and especially the operation of production networks by multinational firms.

The analysis in this chapter investigated the effect of trade in parts and components, as a proxy for production network trade, on a comprehensive index of deep integration that considers all aspects of a trade agreement. The results of the analysis show that production network trade has a positive impact on deep integration commitments, thus contributing to the signing of high-quality agreements that address issue areas such as government procurement, services and intellectual property rights for which the current multilateral trade regime has provided only weak coverage. Production network trade also has a positive impact on investment commitments in PTAs, which this chapter has further examined as a case study. The analysis also controlled for a host of economic and political variables, including trade openness, economic asymmetry, growth, democracy and the political constraints imposed by veto players.

In future studies, the most relevant avenue for gaining a better understanding of regionalism, in Asia and beyond, would be to investigate in greater depth and detail the role of investments in deep integration PTAs. Investments are a key driver in the formation of production networks and would be expected to have a significant role in PTA commitments in this area. Although this chapter employed a basic measure of annual FDI inflows as a percentage of GDP, the effect of FDI may be stronger when there is already a large existing stock of investment that spurs lobbying for deep integration commitments by multinational firms. As to FDI inflows, they may be consequences of deep integration PTAs rather than causes, as the credible commitment provided by the agreement may strongly encourage FDI flows in subsequent years. Future research in this area would also benefit from examining how implementation of deep integration PTAs affects the efficiency of production and networks and, more importantly, whether implementation of these commitments leads to trade gains and the development of mutually compatible domestic trade-related regulatory frameworks in agreement partners.

In addition, the role of multinational firms as political actors in their host countries also calls for closer investigation. A knowledge of how multinational firms, as actors that drive investment and stand to gain much from deep integration, function as an interest group in the political competition over trade policy would provide important insights into the political economy of international supply chains more broadly. Finally, as this study is based on observational data, a general concern regarding unobserved confounders arises. As the randomisation of the treatment – production network trade – is not feasible, future research would also benefit from identifying possible correctives to strengthen the findings of this line of scholarship.

## Appendix to Chapter 6

### Classification of investment provisions in PTAs

This classification is based on Kotschwar (2009) and Miroudot (2011).

1. Sectoral coverage
   a. Definition: is investment defined as FDI, or does it also include portfolio investment?
   b. Is there a separate investment chapter?
   c. Are investment provisions found in the services chapter as mode 3 (commercial presence)?
   d. Endeavours without specified scope: Is there a general commitment to cooperation/liberalisation/promotion of investment (often in the preamble to the agreement) but without specific commitments such as *b* or *c* above?
2. Does the PTA provide for investor–state dispute settlement?
3. MFN and national treatment
   a. Positive-list bindings: PTA investment provisions list sectors to be liberalised; all others remain 'unbound' (not subject to commitments).
   b. Negative-list bindings: PTA investment provisions stipulate MFN and national treatment as general principles applicable across the board but with exemptions for those sectors that are to remain closed.
4. Scope of MFN and national treatment: phases of investment covered by MFN and national treatment:
   a. 'Establishment'
   b. 'Acquisition'

   c. 'Postestablishment'

   d. '(Re)sale' [of investment]'

5. Investment protection: the terms should appear in the provisions.

   a. 'fair and equitable treatment'

   b. Free transfer of funds

   c. Expropriation and compensation: expropriation on a nondiscriminatory basis and with adequate compensation

6. Transfers and payments

   a. Does PTA place restrictions on transfer of funds in the event of balance-of-payments difficulties?

   b. Does PTA place restrictions on transfer of funds in other prescribed circumstances?

7. Performance requirements: obligations (i) to export a particular percentage of goods and services; (ii) to use a particular level or percentage of local content; (iii) to give preference to local goods or services; (iv) to observe trade and foreign exchange balancing requirements; (v) to transfer technology; or (vi) to act as the exclusive supplier of goods and services.

   a. Prohibition of local content, trade or other specified requirements?

   b. Prohibition of local content or trade requirements only? Prohibits any of (i)–(iv) only from preceding list; allows (v) and (vi) and other specified requirements.

   c. Provisions more limited than Trade-Related Investment Measures (TRIMs) (performance requirements not banned/prohibited)? No provisions on local content?

8. Senior management/board of directors: restrictions regarding the nationality of managers and members of the board; hiring of top managerial personnel regardless of nationality; stipulating nationality of majority of board of directors.

   a. Provisions allowing for temporary entry of key personnel? (May be in another part of FTA).

   b. Cannot restrict either senior management/board of directors based on nationality?

   c. Can partially restrict board of directors?

   d. Can partially restrict management or both?

9. Denial of benefits: description: concerns rights of third-party (non-FTA partner country) investors. Issue is whether they enjoy the same rights as investors of a party to the FTA when they have a substantial presence in one member's territory and invest in the other party's territory through this presence. Implies de facto transfer of investment rules to nonparty actors.

a. (Denial of benefits) Only to persons with no substantial business operations in other party?
b. (Denial of benefits) Tougher treatment for specific reasons?
- Examples: denial of benefits in the absence of diplomatic relations between denying party and nonparty or adoption/ maintenance of measures with that nonparty that prohibits transactions with the enterprise
c. (Denial of benefits) Tougher treatment for all reasons?
10. Transparency (in any part of the agreement): GATS obligation to publish all relevant laws and to set up inquiry points that companies/governments can use to obtain information about regulations in the sector. Prior comment: parties notify each other with regard to any proposed or actual matter than might be adopted that might affect other party.
a. 'Prior comment'?
b. Publish (as in GATS)?
c. National inquiry point (as in GATS)? (May also be 'contact point').

Table A6.1 *PTA provisions, UNESCAP categories*

| Goods | tariffs (goods) |  |
|---|---|---|
|  | rules of origin (goods) |  |
|  | contingencies anti-dumping (goods) |  |
|  | contingencies countervailing duties (goods) |  |
|  | contingencies safeguards (goods) |  |
|  | standards (goods) |  |
| Services | liberalisation approach (services) |  |
|  | cross-border supply (mode 1) (services) |  |
|  | consumption abroad (mode 2) (services) |  |
|  | commercial presence (mode 3) (services) |  |
|  | presence of natural persons (mode 4) (services) |  |
|  | (specific chapters) | financial services (services) |
|  | (specific chapters) | telecommunications (services) |
|  | (specific chapters) | movement of natural persons (services) |
|  | (specific chapters) | professional services (services) |
|  | (specific chapters) | other (services) |
|  | most-favoured nation (services) |  |
|  | national treatment (services) |  |
|  | market access (services) |  |
|  | domestic regulation (services) |  |
|  | subsidies covered by services disciplines (services) |  |
|  | denial of benefits for commercial presence (services) |  |

Table A6.1 (cont.)

| | |
|---|---|
| Investment | scheduling approach (investment) |
| | definition of investment (investment) |
| | most-favoured nation (investment) |
| | economic integration exception to mfn (investment) |
| | national treatment (investment) |
| | national treatment provision applies to entry and establishment rights (investment) |
| | fair and equitable treatment (FET) (investment) |
| | clarifying text on FET (investment) |
| | expropriation (investment) |
| | clarifying text (investment) |
| | board of directors and executive personnel (investment) |
| | investor–state arbitration (investment) |
| | denial of benefits (investment) |
| Trade Facilitation | customs procedures (trade facilitation) |
| | customs valuation (trade facilitation) |
| | trade regulations publication and administration (trade facilitation) |
| | use of ICT (trade facilitation) |
| | mobility of business people (trade facilitation) |
| | freedom of transit (trade facilitation) |
| | transport and logistics (trade facilitation) |
| | trade finance (trade facilitation) |
| Other Areas | government procurement (other areas) |
| | investment (other areas) |
| | competition policy (other areas) |
| | intellectual property (other areas) |
| | dispute settlement (other areas) |
| | labour mobility (other areas) |
| | labour and environmental standards (other areas) |
| | technical cooperation (other areas) |
| | institutional mechanism (other areas) |
| Rules of Origin | cumulation (rules of origin) |
| | specific process (rules of origin) |
| | heading change (rules of origin) |
| | de minimis (rules of origin) |
| | minimum content (rules of origin) |
| | drawback (rules of origin) |

Table A6.2 *Depth of integration scores for Asian PTAs*

| PTA | Year of signature | Scope | WTO notification | Depth of integration score |
|---|---|---|---|---|
| Korea–Peru FTA and EIA | 2011 | Bilateral | GATT Article XXIV, GATS Article V | 49 |
| Australia–Chile FTA and EIA | 2008 | Bilateral | GATT Article XXIV, GATS Article V | 47 |
| AANZFTA | 2009 | Country – Bloc | GATT Article XXIV, GATS Article V | 45 |
| Malaysia–Australia FTA | 2012 | Bilateral | GATT Article XXIV, GATS Article V | 45 |
| US–Singapore FTA and EIA | 2003 | Bilateral | GATT Article XXIV, GATS Article V | 44 |
| Japan–Singapore FTA and EIA | 2002 | Bilateral | GATT Article XXIV, GATS Article V | 44 |
| Peru–Singapore FTA and EIA | 2008 | Bilateral | GATT Article XXIV, GATS Article V | 44 |
| Japan–Switzerland FTA and EIA | 2009 | Bilateral | GATT Article XXIV, GATS Article V | 44 |
| Korea–Chile FTA and EIA | 2003 | Bilateral | GATT Article XXIV, GATS Article V | 43 |
| Japan–Thailand FTA and EIA | 2007 | Bilateral | GATT Article XXIV, GATS Article V | 41 |
| Australia–US FTA and EIA | 2004 | Bilateral | GATT Article XXIV, GATS Article V | 41 |
| India–Singapore FTA and EIA | 2005 | Bilateral | GATT Article XXIV, GATS Article V | 41 |
| Australia–Thailand FTA and EIA | 2004 | Bilateral | GATT Article XXIV, GATS Article V | 40 |
| India–Malaysia FTA and EIA | 2011 | Bilateral | Enabling Clause, GATS Article V | 40 |
| Japan–Philippines FTA and EIA | 2006 | Bilateral | GATT Article XXIV, GATS Article V | 40 |
| Japan–Mexico FTA and EIA | 2004 | Bilateral | GATT Article XXIV, GATS Article V | 40 |
| Singapore–Australia FTA and EIA | 2003 | Bilateral | GATT Article XXIV, GATS Article V | 40 |
| Korea–Singapore FTA and EIA | 2005 | Bilateral | GATT Article XXIV, GATS Article V | 39 |

Table A6.2  (cont.)

| PTA | Year of signature | Scope | WTO notification | Depth of integration score |
|---|---|---|---|---|
| Panama–Singapore FTA and EIA | 2006 | Bilateral | GATT Article XXIV, GATS Article V | 39 |
| China–Peru FTA and EIA | 2009 | Bilateral | GATT Article XXIV, GATS Article V | 39 |
| Japan–Indonesia EPA | 2007 | Bilateral | GATT Article XXIV, GATS Article V | 39 |
| Singapore–Costa Rica FTA and EIA | 2010 | Bilateral | early announcement | 39 |
| Japan–Malaysia FTA and EIA | 2005 | Bilateral | GATT Article XXIV, GATS Article V | 38 |
| EFTA–Korea FTA and EIA | 2005 | Country – Bloc | GATT Article XXIV, GATS Article V | 37 |
| ASEAN FTA | 1992 | Regional | Enabling Clause | 37 |
| EFTA– Hong Kong, China | 2011 | Country – Bloc | GATT Article XXIV, GATS Article V | 37 |
| New Zealand– Malaysia FTA and EIA | 2009 | Bilateral | GATT Article XXIV, GATS Article V | 37 |
| New Zealand–China FTA and EIA | 2008 | Bilateral | GATT Article XXIV, GATS Article V | 36 |
| Japan–Brunei Darussalam FTA and EIA | 2007 | Bilateral | GATT Article XXIV, GATS Article V | 36 |
| Japan–Chile FTA and EIA | 2007 | Bilateral | GATT Article XXIV, GATS Article V | 35 |
| Korea–India FTA and EIA | 2009 | Bilateral | GATT Article XXIV, GATS Article V | 35 |
| ACFTA FTA and EIA | 2004 | Country – Bloc | Enabling Clause, GATS Article V | 34 |
| EFTA–Singapore FTA and EIA | 2002 | Country – Bloc | GATT Article XXIV, GATS Article V | 34 |
| New Zealand– Singapore FTA and EIA | 2000 | Bilateral | GATT Article XXIV, GATS Article V | 34 |
| Trans-Pacific SEPA | 2005 | Cross- Continental Plurilateral | GATT Article XXIV, GATS Article V | 32 |

(*cont.*)

Table A6.2 (cont.)

| PTA | Year of signature | Scope | WTO notification | Depth of integration score |
|---|---|---|---|---|
| Singapore–Jordan FTA and EIA | 2004 | Bilateral | GATT Article XXIV, GATS Article V | 31 |
| New Zealand–Hong Kong, China FTA and EIA | 2010 | Bilateral | GATT Article XXIV, GATS Article V | 30 |
| New Zealand–Thailand FTA and EIA | 2005 | Bilateral | GATT Article XXIV, GATS Article V | 30 |
| ANZCERTA FTA and EIA | 1982 | Bilateral | GATT Article XXIV | 30 |
| Japan–Vietnam FTA and EIA | 2008 | Bilateral | GATT Article XXIV, GATS Article V | 29 |
| China–Pakistan FTA and EIA | 2006 | Bilateral | GATT Article XXIV | 27 |
| Malaysia–Pakistan FTA and EIA | 2007 | Bilateral | Enabling Clause, GATS Article V | 27 |
| South Asian FTA | 2004 | Regional | Enabling Clause | 27 |
| China–Hong Kong CEPA | 2003 | Bilateral | GATT Article XXIV, GATS Article V | 26 |
| China–Singapore FTA and EIA | 2008 | Bilateral | GATT Article XXIV, GATS Article V | 25 |
| AKFTA | 2006 | Country – Bloc | GATT Article XXIV | 22 |
| China–Macao CEPA | 2003 | Bilateral | GATT Article XXIV, GATS Article V | 22 |
| China–Chile FTA & EIA | 2005 | Bilateral | GATT Article XXIV | 22 |
| KORUS (Korea–US) | 2007 | Bilateral | GATT Article XXIV, GATS Article V | 21 |
| Gulf Cooperation Council– Singapore FTA | 2008 | Country – Bloc | no notification | 20 |
| Costa Rica–China FTA and EIA | 2010 | Bilateral | GATT Article XXIV, GATS Article V | 18 |
| US–Lao PDR PTA | 2003 | Bilateral | no notification | 16 |

Table A6.2 (cont.)

| PTA | Year of signature | Scope | WTO notification | Depth of integration score |
|---|---|---|---|---|
| Malaysia–Chile FTA | 2010 | Bilateral | GATT Article XXIV | 16 |
| EU–Papua New Guinea–Fiji IEPA | 2009 | Country – Bloc | GATT Article XXIV | 15 |
| South Pacific Regional Trade and Economic Cooperation Agreement | 1980 | Regional | Enabling Clause | 15 |
| AJCEPA | 2008 | Country – Bloc | GATT Article XXIV | 14 |
| Turkey–Mauritius FTA | 2011 | Bilateral | GATT Article XXIV | 13 |
| India–Nepal Treaty of Trade | 2009 | Bilateral | Enabling Clause | 12 |
| ECOTA | 2003 | Regional | no notification | 12 |
| Japan–India FTA and EIA | 2011 | Bilateral | GATT Article XXIV, GATS Article V | 12 |
| Chile–India PTA | 2006 | Bilateral | Enabling Clause | 12 |
| Melanesian Spearhead Group PTA | 1993 | Regional | Enabling Clause | 11 |
| Pacific Island Countries FTA | 2001 | Regional | Enabling Clause | 11 |
| India–MERCOSUR PTA | 2004 | Country – Bloc | Enabling Clause | 11 |
| PATCRA | 1976 | Bilateral | GATT Article XXIV | 10 |
| ASEAN–India FTA | 2009 | Country – Bloc | Enabling Clause | 10 |
| Pakistan–Sri Lanka FTA | 2002 | Bilateral | Enabling Clause | 9 |
| Pakistan–Mauritius PTA | 2007 | Bilateral | no notification | 9 |
| India–Afghanistan PTA | 2003 | Bilateral | Enabling Clause | 9 |
| EU–Korea FTA and EIA | 2010 | Country – Bloc | GATT Article XXIV, GATS Article V | 9 |

(cont.)

Table A6.2 (cont.)

| PTA | Year of signature | Scope | WTO notification | Depth of integration score |
|---|---|---|---|---|
| Asia-Pacific Trade Agreement | 1975 | Regional | Enabling Clause | 9 |
| Group of 8 PTA | 2006 | Cross-Continental Plurilateral | no notification | 9 |
| India–Sri Lanka FTA | 1998 | Bilateral | Enabling Clause | 8 |
| Pakistan–Iran PTA | 2004 | Bilateral | no notification | 6 |
| India–Bhutan FTA | 2006 | Bilateral | Enabling Clause | 6 |
| China–Thailand FTA | 2003 | Bilateral | no notification | 1 |
| Lao PDR-Thailand PTA | 1991 | Bilateral | Enabling Clause | 1 |
| Vietnam–Chile FTA | 2011 | Bilateral | no notification | 0 |
| Korea–Colombia FTA | 2012 | Bilateral | no notification | 0 |
| Japan–Peru FTA | 2011 | Bilateral | GATT Article XXIV, GATS Article V | 0 |
| Turkey–Korea FTA | 2012 | Bilateral | GATT Article XXIV | 0 |
| Indonesia–Pakistan FTA | 2012 | Bilateral | no notification | 0 |
| China–Iceland FTA | 2013 | Bilateral | no notification | 0 |
| Sri Lanka–Iran PTA | 2004 | Bilateral | no notification | 0 |

Note: AANZFTA, ASEAN–Australia–New Zealand Free Trade Agreement; ACFTA, ASEAN–China Free Trade Agreement; AJCEPA, ASEAN Japan Comprehensive Economic Partnership Agreement; AKFTA, ASEAN–Korea Free Trade Agreement; ANZCERTA, Australia-New Zealand Closer Economic Relations Trade Agreement; ASEAN, Association of Southeast Asian Nations; CEPA, Closer Economic Partnership Arrangement; ECOTA, Economic Cooperation Organisation Trade Agreement; EFTA, European Free Trade Association; EIA, economic integration agreement; EPA, economic partnership agreement; FTA, free trade agreement; GATS, General Agreement on Trade in Services; GATT, General Agreement on Tariffs and Trade; IEPA, interim Economic Partnership Agreement; PATCRA, Papua New Guinea–Australia Trade and Commercial Relations Agreement; PTA, preferential trade agreement; SEPA, Strategic Economic Partnership Agreement; WTO, World Trade Organization.

# References

Acharya, Amitav. 2001. *Constructing a Security Community in Southeast Asia: ASEAN and the Problem of Regional Order*. London: Routledge.

Ando, Mitsuyo, and Kimura, Fukunari. 2005. 'The Formation of International Production and Distribution Networks in East Asia.' In *International Trade in East Asia*. National Bureau of Economic Research (NBER)-East Asia Seminar on Economics, vol. 14. Chicago: University of Chicago Press.

ASEAN. 2013. *Asian Investment Report: The Changing FDI Landscape*. Jakarta: ASEAN Secretariat.

Athukorala, Prema-chandra. 2010. 'Production Networks and Trade Patterns in East Asia: Regionalization or Globalization?' ADB Working Papers Series on Regional Economic Integration No. 56. Asian Development Bank, Manila.

Baldwin, Richard. 2011. '21st Century Regionalism: Filling the Gap between 21st Century Trade and 20th Century Trade Rules.' Centre for Economic Policy Research Policy Insight No. 56. Centre for Economic Policy Research, London.

Birdsall, Nancy, and Lawrence, Robert Z. 1999. 'Deep Integration and Trade Agreements.' In *Global Public Goods: International Cooperation in the 21st Century*, edited by Inge Kaul, Isabelle Grunberg and Marc A. Stern, 128–51. Oxford, England: Oxford University Press.

Büthe, Tim, and Milner, Helen V. 2008. 'The Politics of Foreign Direct Investment into Developing Countries: Increasing FDI through International Trade Agreements?' *American Journal of Political Science* 52 (4): 741–62.

Crawford, Jo-Ann, and Fiorentino, Roberto V. 2004. 'The Changing Landscape of Regional Trade Agreements.' WTO Discussion Paper No. 8. World Trade Organization, Geneva.

Elms, Deborah K., and Low, Patrick, eds. 2013. *Global Value Chains in a Changing World*. Geneva: World Trade Organization.

Feenstra, Robert C. 1998. 'Integration of Trade and Disintegration of Production in the Global Economy.' *Journal of Economic Perspectives* 12:31–50.

Feinberg, Richard E. 2006. 'US Trade Arrangements in the Asia-Pacific.' In *Bilateral Trade Agreements in the Asia-Pacific*, edited by Vinod K. Aggarwal and Shujiro Urata, 95–116. New York: Routledge.

Fiorentino, Roberto V., Verdeja, Luis, and Toqueboeuf, Christelle. 2006. 'The Changing Landscape of Regional Trade Agreements: 2006 Update.' WTO Discussion Paper No. 12. World Trade Organization, Geneva.

Fishlow, Albert, and Haggard, Stephan. 1992. *The United States and the Regionalization of the World Economy*. Paris: OECD Development Centre Research Project on Globalization and Regionalization.

Funabashi, Yoichi. 1995. *Asia Pacific Fusion: Japan's Role in APEC*. Washington, DC: Institute for International Economics.

Henisz, Witold J. 2000. 'The Institutional Environment for Multinational Investment.' *Journal of Law, Economics, and Organization* 16 (2): 334–64.

Hoekman, Bernard, and Kostecki, Michel M. 2009. *The Political Economy of the
World Trading System.* 3rd cdn. Oxford, England: Oxford University Press.

Hummels, David, Ishii, Jun, and Yi, Kei-Mu. 2001. 'The Nature and Growth of
Vertical Specialization in World Trade.' *Journal of International Economics*
54:75–96.

Khong, Yuen Foong, and Nesadurai, Helen E. S. 2007. 'Hanging Together, Insti-
tutional Design, and Cooperation in Southeast Asia: AFTA and the ARF.'
In *Crafting Cooperation: Regional International Institutions in Comparative
Perspective,* edited by Amitav Acharya and Alastair Iain Johnston, 32–82.
Cambridge: Cambridge University Press.

Kim, Soo Yeon. Forthcoming. 'Deep Integration and RTAs.' In The Politics of
International Trade, edited by Lisa Martin. Oxford Handbook Series. Oxford,
England: Oxford University Press.

Koremenos, Barbara, Lipson, Charles, and Snidal, Duncan. 2001. 'The Rational
Design of International Institutions.' *International Organization* 55 (4): 761–
99.

Kotschwar, Barbara. 2009. 'Mapping Investment Provisions in Regional Trade
Agreements: Towards and International Investment Regime?' In *Regional
Rules in the Global Trading System,* edited by Antoni Estevadordal, Kati
Suominen and Robert Teh, 365–417. Cambridge: Cambridge University
Press.

Lawrence, Robert Z. 1996. *Regionalism, Multilateralism and Deeper Integration.*
Washington, DC: Brookings Institution.

Manger, Mark. 2009. *Investing in Protection: The Politics of Preferential Trade Agreements between North and South.* Cambridge: Cambridge University Press.

Mansfield, Edward D., and Milner, Helen V. 1999. 'The New Wave of Regionalism.'
*International Organization* 53 (3): 589–627.

———. 2012. *Votes, Vetoes, and the Political Economy of International Agreements.* Princeton, NJ: Princeton University Press.

Mansfield, Edward D., Milner, Helen V., and Pevehouse, Jon C. 2007. 'Vetoing Cooperation: The Impact of Veto Players on Preferential Trading Arrangements.'
*British Journal of Political Science* 37 (3): 403–32.

Mansfield, Edward D., Milner, Helen V., and Rosendorff, B. Peter. 2002. 'Why
Democracies Cooperate More: Electoral Control and International Trade
Agreements.' *International Organization* 56 (3): 477–514.

Miroudot, Sébastien. 2011. 'Investment.' In *Preferential Trade Agreement Policies
for Development: A Handbook,* edited by Jean-Pierre Chauffour and Jean
Christophe Maur, 307–26. Washington, DC: International Bank for Reconstruction and Development/World Bank.

Nesadurai, Helen E. S. 2003. *Globalization, Domestic Politics, and Regionalism: The
ASEAN Free Trade Area.* London: Routledge.

Ng, Francis, and Yeats, Alexander. 1999. 'Production Sharing in East Asia: Who Does What for Whom and Why?' World Bank Policy Research Working Paper No. 2197. World Bank, Washington, DC.

Ravenhill, John. 2008. 'Asia's New Economic Institutions.' In *Asia's New Institutional Architecture: Evolving Structures for Managing Trade, Financial, and Security Relations*, edited by Vinod K. Aggarwal and Min Gyo Koo, 35–58. Berlin: Springer-Verlag.

2009. 'East Asian Regionalism: Much Ado About Nothing?' *Review of International Studies* 35 (1): 215–35.

2010. "The 'New East Asian Regionalism': A Political Domino Effect.' *Review of International Political Economy* 17 (2): 178–208. doi:10.1080/09692290903070887.

Singer, J. David, Bremer, Stuart, and Stuckey, John. 1972. 'Capability Distribution, Uncertainty, and Major Power War, 1820–1965.' In *Peace, War, and Numbers*, edited by Bruce Russett, 19–48. Beverly Hills, CA: Sage.

Tinbergen, Jan. 1954. *International Economic Integration*. Amsterdam: Elsevier.

# PART II

---

## The design of PTAs

# Imitation and innovation in international governance

## The diffusion of trade agreement design

LEONARDO BACCINI, ANDREAS DÜR AND YORAM Z. HAFTEL

### A. Introduction

The growing number of preferential trade agreements (PTAs) is one of the hallmarks of the current global economy. Within and across most, if not all, regions of the world, governments have concluded numerous new agreements or have revised previously signed ones. According to the World Trade Organization (WTO), more than 350 PTAs are currently in force,[1] and many more are under negotiation. Recent studies indicate that these instruments have implications for central concerns in world politics, such as international trade (Baier, Bergstrand and Clance, Chapter 14 in this volume; Dür, Baccini and Elsig 2014), foreign direct investment (Büthe and Milner 2008), foreign aid (Baccini and Urpelainen 2012), human rights (Hafner-Burton 2009), armed disputes (Haftel 2007; Mansfield and Pevehouse 2000) and democratisation (Pevehouse 2005).

A glance over these numerous agreements indicates, however, that they vary a great deal in their scope and design (Dür, Baccini and Elsig 2014). Some PTAs, such as the South Asian Free Trade Agreement (2004), liberalise only trade in goods, whereas others, such as the agreement between Australia and Chile (2008), tackle trade in services, foreign direct investment (FDI), intellectual property rights (IPRs), public procurement and the like. Still others, such as the West African Economic and Monetary Union (WAEMU, 1994), include a common external tariff, free movement of factors of production and a variety of other objectives. PTAs also

We are grateful to Carmela Lutmar, Stephanie Rickard, Johannes Rühl and the participants at the 2013 World Trade Forum for helpful comments on earlier versions of this chapter.
[1] www.wto.org/english/tratop_e/region_e/region_e.htm. Accessed 17 May 2013.

differ in the depth of their members' commitments in any given issue area and the degree to which they allow their members flexibility in the application of substantive provisions. These differences appear to condition the impact of trade agreements on trade flows (Dür, Baccini and Elsig 2014; Kono 2007) and other international interactions (Büthe and Milner 2014; Haftel 2012) in significant ways.

What explains this substantial variation in the design of trade agreements? Research that strives to address this question often assumes that each PTA is conceived independently of other existing agreements. Some studies argue that domestic factors, such as regime type, interest groups or political stability, shape trade rules in important ways (Dür 2007; Kucik 2012; Mansfield, Milner and Rosendorff 2002). Other studies point to regional factors, such as economic interdependence and the balance of power (Haftel 2013; Johns 2013; Smith 2000).

In this study, we relax this assumption and thus contemplate the role of external influences. Specifically, we entertain the possibility that states that form or reform trade agreements do not start from scratch but rather look for an existing institutional model to follow (Kim and Manger 2013; Jetschke and Lenz 2013: 7). We argue that negotiators who bargain over the design of PTAs and look for an existing template can choose from at least three competing models. Specifically, they may

- 'borrow' from a template for a narrow and shallow agreement;
- imitate the European Union (EU), which is purported to be 'the standard model for regional integration' (Börzel and Risse 2012: 197) or
- replicate the North American Free Trade Agreement (NAFTA), which is Washington's preferred model (Grugel 2004; Sbragia 2010).

For countries that want to go beyond shallow cooperation, therefore, 'Pax Americana' and 'Pax Europaea' provide distinct global blueprints for economic integration (Börzel 2013: 518).

Using this observation as a springboard, we ponder its implications for the varying landscape of PTAs worldwide. We develop several conjectures with respect to relational factors that may explain which model the members of a PTA decide to follow. That is, we stress that even when controlling for domestic and regional factors, the relationship between potential PTA members and the EU and the United States matters for model choice. We test these expectations quantitatively with an original data set on the institutional design of a comprehensive sample of PTAs.

Our results, although preliminary, offer a number of insights into the factors that determine PTA design worldwide. First, it appears that more recent PTAs increasingly follow the NAFTA model at the expense of the EU. Second, our findings indicate that as the number of PTA members increases, the design of such agreements becomes more similar to the EU and less similar to NAFTA. In addition, PTAs with members that have close bilateral relations with the United States appear to imitate the NAFTA model. Surprisingly, we do not find an equivalent pattern with respect to the EU. Overall, the empirical analysis suggests that the effect of the EU on the design of trade agreements may have been overstated by the extant research and that even those PTA members that have close ties to the EU are not compelled to adopt EU-like agreements. On the other hand, the American preferred approach carries greater and growing weight in the current global trading system. Nevertheless, the EU still serves as a template for larger and more complex regional economic organisations, which may be the exception to this general rule.

These findings have several broad implications. First, with respect to the study of trade agreements, we show that the design of PTAs tends to cluster. This suggests not only that PTAs are signed in response to existing PTAs (Baccini and Dür 2012, 2013) but also that subsequent PTAs adopt the institutional design of earlier agreements (see also Jo and Namgung 2012). Thus, the design of a trade agreement is not done in isolation but rather is influenced by interdependence among countries and by the preferences of the more powerful players in the international economic system. This does not mean, however, that negotiators simply 'cut and paste' from existing agreements, thereby disregarding their functional needs. Institutional design is still rational (Koremenos, Lipson and Snidal 2001) but shaped by the broader external environment as well as prevailing standards and practices.

This chapter is organised as follows. The second section offers some descriptive evidence of the existence of three distinct PTA models. The third section develops several hypotheses with respect to the sources of model choice. The fourth section elaborates on research design and operationalisation of the dependent and independent variables. The fifth section reports the findings of the empirical analysis. The final section concludes.

## B. Three PTA models

The existence of different approaches to economic integration is perhaps a truism. Observers point to a bifurcation between shallow economic intergovernmental cooperation and deep regional integration (Börzel

2013), between minimalist and interventionist agreements (Duina 2006) or between decentralised and centralised institutional models (Kahler 1995). Indeed, a cursory analysis of agreement texts points to the existence of at least three PTA models. The first model includes a large number of narrow and shallow agreements in which member states agree on the (often partial) reduction of tariffs on a select number of goods. These partial free trade agreements do not contain any provisions that regulate issues such as trade in services or FDI. The agreement between Afghanistan and India (2003), for example, contains only tariff concessions by the two countries on 8 (Afghanistan) and 38 (India) items. Other examples of such agreements, which we label the 'Southern model', are those signed by many Latin American countries under the Treaty of Montevideo (1980).

A second group of agreements resemble the EU. Beginning with the establishment of the European Economic Community (EEC) in 1957, members of this organisation were keen to build powerful and elaborate bodies to shepherd the integration process. Most notable are the European Commission and the European Court of Justice, which enjoy a great deal of independence and can, in some instances, overrule national sovereignty. In line with this focus on institutions, the European project offers a general road map for gradual integration, starting with trade liberalisation and progressing to a customs union, a common market (that is, free movement of labour and capital) and a common economic and monetary union. At the same time, the initial agreement (Treaty of Rome 1957) was vague on many of the fine details of liberalisation. Instead, the task of spelling out these details was delegated to the organisation and its institutions. The subsequent Single European Act (1986) and the Maastricht Treaty (1992) filled in major gaps in important areas, such as trade in services and investment, but left others, such as IPR and government procurement, underspecified. We label this approach, which emphasises institutions at the expense of rules, the 'EU model'.

Several regional agreements resemble the EU model. The Central American Common Market (CACM), especially as revised by the Protocol of Guatemala (1993), is a good example. The aim of this agreement was to create a Central American economic union. The treaty, however, was vague with respect to the specific means by which these goals were to be achieved; many particulars were left to the organisation's bodies – including several ministerial councils – to decide at a later stage. The Caribbean Community (CARICOM), Andean Community and the Economic and Monetary Community of Central Africa also have an elaborate set of institutions but many ambiguous rules. Beyond such regional organisations, many EU agreements with third parties share some characteristics of the former. Such agreements cover a variety of new, nontrade issues, but they frequently do so in a vague and unenforceable manner (Horn, Petros and Sapir 2010). The Stabilization and Association Agreement with Macedonia (2001), for example, specifies that the supply of services should be 'progressively' liberalised; but the only concrete measure contained in the treaty is a provision permitting the temporary movement of natural persons providing a service.

Next to this type of *institutions-based* integration, as exemplified by the EU, one can identify PTAs that engage in *rules-based* integration, exemplified by NAFTA. This PTA was created without the setting up of any meaningful institutions. The parties agreed to establish three national secretariats to oversee the implementation of the agreement but formed neither a corporate secretariat nor a standing tribunal or a parliament. NAFTA is thus an elaborated document that specifies many of the rules in advance and leaves relatively little for future interpretation. Importantly, this agreement stipulates explicit rules in several new, 'behind-the-border' areas, such as nontariff barriers (NTBs), trade in services, FDI, labour standards, technical standards and agriculture (Heydon and Woolcock 2009). Unlike their European counterparts, many of NAFTA's more innovative provisions are not only precise but also reflect strong commitment to enforcing the agreed on rules and regulations (Horn, Petros and Sapir 2010). We label this approach the 'NAFTA model'.

Indeed, many PTAs resemble this model. This is clearly the case for most other agreements signed by the United States, which closely follow the NAFTA template. Perhaps more surprisingly, many agreements signed by Chile, Japan and Mexico show significant parallels to NAFTA as well. The agreement between Australia and Chile, for example, not only covers market access in goods but also includes detailed provisions regarding technical standards, investment, government procurement and IPRs.

A new and original data set on the design of 579 PTAs signed between 1957 and 2009 (Dür, Baccini and Elsig 2014) allows us to undertake a more systematic analysis of model choice. The data set includes 352 bilateral and 88 regional agreements. A further 122 agreements were signed between a region and a single country, and 17 agreements between two regions. The agreements vary widely in terms of type: 169 are partial-scope agreements (that is, they cut tariffs on only a limited number of goods), 351 agreements envisage full free trade areas, 53 provide for the creation of customs unions and 6 are framework agreements.

The data set contains information on more than 100 design features of these agreements, including whether they liberalise trade in services, protect IPRs, foresee a common authority to deal with competition policy, proscribe subsidies and envisage the creation of a dispute settlement body. The provisions can be classified as belonging to three broad aspects of institutional design: the depth of cooperation (a total of 60 items), trade remedies (28 items) and enforcement (27 items). The data were coded manually, with all data coded twice independently, and demonstrate high intercoder reliability. Figure 7.1 shows a sample of provisions included in the data set.

We gauge model membership with cluster analyses of the 115 provisions found in the data set on PTA design. The method of cluster analysis groups more closely together objects that are more similar to each other than objects that are more different (Kaufman and Rousseeuw 2005). As all provisions in the data set are coded as binary variables, we rely on Ward hierarchical cluster analysis. We calculate the distance matrix between agreements using a method appropriate for binary data (Simple Matching Coefficient; see Kaufman and Rousseeuw 2005: 25).[2] The clusters are not sensitive to using a different approach for measuring the distance between agreements (such as the Jaccard coefficient). In fact, very few agreements move from one cluster to another when a different method is applied.[3]

The cluster analysis offers further support for the existence of three PTA models. When dividing the data set into three clusters, we find that one contains mainly agreements concluded by developing countries; another includes agreements concluded by the EU as well as several plurilateral agreements; and the third covers NAFTA and most other PTAs signed by the United States and several Latin American and Asian countries.[4] The three clusters contain 228, 274 and 77 agreements, respectively. Cluster 1 (Southern model) includes more than 80 agreements signed by Latin American countries and approximately 30 PTAs that were signed by African countries. Another substantial part of the cluster includes agreements signed by states that became independent after the dissolution of

---

[2] We use the R package cluster to calculate the distances (Maechler *et al.* 2013).

[3] More precisely, in the three-cluster solution that we calculate, 14 of 579 agreements (2.4 per cent) move from one cluster to another when the Jaccard coefficient is applied. Among them are the US–Jordan (2000), the Algeria–EU (1976) and the Cyprus–EU (1972) agreements.

[4] Hierarchical clustering, in contrast to *k*-means clustering, does not require the researcher to determine the number of clusters *ex ante*. In fact, deciding on the number of clusters to extract is partly discretionary (Ahlquist and Breunig 2012: 96). We opt for the highest level of aggregation because we are interested in explaining broad types of PTAs.

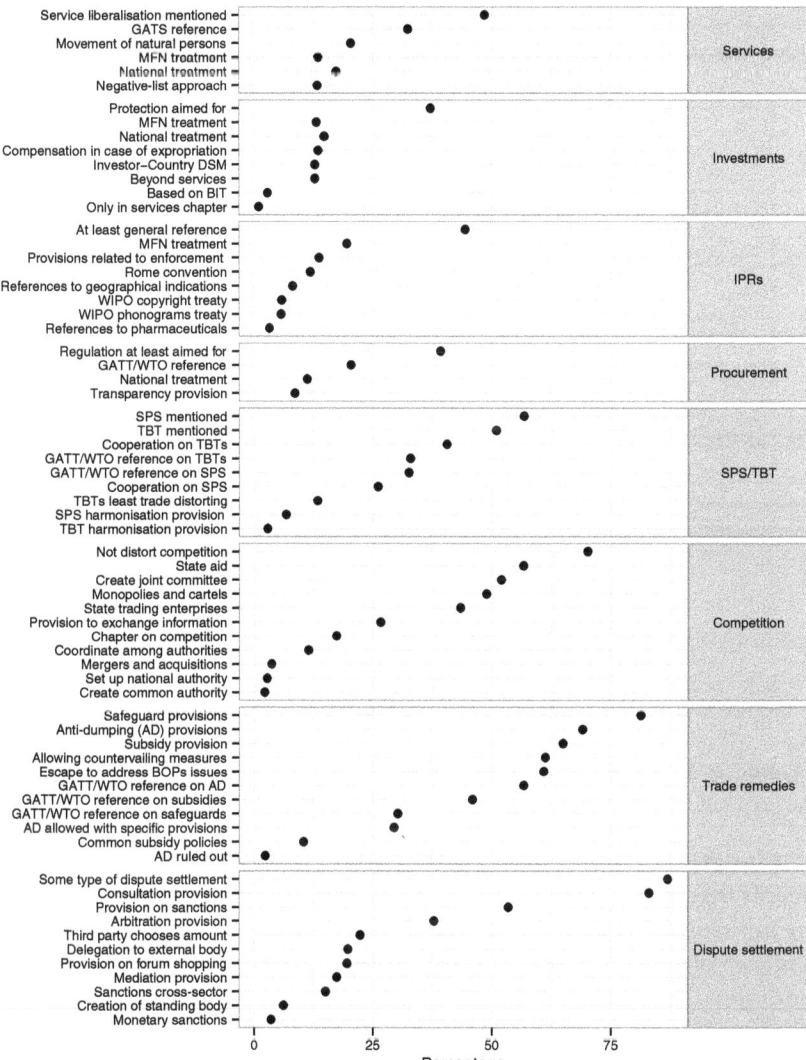

**Figure 7.1** The data on the PTA design
*Source:* Authors' illustration based on data from Dür, Baccini and Elsig 2014.

the Soviet Union. The agreements signed by the EEC and the EU with former colonies in Africa, the Caribbean and the Pacific (the Lomé Conventions and Yaoundé agreements) follow this model as well. A few other agreements that the EEC signed with third countries in the 1960s and 1970s also form part of this cluster.

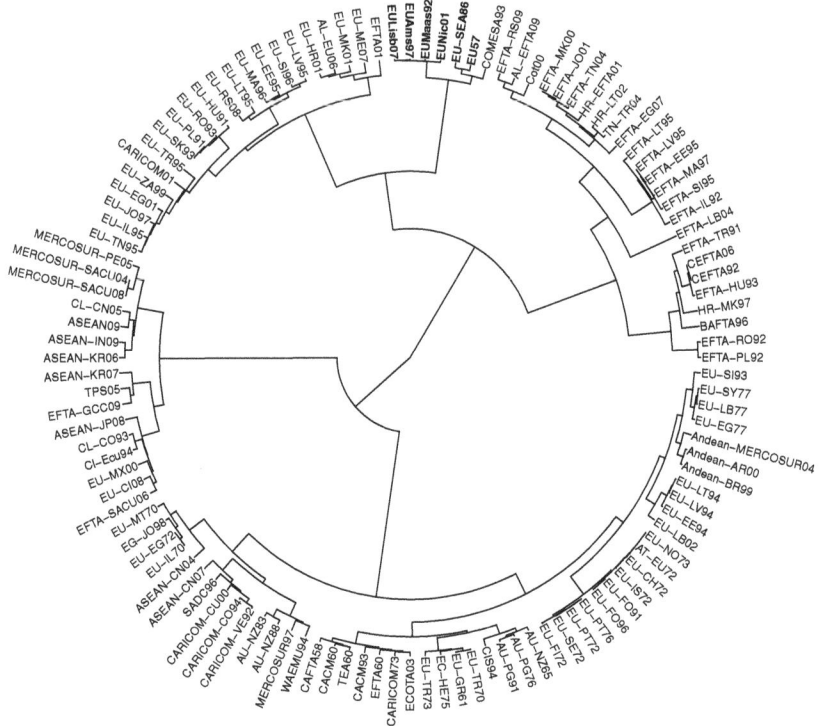

Figure 7.2    EU model (subset of agreements)
Source: Authors' illustration based on data from Dür, Baccini and Elsig 2014.

Cluster 2 (EU model) is composed of all EU treaties and many agreements that the EU signed with third countries. Figure 7.2 presents a part of this cluster graphically.[5] No fewer than 128 of the agreements forming part of this cluster were signed between European countries, with an additional 74 having members from more than one continent. This cluster also contains a substantial number of Latin American and Caribbean agreements. Importantly, the EU's treaties from the Treaty of Rome to the Treaty of Lisbon closely cluster together on the upper part of the plot (highlighted in bold). Interestingly, this part of the cluster also contains the Common Market for Eastern and Southern Africa (COMESA, 1993). Most of the EU's agreements with third countries can also be found in

---

[5] Because of the large number of agreements in this cluster (274), we 'pruned' the dendrograms before producing the graph. This does not affect cluster membership or distances between the 105 agreements shown.

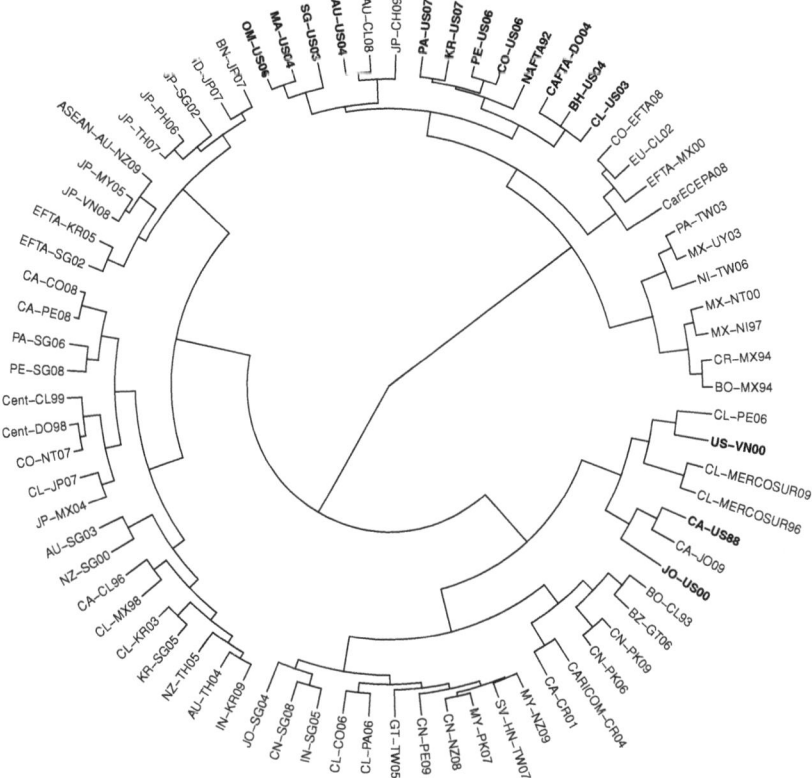

**Figure 7.3** US model
*Source:* Authors' illustration based on data from Dür, Baccini and Elsig 2014.

this cluster. As expected, we find several regional economic organisations, such as the revised MERCOSUR agreement, CARICOM, CACM and West African Economic and Monetary union (WAEMU) in other parts of this cluster.

Cluster 3 (NAFTA model), finally, includes the US agreements and many agreements signed by Asian countries. Figure 7.3 shows that most of the US agreements (highlighted in bold) closely cluster together (upper part of the plot). Twelve of them can be found as close neighbours and three more are on the lower right-hand side of the graph. Only two older US agreements do not form part of this cluster: the Canada–US Automotive Products Trade Agreement and the Israel–US agreement (both are part of cluster 1). The cluster also contains agreements signed by Chile and Mexico with third countries. Moreover, the EU's agreements with the Forum of the Caribbean Group of African, Caribbean and Pacific (ACP) States (CARIFORUM) and Chile cluster with the US agreements (both on the upper right-hand side). By contrast, Asian agreements (especially agreements signed by Japan and Singapore) cluster on the left-hand side of the dendrogram. Interestingly, the European Free Trade Association (EFTA) agreements with South Korea and Singapore are also located in that part of the dendrogram. These two agreements are thus quite different from the other agreements EFTA signed.

Given these differences in membership, it is no wonder that the clusters vary with respect to several attributes. Cluster 1 contains many older agreements. On average, the agreements in this cluster were signed in 1987, whereas the average years for clusters 2 and 3 are 1996 and 2004, respectively. Moreover, the clusters vary in terms of average depth. To show this, we rely on the measure of depth used by Dür, Baccini and Elsig (2014), which is an additive index of the presence or absence of seven key provisions in PTAs.[6] The average depth for agreements in cluster 1 is 0.83, whereas the averages for the other two clusters are 2.33 and 5.34, respectively. As suggested by the distinction between institutions-based and rules-based integration, agreements in cluster 3 contain by far the largest number of provisions: on average, these agreements contain 69 of the provisions contained in the data set (out of 115 considered here), whereas agreements in cluster 1 contain a mean of only 7 provisions. The agreements in the EU cluster are situated in between with 33 provisions.

In summary, both a cursory overview of treaty texts and a cluster analysis substantiate the existence of at least three different PTA models. These can best be described as a Southern model, an EU model, and a NAFTA model. What explains how similar an agreement is to either the Treaty of Rome or NAFTA? The next section provides several potential answers to this question.

## C. Hypotheses about external influences on PTA design

Why are PTAs designed in a certain way and not another? We develop a number of conjectures that stress the relational aspect of model choice.

---

[6] These are whether or not an agreement envisages the creation of a full free trade agreement and whether it contains substantive commitments in the fields of services, FDI, standards, public procurement, IPRs and competition.

We are thus open to the possibility that agreement design is driven not only by considerations that are internal to the PTA and its members but also by the relationships between the PTA members on the one hand and the EU and the United States on the other. In particular, we consider three sets of variables that might matter for model choice: (1) the number of models available at the time of negotiations; (2) the size of membership; and (3) three dyadic variables, namely, international trade, international aid and joint membership in international governmental organisations (IGOs).

*Number of models.* Governments that conclude trade agreements can lower the negotiation costs by employing an existing template as a springboard (Kim and Manger 2013; Jetschke and Lenz 2013). Thus, the number of existing models is likely to affect the influence of a given principal agreement. One could reasonably expect that as the number of models increases, 'newcomers' will gradually come to hold a greater sway over other agreements at the expense of older models. With respect to trade agreements, the European model did not face any meaningful competition between the inception of the EEC in 1957 and the conclusion of NAFTA in 1992. Indeed, it is widely acknowledged that the EEC inspired the creation of several regional economic organisations in the developing world during the 1960s and 1970s (Langhammer and Hiemenz 1990).

Following the conclusion of NAFTA, however, its design was promoted as instrumental in fostering economic liberalisation, especially by the United States (Grugel 2004). Indeed, it quickly became a standard platform for a host of trade agreements between the members of NAFTA and third parties (Horn, Mavroidis and Sapir 2010; Sbragia 2010) as well as between third parties themselves, especially in Latin America. Chile's PTAs, in particular, 'increasingly adopted many NAFTA-like characteristics' (Delvin and Estevadeordal 2001: 21). We therefore expect a temporal change in the impact of the two institutions: the effect of the EU model should decline over time – and especially from the early 1990s on – as it loses 'market share' to NAFTA. Inversely, the latter agreement's influence on other PTAs should grow as time passes (albeit perhaps only up to a point).

*Number of members.* One obvious difference between the EU and NAFTA is the number of participants in these agreements. The former started with six members and then gradually expanded, whereas the latter was designed for three members only. Presumably, plurilateral agreements have to accommodate a greater diversity of interests and perspectives and therefore require an elaborate set of institutions to do so. Bilateral or tri-lateral agreements, on the other hand, may be easier to negotiate and can thus contain more precise rules. Moreover, to the extent that ambiguous rules result in diverse interpretations, they can be discussed bilaterally through conventional diplomatic channels. We therefore surmise that PTAs with few members will find the NAFTA model more attractive than the EU model, but this preference will be reversed as the number of members increases.

Moreover, recent research that examines attempts by the EU to influence integration initiatives around the world (Alter 2012; Börzel and Risse 2012; Farrell 2007; Jetschke and Murray 2012; Lenz 2012) provides empirical evidence mostly with respect to multimember economic IGOs (rather than bilateral agreements) and largely with respect to institutions (rather than rules). Hence, we conjecture that plurilateral agreements will more closely resemble the EU model than the NAFTA model.

*Trade dependence.* Turning to dyadic variables, trade dependence is perhaps the most straightforward determinant of similarity in institutional design. Weaker states that trade extensively with a major power are likely to face substantial costs if they fail to match their policies with those of the more powerful country. Higher transaction costs in exporting to a large power may mean that they lose out compared to other weak states that adjust their policies. Competition between weaker states may then induce them to match the policies of the major power even if domestic considerations speak against doing so (Gruber 2000). Following this line of reasoning, one should expect greater pressure to adjust as commercial interdependence between the hub and the spoke becomes more extensive. Thus, states that trade more with Europe and the United States should find the EU and NAFTA models more appealing, respectively. By contrast, the more the potential member states of a PTA trade among themselves, the lower their dependence on access to the EU and US markets, and thus the less important it is for them to adopt the PTA models of the hubs.

The role of trade dependence should be very visible in agreements between these powerful actors and third parties, where the former can frequently impose their preferred design on the latter. As extant research documents, the United States and the EU use their distinct PTA programmes to spread their favoured regulatory frameworks, at least in part to protect their exporters and investors (Dür 2007; Horn, Mavroidis and Sapir 2010: 43). Perhaps less obviously, trade dependence may also lead third-party governments to sign PTAs among themselves that are similar to one of the predominant models. For countries that already have a PTA link with a major power, this is a sensible strategy: once they have adopted a specific model, they reduce transaction costs by sticking to it. For other countries, doing so can facilitate future negotiations with the potential hub or send a credible signal of interest and readiness.

In summary, we expect higher levels of trade between the PTA members and the EU (United States) to increase the likelihood of the former choosing to adopt the EU (NAFTA) model, but higher levels of intra-PTA trade to decrease the likelihood of adopting either the EU or the NAFTA models. We also anticipate that US trade agreements will resemble NAFTA and those signed between the EU and third parties will share some similarities with the Rome Treaty.

*Financial aid.* The hubs may also derive benefits from the adoption of their preferred approach by other countries (Drezner 2007; Lavenex and Schimmelfennig 2009). Having their rules applied beyond their borders will lower their costs of engaging in trade and FDI. They may then use conditionality to promote their preferred institutional design. Substantial evidence exists that the EU often relies on conditionality in its external relations to achieve its desired policy outcomes (Smith 1998). This may also apply to the realm of PTAs, where powerful actors can link the design of PTAs to financial assistance. In some PTAs between the EU and third countries, such as the Economic Partnership Agreements, aid to regional cooperation projects is part and parcel of the agreement. In other cases, states that rely on financial support may feel compelled to behave in a manner similar to that of their benefactors. The Southern African Development Community (SADC), for example, adopted EU institutions and policies to satisfy the EU's expectations and preserve its financial support (Lenz 2012: 163–4). We therefore conjecture that greater amounts of financial aid from the EU (United States) will result in an increased likelihood of PTA members adopting the EU (NAFTA) model.

*Common membership in IGOs.* Bilateral relationships may work in more subtle ways. In highly technical negotiations in which they have to make decisions regarding complex matters, negotiators may look for a model that has proved to be effective. Consequently, they may be interested in learning from the experience of other countries. Crucially, learning requires the gathering and dissemination of information regarding the model, and thus open channels of communication. The more extensive states' policy ties with a leading actor, therefore, the greater the probability that states will follow the latter's model. This idea is consistent, for example, with the claim that trading groups that receive advice and consultation from EU bureaucrats tend to prefer the European model (Börzel and Risse 2012: 197; Grugel 2004; Lenz 2012). In addition, common membership in IGOs – especially those that address economic issues – may also facilitate the transmission of information about the kinds of policies that have proved effective (Simmons, Garrett and Dobbin 2006). We thus expect that as joint membership in IGOs between the EU (United States) and PTA members increases, so does the likelihood that the PTA will adopt the EU (NAFTA) model.

## D. Research design

In what follows we evaluate our expectations using a reduced-form approach. That is, we do not take into account the fact that the choices whether to adopt the EU or the NAFTA model are taken simultaneously, which would require a structural equation model. Because our outcome variables are continuous, we employ ordinary least squares (OLS) regression techniques. A Breusch–Pagan test indicates that the assumption of constant variance does not hold. We therefore use robust standard errors. In addition, variance inflation factors are always below 10, indicating that the risk of multicollinearity is rather low. In the rest of this section, we elaborate on the dependent, independent and control variables.

### I. Dependent variables

Our dependent variables are the distances between a given agreement and the Treaty of Rome and NAFTA, respectively. These distances are calculated using the approach described previously (simple matching coefficient). The variables potentially range from zero (when two agreements are identical) to one (when two agreements vary in each and every aspect). The actual values of these variables vary from 0.11 to 0.66 for the Rome Treaty and from 0.15 to 0.73 for NAFTA. In the case of the EU, we rely on distances to the Rome Treaty rather than other EU treaties because the evolution from quite a vague treaty (Rome Treaty) to increasingly more precise agreements (most recently, the Lisbon Treaty) is inherent to the EU model. Countries following the EU model should thus imitate the Rome Treaty, leaving the addition of greater precision for later treaty revisions. For NAFTA, we include only PTAs that were signed after 1992 (because we do not expect it to have affected the design of other PTAs before its conclusion).

## II. Explanatory variables

Because our dependent variable is at the PTA level, our unit of analysis is the PTA. When using explanatory variables that are dyadic or monadic, we aggregate them at the PTA level. Consistent with conventional practices, we employ the weakest link assumption. That is, for monadic variables, we always take the minimum value among the PTA members (unless noted otherwise).[7]

We capture the number of models that is available to states considering the design of a new agreement with the year in which a PTA was formed (*Year*). In line with the discussion in the previous section, we expect greater proximity between older PTAs and the EU model and less distance between newer agreements and NAFTA. We employ two variables to test the conjecture relating to the number of members. *Number of members* is a count of the PTA members at the time of the PTA formation. Next, we include a multinomial variable that distinguishes among bilateral agreements, plurilateral agreements, agreements between a regional entity and a third country and agreements between two regional entities (*Plurilateral, Plurilateral & Third Country, Region-Region*). Data for these variables are based on Dür, Baccini and Elsig (2014).

We also use three variables to operationalise our conjectures regarding trade dependence. First, we include the logged volume of trade between the members of a given PTA and the EU and the United States, respectively (*Trade with the EU* and *Trade with the US*). For the EU, we sum trade flows (imports and exports) from (to) each EU member country to (from) third countries. We do not include imports and exports separately because these two measures are highly collinear ($\rho > 0.8$). Trade data come from the International Monetary Fund's Direction of Trade data set integrated with Gleditsch's (2002) imputed data. Second, we include the percentage of intraregional trade of each PTA in our models (*Intra-regional Trade*). Specifically, we divide the total amount of trade (imports and exports) among PTA members by the total amount of trade conducted by the

---

[7] Our results remain unchanged if we substitute the minimum value with the average or median value.

PTA members with all the countries in the world. Finally, we include dummy variables for external PTAs signed by the EU (*EU External PTAs*) and bilateral trade agreements signed by the United States (*US External PTAs*).

With respect to financial aid, we add the logged amount of financial aid received by all members of the PTA from the European Commission and the United States (*Aid from the EU* and *Aid from the US*). In the case of the EU, we use the sum of aid allocated by the European Commission to third countries. We do not include aid allocated individually by each EU member country to third counties. The data are from the World Bank's World Development Indicators (2013).[8] Finally, we include the number of IGOs in which the members of the PTAs share membership with the EU and the United States, respectively (*IGOs with the EU* and *IGOs with the US*). Specifically, we use the mean of joint IGO membership between each EU member and third countries. We rely on the Correlates of War's International Governmental Organizations Data Version 2.0 (Pevehouse, Nordstrom and Warnke 2004).[9]

## III. Control variables

Given that both the EU and NAFTA bring together mostly highly developed and large economies, their models may be more appealing to countries that display similar characteristics. We thus use the logged value of GDP and GDPpc for each PTA (*GDP* and *GDPpc*). The first variable captures market size, whereas the second variable proxies the level of economic development. We use data from the World Bank (2013), Heston, Summers and Aten (2011) and Maddison (2011) to measure these two variables. Previous studies show that democracies are more likely to form PTAs (Mansfield and Milner, 2012; Mansfield, Milner and Rosendorff 2002). Building on that research, one might expect that democratic regimes will be more likely to adopt either the EU model or the NAFTA model, which themselves consist of democratic countries. We

---

[8] Admittedly, foreign aid may be used to promote various objectives that may or may not be related to trade and other economic matters. Ideally, one would employ more fine-grained measures, such as direct financial support devoted to the implementation of the agreement or, more broadly, trade facilitation. Unfortunately, such data are currently not available.

[9] We have also run models with military alliances, that is, third countries sharing an alliance with the EU and the United States. These variables are never statistically significant and are not reported here.

measure this variable with the absolute value of Polity IV for each PTA (*Regime*).

We also account for shared language and religion,[10] which serve as proxies for cultural similarity. We consider a third country *i* having a common language and religion with the EU if country *i* shares language and religion with at least one EU member. Language scores one if and only if all the PTA members share the same language with the EU and the United States. Religion is built in the same way. Data on language and religion come from the Central Intelligence Agency (2013) World Factbook. Furthermore, we include distance from Brussels in the EU models as well as distance from Washington, DC, in the NAFTA model. Data come from the CEPII data set (2007). In general, one should expect that the hubs will have greater influence on model choice in their own backyard than they have on more distant regions (Börzel and Risse 2012).

Next, since EU and US PTAs integrate many WTO provisions, we expect that WTO Members are more likely to choose either the EU model or the NAFTA model rather than the Southern model. Like NAFTA, the multilateral system was expanded to cover rules in several new areas, including trade in services, IPR and FDI, following the Uruguay Round. WTO Members may therefore find it easier to adopt the NAFTA model. We thus include a dummy variable that scores one if all the countries in a PTA are also WTO Members (*WTO*), and zero otherwise. Data come from the WTO website. Finally, we include two dummy variables for North–South PTAs and South–South PTAs as well as region fixed effects. Data for these variables come from DESTA (Dür, Baccini and Elsig 2014).

## E. Results

This section reports the results of the statistical analysis. Table 7.1 reports four models accounting for the sources of the distance between the Rome Treaty and the remainder of PTAs in the sample. Model 1 includes the explanatory variables pertaining to trade relations and a battery of controls. The other three models sequentially add the variables related to

---

[10] We do not include shared colonial heritage because there is little variation on this variable. EU countries colonized much of the rest of the world. The United States, in contrast, hardly colonized any country.

Table 7.1 *Explaining similarity to the EU*

| Variables | (1) EU distance | (2) EU distance | (3) EU distance | (4) EU distance |
|---|---|---|---|---|
| Year | 0.002*** | 0.002*** | 0.002*** | 0.002*** |
|  | (0.001–0.002) | (0.001–0.002) | (0.001–0.003) | (0.001–0.003) |
| Numbers | −0.000 | −0.000 | −0.000 | −0.000 |
|  | (−0.001–0.000) | (−0.001–0.000) | (−0.001–0.000) | (−0.001–0.000) |
| Plurilateral | −0.017* | −0.017* | −0.019* | −0.018 |
|  | (−0.034--0.001) | (−0.033–0.001) | (−0.035--0.003) | (−0.037–0.001) |
| Plurilateral and third country | −0.012 | −0.012 | −0.011 | −0.010 |
|  | (−0.035–0.011) | (−0.035–0.012) | (−0.035–0.013) | (−0.034–0.014) |
| Region-Region | −0.005 | −0.004 | −0.011 | −0.010 |
|  | (−0.052–0.042) | (−0.051–0.043) | (−0.060–0.037) | (−0.058–0.039) |
| ln(Trade) | 0.002* | 0.002* | 0.003** | 0.003 |
|  | (0.000–0.005) | (0.000–0.005) | (0.001–0.006) | (−0.000–0.006) |
| Intra-regional trade | 0.029 | 0.033 | 0.025 | 0.020 |
|  | (−0.129–0.188) | (−0.127–0.193) | (−0.132–0.182) | (−0.134–0.174) |
| EU external PTA | −0.028 | −0.028 | −0.029* | −0.029 |
|  | (−0.058–0.001) | (−0.058–0.001) | (−0.057--0.000) | (−0.059–0.001) |
| ln(Aid) |  | −0.000 | −0.000 | −0.000 |
|  |  | (−0.001–0.001) | (−0.001–0.001) | (−0.001–0.001) |
| IGO membership |  |  | −0.001* | −0.001 |
|  |  |  | (−0.002--0.000) | (−0.002–0.000) |
| ln(GDP) | 0.003 | 0.003 | 0.004 | 0.005 |
|  | (−0.002–0.007) | (−0.002–0.007) | (−0.000–0.009) | (−0.000–0.009) |
| ln(GDPpc) | 0.009 | 0.008 | 0.008 | 0.008 |
|  | (−0.001–0.018) | (−0.001–0.017) | (−0.001–0.017) | (−0.001–0.018) |
| Regime | −0.000 | −0.000 | −0.000 | −0.000 |
|  | (−0.001–0.000) | (−0.001–0.000) | (−0.001–0.000) | (−0.001–0.000) |
| Common language |  |  |  | 0.004 |
|  |  |  |  | (−0.016–0.025) |
| Common religion |  |  |  | −0.004 |
|  |  |  |  | (−0.017–0.009) |
| Distance | 0.053*** | 0.052*** | 0.051*** | 0.050*** |
|  | (0.039–0.067) | (0.038–0.066) | (0.038–0.064) | (0.037–0.064) |
| WTO | 0.022*** | 0.022*** | 0.022*** | 0.021*** |
|  | (0.012–0.033) | (0.012–0.033) | (0.012–0.032) | (0.011–0.032) |
| NorthSouth | 0.043*** | 0.043*** | 0.033** | 0.036** |
|  | (0.019–0.066) | (0.019–0.067) | (0.006–0.060) | (0.007–0.064) |
| SouthSouth | −0.049*** | −0.048** | −0.061*** | −0.057** |
|  | (−0.079--0.020) | (−0.081--0.016) | (−0.096--0.025) | (−0.094--0.020) |

Table 7.1 (cont.)

| Variables | (1) EU distance | (2) EU distance | (3) EU distance | (4) EU distance |
|---|---|---|---|---|
| Asia | −0.010 | −0.010 | −0.013 | −0.015 |
| | (−0.034–0.014) | (−0.034–0.014) | (−0.036–0.009) | (−0.038–0.008) |
| Africa | 0.010 | 0.010 | 0.006 | 0.002 |
| | (−0.015–0.034) | (−0.015–0.034) | (−0.019–0.030) | (−0.023–0.028) |
| Americas | −0.023 | −0.022 | −0.023 | −0.026 |
| | (−0.055–0.009) | (−0.054–0.010) | (−0.054–0.008) | (−0.060–0.009) |
| Oceania | −0.141*** | −0.140*** | −0.146*** | −0.147*** |
| | (−0.184−−0.097) | (−0.183−−0.097) | (−0.189−−0.103) | (−0.190−−0.105) |
| Intercontinental | 0.000 | −0.000 | −0.002 | −0.004 |
| | (−0.014–0.015) | (−0.015–0.015) | (−0.016–0.012) | (−0.020–0.011) |
| Constant | −3.273*** | −3.417*** | −4.251*** | −4.213*** |
| | (−4.303−−2.243) | (−4.530−−2.304) | (−5.508−−2.993) | (−5.545−−2.882) |
| Observations | 519 | 518 | 506 | 500 |
| $R^2$ | 0.522 | 0.522 | 0.534 | 0.531 |

Note: Robust confidence intervals in parentheses.
* $p < 0.1$
** $p < 0.05$
*** $p < 0.01$

financial aid (model 2), IGO membership (model 3) and common language and religion (model 4). Table 7.2 presents the equivalent four models for NAFTA. Table 7.3 reports the substantive effects of the explanatory variables that are statistically significant.

The statistical results offer strong support to our conjecture regarding the number of templates available to governments at the time of PTA negotiations. Year is positive and statistically significant in all EU models and negative and statistically significant in all NAFTA models. Thus, older treaties resemble the Rome Treaty, but newer ones look much more like NAFTA. Table 7.3 indicates that these results are not only statistically significant but also substantively important, especially with respect to NAFTA. Illustratively, a PTA signed in 2006 (e.g. the Chile–Colombia free trade agreement) is closer to NAFTA by about 0.08 points than is a PTA signed in 1996 (e.g. the Canada–Chile free trade agreement). It appears, then, that the early influence of the EU on the design of PTAs diminishes over time and that Washington's preferred model is becoming increasingly influential.

Table 7.2 *Explaining similarity to NAFTA*

| Variables | (5)<br>NAFTA distance | (6)<br>NAFTA distance | (7)<br>NAFTA distance | (8)<br>NAFTA distance |
|---|---|---|---|---|
| Year | −0.008*** | −0.008*** | −0.007*** | −0.007*** |
| | (−0.011−−0.006) | (−0.011−−0.005) | (−0.010−−0.005) | (−0.010−−0.004) |
| Numbers | 0.002** | 0.002** | 0.002** | 0.002** |
| | (0.000−0.004) | (0.001−0.004) | (0.000−0.003) | (0.000−0.004) |
| Plurilateral | 0.042 | 0.047 | 0.039 | 0.039 |
| | (−0.003−0.088) | (−0.003−0.096) | (−0.016−0.094) | (−0.015−0.093) |
| Plurilateral and | 0.043* | 0.061** | 0.051 | 0.051 |
| third country | (0.001−0.085) | (0.011−0.111) | (−0.001−0.103) | (−0.002−0.104) |
| Region-region | 0.072* | 0.069* | 0.051 | 0.049 |
| | (0.001−0.142) | (0.003−0.135) | (−0.017−0.118) | (−0.018−0.115) |
| ln(Trade) | −0.014*** | −0.016*** | −0.013*** | −0.014*** |
| | (−0.021−−0.007) | (−0.023−−0.010) | (−0.021−−0.005) | (−0.022−−0.005) |
| Intra-regional | 0.037 | 0.054 | 0.129 | 0.150 |
| trade | (−0.277−0.352) | (−0.231−0.339) | (−0.150−0.407) | (−0.119−0.419) |
| US external PTA | −0.187*** | −0.196*** | −0.208*** | −0.206*** |
| | (−0.234−−0.139) | (−0.247−−0.145) | (−0.259−−0.157) | (−0.254−−0.159) |
| ln(Aid) | | 0.001 | 0.001 | 0.001 |
| | | (−0.001−0.002) | (−0.001−0.003) | (−0.001−0.002) |
| IGO membership | | | −0.002** | −0.003** |
| | | | (−0.004−−0.000) | (−0.005−−0.001) |
| ln(GDP) | 0.002 | 0.007 | 0.010* | 0.008 |
| | (−0.010−0.013) | (−0.003−0.017) | (0.000−0.019) | (−0.001−0.018) |
| ln(GDPpc) | −0.007 | −0.012 | −0.013 | −0.012 |
| | (−0.026−0.011) | (−0.032−0.007) | (−0.033−0.007) | (−0.033−0.010) |
| Regime | −0.004*** | −0.004*** | −0.003** | −0.004** |
| | (−0.006−−0.002) | (−0.006−−0.001) | (−0.006−−0.001) | (−0.006−−0.001) |
| Common | | | | −0.055* |
| language | | | | (−0.106−−0.005) |
| Common religion | | | | 0.150 |
| | | | | (−0.016−0.317) |
| Distance | 0.015 | 0.019 | 0.015 | 0.046 |
| | (−0.009−0.040) | (−0.010−0.047) | (−0.014−0.045) | (−0.011−0.103) |
| WTO | −0.027** | −0.028** | −0.028** | −0.023* |
| | (−0.048−−0.006) | (−0.048−−0.008) | (−0.048−−0.008) | (−0.043−−0.003) |
| NorthSouth | −0.093** | −0.100** | −0.136*** | −0.138*** |
| | (−0.162−−0.024) | (−0.176−−0.024) | (−0.216−−0.055) | (−0.212−−0.063) |

Table 7.2 *(cont.)*

| Variables | (5) NAFTA distance | (6) NAFTA distance | (7) NAFTA distance | (8) NAFTA distance |
|---|---|---|---|---|
| SouthSouth | 0.011 | −0.007 | −0.055 | −0.056 |
| | (−0.068–0.089) | (−0.095–0.081) | (−0.151–0.040) | (−0.150–0.038) |
| Asia | −0.046** | −0.045** | −0.040* | −0.049** |
| | (−0.082−−0.011) | (−0.082−−0.008) | (−0.077−−0.003) | (−0.089−−0.009) |
| Africa | −0.011 | −0.007 | −0.012 | −0.014 |
| | (−0.059–0.037) | (−0.056–0.042) | (−0.060–0.037) | (−0.063–0.035) |
| Americas | −0.024 | −0.006 | 0.012 | 0.026 |
| | (−0.062–0.014) | (−0.055–0.042) | (−0.041–0.065) | (−0.032–0.084) |
| Oceania | −0.067** | −0.052* | −0.068** | −0.037 |
| | (−0.112−−0.022) | (−0.101−−0.003) | (−0.117−−0.019) | (−0.110–0.035) |
| Intercontinental | −0.022 | −0.012 | −0.006 | −0.005 |
| | (−0.047–0.002) | (−0.037–0.013) | (−0.031–0.020) | (−0.030–0.020) |
| Constant | 17.194*** | 16.892*** | 15.445*** | 15.045*** |
| | (11.913–22.475) | (11.241–22.543) | (9.706–21.183) | (9.202–20.888) |
| Observations | 318 | 274 | 267 | 267 |
| $R^2$ | 0.583 | 0.600 | 0.605 | 0.613 |

*Note:* Robust confidence intervals in parentheses.
$p < 0.1$
* $p < 0.05$
** $p < 0.01$

Table 7.3 *Substantive effects*

| Variable | (Mean − SD) →(Mean + SD) | Lower bound | Upper bound |
|---|---|---|---|
| *EU distance* | | | |
| Year | 0.0880 | 0.0879 | 0.0881 |
| ln(Trade) | 0.0122 | 0.0121 | 0.0124 |
| IGO Membership | − 0.0170 | − 0.0176 | − 0.0163 |
| *NAFTA distance* | | | |
| Year | − 0.083 | − 0.090 | − 0.076 |
| Numbers | 0.025 | 0.024 | 0.027 |
| ln(Trade) | − 0.081 | − 0.086 | − 0.076 |
| IGO Membership | − 0.045 | − 0.047 | − 0.042 |

We also find substantial support for the hypothesis pertaining to PTA membership size, but mainly for the distance to NAFTA. As expected, *Numbers* is positive and statistically significant in the case of NAFTA, indicating that agreements with fewer members follow the NAFTA model more closely than multimember PTAs. The number of member states, however, is not statistically significant in the case of the EU. The results also suggest that the NAFTA model is more appealing to states aiming to sign a bilateral PTA than to states designing agreements between two regions or between a region and a third country. Plurilateral agreements, by contrast, are less distant from the Treaty of Rome than bilateral agreements are. This result corroborates extant research and our conjecture that regional economic organisations tend to follow the EU model.

Results are mixed with respect to the conjecture linking trade dependence to similarity with the EU and NAFTA models. Surprisingly, we find that PTAs signed by countries that are more dependent on access to the EU market are less similar to the EU model than other agreements. The coefficient for *Intra-Regional Trade* is not statistically significant in any model; and the coefficient for *EU External PTA* is significant only in one model, although this coefficient has the expected sign throughout. Results with respect to NAFTA are much more consistent with our expectations. Countries that trade a lot with the United States design PTAs that resemble the NAFTA model more closely than other countries do. In fact, moving from one standard deviation below the mean to one standard deviation above the mean on *Trade with the US* decreases the distance from NAFTA by about 0.08 points. Given that the dependent variable ranges from 0.15 to 0.73, the size of this effect is remarkable. The finding concerning trade with the United States is robust across all four models reported in Table 7.2. The same applies to the coefficient for *US External PTA*; as expected, American PTAs with third countries tend to follow the NAFTA model quite closely. *Intra-Regional Trade* is not statistically significant in the models explaining distance from NAFTA either.

Financial aid from the EU or the United States does not seem to play a role in shaping PTA design. In none of the models is the coefficient for *Aid* statistically significant. By contrast, the results for *IGO Membership* confirm our expectations. In model 3, the coefficient for this variable is negative and statistically significant, suggesting that countries that share membership with the EU in many IGOs design their PTAs following the EU model. This finding, however, is not robust to controlling for common language and common religion (model 4). In regard to the distance to NAFTA, the coefficient for *IGO Membership* is negative and statistically significant in both models 7 and 8. Again, therefore, countries with many joint IGO memberships with the United States design agreements that resemble NAFTA. Presumably, these organisations are instrumental in transmitting useful information regarding institutional design from the hubs to spokes.

Overall, therefore, the findings offer considerable support for the conjectures regarding number of models, number of members, trade dependence and common IGO membership. The conjecture linking financial aid to PTA design, by contrast, is not supported by the analysis. Several of the control variables are statistically significant and have the expected sign. *Distance from Brussels* has a positive sign, indicating that PTAs in the European backyard tend to be closer to the EU model than are PTAs that are farther away. The EU model, however, also seems to appeal to the designers of South–South PTAs. Perhaps unexpectedly, GATT/WTO Member countries design agreements that are less similar to the EU than non-GATT/WTO Members do. With respect to distance from NAFTA, democratic countries sign PTAs that have greater similarity to NAFTA than authoritarian regimes do. GATT/WTO Members are more likely to pick the US model than are nonmembers (given the large distance between NAFTA and the EU, this may explain the negative result for the latter). Not surprisingly, given that NAFTA brings together both developed and developing countries, the NAFTA model particularly inspires the design of North–South PTAs. Interestingly, the recent wave of Asian PTAs seems to emulate the US model. Overall, with an $R^2$ higher than 0.5 in the models including all variables, the predictive power of our models is high. Our working hypotheses perform better for NAFTA than for the EU, however.

Our results are robust to changes in model specifications and operationalisation.[11] First, and most importantly, we estimate seemingly unrelated regression (SUR) models, including all explanatory variables, for both the EU and the United States. The results largely corroborate the OLS estimates. We also exclude outliers according to Cook's distance, drop EU and US PTAs with third countries and replace *Trade with the EU* with *Trade/GDP with the EU* to check whether the positive sign remains

---

[11] These results are not reported here because of space constraints. They are available from the authors upon request.

unchanged.[12] Interestingly, in this last model the sign for *Trade/GDP with the EU* is negative, although the variable is not statistically significant. Overall, however, our results are robust for all these additional specifications.

## F. Conclusion

As trade agreements have mushroomed around the world in recent decades, they have become a primary instrument for the regulation of international commerce. The forces that shape this process are not well understood, in particular with respect to the design of these agreements. In this chapter we take a first crack at this issue. We contend that negotiators do not 'reinvent the wheel' when they bargain over the provisions included in PTAs. Rather, they choose from a limited menu of principal models, specifically a Southern model, an EU model and a NAFTA model. Cluster analysis on a comprehensive and original data set that contains a detailed coding of the institutional design of nearly 600 PTAs allows us to empirically show the existence of these models.

We then develop a theoretical framework that explains variation in similarity between an agreement and the EU and NAFTA, respectively. Our argument is that domestic variables alone are not sufficient to explain similarity to the EU or NAFTA. Rather, variables capturing the relationship between the potential members of a PTA and the EU and the United States, respectively, should also be considered. Our data set allows us to test a series of conjectures derived from this general argument. The empirical results suggest that the choice of PTA model is indeed influenced by the relationship between PTA members and the EU and the United States, respectively. Institutional design, therefore, is not determined by domestic or intraregional factors alone. Most conjectures, however, have more explanatory power for distance to NAFTA than for distance to the EU.

Among the most important implications of our study is that PTAs are not designed in a void; that is, countries imitate existing PTAs when deciding on the contents of new agreements. In other words, they pick off-the-shelf models and then adapt them to the particular circumstances and their specific needs. This observation indicates that institutional design

---

[12]  The Cook's distance statistic is commonly used to estimate the influence of specific observations on the results in a least squares regression analysis.

is driven not only by functional considerations but also is a result of imitation and global interdependence.

## References

Ahlquist, John S., and Breunig, Christian. 2012. 'Model-Based Clustering and Typologies in the Social Sciences.' *Political Analysis* 20 (1): 92–112.

Alter, Karen J. 2012. 'The Global Spread of European Style International Courts.' *West European Politics* 35 (1): 135–54.

Baccini, Leonardo, and Dür, Andreas. 2012. 'The New Regionalism and Policy Interdependence.' *British Journal of Political Science* 42 (1): 57–79.

——— 2013. 'Investment Discrimination and the Proliferation of Preferential Trade Agreements.' *Journal of Conflict Resolution* (online first). doi:10.1177/0022002713516844.

Baccini, Leonardo, and Urpelainen, Johannes. 2012. 'Strategic Side Payments: Preferential Trading Agreements, Economic Reform, and Foreign Aid.' *Journal of Politics* 74 (4): 932–49.

Börzel, Tanja A. 2013. 'Comparative Regionalism: European Integration and Beyond.' In *Handbook of International Relations*, edited by Walter Carlsnaes, Thomas Risse and Beth A. Simmons, 503–31. London: Sage.

Börzel, Tanja A., and Risse, Thomas. 2012. 'When Europeanisation Meets Diffusion: Exploring New Territory.' *West European Politics* 35 (1): 192–207.

Büthe, Tim, and Milner, Helen V. 2008. 'The Politics of Foreign Direct Investment into Developing Countries: Increasing FDI through International Trade Agreements?' *American Journal of Political Science* 52 (4): 741–62.

——— 2014. 'Institutional Diversity in Trade Agreements and Foreign Direct Investment: Credibility, Commitment, and Economic Flows in the Developing World, 1970–2007.' *World Politics* 66 (1): 88–122.

Central Intelligence Agency. 2013. *The World Factbook 2013–14*. Washington, DC: Central Intelligence Agency. https://www.cia.gov/library/publications/the-world-factbook/index.html.

CEPII. 2007. GeoDist data set. www.cepii.fr/CEPII/en/bdd_modele/presentation.asp?id=6. Accessed 3 December 2013.

Delvin, Robert, and Estevadeordal, Antoni. 2001. 'What's New in the New Regionalism in the Americas?' In *Regional Integration in Latin America and the Caribbean: The Political Economy of Open Regionalism*, edited by Victor Bulmer-Thomas, 17–44. London: Institute of Latin American Studies.

Drezner, Daniel W. 2007. *All Politics Is Global*. Princeton, NJ: Princeton University Press.

Duina, Francesco G. 2006. *The Social Construction of Free Trade: The European Union, NAFTA, and MERCOSUR*. Princeton, NJ: Princeton University Press.

Dür, Andreas. 2007. 'EU Trade Policy as Protection for Exporters: The Agreements with Mexico and Chile.' *Journal of Common Market Studies* 45 (4): 833–55.

Dür, Andreas, Baccini, Leonardo, and Elsig, Manfred. 2014. 'The Design of International Trade Agreements: Introducing a New Dataset.' *Review of International Organizations* 9 (3): 353–75.

Farrell, Mary. 2007. 'From EU Model to External Policy? Promoting Regional Integration in the Rest of the World.' In *Making History: European Integration and Institutional Change at Fifty*, edited by Sophie Meunier and Kathleen R. McNamara, 299–315. Oxford, England: Oxford University Press.

Gleditsch, Kristian S. 2002. 'Expanded Trade and GDP Data, 1946–99.' *Journal of Conflict Resolution* 46 (5): 712–24.

Gruber, Lloyd. 2000. *Ruling the World: Power Politics and the Rise of Supranational Institutions*. Princeton, NJ: Princeton University Press.

Grugel, Jean B. 2004. 'New Regionalism and Modes of Governance – Comparing US and EU Strategies in Latin America.' *European Journal of International Relations* 10 (4): 603–26.

Hafner-Burton, Emilie M. 2009. *Forced to Be Good: Why Trade Agreements Boost Human Rights*. Ithaca, NY: Cornell University Press.

Haftel, Yoram Z. 2007. 'Designing for Peace: Regional Integration Arrangements, Institutional Variation, and Militarized Interstate Disputes.' *International Organization* 61 (1): 217–37.

   2012. *Regional Economic Institutions and Conflict Mitigation: Design, Implementation and the Promise of Peace*. Ann Arbor: University of Michigan Press.

   2013. 'Commerce and Institutions: Trade, Scope, and the Design of Regional Economic Organizations.' *Review of International Organizations* 8 (3): 389–414.

Heston, Alan, Summers, Robert, and Aten, Bettina. 2011. Penn World Table Version 7.0. Center for International Comparisons of Production, Income and Prices. University of Pennsylvania, Philadelphia.

Heydon, Kenneth, and Woolcock, Stephen. 2009. *The Rise of Bilateralism: Comparing American, European, and Asian Approaches to Preferential Trade Agreements*. Tokyo: United Nations University Press.

Horn, Henrik, Mavroidis, Petros C., and Sapir, André. 2010. 'Beyond the WTO? An Anatomy of EU and US Preferential Trade Agreements.' *World Economy* 33 (11): 1565–88.

Jetschke, Anja, and Lenz, Tobias. 2013. 'Does Regionalism Diffuse? A New Research Agenda for the Study of Regional Organizations.' *Journal of European Public Policy* 20 (4): 626–37.

Jetschke, Anja, and Murray, Philomena. 2012. 'Diffusing Regional Integration: The EU and Southeast Asia.' *West European Politics* 35 (1): 174–91.

Jo, Hyeran, and Namgung, Hyun. 2012. 'Dispute Settlement Mechanisms in Prefer-ential Trade Agreements: Democracy, Boilerplates, and the Multilateral Trade Regime.' *Journal of Conflict Resolution* 56 (6): 1041–68.

Johns, Leslie. 2013. 'Depth versus Rigidity in the Design of Preferential Trade Agreements.' *Journal of Theoretical Politics.* doi:10.1177/0951629813505723.

Kahler, Miles. 1995. *International Institutions and the Political Economy of Integra-tion.* Washington, DC: Brookings Institution.

Kaufman, Leonard, and Rousseeuw, Peter J. 2005. *Finding Groups in Data: An Introduction to Cluster Analysis.* Hoboken, NJ: Wiley.

Kim, Soo Yeon, and Manger, Mark S. 2013. 'Hubs of Governance: Path-Dependence and Higher-Order Effects of PTA Formation.' Paper presented at the Annual Meeting of the Political Economy of International Organizations, 7–9 Febru-ary, Mannheim and Heidelberg, Germany.

Kono, Daniel Y. 2007. 'When Do Trade Blocs Block Trade?' *International Studies Quarterly* 51 (1): 165–81.

Koremenos, Barbara, Lipson, Charles, and Snidal, Duncan. 2001. 'The Rational Design of International Institutions.' *International Organization* 55 (4): 761–99.

Kucik, Jeffrey. 2012. 'The Domestic Politics of Institutional Design: Producer Pref-erences over Trade Agreement Rules.' *Economics and Politics* 24 (2): 95–118.

Langhammer, Rolf J., and Hiemenz, Ulrich. 1990. *Regional Integration among Devel-oping Countries: Opportunities, Obstacles, and Options.* Kieler Studien 232. Tübingen, Germany: JCB Mohr.

Lavenex, Sandra, and Schimmelfennig, Frank. 2009. 'EU Rules Beyond EU Borders: Theorizing External Governance in European Politics.' *Journal of European Public Policy* 16 (6): 791–812.

Lenz, Tobias. 2012. 'Spurred Emulation: The EU and Regional Integration in Mer-cosur and SADC.' *West European Politics* 35 (1): 155–73.

Maddison, Angus. 2011. Statistics on world population, GDP and per capita GDP, 1–2008 AD, horizontal file. www.ggdc.net/MADDISON/oriindex.htm. Accessed 8 November 2011.

Maechler, Martin, Rousseeuw, Peter, Struyf, Anja, Hubert, Mia, and Hornik, Kurt. 2013. 'Cluster: Cluster Analysis Basics and Extensions (version 1.14.4).' http://cran.r-project.org/web/packages/cluster/.

Mansfield, Edward D., and Milner, Helen V. 2012. *Votes, Vetoes, and the Political Economy of International Trade Agreements.* Princeton, NJ: Princeton Uni-versity Press.

Mansfield, Edward D., Milner, Helen V., and Rosendorff, B. Peter. 2002. 'Why Democracies Cooperate More: Electoral Control and International Trade Agreements.' *International Organization* 56 (3): 477–513.

Mansfield, Edward D., and Pevehouse, Jon C. 2000. 'Trade Blocs, Trade Flows, and International Conflict.' *International Organization* 54 (4): 775–808.

Pevehouse, Jon C. 2005. *Democracy from Above: Regional Organizations and Democratization.* Cambridge: Cambridge University Press.

Pevehouse, Jon C., Nordstrom, T., and Warnke, K. 2004. 'The Correlates of War 2 International Governmental Organizations Data Version 2.0.' *Conflict Management and Peace Science* 21 (2): 101–19.

Sbragia, Alberta. 2010. 'The EU, the US, and Trade Policy: Competitive Interdependence in the Management of Globalization.' *Journal of European Public Policy* 17 (3): 368–82.

Simmons, Beth A., Garrett, Geoffrey, and Dobbin, Frank. 2006. 'Introduction: The International Diffusion of Liberalism.' *International Organization* 60 (4): 781–810.

Smith, James McCall. 2000. 'The Politics of Dispute Settlement Design: Explaining Legalism in Regional Trade Pacts.' *International Organization* 54 (1): 137–80.

Smith, Karen E. 1998. 'The Use of Political Conditionality in the EU's Relations with Third Countries: How Effective?' *European Foreign Affairs Review* 3 (2): 253–74.

World Bank. 2013. *World Development Indicators.* Washington, DC: International Bank for Reconstruction and Development/World Bank.

# 8

# PTA design, tariffs and intra-industry trade

MARK MANGER

## A. Introduction

How does the structure of trade – whether exports and imports are determined by comparative advantage or economies of scale – influence the design of preferential trade agreements (PTAs)? In particular, which trade barriers are immediately eliminated, which are phased out more slowly and what goods are excluded and continue to enjoy protection? Trade can be broadly classified by its determinants, that is, whether it is due to the comparative advantage of countries or due to economies of scale and product differentiation. The latter can be further divided into goods that respond to different consumer tastes and those that are the result of the vertical specialisation of production according to the relative cost of labour and capital in each country. The composition of trade is referred to as the *trade structure*. As a growing body of theoretical and empirical work indicates, it has considerable influence on patterns of trade liberalisation.

This chapter analyses the elimination or reduction of trade barriers in PTAs, focusing on a sample of agreements negotiated by South Korea and Japan with partner countries in Southeast Asia. The diversity of these partners – from high-tech Singapore to resource-rich Indonesia – implies that trade structures vary widely. The analysis in this chapter shows that the more endowment-based the trade in a particular product category – in other words, the more trade is driven by comparative advantage – the longer the liberalisation takes, the higher the remaining tariff is likely to be and the more likely a good is to be wholly excluded from any tariff reductions. Conversely, intra-industry trade is less likely to be excluded, and tariffs on this trade are usually eliminated quickly and thoroughly compared to those applied to endowment-based trade. In other words, trade structure matters for tariff elimination in general and for PTA design in particular. This finding is at odds with a purely economic logic considering that specialisation according comparative advantage offers considerable gains for both countries. It is, however, understandable when we consider the political economy of such agreements. The analysis contributes to the debate around the role of intra-industry trade and its effect on trade policy. The results show that for an important set of PTAs, it is clear that intra-industry trade is much easier to liberalise than is endowment-based trade, regardless of the political or electoral system of the countries involved. Yet beyond this immediate implication, the chapter also underlines that PTAs, in particular between large developed and smaller developing economies, do not accomplish much liberalisation of endowment-based trade at all. This is unfortunate because it leaves economic gains on the table, benefits that apparently could not be realised because of the resistance and political strength of protectionist industries – in particular agriculture.

The next section discusses the theoretical links between trade structure and tariff elimination proposed in the literature. The third section focuses specifically on the question of trade liberalisation in PTAs. The fourth section describes the statistical tests in detail, the fifth, the results and conclusions are drawn in the final section.

## B. Trade structure and tariffs

The central (or at least ostensible) purpose of trade agreements is to eliminate trade barriers, in particular tariffs and duties but also nontariff barriers such as arbitrary or complex standards and regulations. Since the economic case for tariff elimination is so obvious, research in political economy has generally sought to explain the existence of tariffs as a reflection of the political demands of specific interest groups. Such models fall under the rubric of the 'endogenous tariff formation' approach, which suggests that tariffs are endogenously determined given the existing trade and reactions by exporters and importers.

Of the various explanations of endogenous tariff formation, the Grossman–Helpman (1994) model has found particularly strong empirical support. In the Grossman–Helpman model, specific factors in an industry combine to form a lobby with the goal of maximising rents, derived from trade protection net of lobbying effort. Lobby groups are principals bidding in a menu auction, with the items on the menu a vector of trade taxes and subsidies. The menus are presented to the agent, the government, with a mapping onto political contributions. The model has found strong support in work by Gawande and Bandyopadhyay (2000) and Gawande and Hoekman (2006). However, like most models in the endogenous tariff formation literature, it draws on a specific-factors or Ricardo–Viner model. Grossman and Helpman assume the existence of a mobile factor (labour) and a specific factor (capital or land). Hence, the model explains protection for endowment-based trade well but leaves open the question of whether intra-industry trade results would be relatively more or less liberalised.

For endowment-based trade liberalisation in the context of PTAs, the implications are stark. Two countries that primarily trade on the basis of comparative advantage should have considerable difficulty in forming a PTA at all. As long as at least one factor in the predominant industries in each country is specific (not mobile), the cost of adjustment would be so prohibitively high that the resulting lobby effort would be immense. Reciprocal preferential trade liberalisation would really be feasible only under relatively restrictive conditions: factors should at least be somewhat mobile, there must be a lot of industries, that is, bilateral trade has to be quite diversified with many goods exported and imported and, possibly, governments must be in a position to cushion the impact of trade liberalisation, for example, with generous welfare provisions.

These are demanding conditions that make reciprocal trade liberalisation most likely if the partners are relatively rich and their economies quite similar. Unfortunately, this also implies that the economic gains from trade will be modest. By contrast, two countries with a very pronounced difference in comparative advantage, in particular if already 'revealed' in successful exports, will experience difficulties forming PTAs even though the mutual gains from trade would be considerable.

A way out of this problem is to structure tariff liberalisation in a way that exempts the most ardent protectionists. Flexible provisions are a feature of nearly all trade agreements (Pelc 2011; Rosendorff and Milner 2001). Members of the World Trade Organization (WTO), however, are constrained in their ability to exclude their own inefficient industries: Article 24 8(b) of the General Agreement on Tariffs and Trade (GATT 1947) stipulates that the 'duties and other restrictive regulations of commerce ( ... ) are eliminated on substantially all the trade between the constituent territories ( ... ).' What constitutes 'substantially all the trade' is a matter of debate, and the 1994 'Understanding' of the contracting parties is not much clearer: 'eliminated with respect to substantially all the trade between the constituent territories of the union or at least with respect to substantially all the trade in products originating in such territories.' Likewise, duties are to be abolished within a 'reasonable length of time'.

Here, the 1994 'Understanding' at least states that only in exceptional cases should this period exceed 10 years, and if so, a 'full explanation to the Council for Trade in Goods' is necessary.

In principle, other GATT Contracting Parties could challenge those countries forming PTAs that violate these rules by demanding a dispute settlement procedure. In practice, they are reluctant to do so as their own PTAs do not stand scrutiny either. Nonetheless, most countries adhere to the principle that nearly all existing *trade* ought to be tariff free, although this does mean all *tariffs* and other barriers have to be eliminated – some barriers might be so prohibitively high that no trade takes place. The question is thus why some trade is excluded while other trade is fully or mostly liberalised. This leads to a consideration of trade structure and its relationship to the cost of adjustment to tariff elimination.

## *I. Intra-industry trade and ease of adjustment*

According to the 'new trade theory',[1] intra-industry trade should be associated with lower adjustment costs. This view was articulated by the first scholars to investigate the question of economics of scale and trade policy (Aquino 1978; Balassa 1966). Helpman (1981) formalises the argument and predicts intra-industry trade liberalisation may require less adjustment than the liberalisation of endowment-based trade does. In Helpman's model, consumers have a preference for a particular variety of a good. Each firm produces only one variety of a good with increasing returns to scale so that for this particular differentiated product the firm is a monopolist. Consumers are evenly distributed around a circle of product variety, and firms will divide up the market by evenly spacing themselves around the circle.[2] The entry of a foreign firm's imports then leads to an adjustment process, whereby the now greater number of firms is again distributed evenly around the circle. Importantly, if trade is reciprocal, the total volume of trade will not change so that although adjustment costs arise, they are only temporary, and there is 'room' for all firms in the market.

This argument helps explain why the liberalisation of intra-industry trade is far less politically contentious than that of endowment-based

---

[1] The 'new new trade theory' (Melitz 2003) is a refinement of Krugman's (1979, 1980) earlier work. The political economy implications are drawn out in Plouffe (2013).

[2] The 'circle' is merely a mathematical convenience to avoid having to deal with endpoints of a distribution.

trade, and it has been cited to explain why the post–World War II expansion of global trade did not generate much political opposition (Krugman 1981). It also fits nicely with the empirically much more difficult politics of North–South relations, in particular, when trade is largely endowment based and agriculture is an important aspect of trade negotiations.

Milner (1997) offers an extension of this argument to explain the political support for PTAs: firms gain by lowering their costs by achieving greater economies of scale as they expand in a regional market. The key to this is to increase returns to scale at the plant level (Chase 2003) and to export this increase in production to the trade partner. This makes trade liberalisation desirable. At the same time, when products are differentiated by variety to suit consumer tastes (e.g. different brands with minor differences), firms can specialise with relatively low adjustment costs. Rather than exiting an industry completely, firms slightly adapt their products. This does not require much additional investment in the production plant itself and no major allocation of resources.

PTAs are particularly attractive because governments can exchange market-opening offers across different industries, products and (implicitly) firms: 'in industries with differentiated products, this swapping of markets across countries may be possible at low political cost' (Milner 1997: 91). Accordingly, the liberalisation of intra-industry trade becomes an important driver of liberalisation in PTAs.

Two charges have been levelled directly against this view: first, costs are specific to the firm forced to undertake the adjustments. If a small lobbying effort can swing the pendulum against liberalisation, the firm in question can fully internalise the benefit. In other words, there is no collective action cost to lobbying. Second, this view ignores domestic political institutions and their effect on collective action cost more generally. The next section discusses these objections as raised in the literature.

## II. More protection for differentiated goods producers?

As Gilligan (1997) observes, intra-industry trade could lead to more protection because producers of differentiated goods are by definition larger firms (after all, they have to achieve economies of scale) and face fewer collective-action costs than do smaller firms in industries producing undifferentiated goods. Moreover, although the Helpman (1981) model explains well why the overall volume of trade may increase, it tells us nothing about *which firms* may face an adjustment because of imports.

It even allows for the possibility that some may have to come up with wholly new products or exit the industry completely.

As Gilligan points out, while a firm undergoes adjustment, it is by definition experiencing a decrease in returns to scale. This may invite other domestic entrants (Gilligan 1997: 462) – although a counterargument would be that as long as some returns to scale remain, entry could still be deterred (Tirole 1988: 309–11). More importantly, though, because a firm is by definition a monopolist in a particular product variety, imports of a very similar product impose adjustment costs mostly on this individual firm. Hence, it may well pay off to lobby for protection against imports. Adjustment costs, lobbying costs and benefits from protection are all highly specific to the firm. Nonetheless, it is an empirical question if adjustment costs might warrant lobbying efforts to prevent liberalisation. A firm will compare the cost of preventing imports by lobbying with the cost of adjustment through a modification of its products.

Building on this argument, Kono (2009) offers a particularly strong thesis: whether trade is intra-industry in structure should have a greater influence on the incentives to lobby, with the more electoral institutions favouring particularistic interests. Single-member-district plurality systems often allow candidates to compete successfully for seats without party support, so they cultivate only a small, localised constituency necessary to win a district. At the other extreme, proportional representation systems in which candidate lists are drawn up by parties incentivise candidates to maximise the vote share of their party and to appeal to a large constituency (Carey and Shugart 1995). Applied to trade policy, this means that protectionism should fall with constituency size (Rogowski 1987). There is considerable empirical support for this claim (Hankla 2006; Nielson 2003).

However, Kono's modification of Gilligan's model does not predict the qualitative impact of intra-industry trade either – that is, whether firms will demand protection or trade liberalisation – but merely predicts the effect of different electoral institutions on the magnitude: if intra-industry trade also coincides with demands for greater protection, and the payoff from lobbying is greater in an electoral system, we will observe more protectionism.

In other words, the empirical question remains. Gilligan focuses on demands by industry groups in the United States that request action from the International Trade Commission (ITC). Such demands launch a quasi-judicial process involving hearings that can lead to the imposition of anti-dumping duties and other trade remedies. His study of requests made to the ITC between 1988 and 1992 reveals that industries with a high degree of intra-industry trade were also more likely to demand action from the ITC (Gilligan 1997: 470).

Kono opts for a far more encompassing approach. He tests his results using a data set assembled by Kee, Nicita and Olarreaga (2009) that provides a cross-sectional index of trade barriers imposed by 65 countries in the year 2005–6, capturing both tariff and nontariff barriers as well as subsidies. Kono finds strong evidence that import-competing firms engaged in intra-industry trade obtain protection for their products, provided the election system is sufficiently favourable to particularistic interests. Yet it is unclear whether much of this is driven by import-competing industries or whether demands could swing the other way if electoral institutions were different. More important, however, are two other problems that make these results slightly inconclusive: first, intra-industry trade is a bilateral phenomenon, whereas the trade barrier data used are multilateral, that is, they provide an average of the various trade barriers against imports from all countries. Second, the trade restrictiveness index is itself estimated using the same import data, so although Kono's findings are plausible, an adjustment for this uncertainty is required before we can have confidence in the statistical results.

PTAs present the opportunity for a more direct test. Tariff and trade barrier reduction in PTAs is usually bilateral, or at least restricted to a small number of states. Even in regional agreements, negotiations (as the objective of lobbying) are often bilateral (Cameron and Tomlin 2000). Moreover, by studying the liberalisation within PTAs, we can home in on the question of whether intra- or interindustry trade leads to more or less liberalisation between two countries, conditional on other variables, holding the electoral systems in the individual states constant by virtue of the research design. The next section proposes such a test.

## C. Intra-industry trade and tariff liberalisation in PTAs

Whether multilaterally or in PTAs, the most obvious gains from trade can be achieved when countries export those goods in which they have a comparative advantage. Yet such specialisation by definition implies considerable adjustment costs. As a country ceases to export a good because it has a lower opportunity cost in the production of other goods, inefficient producers will have to shut down, and capital and labour will have to find a new use. Such adjustment costs are highly concentrated – recall that, unlike in the case of intra-industry trade, comparative advantage

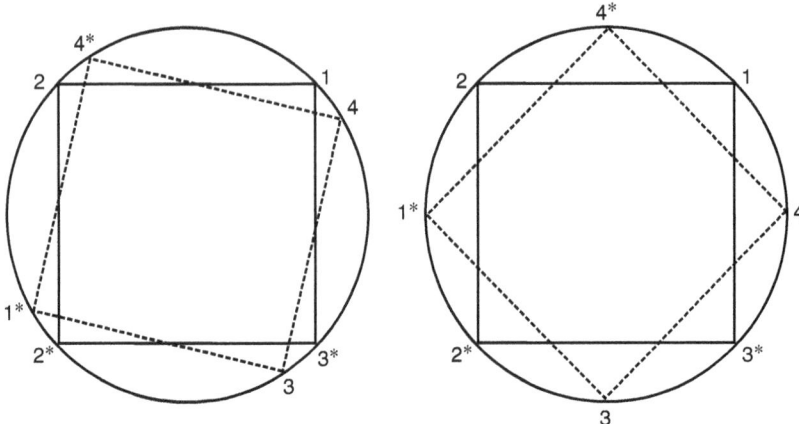

Figure 8.1   Adjustment and product differentiation

implies that, in many cases, a country will no longer produce a particular good.

In the case of intra-industry trade, it is easy to construct a scenario in which adjustment costs to firms are indeed low: if both countries already have sufficient, perhaps growing intra-industry trade in a particular product category, then this suggests that adjustment costs would be low. We might see an increase in the volume of intra-industry trade, but since both products are already exported to the respective partner country, there is at least some demand for the variety.

By contrast, if there is little intra-industry trade, adjustment costs *may* be higher postliberalisation. Consider a situation in which two firms begin to trade reciprocally for the first time, as depicted in Figure 8.1, which draws on Gilligan (1997) and Helpman (1981). If firm 1 and 1* (respectively, the domestic firm and its foreign competitor) produce minimally differentiated goods prior to liberalisation as in the left-hand panel of Figure 8.1, then the adjustment cost may be considerable, even though both firms would end up producing the same volume of goods after differentiating them again (*ceteris paribus* and, in particular, always assuming that they are equally successful at exporting to each other's markets). If they happen to produce highly differentiated goods as in the right-hand panel of Figure 8.1, no adjustment is required, except both will need to learn how to export.

The original impetus for the development of the intra-industry trade model was that most trade flowed between countries with a similar level of development and often (but not always) similar factor endowments, at least with respect to capital and labour. The decades since 1990, however, have seen a general shift of manufacturing from the developed to the developing world, leading to a considerable increase in intra-industry trade between countries in the North and the South. The shift of manufacturing has coincided with the formation of numerous North–South PTAs (Manger 2009; Shadlen 2005). In particular, in the Asia-Pacific region, large, developed countries have formed such trade agreements with smaller, developing economies.

As the factor endowments of these countries often differ greatly, such trade agreements could be expected to be much less common, and liberalisation in those that materialise to proceed slowly. The considerable adjustment required when very different economies eliminate bilateral trade barriers would either lead to highly contentious politics or alternatively result in superficial agreements without much actual liberalisation, as predicted by Ravenhill (2010). Yet if intra-industry trade comes to dominate the economic exchange between these countries, adjustment costs are low and the political systems do not impede liberalisation as predicted by Kono (2009), we might observe substantially important agreements and considerable liberalisation.[3]

To understand the driving forces of intra-industry trade between countries with different factor endowments and per capita income, we need to separate horizontal and vertical intra-industry trade. Horizontal intra-industry trade (HIIT) arises as described by the models in Milner (1997) and Chase (2005). Here, firms prefer to produce more in plants in their home country, achieve greater returns to scale and export the additional production to the partner country. Goods will be differentiated according to consumer preferences, but they are not very different in terms of unit values. An example of this kind of trade is fashion products exported by France and Italy to each other. Most of these goods are of equal, high unit value, but some consumers might prefer an Ermenegildo Zegna suit over a Dior suit or vice versa even though the suits are similarly priced.[4]

Vertical intra-industry trade (VIIT) (Abd-el-Rahman 1991; Greenaway, Hine and Milner 1994; Krugman 1981), on the other hand, is trade differentiated by unit value or 'quality'. Examples of this type of trade

---

[3] Elsewhere, I have analysed how intra-industry trade contributes to PTA formation (Manger 2012).

[4] Sadly, both are priced well above the monthly take-home pay of the average academic.

would be a pair of handcrafted Italian shoes with an import value of €150 in Shanghai, equivalent to the import of 10 pairs of running shoes from China to Italy. These examples also remind us that intra-industry trade is not necessarily exclusive to high-technology manufacturing.

Often, different segments of a market correspond to different characteristics of exporting countries. For example, relatively more people can afford high-value goods in countries with a higher per capita income, whereas the market for low-value goods is bigger in poorer countries. Moreover, as the production of goods with a higher unit value is often more capital intensive (although not necessarily in their manufacturing, but perhaps in their design, as the shoe example underlines), production of high-value goods in richer countries tends to be more efficient than production of low-value goods is, with the reverse being true for poorer countries. Through this effect, factor endowments, in particular, relative abundance of capital and labour, influence the specialisation that occurs within intra-industry trade.

Recent research has focused on a related question: how PTAs affect the structure of trade. Various studies suggest that PTA formation is associated with an increase in intra-industry trade – in fact, most of the trade volume increase appears due to this change in the trade relationship (Egger, Egger and Greenaway 2008; Foster and Stehrer 2011). Yet this does not take into consideration that trade structures already change considerably prior to PTA formation.

In the sample of PTAs used in this study, there is much evidence for the rapid growth of VIIT between the two countries involved. Figure 8.2 shows the growth in VIIT for six PTAs between 1998 and 2006. In several cases, almost all of the expansion in trade volume between the partners results from more VIIT rather than from other types of trade. The vertical line in the graphs shows the year in which the PTA between the two countries was signed. As discussed earlier, such preexisting intra-industry trade would imply that the elimination or reduction of trade barriers in the PTA should be relatively painless compared to the liberalisation of endowment-based trade in the same agreement. Moreover, much of this trade is likely to be part of the production networks that encompass the region, as Soo Yeon Kim (Chapter 6 in this volume) emphasises.

VIIT is not necessarily as easy to liberalise as HIIT because a shift in consumer preferences in a rich country towards a low-cost variety of a product can create considerable adjustment pressure. However in practice, it is often the same firms, having spread their production across different countries, that will export goods back and forth. For example,

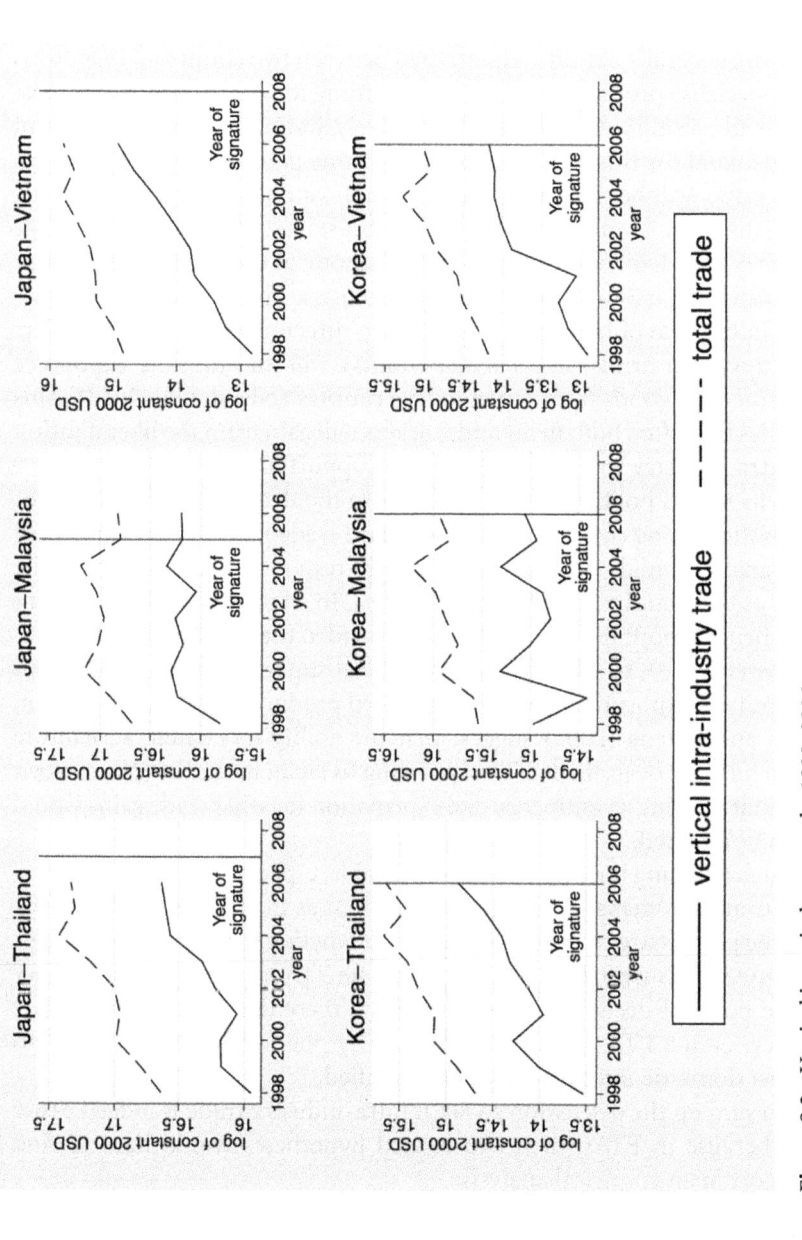

**Figure 8.2** Vertical intra-industry trade, 1998–2006
*Source:* CEPII BACI, author's calculations.

Ford USA will have few objections to imports of vehicles produced by
Ford Mexico – in fact, in this instance the firm is likely to become a
supporter of such liberalisation.

More generally, if trade is liberalised between two countries, then firms
will specialise production vertically according to where a product is most
efficiently produced and where (most likely, but not necessarily) most of
the demand for this product exists. The same good, but with a different
unit value, will be traded back and forth. It can be shown that vertically
specialised firms will create demand for less-skilled labour in the low-wage
country and demand for highly skilled labour in the high-wage country
(Feenstra 2004: 386). Recent empirical work at the product level shows
that in the case of Japanese firms, foreign direct investment by suppliers
(or 'upstream firms') in a partner country will lead to more exports of
intermediate goods from Japan to this country (Nishitateno 2013). This
implies that often both firms and workers will gain from the liberalisation
of intra-industry trade and are likely to support it.

Why would politicians be responsive to the demands of firms for liberalisation along these lines? The standard trade policy model on which
this analysis builds suggests that they will respond to lobbying from the
groups that stand to gain from such a deal. In a bilateral trade agreement
that benefits both firms and workers (provided they are engaged in intra-
industry trade), to obtain enough political support it may be sufficient
to limit the exposure of endowment-based producers. Indeed, Pekkanen,
Solís and Katada (2007) suggest that the ability to exclude agriculture
from bilateral deals made PTAs appealing to Japan in the first place, albeit
without offering a commensurate explanation for what trade gains would
then be attained.

Such lobbying is rarely directly observable, especially since few political
environments make lobbying as transparent as the US system. However,
for the present argument it is less relevant whether firms lobby politicians
or bureaucrats who then proceed to initiate PTA negotiations or whether
these political decision-makers anticipate these demands in their trade
policy: even a PTA proposed top-down by political leaders will have to
reflect domestic interests if it is to be ratified.

To sum up the discussion so far, if intra-industry trade is indeed easier
to liberalise in PTAs, then two related hypotheses would have to find
support in an empirical analysis:

1. tariff reductions should be quicker and deeper for differentiated goods
   than for goods traded as a result of comparative advantage and

2. intra-industry goods should be less likely to be excluded from tariff reductions than other goods are.

In the next section, I provide empirical evidence in support of these hypotheses.

## D. Testing the argument: intra-industry trade and tariffs in PTAs

This section presents an empirical test of the two hypotheses. I use tariff elimination data drawn from the most-favoured-nation (MFN) tariffs and PTA schedules of Japan and South Korea with several important partners in the Asia-Pacific region. The research design implies that within each 'case' of PTA, there are thousands of tariff lines representing different products, each with its own tariff, and a fixed period until the tariff is eliminated or (occasionally) not eliminated at all but rather excluded from any tariff changes. At the same time, the approach allows for a tentative test of how different election systems affect elimination of tariffs on intra-industry trade. Whereas South Korea has a semipresidential system of government and Japan a parliamentary system, the election systems of the two countries are quite similar. Both elect most of their members of parliament (MPs) with a first-past-the-post system and a smaller number through proportional representation of the votes won. In South Korea, 245 MPs for the only chamber are elected in single-seat constituencies and 54 by proportional representation. In Japan, two chambers are elected, 480 in single-seat constituencies and 180 by proportional representation in the lower house, and 146 in single- and multiseat constituencies by single nontransferable vote and 96 by proportional representation in the upper house. Although these are mixed systems, the majoritarian element dominates. Following Kono's (2009) predictions, we could thus expect intra-industry trade to lead to greater protection.

### I. Operationalisation and data

The analysis is focused on variation on two dependent variables. First, *PreferenceMargin* denotes the difference between the applied MFN tariff of a product at the time when a PTA is signed and the preferential tariff (if any) levied on the good after the full implementation of the PTA. Of course, it is possible that either a lower MFN tariff is applied between the time of signature and full implementation or that a future WTO negotiating agreement might lower MFN tariffs across the board, but neither can be reliably predicted at the point of PTA signature. In fact, the preference margin might increase with a higher applied MFN tariff, provided there is some room between bound and applied rates. Even developed countries occasionally make such fatuous choices, as shown by the increase of applied MFN tariff rates by Canada in 2013. While this variable does not capture the benefit of certainty that a low or zero PTA tariff confers, it should be closely linked to the lobbying efforts of groups with an interest in trade. The variable reaches its maximum when tariff concessions are greatest and has two possible reasons for reaching its minimum of zero: when the MFN tariff was already zero and when there is an existing high applied MFN tariff but exporters have not gained any improved market access, either because they did not ask for it or because protectionist, import-competing groups in the partner country resisted such concessions.

The second dependent variable is a dummy that equals one if a particular good has been *Excluded* from liberalisation, is left for 'renegotiation' at some future date or retains a tariff-rate quota (TRQ).[5]

The key independent variable is the trade type. I use the classification scheme developed by Fontagné and Freudenberg (Fontagné and Freudenberg 1997; Fontagné, Freudenberg and Gaulier 2006).[6] The calculation is performed as follows: first, I check whether trade in a particular good, defined as a six-digit tariff line in the 1992 Harmonized System of the World Customs Organization, is two-way. If the flow of goods in one direction is less than 10 per cent of the value of the goods flowing in the other direction, then trade is clearly one-way. One-way trade is endowment based, but it is important to allow for small amounts of exports that are the extreme opposite of their comparative advantage but that should not be considered a structural characteristic of a bilateral trade relationship. To take a concrete example, the UK exports cheese to

---

[5]  A tariff-rate quota (TRQ) provides for a limited import volume at a lower tariff, and a much higher tariff when the quota is exceeded. TRQs are common for agricultural products and often result in higher prices once the quota is exceeded than those charged by domestic producers in the importing country. In other words, they are often insurmountable barriers.

[6]  This classification is referred to as the 'threshold method' in the applied economics literature. Theoretically more precise alternatives use hedonic pricing (Cooper, Greenaway and Rayner 1993) or price elasticities (Brenton and Winters 1992), but the necessary data are not available for developing countries. See Flam and Helpman (1987) for further discussion of the underlying theory. Important applications of the decomposition into trade types using thresholds are Fukao, Ishido and Ito (2003) and Kimura and Ando (2005).

France, and France ale to the UK, but the values are so small that neither is a systematically important feature of trade.

The remaining trade is bidirectional trade in the same products differentiated by some product characteristic. By separating goods that are VIIT and HIIT, we can explore whether firms will react differently to the required adjustment. For example, if HIIT is liberalised more quickly, then this speaks strongly in favour of the original argument by Milner and against Gilligan's proposition.

To separate goods into HIIT and VIIT, I rely on Fontagné and Freudenberg's (1997) threshold of 25 per cent difference in the value of the units traded. Bilateral trade in the same tariff category but with unit value differences greater than 25 per cent is classified as VIIT, whereas goods with unit value differences lower than 25 per cent fall into the HIIT category. Importantly, their classification is merely a refinement of the commonly used Grubel–Lloyd (1971) index, so the sum of VIIT and HIIT is approximately equal to the Grubel–Lloyd index.

Because horizontal and vertical intra-industry trade might differ in the opposition to liberalisation they create, I use two separate dummy variables, called *VIIT* and *HIIT*, to indicate whether a good is respectively either VIIT or HIIT, with endowment-based trade as the reference category. In the first of my models, I test whether goods that comprise the different trade types receive greater tariff preferences. In the second model, I test whether endowment-based trade is more or less likely to be excluded completely from liberalisation in the PTA.

Following Achen (2002) and Schrodt (2014), I 'test up', drop control variables that are not significant even at the 10 per cent level in any specification, and focus on a minimal model.

In any political economy model, it is essential to control for the degree to which an industry is import competing – in particular, higher levels of import penetration will lead to greater protection (Trefler 1993). To this end, I match the International Standard Industrial Classification (ISIC) four-digit industry classification to the HS6 tables, using the concordance tables provided by CEPII.[7] With this, I calculate the variable *ImportCompetition* as the ratio of imports of goods produced by this industry divided by the domestic consumption of such a good. These data are drawn from the United Nations Industrial Development Organization (UNIDO) database on supply and demand. Unfortunately, data

---

[7] See www.cepii.fr/anglaisgraph/bdd/baci/non_restrict/sector.asp.

coverage is patchy, with countries not consistently reporting all sectors and all years. The variable ranges from zero, when all goods produced by an industry are imported (and hence produced by this industry abroad), to one, when all consumed goods are produced at home. Lower values of *ImportCompetition* indicate that an industry is relatively less competitive than the industry in the country from where imports arrive. Note that small values, however, do not indicate automatically that an industry is politically weak: industries that employ few people and contribute little to GDP are regularly among the most powerful actors in trade policy (Gawande, Krishna and Olarreaga 2012). Examples are industries such as textiles in industrialised countries. As industries that are highly competitive compared to exports are less likely to seek protection, the expected coefficient is negative in the first model (goods from import-competing industries should see less tariff reduction) and positive in the second model (such goods are more likely to be excluded from liberalisation).

I also control for the total value of the *Exports* (in log of constant 2005 USD) in the specific tariff category: if exports are already substantial, the producers of this good have already been 'revealed' as more competitive. The data are from the UN COMTRADE database. Again, the expected sign of the coefficient is negative in the liberalisation model and positive in the exclusion model.

For the controls, I take five-year averages from *t-5* to *t-1*, as trade values often fluctuate greatly from year to year, but lobbying for protection is likely only if industries experience pressure over longer periods (although using only the most recent year does not change the substantive results).

In principle it would be possible for countries to set a final tariff for a specific good in a PTA that exceeds the MFN tariff when the PTA is signed. However, this is never the case in my sample, and the variable *PreferenceMargin* never takes values smaller than zero. It is therefore appropriate to consider it a latent variable, as the truly intended tariff margin is not directly observable. The appropriate estimation approach is thus a Tobit model for the first model. The dependent variable in the second model is binary, so I estimate a logit model. Observations within a specific country pair will clearly not be independent – as the tariff negotiation is undertaken as one package deal – so I cluster over the specific PTA.

The tariff data are drawn from 10 PTAs, namely, the agreements between South Korea and Singapore, Malaysia, Indonesia, Thailand and the Philippines; Japan's PTAs with the same countries as well as the PTA with Vietnam and from the World Bank's World Integrated Trade Solution (WITS) database for the MFN tariffs applied in a given year. Although the South Korea–Association of Southeast Asian Nations (ASEAN) PTA is a single agreement, it lists individual schedules for each country, so I treat the PTAs as independent, but not the observations within each PTA.

In the tariff schedules in these agreements, goods are assigned to various categories. For example, in Japanese FTAs, category 'A' typically stands for 'tariff-free from the time the agreement enters into force', whereas 'B7' denotes that the tariff on a good shall be eliminated in equal annual steps over a period of seven years. Most agreements stipulate a base rate. I compared this base rate with the data for the applied MFN rate for the year and chose the lower of the two, and then subtracted the final rate in the PTA after full implementation from the latter to calculate the preference margin. 'Excluded' denotes that a good is not being liberalised it is left for renegotiation or it continues to be restricted with a tariff-rate quota.

## E. Results

The results are shown in Table 8.1. Recall that a positive coefficient on VIIT and HIIT indicates that these two trade types have received a greater preference margin, that is, liberalisation is relatively deeper than for the referent category of endowment-based trade, even after controlling for a greater volume of trade and the import-competing character of the good. This prediction is borne out. The coefficients on both dummy variables are positive and significant.

The substantive effects are considerable. To illustrate, according to model 1, if a good in a particular tariff category was VIIT rather than endowment-based trade, then the tariff preference obtained would be about one-fifth greater and, for HIIT, about one-third greater. In this particular sample, VIIT is more common than HIIT, so the liberalisation of VIIT is substantively much more important. However, the relatively greater tariff preference negotiated for HIIT does not clearly indicate that VIIT is more difficult to liberalise; it may simply reflect that tariffs on HIIT were already lower before the respective PTAs were signed. The two control variables ImportCompetition and Exports have the expected sign

Table 8.1 *Regression results*

| Independent variable | Preference margin | Excluded category |
|---|---|---|
| HIIT | 2.915** | −0.782** |
| | (0.623) | (0.272) |
| VIIT | 2.000** | −0.387** |
| | (0.530) | (0.141) |
| *ImportCompetition* | −16.553** | −0.932 |
| | (3.720) | (0.481) |
| *lnExports* | −0.513* | 0.119* |
| | (0.230) | (0.049) |
| *Constant* | 16.792** | −4.645** |
| | (3.004) | (0.379) |
| Observations | 15 569 | 18 865 |
| Clusters | 9 | 10 |

*Note:* Robust standard errors clustered by PTA in parentheses. (1) is a tobit estimator; (2) a logit estimator. Standard errors are clustered over the PTA.
* significant at 5 per cent
** significant at 1 per cent

Table 8.2 *Conditional marginal effects (Tobit model)*

| | $dy/dx$ | SE | [95% CI] | |
|---|---|---|---|---|
| HIIT | 1.217 | 0.289 | 0.652 | 1.783 |
| VIIT | 0.763 | 0.325 | 0.127 | 1.400 |
| *LnExports* | −0.178 | 0.100 | −0.374 | 0.017 |
| *ImportCompetition* | −8.571 | 1.877 | −12.250 | −4.892 |

and are statistically significant in model 1. Marginal effects of the expected value of *PreferenceMargin* are shown in Table 8.2.

   Column 2 shows the estimated coefficients for the logit model that tests whether VIIT and HIIT are more or less likely to be excluded from liberalisation than endowment-based trade is. The results in column 2 indicate that goods that belong to the endowment-based trade category are indeed more likely to be excluded than either VIIT or HIIT is. To offer a sense of the substantive contribution, we can calculate the 'relative risk contribution'. To do so, we divide the estimated probability of exclusion when the respective intra-industry dummy is zero by the estimated

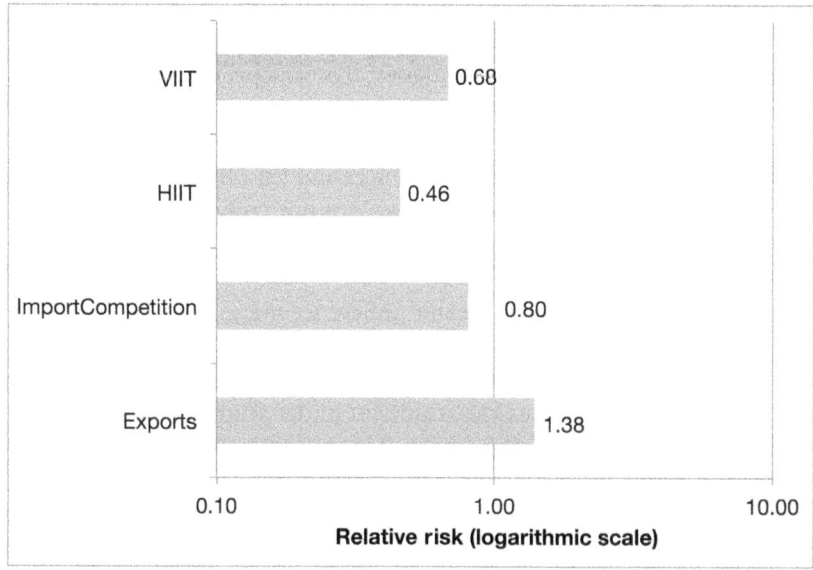

Figure 8.3  Contribution to relative risk of exclusion (model 2)

probability when it is equal to one and divide the probability when a continuous variable is at its mean by the probability at its mean plus one standard deviation. Compared to the baseline category of interindustry trade, VIIT is only 0.68 times as likely and HIIT 0.46 times as likely to be excluded.

This again suggests that intra-industry trade of either type is easier to liberalise than endowment-based trade. Exclusions are 'costly' because they completely prevent market access gains for a particular group of exporters in the partner country and will generally be negotiated only when protectionist forces are strong and well organised. Figure 8.3 shows the point predictions of this relative risk contribution.

In model 2, *LnExports* is correctly signed and statistically significant, but the variable *ImportCompetition* fails to reach significance. It is possible that this reflects 'complete protection' so that there are next to no imports in the product category, and the effect cannot be estimated.

## F. Conclusion

At least as far as this sample of PTAs is concerned, the statistical results suggest that intra-industry trade is associated with more liberalisation and a greater preference margin over the MFN tariff. Conversely, endowment-based trade is much more likely to be excluded completely from any tariff reductions. These findings suggest that irrespective of the electoral system, intra-industry trade necessitates relatively less adjustment. There is a slight difference between HIIT and VIIT, with the former being most likely to receive generous tariff preferences and least likely to be excluded from liberalisation, but these estimates are not truly comparable since VIIT makes up a much greater share of the bilateral trade among the countries studied here.

Importantly, however, the greater preference margin is conditional on the extent to which an industry is import competing. Substantively, this is by far the strongest effect in the first model. Irrespective of the different natural endowments of the countries under study here, whether an industry is competitive matters most. It is entirely possible that an industry trading differentiated goods – for example, the French and Japanese motor vehicle industries – can have very lopsided trade balances. Although such trade might strictly speaking be intra-industry, underlying it is either a failure in marketing a product to consumers (few Japanese consumers purchase French cars, despite the popularity of other European vehicles in Japan) or considerable differences in the productivity of the firms involved.

With relatively lower productivity as the likely reason why some firms find themselves competing with imports, future research efforts should tackle the implications head-on. Collecting systematic data on lobbying efforts will be challenging, when the cost calculations of firms themselves are dependent on data that are not easily accessible. A focus on PTAs, however, could prove useful for such studies, since the (usually) bilateral nature of the agreements allows researchers to isolate the specific effects of the determinants of trade and their link to outcomes via the political economy of trade liberalisation bargains.

### References

Abd-el-Rahman, Kamal. 1991. 'Firms' Competitive and National Comparative Advantages as Joint Determinants of Trade Composition.' *Weltwirtschaftliches Archiv* 127 (1): 83–97.

Achen, Christopher H. 2002. 'Toward a New Political Methodology: Microfoundations and ART.' *Annual Review of Political Science* 5 (1): 423–50.

Aquino, Antonio. 1978. 'Intra-Industry Trade and Inter-Industry Specialization as Concurrent Sources of International Trade in Manufactures.' *Weltwirtschaftliches Archiv* 114 (2): 275–96.

Balassa, Bela. 1966. 'Tariff Reductions and Trade in Manufacturers among the Industrial Countries.' *American Economic Review* 56 (3): 466–73.

Brenton, Paul A., and Winters, L. Alan. 1992. 'Estimating the International Trade Effects of "1992": West Germany.' *Journal of Common Market Studies* 30 (2): 143–56.

Cameron, Maxwell A., and Tomlin, Brian W. 2000. *The Making of NAFTA: How the Deal Was Done*. Ithaca, NY: Cornell University Press.

Carey, John M., and Shugart, Matthew S. 1995. 'Incentives to Cultivate a Personal Vote: A Rank Ordering of Electoral Formulas.' *Electoral Studies* 14 (4): 417–39.

Chase, Kerry A. 2003. 'Economic Interests and Regional Trading Arrangements: The Case of NAFTA.' *International Organization* 57 (1): 137–74.

2005. *Trading Blocs: States, Firms, and Regions in the World Economy*. Ann Arbor: University of Michigan Press.

Cooper, Douglas, Greenaway, David, and Rayner, Anthony J. 1993. 'Intra-Industry Trade and Limited Producer Horizons: An Empirical Investigation.' *Review of World Economics* 129 (2): 345–66.

Egger, Hartmut, Egger, Peter, and Greenaway, David. 2008. 'The Trade Structure Effects of Endogenous Regional Trade Agreements.' *Journal of International Economics* 74 (2): 278–98.

Feenstra, Robert C. 2004. *Advanced International Trade: Theory and Evidence*. Princeton, NJ: Princeton University Press.

Flam, Harry, and Helpman, Elhanan. 1987. 'Vertical Product Differentiation and North–South Trade.' *American Economic Review* 77 (5): 810–22.

Fontagné, Lionel, and Freudenberg, Michael. 1997. 'Intra-Industry Trade: Methodological Issues Reconsidered.' CEPII Working Paper No. 1997-01. Centre d'Etudes Prospectives et d'Informations Internationales, Paris.

Fontagné, Lionel, Freudenberg, Michael, and Gaulier, Guillaume. 2006. 'A Systematic Decomposition of World Trade into Horizontal and Vertical IIT.' *Review of World Economics* 142 (3): 459–75.

Foster, Neil, and Stehrer, Robert. 2011. 'Preferential Trade Agreements and the Structure of International Trade.' *Review of World Economics* 147 (3): 385–409.

Fukao, Kyoji, Ishido, Hikari, and Ito, Keiko. 2003. 'Vertical Intra-Industry Trade and Foreign Direct Investment in East Asia.' RIETI Discussion Paper Series 03-E-001. Research Institute of the Ministry of Economy, Trade and Industry, Tokyo.

Gawande, Kishore, and Bandyopadhyay, Usree. 2000. 'Is Protection for Sale? Evidence on the Grossman–Helpman Theory of Endogenous Protection.' *Review of Economics and Statistics* 82 (1): 139–52.

Gawande, Kishore, and Hoekman, Bernard. 2006. 'Lobbying and Agricultural Trade Policy in the United States.' *International Organization* 60 (3): 527–61.

Gawande, Kishore, Krishna, Pravin, and Olarreaga, Marcelo. 2012. 'Lobbying Competition over Trade Policy.' *International Economic Review* 53 (1): 115–32.

Gilligan, Michael J. 1997. 'Lobbying as a Private Good with Intra-Industry Trade.' *International Studies Quarterly* 41 (3): 455–74.

Greenaway, David, Hine, Robert, and Milner, Chris. 1994. 'Country-Specific Factors and the Pattern of Horizontal and Vertical Intra-Industry Trade in the UK.' *Weltwirtschaftliches Archiv* 130 (1): 77–100.

Grossman, Gene M., and Helpman, Elhanan. 1994. 'Protection for Sale.' *American Economic Review* 84 (4): 833–50.

Grubel, Herbert G., and Lloyd, P. J. 1971. 'The Empirical Measurement of Intra-Industry Trade.' *Economic Record* 47 (4): 494–517.

Hankla, Charles R. 2006. 'Party Strength and International Trade: A Cross-National Analysis.' *Comparative Political Studies* 39 (9): 1133–56.

Helpman, Elhanan. 1981. 'International Trade in the Presence of Product Differentiation, Economies of Scale and Monopolistic Competition: A Chamberlin-Heckscher-Ohlin Approach.' *Journal of International Economics* 11 (3): 305–40.

Kee, Looi Hiau, Nicita, Alessandro, and Olarreaga, Marcelo. 2009. 'Estimating Trade Restrictiveness Indices.' *Economic Journal* 119 (534): 172–99.

Kimura, Fukunari, and Ando, Mitsuyo. 2005. 'Two-Dimensional Fragmentation in East Asia: Conceptual Framework and Empirics.' *International Review of Economics and Finance* 14 (3): 317–48.

Kono, Daniel Y. 2009. 'Market Structure, Electoral Institutions, and Trade Policy.' *International Studies Quarterly* 53 (4): 885–906.

Krugman, Paul R. 1979. 'Increasing Returns, Monopolistic Competition, and International Trade.' *Journal of International Economics* 9 (4): 469–79.

——— 1980. 'Scale Economies, Product Differentiation, and the Pattern of Trade.' *American Economic Review* 70 (5): 950–9.

——— 1981. 'Intraindustry Specialization and the Gains from Trade.' *Journal of Political Economy* 89 (5): 959–73.

Manger, Mark S. 2009. *Investing in Protection: The Politics of Preferential Trade Agreements between North and South*. Cambridge: Cambridge University Press.

——— 2012. 'Vertical Trade Specialization and the Formation of North–South PTAs.' *World Politics* 64 (4). 622–658.

Melitz, Marc J. 2003. 'The Impact of Trade on Intra-Industry Reallocations and Aggregate Industry Productivity.' *Econometrica* 71 (6): 1695–725.

Milner, Helen V. 1997. 'Industries, Governments, and the Creation of Regional Trade Blocs.' In *The Political Economy of Regionalism*, edited by Edward D. Mansfield and Helen V. Milner, 77–106. New York: Columbia University Press.

Nielson, Daniel L. 2003. 'Supplying Trade Reform: Political Institutions and Liberalization in Middle-Income Presidential Democracies.' *American Journal of Political Science* 47 (3): 470–91.

Nishitateno, Shuhei. 2013. 'Global Production Sharing and the FDI–Trade Nexus: New Evidence from the Japanese Automobile Industry.' *Journal of the Japanese and International Economies* 27 (1): 64–80.

Pekkanen, Saadia M., Solís, Mireya, and Katada, Saori N. 2007. 'Trading Gains for Control: International Trade Forums and Japanese Economic Diplomacy.' *International Studies Quarterly* 54 (4):945–70.

Pelc, Krzysztof J. 2011. 'How States Ration Flexibility: Tariffs, Remedies, and Exchange Rates as Policy Substitutes.' *World Politics* 63 (4): 618–46.

Plouffe, Michael. 2013. 'The New Political Economy of Trade: Heterogeneous Firms and Trade Policy.' Working Paper. University College London, London.

Ravenhill, John. 2010. 'The "New East Asian Regionalism": A Political Domino Effect.' *Review of International Political Economy* 17 (2): 178–208.

Rogowski, Ronald. 1987. 'Political Cleavages and Changing Exposure to Trade.' *American Political Science Review* 81 (4): 1121–37.

Rosendorff, B. Peter, and Milner, Helen V. 2001. 'The Optimal Design of International Trade Institutions: Uncertainty and Escape.' *International Organization* 55 (4): 829–57.

Schrodt, Philip A. 2014. 'Seven Deadly Sins of Contemporary Quantitative Political Analysis.' *Journal of Peace Research* 51 (2): 287–300.

Shadlen, Kenneth C. 2005. 'Exchanging Development for Market Access? Deep Integration and Industrial Policy under Multilateral and Regional-Bilateral Trade Agreements.' *Review of International Political Economy* 12 (5): 750–75.

Tirole, Jean. 1988. *The Theory of Industrial Organization.* Cambridge, MA: MIT Press.

Trefler, Daniel. 1993. 'Trade Liberalization and the Theory of Endogenous Protection: An Econometric Study of U.S. Import Policy.' *Journal of Political Economy* 101 (1): 138–60.

# 9

## Audiovisual goods and services in preferential trade agreements

KERRY A. CHASE

### A. Introduction

Preferential trade agreements (Ptas) govern a wide range of commercial issues. Few receive so much attention, relative to their commercial value, or generate so much friction as audiovisual media. In a few instances, audiovisual trade has become highly politicised – especially when the United States has forced the issue. An exception for Canada's 'cultural industries' was a major sticking point in the North American Free Trade Agreement (NAFTA). The relaxation of South Korea's screen quota at cinemas, a precondition for trade talks with the United States, incited protest rallies by movie industry professionals. Australian concessions on broadcasting policy sparked a similar, if less riotous, hue and cry over a US trade pact. In the summer of 2013, a ruckus over audiovisuals held up the launch of trade talks between the United States and the European Union (EU).

Many of these stories have been well publicised. The audiovisual sector – film, video, broadcast media and sound recordings – has long been an intractable issue at the multilateral level. PTA negotiations sometimes rekindle these controversies (Choi 2008; Roy 2009). Not many sectors are singled out for special status in PTAs with any regularity. Audiovisuals are one such area, and a high-profile one at that. Several PTAs, however, have achieved advances over commitments in the World Trade Organization (WTO) for audiovisual media, often with little fanfare. Recent research documents improvements over the WTO in PTAs, notably in services

Thanks to Manfred Elsig and Andreas Dür for their comments. I also thank Catherine Worsnop for research assistance and Margarita Corral for Spanish translation. The Theodore and Jane Norman Fund at Brandeis University provided research funding. All errors are my own.

(Fink and Jansen 2009; Marchetti and Roy 2009; Miroudot, Sauvage and Sudreau 2010; Roy, Marchetti and Lim 2008). Audiovisual media are a prominent example where deadlock in the WTO has displaced the action to the bilateral and regional levels. The upshot is that audiovisuals gain markedly varied treatment in PTAs. Some PTAs contain far-reaching guarantees; others carve audiovisuals out of trade obligations entirely; and the majority of cases fall somewhere in between.

This chapter takes a close look at the audiovisual sector and its treatment in PTAs. PTAs, I will explain, are differentiated primarily in their rules for audiovisuals as services, though audiovisual media can be traded as goods as well. Yet little is known about how and why PTA design varies, in audiovisuals specifically or across services generally. Surveys such as Mattoo and Sauvé (2011) detail the rules and modalities of services PTAs separate from actual commitments, whereas other studies, including those cited earlier, take up services commitments qualitatively. My analysis presents one of the first quantitative assessments of PTA design in a service sector. Using a data set of 116 services PTAs, I construct an index of audiovisual services commitments contracted by 360 signatories.

The first part of the study is descriptive – this part explores the pattern of PTA commitments in the audiovisual sector. I find that countries make greater commitments when they have scheduled audiovisual services in the WTO, when the PTA is oriented to deep integration, when the PTA uses a negative-list format for services and when the United States is a party. Fewer commitments result from positive-list modalities, PTAs between developing and developed countries and PTAs involving Canada or the EU, which exclude audiovisual services.

The second part of the study is more conceptual – this part seeks to account for variation in services commitments across countries and their trade partners. Although the literature on trade protection is extensive, only lately have services attracted much scrutiny (see Francois and Hoekman 2010; Hoekman 2006; Hoekman and Primo Braga 1997). The determinants of services trade policies therefore remain an important unanswered puzzle. My analysis of audiovisual services in PTAs bears out three propositions. First, audiovisual services commitments are strongly related to a country's trade balance in the sector. Second, a few countries with an intense interest in improved access, especially the United States, have exploited bargaining leverage to extract assurances from PTA partners. Third, cultural ties appear to play a role in commitment coverage. In particular, the evidence uncovers a tendency for countries to offer the best commitments in PTAs with trade partners that are culturally close to them. Why culture matters in this way is a puzzle for future research. Section B contextualises trade in audiovisual media and reviews the array of terms and provisions for audiovisuals in PTAs. Section C evaluates some initial statistical models to illuminate the sources of variation in audiovisual services commitments. The last section considers implications for services generally in PTAs and for audiovisuals in the WTO.

## B. The treatment of audiovisual media in PTAs

Audiovisual media can be traded as goods and as services. Film prints, videotapes and audio and video discs cross borders packaged in the form of goods, while movie exhibition, television transmission and the rental or sale of videos and sound recordings are services delivered to consumers. Traditionally, the supply of a service across borders required the movement of a physical good: the distribution of imported film prints to cinemas, videotapes to television stations and records, tapes and discs to retailers. However, technological advances have made the delivery of services electronically via the Internet, satellite and cable practicable – not to mention increasingly lucrative. These advances give distributors of audiovisual media multiple delivery platforms to exploit while offering consumers myriad ways to access content of their choice, at the touch of a button, at home and on the go. Accordingly, production, consumer spending and trade – in packaged audiovisual goods and even more in electronically delivered services – have all grown briskly of late.

Trade in goods is scrupulously recorded at customs, whereas figures on trade in services remain patchy. The United Nations (United Nations 2010) reports world trade in audiovisual goods of US$59.9 billion in 2008, 2.5 times higher than the US$24.2 billion in world trade in audiovisual services. These numbers are deceptive, however. The services figure counts cross-border supply, but not sales by foreign affiliates, and no data are available for more than one hundred countries that together comprise a quarter of the global economy. The goods figure, furthermore, includes all kinds of unrecorded media that carry no images or sound.[1]

---

[1] Harmonized System (HS) code 8523 covers cards, tapes, discs, records and other media for use in electrical and electronic accessories, so the data combine audio and video (such as movie DVDs and music CDs) with blank discs, cassettes, tapes, smart cards and myriad storage devices.

Trade data from the United States, the leading exporter of entertainment, provide a fuller picture of how audiovisual media are traded. In 2011, foreign receipts for the distribution of film, video and broadcasting services totalled US$15.3 billion compared to US$92 million in exports of film and video as goods; payments to overseas suppliers amounted to US$2.5 billion, while imports, mainly due to offshore production of US television programmes in Canada, totalled US$273 million. For audio recordings, services credits were US$1.5 billion and exports US$111 million; services debits were US$1.0 billion and imports US$191 million.[2] Although the groupings are not identical, the data point to two conclusions: first, audiovisual media are traded as services more than as goods and, second, this propensity is growing as digital delivery becomes faster and cheaper. Whereas movies and broadcast material have always been distributed as services foremost, a shift towards services delivery, at least to and from the United States, is evident in audio recordings and home video as a result of the ease and speed of digital download.

Because audiovisual media are traded both as goods and as services, they are handled in twofold and somewhat confusing ways in international trade agreements. In multilateral trade rules, the General Agreement on Tariffs and Trade (GATT) of 1947 allows states to regulate screen time at cinemas as an exception to national treatment under Article III, in effect displacing the supply of a service to trade rules for goods. Because this article is limited to 'cinematograph films', however, the GATT does not apply to newer platforms for delivering content, such as television broadcasting or streaming video over the Internet. Electronic media instead fall under the General Agreement on Trade in Services (GATS) of 1994. Other formats, for example, home video and sound recordings, can be subject to GATT or GATS, or both, depending on the method of delivery to the consumer. And though cinema exhibition is specially provided for in the GATT, motion picture projection is also included in the GATS but with no corresponding national treatment exception (Chase 2013).

---

[2] Data for goods were obtained from the US International Trade Commission's Interactive Tariff and Trade DataWeb at http://dataweb.usitc.gov. Product codes are HS 3706 for films and parts of HS 8523 for audio and video. Data for services are from the US Bureau of Economic Analysis, US International Services, Table 4 – Royalties and License Fees at www.bea.gov/international/international_services.htm. Services categories are 'film and television tape distribution' and 'broadcasting and recording of live events' for film, video and broadcasting; for audio recordings, the category is 'books, records, and tapes' (which includes audiobooks).

PTAs, in contrast, attend to audiovisuals almost entirely as services – with one anomaly, Canadian PTAs, described later. PTAs, generally speaking, come in two forms: some cover goods only; others include services together with provisions for goods.[3] The universe of PTAs therefore consists of goods-only and goods-services agreements. To investigate the treatment of audiovisual media in PTAs, I surveyed 251 PTAs notified to the WTO and in force at year-end 2013.[4] Of the total, 134 (53 per cent) are goods-only agreements and 117 (47 per cent) are goods-services agreements. In all, 209 countries and territories, counting EU members individually, are a party to at least one PTA. An electronic text search of every agreement, including annexes and side letters, uncovered entries with root words related to audiovisual media. Provisions applicable to the audiovisual sector were extracted and categorised.

Goods-only PTAs rarely single out audiovisual media for special treatment. Audiovisual goods are usually treated like any other merchandise in these agreements, subject to market-opening commitments and national treatment. These product lines routinely appear in negotiated tariff schedules, which specify the time span for tariff reduction for PTA participants. There is nothing unusual about origin requirements. There is no case of a PTA preferentially liberalising quantitative restrictions for audiovisual goods.

The one irregularity in goods-only PTAs is Canada. Canada's PTAs include an exception for 'cultural industries', which covers not only the audiovisual sector but also books, magazines, periodicals, newspapers and sheet music. A cultural industries exception is present in all 10 PTAs that Canada has signed, 4 of them goods-only and 6 goods-services. Under this clause, the cultural industries remain subject to commitments on tariff elimination, but they are exempt from the other terms of the PTA. By design, the cultural industries exception applies mutually to Canada's trade partners,[5] several of which have contracted commitments

---

[3] In GAT3 terminology, PTAs for services are 'economic integration agreements'. In some instances, services agreements were negotiated and put into effect after a goods agreement, with time lags ranging from a few months up to 42 years in the case of the European Free Trade Association (EFTA).

[4] The list is available on the WTO website at http://rtais.wto.org/UI/PublicAllRTAList.aspx. My inventory excludes the Global System of Trade Preferences among Developing Countries and accessions to existing agreements (such as the EU), which I do not count as separate PTAs.

[5] Except for NAFTA – the United States and Mexico exchanged commitments, as the cultural industries exception is for Canada only.

on audiovisual services in other PTAs. In Canada's first PTA, with the United States, the US government relented and accepted the cultural exception but countered by insisting on a clause reserving US rights to retaliate against Canadian policies towards the cultural industries with 'measures of equivalent commercial effect'.[6] Canada's other PTA partners have not attached any strings to the cultural industries exception.

Unlike Canada, the EU has not excluded audiovisual media, much less cultural industries more widely, in any of its 23 goods-only PTAs. This may seem surprising insofar as Canada and the EU led the charge for special status for audiovisuals in the Uruguay Round. Yet audiovisual exceptions are absent even in the EU's 17 goods-only PTAs initialled since 1996. In fact the different approaches of Canada and the EU accord with the position each has adopted in multilateral negotiations. In the GATS, Canada advocated a wholesale exclusion of the cultural industries, just as in the NAFTA, whereas the EU rejected this stand in favour of a sector annex to accommodate the 'cultural specificity' of audiovisual services. Over a longer time span, the EU has maintained, since the first GATT debates on trade in television programmes in the 1960s, that audiovisual media are services and should be treated accordingly (Chase 2013). In contrast, Canada's concerns have extended beyond broadcasting services to encompass traditional cultural goods such as publications and recorded music as well (Acheson and Maule 1999).

Although the EU has not excluded audiovisual media in goods-only PTAs, its seven services PTAs exempt the audiovisual sector from the services provisions of these accords. As inscribed, the rules for services apply to 'all service sectors with the exception of' audiovisual services and a handful of other activities, shielding audiovisual media from PTA obligations.[7] This exception in the core services provisions of these PTAs resembles the sort of exclusion that the EU opposed in the GATS. However, the Stabilization and Association Agreements between the EU and candidate countries for future EU accession do not exclude audiovisual services. These four PTAs instead stipulate that PTA partners must harmonise their legislation with EU law and align content requirements in broadcasting with EU policy.

---

[6] Article 2005, Canada–US Free Trade Agreement; this clause governs US–Canada interactions under NAFTA.

[7] In these clauses, audiovisual services keep unusual company: also excluded are nuclear materials, arms and munitions, maritime and air transport, computer reservation systems and, in one instance, toxic wastes.

In the EU's services PTAs after 2008, the audiovisual exclusion coexists with a 'Protocol on Cultural Cooperation'. The EU launched this initiative in its PTA with the Caribbean Forum (CARIFORUM), and it has continued the approach since then (the recent EU–Singapore PTA, however, does not presently include a cultural protocol). Building from earlier EU agreements, which call for cultural cooperation in general terms, this design affirms the Convention on the Diversity of Cultural Expressions, adopted in 2005 by the United Nations Educational, Scientific and Cultural Organization (UNESCO).[8] In effect the protocols are nonbinding pledges to pursue various cooperative endeavours, including cultural exchanges and dialogue (such as professional contacts between artists, creators and other cultural professionals); co-production and other collaborations, within the parameters of existing laws, in audiovisuals, the performing arts and publishing; and joint efforts to protect historic monuments and heritage sites. In this manner, the EU undertakes to encourage and facilitate cultural interchange while maintaining full discretion over audiovisual regulation – in line with its multilateral strategy of championing the UNESCO Convention while neither requesting nor offering commitments on audiovisuals in the WTO.

Cultural cooperation crops up sporadically in PTAs not involving the EU. Three African PTAs for goods – the Economic Community of West African States, the Common Market for Eastern and Southern Africa and the Economic and Monetary Community of Central Africa – call for closer cooperation in radio and television (the third one also cinema). A few PTAs take language straight from EU agreements (the Chile–China PTA, for example, encourages 'co-production, training, development and distribution activities') or incorporate soft-law provisions for training visits, information sharing, joint events and personnel exchanges in the audiovisual sector. Occasionally the terms are more robust if still nonbinding. A 'Framework for Media Cooperation' annexed to the India–Singapore PTA extends dialogue beyond the private sector to the 'exchange of views between regulatory authorities'.[9] A handful of PTAs – South Korean agreements with Singapore, India and Peru and the

---

[8] The UNESCO Convention promotes cooperation and dialogue on cultural matters while safeguarding the rights of states to act as they see fit to protect and promote cultural diversity within their territory (United Nations Educational, Scientific and Cultural Organization 2005).

[9] Annex 14A, Framework for Media Cooperation, India–Singapore PTA.

New Zealand–Taiwan accord – outline terms and procedures for film and television co-productions. In total, about three dozen PTAs, more than half involving the EU, include cultural cooperation clauses in some form. Whereas several PTAs emulate the EU on cultural cooperation, not one other services PTA has followed the EU lead by excluding audiovisual media from trade rules for services. In PTAs to date, the only other example of note where the core text conceivably affords some flexibility to employ otherwise prohibited measures in the audiovisual sector is a 'soft' cultural exception in New Zealand's PTAs. This clause permits regulations 'necessary to protect national works, items or specific sites of historical or archaeological value, or to support creative arts of national value'.[10] An illustrative list of 'creative arts' specifies 'film and video', 'digital interactive media' and 'creative online content'. Modelled on GATT Article XX, this exception adds the proviso that regulatory interventions must not create 'arbitrary or unjustifiable discrimination' or function as 'a disguised restriction on trade'. In five PTAs, the exception applies to goods and services alike; three others restrict its scope to services. It is difficult to judge from the wording what actions this clause permits or how its requirements might be interpreted in dispute settlement. New Zealand, in any case, has made some of the most liberal audiovisual services commitments in PTAs.

The omission of audiovisual-sector exclusions and cultural industries exceptions in PTAs not involving the EU or Canada does not mean that these other arrangements have lifted trade barriers. To the contrary, several countries have been as hesitant to open up audiovisual services in PTAs as they are in the WTO. But where the EU and Canada exclude audiovisuals in the core text, others have qualified their promises, or declined to extend any, in the fine print – the annexes, where services commitments are documented. Evaluating the coverage and content of these commitments therefore requires a close analysis of service-sector annexes in PTAs.

*I. Audiovisual Services Commitments in PTAs*

Services PTAs follow one of two approaches. One format is a positive-list approach. Under the positive-list format, states opt in to services commitments on a sector-by-sector basis. In this approach, annexes to

---

[10] This wording is from Chapter 19, Transpacific Strategic Economic Partnership. One of New Zealand's eight PTAs, with Australia, does not specify 'creative arts' in the exceptions.

the services chapter list each participant's scheduled commitments; a party makes no guarantees in any sector that is not listed in its schedule or that is listed as 'unbound'. Participants have further leeway to qualify their commitments by inscribing limitations in their schedules for restrictive and discriminatory measures that they intend to maintain. The GATS exemplifies the positive-list approach. Many PTAs follow the GATS model for listing services commitments.

A second format is a negative-list agreement. Under the negative-list format, states must opt out of obligations by notifying specific noncompliant policies in a sector; otherwise, they are held to the services chapter's terms. In practice, nonconforming measures are itemised in two PTA annexes, one for regulations already in force and the other for potential future measures.[11] Through the process of cataloguing nonconforming measures, the parties essentially set an upper limit, or bound maximum, on present and future trade restrictions, except for situations where a state reserves its rights to adopt any measures in a sector. NAFTA, signed in 1992, is the oldest negative-list agreement, and several PTAs use a similar format.

The two approaches to services PTAs – positive-list and negative-list – differ both in form and in effect. In the positive-list format, no commitment exists unless a state positively consents to be bound in a sector. Governments may keep existing trade measures, and preserve leeway for future ones, by declining to list a service in their schedule or by listing a service as unbound. All of the EU's PTAs are positive-list, and the EU could have left audiovisual services off its schedule to shelter the broadcasting regulations it is keen to preserve. In the negative-list format, nonconforming measures must be eliminated unless they have been notified or rights to regulate in the sector have been reserved. Canada could have reserved all rights in its negative-list PTAs to regulate cultural services (though additional reservations would have been needed for cultural goods). Several governments have chosen these routes not taken by the EU or Canada to retain a free hand in audiovisual services. They achieved this not by way of exclusions in the PTA core text but through scheduling in the annexes.

This section analyses scheduled commitments in audiovisual services in PTAs. For this analysis, I have coded commitments in 116 services

---

[11] Usually, the annexes apply to two sections of the PTA, a chapter on services and a corresponding chapter on investment. Sometimes there are additional annexes for added transparency.

PTAs involving 73 countries and territories (counting EU members individually).[12] The unit of analysis is not a PTA; it is a PTA signatory. More than two-thirds of PTAs involve 2 parties; others involve more than 2 all the way up to 16 parties in the EU–CARIFORUM PTA. In this set-up, 'signatory' or 'party' is every participant with its own commitment schedule (positive-list) or nonconforming measures list (negative-list). Thus, the EU is counted as one because its members negotiate a single list. In PTAs involving other regional groupings, namely, the Association of Southeast Asian Nations (ASEAN), CARIFORUM, European Free Trade Association (EFTA), Gulf Cooperation Council (GCC) and the Southern Common Market (MERCOSUR), every member contracts its own list, so each is counted once. The number of signatories in 116 services PTAs adds up to 360 observations. No annex could be located in 17 cases, leaving a final total of 343.

In the WTO, service sectors are defined by Central Product Classification (CPC) code (World Trade Organization 2010). Audiovisual services are composed of five sectors:

CPC 9611   Motion picture and video tape production and distribution services
CPC 9612   Motion picture projection service
CPC 9613   Radio and television services
CPC 7524   Radio and television transmission services
No CPC     Sound recording

Commitments are coded by subsector (five-digit CPC), counting sound recording as one sector and subsector; I omit two subsectors, CPC 96111 (promotion or advertising services) and CPC 96133 (combined programme making and broadcasting services), which are hardly ever listed

---

[12] The universe is the 117 services PTAs referenced earlier plus 2 services PTAs presently in force but not notified to the WTO (Chile–MERCOSUR; Singapore–Gulf Cooperation Council) and 7 services PTAs signed and published but awaiting ratification (Canada–Honduras, Costa Rica–Colombia, EFTA–Gulf Cooperation Council, EFTA–Costa Rica and Panama, EU–Singapore, Switzerland–China and Iceland–China). From this list of 126 services PTAs, I exclude the EC Treaty (which did not cover audiovisuals), plus the EU's four Stabilization and Association Agreements and the European Economic Area (which simply require EU trade partners to align audiovisual policies with EU law). Mexico's PTAs with Central American countries are listed in the WTO database as five bilateral agreements, but in fact they were consolidated into one in 2011, bringing the total number of services PTAs to 116. Of this total, no services annexes could be located for 3 PTAs (Dominican Republic–Central America, EFTA–Mexico and Mexico–Uruguay), so the number of PTAs coded is 113.

in positive-list PTAs or referenced in negative-list PTAs. This leaves two subsectors per sector, plus sound recording, yielding nine subsectors in audiovisual services.

The principal obligations in services agreements are to grant market access and observe national treatment. Most PTAs, especially those signed in the past decade, define market access by reference to GATS Article XVI, which specifies six prohibited classes of measures (primarily quantitative restrictions). National treatment, which prohibits discrimination between foreign and domestic suppliers of the same service, is also generally understood in the context of the GATS, though Article XVII does not identify specific measures. For all 343 country-PTA cases, I code market access and national treatment commitments in all nine audiovisual services subsectors.[13]

Internationally traded services can be delivered from one market to another in different ways. The GATS framework distinguishes four modes of supply: cross-border supply (mode 1); consumption abroad (mode 2); commercial presence (mode 3); and presence of natural persons (mode 4).[14] In line with earlier studies of services commitments in trade agreements, I code commitments in mode 1 and mode 3 only. According to Magdeleine and Maurer (2008), 80–90 per cent of all world services trade falls into these two categories, and cross-border supply and local presence are the dominant modes of delivering audiovisual services. Coding market access and national treatment at mode 1 and mode 3 across nine subsectors produces 36 commitments (2 × 2 × 9) in audiovisual services for each PTA signatory.

My coding method follows past research on services commitments (Egger and Lanz 2008; Harms, Mattoo and Schuknecht 2003; Hoekman 1996; Marchetti and Roy 2009; Roy, Marchetti and Lim 2008). For each subsector, obligation and mode of supply, a signatory may commit fully, partially or not at all. Standard practice is to code no commitment as zero and full commitment as one. No commitment means that a government

---

[13] Negative-list PTAs establish a set of auxiliary obligations for services and investment. The most common are to eliminate performance requirements, restrictions on local presence and limitations on senior management and boards of directors. These obligations essentially represent supplements to or elaborations of the general principles of market access and national treatment.

[14] In mode 1, cross-border supply, the supplier and the buyer remain in separate countries; in mode 2, consumption abroad, the buyer travels to the supplier's country to consume the service; in mode 3, commercial presence, the supplier establishes a business enterprise in the buyer's country to deliver the service; and in mode 4, presence of natural persons, the supplier travels to the buyer's country to deliver the service.

Table 9.1 *Partial commitments for audiovisual services in PTAs*

| Type of measure | Coded value |
| --- | --- |
| 1. Quantitative restrictions | 0.25 |
| Import quotas | |
| Screen quotas | |
| Transmission quotas | |
| Local content requirements | |
| 2a. Restrictions on foreign capital participation | 0.50 |
| Foreign equity limitations | |
| 2b. Licensing, qualification, and other entry restrictions | 0.50 |
| Nationality requirements | |
| Residency requirements | |
| Commercial presence required for cross-border supply | |
| 3. Other limitations and requirements | 0.75 |
| Dubbing or subtitling requirements | |
| Transmission in the local language required | |
| Minimum expenditure requirements on local productions | |
| Discriminatory taxes on royalties | |
| Discriminatory fees on distribution revenues | |
| Imports subject to administrative approval | |
| Local participation (joint venture) requirements | |
| Requirements on the form of legal entity | |

retains full discretion to employ measures that contravene the obligation in question; full commitment means that it is obliged to guarantee open access and nondiscrimination. Coding depends in part on negotiating modalities. In a positive-list format, every entry is zero (no commitment) unless the sector is listed and it is not 'unbound' for that obligation and mode of supply. In a negative-list format, every entry is one (full commitment) unless a nonconforming measure for that sector is on file or the party reserves its rights in whole or in part.[15]

The coding of partial commitments is more complicated. Table 9.1 categorises three sets of limitations for audiovisual services contained in

---

[15] A handful of negative-list PTAs are hybrids in which market access is subject to positive listing in a clause that reserves a party's right to restrict access in any service except those named. In that case, market access is zero (no commitment) unless the sector is catalogued in the list or a partial commitment is contracted in another entry. In the few instances in which market access is listed positively and national treatment negatively, I reduce the coded value for national treatment by half if market access is not committed for that sector and mode of supply.

PTA annexes.[16] The first set is quantitative restrictions – quotas and other numerical limits, principally on foreign content. The second set consists of equity restrictions on foreign capital and various nonquantitative access restrictions. The third set is a catch-all for measures not included in the first two categories. Following the example of past research on services commitments, I order the groups according to severity, assigning 0.25 to the most restrictive (group 1), 0.5 to measures of intermediate restrictiveness (group 2) and 0.75 to the least restrictive (group 3). Some limitations are more trade distorting than others, and to an extent these groupings are judgement calls. The coding is intended as a first approximation of the extent and coverage of PTA commitments in audiovisual services.

The final product of these coding rules is an ordered scale that ranges from 0 if a party contracts no commitments at all to 36 if both market access and national treatment are fully committed for all nine subsectors and the two modes of supply. For simplicity, I divide by 36 to index the scale to 1. The index in essence reflects the proportion of sectors and modes of supply for which a country locks in guarantees. After presenting some descriptive characteristics, I use the index to probe the determinants of audiovisual services commitments in PTAs.

One noteworthy result is that PTA participants make no guarantees at all in 124 cases, 36 per cent of the time.[17] Canadian and EU PTAs, which shelter PTA partners from commitments because the exclusions apply in both directions, account for 45 of these 'no commitment' cases. Of the other 79 cases, 67 are positive-list PTAs with audiovisual services left off the services schedule; in the 12 remaining cases, a country reserved all rights in audiovisual services in a negative-list PTA. The majority of services PTAs are negative-list, so the positive-list modality appears much more likely to produce de facto exclusion. All told, positive-list PTAs return no commitments 53 per cent of the time, compared to 15 per cent of the time for negative-list PTAs.

Although countries have often avoided audiovisual services commitments, advances over GATS coverage have been achieved in PTAs. Audiovisual services remain a sensitive area for multilateral negotiations: only 32 of 159 WTO Members have listed any part of the sector in their

---

[16] In categorising measures by obligation and mode of supply, I use the guidelines in World Trade Organization, Council for Trade in Services (2001).
[17] In 12 such cases, the country had listed audiovisual services in the GATS, resulting in negative preferences.

GATS schedules.[18] Governments that committed audiovisual services in the GATS almost always do the same in PTAs – 91 per cent of the time. More remarkably, WTO Members whose GATS schedules omitted audiovisual services have undertaken commitments in PTAs 44 per cent of the time. Besides the EU and Canada, just five WTO Members with services PTAs have refused to tie their hands at all in audiovisual services: Norway (9 PTAs); Kuwait, Qatar and the United Arab Emirates (2 each); and Pakistan (1). All told, 38 WTO Members with no GATS listing for audiovisual services have contracted commitments in PTAs. Some, it is true, are unlikely to now change course in the WTO: 20 of the 38 only scheduled audiovisuals in PTAs joining nearby areas into a common market (MERCOSUR, the Caribbean Community and Common Market and the East African Community). In other cases, however, governments may be more inclined to entertain new GATS commitments, having signed on in PTAs – though some may continue to withhold audiovisual services to preserve bargaining currency in PTA talks.

New commitments in audiovisual services often share a common thread: they seem to be most prevalent when a PTA partner is intent on gaining improved access. Six countries – Hong Kong, Japan, Mexico, Singapore, Taiwan and the United States – submitted a collective request on audiovisual services to WTO Members in 2006, asking for bindings in motion picture and videotape production and distribution, motion picture projection and sound recording. Though the sponsors have made little headway in the Doha Round, PTAs provide an alternative means to these ends.[19] The United States, most of all, has used PTAs to extract new guarantees – not only in motion pictures, video and sound but also in broadcasting, which was not part of the collective request. Of the 38 WTO Members with audiovisual commitments in PTAs only, 9 have struck PTAs with the United States, whose only PTA partner to grant no guarantees in audiovisuals is Canada. Table 9.2 compares the commitments index in the PTAs of the sponsors of the collective request to their PTA partners' average GATS commitments for audiovisual services. Along with the United States, Mexico and Taiwan have gained improvements in PTAs, whereas Japan has bargained first-time commitments from the Philippines, Indonesia and Switzerland.

---

[18] GATS schedules are available on the WTO website at http://i-tip.wto.org/services.

[19] The sponsors later reported 'disappointment with the responses provided so far and the absence of ambition in most recipients' responses for this under-committed sector' (World Trade Organization, Council for Trade in Services 2007).

Table 9.2 *Improvements over GATS for audiovisual services in PTAs*

| Country | Number of PTA partners | Audiovisual services index for PTA partners | Audiovisual services index of PTA partners in GATS | Ratio of PTAs vs. GATS |
|---|---|---|---|---|
| United States | 19 | 0.725 | 0.168 | 4.31 |
| Mexico | 12 | 0.441 | 0.155 | 2.84 |
| Japan | 12 | 0.245 | 0.090 | 2.72 |
| Taiwan | 6 | 0.838 | 0.313 | 2.68 |
| Hong Kong | 6 | 0.321 | 0.161 | 1.99 |
| Singapore | 24 | 0.223 | 0.180 | 1.24 |

Regression analysis allows a more systematic examination of PTA commitments in audiovisual services. Leaving theoretical approaches for the next section, the model in Table 9.3 provides a general picture of negotiated commitments across PTAs.[20] One clear result is that GATS schedules, calculated the same way as for PTAs, are a strong predictor of PTA commitments. Countries have little reason to grant negative preferences – worse treatment than is already granted in the GATS – though it does sometimes happen (see Adlung and Morrison 2010). It is therefore logical that services commitments in PTAs track GATS commitments. Only NAFTA of all services PTAs preceded the WTO agreements,[21] making GATS schedules a natural starting point for negotiations. PTA type and negotiating modality matter too. PTAs to form a common market produce wider coverage on average, though a few states (Paraguay and Uruguay in MERCOSUR; Tanzania in the East African Community) tightly circumscribe their assurances. The negative-list format also yields guarantees over and above what was contracted in the GATS.

The identity of PTA participants is another factor. Because Canada and the EU exclude audiovisual services in their PTAs, neither offering nor

---

[20]  Because the commitments index is a proportion bounded at 0 and 1, all of the statistical analyses in this chapter are estimated in a generalized linear model using binomial family variance with a logistic link. The data set takes the form of an unbalanced panel in which several countries are observed in multiple PTAs. To correct for the nonindependence of country observations, I use a panel-data approach with signatory country as the panel variable and country-clustered standard errors. No time component is modelled.

[21]  The Australia New Zealand Closer Economic Relations Trade Agreement protocol on trade in services was signed and in force from 1988, but it did not cover market access. A protocol on investment, completed in 2013, extended services obligations and added new reservations.

Table 9.3 *Correlates of audiovisual services commitments in PTAs*

| Variable | Coefficient |
| --- | --- |
| GATS commitments | 3.713** |
| | (0.666) |
| Negative-list format | 1.724** |
| | (0.380) |
| Common market | 2.838** |
| | (0.380) |
| EU and Canada PTA partners | −1.987** |
| | (0.605) |
| US PTA partners | 1.780** |
| | (0.324) |
| Mexico PTA partners | −0.083 |
| | (0.381) |
| Japan PTA partners | 0.536 |
| | (0.354) |
| Taiwan PTA partners | 1.344 |
| | (0.690) |
| Hong Kong PTA partners | −0.100 |
| | (0.712) |
| Singapore PTA partners | −0.469* |
| | (0.233) |
| North–South PTAs | −0.688* |
| | (0.289) |
| Constant | −2.157** |
| | (0.243) |
| Wald chi-square | 239.33** |

*Note:* Standard errors, adjusted for clustering by country, are in parentheses. $N = 343$.
* $p < 0.05$
** $p < 0.01$

requesting any commitments, their PTA partners grant fewer guarantees. The United States, however, gets better audiovisual services commitments from its trade partners than the norm. None of the other five sponsors of the WTO collective request on audiovisual services fares so well; Singapore's PTAs actually yield fewer commitments from PTA partners. North–South PTAs, which comprise the majority of all PTAs, also produce lower commitment coverage. One interpretation is that developing countries dig in their heels in bargaining with developed countries. Although that could be so, it is also true that the EFTA states and Australia, in addition to the EU and Canada, generally have not pushed PTA partners on audiovisual services.

The purpose of this exercise is descriptive – to map the landscape of PTA commitments in audiovisual services. Causal inference is more demanding, and this first model is ill-suited for it. GATS schedules provide a baseline for PTAs, but the same factors that led governments to schedule audiovisual services in the first place condition their choices later. If audiovisuals are a sacred cow for the EU and Canada in all trade agreements, the deeper puzzle is to get at why these two powers and some like-minded countries resist all concessions in this area, while other governments are more flexible. Why states seeking improved access through PTAs manage to strike better deals with some trade partners than with others is another question in need of answers. The next section takes a first crack at a deeper conceptual understanding of the pattern of audiovisual services commitments in PTAs.

## C. Explaining variation in services commitments in the audiovisual sector

What accounts for the varied treatment of services in trade agreements? The literature on the structure of trade protection in manufactures is extensive. Applied trade restrictions in services are difficult to identify and harder still to quantify; as a result, the determinants of services trade policies have not gained enough attention. Trade agreements, however, represent a goldmine of information about bound trade measures.

Services encompass a heterogeneous group of activities, and sector-specific regulatory interventions represent the primary impediments to trade. If services are highly diverse to start with, audiovisual services are unlike many other services. For one thing, films, videos, broadcast material and sound recordings can be stored – inside a physical package or in digital memory – and moved to where consumers (or content providers) reside. This indefinite shelf-life and the capacity for repeated play permit cross-border trade that is inconceivable for services that require buyer and seller to meet in person. Moreover, though audiovisual media are, like most commodities, exchanged for their commercial value, they also represent an essential form of cultural expression, and in that sense they serve as carriers of cultural ideas, symbols and values. Because of this duality, the audiovisual sector poses unusual trade problems, and this has made common ground at the multilateral level unusually difficult to locate (Chase 2013).

In this section, I develop three main ideas and present preliminary statistical appraisals of each one, using the index, data set and modelling assumptions described previously. One idea is that services commitments may respond to trade flows – export dependence and import competition – in the same way as studies have found for trade protection in manufactures. Even if audiovisuals are carriers of culture, it stands to reason that export dependence and import competition are liable to condition a government's readiness to make binding commitments in the sector. A second idea is that cultural concerns may supersede commercial considerations in negotiations regarding audiovisual services. Culture receives short shrift in the study of political economy, yet the pervasiveness of cultural rationales in trade debates involving audiovisuals calls for theoretical assessment. A third idea is that politics should matter too, making outcomes dependent, to some extent, on how hard countries push trade partners for concessions and how much leverage they can bring to bear.

The first proposition is that countries that are net importers of audiovisual services have incentives to refuse commitments in this sector, whereas net-exporting countries have less to lose and more to gain from locking in guarantees. This conjecture is not novel; whether trade flows affect services commitments remains an unknown, however. One problem is that services trade data cover countries and sectors unevenly. For this analysis, I merged audiovisual services trade data from the WTO, the International Monetary Fund (IMF), the United Nations (UN), and the UN Conference on Trade and Development (UNCTAD).[22] To capture a country's trade orientation, I use the dollar value of net exports per capita – exports minus imports divided by population – averaged over the five years preceding the signing of a PTA.[23] Past research finds the highest import penetration where policy is most restrictive (Marvasti and Canterbery 2005), suggesting that regulatory interventions do not

[22] The data sets are Trade in Commercial Services (WTO), Balance of Payments Statistics (IMF), Statistics on International Trade in Services (UN) and Creative Services (UNCTAD). Governments are the original sources of these data, but the data sets are not identical: small differences exist in country-year coverage, and reported values occasionally disagree. However, the four data sets are correlated at 0.991 on average. To reduce potential errors, I average reported values across all the data sets.
[23] If fewer than five years of trade values were reported, I average over the available years.

shift a country to an export footing (at least in motion pictures, a major component of the sector).[24] Trade values are available for approximately 40 per cent of observations, skewing the sample towards developed countries, which are more likely to report services trade.

In this exercise, I also evaluate the third proposition – that negotiating leverage matters. To capture a country's power over PTA partners, I consider two possibilities. First, economic size could be a source of clout: large countries have more economic and political resources at their disposal than do small countries, and they can use these assets to extract concessions of value. Second, bilateral trade ties could provide leverage. Trade linkages between goods and services appear to be a common means of balancing concessions in PTAs to overcome domestic backlash (Fink and Jansen 2009; Roy *et al.* 2008). In that case, governments may be able to bargain concessions from PTA partners that rely on exports to their market. For economic size, I take the ratio of gross domestic products (GDPs) of PTA partners; for trade dependence, I use a country's gross exports to the PTA partner in dollars per person.[25] In each scenario, leverage will influence services commitments only insofar as a country bargains for concessions in that sector. Thus, I add an interaction term, the product of the leverage measure and a binary variable for PTA partners of the sponsors of the WTO collective request in audiovisual services.

Estimates appear in Table 9.4. Both models include audiovisual services net exports. The first model includes economic size, and the second uses trade dependence. In both models, net exports of audiovisual services are a major factor in commitments in the sector: net exporters show greater commitment coverage, suggesting that net importers are more resistant to issuing guarantees. The effects of bargaining leverage are less clear-cut. Larger countries, not smaller ones, make more

---

[24] In practice, using imports per capita makes little difference, except that the export-oriented United States becomes indistinguishable from less trade-involved economies. The only countries with audiovisual net exports greater than $1 per capita on average are the United States (US$35.0) and Hong Kong (US$15.5). Net exports are strongly correlated with GATS commitments in audiovisual services (0.660), so these models omit this latter variable.

[25] GDP and population data are from the World Bank's World Development Indicators database. Trade data are from the UN COMTRADE database. EU Members are aggregated into one. For PTAs with more than two parties, I take GDP relative to the largest (or next largest) PTA partner and exports to the PTA partner that receives the largest amount of a country's goods on the thinking that leverage is still exerted bilaterally in multiparty PTAs.

Table 9.4 *Trade flows and leverage in audiovisual services commitments*

| Variable | (1) | (2) |
|---|---|---|
| Audiovisual services net exports | 0.067** | 0.083** |
| | (0.023) | (0.028) |
| GDP relative to PTA partner | 0.002* | |
| | (0.001) | |
| Exports to PTA partner | | 0.002 |
| | | (0.002) |
| Negative-list format | 1.912** | 1.788** |
| | (0.626) | (0.548) |
| Common market | 2.312** | 2.133** |
| | (0.498) | (0.466) |
| EU and Canada PTA partners | −0.797 | −1.602 |
| | (1.114) | (1.199) |
| US PTA partners | 2.577** | 2.313** |
| | (0.935) | (0.709) |
| US PTA partners × relative GDP | −33.794** | |
| | (12.814) | |
| US PTA partners × exports to | | −0.004* |
| PTA partner | | (0.002) |
| North–South PTAs | −0.678 | −0.511 |
| | (0.774) | (0.727) |
| Constant | −1.383** | −1.287** |
| | (0.449) | (0.390) |
| Wald chi-square | 221.97** | 105.59** |

*Note:* Standard errors, adjusted for clustering by country, are in parentheses. $N = 131$.
* $p < 0.05$
** $p < 0.01$

commitments overall; so do countries exporting a lot to PTA partners, though this result is not statistically significant. The interaction terms are more revealing. In PTAs with the United States, smaller economies make bigger concessions in audiovisual services, in line with expectations. However, PTA partners dependent on the US market offer less generous treatment. On this count, it is notable that Canada held out despite sizeable trade dependence, whereas less trade-dependent countries such as Morocco and Jordan offered large improvements. Neither economic size nor export dependence appears to fully capture US leverage: the dummy variable for PTA partners of the United States is still statistically significant. As in the model in the last section, negative-list PTAs and common markets produce greater commitment coverage. Effects for PTA partners of the EU and Canada, and for North–South PTAs, remain negative but are no longer statistically significant.

These findings testify to the importance of a country's trading position in audiovisual services for its audiovisual-sector commitments in PTAs. Although this may seem unsurprising, a connection between trade flows and services commitments has not been broadly demonstrated. That trade would have this impact even in an area as unusual as audiovisuals, where cultural as well as commercial considerations predominate, is interesting and significant.

The puzzle that remains is whether cultural factors independently shape commitments in PTAs. One view is that regulating trade to serve cultural objectives represents protectionism in disguise. However, garden-variety protectionism can be difficult to disentangle from genuinely held government concern for community needs. When entertainment is traded, not only is material gain at stake. Import competition can reduce the availability of native fare in the market or restrict consumer access to local alternatives; it can also compel domestic industries to model foreign styles as a survival strategy, sacrificing the national distinctiveness of their craft. These kinds of adjustments conceivably could cause people, as consumers of entertainment, to lose touch with their heritage, weakening the collective sense of identity (Voon 2007).

The challenge is to define the sources of these cultural influences and to devise credible measures. Culture is a difficult concept to operationalise for empirical research. In audiovisual media, the most forceful cultural pressure impinging on many societies, since the days of silent films, has been mass entertainment from the United States. Japanese animation, British dramas, Bollywood movies, Mexican and Brazilian soap operas and Swedish pop music all reach global audiences. Yet the United States remains a commanding presence in film, television and music. Moreover, the case for cultural policy is often stated in terms of blunting US dominance or resisting Americanisation.

A logical starting point is that the impact of US mass culture on a society is a function of exposure, while exposure is a function of receptiveness to it. Cultural distance is a potential means to capture these influences. This concept situates the cultural relationship between two societies on a continuum ranging from close (similar or alike) to distant (different or unlike). When societies are in close cultural proximity, information and ideas travel easily between them; over longer distances, however, more is lost in translation. The best measure of cultural distance is linguistic ancestry (Fearon 2003; Spolaore and Wacziarg 2009). Language phylogenies, or family trees, organise kindred languages into strings of nested genealogical classifications. The closer the nearest common ancestor on the family tree, the less the time elapsed since two languages branched apart and hence the closer they are genealogically. This yardstick makes the 'distance' between languages measurable. Language pairs can be aggregated into country dyads by averaging these distances, summed over the languages spoken in each country and weighted by the population share of each language. Hanson and Xiang (2009) uncover a strong connection between linguistic measures of cultural distance and trade in feature films, evidence that language taps deeper structures that guide flows of information and ideas between societies. Moreover, there is no chance of reverse causation: language families are much too old for modern-day forces to alter their make-up, so trade cannot make countries any culturally closer by this measure.

The last set of models evaluates two propositions. The first is that countries with cultural proximity to the United States contract fewer audiovisual services commitments in PTAs. These societies will tend to be more exposed to US mass culture in the first place; their governments are likely to engage in more interventions in the audiovisual sector, both to protect industry and to blunt US cultural influences; liberalising or binding these policies, in the GATS or in PTAs, imposes undesirable limits on state regulation for industrial and cultural objectives while also inviting further pressure for guarantees in future PTAs. Inconsistencies do exist – New Zealand's scheduled commitments are some of the most liberal of any country, and Australia even made preferential concessions to the United States – yet it is unclear how anomalous these examples are. In other research (Chase 2011), I have shown that cultural proximity to the United States, conditional on national market size in feature films and television programming, effectively accounts for governments' positions on special rules for audiovisuals in the GATS. It is therefore worth testing whether similar effects hold up in PTAs, too.

The second proposition is that cultural proximity to PTA partners is likely to condition commitment coverage in audiovisual services. Logically, this effect could go either way. If countries that are culturally close to one another trade more audiovisual services than do countries that are culturally far apart, then commercial pressures and cultural influences will be more intense in these dyads. This could create reluctance to limit discretion in the audiovisual sector.[26] But cultural influences could also push in the other direction – commitment may be easier with PTA partners whose entertainment is culturally more compatible. Thus, I assess this proposition with no strong preconceptions about the direction of the effect, if any.

An initial test of these propositions about cultural proximity yields interesting results and poses new puzzles.[27] Table 9.5 presents three models, the first for the entire audiovisual sector, the second for film and video and the third for television and radio broadcasting. In the sector as a whole and in film and video, countries that are culturally close to the United States undertake fewer commitments, but this effect is not statistically significant. In television and radio, in contrast, cultural proximity to the United States leads to greater commitments, not fewer, and this result is marginally significant. Also noticeable in the third model is that commitment coverage in broadcasting declines with total exports to PTA partners (a relationship that is marginally significant in the whole-sector model).

These findings call attention to Asian countries that are culturally insulated from the United States and export oriented in manufactured goods. Japan, Hong Kong and Singapore, all participants in the WTO collective request (which included film, video and sound recording, but not television and radio), have refused to schedule broadcasting services either in the WTO or in PTAs; Taiwan made some GATS commitments in radio and television, but it has not extended these guarantees into its PTAs. Broadcasting on the whole attracts many fewer commitments: the average index across all observations is 0.252 compared to 0.447 for film and video. A primary reason is that a number of Asian countries continue to hold television and radio out of PTAs (and the WTO) despite undertaking commitments in film and video. Why these governments have been willing to bind policies towards film and video but not radio and television is not easily explained.

---

[26] In Chase (2011), the competitive effect is conditional on national consumption of entertainment: cases of close cultural proximity favour the larger market over the smaller market. It is worth noting that some major audiovisual producers, namely, Japan, South Korea and India, lack cultural proximity (as measured by linguistic ties) to their trade partners, even geographically nearby ones.

[27] Cultural proximity data are from Spolaore and Wacziarg 2009. In PTAs involving regional groupings, including the EU, I average the cultural proximity measures across all PTA partners.

Table 9.5 *Cultural distance and audiovisual services commitments*

| Variable | (1) Audiovisuals | (2) Film and video | (3) Broadcasting |
|---|---|---|---|
| Cultural proximity to United States | −0.034 | −0.084 | 0.109*** |
| | (0.025) | (0.052) | (0.063) |
| Cultural proximity to PTA partner(s) | 0.093** | 0.086** | 0.107** |
| | (0.020) | (0.027) | (0.030) |
| GATS commitments | 3.844** | 6.304** | 2.625** |
| | (0.680) | (1.554) | (0.711) |
| Negative-list format | 1.133** | 1.443* | 1.342* |
| | (0.430) | (0.644) | (0.578) |
| Common market | 2.259** | 2.340** | 3.003** |
| | (0.445) | (0.625) | (0.646) |
| EU and Canada PTA partners | −2.431** | −3.802** | −1.367*** |
| | (0.874) | (1.048) | (0.828) |
| US PTA partners | 2.089** | 2.341** | 3.170** |
| | (0.375) | (0.691) | (0.794) |
| North–South PTAs | −0.074 | −0.003 | −0.666 |
| | (0.216) | (0.296) | (0.498) |
| GDP relative to PTA partner | 0.001 | 0.001 | −0.096 |
| | (0.002) | (0.002) | (0.059) |
| Exports to PTA partner | −0.000*** | −0.000 | −0.003** |
| | (0.000) | (0.000) | (0.001) |
| Constant | −2.432** | −2.213** | −3.090** |
| | (0.254) | (0.353) | (0.523) |
| Wald chi-square | 229.99** | 124.31** | 288.40** |

*Note:* Standard errors, adjusted for clustering by country, are in parentheses. $N = 286$.
* $p < 0.05$
** $p < 0.01$
*** $p < 0.1$

Though cultural proximity to the United States appears not to carry much weight, cultural proximity between PTA partners positively affects audiovisual services commitments. In the sector overall and in the two main subsectors, film and video and television and radio, cultural proximity to PTA partners increases commitment coverage. Why governments would be more inclined to commit to bindings in PTAs with culturally close trade partners warrants further examination. Finally, even after controlling for GATS commitments, negotiating modality and PTA type, still the United States always gets the best deals in audiovisual services, as all of the models in this chapter have consistently confirmed.

## D. Audiovisuals, PTAs and the WTO

PTAs of all kinds have grown impressively in number of late. Enhanced agreements that cover services are appearing at an especially rapid pace. Trade in services has been increasing anyway by means of new technologies, and the expansion of preferential trading links eases markets open and improves the transparency and predictability of policy regimes. Services PTAs are therefore a new and ongoing development with important effects on this flourishing segment of trade. This is especially so because progress on services in the WTO has been slow. The GATS therefore has provided a foundation to build on – not in a swift sequel to the Uruguay Round, but in the profusion of services PTAs, most of them modelled on GATS obligations.

Services PTAs are particularly significant for difficult sectors, such as audiovisual media, with limited commitments in the GATS. Countries seeking greater access and more certainty in audiovisual services have turned out of necessity to PTAs to negotiate better deals preferentially. The United States has accomplished this most effectively; other parties to the WTO collective request on audiovisual services have achieved some gains via PTAs as well. How these countries managed to get the concessions they did and the extent of the improvements in specific subsectors and modes of supply are important issues, and this chapter presents some preliminary answers.

My survey of audiovisual services commitments in PTAs points to conclusions about PTA design. Although exceptions and exclusions for the audiovisual sector in Canadian and EU PTAs are widely known, these carve-outs are not the only way for states to keep a sector off the table. Nonlistings in positive-list PTAs and targeted reservations in negative-list PTAs are more common methods for evading services commitments. Several governments have selected these lower-profile alternatives for audiovisual services and a few, besides Canada and the EU, have maintained full discretion in their PTAs. However, there is powerful evidence that negotiating modality matters: the negative-list simply makes commitments harder to avoid. It is reasonable to infer that keeping a sector off limits comes at a higher price in negative-list PTAs, especially when dealing with trade partners that are keen on improving access.

In audiovisual media specifically, trade patterns and deeper cultural relationships could condition PTA commitments in the future. Net importers of audiovisual services have resisted offering guarantees in any forum, the GATS or PTAs. Countries culturally close to the United States have made some concessions in PTAs, but governments of all kinds appear more inclined to contract audiovisual services commitments when PTA partners are in close cultural proximity. Import exposure and cultural ties may be limiting factors in future PTAs as well. Yet further improvements are likely, especially in film and video. In television and radio, in contrast, many governments remain inflexible – even Asian countries, whose airwaves are harder for American cultural fare to conquer. Why broadcasting looms as the toughest nut to crack in this difficult sector is an issue worthy of further research.

## References

Acheson, Keith, and Maule, Christopher J. 1999. *Much Ado about Culture: North American Trade Disputes.* Ann Arbor: University of Michigan Press.

Adlung, Rudolf, and Morrison, Peter. 2010. 'Less Than the GATS: "Negative Preferences" in Regional Services Agreements.' *Journal of International Economic Law* 13 (4): 1103–43.

Chase, Kerry A. 2011. 'Culture and Politics in the Trade Regime: Designing the General Agreement on Trade in Services.' Unpublished manuscript, on file with author.

  2013. 'Trading Cultural Goods: The Contentious Politics of Filmed Entertainment.' Unpublished manuscript, on file with author.

Choi, Byung-il. 2008. 'Trade Barriers or Cultural Diversity? The Audiovisual Sector on Fire.' In *Governing Global Electronic Networks: International Perspectives on Policy and Power*, edited by William. J. Drake and Ernest J. Wilson III, 233–73. Cambridge, MA: MIT Press.

Egger, Peter, and Lanz, Rainer. 2008. 'The Determinants of GATS Commitment Coverage.' *World Economy* 31 (12): 1666–94.

Fearon, James D. 2003. 'Ethnic and Cultural Diversity by Country.' *Journal of Economic Growth* 8 (2): 195–222.

Fink, Carsten, and Jansen, Marion. 2009. 'Services Provisions in Regional Trade Agreements: Stumbling Blocks or Building Blocks for Multilateral Liberalisation?' In *Multilateralising Regionalism: Challenges for the Global Trading System*, edited by Richard Baldwin and Patrick Low, 221–61. Cambridge: Cambridge University Press.

Francois, Joseph, and Hoekman, Bernard. 2010. 'Services Trade and Policy.' *Journal of Economic Literature* 48 (3): 642–92.

Hanson, Gordon H., and Xiang, Chong. 2009. 'International Trade in Motion Picture Services.' In *International Trade in Services and Intangibles in the Era of Globalisation*, edited by Marshall Reinsdorf and Matthew J. Slaughter, 203–22. Chicago: University of Chicago Press.

Harms, Philipp, Mattoo, Aaditya, and Schuknecht, Ludger. 2003. 'Explaining Liberalisation Commitments in Financial Services Trade.' *Review of World Economics* 139 (1): 82–113.

Hoekman, Bernard. 1996. 'Assessing the General Agreement on Trade in Services.' In *The Uruguay Round and the Developing Countries*, edited by Will Martin and L. Alan Winters, 84–124. Cambridge: Cambridge University Press.

    2006. 'Liberalizing Trade in Services: A Survey.' World Bank Policy Research Working Paper 4030. World Bank, Washington, DC. www-wds.worldbank. org/servlet/WDSContentServer/WDSP/IB/2006/10/06/000016406_ 20061006151055/Rendered/PDF/wps4030.pdf. Accessed 17 September 2013.

Hoekman, Bernard, and Primo Braga, Carlos A. 1997. 'Protection and Trade in Services: A Survey.' *Open Economies Review* 8 (3): 285–308.

Magdeleine, Joscelyn, and Maurer, Andreas. 2008. 'Measuring GATS Mode 4 Trade Flows.' WTO Economic Research and Statistics Division, Staff Working Paper ERSD-2008–05. World Trade Organization, Geneva. www.wto.org/english/ res_e/reser_e/ersd201216_e.pdf. Accessed 13 November 2013.

Marchetti, Juan A., and Roy, Martin. 2009. 'Services Liberalisation in the WTO and in PTAs.' In *Opening Markets for Trade in Services: Countries and Sectors in Bilateral and WTO Negotiations*, edited by Juan A. Marchetti and Martin Roy, 61–112. Cambridge: Cambridge University Press.

Marvasti, Akbar, and Canterbery, E. Ray. 2005. 'Cultural and Other Barriers to Motion Pictures Trade.' *Economic Inquiry* 43 (1): 39–54.

Mattoo, Aaditya, and Sauvé, Pierre. 2011. 'Services.' In *Preferential Trade Agreement Policies for Development*, edited by Jean-Pierre Chauffour and Jean-Christophe Maur, 235–74. Washington, DC: World Bank.

Miroudot, Sébastien, Sauvage, Jehan, and Sudreau, Marie. 2010. 'Multilateralising Regionalism: How Preferential Are Services Commitments in Regional Trade Agreements?' OECD Trade Policy Papers No. 106. Organisation for Economic Co-operation and Development, Paris. http://dx.doi.org/10.1787/ 5km362n24t8n-en. Accessed 14 November 2013.

Roy, Martin. 2009. 'Beyond the Main Screen: Audiovisual Services in PTAs.' In *Opening Markets for Trade in Services: Countries and Sectors in Bilateral and WTO Negotiations*, edited by Juan A. Marchetti and Martin Roy, 340–77. Cambridge: Cambridge University Press.

Roy, Martin, Marchetti, Juan, and Lim, Aik Hoe. 2008. 'The Race Towards Preferential Trade Agreements in Services: How Much Market Access Is Really Achieved?' In *GATS and the Regulation of International Trade in Services*, edited by Marion Panizzon, Nicole Pohl and Pierre Sauvé, 77–110. Cambridge: Cambridge University Press.

Spolaore, Enrico, and Wacziarg, Romain. 2009. 'The Diffusion of Development.' *Quarterly Journal of Economics* 124 (2): 469–529.

United Nations. 2010. *Creative Economy Report 2010 – Creative Economy: A Feasible Development Option.* unctad.org/en/Docs/ditctab20103_en.pdf. Accessed 12 September 2013.

United Nations Educational, Scientific and Cultural Organization. 2005. *Convention on the Protection of the Diversity of Cultural Contents and Artistic Expressions.* http://unesdoc.unesco.org/images/0014/001429/142919e.pdf. Accessed 13 September 2013.

Voon, Tania. 2007. *Cultural Products and the World Trade Organization.* Cambridge: Cambridge University Press.

World Trade Organization, Council for Trade in Services. 2001. *Guidelines for the Scheduling of Specific Commitments under the General Agreement on Trade in Services (GATS).* S/L/92, 28 March. www.wto.org/english/tratop_e/serv_e/sl92.doc. Accessed 22 October 2013.

2007. *Special Session, Communication from Mexico – Review of Progress in Audiovisual Services.* JOB(07)/195, 5 December. www.wtocenter.org.tw/SmartKMS/fileviewer?id=92119. Accessed 20 November 2013.

2010. *Audiovisual Services: Background Note by the Secretariat.* S/C/W/310, 12 January. https://docs.wto.org/dol2fe/Pages/FE_Search/DDFDocuments/101492/Q/S/C/W310.pdf. Accessed 9 September 2013.

# 10

# Competition policy and free trade

## Antitrust provisions in Ptas

ANU BRADFORD AND TIM BÜTHE

## A. Introduction

Trade agreements increasingly contain provisions concerning 'behind-the-border' barriers to trade, often beyond current World Trade Organization (WTO) commitments (Dür, Baccini and Elsig 2014). Today's preferential trade agreements (PTAs) may include, for instance, rules regarding 'technical' barriers to trade that go beyond the WTO's Agreement on Technical Barriers to Trade (TBT Agreement), accelerating the replacement of differing national product safety standards with common international standards and thus reducing the trade-inhibiting effect of regulatory measures (Büthe and Mattli 2011; World Trade Organization 2012). Today's PTAs may also go beyond WTO rules in prohibiting preferences for domestic producers in government procurement (Arrowsmith and Anderson 2011; Dawar and Evenett 2011), although here the effectiveness of the PTA provisions is in question (Rickard, Chapter 11 in this volume). PTA provisions concerning trade in services (Trebilcock and Howse 2005: 349ff.), restrictions on the use of trade remedies and anti-dumping (Bown 2011; Bown and Wu 2014) and provisions concerning the treatment of foreign investment (Büthe and Milner 2014;

For comments, we are grateful to Todd Allee, Andreas Dür, Manfred Elsig, Simon Evenett, Bernard Hoekman, Helen Milner and participants of the September 2013 conference 'Trade Cooperation: The Purpose, Design and Effects of Preferential Trade Agreements' at the World Trade Institute, Bern. We gratefully acknowledge financial support from the US National Science Foundation, Law and Social Science Program, collaborative research grants SES-1228453 and SES-1228483, supplemented by grants from Columbia Law School, Duke University Arts & Sciences Council's Committee on Faculty Research, and the University of Chicago Law School. For excellent research assistance, we thank Taimoor Aziz, Alexander Bergersen, Justin Epner, Yian Huan, Dushyant Manocha, Shahryar Minhas, Mark Sater, Philippe Thill and especially Cindy Cheng and Margarita Kelrikh.

United Nations Conference on Trade and Development 2006) have similarly attracted substantial attention, as they often go beyond the rules in the multilateral trade regime. All of these measures involve governments committing to adopt – or to refrain from – particular policies. The stated objective of such commitments usually is to eliminate or at least reduce the trade-distorting effects of domestic policies (Bhagwati and Hudec 1996), though linking particular policy choices to trade might also serve other purposes. Linkage may, for instance, increase the bargaining space for 'getting to yes' on trade liberalisation (see Axelrod and Keohane 1986; Davis 2004) or reduce the bargaining space, arguably with the intent of retaining a higher level of protectionism (e.g. Salazar-Xirinachs 2000). PTA commitments on behind-the-border measures may also be adopted to 'lock in' policies by making it politically and economically more costly for the current government or its successors to depart from the policy choices specified in the trade agreement (Büthe and Milner 2008; Mansfield and Milner 2012; Moe 2005).

Competition policy – the enforcement of laws against various forms of anticompetitive behaviour, including cartels and the abuse of market power, as well as the regulation of mergers, acquisitions and joint ventures – has similarly been the focus of articles and even entire chapters of numerous international trade agreements.[1] Yet, these competition policy provisions in PTAs have only in recent years attracted the attention of scholars and practitioners, mostly after competition policy was removed from the negotiating agenda of the WTO Doha Round in 2004 (Anderson and Holmes 2002; Baldwin, Evenett and Low 2009: 94). Only since Solano and Sennekamp's (2006) study of the competition chapters of 86 PTAs for the Organisation for Economic Co-operation and Development (OECD) and Anderson and Evenett's (2006) critique have competition policy provisions been included among the behind-the-border issues regularly considered in analyses of the international trade regime (Baccini et al. 2011: 25–8; Teh 2009; World Trade Organization 2011: 142–5).

Competition policy is one of the most powerful policy instruments governments have to shape the structure and operation of market economies. Competition provisions in PTAs, however, present a puzzle because the literature on the political economy of trade has, since Smith and Ricardo, traditionally emphasised that trade openness inherently increases competition by lowering barriers to entry into previously closed markets (see,

---

[1] We will use 'competition policy' throughout this chapter for what in the United States is generally known as 'antitrust' law and policy.

e.g., the Smith and Ricardo selections in Crane and Hovenkamp 2013: 5–40). Indeed, trade economists who advocate liberal foreign economic policies still regularly argue that one of the inherent benefits of free trade is that it drives out anticompetitive practices (Blackhurst 1991; Irwin 2009). The institutionalisation of more liberal trade policies in trade agreements should thus reduce the need for competition policy. What then is actually covered by these competition policy provisions in PTAs? And why do we find them in PTAs at all?

This chapter provides a first, preliminary answer to these questions, based on a major new and ongoing research project directed by the authors. We start with a review of the small existing literature on competition provisions in PTAs. We then examine how competition policy is covered in PTAs and how that coverage has changed over time based on detailed coding of a random sample of 182 PTAs from the Design of Trade Agreements (DESTA) Database.[2] We then turn to some possible explanations for the far more frequent inclusion of competition policy provisions in PTAs over the past two decades. Here, we first contemplate the possibility that the inclusion of competition provisions is simply part of a more general tendency to sign 'deeper' (more comprehensive) trade agreements (Dür and Elsig, Chapter 1 in this volume) but find this line of reasoning raises at least as many questions as it answers. We then consider the hypothesis that such provisions are attempts to forestall a strategic use of domestic competition policy for protectionist purposes. This would appear warranted if governments were above all concerned about discriminatory enforcement of competition law, as one prominent school of thought suggests. We challenge this account by offering an alternative rationale for the inclusion of competition provisions in PTAs, which suggests that such provisions reflect a genuine desire by governments – or at least by competition regulators – to safeguard market competition when the boundaries of markets no longer coincide with the borders of the polity. Our analysis of the specific competition policy provisions included in our sample of PTAs shows that provisions to promote transgovernmental regulatory cooperation and more generally effective competition law enforcement (consistent with our theoretical approach) are substantially more common than provisions aimed at constraining competition regulators (as should be expected by the conventional wisdom).

---

[2] This sample is substantially larger (and more clearly a probability sample) than the samples used in previous work. For more information about the DESTA data, see www.designoftradeagreements.org.

## B. Prior studies of competition provisions in PTAs

Although the increase in competition policy provisions in PTAs had previously been noted,[3] Solano and Sennekamp's (2006) study for the OECD was, to the best of our knowledge, the first attempt to systematically take stock of competition provisions in a large sample of PTAs.[4] Solano and Sennekamp examine 86 PTAs, a sample that appears to have consisted of all PTAs that were notified to the WTO Secretariat between January 2001 and July 2005 and that contained a competition chapter. In addition, this sample includes an unspecified number of earlier PTAs as well as some unnotified agreements, chosen because of their 'importance to trade' (again conditional on having a competition policy chapter) or because of the special 'relevance of their competition provisions' (Solano and Sennekamp 2006: 6).[5]

Solano and Sennekamp record information about 24 aspects of each of those 86 PTAs. Most prominently, they record the type of competition issue or anticompetitive behaviour addressed (using five very broad categories); whether and to what extent the competition chapter included provisions for coordination and cooperation between national competition regulators; whether the PTA contains provisions on issues often seen as linked to competition policy, such as anti-dumping; and whether the PTA's dispute settlement mechanism (if any) is applicable to its competition policy provisions. Developing the first explicit coding scheme for PTA competition chapters was an important contribution, but the resulting data lack precision and detail. Solano and Sennekamp's coding, for instance, makes no distinction between a PTA that permanently exempts substantial portions of the economy from its competition provisions and a PTA whose competition provisions apply to the entire economy but only after a transition period (both are simply coded as 'flexible' commitments). It also does not allow us to differentiate between horizontal anticompetitive agreements (e.g. price-fixing agreements among competitors) and vertical anticompetitive agreements (e.g. agreements between a

---

[3] See, for example, Brusick, Alvarez and Cernat (2005) and Silva (2004).

[4] In addition, the question of whether the GATT/WTO needed an antitrust agreement had been extensively debated; see Bradford (2007), Clarke and Evenett (2003), Fox (1997), Guzman (2004), Marsden (2003) and Stephan (2004). See also the document collection of the WTO Working Group on the Interaction between Trade and Competition Policy at www.wto.org/english/tratop_e/comp_e/wgtcp_docs_e.htm.

[5] A substantial (though unspecified) portion of their sample thus appears to have been selected through nonprobabilistic methods, including selection on the dependent variable.

firm and its distributors to deny competitors market access). Beyond their coding and its limitations, Solano and Sennekamp come to the overarching qualitative assessment that competition policy provisions in PTAs are generally intended to support trade liberalisation, as evidenced by an often explicit recognition that 'anti-competitive practices can undermine the trade objective' or an express objective 'to combat anti-competitive behavior [in order to] enhance the trade objectives of the agreement' (Solano and Sennekamp 2006: 9).

Anderson and Evenett (2006) build on Solano and Sennekamp's analysis, above all, to examine whether PTAs and competition policy provisions in PTAs affect the behaviour of the private sector, especially private-sector cross-border mergers and acquisitions (Anderson and Evenett 2006: esp. 29ff.).[6] Importantly, they also criticise Solano and Sennekamp's methodology, in particular, the exclusive focus on competition chapters. As Anderson and Evenett point out, sector-specific PTA chapters concerning industries such as financial services, telecommunications or transportation may contain competition policy provisions distinct from, and going beyond, the provisions in a PTA's competition policy chapter. In fact, a PTA may contain such substantial, albeit industry-specific competition provisions even if it does not have a chapter devoted to competition policy (Anderson and Evenett 2006: 21f.).

Anderson and Evenett's warning, based primarily on a close reading of a few PTAs, that important competition-related PTA provisions appear frequently outside a designated competition policy chapter, is confirmed by Teh's systematic analysis of 'all competition-related provisions' of 74 PTAs (Teh 2009: 418). Selected for geographical diversity, economic importance (presumably of the signatories to overall world trade) and representativeness over time (Teh 2009: 420f.), this sample of PTAs is intended to be better suited to generalisation than the Solano and Sennekamp sample is, although it remains somewhat unclear how the author implemented the

---

[6] Their analysis covers cross-border mergers and acquisitions (M&As) for 116 countries over 15 years (1989–2004). Controlling for the size of the M&A-receiving economy and standard economic covariates, they find that PTAs as such have no statistically significant effect (except when US and EU participation in the PTA is instrumented, in which case PTAs actually reduce inward M&A investment), whereas having a national competition policy law that includes merger regulation significantly reduces cross-border M&As (possibly because it simply reduces M&As in general). At the same time, PTA provisions that commit the parties to transparency in their application of competition policy significantly increase cross-border M&As, whereas other characteristics of PTA competition policy chapters (including whether the PTA competition chapter includes provisions regarding mergers) have no significant effect (Anderson and Evenett 2006: esp. 39ff.).

selection criteria. Based on a very detailed coding of sectoral provisions for the telecommunications, financial and maritime transport services industries, as well as general substantive provisions for the treatment of investments, government procurement and intellectual property rights, Teh shows that competition-related rules can indeed be found in many different places in PTAs.

Finally, Sokol (2008) complements this research with an analysis of the 36 PTAs noted in the Organization of American States' trade database as having been signed between 1992 and 2006 and to which 'at least one Latin American country [was] a party' (Sokol 2008: 253). Focusing on this smaller Latin American sample enabled him to code each PTA in considerable depth and to examine its context, allowing for greater internal validity albeit at the recognised cost of reduced generalisability.[7] His key finding is that all 24 Latin American PTAs that include a competition policy chapter[8] exclude those chapters from their dispute settlement mechanism. He then discusses numerous possible reasons for the apparent hesitation to subject competition policy to external dispute settlement – an important issue (see also Teh 2009: 481f.), but beyond the scope of this chapter.

In sum, existing scholarship on competition policy provisions in PTAs yields a number of important findings, which are, however, more suggestive than conclusive as a result of small or nonprobability samples of PTAs and insufficiently fine-grained coding. Our current research, from which we here report initial, preliminary results, is the first attempt to code the comprehensive set of PTAs identified by the DESTA project at the level of detail needed to overcome these limitations of previous research and provide an accurate picture of competition policy provisions in PTAs.

## C. Competition provisions in a sample of 182 PTAs

To overcome the problems that arise from the use of nonprobability samples of PTAs in most of the research reviewed earlier, we follow

---

[7] He finds, for instance, that the prior adoption of a competition law at the national level has been virtually a prerequisite for Latin American countries to be willing to include a competition chapter (found in 24 of the 36 PTAs) – a finding that does not hold true in other regions. Only the three plurilateral PTAs involving the group of 'Central American States' (Costa Rica, El Salvador, Guatemala, Honduras and Nicaragua) with the Dominican Republic (1998), Chile (2002) and Panama (2002) contain a competition chapter without prior adoption of a national competition law by all signatories.
[8] Notwithstanding Anderson and Evenett's critique of the earlier work, Sokol (2008: 253) excludes from consideration 'provisions in other chapters that have competition impact'.

Koremenos's (2005, 2007) random sampling approach to the analysis of international treaties. Specifically, we used a random number generator to select a random sample of 182 PTAs from the maximally comprehensive list of post–World War II PTAs compiled by Baccini, Dür, Elsig and Milewicz (see Dür, Baccini and Elsig 2014).[9]

The following process was used to generate the data reported here. Each PTA in our sample was independently coded by at least two students at the University of Chicago or Columbia Law Schools under the guidance and supervision of the authors.[10] For each PTA, coders recorded basic information, such as the parties to the treaty and when the agreement was signed. Coders then undertook a thorough content analysis of the treaty text, including preambles, annexes, appendices and linked implementation agreements, if any. Specifically, coders were asked to answer numerous questions about each PTA, through which they generated more than 100 variables per PTA, assisted by survey software that ensured coders would be asked only the questions that were pertinent, given their prior answers and known contextual information. The coders thus recorded a wealth of information about each PTA's competition chapter (if any), competition articles (if any) and other competition-related provisions (discussed later), including the specific kinds of competition policy issues covered by the PTA (unilateral anticompetitive behaviour, anticompetitive behaviour by two or more firms, mergers, government subsidies ('state aid'). The goals of competition policy as well as any permissible exemptions from the PTA's competition policy rules were also coded, as well as the nature and scope of commitments for cooperation among competition enforcement agencies. Coders further recorded information about related aspects of each PTA, such as whether the PTA includes a dispute settlement mechanism (DSM), whether the DSM applies to the competition provisions and whether the PTA includes provisions

---

[9] At the time of the sample selection, the collection contained the texts of 395 PTAs. It now contains 587, and our ultimate goal is to code all of them. The initial sample consisted of 200 PTAs, of which, however, 2 were not in fact double-coded as a result of coder error, 16 were omitted as a result of lack of an English-language text. Translations or foreign language coding and supplemental coding work to complete the sample of 200 are under way.

[10] Most of the coders had prior academic training in antitrust law, international trade law or both; many of the LLM student coders had practised antitrust law prior to embarking on an LLM. All of the coders received extensive training, including the test coding of multiple full-length PTAs. Moreover, all coding was conducted using plain-text online surveys (with quantification automated using the Qualtrics survey software) – a methodological innovation for content analysis described in greater detail elsewhere.

concerning intellectual property rights, anti-dumping, government procurement or nontariff barriers (Ntbs). Upon completion of the coding,
we conducted an analysis of intercoder reliability and closely re-reviewed,
with a team of coders, every aspect of every PTA where the original coders
had differed to arrive at a final consensus data set.[11]

*I. The form of competition policy provisions across 182 PTAs*

To what extent is competition policy covered across the 182 PTAs in
our sample? We take Anderson and Evenett's critique of Solano and
Sennekamp's work into account and therefore allow for the possibility
of competition policy provisions occurring in any part of the PTAs we
code. To do so, we asked, first: 'Does the PTA have a separate chapter
devoted to competition law/policy?' To qualify, a chapter (or cohesive
group of articles) did not have to have the word 'competition' in the title
but had to be substantively about competition law or policy, possibly in
conjunction with closely related issues (such as in a chapter on 'Business
Practices'). For 50 of the PTAs in our sample, the answer was yes (27.5
per cent of our sample). If the PTA did not contain such a chapter, coders
were asked: 'Does the PTA have a separate article or articles devoted to
competition law/policy?' Here, too, we counted any article specifically
devoted to business practices that restrain competition, as well as articles
using the language of 'antitrust' or referring to merger review, control
or regulation.[12] The answer was yes for 78 of the PTAs in our sample
(42.9 per cent). Across the full sample of the 182 PTAs, we thus find at
least one article, and often several articles or an entire chapter, devoted to
competition policy in 128 PTAs (just over 70 per cent of our sample), as
shown in Figure 10.1.

Anderson, Evenett and Teh advocate an even more inclusive approach.
We allow for such inclusiveness but caution that Teh's analysis in fact
shows that 'competition-related' provisions vary tremendously in how
closely they are related to what might legitimately be considered competition *law* or *policy*. Article 39(1)b of the 1997 EC–Jordan PTA, for instance,
states that: 'The Parties affirm their commitment to a freely competitive
environment as being an essential feature of the dry and liquid bulk

---

[11] Such meticulous review of discrepancies is extremely time consuming. We are therefore
only able to draw on fully reliable final data for a subset of the variables so far, making
the empirical analysis consciously preliminary.

[12] Articles solely concerned with government subsidies or other forms of 'state aid' did not
count.

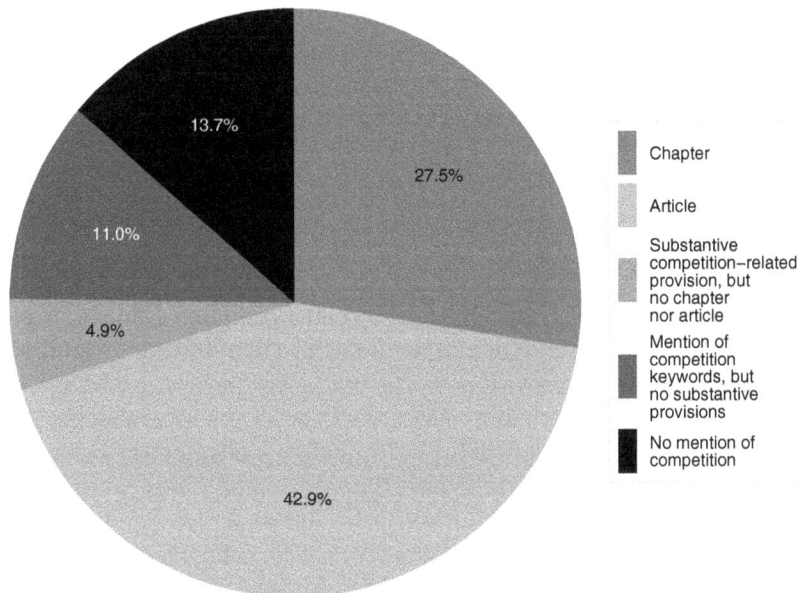

**Figure 10.1**   How competition policy is addressed

trade.' This part of Article 39 (an article devoted to the 'Cross-Border Supply of Services') is highlighted by Teh as an example of competition provisions outside competition chapters. And the article certainly may be interpreted as a commitment, in principle, to take action against anti-competitive practices in the transport industry. It is qualitatively different, however, from PTAs in which a competition policy chapter includes, for instance, commitments to adopt or maintain a competition law[13] (which makes the prohibition of anticompetitive conduct enforceable by domestic agencies and courts) or maybe even to have or maintain an independent competition law enforcement agency.[14]

---

[13]   As stipulated, for instance, in Articles 14.3(1) and 14.3(2) of the 2008 Australia–Chile PTA, according to which: 'Each Party shall maintain or adopt measures consistent with its domestic law to proscribe anticompetitive activities and take appropriate action with respect thereto, recognising that such measures will help realise the objectives of this Agreement. [ ... ] Each Party shall ensure that all businesses operating in its territory are subject to its competition laws.'

[14]   As stipulated, for instance, in Article XI.2.5 of the 2002 Canada–Costa Rica PTA, according to which: 'Each Party shall establish or maintain an impartial competition authority that is: (a) authorized to advocate pro-competitive solutions in the design, development and implementation of government policy and legislation; and (b) independent from political interference in carrying out enforcement actions and advocacy activities.'

We therefore ask two questions that allow us to differentiate between various references to competition and related issues in PTAs that do not contain designated articles or chapters on competition policy. First, we ask: 'Does the PTA contain any mention of competition, any mention of antitrust or any mention of the regulation of cartels, monopolies or mergers/acquisitions?' If the answer is yes (as it is for 29 of the PTAs without competition article or chapter), we then ask: 'Is antitrust/competition *policy* recognized anywhere in the PTA as a (trade-related but) distinct issue, that is, not just competition as a characteristic of trade in the sense that trade inherently entails foreign goods competing with domestic ones?' In our assessment, only PTAs that warrant an affirmative answer to the second question (9 PTAs, accounting for 4.9 per cent of our sample) may be said to contain a substantive discussion of competition policy even when they contain neither a chapter nor an article devoted to competition policy. Figure 10.1 summarises this information about the ways competition policy is addressed in our sample of PTAs.

Anderson and Evenett also note that general 'national treatment' or nondiscrimination clauses, which are found in many PTAs as well as in the General Agreement on Tariffs and Trade (GATT) and the 1994 WTO treaties, may be read as already prohibiting discriminatory enforcement of competition laws.[15] This point is underscored in the section on competition policy in the 2011 *World Trade Report*, which is devoted to the relationship between PTAs and the multilateral trade regime (World Trade Organization 2011). Teh (2009: esp. 464–6) goes further in his interpretation of commitments to the 'horizontal principles' of nondiscrimination (rare), procedural fairness (moderately common) and transparency (widespread) among the general principles or in the general administrative provisions of PTAs. Teh attributes to such commitments an effect on competition (maybe even intentional) that has a similar thrust to competition policy provisions so that 'these general horizontal principles may represent significant competition-related elements of [P]TAs' (Teh 2009: 464). We reject this interpretation as it risks going too far in broadening the notion of 'competition[-related] provisions' to the point where the concept of competition policy loses its analytical usefulness.

---

[15] They give Article 2 of the 2002 Chile–EU Interim Agreement as an example (emphasis added by Anderson and Evenett): 'Imported products of the territory of the other Party shall be accorded treatment no less favourable than that accorded to domestic products in respect of *all laws, regulations and requirements affecting their internal sale, offering for sale, purchase, transportation, distribution or use.*'

Although it is technically correct that general PTA provisions for transparency, procedural fairness and national treatment *might* be applicable to the enforcement of domestic competition laws and might even be read to articulate *some* of the core principles of competition policy, this potentially vast reinterpretation of general PTA provisions remains at best untested. To avoid problems of overinclusion, we therefore focus on the first three categories identified previously, and in particular on the 128 PTAs with at least one article devoted specifically to competition policy. In the many analyses where it makes virtually no difference to the results, we also consider the 9 additional PTAs that contain substantive provisions concerning competition policy without devoting a distinct article to the topic (for a total of 137 PTAs).

## II. Competition policy provisions in PTAs over time

The distribution of our sample of PTAs over time is highly uneven, reflecting in part the explosive increase in PTA formation over the past 20 years but also an inherent limitation of random sampling from a highly unevenly distributed population: only 26 of our 182 PTAs were signed before 1991. We therefore hesitate to draw strong inferences about trends over time prior to 1991, but regressing the share of a year's PTAs with either a competition article or chapter on a simple trend term (using logit) shows a clearly statistically significant increase over time. In fact, before 1991, both competition articles and chapters were very rare, each found in just 3 of the 26 PTAs. By contrast, during the period of the most intensive institutionalisation of free trade during the last two decades, competition provisions in PTAs have generally become more detailed, warranting in many cases the inclusion of not just a separate article but even an entire chapter. Figure 10.2 captures this pattern over time by showing the percentage of newly signed PTAs with at least a distinct article devoted to competition policy (solid line, left-hand scale), as well as the number of PTAs signed in a given year[16]

---

[16] Given the small number of observations per year, we use a five-year moving average for Figure 10.2 to focus on the overall pattern rather than year-to-year variability. In order not to show the effect of a new PTA before it is signed, the moving five-year window consists of the current year and the immediately preceding four years. We start the time series displayed in 1958 since it is the first year for which there are continuously at least 2 PTAs in the five-year window (with the exception of 1990, where the moving average is based on a single PTA (the 1988 Canada–US PTA), which accounts for the spike).

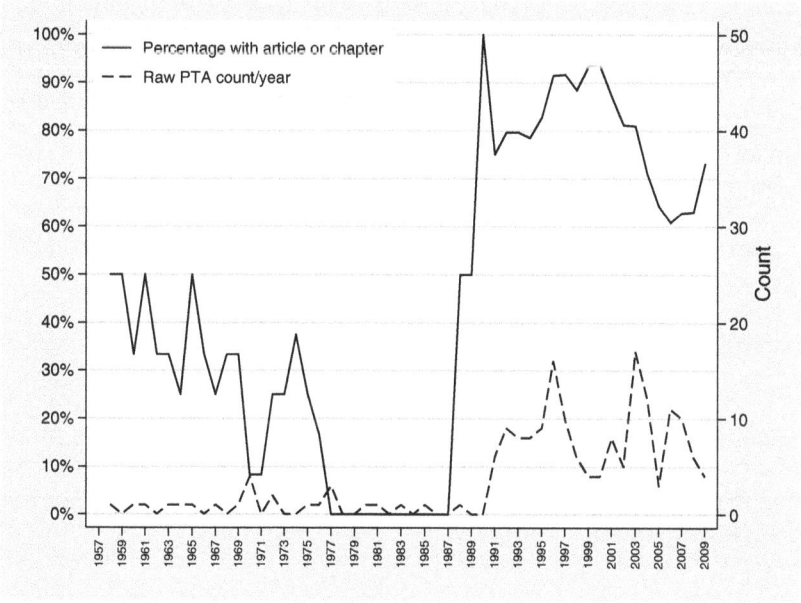

**Figure 10.2**   Percentage of PTAs with a competition article or chapter, five-year moving average

## D. Explaining the pattern of competition policy articles and chapters in PTAs

Before turning to the variation in substantive provisions contained in the competition policy articles and chapters of PTAs, we take up one of the issues raised by Dür and Elsig (Chapter 1 in this volume) about the increasing scope and depth of PTAs in recent decades. Based on previous work with Baccini, Dür and Elsig show that the 'depth' of PTAs has generally increased over time, which may account for much of the increasing formalisation, length and detail of PTA provisions in any particular issue area without the need to resort to issue area–specific explanations. To be sure, a general trend is inherently dissatisfying as an 'explanation'. Similarly to explanations of institutional change that invoke institutional isomorphism as an explanation, it raises the questions of where the trend comes from, what sustains it and why we should expect it to affect a diverse set of issue areas covered in PTAs. It is also not clear whether PTA competition provisions, even when we focus simply on their presence or absence or on their form as captured by Figure 10.2 (chapter vs. article

Table 10.1 *All good things go together? Format of competition provisions as a function of PTA depth*

|  | Model 1 | Model 2 | Model 3 | Model 4 | Model 5 | Model 6 |
|---|---|---|---|---|---|---|
| Baccini *et al.* | 0.542*** | 0.889*** | 0.899*** |  |  |  |
| Depth Index | (0.142) | (0.126) | (0.125) |  |  |  |
| Rasch Depth |  |  |  | 1.27*** | 1.71*** | 1.70*** |
| Index |  |  |  | (0.240) | (0.217) | (0.209) |
| Constant | −0.275 |  |  | 0.595*** |  |  |
|  | (0.321) |  |  | (0.185) |  |  |
| Estimation | logit | ordered logit | ordered logit | logit | ordered logit | ordered logit |
| N | 180 | 180 | 180 | 180 | 180 | 180 |
| Pseudo-$R^2$ | 0.0897 | 0.1724 | 0.1633 | 0.1711 | 0.2130 | 0.1974 |

*Note:* Dependent variable differs for models 1 and 4 vs. 2 and 5 vs. 3 and 6; see text for details. All estimates in Stata 12.1.
* $p < 0.1$, ** $p < 0.05$, *** $p < 0.01$

vs. no/indirect coverage), are well captured by any single global trend. At the same time, trends can cause inferential problems even when they are unexplained, so we briefly explore the issue in this section.

In Table 10.1, we report $3 \times 2$ sets of bivariate logistic regressions, conducted as very basic, preliminary tests of the hypothesis, given the absence of an established econometric model that would provide a proper benchmark. The dependent variable for models 1 and 4 is a dichotomous variable coded 1 if the PTA contains either an article or a chapter and coded 0 otherwise. Since that measure ignores the potentially important difference between chapters and articles, we use a second dependent variable (models 2 and 5). It is an ordinal measure coded 2 for PTAs with a competition policy chapter; 1 for PTAs with a competition policy article; 0 for all other PTAs. Finally, a third dependent variable (models 3 and 6) takes into account the PTAs with a substantive discussion of competition issues yet no article or chapter by assigning a 1 to such PTAs, a 2 to PTAs with a competition article and a 3 to PTAs with a competition chapter. The independent variable for the first three models is the basic depth index of Dür, Baccini and Elsig (2014), which, for the 180 PTAs covered here, ranges from 0 to 6 with a mean of 2.5 and a standard deviation of

1.6.[17] For the second three models, we consider the Rasch depth measure, which for the 180 PTAs ranges from −1.03 to 2.31 with a mean of 0.443 and a standard deviation of 0.918; all else remains the same.[18] The estimated coefficients, which are strongly statistically significant for either of the measures of depth and all three of the dependent variables, support the hypothesis that the format of competition provisions might be a function of the general depth of PTAs, though the finding is tentative given the caveats noted previously. At the same time the pseudo-$R^2$ – an imperfect approximation of model fit for logistic models – suggests that there is much variance left to be explained. Moreover, we observe tremendous variation in the particular elements of competition policy that are covered, even just within the subset of PTAs with a competition chapter. We turn to some of that interesting variation in the next section.

## E. Explaining the presence and specific content of competition provisions in trade agreements

A comprehensive account of the variation in competition provisions is beyond the scope of this chapter, but we observe much, often striking, variation among the PTAs with substantive competition policy provisions (the 137 PTAs in the first three pie chart segments in Figure 10.1). The coverage of the traditional core antitrust concerns illustrates this well: 69 per cent of these 137 PTAs contain provisions concerning cartels or similar horizontal anticompetitive agreements or practices (between ostensibly competing firms in the same market). Sixty-three per cent contain provisions concerning anticompetitive vertical agreements or vertical cooperation (between a firm and its suppliers or its immediate customers/distributors). And yet, a striking 89 per cent contain provisions against unilateral anticompetitive conduct (monopolisation or abuse of dominance by a single firm).[19] This variation is puzzling, at a minimum insofar as the prohibition of cartels is usually considered far more widely

---

[17] Dür et al. excluded accession agreements from their index calculation. Hence, we lose from our sample of 182 PTAs the CEFTA–Croatia accession treaty and the 2003–4 EU enlargement treaty, which increased the number of EU members from 15 to 25.

[18] For details about both measures, see Dür, Baccini and Elsig (2014). We thank Andreas Dür for recalculating the two indices without consideration of competition provisions (so as to safeguard against rendering the hypothesis true by definition) and for making the measures available to us.

[19] If the sample is restricted to the PTAs with a competition article or chapter, the percentages rise to 73 per cent, 66 per cent and 94 per cent, respectively.

accepted than regulatory intervention against anticompetitive behaviour by a single firm.

In an attempt to explain this variation, we turn to two general schools of thought regarding the relationship between trade openness and competition policy. These theoretical approaches provide possible explanations for the prevalence of competition provisions in PTAs, which traditional trade economics – positing trade liberalisation and competition policy as substitutes in their capacity to enhance market competition – would not expect. Although both theoretical perspectives we discuss see trade and competition law and enforcement as complements, they yield distinctive observable implications regarding the content of competition provisions in PTAs, which makes it worthwhile to derive those hypotheses explicitly. Deductively, the difference between the two approaches turns in large part on how governments view the relationship between trade and competition policy and their respective roles in generating and preserving market competition. We submit that PTAs offer distinctly good and direct insights into this question.

## I. Competition policy as protectionism

The first theoretical perspective sees competition policy as a substitute for trade restrictions. It assumes that governments want to protect domestic producers (and that they suspect each other of wanting to do so). It further assumes that competition law can be selectively enforced to the benefit of domestic firms and the detriment of their foreign competitors. There are two variants of this 'competition-policy-as-protectionism' perspective.

What may be called the aggregate national welfare variant, with strong affinities to statist theories of international relations, treats governments as unitary actors and assumes that each government seeks to maximise the country's aggregate (consumer + producer) welfare. Under this assumption, (net) imports create an incentive for excessively stringent competition laws and enforcement (relative to what would maximise global economic welfare), because such an 'oversupply' of competition policy creates benefits for domestic consumers, whereas the costs are borne disproportionately by foreign producers. By contrast, (net) exports create an incentive for excessively lax competition law and enforcement because the gains from tolerated anticompetitive behaviour are disproportionately enjoyed by domestic producers, whereas the costs are disproportionately borne by foreign consumers (Guzman 1998, 2004; Horn and Levinsohn 2001; Iacobucci 1997; Richardson 1999; Williams and Rodriguez 1995).

Such selective enforcement is particularly attractive for economically large countries, that is, countries whose markets are sufficiently large that enforcement-induced changes in their production or consumption affect the world price and hence the country's terms of trade. Strategic enforcement is attractive for them because it can yield a gain in aggregate welfare rather than just redistribution among domestic consumers and producers.

The domestic political economy variant of the competition-policy-as-protectionism perspective, with strong affinities to the public choice perspective on regulation, starts from the assumption that firms will seek alternative ways to protect their market share or profits when faced with increased foreign competition resulting from trade liberalisation. Firms' 'actions aimed at effectively locking competing imports or foreign investors out of their domestic market' (Trebilcock and Howse 2005: 591) can include the 'use of antitrust to subvert competition' (Baumol and Ordover 1985: 247).[20] This argument lacks an explicit theory of politics or policymaking but implicitly usually assumes a pluralistic responsiveness of policymakers to political lobbying (e.g. Shughart, Silverman and Tollison 1995). Consequently, it yields similar observable implications to those noted for the aggregate national welfare variant but for all countries (rather than primarily for economically large countries) because there is no assumption that policymakers seek to maximise aggregate welfare and therefore may readily engage in selective enforcement that is 'inefficient' for the national economy.

Both variants of the competition-policy-as-protectionism perspective remain empirically largely untested.[21] We have discussed them together because they have similar implications for the kind of competition

---

[20] This starting point is consistent with Bhagwati's (1988) 'law of constant protection', according to which firms will always find a way to replace a barrier to trade that has been negotiated away with a new one.

[21] Limited anecdotal evidence exists, suggesting that both US and European competition regulators have in some cases enforced competition laws in ways that discriminated against foreign stakeholders (e.g. Guzman 1998: esp. 1532f.), and China's 2007 antimonopoly law has, almost from the beginning, prompted vocal concerns about selective and discriminatory enforcement (Huang 2008, but cf. Faure and Zhang 2013). Shughart, Silverman and Tollison (1995) present a statistical analysis of antitrust enforcement budgets for the US Department of Justice and the Federal Trade Commission, in which the US enforcement agencies' resources are significantly correlated with the US trade deficit, suggesting more vigorous antitrust enforcement at times when the United States in the aggregate was a net importer. Ecological inference and other methodological problems, however, raise questions about these findings, which we have also been unable to replicate with their aggregate data.

provisions we should expect to find in PTAs. This yields our first hypothesis, which we will further operationalise in the next section:[22]

H$_1$: *To the extent that trade agreements contain competition provisions, they should reflect concern about selective enforcement and contain measures to prevent or discipline such enforcement against firms from the other Parties.*

## II. Free trade and competition policy as complements

Dissatisfied with the theoretical approach sketched previously, we have developed an alternative theoretical account, which views trade openness and competition policy as genuine complements. We start from the observation that the progressively denser web of PTAs and the shift from the GATT to the more legalised WTO have institutionalised trade liberalisation in such a way that governments' ability to protect domestic producers through traditional trade barriers has been severely compromised (Bagwell and Staiger 1999). Domestic producers – now exposed to increased foreign competition – might, of course, still turn to their governments to clamour for protection, and governments might yet find new covert means of protecting domestic firms from foreign competitors (e.g. Kono 2006). If the governments' hands, however, truly are increasingly tied by trade agreements, firms have an incentive to pursue what has become known as 'private protection' (Ludema 2001; Trebilcock 1996; Williams and Rodriguez 1995): protecting themselves from the consequences of market competition through collusion with their ostensible competitors or other anticompetitive practices. In fact, trade liberalisation creates opportunities and incentives for engaging in anticompetitive practices transnationally for at least two reasons. First, the integration of product markets creates opportunities for gain from collusion *across borders*, which did not exist when the boundaries of states and markets largely coincided. Second, integration creates additional incentives for such anticompetitive behaviour by lowering the risk of getting caught. International cartels, for instance, may be harder to detect or prosecute because antitrust agencies may find it more difficult to monitor global markets and pursue enforcement against them as most of the evidence can be kept out of reach of any one enforcement agency (e.g. Connor 2007).

---

[22] Elsewhere (e.g. Bradford 2007; Büthe 2014), we critique the deductive logic of these arguments. Here, we simply focus on the empirical implications.

Assessing this argument is made more difficult by the fact that such private protection is illegal in many countries. Consequently, changing patterns of anticompetitive behaviour are virtually impossible for scholars to observe directly. The argument, however, also has observable implications for what governments should write into PTAs, provided that we are able to assume that governments generally:

1. understand the international political economy of market competition and anticompetitive behaviour in open economies at least sufficiently well to recognise that trade openness creates opportunities and incentives for private protection and
2. in fact, seek to safeguard market competition against the accumulation and abuse of market power (at least in countries with an independent enforcement agency).[23]

Under these assumptions, governments should see trade openness and the *need for* vigorous competition policy as complements.[24] Governments can attempt to increase enforcement unilaterally, for example, through intensified monitoring. Alternatively, or in addition, they should be expected to counteract transnational collusion through corresponding transgovernmental collaboration. Such regulatory cooperation may and does take place informally, but we would also expect to find evidence of a trade-related increase in substantively meaningful antitrust provisions in trade agreements or in separate antitrust enforcement agreements.

In sum, this alternative theoretical perspective implies for PTAs:

H₂: *If trade agreements contain competition provisions, they will focus on enhancing the capacity and procedures for detecting transnational anticompetitive behaviour and strengthening transgovernmental enforcement cooperation.*

---

[23] The argument does not depend on any particular assumption about the goals of competition policy. We merely allow for the possibility that competition regulators mean it when they claim that safeguarding market competition is their primary goal. The effectiveness of such normative commitment is at least a real possibility since antitrust regulators form a tight transnational peer network, which provides mechanisms for reenforcing shared professional norms through the reputational and social dynamics identified by Sabel and Zeitlin's (2010) notion of 'experimentalist' governance (see also Ansell 2011).

[24] Strictly speaking, the logic of our argument requires governments or national regulators only to *observe* (rather than anticipate) increased anticompetitive activity and attribute it to trade openness.

## F. Empirical analysis, part 2: PTA competition provisions, 1945–2010

In this overview of the specific content of PTAs, we focus on those competition provisions that allow us to distinguish between the two theoretical approaches discussed in Section E. Some common competition policy provisions, however, are worth noting even though they do not allow us to assess the relative explanatory power of the two theoretical approaches. Specifically, of the 137 PTAs that contain any substantive competition provisions, 40 PTAs (29.2 per cent) contain an obligation to have or adopt a competition law – or other obligations that are predicated upon having or maintaining a competition law.[25] A considerably smaller number, 24 PTAs (17.5 per cent), contain an obligation for 'transparency' in the implementation of the national competition law's enforcement policies and practices.[26]

Very common, by contrast, are provisions that commit the signatories to establishing a working group, study group or committee of representatives of parties' governments (or competition authorities) to discuss competition policy issues. PTAs may include such a commitment in one of two ways:

1. The PTA may establish such a committee or working group for the PTA as a whole and include competition policy within its purview, usually in this case along with most or all other subjects covered in the PTA.
2. The PTA may establish a separate working group specifically for competition policy discussion.

Figure 10.3 shows the distribution of these options (vis-à-vis each other and vis-à-vis having no such provision in the PTA at all), illustrating the overwhelming prevalence of the first option. The near-universal inclusion of provisions for the institutionalisation of inter- or transgovernmental dialogue is certainly interesting. However, since such a working group may be used not only to coordinate policies or cooperate in enforcement (consistent with $H_2$) but also to address accusations of selective,

---

[25] For PTAs in which one party did not previously have a competition law (a piece of information that we are still gathering), such a provision might be considered evidence against $H_1$, since a government that is concerned about selective enforcement should hardly want to commit other governments to having such laws.

[26] Here, we specifically coded for whether the word *transparency* appeared in the PTA provision given its prominence in the literature.

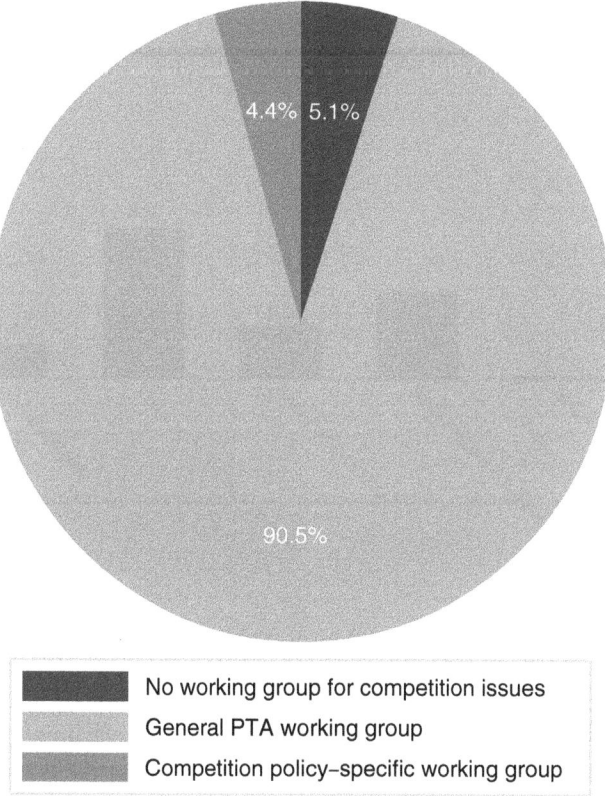

**Figure 10.3**    PTA-established working groups for the discussion of competition policy

discriminatory enforcement (consistent with $H_1$), the presence or absence of these provisions does not allow us to distinguish between the two theoretical positions.

## I. Testing $H_1$

If governments include competition policy provisions in PTAs primarily out of a concern that other governments may enforce their competition laws selectively and for protectionist purposes, we would expect to find – frequently and prominently – provisions that seek to safeguard against such discrimination. The risk of selective enforcement might be reduced, for instance, through mutual commitments that competition regulators and courts must provide full legal reasoning to those against

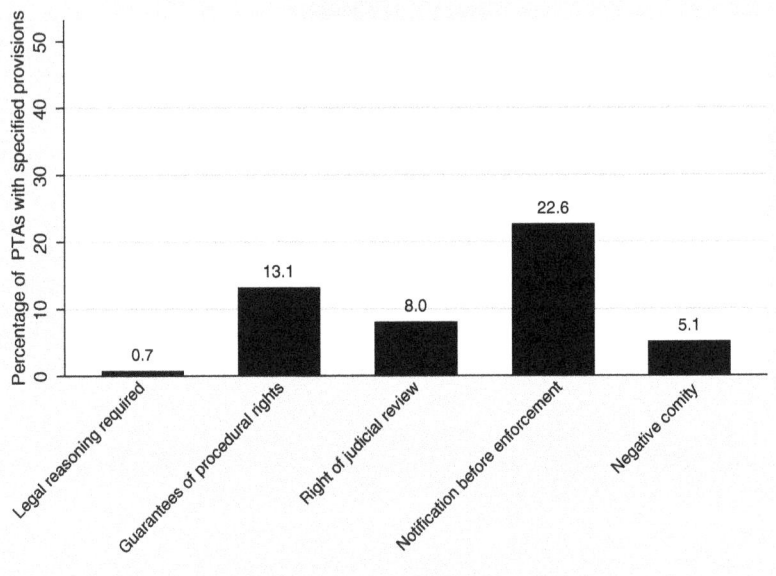

**Figure 10.4**    Provisions indicating concerns about selective enforcement

whom they bring competition policy enforcement actions. $H_1$ would also lead us to expect committing the parties to provide various procedural rights in competition law enforcement cases or to guarantee the right to judicial review or appeal following initial (often administrative) decisions in competition enforcement cases or merger review.[27] We therefore asked coders to record for each PTA whether it included such provisions. As shown by the first three bars in Figure 10.4, they are quite rare. An obliga tion to provide legal reasoning is found in only one of the 137 PTAs with substantive competition provisions. The other commitments are found in 18 and 11 PTAs, respectively.

[27]  The coding question and response options were:

Does the PTA establish any of the following obligations for the governments of the member countries in the implementation of their antitrust/competition law? Please check all that apply.

☐  to provide the legal reasoning behind any decisions;
☐  to provide for procedural rights for the defendant in antitrust proceedings, such as opportunities to present evidence, to be heard, to cross-examine witnesses;
☐  to provide for judicial review (appeal) of an antitrust enforcement or merger review decision.

An even stronger safeguard against selective enforcement with protectionist intent might be created by a requirement to notify the other party before an enforcement action is taken against one of its firms or citizens.[28] Finally, a 'negative comity' provision would have the same thrust – and arguably provides the strongest safeguard. Negative comity, as Dabbah (2011: 288) puts it well, seeks to 'prevent jurisdictional conflict'. Such a provision in a PTA would entail each party committing to take the actions and important interests of the other parties into consideration before taking any actions that may affect the interests of those other parties. As shown by the last two bars in Figure 10.4, a commitment to alert the other party *before* taking enforcement actions against one of its firms or citizens is relatively common, found in 22.6 per cent of the 137 PTAs. By contrast, and very surprisingly, negative comity provisions – which we would have expected to be quite common – are very rare in our sample, found in just over 5 per cent of the PTAs.

## II. Testing H₂

What would we expect instead if hypothesis 2 were borne out? If the inclusion of competition policy provision in PTAs were largely or predominantly motivated by a desire to improve the efficiency and effectiveness of competition law enforcement in the face of increasingly internationally integrated markets, we would expect a very different emphasis in the specific provision. In our theoretical discussion in Section E.II, we focused on transgovernmental cooperation among competition regulators to facilitate the detection of increasingly transnational anticompetitive practices and possible cooperation in enforcement. But such transgovernmental cooperation presupposes not just the existence but also substantial capacity on the part of the competition regulator. We would therefore expect, first, provisions that ensure or increase regulatory capacity at the national level through commitments to

- devote resources to enforcement,
- establish and maintain an independent enforcement agency and
- provide reciprocal or (in North–South PTAs) unilateral technical capacity-building assistance.[29]

---

[28] We note as a caveat that such an obligation impinges on the other country's sovereignty and might therefore be resisted.

[29] The exact question and response option wording here was: 'Does the PTA establish an obligation to cooperate on antitrust or competition matters in any of the following

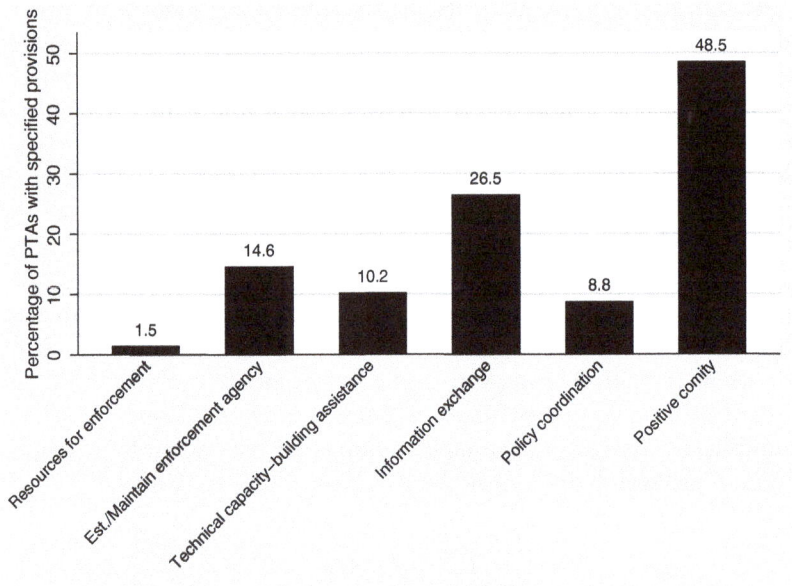

**Figure 10.5**   Provisions indicating desire to enhance enforcement

As shown by the first three bars in Figure 10.5, provisions that commit the parties to devote ancillary resources to enforcement are quite rare, found in only 2 of the 137 PTAs (possibly because such provisions impinge upon the sovereignty over budgetary matters of the parties' legislatures), but the other types of provisions are more common, found in 20 (14.6 per cent) and 14 (10.2 per cent) of the PTAs, respectively.

Given the existence, or at least the promise, of capable enforcement agencies, we would then expect an emphasis on information exchange, possibly policy coordination (subject to a caveat similar to the caveat that applied to the funding commitment earlier) and, especially, 'positive comity' provisions, under which each party, acting at that moment as the so-called requesting party, 'can ask the other party (known as the requested party) to address anticompetitive behavior within the latter's boundaries [based solely on the claim that the behavior] has a [detrimental] effect on the interest of the former' (Dabbah 2011:

ways? . . . For one or more of the Parties to provide technical assistance or resource transfer to another Party to help it finance its enforcement activity or build its competition-regulatory capacity.'

288). Such a positive comity provision constitutes the clearest and most far-reaching commitment to assist each other in competition law enforcement.

As shown by the last three columns in Figure 10.5, information exchange provisions (about both enforcement actions and merger reviews) are quite common, found in 26.5 per cent of PTAs. Commitments to policy coordination are less common, found in 8.8 per cent of PTAs (though they are still more common than what should have been the theoretically strongest type of provisions for $H_1$). Most strikingly, positive comity – considered a very demanding commitment from a legal point of view – is more common than any other commitments, as it is found in almost half (48.5 per cent) of the PTAs.

# G. Conclusion

In this chapter, we have examined competition policy provisions in PTAs. Such provisions are a puzzle from a traditional trade economics perspective and have only recently begun to attract systematic scholarly attention. We have sought to provide an initial sketch of some of the key variation in competition policy provisions in PTAs – including the form such provisions take and how their role has changed over time – based on a large random sample of 182 PTAs drawn from the DESTA Database. We have also briefly explored the extent to which the increased formalisation of the treatment of competition issues in PTAs might be merely a reflection of a general trend towards deeper PTAs and found this to be only modestly so and with several caveats. Most importantly, we introduced two alternative and quite general theoretical approaches for thinking about the relationship between trade openness and competition policy, from which we have derived two rather different hypotheses about the kinds of competition policy provision we should expect to find in PTAs. Our final (though still explicitly preliminary) empirical analysis has yielded some support for both, although on balance we observe with greater frequency provisions that suggest a deep concern with and interest in enhanced enforcement cooperation rather than concern about the protectionist selective enforcement by the other side in the PTA.[30]

---

[30] Numerous further provisions are yet to be examined in future work when the content analysis is fully completed. Dispute settlement mechanisms of the PTAs, for example, should be very telling, since subjecting competition policy to a DSM should be very important if governments are concerned about selective, discriminatory enforcement.

The research presented is drawn from work in progress, which itself is part of a larger research agenda that also entails collecting and coding in detail all national competition laws since the first such law for each country. This will allow us to examine, for instance, whether PTAs create new obligations or simply codify what countries are already doing. As part of that larger project, we are also collecting and coding bilateral competition enforcement agreements (a potential substitute for competition provisions in PTAs, which could be a source of omitted variable bias for the analysis of PTAs). And we are collecting enforcement data to allow us to test whether countries only commit to competition provisions in PTAs if they are undertaking serious enforcement already.

Beyond this work in progress, the research presented here suggests several promising avenues for future research. In particular, we know little about the details of the treaty-writing process. Who actually writes PTAs? Who exerts influence over what competition provisions get written into a PTA – and who is unsuccessful when they attempt to influence such content of PTAs? We should also want to know more about the consequences of these provisions, including whether they are enforced in practice, and what their effects are on actual competition law and enforcement, as well as on the behaviour of private economic actors.

## References

Anderson, Robert D., and Evenett, Simon J. 2006. 'Incorporating Competition Elements into Regional Trade Agreements: Characterization and Empirical Analysis.' Unpublished manuscript, WTO and University of St. Gallen.

Anderson, Robert D., and Holmes, Peter 2002. 'Competition Policy and the Future of the Multilateral Trading System.' *Journal of International Economic Law* 5 (2): 531–63.

Ansell, Christopher. 2011. *Pragmatist Democracy: Evolutionary Learning as Public Philosophy.* New York: Oxford University Press.

Arrowsmith, Sue, and Anderson, Robert D., eds. 2011. *The WTO Regime on Government Procurement: Challenge and Reform.* Cambridge: Cambridge University Press.

Axelrod, Robert, and Keohane, Robert O. 1985. 'Achieving Cooperation under Anarchy: Strategies and Institutions.' *World Politics* 38 (1): 226–54.

Baccini, Leonardo, Dür, Andreas, Elsig, Manfred, and Milewicz, Karolina. 2011. 'The Design of Preferential Trade Agreements: A New Dataset in the Making.' WTO Staff Working Paper No. ERSD 2011–10 (Economic Research and Statistics Division). World Trade Organization, Geneva.

Bagwell, Kyle, and Staiger Robert W. 1999. 'An Economic Theory of GATT.' *American Economic Review* 89 (1): 215–48.

Baldwin, Richard, Evenett, Simon, and Low, Patrick. 2009. 'Beyond Tariffs: Multilaterising Non-Tariff RTA Commitments.' In *Multilateralising Regionalism: Challenges for the Global Trading System*, edited by Richard Baldwin and Patrick Low, 79–141. Cambridge: Cambridge University Press.

Baumol, William J., and Ordover, Janusz A. 1985. 'Use of Antitrust to Subvert Competition.' *Journal of Law and Economics* 28 (2, special issue on Antitrust and Economic Efficiency): 247–65.

Bhagwati, Jagdish. 1988. *Protectionism*. Cambridge, MA: MIT Press.

Bhagwati, Jagdish, and Hudec, Robert E., eds. 1996. *Fair Trade and Harmonization*. 2 vols. Cambridge, MA: MIT Press.

Blackhurst, Richard. 1991. 'Trade Policy Is Competition Policy.' In *Competition and Economic Development*, 253–8. Paris: OECD.

Bown, Chad P. 2011. 'Taking Stock of Antidumping, Safeguards, and Countervailing Duties, 1990–2009.' *World Economy* 34 (12): 1955–98.

Bown, Chad P., and Wu, Mark. 2014. 'Safeguards and the Perils of Preferential Trade Agreements: Dominican Republic – Safeguard Measures.' *World Trade Review* 13 (2): 179–227.

Bradford, Anu. 2007. 'International Antitrust Negotiations and the False Hope of the WTO.' *Harvard International Law Journal* 48 (2): 383–440.

Brusick, Philippe, Alvarez, Ana Maria, and Cernat, Lucian, eds. 2005. *Competition Provisions in Regional Trade Agreements: How to Assure Development Gains*. New York: United Nations Conference on Trade and Development.

Büthe, Tim. Forthcoming. 'The Politics of Market Competition: Trade and Antitrust in a Global Economy.' In *Oxford Handbook of the Politics of International Trade*, edited by Lisa L. Martin. New York: Oxford University Press, 2015.

Büthe, Tim, and Mattli, Walter. 2011. *The New Global Rulers: The Privatization of Regulation in the World Economy*. Princeton, NJ: Princeton University Press.

Büthe, Tim, and Milner, Helen V. 2008. 'The Politics of Foreign Direct Investment into Developing Countries: Increasing FDI through International Trade Agreements?' *American Journal of Political Science* 52 (4): 741–62.

——— 2014. 'Institutional Diversity in Trade Agreements and Their Effects on Foreign Direct Investment: Credibility, Commitment, and Economic Flows in the Developing World, 1971–2007.' *World Politics* 66 (1): 88–122.

Clarke, Julian L., and Evenett, Simon J. 2003. 'A Multilateral Framework for Competition Policy?' In *The Singapore Issue and the World Trading System: The Road to Cancun and Beyond*, 77–168. Berne, Switzerland: Swiss State Secretariat of Economic Affairs (Seco Publikation Welthandel).

Connor, John M. 2007. *Global Price Fixing*. 2nd updated and revised edn. Berlin/New York: Springer.

Crane, Daniel A., and Hovenkamp, Herbert, eds. 2013. *The Making of Competition Policy: Legal and Economic Sources*. New York: Oxford University Press.

Dabbah, Maher M. 2011. 'Future Directions in Bilateral Cooperation.' In *Cooperation, Comity, and Competition Policy*, edited by Andrew T. Guzman, 287–99. Oxford, England: Oxford University Press.

Davis, Christina L. 2004. 'International Institutions and Issue Linkage: Building Support for Agricultural Trade Liberalization.' *American Political Science Review* 98 (1): 153–69.

Dawar, Kamala, and Evenett, Simon J. 2011. 'Government Procurement.' In *Preferential Trade Agreement Policies for Development: A Handbook*, edited by Jean-Pierre Chauffour and Jean-Christophe Maur, 367–85. Washington, DC: World Bank.

Dür, Andreas, Baccini, Leonardo, and Elsig, Manfred. 2014. 'The Design of International Trade Agreements: Introducing a New Dataset.' *Review of International Organizations* 9 (3): 353–75.

Faure, Michael, and Zhang, Xinzhu, eds. 2013. *The Chinese Anti-Monopoly Law: New Developments and Empirical Evidence*. Cheltenham, England: Edward Elgar.

Fox, Eleanor M. 1997. 'Toward World Antitrust and Market Access.' *American Journal of International Law* 91 (1): 1–25.

Guzman, Andrew T. 1998. 'Is International Antitrust Possible?' *New York University Law Review* 73 (5): 1501–48.

2004. 'The Case for International Antitrust.' *Berkeley Journal of International Law* 22 (3): 355–74.

Horn, Henrik, and Levinsohn, James. 2001. 'Merger Policies and Trade Liberalisation.' *Economic Journal* 111 (470): 244–76.

Huang, Yong. 2008. 'Pursuing the Second Best: The History, Momentum, and Remaining Issues of China's Anti-Monopoly Law.' *Antitrust Law Journal* 75 (1): 117–31.

Iacobucci, Edward M. 1997. 'The Interdependence of Trade and Competition Policies.' *World Competition* 21 (2): 5–33.

Irwin, Douglas A. 2009. *Free Trade Under Fire*. 3rd edn. Princeton, NJ: Princeton University Press.

Kono, Daniel Y. 2006. 'Optimal Obfuscation: Democracy and Trade Policy Transparency.' *American Political Science Review* 100 (3): 369–84.

Koremenos, Barbara 2005. 'Contracting Around International Uncertainty.' *American Political Science Review* 99 (4): 549–65.

2007. 'If Only Half of International Agreements Have Dispute Resolution Provisions, Which Half Needs Explaining?' *Journal of Legal Studies* 36 (1): 189–212.

Ludema, Rodney D. 2001. 'Market Collusion and the Politics of Protection.' *European Journal of Political Economy* 17 (4): 817–33.

Mansfield, Edward D., and Milner, Helen V. 2012. *Votes, Vetoes, and the Political Economy of International Trade Agreements.* Princeton, NJ: Princeton University Press.

Marsden, Philip. 2003. *Competition Policy for the WTO.* London: Cameron May.

Moe, Terry M. 2005. 'Power and Political Institutions.' *Perspectives on Politics* 3 (2): 215–33.

Richardson, Martin. 1999. 'Trade and Competition Policy: Concordia Discors?' *Oxford Economic Papers* 51 (4): 649–64.

Sabel, Charles F., and Zeitlin, Jonathan, eds. 2010. *Experimentalist Governance in the European Union: Towards a New Architecture.* New York: Oxford University Press.

Salazar-Xirinachs, Jose M. 2000. 'The Trade-Labor Nexus: Developing Countries' Perspectives.' *Journal of International Economic Law* 3 (2): 377–84.

Shughart, William F., Silverman, Jon D., and Tollison Robert D. 1995. 'Antitrust Enforcement and Foreign Competition.' In *The Causes and Consequences of Antitrust: The Public Choice Perspective,* edited by Fred S. McChesney and Willam F. Shughart II, 179–87. Chicago: University of Chicago Press.

Silva, Verónica. 2004. *Cooperation on Competition Policy in Latin American and Caribbean Bilateral Trade Agreements.* Geneva: United Nations Conference on Trade and Development.

Sokol, D. Daniel. 2008. 'Order Without (Enforceable) Law: Why Countries Enter into Non-Enforceable Competition Policy Chapters in Free Trade Agreements.' *Chicago-Kent Law Review* 83 (1): 231–92.

Solano, Oliver, and Sennekamp, Andreas. 2006. 'Competition Provisions in Regional Trade Agreements.' OECD Trade Policy Working Paper Series No. 31. Organisation for Economic Co-operation and Development, Paris.

Stephan, Paul B. 2004. 'Against International Cooperation.' In *Competition Laws in Conflict: Antitrust Jurisdiction in the Global Economy,* edited by Richard A. Epstein and Michael S. Greve, 66–98. Washington, DC: American Enterprise Institute Press.

Teh, Robert. 2009. 'Competition Provisions in Regional Trade Agreements.' In *Regional Rules in the Global Trading System,* edited by Anti Estevadeordal, Kati Suominen and Robert Teh, 418–91. Cambridge: Cambridge University Press.

Trebilcock, Michael J. 1996. 'Competition Policy and Trade Policy: Mediating the Interface.' *Journal of World Trade* 30 (4): 71–106.

Trebilcock, Michael J., and Howse, Robert. 2005. *The Regulation of International Trade.* 3rd edn. New York: Routledge.

United Nations Conference on Trade and Development. 2006. *Investment Provisions in Economic Integration Agreements.* New York: United Nations.

Williams, Mark D., and Rodriguez, A. E. 1995. 'Antitrust and Liberalization in Developing Countries.' *International Trade Journal* 9 (4): 495–518.

World Trade Organization. 2011. *World Trade Report 2011: The WTO and Preferential Trade Agreements: From Co-Existence to Coherence.* Geneva: World Trade Organization.

  2012. *World Trade Report 2012: Trade and Public Policies – A Closer Look at Non-Tariff Measures in the 21st Century.* Geneva: World Trade Organization.

# 11

# PTAs and public procurement

STEPHANIE J. RICKARD

## A. Introduction

Public procurement increasingly features in international trade negotiations. Public procurement is the process by which governments purchase goods and services from the private sector for their own use. Governments buy everything from routine items such as stationery to highly complex objects such as aircraft carriers. These purchases add up. Public procurement represents between 13 and 20 per cent of gross domestic product (GDP) on average worldwide (Ueno 2013). In virtually all countries, procurement accounts for a large share of the total value of commercial activity. Given the vast sums of money at stake, it is not surprising that public procurement is part of international trade negotiations.

The first multilateral procurement rules were adopted in 1979 and came into force as the Tokyo Round Government Procurement Code in 1981. The World Trade Organization (WTO) Agreement on Government Procurement (GPA) was adopted in 1994 and entered into force in 1996. In March 2012, the WTO Committee on Government Procurement adopted revisions to the 1994 GPA text that expanded the coverage of the WTO procurement rules (Ueno 2013). The GPA provisions generally seek to eliminate bias against foreign firms bidding for government contracts. The GPA also includes provisions that aim to ensure that procurement is carried out in a transparent and competitive manner.

Not all WTO Members are bound by the GPA. The GPA is a plurilateral agreement and consequently applies only to countries that choose to sign it. Only 42 of the WTO's 157 Members are currently signatories to the GPA.[1] Even for these 42 signatories, the GPA does not cover all

---

[1] As of the end of 2012, GPA signatories include the 28 Member States of the European Union (which I refer to here as 28 individual countries for ease of presentation), Armenia, Canada, Hong Kong, China, Iceland, Israel, Japan, Korea, Liechtenstein, the Netherlands with respect to Aruba, Norway, Singapore, Switzerland, Chinese Taipei and the United States.

public procurement. Only certain government entities are regulated by the agreement, and only purchases above a specified monetary value are subject to the rules. Perhaps for these reasons, questions exist about the effectiveness of the GPA.

Doubts about the GPA's effectiveness may have helped to fuel the proliferation of procurement chapters in preferential trade agreements (PTAs). More and more PTAs include explicit rules that aim to increase the competitiveness of government procurement. This trend raises important and interesting questions, several of which are highlighted in this chapter. Why, for example, do governments sign PTAs with procurement rules when research shows that such rules have limited success in liberalizing procurement markets? One possible reason is that PTA procurement rules represent a win–win situation for governments. Governments can sign procurement PTAs safe in the knowledge that they can still 'buy national' with relative impunity because of the opacity of public procurement. At the same time, when a government needs to buy foreign, the PTA's procurement rules give them political cover. Governments can point to the PTA and argue that their hands are tied. In effect, the agreement serves as a 'scapegoat' for unpopular foreign purchases.

## B. Discrimination in public procurement

In theory, the procurement chapters included in an increasing number of PTAs seek to ensure competitive public procurement. Competitive public procurement has two main benefits. The first is that it allows governments to choose between multiple suppliers. This should establish price competition and thus reduce the costs to taxpayers. The other main argument for competitive procurement is that it allows for the use of specialists rather than work being carried out by in-house public-sector employees who may lack the requisite expertise for a specific project or task.

Despite the benefits of competitive procurement, governments frequently discriminate against foreign firms (Lowinger 1976; Trionfetti 2000). In Norway, for example, only 7 per cent of government contracts were awarded to foreign suppliers in 2009 (Rickard and Kono 2013). On average, 98 per cent of all local authority contracts were awarded to domestic firms in European Union (EU) countries in 1993 (Martin, Hartley and Cox 1999). Forty-six per cent of businesses surveyed by the EU believe that local preferences significantly influence the outcome of public procurement procedures (European Commission 2011). In fact, direct cross-border procurement accounts for only 1.6 per cent of contracts awarded by the governments of EU Member States, or roughly 3.5 per cent of the total value of contract awards during 2006–9. Taken together, these numbers illustrate the extent to which public procurement markets remain closed to foreign firms.

## C. Procurement rules in PTAs

International trade negotiators are working hard to try to pry open public procurement markets. More and more PTAs explicitly regulate public procurement. Forty-three PTAs notified to the WTO before 2010 and currently in force include meaningful procurement rules. Nearly 80 per cent of these procurement PTAs have entered into force since 2000, as illustrated in Table 11.1.[2] Only PTAs with explicit rules regulating government procurement are included in Table 11.1. This criterion excludes, for example, agreements that are merely aspirational in nature: for example, the European Community–Montenegro agreement states, 'The Community and Montenegro consider the opening up of the award of public contracts on the basis of non-discrimination and reciprocity to be a desirable objective.' However, no further mention of procurement is made in the agreement.

Although the specific rules differ across PTAs' procurement chapters, they generally aim to increase competition by offering fair access to all prospective bidders, whether foreign or domestic. Many procurement chapters include market access for each party to the government procurement market of the other party, national treatment for foreign firms and products, a list specifying which levels of government (national, regional and municipal) are bound by the agreement and a specification of monetary 'threshold levels' above which the agreement applies.

Some PTAs explicitly forbid certain forms of discrimination in public procurement. Many, for example, forbid explicit 'buy national' policies,

---

[2]  Many agreements begin at the start of the year: for example, the North American Free Trade Agreement (NAFTA) entered into force on 1 January 1994. However, this is not always the case. For example, the European Free Trade Agreement (EFTA)–Chile agreement came into force on 1 December 2003. As a rule, I code the year of entry into force as $t + 1$ when agreements come into force after 1 October in year $t$. I thus code the EFTA–Chile agreement as entering into force in 2004. This coding acknowledges that in such cases governments may continue discriminating for most of year $t$.

## Table 11.1 *PTAs with procurement rules*

| Year | Agreement |
|------|-----------|
| 1983 | Australia–New Zealand |
| 1985 | US–Israel |
| 1994 | European Community (EC) |
| 1994 | European Economic Area (EEA) |
| 1994 | North American Free Trade Agreement (NAFTA) |
| 1995 | Costa Rica–Mexico |
| 1997 | Canada–Israel |
| 1998 | Mexico–Nicaragua |
| 1999 | Chile–Mexico |
| 2000 | EC–Mexico |
| 2000 | Israel–Mexico |
| 2001 | European Free Trade Association (EFTA)–Mexico |
| 2001 | New Zealand–Singapore |
| 2002 | Chile–El Salvador |
| 2002 | Chile–Costa Rica |
| 2003 | Japan–Singapore |
| 2003 | EC–Chile |
| 2003 | EFTA–Singapore |
| 2003 | Panama–Costa Rica |
| 2003 | Panama–El Salvador |
| 2003 | Singapore–Australia |
| 2004 | Korea–Chile |
| 2004 | US–Singapore |
| 2004 | US–Chile |
| 2005 | EFTA–Chile |
| 2005 | Japan–Mexico |
| 2005 | US–Australia |
| 2006 | Dominican Republic–Central America FTA (CAFTA-DR) |
| 2006 | EFTA–South Korea |
| 2006 | South Korea–Singapore |
| 2006 | Panama–Singapore |
| 2006 | US–Bahrain |
| 2006 | US–Morocco |
| 2007 | Chile–Japan |
| 2008 | EC–Caribbean Forum of African, Caribbean and Pacific (CARIFORUM) States |
| 2009 | Australia–Chile |
| 2009 | Canada–EFTA |
| 2009 | Canada–Peru |
| 2009 | Chile–Colombia |
| 2009 | Japan–Switzerland |
| 2009 | Peru–Singapore |
| 2009 | US–Peru |
| 2009 | US–Oman |

*Source:* Rickard and Kono (2013).

such as the 2009 Buy American provisions. However, explicitly discriminatory rules, such as the 2009 Buy American provisions, are rare. Instead, governments tend to discriminate against foreign firms using less obvious measures. PTAs attempt to regulate these less formal means of discrimination. For example, some PTA procurement chapters explicitly prohibit price discrimination (i.e. choosing higher-priced domestic bids over lower-priced but otherwise identical foreign bids). Beyond this, PTAs' procurement rules typically ban a range of other policies that favour domestic firms. For example, they often outlaw local-content requirements, since local firms are much more likely to source their inputs domestically (Grier 1996).

One of the earliest and most comprehensive sets of PTA procurement rules was agreed by the European Community (EC). Harmonised procurement rules were established to create a level playing field for all businesses across Europe. Businesses registered in an EU country have the right to compete for public contracts in other EU countries. Governments and other public authorities may not discriminate against a business simply because it is registered in another EU country. EU procurement rules also require that governments make all information regarding tenders available to all interested companies, regardless of what EU country they are registered in. Like the WTO's GPA, however, these rules apply only to contracts whose monetary value exceeds a certain amount. These 'above threshold' tenders are, presumably, of cross-border interest; in other words – the tender value makes it worthwhile for a business to submit a tender abroad.

A more recent example of a procurement PTA is the 2004 bilateral trade agreement between the United States and Chile. The stated objective of this PTA's procurement chapter is to 'provide comprehensive coverage of procurement markets by eliminating market access barriers to the supply of goods and services, including construction services'. The chapter, however, goes beyond aspirations. It stipulates rules for purchases by 20 Chilean federal ministries, many regional governments and 341 municipalities, as well as 79 federal US departments and many offices of state governments. The main principles are national treatment and nondiscrimination. The chapter states: 'Each Party shall accord to the goods and services of the other Party . . . treatment no less favorable than the most favorable treatment the Party accords to its own goods, services, and suppliers.' The chapter goes further, stipulating that 'neither Party may treat a locally established supplier less favorably than another locally established supplier on the basis of degree of foreign affiliation or owner-ship'. These provisions aim to reduce discrimination against foreign firms in government procurement.

## D. Why procurement rules?

Recent research suggests at least two possible explanations for the prolif-eration of procurement chapters in PTAs. First, procurement rules may have become part of 'boilerplate' PTA language. Countries need not 'start from scratch' when negotiating a new PTA (Baccini, Dür and Haftel, Chapter 7 in this volume). Instead, negotiators can use an existing PTA template as the basis for their negotiations (Baccini, Dür and Haftel, Chapter 7 in this volume; Kim and Manger 2013; Jetschke and Lenz 2013BIB-11'19: 7). Baccini, Dür and Haftel (Chapter 7 in this volume) contend that three broad templates exist. Two of the three templates iden-tified include public procurement rules. Once procurement becomes part of a PTA 'template', all subsequent PTAs may include procurement rules simply because they were modelled on an existing 'template' that included procurement.

A second possible explanation for the increased popularity of pro-curement rules is that recent PTAs tend to be 'deeper' agreements (Kim, Chapter 2 in this volume). As trade negotiators pursue deeper market inte-gration, procurement rules may become indispensable. Discriminatory procurement can substitute for other barriers to trade, such as subsidies or tariffs (Kono and Rickard 2013). If subsidies are restricted by interna-tional agreements, for example, governments can instead buy products from domestic firms at above-market rates via discriminatory public procurement. By doing so, the government effectively subsidises the firm. Deep market integration therefore cannot be achieved by the elimination of tariffs and subsidies alone. Negotiators must also tackle discriminatory procurement practices.

Procurement rules may therefore be an important feature of deep trade agreements, which characterise many of the more recent PTAs. Evidence suggests that PTAs with procurement chapters do, in fact, tend to be deeper agreements than those without procurement chapters are. The depth of PTAs is measured using an index developed by Dür, Baccini and Elsig (2014). This additive index combines seven key provisions that can be included in PTAs. The first captures whether the agreement foresees that all tariffs (with limited exceptions) should be reduced to zero (that is,

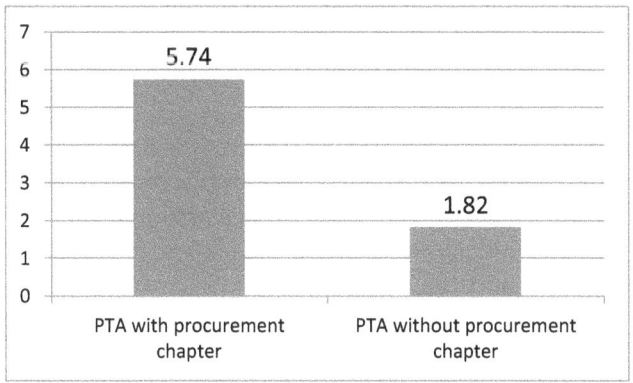

<figure>Figure 11.1    Depth of PTAs</figure>

whether the aim is to create a full free trade area). The other six provisions capture cooperation that goes beyond tariff reductions.[3]

Using this index, I calculate the average depth of PTAs with and without procurement chapters. These results are reported in Figure 11.1.

PTAs identified by Rickard and Kono (2013) as having substantive procurement chapters are, on average, deeper agreements than are PTAs without procurement chapters. PTAs with procurement chapters score 5.7, on average. This is a relatively high score given that the maximum possible value is 7. PTAs without explicit procurement rules, however, score only 1.8, on average. This difference is substantively large (3.9 units) and statistically significant at the 1 per cent level in a two-sample $t$-test with equal variances. In short, procurement rules tend to appear in deeper PTAs. Arguably, procurement rules are included in deep agreements because discriminatory procurement can substitute for other barriers to trade, such as subsidies or tariffs (Kono and Rickard 2013). Deep market integration therefore cannot be achieved by the elimination of tariffs and subsidies alone; negotiators must also tackle discriminatory procurement practices.

This argument assumes that PTAs with procurement rules foster the liberalisation of public procurement markets. However, scant evidence exists to suggest that PTAs' procurement rules are effective in reducing discrimination against foreign bidders. Rickard and Kono (2013), for

---

[3] One of these areas is public procurement, and as a result, the reported differences must be treated with some caution.

example, find no evidence that PTAs' procurement rules reduce discrimination against foreign firms. Discrimination is difficult to measure. For this reason, Rickard and Kono (2013) use a necessarily indirect method to estimate procurement discrimination. They use the elasticity of imports to procurement spending, controlling for other determinants of imports, as an estimate of the extent of procurement discrimination. They then investigate whether joining a PTA with explicit procurement rules reduces procurement discrimination against fellow PTA members. Rickard and Kono (2013) find discouraging results; the procurement–imports relationship is no different in country pairs in which both countries are members of the same procurement PTA than when they are not. In other words, PTAs' procurement rules do not significantly reduce discrimination in government procurement.

This null result holds for PTAs both collectively and individually. Rickard and Kono (2013) investigate the individual effects of various PTAs with explicit procurement rules, including the North American Free Trade Agreement (NAFTA), the Central American Free Trade Agreement (CAFTA), the European Economic Area (EEA), as well as the collective effect of all bilateral agreements between the EU and non-EEA countries, bilateral agreements between the European Free Trade Association (EFTA) and non-EEA countries and purely bilateral public procurement documents (PPAs) that are not associated with any regional agreement.[4] The results are easily summarised: none of the PTAs meaningfully affect the elasticity of imports to procurement spending. To sum up, Rickard and Kono (2013) find no evidence that PTAs with procurement rules liberalise government procurement.[5]

The null results reported by Rickard and Kono (2013) are consistent with those of other studies. Crozet and Trionfetti (2002) find that public procurement has a negative impact on trade flows using intra-European trade data from 1975 to 1985. Shingal (2011) finds that the GPA has not increased foreign access to procurement markets in Switzerland and Japan. The WTO itself concedes that many 'members still use their purchasing decisions to achieve domestic policy goals, such as the promotion

---

[4] Rickard and Kono (2013) do not include the EU and EFTA themselves because together they constitute the EEA. The EU provides most of the EEA's membership; hence, the correlation between the two groupings is more than 0.9. When the EEA is dropped and the EU and EFTA are included separately, both are insignificant.

[5] The WTO GPA appears to be equally ineffective in reducing procurement discrimination (Rickard and Kono 2013).

of specific local industry sectors or social groups' (World Trade Organization 2013).

## E. Ineffectiveness of procurement rules

Why are PTA procurement rules ineffective? Several possible explanations exist. First, procurement agreements may allow governments too much flexibility. Take for example the EU's procurement rules. These rules are some of the most stringent agreed to date. Yet, significant variation exists in the procurement procedures of EU countries. EU procurement rules allow governments to select tenders using two criteria: either the lowest price criterion or a combination of qualitative and quantitative aspects, known as Most Economically Advantageous Tender (MEAT). Considerable variation exists in Member States' use of these criteria. In Lithuania, for example, 87 per cent of tenders are selected using the lowest price criterion, as reported in Table 11.2. In Germany, however, 31 per cent of tenders are selected using the lowest price criterion, and in the UK, only 3 per cent of tenders using the lowest price criterion.

Ninety-seven per cent of tenders in the UK are selected using a combination of qualitative and quantitative aspects that could include quality, technical merit and delivery times. These criteria allow the government discretion over to whom to award the contract and, thus, opportunities exist for discrimination again foreign bidders. The UK's use of MEAT criteria is higher than the EU average (see Table 11.2) and seems to be at odds with the UK government's own insistence that 'value for money is the primary driver for procurement'. The British government has stated that 'given the limited resources available to government, ensuring value for money in procurement is key to ensuring the optimum utilisation of scarce budgetary resources' (Office of Government Commerce 2008). Despite this assertion, only 3 per cent of tenders are selected using the lowest price criterion. In contrast, many other EU countries, bound by identical procurement rules, exhibit far more frequent use of the lowest price criterion.

Other procurement practices also vary across EU Member States. For example, Member States remain free to decide whether public contracts are awarded on an anonymous basis. Some EU Member States have put in place rules to protect the anonymity of the bidders, at least up to a certain stage of the procedure. In Portugal, for example, anonymity is observed until the opening of the offers. Similar practice is also reported in Cyprus.

Table 11.2 *Tender criteria*

| Country | Lowest price (%) | MEAT (5%) |
|---|---|---|
| Belgium | 25 | 75 |
| Bulgaria | 36 | 64 |
| Czech Republic | 38 | 62 |
| Denmark | 24 | 76 |
| Germany | 31 | 69 |
| Estonia | 76 | 24 |
| Ireland | 3 | 97 |
| Greece | 66 | 34 |
| Spain | 5 | 95 |
| France | 3 | 97 |
| Italy | 33 | 67 |
| Cyprus | 81 | 19 |
| Latvia | 61 | 39 |
| Lithuania | 87 | 13 |
| Luxembourg | 44 | 56 |
| Hungary | 41 | 59 |
| Malta | 59 | 41 |
| The Netherlands | 27 | 73 |
| Austria | 43 | 57 |
| Poland | 83 | 17 |
| Portugal | 43 | 57 |
| Romania | 67 | 33 |
| Slovenia | 68 | 32 |
| Slovakia | 84 | 16 |
| Finland | 33 | 67 |
| Sweden | 37 | 63 |
| United Kingdom | 3 | 97 |
| EU average | 29 | 71 |

*Source:* Hansard (2012) HC 1453 Transport Committee Supplementary written evidence from the European Commission (RSP 12a).

In others Member States, however, such as Greece and Spain, anonymity is not practised.

These examples suggest that procurement rules agreed as part of PTAs may be ineffective because they are flexible. Ironically, such flexibility may make it possible for governments to commit to these agreements

(Rosendorff 2005). PTAs can have multiple member countries with potentially different interests in public procurement. For example, PTAs may be agreed by two economically asymmetric countries, such as the United States and Oman. In these cases, the country with the larger economy, here the United States, may want stringent procurement rules, whereas the smaller economy may want no procurement rules or only shallow rules as a function of how much it can supply to a large economy like the United States. In bilateral negotiations, the two states may compromise on some middle ground, and often such compromises take the form of flexible rules. Flexibility may make an agreement palatable to both states. Yet, this flexibility may ultimately undermine the effectiveness of PTA procurement chapters.

Second, international rules may be ineffective because procurement is fragmented across many government agencies. For example, in the UK, police procurement is fragmented across the 43 police forces in England and Wales. The huge range of definitions for basic items is striking. Something as simple as a high-visibility jacket has 20 different specifications, with associated prices that differ by as much as £80 (Hansard 2013). Similarly, recent research by Peto and Ernst & Young has shown that prices charged by suppliers for the same products vary by as much as 200 per cent from one hospital to another in the United Kingdom (Trent 2013).

Finally, the ineffectiveness of international procurement rules may be due to the opaque, complex nature of public procurement. Observing and proving procurement discrimination are difficult because many aspects of procurement decisions are inherently nontransparent (Evenett 2002). The opacity of public procurement makes it difficult to prove violations of international rules. The European Commission itself recently concluded that 'discrimination in public procurement is very difficult to detect or prove' after an evaluation of the effectiveness of EU procurement legislation (European Commission 2011). Although 46 per cent of EU businesses reported that local preferences influence the outcome of public procurement procedures to a large extent, none could provide concrete evidence of discrimination (European Commission 2011).

One reason for the lack of tangible evidence of discrimination is the fact that governments can discriminate against foreign suppliers in many nonobvious ways. For example, governments may provide information necessary to draft a competitive bid only to domestic firms. An example of such selective information provision recently emerged in the EU, when in 2012 the European Commission called on Romania to comply with EU procurement rules in connection with a contract awarded by the municipal authorities (European Union 2013). The contract, worth around €110 million, was allegedly awarded without allowing potential applicants sufficient time to prepare their bids. Furthermore, during the procedure the Romanian authorities made changes to a number of mandatory conditions in the procurement notice, including the selection criteria, which were announced at national level but not internationally. As a result, crucial information was available to domestic bidders, but not to foreign bidders, which subsequently gave local bidders an advantage in the process. By providing information selectively to domestic firms, the Romanian authorities were able to covertly discriminate against foreign firms.

Myriad opaque methods exist to discriminate against foreign firms. For example, governments can tailor technical requirements specifically to local suppliers (Beviglia-Zampetti 1997). In this case, discrimination would be exceedingly hard to prove. Moreover, governments can always invoke 'quality' as a reason to favour domestic bids over foreign ones (Vagstad 1995). Without overtly violating international rules, governments can split up large contracts so that the value of each of the constituent parts falls below the threshold stipulated in the procurement agreement. Contracts below stipulated thresholds use less formal procurement procedures. For example, supplies or services with a value of less than €5000 may be purchased on the basis of verbal quotes from one or more competitive suppliers in Ireland (Environmental Protection Agency 2013). Such informal procedures give governments significant leeway to discriminate in favour of local suppliers. In short, the opacity of procurement makes it difficult to verify violations of international rules. The difficultly of proving violations may allow governments to discriminate in favour of domestic bidders with impunity – even as signatories to PTAs with explicit procurement rules.

If PTAs' procurement rules are ineffective, why do governments negotiate them? Negotiating procurement chapters is costly and time consuming. Complying with such rules may incur further expense. Why then do an increasing number of PTAs include procurement chapters?

## F. A win–win situation for governments

Governments may have incentives to sign procurement PTAs even though they face compelling reasons to privilege domestic firms over foreign ones when purchasing otherwise similar goods and services. Awarding contracts to local firms shifts profits from foreign firms to domestic ones (Branco 1994; Vagstad 1995). Domestic firms may consequently reward politicians who discriminate in their favour by providing them with votes or campaign contributions. Government contracts may also allow local firms to create new jobs and generate higher tax revenues. For these reasons, governments value the freedom to discriminate against foreign firms in favour of domestic firms.

In theory, signing a procurement PTA limits governments' ability to buy national. In practice, however, governments often discriminate against foreign firms even as signatories to international procurement agreements (Rickard and Kono 2013). Governments may therefore sign PTAs with procurement chapters safe in the knowledge that they can still buy national with relative impunity.

PTAs' procurement chapters have additional advantages for signatory governments. Governments can claim to be working on behalf of domestic firms by providing better access to foreign procurement markets. When speaking in support of the Australia–Chile Free Trade Agreement, for example, the Australian trade minister said, 'The agreement provides greater certainty for Australians looking to participate in the Chilean government procurements market. The agreement will provide access to a nondiscriminatory regime which puts Australian suppliers' goods and services on an equal footing with competitors from other countries.' The minister made this statement in a speech encouraging legislators to vote for the agreement. Access to foreign procurement markets was understood by the minister to be a 'vote-winning' characteristic of the agreement – one that merited discussion on the floor of the legislature.[6]

A further attraction of international procurement rules may be that they provide 'political cover' for governments when they choose to 'buy foreign'. Governments that reject domestic bids in favour of foreign ones often face criticism. Domestic firms may make life difficult for vote-sensitive politicians when they lose out to foreign bidders (Martin, Hartley and Cox 1999: 390). For example, a recent decision by the British government to award a train-building contract to Siemens of Germany

---

[6] The Australian example suggests that governments may expect to gain politically from securing improved access to foreign procurement markets. If procurement agreements do not liberalise procurement markets, however, then the value to local firms of international procurement agreements may be small.

rather than to the UK-based arm of Bombardier was widely criticised by opposition parties and national trade unions. Trade unions loudly criticised this decision, and for days it was widely covered by the national media. The government responded to the vociferous criticism of this decision by citing international procurement rules. Minister Theresa Villiers stated in the House of Commons that the government was 'legally bound by European law to judge bids on a completely blind basis'. She went on to explain, 'Under EU law, domestic and overseas suppliers must be judged impartially and on a wholly equal footing' (Hansard 2011). In effect, the British government used its international obligations as a signatory to the EU's procurement rules to provide political cover for an unpopular purchase. This illustration suggests that governments might sign procurement PTAs knowing that they can be used as political cover when necessary, that is, when governments have to buy foreign.

Previous studies demonstrate how international agreements can provide political cover for unpopular governmental actions. It is often argued, for example, that the International Monetary Fund (IMF) provides political cover for governments that want to reform their economies but that face opposition at home (Haggard and Kaufman 1995; Putnam 1988; Vreeland 2003). In these arguments, governments seek to deflect the blame for unpopular policy decisions by using the international agreement as a 'scapegoat' (Steinwand and Stone 2008: 127).[7] PTAs with procurement chapters may serve such a role – acting as a scapegoat for governments when they have to buy foreign.

Governments may have to purchase from foreign suppliers for reasons of cost or supply limitations. If a required good or service is not supplied domestically, the government will have to buy from foreign suppliers. In Brazil, for example, the domestic capacity to produce oilfield equipment is limited (Economist 2013). Thus, it would be rational for the government to seek a foreign supplier from whom to buy the necessary equipment. However, it is unable to do so because of its own buy-national policies. The limited domestic capacity in combination with Brazil's buy-national policies has hampered the partially state-owned Petrobras's ability to exploit new deep-sea oil deposits (Economist 2013). An international procurement agreement could help governments in such situations. After

---

[7] Of course, scapegoating may not work under all circumstances. In the run-up to democratic elections, for example, voters may not find governments' scapegoating claims credible (Rickard and Caraway 2014).

signing a PTA with procurement rules, a government could buy foreign without fear of retaliation from any domestic suppliers that exist or voters who resent their tax monies being spent abroad.

Cost saving may also lead governments to buy foreign. For example, when speaking in the House of Representatives about public procurement, Australia's minister for finance said in 2009, 'We are saving around $15 million per year through a volume-sourcing arrangement with Microsoft' (Hansard 2009b). In this illustrative example, the government decided to buy foreign explicitly for cost-saving reasons. Highlighting these savings may have been an attempt to make a foreign purchase more palatable to voters. Yet despite the potential cost savings, choosing a cheaper foreign bid over a domestic bid may provoke criticism from voters and producers alike. When governments choose to buy from foreign suppliers, the domestic producers in competition for the contract face tangible economic losses. Such losses may incite firms to make their resentment known to the government. A company passed over for a lucrative government contract in the United Kingdom, for example, subsequently announced 1400 job losses. The company also stated publicly that it would now have to 'review its factory's future' in Britain (Economist 2011).

Domestic suppliers not directly affected by a government's decision to buy foreign in any particular case are likely to oppose their government's decision to buy foreign as well for fear that it might increasingly become standard practice. Taxpayers may also resent their hard-earned taxes being spent abroad. In sum, buying from foreign suppliers is politically costly for governments, and this may explain the well-documented evidence of discrimination against foreign firms by governments.

International procurement rules can provide political cover for governments that choose to buy foreign. Criticism of foreign purchases can be deflected by the government saying that its hands are tied by international rules. PTA obligations require governments to evaluate bids blindly without giving any special consideration to domestic suppliers. For example, the Australian minister of defence invoked international procurement procedures in a speech on the floor of the House of Representatives. The minister was speaking in defence of the government's decision to award a contract to an international archaeological firm. Media reports criticised the decision, alleging that the firm had misrepresented its costs in order to undercut local bids. The minister responded by saying, 'I would like to say a few words about the selection of Oxford Archaeology . . . as there has been some extremely inaccurate media representation of their contract. The choice to engage Oxford Archaeology was an international decision, reached using an open and transparent tender process that was in accordance with Commonwealth Procurement Guidelines' (Hansard 2009a).

Similarly, following an announcement that 1775 shipbuilders would lose their jobs, the British government came under pressure to explain its decision to award a contract to build four new British military super tankers for the Royal Fleet Auxiliary to a Korean shipyard at a cost of £450 million. To justify this decision, government ministers made reference to EU procurement rules. When an astute constituent wrote the Department of Defence to query why a defence-related contract, which is exempt from EU procurement rules, was put out for competitive tender, the minister of defence responded that a tanker 'didn't qualify as a warship' and therefore the contract had to be put out to tender (Prestwich 2013). In this example, the government used international procurement rules as political cover for a decision that became controversial with voters following news that British workers in the shipbuilding sector were being laid off.

These illustrative examples suggest that governments may sign procurement PTAs safe in the knowledge that they can violate them with little fear of reprisal when it is in their interest to buy national and at the same time use the agreement as political cover when it is necessary to buy foreign. This valuable characteristic may explain why an ever-growing number of governments sign international procurement agreements, despite (or indeed because of) the agreements' apparent ineffectiveness.

## G. Conclusion

Increasingly, PTAs include rules regulating governments' purchases of goods and services. The inclusion of public procurement rules in ever more PTAs raises important and interesting questions. This chapter has highlighted several such questions and offered preliminary thoughts as to their answers. It seems puzzling, for example, that governments rush to sign such agreements when research shows they have little success in liberalizing procurement markets. Why would governments sign procurement agreements in ever greater numbers if these agreements are ineffective?

A possible reason is that PTA procurement rules represent a win–win situation for governments. On one hand, governments are able to sign such agreements safe in the knowledge that they can still buy national with relative impunity because of the opacity of public procurement. On the other hand, when governments need to buy foreign, international procurement rules give governments political cover. Governments can point to the PTA and argue that their hands are tied. The agreement in effect serves as a scapegoat for unpopular foreign purchases by signatory governments.

This interpretation of PTAs' procurement chapters is consistent with existing arguments about international agreements acting as scapegoats for unpopular government actions. It suggests a potential explanation for why governments rush to sign PTAs with procurement rules, despite having strong political incentives to spend taxpayers' money at home by purchasing locally produced goods and services. However, this explanation does not explain why governments rush to sign PTAs with procurement chapters rather than accede to the WTO's GPA. The stampede to sign PTAs with procurement chapters has not been matched by a similar rush to sign the GPA. In fact, since 2000, only three new parties joined the GPA (Ueno 2013). Only 10 countries are currently negotiating accession to the GPA. If international procurement rules are a win–win for governments, why are so few countries willing to sign the GPA? One possibility is that PTAs allow for negotiation over procurement rules, whereas countries that accede to the GPA cannot negotiate the terms of the agreement. The potential trade-offs between signing the GPA and signing a procurement PTA are yet another interesting question for future study. Thus, international procurement agreements present an important area for future research – one that can shed new light on the reasons why governments sign such agreements and when and under what conditions they comply with the agreed rules.

## References

Beviglia-Zampetti, Americo. 1997. 'The UNCITRAL Model Law on Procurement of Goods, Construction and Services.' In *Law and Policy in Public Purchasing*, edited by Bernard Hoekman and Petros Mavroidis, 273–87. Ann Arbor: University of Michigan Press.

Branco, Fernando. 1994. 'Favoring Domestic Firms in Procurement Contracts.' *Journal of International Economics* 37 (1): 65–80.

Crozet, Matthieu, and Trionfetti, Federico. 2002. 'Effets-frontières Entre les Pays de l'Union Européenne: le Poids des Politiques d'Achats Publics.' *Economie International* 1:189–208.

Dür, Andreas, Baccini, Leonardo, and Elsig, Manfred. 2014. 'The Design of International Trade Agreements: Introducing a New Dataset.' *Review of International Organizations* 9 (3): 353–75.

Economist. 2011. 'Rolling on and on.' 7 September. www.economist.com/blogs/blighty/2011/09/rail-procurement. Accessed 3 March 2014.

Economist. 2013. 'Special Report World Economy.' 12–18 October , 17–19.

Environmental Protection Agency. 2013. 'Public Procurement.' www.epa.ie/about/procurement/#.UpeBQ8RDtqU. Accessed 15 November 2013.

European Commission. 2011. 'On the Modernisation of EU Public Procurement Policy: Towards a More Efficient European Procurement Market.' Green Paper. European Commission, Brussels. http://eur-lex.europa.eu/LexUriServ/LexUriServ.do?uri=COM:2011:0015:FIN:EN:PDF.

European Union. 2013. 'Infringement Cases (Public Procurement).' http://ec.europa.eu/internal_market/publicprocurement/infringements/cases/index_en.htm. Accessed 15 November 2013.

Evenett, Simon J. 2002. 'The WTO Government Procurement Agreement: An Assessment of Current Research and Options for Reform.' Paper prepared for the World Bank Conference 'Informing the Doha Process: New Trade Research for Developing Economies,' Cairo, Egypt.

Grier, Jean H. 1996. 'Japan's Implementation of the WTO Agreement on Government Procurement.' *University of Pennsylvania Journal of International Economic Law* 17:605–58.

Haggard, Stephan, and Kaufman, Robert R. 1995. *The Political Economy of Democratic Transitions.* Princeton, NJ: Princeton University Press

Hansard Australia HC, 19 August 2009a. Combet, Greg, MP (Charlton), Minister for Defence Personnel, Material and Science and Minister Assisting the Minister for Climate Change. House of Representatives Ministerial Statements. Fromelles Project Update Speech. www.aph.gov.au/Parliamentary_Business/Hansard/Search&?q=&expand=true&drvH=0&drt=2&pnu=43&pnuH=43&pi=0&pv=&chi=2&coi=0.

Hansard Australia HC. 16 September 2009b. Tanner, Lindsay, MP (Melbourne), Minister for Finance and Deregulation. House of Representatives Ministerial Statements. Fiscal Policy Speech. www.aph.gov.au/Parliamentary_Business/Hansard/Search&?q=&expand=true&drvH=0&drt=2&pnu=43&pnuH=43&pi=0&pv=&chi=2&coi=0.

Hansard UK HC 1453 Transport Committee Supplementary Written Evidence from the European Commission (RSP 12a) 2012. www.publications.parliament.uk/pa/cm201314/cmselect/cmtran/850/85015.htm.

Hansard UK HC 12 July 2011. www.publications.parliament.uk/pa/cm201011/cmhansrd/cm110712/halltext/110712h0001.htm.

Hansard UK HL 26 March 2013. A statement from The Rt Hon Margaret Hodge MP, Chair of the Committee of Public Accounts. www.parliament.uk/business/

committees/committees-a-z/commons-select/public-accounts-committee/
news/chairs-statement-on-police-procurement.

Jetschke, Anja, and Lenz, Tobias. 2013. 'Does Regionalism Diffuse? A New Research Agenda for the Study of Regional Organizations.' *Journal of European Public Policy* 20 (4): 626–37.

Kim, Soo Yeon, and Manger, Mark S. 2013. 'Hubs of Governance: Path-Dependence and Higher Order Effects of PTA Formation.' Paper presented at the Annual Meeting of the Political Economy of International Organizations, 7–9 February, Mannheim and Heidelberg, Germany.

Kono, Daniel Y., and Rickard, Stephanie J. 2014. 'Buying National: Democracy and Public Procurement.' 'International Interactions' DOI:10.1080/03050629.2014.899220 Published online: 8 August 2014.

Lowinger, Thomas. 1976. 'Discrimination in Government Procurement of Foreign Goods in the US and Western Europe.' *Southern Economic Journal* 42:451–60.

Martin, Stephen, Hartley, Keith, and Cox, Andrew. 1999. 'Public Procurement Directives in the European Union: A Study of Local Authority Purchasing.' *Public Administration* 77 (2): 387–406.

Office of Government Commerce. 2008. 'An Introduction to Public Procurement.' http://webarchive.nationalarchives.gov.uk/20110601212617/http:/www.ogc.gov.uk/documents/Introduction_to_Public_Procurement.pdf.

Prestwich, Alan Quinn. 2013. Letters to the *Daily Telegraph*, 9 November.

Putnam, Robert D. 1988. 'Diplomacy and Domestic Politics: The Logic of Two-Level Games.' *International Organization* 42 (3): 427–60.

Rickard, Stephanie J., and Caraway, Teri. 2014. 'International Negotiations in the Shadow of National Elections.' *International Organizations* 68 (3): 701–20.

Rickard, Stephanie J., and Kono, Daniel Y. 2014. 'Think Globally, Buy Locally: International Agreements and Government Procurement.' *Review of International Organizations* 9 (3): 333–52.

Rosendorff, B. Peter. 2005. 'Stability and Rigidity: Politics and Design of the WTO's Dispute Settlement Procedure.' *American Political Science Review* 99 (3): 389–400.

Shingal, Anirudh. 2011. 'Services Procurement under the WTO's Agreement on Government Procurement: Whither Market Access?' *World Trade Review* 10 (4): 527–49.

Steinwand, Martin C., and Stone, Randall W. 2008. 'The International Monetary Fund: A Review of the Recent Evidence.' *Review of International Organizations* 3 (2): 123–49.

Trent, Julian. 2013. 'The Government's Procurement Strategy Does Not Address Lack of Transparency.' *Guardian*, 29 October.

Trionfetti, Federico. 2000. 'Discriminatory Government Procurement and International Trade.' *World Economy* 23:57–76.

Ueno, Asako. 2013. 'Multilateralising Regionalism on Government Procurement.' OECD Trade Policy Papers No. 151. OECD Publishing, Paris.

Vagstad, Steinar. 1995. 'Promoting Fair Competition in Public Procurement.' *Journal of Public Economics* 58:283–307.

Vreeland, James R. 2003. *The IMF and Economic Development.* Cambridge: Cambridge University Press.

World Trade Organization. 2013. 'Government Procurement.' www.wto.org/english/tratop_e/gproc_e/gproc_e.htm. Accessed 15 November 2013.

# 12

## Trade agreements, violent conflict and security

YORAM Z. HAFTEL

### A. Introduction

According to Article 5 of the 2007 treaty of EAC,[1] one of the organisation's main goals is 'the promotion of peace, security, and stability within, and good neighborliness among, the Partner States'. Article 3 of the Central American Integration System's (SICA) 1991 Tegucigalpa Protocol lists 'the eradication of violence, corruption, terrorism, and trafficking in drugs and arms' as one of its fundamental objectives. One objective of the Association of Southeast Asian Nations (ASEAN) 1967 Bangkok Declaration is to 'promote regional peace and stability through abiding respect for justice and the rule of law in the relationship among countries of the region and adherence to the principles of the United Nations Charter'.

These are but three of the many examples of trade agreements that make a direct link between economic cooperation and integration, on the one hand, and peace, security and stability on the other. Furthermore, the rising number and prominence of these instruments (Baccini, Dür and Haftel, Chapter 7 in this volume) are accompanied by a widespread perception that they are indispensable in reducing frictions between their members. At the same time, their vision of how to promote regional security and the manners by which they are expected to achieve this goal are remarkably diverse. Several agreements, such as SAARC and SACU, are essentially designed to tackle economic affairs. Presumably, member states believe that cooperation on trade and development will produce economic benefits, familiarity and mutual trust, thereby preventing armed conflict.

The Hebrew University's Davis Institute of International Relations provided financial support for this project. I thank Susanna Campbell, Andreas Dür, Magnus Lundgren, Edward Mansfield and the participants of the 2013 World Trade Forum for helpful comments and suggestions. Daniel Wajner provided helpful research assistance.

[1] Full names of this and other trade agreements are reported in the appendix.

Notably, however, many commercial institutions have been gradually expanding their mandates to include agreements and mechanisms that address security concerns more directly. Thus, the combination of economic and security arrangements under one institutional umbrella is currently rather common. A closer look at the security components of regional organisations indicates that they are very different in terms of purpose, design and level of activity. Organisations such as ECOWAS and SADC have developed multilateral armed forces capable of conducting military and peacekeeping operations. Others, MERCOSUR and MRU, for example, emphasise confidence-building measures (CBMs), joint military exercises or mechanisms for the resolution of bilateral disputes. Still others address 'nontraditional' security challenges, which include terrorism, organised crime and cross-border trafficking of drugs and arms.

Despite the rising significance of this development, the spillover of regional economic organisations into the military/security sphere and its consequences for political stability have attracted only scant scholarly attention. To be sure, new theoretical insights, methodological innovations and accumulation of new data in the last two decades shed light on the links between trade agreements, violent conflict and national security. Nevertheless, much of the extant research on the links between trade agreements and violent conflict focuses almost exclusively on economic integration and functional cooperation and overlooks other areas of cooperation. This chapter begins to bridge this gap in our understanding of the nexus between trade agreements and regional security. Zeroing in on one important type of trade agreements – regional economic organisations (REOs) – it examines the conditions necessary for nesting deep security substructures within economic institutions.

The next section takes stock of extant research on trade agreements and conflict and highlights some of the main advances and lacunae in this field of inquiry. The section following that describes the phenomenon of security substructures within trade and economic agreements and analyzes three necessary conditions for their existence. The final section concludes.

## B. Extant research on trade agreements and armed conflict

This section provides an overview of recent research on the relationship between trade agreements and violent conflict. It shows that much progress in our understanding of this issue has been made in the last two decades. Even so, it underscores the insufficient attention paid to the role of security institutions embedded in these agreements. I define trade agreements broadly to include all international agreements that promote trade policy cooperation or integration among their members. Thus, elimination of barriers to trade is an important part – but not necessarily an exclusive one – of the agreement's formal objectives (Mansfield and Milner 1999). This definition includes a range of international institutions, starting with bilateral trade agreements with limited coverage, such as the Bahrain–Jordan agreement, and ending with regional organisations that tackle a variety of issue areas, such as ASEAN and the European Union (EU).

The nexus of trade agreements and conflict is best understood within the context of the Kantian peace framework (Russett and Oneal 2001). This framework, which is rooted in liberal economic and political thought, identifies three factors that purportedly mitigate interstate armed conflict: democratic governments, high levels of international interdependence and shared membership in international organisations. As can be seen from the preceding definition, trade agreements are located at the intersection of the last two of these factors. Indeed, most, if not all, arguments about the pacifying effect of trade agreements can be linked to the alleged pacifying effect of either economic interdependence or international organisations (or both).[2] I discuss each in turn.

The notion that commercial exchange promotes peace is not new and can be traced back to at least eighteenth- and nineteenth-century liberal thought (Mansfield and Pevehouse 2000; Schiff and Winters 1998). Given their ability to boost trade, investment and development as well as to inject predictability and stability into cross-border economic exchange, it is argued, trade agreements should promote economic interdependence and, in turn, increase the opportunity cost of violent conflict. This line of reasoning was part and parcel of the neofunctionalist perspective, which emerged in the 1950s and 1960s in the wake of integration efforts and relative stability in western Europe (Haas 1964; Nye 1971). This research often assumed rather than demonstrated, however, the spillover of functional and economic cooperation into the security realm (Bearce 2003).

In a series of pioneering studies, Edward Mansfield and his co-authors revived interest in this largely neglected issue. They spelled out several mechanisms by which preferential trade agreements (PTAs) can

---

[2] The two factors are, of course, closely intertwined. Extant research indicates that greater economic interdependence and broader economic scope lead to greater institutionalization of trade agreements (Egger and Nigai, Chapter 15 in this volume; Haftel 2013; Vicard 2012).

mitigate conflict and demonstrated empirically that PTAs reduce the risk of a militarised conflict (Mansfield 2003; Mansfield and Pevehouse 2000, 2003; Mansfield, Pevehouse and Bearce 1999/2000). Theoretically, they call attention to the commitment to enduring economic liberalisation enshrined in PTAs (compared to unilateral or ad hoc liberalization). Going beyond the traditional emphasis on international trade, they highlight the positive effect of PTAs on cross-border investment and on bargaining leverage during negotiations with third parties. The empirical analyses reported in these studies treat PTAs as homogeneous 'black boxes', however, thereby overlooking differences in their design and actual performance.[3] Thus, even though these studies acknowledge the substantial variation across trade agreements, they stop short of teasing out its empirical implications.

Subsequent research has begun to unpack this variation and to look inside these institutions to identify specific features that make a difference. Bearce and Omori (2005), Mansfield and Pevehouse (forthcoming), Vicard (2012) and Haftel (2007, 2012) take a first look at the relationships between the depth of regional integration and conflict. The first three of these studies take account of a large number of trade agreements and employ Balassa's (1961) ordinal scale – a free trade agreement, a customs union, a common market and a monetary union – to measure the variation in the scope of economic activity.[4] The results reported in these studies are rather mixed. Vicard (2012) finds that deeper planned integration is indeed associated with less conflict, but Bearce and Omori (2005) and Mansfield and Pevehouse (2013) do not.

These studies suffer from several limitations. First and foremost, the Balassa indicators are rather crude and fail to account for many of the issues covered by modern trade agreements, such as foreign investment, trade in services and economic development.[5] Second, they largely consider institutional design and overlook the degree of implementation.[6] Given the wide and varying gap between aspirations and actual achievements of existing trade arrangements (Gray 2014; Haftel 2012), this is a significant oversight. In my own work (Haftel 2007, 2012), I have begun to

---

[3] See Hafner-Burton and Montgomery (2012) for a similar approach.
[4] Mansfield and Pevehouse (forthcoming) consider only free trade agreements and customs unions.
[5] See Haftel (2012: Chap. 3) for a fuller discussion of this point.
[6] Bearce and Omori (2005) do make a distinction between proposed and achieved integration. They do not elaborate on the manners by which they measure the two concepts and code specific agreements, however.

tackle these shortcomings by developing a comprehensive and nuanced coding scheme that captures the main economic activities covered by REOs and distinguishing between their design and implementation. My analysis indicates that greater scope of economic activity, when implemented, results in fewer armed disputes. Like most of the aforementioned research, however, it overlooks cooperation on noneconomic matters.

Only a handful of recent studies have begun to explore security aspects of trade agreements in a systematic manner. Bearce (2003) argues that commercial institutions with security substructures mitigate violent conflict and finds support for this conjecture in two case studies. A subsequent study that employs a quantitative analysis (Bearce and Omori 2005) fails to corroborate this conclusion, however. Powers (2006) finds that African commercial institutions that include an alliance reduce militarised disputes. These studies do not account for the variation in the nature of security arrangements and have a limited temporal and spatial coverage. They are also silent on the conditions under which governments choose to interweave economic and security elements in a unified institutional framework.

Other studies examine REOs in the broader context of regional or international security. Tavares (2009) and Kirchner and Domínguez (2011), for example, provide excellent accounts of the rising phenomenon of regional security governance as well as a useful depiction of several key organisations. In another study, Boehmer, Gartzke and Nordstrom (2004) assess the pacifying effect of a large sample of international organisations. They find that those organisations that have a security mandate dampen violent conflict. Like much of the research thus far discussed, such studies focus on the ability of these organisations to shape international politics and have less to say about the sources of their institutional structure and functions. In addition, they focus on organisations that have security components, whether they have economic dimensions or not. Consequently, they are not well positioned to shed light on the sources and consequences of security institutions nested within economic ones.

Turning to the 'third leg' aspect of the Kantian tripod – international organisations – one should look beyond the kind and degree of cooperation trade agreements foster and instead examine their institutional set-up. Like other types of international organisations, REOs commonly have organisational features that are allegedly conducive to peace. I briefly consider three organs that are pertinent to the issue at hand: a dispute settlement mechanism (DSM), a corporate secretariat and regular meetings of high-level officials.

Perhaps unsurprisingly, the existence and legalisation of a DSM take a pride of place in studies on the link between institutions and peace. The perceived neutrality of this adjudicating body injects its ruling with legitimacy and increases the cost of unilateral action (Boehmer, Gartzke and Nordstrom 2004). As a result, it is often argued, it advances an amicable resolution of existing disagreements and prevents their escalation (Mansfield and Pevehouse 2000; Russett and Oneal 2001). Given the marked variation in the authority of DSMs (Allee and Elsig, Chapter 13 in this volume; Dür, Baccini and Elsig 2014; Haftel and Thompson 2006), one might expect more legalised bodies to be more effective in the mitigation of discord and conflict. At the same time, some caution is warranted: some DSMs embedded in trade agreements lack the ability to deal with security issues or to settle militarised disputes, whereas others are designed to resolve political and military disputes. In this context, it is noteworthy that extant empirical research indicates that strictly economic DSMs have a limited impact on security issues regardless of the level of legalisation (Bearce and Omori 2005; Haftel 2012; Mansfield and Pevehouse forthcoming). It is therefore important to account not only for these bodies' level of legalisation but also for their mandate.

A second organ that is purported to dampen conflict is the corporate secretariat that manages the operation of the organisation. One important function of such a body is to amass and disseminate unbiased information on the members' activities, thereby allowing governments to scrutinise the actions of their partners as well as to assure others of their own good behaviour (Haftel and Thompson 2006; Pevehouse and Russett 2006; Russett and Oneal 2001). In so far as facts provided by this bureaucratic body pertain to members' disputes, it can reduce a potential 'information arbitrage' and improve the prospects of a peaceful resolution to the conflict (Boehmer, Gartzke and Nordstrom 2004). Like DSMs, however, secretariats of economic organisations appear to be in a better position to collect and disseminate information on trade and investment than on military capabilities and other strategic factors (Boehmer, Gartzke and Nordstrom 2004). Indeed, empirical studies that examined this issue did not uncover evidence of the pacifying effect of regional secretariats (Bearce and Omori 2005; Haftel 2012). As with respect to DSM, a more nuanced treatment of secretariats' areas of competence and authority, especially those that touch on matters of national security, may offer new insights into their contribution to regional peace and stability.

Finally, as I have argued elsewhere (Haftel 2007, 2012), economic organisations frequently – but not always – call for regular meetings of top-level officials, which usually operate as the highest body of decision-making. This organ is perhaps the most security oriented of the three examined here: while the formal agenda of such meetings often addresses economic cooperation, it gives senior policymakers the opportunity to discuss political issues directly and openly. These face-to-face interactions can be conducive to peaceful management of disputes between member states. As such, they foster interpersonal familiarity, trust and mutual confidence (Bearce 2003; Martin, Mayer and Thoenig 2010; Schiff and Winters 1998). Such meetings also provide members that are not directly involved in the conflict with an opportunity to act as third-party mediators or honest brokers. In this capacity, these policymakers can provide additional information to the rival parties and introduce creative solutions to the dispute (Dorussen and Ward 2008, 2010). Consistent with these expectations, Bearce and Omori (2005) as well as my own research (Haftel 2007, 2012) find that REOs that hold regular meetings of high-level officials experience fewer armed conflicts. The extent to which top officials who gather in such meetings engage in security matters directly is not entirely clear, however. In addition, extant research pays insufficient attention to meetings of high-level security and defence officials.

In short, research on the links between trade agreements and armed disputes has come a long way since the 1990s. We now have a good grasp of the manners in which these instruments mitigate conflict, the conditions under which they do so and the pacifying effect of specific institutional features. Even so, this brief review shows that the focus thus far was mostly on those activities and organs that regulate trade and economic issues and much less on those that engage more directly in military and security affairs. In light of the growing tendency to amalgamate economic and security issues in a unified institutional framework, it is high time to contemplate the roots of this phenomenon. The next section takes a preliminary step in this direction.

## C. Trade agreements and nested security institutions

As the discussion thus far makes clear, extant research focuses almost exclusively on the economic aspects of trade agreements and cross-border armed conflict. Consequently, it overlooks significant trends in the development of both phenomena. National security is no longer one-dimensional (if it ever was). Many governments around the world have to deal with civil wars, insurgency and terrorism. And, as described in greater detail later, especially since the 1990s, many trade agreements cover not only economic issues but also security ones. This section first conceptualises and describes the variation in security cooperation within one type of trade agreement, namely, REOs. It then employs a set-theoretic method to briefly examine the conditions necessary for a meaningful security substructure within the economic organisation.

### I. The landscape of security institutions within REOs

The combination of economic and security arrangements under one institutional umbrella is currently rather common. A glance at the security components of regional organisations indicates that they are very different in terms of purpose, design and level of activity, however. Organisations such as ECOWAS and SADC have developed multilateral armed forces capable of conducting military and peacekeeping operations. Other organisations, MERCOSUR and MRU, for example, emphasise CBMs, joint military exercises or mechanisms for the resolution of bilateral disputes. Still others, such as the AMU and ASEAN, signed agreements on neutrality, collective security, a nuclear-free zone and the like. In parallel to economic agreements, some of these agreements and mechanisms were implemented while others remain on paper.

The examples just mentioned indicate that the design of security arrangements can be very diverse, thereby complicating a structured comparison across regions. Nevertheless, a preliminary distinction between those REOs that include meaningful security cooperation and those that do not is still possible. I thus create an ordinal variable that ranges from zero to one with four categories of security cooperation:[7]

- *None (0)* – no security agreement or institution.
- *Low (0.33)* – passive security cooperation. This includes general statements about security cooperation or reactive security agreements (e.g. a nonaggression pact, a nuclear-free zone, a DSM) or unimplemented agreements.
- *Medium (0.66)* – active security cooperation. This includes either regular meetings of security officials or an operational organ that addresses security affairs or an agreement on and execution of joint military exercises.

---

[7] The specific values of the different categories of this and other variables were selected to facilitate the empirical analysis. A more detailed discussion of this issue is provided later.

• *High (1)* – use of force. This includes the establishment and actual deployment of joint military forces capable of executing peacekeeping operations and other active security missions.

With this metric, I measure the degree of security cooperation in 32 REOs. The appendix to this chapter provides a list of these organisations. Although a complete description of the rationale for this sample is beyond the scope of this chapter, it is worth noting that it is very comprehensive, spans all continents and includes the majority of states worldwide. In addition, given my interest in the expanding mandate of economic agreements, I exclude organisations that deal exclusively with political and security issues (e.g. NATO and the Organisation of American States) or security organisations that 'trespassed' into the economic realm (e.g. the League of Arab States that established the Greater Arab Free Trade Area). Thus, the sample includes REOs, such as the EU, ECOWAS and MERCOSUR, whose initial emphasis was on economic cooperation and REOs in which both economic and security matters were central components of the original mandate (e.g. EAC and CIS).

To code the 32 REOs on the depth of their security cooperation, I first surveyed all their agreements and protocols and recorded the articles that deal with security matters. These texts provide a very good sense of the kind of planned security arrangements and institutions. I complemented this survey with an examination of additional secondary sources, which included the REOs' own websites and scholarly articles and reports. These sources offered a good picture of the actual organs established and activities taking place in relation to regional security. Many of the activities – for example, annual meetings of security officials or military exercises – take place regularly. The more demanding undertakings, those falling within the realm of the use of force, occur more haphazardly, often in response to unfolding events on the ground. To allow a fruitful comparison, I restricted the coding of such operations to the post–Cold War era.

Table 12.1 reports the value on security cooperation – labelled *Security* – for all the REOs included in the sample. It indicates that almost 70 per cent (22 out of 32) include a security substructure of some kind. This observation affirms the assertion that the mandate of many regional institutions is no longer either strictly economic or exclusively security related. Instead, a growing number of REOs link these issues in a unified institutional framework. This phenomenon is widespread and not confined to one region or continent. Security substructures

Table 12.1 *Fuzzy-set membership scores on four variables*

| REO | Security | Conflict | Hegemony | Nonrivalry |
|---|---|---|---|---|
| AMU | 0.33 | 0.33 | 0.00 | 0.00 |
| ASEAN | 0.66 | 1.00 | 0.33 | 1.00 |
| CACM | 0.66 | 0.33 | 0.00 | 1.00 |
| CAN | 0.33 | 0.66 | 0.00 | 0.00 |
| CARICOM | 0.33 | 0.00 | 0.33 | 1.00 |
| CEFTA | 0.00 | 0.66 | 0.33 | 0.00 |
| CEMAC | 0.33 | 0.33 | 0.33 | 1.00 |
| CEPGL | 0.33 | 0.66 | 0.66 | 1.00 |
| COMESA | 0.33 | 1.00 | 0.00 | 0.00 |
| EAC | 0.66 | 0.33 | 0.33 | 1.00 |
| ECCAS | 0.66 | 0.66 | 0.00 | 1.00 |
| ECO | 0.00 | 1.00 | 0.33 | 0.00 |
| EU | 1.00 | 0.00 | 0.00 | 1.00 |
| LAIA | 0.00 | 0.66 | 0.33 | 1.00 |
| OECS | 0.33 | 0.00 | 0.00 | 1.00 |
| WAEMU | 0.00 | 0.33 | 0.00 | 1.00 |
| EFTA | 0.00 | 0.00 | 0.33 | 1.00 |
| UNASUR | 0.66 | 0.66 | 0.66 | 1.00 |
| APTA | 0.00 | 1.00 | 1.00 | 0.00 |
| ECOWAS | 1.00 | 0.66 | 0.66 | 1.00 |
| GCC | 0.66 | 0.00 | 0.66 | 1.00 |
| IOC | 0.00 | 0.00 | 0.66 | 1.00 |
| MSG | 0.33 | 0.00 | 0.66 | 1.00 |
| CIS | 1.00 | 1.00 | 1.00 | 1.00 |
| MERCOSUR | 0.66 | 0.00 | 1.00 | 1.00 |
| MRU | 0.33 | 0.33 | 0.66 | 1.00 |
| NAFTA | 0.00 | 0.00 | 1.00 | 1.00 |
| PIF | 0.66 | 0.00 | 1.00 | 1.00 |
| SAARC | 0.00 | 1.00 | 1.00 | 0.00 |
| SACU | 0.00 | 0.00 | 1.00 | 1.00 |
| SADC | 1.00 | 0.66 | 0.66 | 1.00 |
| SCO | 0.66 | 0.66 | 1.00 | 1.00 |

exist within REOs in Europe, Africa, Latin America and the Asia-Pacific region.

A finer distinction between shallow and deep security cooperation sheds additional light on the varying landscape of regional institutions.

As one might expect given the high material and sovereignty costs associated with peacekeeping and enforcement, only four REOs developed the required legal framework and institutions for, as well as engaged in, actual military operations. Table 12.2 lists these organisations and summarises their main security-related agreements, organs and activities. A glance at this list indicates that deep security cooperation is not circumscribed to one geographical area and can be found in sub-Saharan Africa and Europe (but not in the Americas and the Asia-Pacific region). Nine additional organisations have active security cooperation, either through joint military exercises (e.g. MERCOSUR and the GCC) or regular meetings of security officials, exchange of information, CBMs and the like (e.g. ASEAN, PIF and the CACM). The remaining nine REOs have either passive security institutions (e.g. CARICOM and COMESA) or have failed to implement signed agreements (e.g. AMU and CEPGL). To facilitate a preliminary account of the observed variation, I consider only medium and high levels as instances of meaningful security institutions.

## II. Three explanations for the nesting of security institutions

It is useful to contemplate the sources of institutional differences with 'demand-side' and 'supply-side' logics. The former views international institutions as a solution to challenges states cannot overcome on their own and thus emphasises the needs and incentives for cooperation. The latter emphasises the constraints faced by states that consider institutionalized cooperation with their neighbours and underscores the obstacles to collective action in a political arena lacking a central government.

Demand-side considerations are best understood in context of a region's security situation. One might reasonably expect zones of conflict to face pressure to set up security institutions. There, governments may have to take notice of calls to intervene in instances of domestic strife and civil wars, which tend to have negative security, political and economic 'externalities' for their neighbouring states. Zones of long-lasting peace and stability or REOs whose members are not contiguous (small island states, for example), on the other hand, are in less need of security arrangements. In such regions, security cooperation is unlikely to yield many benefits and will render investment in security institutions undesirable. We can therefore hypothesise that high levels of intraregional violent conflict will result in the inclusion of a meaningful security component in the REO's institutional structure.

Table 12.2 *Main instruments and activities of REOs with a high level of security cooperation*

| REO | Legal instruments | Organs | Operational activity |
|---|---|---|---|
| CIS | • CIS Charter (1993)<br>• Concept of Prevention of Resolution of Conflicts in the Territories of Member States of the CIS (1996) | • Council of Heads of State & Heads of Government<br>• Chief Command of the United Armed Forces | • Peacekeeping in Moldova (1992), Georgia (1994–2008) and Tajikistan (1993–2000) |
| ECOWAS | • Protocol on Non-Aggression (1978)<br>• Protocol on Mutual Assistance in Defence (1981)<br>• Protocol relating to the Mechanism for Conflict Prevention, Management, Resolution, Peace-keeping and Security (1999)<br>• ECOWAS Conflict Prevention Framework (2008) | • The Authority<br>• The Defence Council<br>• ECOWAS Monitoring Group (ECOMOG)<br>• ECOWAS Standby Force (ASF) | • Peacekeeping forces in Liberia (1990–7, 2003), Sierra Leone (1997–9), Guinea Bissau (1998–9) and Côte D'Ivoire (2003–4) |
| EU | • European Union Treaty (1999–2010) | • European Council<br>• High Representative of the Union for Foreign Affairs and Security Policy | • Peacekeeping forces in Macedonia (2003), Bosnia (2004–), Democratic Republic of the Congo (2005–), Chad/Central African Republic (2008–9)<br>• Antipiracy operations off the coast of Somalia<br>• Monitoring forces in Aceh (Indonesia, 2005–6) |
| SADC | • Protocol on Politics, Defence and Security Cooperation, entire (2001)<br>• SADC Mutual Defence Pact (2003) | • Organ on Politics, Defence and Security Cooperation<br>• SADC Standby Brigade | • Peacekeeping in Lesotho (1998) and Democratic Republic of the Congo (1998) |

To be sure, neighbouring states can establish separate security and economic institutions to deal with these diverse problems rather than embedding them in one unified institutional framework. Why nest them, then? Here, we could rely on the institutionalist perspective, which points to the benefits of expanding the mandate of an existing arrangement rather than creating a new one. Doing so reduces the cost of the initial set-up, decreases the transaction costs involved in side payments and facilitates issue linkage (Aggarwal 1998; Keohane 1984). For example, the EU's Common Security and Defence Policy benefits from the EU's existing institutional framework and the familiarity of its members with each other's interests (Hofmann 2011, 2013; Kirchner 2011).

The intensity of regional violence is measured with the number of armed conflicts as reported in the Uppsala Conflict Data Program's (UCDP) Armed Conflict Dataset (Gleditsch et al. 2002; Themnér and Wallensteen 2012). This data set distinguishes among three levels of intensity: minor armed conflict (1), intermediate armed conflict (2) and war (3).[8] I count all violent conflicts within member states and between member states of a given REO from 1990 to 1999.[9] I then multiply the number of conflict years by the level of intensity and aggregate these sums for the entire region. Disputes between member states and third parties are excluded from the counting. I used the raw values to differentiate among very low (10 or below), low (11 to 20), medium (21 to 40) and high (more than 40) levels of violent conflict. Accordingly, this variable – labelled Conflict – takes values of 0, 0.33, 0.66 and 1. Table 12.1 reports the values on this variable (and the two other explanatory variables) for each REO in the sample.

Turning to supply-side dynamics, the existence of a powerful member – often labelled a regional 'hegemon' – in the REO is thought to be conducive to regional cooperation (Mattli 1999; Yarbrough and Yarbrough 1992: 61–6). Presumably, such a regional power has both the willingness and capabilities required to sustain the activities associated with the REO. This is especially true with respect to security cooperation, which can be rather demanding in terms of physical and human resources. In

---

[8] A minor armed conflict involves at least 25 battle-related deaths per year and fewer than 1000 battle-deaths during the course of the conflict. An intermediate conflict involves at least 25 but fewer than 1000 battle-related deaths per year and an accumulated total of at least 1000 battle-deaths during the course of the conflict. War involves at least 1000 battle-deaths per year.

[9] I exclude conflicts that took place in the 2000s to reduce the risk of reversed causality, that is, that security cooperation affected the level of conflict.

addition, the participation in security institutions may allow the hegemon to demonstrate its benign intentions vis-à-vis the weaker members
and project an image of a responsible regional player (Ikenberry 2001;
Thompson 2006). I therefore expect REOs with a hegemonic state to
develop deeper security substructures than REOs that lack an undis-
putable leader do.

The regional balance of power is measured with the so-called concentration ratio, which takes into account both the relative economic
size of all members and the number of members in the organisation
(Mansfield and Pevehouse 2000). The value of this variable increases with
power asymmetry and is bounded between zero and one. This variable –
labelled *Hegemony* – is divided into four categories. Values above the third
quartile indicate a strongly hegemonic REO and score 1; those that fall
between the third quartile and the median indicate a weakly hegemonic
REO and score 0.66; values lower than the median but higher than the
first quartile indicate a weakly balanced REO and score 0.33; and those
that fall below the first quartile indicate a strongly balanced REO and
score 0. I employ Penn World Tables' gross domestic product (GDP) data
from 1990 to 1999 to calculate this variable (Heston, Summers and Aten
2002).

An uneven distribution of power may not always facilitate cooperation.
Hegemons and other major states can be threatening to their neighbours.
Security cooperation, in particular, can be perceived as an instrument
used by the more powerful members to promote their own national
interests in the region. To the extent that other REO members distrust the
intentions of such powerful countries, they will be reluctant to include
security arrangements that infringe on their national sovereignty in REOs.
Thus, where major regional powers have tense relationships with other
members, the organisation is unlikely to enjoy a 'hegemonic dividend'. I
thus hypothesise that the inclusion of a meaningful security component in
the REO's institutional structure requires the absence of regional rivalries
between major regional powers and other members.

The divergence (or congruence) of interests is captured with the existence of strategic rivalries between the regional hegemon or major member states, on the one hand, and their counterparts, on the other. I use
Colaresi, Rasler and Thompson's (2007) list of rivalries to identify all the
strategic rivalries within any given REO. I then distinguish between major
rivalries and minor rivalries. The former involve the regional hegemon or,
if no clear hegemon can be identified, the more powerful state or states.
Given my expectation that nonrivalry will result in meaningful security

institutions, this variable – labelled *Non-Rivalry* – scores one if the REO is free of major rivalries and zero otherwise.

## III. A preliminary analysis of necessary conditions

Given the small number of observations and the potential for causal complexity, the fuzzy-set qualitative comparative analysis (fsQCA) is an appropriate technique to evaluate the hypotheses thus far discussed. This method is designed to identify necessary and sufficient conditions for the occurrence of a certain phenomenon (Ragin 2008; Schneider and Wagemann 2012), the presence of meaningful security institutions within REOs in this study. The method of fsQCA requires that we identify the observations that are members of a particular 'set', meaning that they have a certain trait (or not), and assign them a value that ranges from zero to one. REOs that have this trait are full members of the set, thereby scoring one, and those that lack it score zero. REOs can also be partial members of a given set; that is, they score less than one but more than one-half. Or, they can be partial members of the set's negation, scoring more than zero but less than one-half. The values on the four variables are already calibrated accordingly (revisit Table 12.1). In the rest of this section, I consider the possibility that any of the three conditions is a necessary (but not sufficient) condition for meaningful security institutions (Goertz and Starr 2003).[10]

I gauge the three hypotheses with two measures: *consistency* and *coverage*.[11] Consistency, the more important parameter, accounts for the degree of the data's compatibility with necessity. In so far as all the values on the condition variables are equal to or smaller than the values on the outcome variable, the level of consistency equals one. If, on the other hand, the value of the condition variable is higher than the outcome, the expectation of necessity is violated, resulting in a consistency value that is lower than one.[12] According to conventional practice, consistency levels of 0.9 and higher indicate necessity (Schneider and Wagemann 2012: 143). Shown graphically with a two-way plot, the value of necessity consistency increases as the number of observations that fall under the diagonal that runs from bottom left to upper right becomes larger.

Coverage captures the relevance of the condition to the outcome. That is, it accounts for the number of observations that belong to both

---

[10]  I intend to examine sufficient conditions in future research.
[11]  Analysis is conducted with FS/QCA 2.0 (Ragin, Drass and Davey 2006).
[12]  For a more complete discussion, see Schneider and Wagemann (2012: 139–50).

Table 12.3 *Levels of consistency and coverage*
*for conflict, hegemony and nonrivalry*

| Condition | Consistency | Coverage |
|-----------|-------------|----------|
| Conflict | 0.59 | 0.54 |
| Hegemony | 0.61 | 0.50 |
| Nonrivalry | 0.92 | 0.48 |

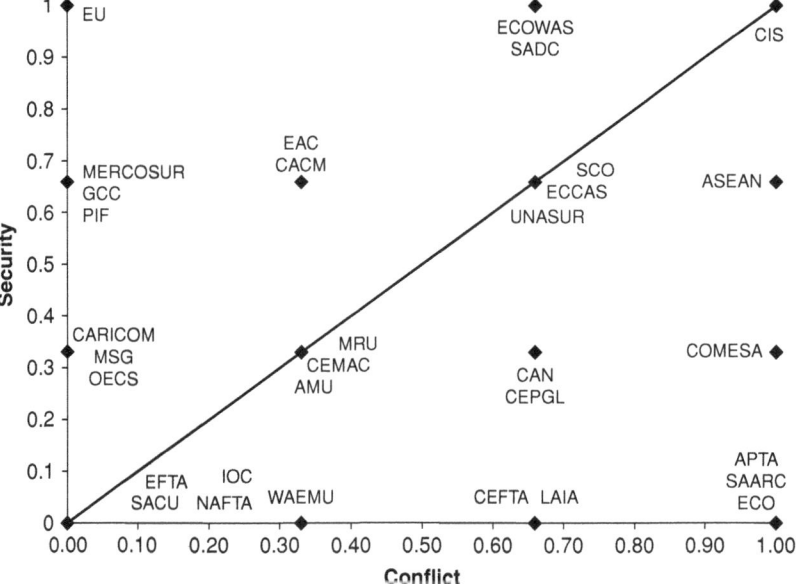

Figure 12.1   A two-way graph of conflict and security

sets out of those that belong to the condition. In addition, it is possible that the necessary condition will cover only a small number of
cases, but that these cases are nevertheless intrinsically important. This
requires close attention to and qualitative analysis of specific observations.
Table 12.3 reports the consistency and coverage values for each of the three
conditions. Figures 12.1, 12.2 and 12.3 present two-way plots of security
institutions and conflict, hegemony and nonrivalry, respectively.

It is apparent from the low consistency value that high levels of violent conflict are unnecessary for the creation of meaningful security
institutions within REOs. Whereas in some instances of deep security

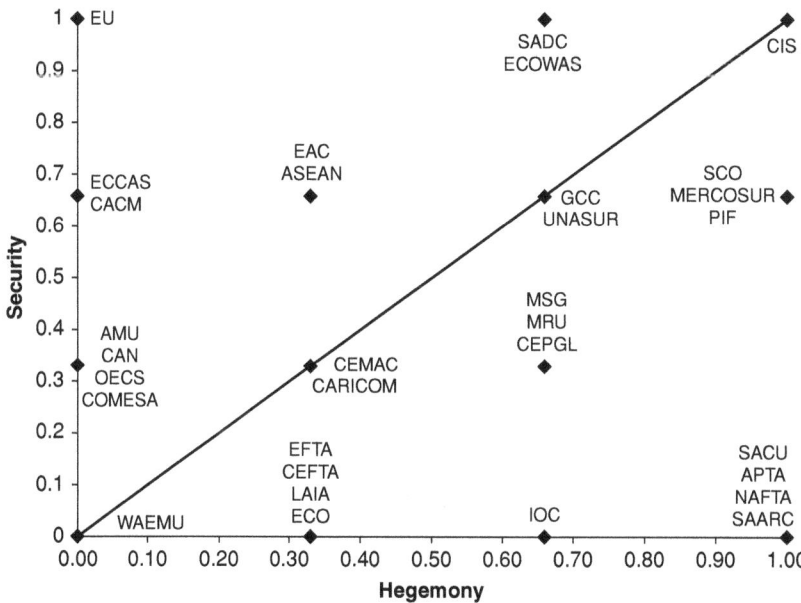

Figure 12.2    A two-way graph of hegemony and security

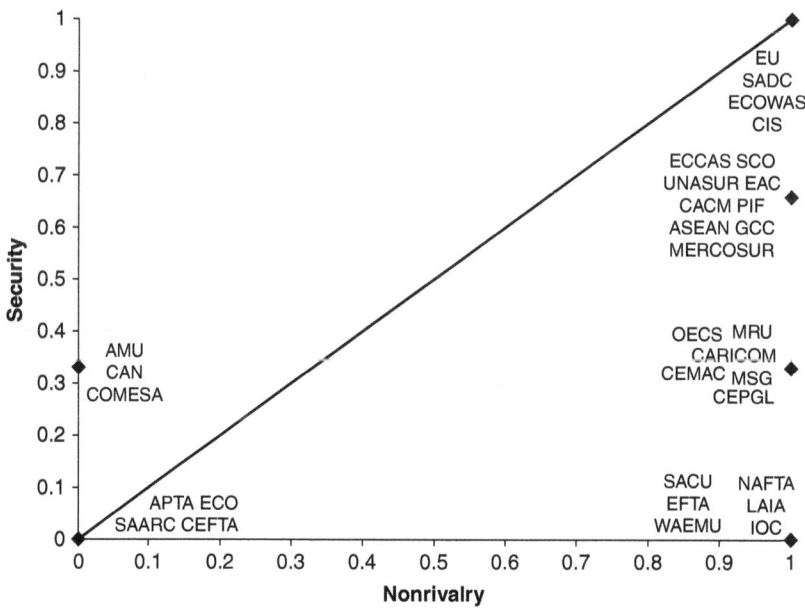

Figure 12.3    A two-way graph of nonrivalry and security

cooperation conflict is clearly present (e.g. ASEAN and CIS), in other cases governments invest in such instruments despite enjoying relative calm. Figure 12.1 offers some clues to this, perhaps surprising, result. Two organisations contradict the conflict hypothesis most clearly: the EU and, to a lesser extent, GCC. Members of both REOs have experienced low levels of violent conflict but nevertheless engaged in rather extensive security cooperation. A closer look indicates that in both cases these capabilities were developed to address external, rather than internal, security concerns. All of the EU's operations took place outside its borders (revisit Table 12.2), and most of GCC's (minor) operations, military exercises and the like were designed to fend off security threats from Iran and Iraq (Kuffel 2000).[13] These two cases point to the need to account for factors outside the region, such as external threat and instability, in a more systematic manner.

The consistency level of *Hegemony* is a little higher but still well below conventional thresholds, suggesting that extensive security cooperation can develop even without an undisputed leader. In some regions the hegemon was essential, for example, South Africa in SADC and Australia in PIF. In others, member states were able to overcome the collective action problem in a more balanced setting. Figure 12.2 shows that the EU stands out in this regard. Despite lacking a clear hegemonic state, it takes on security and military missions regularly. Possibly, this can be explained by its supranational nature, which obviates the need for a regional hegemon.[14] Four other REOs – ASEAN, CACM, EAC and ECCAS – developed medium levels of security cooperation despite the absence of a hegemon. Their experience suggests that such levels of security cooperation are achievable in nonhegemonic regions. One should keep in mind, of course, that the difference between medium and high levels of security cooperation can be quite substantial. Engagement in joint operations and allocation of resources to peacekeeping frequently carry serious sovereignty concerns and require the costly provision of troops, military equipment and logistical support.

---

[13] This has changed since the eruption of the Arab Spring and associated domestic challenges to some GCC governments.

[14] Alternatively, one could argue that the EU is a hegemonic REO. Mattli (1999), for example, maintains that Germany was the undisputed leader of the EU and provided much of the impetus for integration. This assertion rests more on the proactive leadership role Germany plays in the EU, however, and less on objective measures of power differentials, which are rather modest in the EU compared to other REOs.

In contrast to the first two variables, nonrivalry proves to be a necessary condition for meaningful security cooperation. Its consistency level easily passes conventional thresholds. In the most notable cases of security cooperation, the EU, ECOWAS, SADC and CIS, there are no major political rivalries. On the other hand, such rivalries were significant impediments in REOs such as SAARC (India vs. Pakistan). Figure 12.3 indicates that three REOs – AMU, CAN and COMESA – established security institutions despite having major rivalries in the organisation. Given that none of the three REOs are members of the set of meaningful security cooperation, they do not contradict the expectation of necessity (or, in the language of fsQCA, they are not logically inconsistent). In line with the hypothesis, in at least two of these cases, political rivalries presented major obstacles to security cooperation: Algeria versus Morocco in AMU, and Peru versus Ecuador and Venezuela versus Colombia in CAN. Thus, the existence of intraregional political enmity appears to be an important impediment to a meaningful expansion of economic organisations into the security realm.

Overall, the empirical assessment provides suggestive evidence regarding the determinants of nesting security institutions within economic agreements. It suggests that such spillover does not necessarily require regional instability or an undisputed hegemon, but it does require good political relations between the organisation's leading members. Future research ought to consider not only necessary but also sufficient conditions for this phenomenon as well as other factors that might affect the creation and design of nested security institutions. In addition, an inquiry into the effect of security cooperation on regional stability and peace is sorely needed. Only a handful of studies have begun to tackle this issue (Bearce 2003; Powers 2006), and many questions remain unanswered.

## D. Conclusion

The new wave of trade agreements is central to the contemporary world economy. Currently, most industrial and less developed states have signed at least one of the several hundred trade agreements in existence. Governments that concluded them envisioned them not only as vehicles of economic prosperity but also as instruments of stability and peace. This aspiration has become ever more pronounced in the aftermath of the Cold War rivalries and the growing autonomy of regions around the world.

This chapter has highlighted recent advances in our understanding of the links between trade agreements and conflict, with particular attention to variation across these instruments. It has shown that extant research is becoming increasingly sensitive to differences in the economic scope and institutional make-up of these agreements, thereby providing a nuanced account of the conditions under which they mitigate conflict. An overview of the literature also pointed to the scant attention thus far paid to security cooperation within these economic agreements as well as to the nexus of trade agreements and civil wars.

Beginning to remedy this shortcoming, this chapter has provided a pre-liminary enquiry into the growing, but little understood, trend of nested security institutions. In describing this seemingly puzzling phenomenon, it examined possible conditions necessary for meaningful security coop-eration within REOs. The results indicate that regions mired in bilateral rivalries will face insurmountable obstacles in this respect. The presence of high levels of conflict or a regional hegemon, on the other hand, is not necessary for the spillover of economic cooperation into the security realm. This is only a first, and modest, step towards a better grasp of this phenomenon, however. The examination of nontraditional security issues, the relevance of general institutional capacity and domestic fac-tors to the depth of security institutions and, perhaps most importantly, the impact of security cooperation on peace and stability are promising avenues of future research.

## Appendix to Chapter 12

### List of regional economic organisations

1. Arab Maghreb Union (AMU)
2. Asia Pacific Trade Agreement (APTA)
3. Association of Southeast Asian Nations (ASEAN)
4. Caribbean Community (CARICOM)
5. Central American Common Market (CACM)
6. Central European Free Trade Agreement (CEFTA)
7. Common Market for Eastern and Southern Africa (COMESA)
8. Community of Andean Nations (CAN)
9. Community of Independent States (CIS)
10. Community of the Countries of the Great Lakes (CEPGL)
11. East African Community (EAC)
12. Economic and Customs Union of the Central African States (CEMAC)
13. Economic Community of Central African States (ECCAS)
14. Economic Community of West African States (ECOWAS)

15. Economic Cooperation Organisation (ECO)
16. European Free Trade Association (EFTA)
17. European Union (EU)
18. Gulf Cooperation Council (GCC)
19. Indian Ocean Commission (IOC)
20. Latin American Integration Association (LAIA)
21. Mano River Union (MRU)
22. Melanesian Spearhead Group (MSG)
23. Mercado Común del Sur (MERCOSUR)
24. North American Free Trade Agreement (NAFTA)
25. Organisation of Eastern Caribbean States (OECS)
26. Pacific Islands Forum (PIF)
27. Shanghai Cooperation Organisation (SCO)
28. South African Customs Union (SACU)
29. South Asian Association for Regional Cooperation (SAARC)
30. Southern African Development Community (SADC)
31. Union of South American Nations (UNASUR)
32. West African Economic and Monetary Union (WAEMU)

## References

Aggarwal, Vinod K. 1998. *Institutional Design for a Complex World: Bargaining, Linkages, and Nesting*. Ithaca, NY: Cornell University Press.

Balassa, Bela. 1961. *The Theory of Economic Integration*. Homewood, IL: Richard D. Irwin.

Bearce, David H. 2003. 'Grasping the Commercial Institutional Peace.' *International Studies Quarterly* 47 (3): 347–70.

Bearce, David H., and Omori, Sawa. 2005. 'How Do Commercial Institutions Promote Peace?' *Journal of Peace Research* 42 (6): 659–78.

Boehmer, Charles, Gartzke, Erik, and Nordstrom, Tim. 2004. 'Do Intergovernmental Organizations Promote Peace?' *World Politics* 57 (1): 1–38.

Colaresi, Michael P., Rasler, Karen, and Thompson, William R. 2007. *Strategic Rivalries in World Politics: Position, Space, and Conflict Escalation*. Cambridge: Cambridge University Press.

Dorussen, Han, and Ward, Hugh. 2008. 'Intergovernmental Organizations and the Kantian Peace.' *Journal of Conflict Resolution* 52 (2): 189–212.

2010. 'Trade Networks and the Kantian Peace.' *Journal of Peace Research* 47 (1): 29–42.

Dür, Andreas, Baccini, Leonardo, and Elsig, Manfred. 2014. 'The Design of International Trade Agreements: Introducing a New Dataset.' *Review of International Organizations* 9 (3): 353–75.

Gleditsch, Nils Peter, Wallensteen, Peter, Eriksson, Mikael, Sollenberg, Magareta, and Strand, Harvard. 2002. 'Armed Conflict 1946–2001: A New Dataset.' *Journal of Peace Research* 39 (5): 615–37.

Goertz, Gary, and Starr, Harvey, eds. 2003. *Necessary Conditions: Theory, Methodology, and Applications*. Lanham, MD: Rowman & Littlefield.

Gray, Julia. 2014. 'Domestic Capacity and the Implementation Gap in Regional Trade Agreements.' *Comparative Political Studies* 47 (1): 55–84.

Haas, Ernest B. 1964. *Beyond the Nation-State*. Stanford, CA: Stanford University Press.

Hafner-Burton, Emily M., and Montgomery, Alexander H. 2012. 'War, Trade, and Distrust: Why Trade Agreements Don't Always Keep the Peace.' *Conflict Management and Peace Science* 29 (3): 257–78.

Haftel, Yoram Z. 2007. 'Designing for Peace: Regional Integration Arrangements, Institutional Variation, and Militarized Inter-state Disputes.' *International Organization* 61 (1): 217–37.

2012. *Regional Economic Institutions and Conflict Mitigation: Design, Implementation, and the Promise of Peace*. Ann Arbor: University of Michigan Press.

2013. 'Commerce and Institutions: Trade, Scope, and the Design of Regional Economic Organizations.' *Review of International Organizations* 8 (3): 389–414.

Haftel, Yoram Z., and Thompson, Alexander. 2006. 'The Independence of International Organizations: Concept and Applications.' *Journal of Conflict Resolution* 50 (2): 253–75.

Heston, Alan, Summers, Robert, and Aten, Bettina. 2002. *Penn World Table Version 6.1*. Philadelphia, PA: Center for International Comparisons at the University of Pennsylvania (CICUP).

Hofmann, Stephanie C. 2011. 'Why Institutional Overlap Matters: CSDP in the European Security Architecture.' *Journal of Common Market Studies* 49 (1): 101–20.

2013. *European Security in NATO's Shadow: Party Ideologies and Institution Building*. Cambridge: Cambridge University Press.

Ikenberry, John G. 2001. *After Victory: Institutions, Strategic Restraint, and the Rebuilding of Order after Major Wars*. Princeton, NJ: Princeton University Press.

Keohane, Robert O. 1984. *After Hegemony: Cooperation and Discord in the World Political Economy*. Princeton, NJ: Princeton University Press.

Kirchner, Emil. 2011. 'The EU as a Regional and Global Security Provider.' In *The Security Governance of Regional Organizations*, edited by Emil Kirchner and Roberto Domínguez, 25–45. London: Routledge.

Kirchner, Emil, and Domínguez, Roberto, eds. 2011. *The Security Governance of Regional Organizations*. London: Routledge.

Kuffel, Glenn P. 2000. 'The Gulf Cooperation Council's Peninsular Shield Force. New Port: Naval War College and Joint Military Operations Department.' Paper submitted to the Faculty of the Naval War College, Newport, RI. www.dtic.mil/cgi-bin/GetTRDoc?Location=U2&doc=GetTRDoc. pdf&AD=ADA378521. Accessed 14 February 2013.

Mansfield, Edward D. 2003. 'Preferential Peace: Why Preferential Trade Arrangements Inhibit Inter-state Conflict.' In *Economic Interdependence and International Conflict: New Perspectives on an Enduring Debate*, edited by Edward D. Mansfield and Brian M. Pollins, 222–36. Ann Arbor: University of Michigan Press.

Mansfield, Edward D., and Milner, Helen V. 1999. 'The New Wave of Regionalism.' *International Organization* 53 (3): 529–627.

Mansfield, Edward D., and Pevehouse, Jon C. 2000. 'Trade Blocs, Trade Flows, and International Conflict.' *International Organization* 54 (4): 775–808.

2003. 'Institutions, Interdependence, and International Conflict.' In *Globalization and Armed Conflict*, edited by Gerald Schneider, Katherine Barbieri and Nils Petter Gleditsch, 233–50. Lanham, MD: Rowman & Littlefield.

Forthcoming. 'The Institutional Design of Preferential Trade Agreements and the Outbreak of Conflict.' In *The Political Economy of Regional Peacemaking*, edited by Steven Lobell and Norrin Ripsman. Ann Arbor: University of Michigan Press.

Mansfield, Edward D., Pevehouse, Jon C., and Bearce, David H. 1999/2000. 'Preferential Trading Arrangements and Military Disputes.' *Security Studies* 9 (1–2): 96–118.

Martin, Philippe, Mayer, Thierry, and Thoenig, Mathias 2010. 'The Geography of Conflicts and Free Trade Agreements.' CEPR Discussion Papers No. 7740. Centre for Economic Policy Research, London.

Mattli, Walter. 1999. *The Logic of Regional Integration: Europe and Beyond.* Cambridge: Cambridge University Press.

Nye, Joseph S. 1971. *Peace in Parts: Integration and Conflict in Regional Organizations.* Boston: Little, Brown.

Pevehouse, Jon C., and Russett, Bruce. 2006. 'Democratic International Governmental Organizations Promote Peace.' *International Organization* 60 (4): 969–1000.

Powers, Kathy L. 2006. 'Dispute Initiation and Alliance Obligations in Regional Economic Institutions.' *Journal of Peace Research* 43 (4): 453–71.

Ragin, Charles C. 2008. *Redesigning Social Inquiry: Fuzzy Sets and Beyond.* Chicago: University of Chicago Press.

Ragin, Charles C., Drass, Kriss A., and Davey, Sean. 2006. *Fuzzy-Set/Qualitative Comparative Analysis 2.0.* Tucson: Department of Sociology, University of Arizona.

Russett, Bruce, and Oneal, John R. 2001. *Triangulating Peace: Democracy, Interdependence, and International Organizations.* New York, NY: Norton.

Schiff, Maurice, and Winters, Alan. 1998. 'Dynamics and Politics in Regional Integration Arrangements: An Introduction.' *World Bank Economic Review* 12 (2): 177–95.

Schneider, Carsten Q., and Wagemann, Claudius. 2012. *Set-Theoretic Methods in the Social Sciences. A Guide to Qualitative Comparative Analysis.* Cambridge: Cambridge University Press.

Tavares, Rodrigo. 2009. *Regional Security: The Capacity of International Organizations.* New York: Routledge.

Themnér, Lotta, and Wallensteen, Peter. 2012. 'Armed Conflict 1946–2011.' *Journal of Peace Research* 49 (4): 465–75.

Thompson, Alexander. 2006. 'Coercion through IOs: The Security Council and the Logic of Information Transmission.' *International Organization* 61 (1): 1–34.

Vicard, Vincent. 2012. 'Trade, Conflict, and Political Integration: Explaining the Heterogeneity of Regional Trade Agreements.' *European Economic Review* 56 (1): 54–71.

Yarbrough, Beth, and Yarbrough, Robert. 1992. *Cooperation and Governance in International Trade: The Strategic Organizational Approach.* Princeton, NJ: Princeton University Press.

# 13

## Dispute settlement provisions in PTAs

### New data and new concepts

TODD ALLEE AND MANFRED ELSIG

## A. Introduction

Dispute settlement occupies a central role within the study of international institutions. The fact that state parties have signed a treaty or joined a regime signifies not so much an end but a beginning. Whether one conceptualises the important posttreaty (or postaccession) process as compliance or enforcement, the question of how future disputes between state parties will be resolved is crucial. In fact, within the economic realm one would be justified in claiming that academic research on the World Trade Organization (WTO) is dominated by studies of its noteworthy dispute settlement system (see Bernauer, Elsig and Pauwelyn 2012). If one looks more narrowly at something like bilateral investment treaties (BITs), perhaps the best analogy for preferential trade agreements (PTAs), it also becomes clear that how treaty-related disputes will be resolved is the most important aspect of the agreements (Allee and Peinhardt 2014).

PTAs increasingly dominate the trade policymaking landscape as they continue to be negotiated and their numbers rise. The increasing acknowledgement that PTAs are not only prevalent but vary in important ways has resulted in the current wave of scholarship on PTA design (e.g. Dür, Baccini and Elsig 2014; Hicks and Kim 2012; Kucik 2012). Recent studies have focused on certain design features of PTAs (such as depth and flexibility) and how these features interact (i.e. depth with flexibility). What has received relatively less attention, however, is how states decide on the architecture of dispute resolution provisions. This is surprising given the importance of dispute settlement mechanisms in other international

We wish to thank Maura Iliuteanu for excellent research assistance. Financial support from the NCCR Trade Regulation (www.nccr-trade.org) is greatly acknowledged.

institutions (e.g. WTO, the European Union (EU), regional human rights bodies) as well as the greater-than-realised use of dispute settlement mechanisms in regional PTAs.[1] Dispute settlement design in regional PTAs was actually one of the first aspects of PTAs to be unpacked and explored (Smith 2000). Yet despite one other attempt to update this early study (Jo and Namgung 2012) and valuable descriptive contributions from international law scholars on variation in dispute settlement processes (e.g. Chase *et al.* 2013; Donaldson and Lester 2009; Porges 2011), we argue that our understanding of dispute settlement provisions (Dsps) in PTAs needs substantial revisiting, both in terms of conceptualisation and data collection.

This chapter aims to broaden our conceptualisation and to illuminate the richness of the agreements' DSPs using a much more complete universe of PTAs and showcasing far more variables than have been employed in earlier analyses. In the remainder of the chapter we first discuss how the international relations (IR) literature has conceptualised dispute settlement solely in terms of 'legalisation', thus misclassifying dispute settlement in PTAs into a binary categorisation between legal versus diplomatic. Second, we present new empirical evidence on the considerable variation in DSPs across PTAs, relying on novel data from the Design of Trade Agreements Database (Dür, Baccini and Elsig 2014). We show data on 30 dispute settlement variables, for nearly 600 PTAs, and discuss patterns and trends. In the third and final section, we draw upon these new data and put forward general concepts that might characterise DSPs, such as enforceability, settlement promotion and (dispute settlement) flexibility, as well as expanding upon concepts such as delegation.

## B. Previous research on PTA dispute settlement

Since the end of the 1990s, scholarship on international institutions has often focused on the question of how 'legalised' international cooperation

---

[1] PTA dispute settlement procedures have been actively used across the Americas, for instance. The North American Free Trade Agreement (NAFTA)'s dispute settlement mechanisms related to investment, trade remedies and disputes generally have been used multiple times, and many trade-related conflicts in MERCOSUR and the Andean Community, and to a lesser extent the Central American Common Market, have been resolved through the organisations' legal dispute settlement procedures. Additionally, and by contrast, the EU has addressed several disputes with its trading partners through formal consultations, the first step of formal dispute settlement procedures. Similarly, multiple European Free Trade Association (EFTA) disputes have been resolved at the level of committees, which is part of the agreement's dispute settlement procedures.

has become over time (Abbott *et al.* 2000). This is a logical starting point because the rich legalisation framework emphasises treaty design elements such as obligation, precision and delegation that can be linked in some way to DSPs. The result is that virtually all scholarship that attempts to understand dispute settlement in PTAs thinks in terms of a single dimension of legalisation. That is, is a DSP 'legal' or is it instead merely 'political' or 'diplomatic' (Jo and Namgung 2012; Smith 2000; also Chase *et al.* 2013; Porges 2011).

The literature on the 'rational design' of international institutions (Koremenos, Lipson and Snidal 2001) likewise has informed existing scholarship on dispute settlement in indirect ways that reinforce the focus on a single dimension of dispute settlement. Two of the design features, 'centralisation' (Koremenos, Lipson and Snidal 2001) and 'delegation' (Koremenos 2007), can be used as ways to classify DSPs in PTAs or other agreements (see Allee and Peinhardt 2014). Despite the differing nomenclatures, the conceptual focus remains on a one-dimensional conceptualisation of whether disputes shall be settled by the parties informally or are to be addressed more formally using a (legal) third party (see Koremenos 2007).

One major challenge lies in moving these conceptualisations from abstract theory to empirical reality. One limitation is the lack of rigorous empirical testing of these otherwise thoughtful conceptualisations of international institutions (Duffield 2003; also Allee and Peinhardt 2014; Copelovitch and Putnam, 2014). Moreover, the empirical tests we observe tend to measure dispute settlement in a fairly simplistic way. For instance, Koremenos (2007) conducts a basic multivariate regression analysis to predict whether a random sample of all international treaties contains a DSP. This is somewhat problematic in the PTA context, since nearly all PTAs, like most other important treaties, contain such a provision. The more important question, then, is what is contained in those provisions?

By far the most important study that informs this chapter is that of Smith (2000), who was the first to open up the black box of DSPs in PTAs. He focuses on 62 regional trade pacts and differentiates levels of legalism ranging from diplomatic to legalistic types. He collects data on five specific elements, all of which are tied to the dimension of legalism. The first three emphasise the existence and basic form of third-party, legal dispute settlement:

1. Are states able to utilise legal, third-party dispute settlement without being blocked (third-party review)?

2. Is the judgment by a third party binding (third-party ruling)?
3. Is the body ad hoc or standing (judges)?

The fourth variable captures whether actors beyond the state have standing in legal proceedings (standing), and the fifth captures whether rulings have direct effect (type of remedy).

It is important to note that Smith's fourth and fifth variables seem less relevant today and in the more general context of PTAs (as compared to regional trade agreements (RTAs)). One reason is that regional agreements have become highly integrated political and legal entities, and thus direct effect is a common feature of regional agreements. Furthermore, relatively few PTAs provide private standing, and when they do, it is typically for investment arbitration, which almost always is derived from a BIT as opposed to a PTA. Interestingly, a more recent study, which builds directly on Smith, effectively collapses his five-factor indicator into three elements. Following Smith's (2000) lead, Jo and Namgung (2012) similarly code:

1. whether third-party review is allowed (third-party review),
2. whether the review has any legal effect (bindingness of decisions) and
3. whether there are institutionalised bodies such as standing courts (institutionalisation).

From this coding they derive three degrees of legalism (low, medium, high) – maintaining the same overall dimension as Smith – and put forward an expanded theoretical discussion and conduct more extensive quantitative tests.

Smith's study, and Jo and Namgung's more recent update, are essential contributions and directly inform our efforts. However, we identify some possible limitations of their approaches. The first is that the three common variables (third-party review, bindingness, institutionalisation) are highly correlated and overlap in important ways. For example, a system with a standing body, which captures the degree of institutionalisation, certainly comes with the right to third-party resolution. At the same time, this standing body is almost certain to render verdicts that are binding. A second concern is with the concept of 'bindingness' as a variable, which we suggest is actually more of a constant. From a legal standpoint, we would expect any ruling that arises from an arbitral or adjudicatory body to be legally binding on the parties unless explicitly stated otherwise. As we discuss later, we find virtually no cases in which the parties agree that a panel ruling is not binding. A third issue is with the exclusive focus on legalism. Although this concept is undoubtedly important, we believe its overuse obscures other important concepts and other components of the dispute settlement process. A related concern is with the overall lack of variables that are coded. Coding data is a time-intensive process, but we suggest that more than three, or even five, variables are relevant to DSPs. A fifth and final issue is the narrow scope of the cases in Smith's study, which is not necessarily a criticism of Smith's work but rather a concern about generalisability. RTAs are clearly important in international affairs, but there are only 62 of them in Smith's study. Jo and Namgung (2012) broaden the focus to all PTAs and analyse 221 of them, yet a pervasive concern is that they, like the rest of the literature, are missing a significant number of PTAs in their samples.

Recent descriptive studies from legal scholars address some of these gaps. Some research has looked comparatively at DSPs in PTAs from a primarily legal viewpoint (Donaldson and Lester 2009; Morgan 2008; Porges 2011). Porges (2011), for instance, discusses a broad set of DSPs in PTAs while continuing to conceptualise dispute settlement along a unidimensional scale from diplomatic to legal (with a distinction among the latter made between ad hoc and standing arbitration). The most noteworthy recent study is an exhaustive WTO working paper from Chase *et al.* (2013). The majority of their paper is a careful cataloguing of all of the major DSPs in PTAs. Despite the richness of their study, we see two possible limitations of their approach. First, at a broader analytical level, they default to thinking about PTAs on a familiar three-part continuum from 'political' to 'judicial', in which nearly all recent PTAs are classified in the middle category of quasi-judicial. Second, they consider an incomplete set of 226 PTAs – only those notified to the WTO – compared to the nearly 600 for which we have compiled and analysed data. Nevertheless, all of the aforementioned valuable studies push scholarship on PTAs, and institutional design, in a useful direction.

## C. Dispute settlement in PTAs: the data

Our new data on DSPs in PTAs are part of a larger project to systematically collect detailed data on PTAs (Dür, Baccini and Elsig 2014). The data set currently includes 589 PTAs concluded between 1947 and 2009. The collection of agreements includes customs unions, free trade agreements that promise to liberalise substantially all trade and partial trade agreements. In the following section we present data focused specifically on DSPs; that is, those variables that capture the ways treaty-makers foresee the solution of future disputes when they arise. Significant steps have been taken to ensure the validity of these data.[2]

Our data on dispute settlement currently include 30 variables related to how dispute settlement is designed across PTAs. These capture a multitude of dimensions ranging from types of mechanisms envisaged, the use of multiple fora, procedural issues, the scope of dispute settlement (i.e. exclusions and exceptions) and instruments to improve implementation (i.e. sanctions). Sizeable literatures across international law and international relations inform the coding scheme, as do discussions with legal experts and trade negotiators. Our coding overlaps to some degree with the taxonomy offered by the WTO Secretariat in its recent staff working paper (Chase *et al.* 2013). A distinguishing feature of our research on dispute settlement is that we move beyond the single dimension of *legalisation* and instead consider how the dispute settlement components can be characterised by the degree to which they aid *enforceability*, entail greater *delegation* (as compared to *control*), specify *flexibility* or *promote overall settlement* of the dispute (see Section D).

## I. Dispute settlement provisions

Digging into the data, we explore whether DSPs are typically included in PTAs as our first question. That is, are there any explicit rules to regulate potential conflicts that may arise out of the interpretation of treaty and, more importantly, parties' behaviour? The answer is a resounding yes.

Table 13.1 shows that more than 83 per cent of PTAs (488 of 589) in our data set include a provision on dispute settlement, and among the newest

Table 13.1 *PTAs with a dispute settlement provision*

| Provision | Number | As a % of all PTAs |
| --- | --- | --- |
| Dispute settlement | 488 | 83 |

[2] All coders are trained in advance to ensure appropriate knowledge of the coding scheme. Given that many of the original treaty texts are in languages other than English (e.g. Spanish, French, Arabic, Russian), we relied on students with the necessary language skills to code non-English-language treaties. All variables on dispute settlement were double-coded during two waves of coding. Intercoder reliability has been found to be high: 92.2 per cent is the average overlap for the variables. A referee (one of the authors) has acted as a judge regarding which coding prevails in the cases of different interpretation by coders.

and most relevant PTAs, this number approaches 100 per cent.[3] More than 97 per cent of PTAs in the 2000s, for instance, explicitly mention how disputes should be resolved, whereas only 5 of 212 fail to include a DSP. The percentages are similarly striking if one considers 'meaningful' agreements; that is, PTAs that move in at least modest ways towards trade liberalisation. Using a simple, 0–7 index of PTA 'depth' drawn from Dür, Baccini and Elsig (2014), we see that among PTAs at or above modest levels of depth (2 or higher), more than 98 per cent contain a DSP. In contrast, almost all (more than 90 per cent) of the PTAs without a DSP are concentrated at the bottom of the depth scale, with either a score of 0 (40 of 73) or a score of 1 (26 of 73). To sum up, PTAs almost universally specify some type of rules for settling disputes – which means attention now turns to understanding important differences between these rules.

## II. Types of dispute settlement

### 1. Consultations

As a starting point, nearly all DSPs encourage parties to engage in *consultations* at the first stage of a dispute. In total, 450 PTAs specify a consultation mechanism for responding to problems and disputes arising from the agreement (see Table 13.2), which represents more than 76 per cent of all PTAs in our data set and, more relevantly, 92 per cent of all PTAs with a DSP (450 of 488). Almost universally, then, having the parties discuss the issue without formal third-party involvement is therefore seen as an integral first step in the dispute settlement process – an attempt to exchange viewpoints and potentially resolve all or at least some issues before the dispute goes to a more formal channel. Oddly, many of the

Table 13.2 *PTAs with a consultation provision*

| Provision | Number | As a % of all PTAs | As a % of PTAs with a DSP |
|---|---|---|---|
| Consultation | 450 | 76 | 92 |

[3] Often there is an explicit article on dispute settlement, yet in some cases the relevant language can be found in chapters on committees (e.g. 'joint committees') that are mandated to manage the implementation of the treaty obligations or to serve as a forum in case of disagreement or dispute.

38 PTAs that do not explicitly mention consultations, and instead directly guide members towards legal dispute settlement, are customs unions. Given their otherwise extensive dispute settlement operations, it seems that in many of these cases consultation is probably seen as too obvious an initial step to need to put it into the DSP explicitly.

## 2. Mediation

An obvious next place to look is for language on what we label *mediation*, which entails bringing in a third party to assist the parties in reaching a negotiated solution.[4] Mediation is the first of four types of third-party dispute settlement and the only one that relies on assisted negotiations instead of legal proceedings. Eighty-eight PTAs include a mediation provision, always in conjunction with a consultation provision. Sometimes the treaties list titles of leaders of international organisations to serve in their capacity. Table 13.3 depicts the frequency of mediation as well as the percentage of DSPs that include mediation (along with similar data on the three other types of third-party settlement, which we discuss shortly). Provisions usually stress that mediation is undertaken voluntarily and can be terminated at any time and that positions taken by the parties during these proceedings shall be confidential and without prejudice to the rights of either party in any further proceedings under these procedures.

In terms of patterns, mediation is a relatively new innovation. Although mediation in PTAs dates back to 1969, half (50 of 100) of PTAs with mediation provisions are in the last five years of our data set (2005–9). This upsurge results not only from the preponderance in the data set of PTAs signed in the past 10–15 years but also perhaps from increasing emphasis in legal circles on alternative dispute resolution (ADR) and the

Table 13.3 *PTAs with various types of dispute settlement*

| Provision | Number | As a % of PTAs with a DSP |
|---|---|---|
| Mediation | 88 | 18 |
| Arbitration | 224 | 46 |
| Standing body | 31 | 6 |
| Reference to external body | 113 | 23 |

[4] This category also includes 'good offices' and 'conciliation'.

prominence of mediation in other domestic and international settings. There are important regional differences. European states rarely rely on mediation procedures, yet, by contrast, mediation is a prominent tool in PTAs in Asia (22 of 67, or 33 per cent) and the Americas (38 of 143, or 27 per cent) as well as in treaties involving the United States. It is possible that the motivation might differ across these treaties. In the US treaties it might reflect a general trend in US legal circles towards alternative dispute resolution or multiple dispute options, whereas in Asian agreements it might be interpreted as an 'Asian way' of attempting to settle conflicts without resorting to legalism. An important caveat, which we discuss later, is that some of these same treaties (Asia, Americas, United States) also include resort to legal dispute settlement – an indication that dispute settlement venues are not zero-sum and the multiple types of dispute settlement often co-exist.

## 3. Arbitration

The first, and most frequently specified, of three legal dispute settlement options is arbitration, typically using ad hoc panels of three or sometimes five panellists. Any of the parties may request the establishment of an arbitration panel, and its establishment cannot be blocked by the defending party. Usually, the award (decision) by the panellists is final and binding for the parties. Arbitration provisions can be quite lengthy and may include specific information, for example, on time frames, the selection of panellists, rules of procedures, cost distribution. A total of 224 PTAs include an arbitration provision, which represents 38 per cent of PTAs and 46 per cent of PTAs with DSPs (see Table 13.3). Arbitration dates back to the very earliest PTAs but has become a more common feature in recent years. About 20–25 per cent of PTAs before 1995 include an arbitration provision, a figure which jumps to 35–40 per cent for the years between 1995 and 2004. Since 2005, nearly 80 per cent of PTAs have specified ad hoc arbitration as an option.

The patterns around the globe are notable and mirror those for mediation. Seventeen of 18 PTAs involving the United States include arbitration, as do two-thirds of North–South PTAs – a far greater percentage than for North–North and South–South agreements. Forty-five per cent of PTAs in both Asia and the Americas include arbitration provisions, and cross-region agreements include ad hoc arbitration 55 per cent of the time. Half of EU agreements include arbitration. The laggard this time is Africa, since only 2 of 35 African PTAs allow for arbitration.

## 4. Standing body

In contrast to the more common option of ad hoc arbitration, some PTAs also specify the creation of a standing dispute settlement body to which disputes are delegated. These agreements generate some of the most notable dispute settlement bodies around the globe, such as the European Court of Justice, Court of Justice of the Andean Community, East African Court of Justice and the Caribbean Court of Justice. Only 31 PTAs, however, specify the creation of such bodies (see Table 13.3). The clearest pattern is that standing bodies emerge out of regional economic integration agreements. Twenty-seven of the 31 standing bodies are spawned by regional efforts at greater economic cooperation.

In general, the patterns for standing body creation are very different from those for arbitration as well as the other third-party options. In this case, Northern agreements (6 of 44, or 18.2 per cent) are more likely to generate standing bodies than are Southern agreements (6.4 per cent) or North–South PTAs (2.1 per cent). Noteworthy is the trend towards adoption by African countries: PTAs in Africa have by far the highest rate (11 of 36, or 31 per cent) of standing body creation. All of this probably reflects that agreements among certain subsets of states reflect those states' desires to build deeper institutions among regional or similar peers.

## 5. Reference to external body

A final scenario is one in which PTAs encourage parties to refer to an outside dispute settlement mechanism, body or court. A total of 113 PTAs do so (all of which also include consultation), which represents just less than 20 per cent of PTAs and more than 23 per cent of those with DSPs. By far the most common external body specified is the WTO (and the former General Agreement on Tariffs and Trade (GATT)) and its dispute settlement mechanism (DSM). This reference can take different forms, such as suggesting that certain WTO provisions and their interpretation through WTO DSMs (e.g. on anti-dumping) be incorporated into the PTA obligations or encouraging the use of WTO dispute settlement in certain issue areas. Some PTAs also make a reference to the use of other treaties' dispute mechanisms to which contracting states are party (which can also mean other PTAs). In earlier PTAs, such as the Benelux Economic Union of 1958, reference is made to the International Court of Justice (ICJ), for instance.

There are some interesting and familiar patterns in terms of reference to an external body. Not surprisingly, there is an upward trend over time, driven largely by the creation of the WTO DSM as an obvious outside option from 1995 onward. A total of 11 PTAs in force before 1994 made reference to external dispute settlement institutions (to the ICJ or the GATT), whereas since 1994 an average of 11 PTAs annually have specified that disputes could be referred to bodies such as the WTO DSM. Similarly to ad hoc arbitration, reference to an external body is more likely among North–South agreements (55 of 141, or 39 per cent) and within US agreements (16 of 18). Among regions, about one-third of cross-regional agreements include these possibilities, as do approximately one-quarter of PTAs in the Americas and Asia.

## 6. Overlap

The preceding patterns raise the important issue of overlap in types of dispute settlement. For each of the four types of third-party dispute settlement (mediation, ad hoc arbitration, creation of standing body and reference to external dispute settlement body), Table 13.4 shows how many PTAs that include a given type of dispute settlement also allow for each of the other types of dispute settlement.

One clear pattern is the considerable overlap between arbitration provisions and those on mediation and reference to an external body. PTAs that allow for mediation also specify the option of ad hoc arbitration 92 per cent of the time (81 of 88 agreements) and frequently also make reference to external bodies (80 per cent of the time). Similarly, nearly all PTAs that refer to an external body such as the WTO allow for ad hoc

Table 13.4 *Overlap between types of dispute settlement*

| Provision | Number that include the provision | Number (percentage) that also include | | | |
|---|---|---|---|---|---|
| | | Mediation | Arbitration | Standing body | Reference to external body |
| Mediation | 88 | | 81 | 6 | 70 |
| | | | (92%) | (7%) | (80%) |
| Arbitration | 224 | 81 | | 7 | 108 |
| | | (36%) | | (3%) | (48%) |
| Standing body | 31 | 6 | 7 | | 2 |
| | | (19%) | (23%) | | (6%) |
| Reference to external body | 113 | 70 | 108 | 2 | |
| | | (62%) | (96%) | (2%) | |

arbitration (108 of 113; 96 per cent). Arbitration provisions are by far the most popular dispute settlement option in PTAs, occurring in 224 agreements, yet a sizeable number of PTAs that allow for arbitration also specify mediation (36 per cent) as an option or refer to an external body (48 per cent). These patterns suggest that for many PTAs, both mediation and legal dispute settlement will be an option, and multiple venues for legal dispute settlement may be available.

A second clear pattern in Table 13.4 is that standing bodies tend to 'stand alone' compared to other types of PTA dispute settlement. Only 7 of 224 PTAs that specify ad hoc arbitration also provide for settlement before a standing body. Or fewer than one-quarter (7 of 31) of the agreements that create a standing body also allow for ad hoc arbitration. Thus these two types of dispute settlement – ad hoc arbitration and the creation of an internal, standing body – function more as substitutes than as complements. Moreover, only 6 of the 31 also allow for the relatively common option of mediation (see Table 13.4). In fact, not only is there little overlap between the creation of a standing body and other options but the discussion in the preceding pages suggests very distinct patterns for PTAs that create standing dispute settlement bodies. Overall, then, PTAs that channel dispute settlement to an internal, standing body look quite different from the majority of PTAs that rely on other, overlapping types of dispute settlement.

## 7. Legal dispute settlement

Table 13.4 also suggests the need to consider the total number of PTAs that allow for any type of *legal dispute settlement*; that is, PTAs which allow ad hoc arbitration allow the use of a standing dispute settlement body or suggest WTO or other outside dispute settlement mechanisms. In total, 252 PTAs contain a provision allowing some type of legal dispute settlement. Once again, put in the proper context, this number appears even more sizeable. Overall, since 1990, between 5 and 20 PTAs that include legal dispute settlement have been signed annually. Moreover, among PTAs of moderate or higher (greater than or equal to 3) integration on the 0–7 depth index noted earlier, five-sixths include at least one form of legal dispute settlement. Thus, one conclusion is that to really understand contemporary dispute settlement, one must unpack the 'legalisation' that characterises many DSPs in PTAs to uncover what options are available, how they are chosen, the rules governing proceedings and how awards are implemented. Most of the following variables, then, use the total number of PTAs with legal dispute settlement (252) as the reference point or baseline.

## II. Forum choice

The earlier discussion about overlapping legal dispute options raises the issue of forum choice, particularly as related to intra-PTA mechanisms and outside options (e.g. Busch 2007; Pauwelyn 2009). Building on the discussion in the previous section, we identify 109 PTAs that contain an internal dispute settlement mechanism (through arbitration or a standing body) and also specify an external option such as the WTO DSM. The question becomes one of whether and how these agreements address the fact that they specify multiple legal fora for settling disputes. An initial answer is seen in the number of PTAs that include a provision on the choice of forum. A sizeable number of agreements, 104 in total, include such a provision (see Table 13.5). This suggests that treaty designers are quite conscious of the multiple-fora issue and attempt to address it with provisions on forum choice.

It is interesting to note that all 104 of these agreements allow the complainant to choose the forum, seemingly giving the complainant state significant power to choose a favourable venue. However, nearly all PTAs with forum choice provisions (100 of them; see Table 13.5) also place restrictions on the use of more than one forum at any given time. Thus in the overwhelming majority of potential forum-shopping situations, the forum choice provision significantly curtails the complainant's ability to 'shop' between the PTA and an external venue in a manner that might be disproportionately advantageous.

## III. Proceedings

We now explore several variables that address how dispute settlement proceeds after it has been set in motion, an aspect of DSP design that

Table 13.5 *Forum choice in PTA dispute settlement*

| Provision | Number | As a % of PTAs that specify multiple venues |
| --- | --- | --- |
| Forum choice | 104 | 95 |
| Restrictions on multiple fora | 100 | 92 |

Table 13.6 *Features of dispute settlement proceedings*

| Provision | Number | As a % of PTAs with legal dispute settlement |
|---|---|---|
| Joint committee action | 138 | 55 |
| Chairperson selection (through consultations) | 114 | 45 |
| Chairperson selection (by third party) | 89 | 35 |
| Chairperson selection (by lot) | 69 | 27 |
| Chairperson selection (jointly by arbitrators) | 35 | 14 |
| Interim report | 74 | 29 |
| Separate opinions | 28 | 11 |
| Time limits | 203 | 81 |
| Refer to MAS (total) | 106 | 42 |
| Refer to MAS (pre-award) | 76 | 30 |
| Refer to MAS (postaward) | 104 | 41 |

also has been largely overlooked. All of these 'proceedings' variables are depicted in Table 13.6.

### 1. Joint committee action

The first issue is whether there is a provision allowing for a joint committee comprising representatives of PTA partners to address the dispute before the establishment of the arbitral panel. This can be thought of as an additional procedural step between consultations and the actual panel process, the intent of which is to resolve the dispute without litigation. All in all, 138 PTAs include this type of joint committee measure, which represents approximately 55 per cent of agreements with some form of legal dispute settlement (see Table 13.6). There is relatively little variation in the inclusion of this provision over time, and it does not correlate highly with depth or type of agreement. Most notable is the relatively high rate of inclusion in US PTAs (14 of 18).

### 2. Chair selection

At the outset of any arbitral proceedings, the selection of the chairperson becomes important because arbitration panels take decisions by majority and the chair often plays a pivotal role. In ad hoc arbitration with a three-person panel, a common scenario is for each side to appoint one panellist, and then there must be some process for determining who will serve as the additional (seemingly neutral) panellist who will also chair the panel. There are four potential, not mutually exclusive, methods for determining the chair:

1. existing arbitrators select the chair *jointly,*
2. chair is selected *by lot,*
3. chair is selected by *third party* and
4. chair is selected through *consultation* of the parties.

The basic data for each of the selection methods, shown in Table 13.6, illustrates that 'consultation' (114) is the most common method of chairperson selection, followed by 'third party' (89) and 'by lot' (69), with 'jointly by arbitrators' (35) being the least common. In total, 169 agreements contain a provision on chair selection. All four methods are evident throughout the time period covered by our data set. If anything, we observe a pattern of third-party selection becoming less common and selection by lot and through consultation becoming relatively more prevalent. Since chairperson selection is a consequential and politically charged decision, there may be some learning going on that is leading designers to take this power out of the hands of individual actors and international organisations (third party) and instead to allow chairperson selection to be determined randomly (by lot). Among the cross-sectional patterns that stand out, the EU tends to use third-party selection, whereas the United States, and agreements across the Americas, tend to specify consultations and selection by lot (in that order). Some potential explanations for these patterns are possible regional diffusion and a US aversion to delegating authority to international organisations or both.

Multiple methods of chair selection can be specified, and the combinations and sequencing are quite interesting. Overall, the three most common outcomes for this variable are:

1. consultations, then by lot (27 per cent of cases in which a method is specified),
2. consultations, then by third party (20 per cent) and
3. third party only (16 per cent).

The first two outcomes reflect that selection by consultation is the starting point in 60 per cent of instances for selecting arbitral chairpersons. It is viewed as an initial and hopefully amicable attempt, which, if unsuccessful, is followed by a more definitive method of selection, either by drawing lots or allowing a third party to choose. Interestingly, among the four options, lot and third party exhibit the least overlap and seem to function as 'last resort' substitutes.

## 3. Interim report

Once the legal proceedings are well under way and arguments have been presented, the next question is whether the panel issues some type of interim (draft, initial) report prior to issuance of the final report. Such a report conveys an initial determination of whether measures are inconsistent and whether the party has failed to meet its obligations, resulting in the nullification or impairment of benefits otherwise due. It potentially helps parties to learn from and possibly correct parts of the report and to prepare for the overall decision that is expected.

In general, this *interim report* variable is the first of two indicators of whether additional, clarifying information is conveyed during the proceedings. A total of 74 agreements call for this type of interim report, which represents approximately 30 per cent of PTAs with legal dispute settlement (see Table 13.6). Interim reports are a relatively new phenomenon, with all but three instances occurring since 1995, possibly reflecting the influence of the WTO DSM or NAFTA, both of which also provide for interim panel reports.

Another clear pattern is that interim reports occur overwhelmingly in connection with arbitration (72 of 74 positive codings) rather than with standing bodies (two positive codings). There is also a heavy regional concentration: all but one of the cases of an interim report provision occur in Asian, Americas, or cross-region PTAs. In contrast, none of the 134 European PTAs (including but not limited to EU agreements) allows for interim reports.

## 4. Separate opinions

Whether the arbitration process allows separate options is the second of two variables that capture whether additional information is provided during the dispute settlement proceedings. This variable is coded as present when members of the panel are allowed to form and draft separate, anonymous opinions that are to be included in the panel report. Twenty-eight agreements allow for separate opinions (see Table 13.6). This relatively rare provision is found only in agreements that specify ad hoc arbitration. The lack of separate opinions in standing bodies is not particularly surprising because many standing bodies are based on the EU model, the ECJ does not allow separate opinions and the EU is suspicious about allowing separate opinions in WTO dispute settlement (Flett

2010). As such, separate opinions are the exclusive domain of cross-region (8) and Americas (20) agreements, although only a minority of US PTAs (4 of 14) includes them.

## 5. Time limits

The next variable captures whether the DSP in a given treaty sets time limits for the dispute settlement process, whether overall or for particular stages (i.e. pre- and postaward). The specification of time frames encourages a (comparatively) faster dispute settlement process and should aid enforceability of obligations. A total of 203 agreements specify time limits (see Table 13.6). Some familiar, emerging patterns are evident. Region–region and region–country agreements include them at a higher rate, as do North–South agreements and those across Asia, the Americas and multiple regions. This time the EU, and European agreements more generally, tend to include them with greater frequency, as does the United States.

## 6. Mutually agreeable solution (pre-award, postaward)

The final set of variables captures how many times the parties evoke the concept of reaching a 'mutually agreeable solution' (MAS) throughout the text of the dispute settlement chapter, both before and after the award is rendered. A high count is an indication of the parties' commitment to reaching an amicable settlement to the dispute throughout the entire litigation process. A total of 106 agreements (out of 252 with some form of legal dispute settlement) make some reference to trying to conclude a MAS, even while the litigation process is pending or an award has been rendered (see Table 13.6). Table 13.7 further shows that the total number of MAS references is quite high, ranging from 1 to 11 per agreement, with a relatively uniform distribution between 1 and 5 references. We

Table 13.7 *Number of references per agreement to mutually agreeable solutions (MAS)*

|  | Number of references | | | | | | | | | |
|---|---|---|---|---|---|---|---|---|---|---|
| Provision | 1 | 2 | 3 | 4 | 5 | 6 | 7 | 8 | 9 | 10+ |
| Total MAS | 14 | 16 | 18 | 13 | 11 | 5 | 10 | 9 | 5 | 5 |
| Pre-award MAS | 29 | 19 | 9 | 12 | 5 | 2 | 0 | 0 | 0 | 0 |
| Postaward MAS | 24 | 24 | 25 | 18 | 6 | 5 | 1 | 0 | 0 | 1 |

further distinguish between references to amicable solutions prior to the award and after the award.[5] Slightly more agreements mention postawards MAS (104) than similar pre-award settlements (76), although more than two dozen agreements make 4 or more of each type of reference (see Table 13.7).

There are very clear regional patterns for these MAS variables. Agreements in Africa (0) and Europe (3), even those that include legal dispute settlement, rarely evoke MAS. In contrast, more than half of the PTAs with some legal dispute settlement process within Asia (20 of 31; 65 per cent) and the Americas (38 of 69; 55 per cent) do so. PTAs in the Americas focus mostly on pre-award MAS references (38 agreements) rather than postaward MAS (22 agreements). All Asian agreements with MAS (20 agreements) include the language for the pre-award phase; in fact, 16 of the 20 of them make three or more references to pre-award MAS. Yet 18 of these 20 also include postaward MAS references, suggesting that Asian PTAs encourage parties to reach an amicable solution throughout the dispute settlement process.

## IV. Implementation

In regard to implementation of arbitration and adjudication awards, the first issue to consider is whether an award is legally binding – which is the default – or whether the treaty specifies that rulings are explicitly nonbinding. As noted earlier, the question of whether a ruling is legally binding has been an integral part of previous, legalisation-based conceptions of PTA dispute settlement.

According to our data, 224 PTAs, which includes the overwhelming majority of those that contain legal dispute settlement (89 per cent), have a provision on bindingness. Among these 224 cases, a near-universal 222 (99 per cent) of them include language that explicitly states that tribunal decisions are binding.[6] In fact, only two agreements explicitly state that a panel or tribunal ruling is not binding (Jordan–US 2000 and Israel–US 1985). Moreover, for the relatively few instances in which there is no provision at all on bindingness, one would consider any legal award to be

---

[5] More information on the coding can be found at www.designoftradeagreements.org.
[6] Although in some treaties the language unambiguously states that the awards are final and binding, many PTAs are worded less strongly, saying that the parties shall agree on the resolution of the dispute, which shall be in conformity with the determinations and the recommendations of the panel. Nevertheless, we interpret both types of obligations as binding.

legally binding based on customary international law. Thus, by our count, in only two cases, representing less than 1 per cent of all PTAs, should one consider any outcomes not to be binding. We therefore conclude that the past focus on bindingness is misguided and that efforts should be directed elsewhere, such as at the procedures for actually carrying out and enforcing awards.

### 1. Sanctions provisions

Next we consider the various sanctioning tools that are available in the case of nonimplementation of a legal award. Sanctions are a prominent and largely unexplored component of PTA dispute settlement design, one which has attracted great attention in the WTO context (Bown and Pauwelyn 2010).[7] As a starting point, the data reveal that 163 PTAs have a sanctions provision that spells out the rules governing how retaliation can be used to try and address noncompliance with an award (see Table 13.8). This represents more than 65 per cent of agreements that contain legal dispute settlement. Overall a sanctions provision is present in nearly 60 per cent of agreements reached during the past decade. This may be partly attributable to a learning or diffusion effect from the prominent WTO sanctions mechanism. Yet sanctions clauses are not entirely a new phenomenon: they are included in PTAs dating back to the 1950s, and 40 agreements signed before the WTO came into being included a sanctions provision. As for other patterns, sanctions provisions appear

Table 13.8 *Sanctions in PTA dispute settlement*

| Provision | Number | As a % of PTAs with legal dispute settlement |
|---|---|---|
| Sanctions provision | 163 | 65 |
| Retaliation determined jointly by parties | 91 | 36 |
| Retaliation chosen by complainant | 152 | 60 |
| Retaliation chosen by third party | 115 | 46 |
| Same-sector retaliation | 88 | 35 |
| Cross-retaliation | 83 | 33 |
| Monetary sanctions | 20 | 8 |

[7] In international law, the expression more widely used for sanctions is retaliation. We use these expressions interchangeably.

to a notable degree in all types of agreements but are virtually absent in North–North agreements (13 of 186, or 7 per cent) as compared to North–South and South–South agreements. They also appear to a greater degree in US agreements (16 of 18), cross-region agreements and PTAs across all regions except Africa.

## 2. Selection of sanctions

Perhaps the single biggest issue within sanctions-provision design is who determines the appropriate level of retaliation. Across PTAs we see three options, in which retaliatory sanctions are: (1) determined jointly by the two parties, (2) chosen by the complainant and (3) chosen by a third party.[8] Each method appears with some regularity, as each is included in 91, 152 and 115 agreements, respectively (see Table 13.8). Moreover, the options are not mutually exclusive (see following discussion of sequencing). In terms of geographical patterns, cross-region and pan-American PTAs allow the complainant to choose sanctions at a slightly higher rate. North–South (83 of 141; 59 per cent), EU (30 of 67; 45 per cent) and US (16 of 18; 89 per cent) PTAs also allow complainants to choose sanctions in the large majority of cases, although US agreements also typically allow for joint (13 of 18; 72 per cent) and third-party-determined (13 of 18; 72 per cent) sanctions as well.

Table 13.8 suggests that when one particular method is specified for 'who chooses', it is also highly likely that either or both of the other methods of selection will be specified, thus raising the issue of sequencing. Most PTAs with sanctions provisions (114 of 163) also specify an order. A large majority of US agreements (14 of 18; 78 per cent) contain language on sequencing, as do sizeable numbers of North–South (53 of 141; 38 per cent), Asian (21 of 67; 31 per cent), cross-region (46 of 155; 30 per cent) and Americas (41 of 146; 28 per cent) agreements.[9] The most common sequencing pattern is that after receiving the award the parties jointly try to come up with mutually accepted compensation in case of nonimplementation; if this fails, the complainant may choose the level and type of retaliation. Likewise, if the defendant party considers the amount to be disproportionate, the original panel is often called upon to make a recommendation regarding the right value.

---

[8] The third party is usually the original panel that is being reconvened.
[9] The EU, for instance, includes sanctions in just under half of its agreements. But it tends to specify that the complainant should choose the appropriate level of sanctions, and thus it has less need to include language on sequencing given its emphasis on a single method of selection.

## 3. Forms of sanctions

We now consider the different forms of sanctions that may be used. The most common type of retaliatory measure is called the 'suspension of benefits of equivalent effect', which means that the complainant is encouraged to suspend benefits (by raising tariffs) in the same sector (goods or services). Retaliation in other sectors (cross-sector) also may occur if same-sector retaliation is impractical or likely to be ineffective. Despite this conceptual distinction, in reality agreements that specify one form almost always also specify the other. Table 13.8 shows that 88 PTAs include same-sector retaliation, and 83 of them also include cross-sector retaliation, which is never specified in isolation. Considering these two forms as a 'package deal', we see an increase in the specification of both in recent years, which is a logical outgrowth of not only the greater number of agreements but also the increasing diversification of retaliation described earlier. Among various patterns, the most notable is that cross-retaliation is most common in Asian PTAs – perhaps surprisingly – with 21 of 58 (36 per cent) allowing for it.

Monetary sanctions, in contrast, are far less common. They are included in only 20 PTAs (see Table 13.8) and are almost exclusively found in US and EU agreements. In fact, two-thirds of US agreements specify the use of 'monetary sanctions', which comprise 60 per cent of the universe of cases. In EU agreements, this type of sanction is used in intra-EU integration, but not in EU agreements with outside parties. In a number of agreements, monetary sanctions are related to labour and environmental obligations, and so-called financial compensation payments may go into a special fund for addressing regulatory concerns.

## V. Exceptions and exemptions

Nearly 100 PTAs also include some form of exception or exemption in terms of what can and cannot be subject to dispute settlement (see Table 13.9). There are two types of exceptions: negative exemptions, in which the areas not subject to dispute settlement are explicitly listed, and positive inclusions, in which specific mention is made of the areas for which there is a theme-specific dispute settlement mechanism. Overall, some form of exception is included in 96 agreements, with 62 PTAs including positive and negative exceptions and 34 specifying only one type. Most agreements with positive inclusions specify one unique area, whereas negative exceptions specify one, two, three or four areas with roughly equal regularity. Areas most commonly excluded from dispute

Table 13.9 *Exceptions in PTA dispute settlement*

| Provision | Number | As a % of PTAs with legal dispute settlement |
|---|---|---|
| Any type of exception | 96 | 38 |
| Positive and negative | 62 | 25 |
| Positive only | 17 | 7 |
| Negative only | 17 | 7 |

settlement are trade remedies, safeguards, some forms of services, temporary entry of workers, sanitary and phytosanitary measures and technical
barriers to trade, competition policy and investment. As to positive lists
indicating substantially different dispute settlement procedures, investment stands out. Also, labour and environment-related cases often receive
a special process.

Exceptions tend to be included in US (16 of 18), North–South (51),
cross-region (43), Americas (36) and Asian (16) agreements. In terms of
the first two of these, one important question is whether the exceptions
are inserted by Northern states such as the United States to exclude certain
sensitive sectors from dispute settlement. This also raises the broader issue
of whether these exceptions, which tend to coincide with strong sanctions
and a choice among legal venues, represent a weakening of the ability
of states to enforce obligations in the PTAs. Future work is needed to
investigate these dynamics more thoroughly.

## D. Conceptualising dispute settlement in PTAs

We now take a step back to contemplate what these variables can tell us
about the role and function of dispute settlement, in PTAs and other types
of agreements. Although interesting in their own right, these 30 variables
can serve as building blocks for higher-level theorising and corresponding empirical measures. We identify several theoretical concepts to which
our data can speak, many of which are the subject of lively debates in
the dispute settlement literature in international relations and beyond.
For instance, selected variables from our data set can be combined to tell
us something about the degree of *flexibility* within dispute settlement,
the amount of *delegation* of dispute settlement authority states are willing to grant or the degree to which the DSP facilitates *enforcement* of

treaty obligations or promotes an effective *settlement* of the dispute. In the following section we put forward five theoretical concepts, discuss their relevance and identify the variables from our data that reflect each concept. The ultimate goal is to generate composite empirical measures of important concepts that can be used – by us and by others – to test important arguments within international relations, economics and law.

## *I. Delegation*

In existing work on dispute settlement, one sometimes encounters the concept of 'delegation', a subcomponent of legalisation (Abbott *et al.* 2000) that has been applied previously to dispute settlement design (e.g. Allee and Peinhardt 2010; Koremenos 2007; Koremenos and Betz 2013). Delegation entails placing authority for settling disputes into the hands of a third party that pursues resolution according to defined processes and following legal principles. In simple terms, any PTA that contains a provision on arbitration, creates a standing body or makes reference to the WTO or ICJ is effectively 'delegating' dispute settlement authority. Yet as our data show, a more complete way to think about delegation is to consider not just whether legal dispute settlement is allowed but rather how much power or authority is given ('delegated') to a third party throughout the process.

This expanded notion of delegation speaks directly to realism-inspired debates about state power as well as scholarship on principal–agent approaches to international organisations. The frequency of delegation in PTAs calls into question realist assertions that states will be hesitant to delegate authority to third parties to resolve interstate disputes. Perhaps a better course of action, then, is to examine how much (as opposed to whether) control over important issues is ceded by states and which states are most likely to delegate. Moreover, as applied to dispute settlement in trade institutions (e.g. Elsig and Pollack 2014), the principal–agent approach suggests that designers are aware of the possible lack of control that delegation through legal dispute settlement might entail. When countries are concerned about the distributional consequences of third-party treaty interpretation, we might expect to see *ex ante* control (selection of panellists or court members) or on-the-spot control mechanisms (e.g. interim reviews) become more important. In principal–agent terms, then, what is important is not just the absolute 'size' of delegation but also the relative 'size', which is affected by the amount of control designed into the treaty.

Table 13.10 *Conceptualising degree of* delegation *in PTA dispute settlement provisions*

| Concept | Variables |
|---|---|
| DELEGATION (simple) | *Legal dispute settlement* (yes) |
| DELEGATION (expanded) | *Legal dispute settlement* (yes) |
| | *Chairman selection* (third party or lot) |
| | *Sanctions selection* (third party) |

Drawing upon our new variables, we propose a more comprehensive empirical measure to capture the amount of *delegation* in PTAs. (See Table 13.10.) It builds upon a simpler notion of delegation, reflected in the extant literature, which captures whether the PTA allows for any type of delegation (ad hoc arbitration, reference to external body, standing body). The expanded conceptualisation also considers whether the states or a third party select the panel chairman and whether the states or a third party choose the level of sanction. All of these variables capture whether third parties hold primary authority for important decisions or whether states maintain a degree of control over the process.

## II. Information provision

The next two concepts reflect important theoretical debates about the role of dispute settlement within international cooperation. A common distinction, which we follow here, is that dispute settlement institutions serve either as information provision mechanisms to the state parties (e.g. Johns and Rosendorff 2009) or as enforcement devices (e.g. Downs, Rocke and Barsoom 1996; Yarborough and Yarborough 1997). They might also perform both functions (Sattler and Bernauer 2010) or a type of hybrid function (Johns 2012), perhaps in a manner that addresses incomplete contracts (Maggi and Staiger 2011). Nevertheless, this distinction between information provision and enforcement is also at the heart of long-standing debates on treaty compliance.[10]

From the information provision perspective, the dispute settlement process is designed to provide new information to the parties and clarify state obligations. In this respect, the DSM is seen, first and foremost, as a source of new knowledge. It might provide clues to the parties to help them

---

[10] See von Stein (2013) for an excellent overview.

resolve a current dispute, and it can also provide information about how courts deliberate and how they balance different legal principles in general (Pauwelyn and Elsig 2013). This may affect the cost–benefit calculations of actors when launching new cases and influence how parties comply with treaty obligations overall. Whereas the content of legal opinions conveys direct information from courts to states, the design of the DSM with regard to certain variables gives indirect clues about the possibility of increasing the amount and quality of information.

A few variables in our data set capture the extent to which the DSP in an agreement truly fulfils an *information provision* function. (See Table 13.11.) For a DSP to be considered one that encourages the provision of a large amount of information, a necessary condition is that it must include some type of legal dispute settlement, since the arbitration or adjudication body is a necessary actor in information provision. One important variable that indicates information provision is whether the treaty allows for an *interim report* prior to the issuance of any final report. The interim report serves primarily an informational function by providing facts to the parties about the panel's initial judgments, to which the parties may respond. A second variable that reflects this information provision function is whether the agreement allows members of the panel to form and draft *separate or concurrent opinions* that are to be included in the panel report. This indicates the extent of unanimity of the panel members and also provides additional viewpoints on the matters in question apart from what is provided in the panel report. A common thread between the interim report and separate opinion is that, although neither has any legal effect, they may have an impact as a result of the factual information they provide.

### III. Enforcement

A quite different perspective on DSMs is to think of them primarily as enforcement devices. The enforcement concept as applied to

Table 13.11 *Conceptualising amount of information provision in PTA dispute settlement provisions*

| Concept | Variables |
| --- | --- |
| INFORMATION PROVISION | *Legal dispute settlement* (yes) |
| | *Interim report* (yes) |
| | *Separate opinions* (yes) |

international agreements is often linked with formalised arguments about the need to include strong, legal enforcement as a way to ensure compliance with deep, meaningful treaties (e.g. Downs *et al.* 1996; Yarbrough and Yarbrough 1997). The purpose of a DSM, then, is to ensure that state signatories fulfil their trade obligations as enshrined in the trade agreements. Any resulting 'disputes' will revolve around claims by one signatory or member (a complainant) that another is not meeting its obligations. The litigation process and the prospect of it working swiftly and effectively by inducing the noncomplaining party into compliance are what constitute enforcement. From an enforcement standpoint, PTAs should work well when they provide complainants with the tools to push their claims and make important decisions, and facilitate a relatively swift resolution to the dispute.

Once again, the precursor to all of this is that the PTA must allow for some type of legal dispute settlement, or 'enforcement process'. Assuming this exists, several additional features would reflect a strong enforcement provision within the PTA. The first is when the complainant is explicitly given power over *forum choice*, namely, when the treaty specifies that the complainant is allowed to choose the venue. This would be particularly true when there are *no restrictions on multiple fora*, although, as noted previously, this is relatively rare. Retaliatory sanctions are another powerful tool that can enhance enforcement. In the simplest terms, enforcement in a PTA will be more effective, *ceteris paribus*, when the agreement contains a *sanctions provision*. The strength of enforcement might also depend in part on who selects the retaliatory measure. When the form of *retaliation is selected by the complainant*, and to a lesser extent by a third party, we expect the enforcement effect to be greater as a result of the potential for larger sanctions. Furthermore, sanctions devices that allow for tangible, cost-imposing measures to be levied should enhance enforcement even more. These would include the potential for *same-sector and cross-retaliation* as well as *monetary sanctions*. Overall, treaties that proscribe the use of sanctions give the complainant the legitimacy to drive the enforcement process, and greater choice in the use of sanctions allows the complainant to use targeted sanctions that will increase the likelihood of compliance. Likewise, enforcement might also depend on who chooses the all-important panel chairperson. Unless the treaty specifies selection by lot or third party, the respondent may block the composition endlessly. A final component of enforceability would be the ability to carry out the process in a relatively swift manner, since one of the greatest impediments to enforcement is the ability to delay. PTAs that

Table 13.12 *Conceptualising level of* enforcement *in PTA dispute settlement provisions*

| Concept | Variables |
| --- | --- |
| ENFORCEMENT | *Legal dispute settlement* (yes) |
| | *Forum choice* (yes) |
| | *Restrictions on multiple fora* (no) |
| | *Sanctions selection* (complainant) |
| | *Sanctions provision* (yes) |
| | *Same-sector retaliation* (yes) |
| | *Cross-retaliation* (yes) |
| | *Monetary sanctions* (yes) |
| | *Chairman selection* (by lot, third party) |
| | *Time limits* (yes) |

impose *time limits* reflect agreements that are more easily enforced. (See Table 13.12.)

### IV. Settlement promotion

The next concept captures the idea that the purpose of a dispute settlement mechanism should be to promote the effective *settlement* of a dispute; that is, to specify a set of rules that are most likely to resolve the disagreement in a way that is acceptable to both parties. This may seem obvious, yet the idea of a DSM trying to promote settlement should be contrasted with the previous ideas about a DSM as an enforcement device or as an institution that provides information – neither of which necessarily promotes settlement. The key distinguishing feature of a settlement-promoting DSM is that the rules are agnostic about how and when the dispute is settled as long as an effective and acceptable resolution is reached. States may wish to specify a range of options and pathways to a resolution because they have limited knowledge about how future dispute settlement fora will work. Having recourse to multiple fora, both internal (consultations, mediation, arbitration) and external (e.g. WTO, ICJ), will provide the greatest opportunity in the future to seek out settlements in the venue that seems most appropriate to the parties at the time a particular dispute occurs.

A core component of this idea of the DSM as a settlement-promotion device is the ability of the parties to reach an informal or negotiated settlement at any point in time. Most disputes, trade or otherwise, are resolved through a negotiated settlement, even well after legal proceedings have been launched. These 'out of court' or 'mutually agreeable' settlements may be preferable because they reduce tensions and consume fewer legal resources. Past research tends to label these settlements as 'diplomatic' or 'political' and to consider them the opposite of 'legalisation' in terms of dispute settlement design. But an amicable settlement can happen at any time; indeed, many WTO disputes are settled in this manner, often well after the formal 'legalised' process has begun. Therefore, we consider the potential for such settlements at all stages of dispute settlement.

The starting point for measuring the extent to which the DSP in a PTA *promotes settlement* of disputes is to count the *total number of types of dispute settlement* that are specified (consultation, mediation, ad hoc arbitration, standing body, mentioning of external bodies), which captures the range of dispute resolution options that may be pursued. Within the context of legal dispute settlement, another important variable is whether the agreements specify a *Joint Committee* or *Association Commission* composed of high-ranking officials of the PTA member governments to address the dispute before the establishment of a legal panel. This provides for a mandatory step during which an acceptable resolution might be reached. The final collection of variables is for the number of references in the DSP to *mutually agreeable solutions, pre-award, postaward,* and *overall.* These are perhaps the most direct and most novel indicators of the degree to which the parties have tried to design a mechanism that promotes the settlement of disputes. (See Table 13.13.)

## V. Flexibility

The final way to conceptualise dispute settlement in PTAs is to contemplate the degree to which the contents of the DSP provide flexibility to the parties. The general idea of flexibility has been central to studies of

Table 13.13 *Conceptualising* settlement promotion *in PTA dispute settlement provisions*

| Concept | Variables |
| --- | --- |
| SETTLEMENT PROMOTION | *Types of dispute settlement* (number specified) *Joint commission* (yes) *Pre-award references to MAS* (number) *Postaward references to MAS* (number) *Total references to MAS* (number) |

trade agreements (Kucik and Reinhardt 2008; Pelc 2009) and other types of international agreements (Helfer 2013; Koremenos, Lipson and Snidal 2001), with the basic idea being that providing some flexibility or 'wiggle room' to the parties will help them to make costly commitments. In relation to trade agreements, flexibility is typically portrayed as tools 'that allow states to anticipate and respond to domestic contingencies or to adjust their policies for other purposes without violating the terms of an agreement' (Baccini, Dür and Elsig 2014). When applying the concept of flexibility to dispute settlement, we see two interesting flexibility tools. One way to think about flexibility in dispute settlement is in terms of the number of ways that states can pursue a resolution to the dispute, or the number of types of dispute settlement. This notion of 'procedural' flexibility was discussed in the previous subsection as part of the concept of settlement promotion but could also be incorporated here as part of the general idea of flexibility.

A second way to conceptualise flexibility, and the one we emphasise here, is to consider which areas are excluded from (or included in) dispute settlement. Flexibility understood as exemptions may be demanded by import-competing firms, which, if they cannot derail the agreement, may wish to exclude a certain area from dispute settlement (e.g. standards, trade remedies). To sum up, flexibility provisions help maintain the overall stability (and balance of commitments) and are conducive to concluding the agreements.

To examine the degree to which the DSP of a PTA provides this type of *flexibility*, we turn to our new variables on exceptions within dispute settlement. All three *exceptions* variables should be relevant. In the simplest terms, whether a PTA lists any *exemptions* at all provides an initial indicator of flexibility. The next is whether there is an explicit list of *negative exemptions* from dispute settlement (and if so, how many?). The removal of certain areas from dispute settlement, particularly sensitive ones, would reflect greater flexibility in dispute settlement. Finally, a *positive list of inclusions in dispute settlement*, either in the form of explicit mentions or theme-specific dispute settlement mechanisms, might also indicate flexibility to tailor dispute settlement towards specific issue areas. (See Table 13.14.)

## E. Next steps

The most obvious immediate step is to engage more fully the operationalisation of the aforementioned five concepts – for their ultimate inclusion in empirical tests. The list of variables associated with each concept is

Table 13.14 *Conceptualising* flexibility *in PTA dispute settlement provisions*

| Concept | Variables |
| --- | --- |
| FLEXIBILITY | *Dispute settlement exceptions* (yes) |
| | *Negative list of exemptions* (yes) |
| | *Count of negative exemptions* (number) |
| | *Positive list of exemptions* (yes) |
| | *Count of positive exemptions* (number) |

currently somewhat broad, and it is possible that some variables might be deemed to reflect the overarching concept more closely than others do. In terms of measurement, many of the variables that comprise the concepts discussed previously are indicator variables, which makes using simple, additive indices an obvious option. More nuanced methods of variable aggregation, such as types of factor analysis, are also an option, but this is complicated by the binary form of many of the variables.

Another issue is to determine how any empirical strategy maps on to the most obvious differences between treaties in terms of their DSP. It is apparent that a major dividing line exists between those now-rare PTAs that have no legal dispute settlement whatsoever and the increasing number that specify some form of legal dispute settlement, which to us are by far the most interesting and relevant. One way to do this is with various two-stage models. The first step would be to predict which PTAs are in the first group rather than in the second group, which is likely to be a simple function of treaty depth and time. This initial sorting would allow us to concentrate on the richer and more important variation among treaties in the second group. In other words, it would allow us to focus on the unpacking of *legalisation* in dispute settlement. Most of the variation we have discussed in this chapter, for both variables and the broader concepts, is variation among PTAs with some form of legal dispute settlement.

Another important task is to contemplate possible explanations for some of the variation we see across both variables and concepts. We are particularly interested in explaining variation across DSPs in PTAs in terms of the amount of delegation, information provision, enforcement, settlement promotion and flexibility. One starting point is to probe further some of the differences we uncovered when examining variation across individual variables. There we identified some initial patterns across different types of treaties and treaties with varying degrees of depth. Regional and North–South differences were also apparent. These could reflect several mechanisms, including but not limited to regional norms, diffusion or contracting problems among dissimilar actors. Country-specific patterns for the United States, and to a lesser extent the EU, might also play a role and may be distinct from or a part of the same dynamics that characterise the regional variation.

There is also room for the inclusion and refinement of other dispute settlement concepts beyond the five presented in the second half of this chapter. One possible addition is the idea of whether the DSP contains elements that make dispute resolution *adversarial* as compared to more cooperative or *amicable*. This overlaps somewhat with the concept of *settlement promotion*, yet we consistently see that some dispute rules reflect a more adversarial approach, whereas others attempt to have the parties cooperate on issues such as the selection of sanctions and panel chairs. Another direction is to think in terms of *interest group* influence, or a *pluralist* conceptualisation of DSPs. If we take a political economy view of PTA design, we might expect to see DSPs reflect the influence of powerful interests (in powerful countries), which should be apparent in variables such as dispute settlement exceptions.

## F. Conclusion

Our goals in this chapter were threefold. The first was to consider dispute settlement across a wide range of PTAs, which we are able to do by being part of a broader effort to systematically collect data across a much more comprehensive collection of agreements (Dür, Baccini and Elsig 2014). The second was to collect data on a wide range of variables from all aspects of the dispute settlement process. We compiled data on 30 variables, many of which have been acknowledged as important but had been neglected from an empirical standpoint. The third goal was to reorient the conceptual discussion away from a myopic emphasis on legalism and instead to consider what other concepts might characterise the DSPs of PTAs. We believe this 'unpacking' of legalisation is an important part of the future research trajectory, particularly as more DSPs are being used with greater frequency.

Overall this work on dispute settlement is part of a more general move to identify differences among seemingly similar treaties such as PTAs. This trend towards differentiation is likely to continue and to spread to the study of other types of international agreements. For us, distinguishing between DSPs in PTAs is more than an empirical endeavour or data collection exercise. Indeed, we view this collection and presentation of data as a first step towards thinking about how PTAs are designed and linking those differences in the practical negotiation of treaties to academic debates about the purpose of dispute settlement institutions in international affairs.

## References

Abbott, Kenneth W., Keohane, Robert O., Moravcsik, Andrew, Slaughter, Anne-Marie, and Snidal, Duncan. 2000. 'The Concept of Legalization.' *International Organization* 54 (3): 401–19.

Allee, Todd, and Peinhardt, Clint. 2010. 'Delegating Differences: Bilateral Investment Treaties and Patterns of Dispute Resolution Design.' *International Studies Quarterly* 54 (1): 1–26.

2014. 'Evaluating Three Explanations for the Design of Bilateral Investment Treaties.' *World Politics* 66 (1): 47–87.

Baccini, Leonardo, Dür, Andreas, and Elsig, Manfred. 2014. 'Depth, Flexibility and International Cooperation: The Politics of Trade Agreement Design.' *International Studies Quarterly*, forthcoming.

Bernauer, Thomas, Elsig, Manfred, and Pauwelyn, Joost. 2012. 'The Dispute Settlement Mechanism: Analysis and Problems.' In *Oxford Handbook on the World Trade Organization*, edited by Amrita Narlikar, Martin Daunton and Robert M. Stern, 485–506. Oxford, England: Oxford University Press.

Bown, Chad, and Pauwelyn, Joost, eds. 2010. *The Law, Economics and Politics of Retaliation in WTO Dispute Settlement*. Cambridge: Cambridge University Press.

Busch, Marc. 2007. 'Overlapping Institutions, Forum Shopping, and Dispute Settlement in International Trade.' *International Organization* 61 (4): 735–61.

Chase, Claude, Yanovich, Alan, Crawford, Jo-Ann, and Ugaz, Pamela. 2013. 'Mapping of Dispute Settlement Mechanisms in Regional Trade Agreements – Innovative or Variations on a Theme?' WTO Staff Working Paper ERSD-2013-07. World Trade Organization, Geneva.

Copelovitch, Mark, and Putnam, Tonya. Forthcoming. 'Design in Context: Existing International Agreements and New Cooperation.' *International Organization* 68 (2): 471–93.

Donaldson, Victoria, and Lester, Simon. 2009. 'Dispute Settlement.' In *Bilateral and Regional Trade Agreements: Commentary and Analysis*, edited by Simon Lester and Bryan Mercurio, 367–414. Cambridge: Cambridge University Press.

Downs, George W., Rocke, David M., and Barsoom, Peter N. 1996. 'Is the Good News about Compliance Good News about Cooperation?' *International Organization* 50 (3): 379–406.

Duffield, John. 2003. 'The Limits of "Rational Design".' *International Organization* 57 (2): 411–30.

Dür, Andreas, Baccini, Leonardo, and Elsig, Manfred. 2014. 'The Design of International Trade Agreements: Introducing a New Dataset.' *Review of International Organizations* 9 (3): 353–75.

Elsig, Manfred, and Pollack, Mark. 2014. 'Agents, Trustees, and International Courts: Nomination and Appointment of Judicial Candidates in the WTO Appellate Body.' *European Journal of International Relations* 20 (2): 391–415.

Flett, James. 2010. 'Collective Intelligence and the Possibility of Dissent: Anonymous Individual Opinions in WTO Jurisprudence.' *Journal of International Economic Law* 13 (2): 287–320.

Helfer, Laurence R. 2013. 'Flexibility in International Agreements.' In *Interdisciplinary Perspectives on International Law and International Relations*, edited by Jeffrey Dunoff and Mark Pollack, 175–96. Cambridge: Cambridge University Press.

Hicks, Raymond, and Kim, Soo Yeon. 2012. 'Reciprocal Trade Agreements in Asia: Credible Commitment to Trade Liberalization or Paper Tigers?' *Journal of East Asian Studies* 12: 1–29.

Jo, Hyeran, and Namgung, Hyun. 2012. 'Dispute Settlement Mechanisms in Preferential Trade Agreements: Democracy, Boilerplates, and the Multilateral Trade Regime.' *Journal of Conflict Resolution* 56 (6): 1041–68.

Johns, Leslie. 2012. 'Courts as Coordinators: Endogenous Enforcement and Jurisdiction in International Adjudication.' *Journal of Conflict Resolution* 56 (2): 257–89.

Johns, Leslie, and Rosendorff, Peter. 2009. 'Dispute Settlement, Compliance and Domestic Politics.' In *Trade Disputes and the Dispute Settlement Understanding of the WTO: An Interdisciplinary Assessment*, edited by James C. Hartigan, 140–63. Bingley, UK: Emerald Group Publishing.

Koremenos, Barbara. 2007. 'If Only Half of International Agreements Have Dispute Resolution Provisions, Which Half Needs Explaining?' *Journal of Legal Studies* 36 (1): 189–212.

Koremenos, Barbara, and Betz, Timm. 2013. 'The Design of Dispute Settlement Procedures in International Agreements.' In *Interdisciplinary Perspectives on International Law and International Relations*, edited by Jeffrey Dunoff and Mark Pollack, 371–93. Cambridge: Cambridge University Press.

Koremenos, Barbara, Lipson, Charles, and Snidal, Duncan. 2001. 'The Rational Design of International Institutions.' *International Organization* 55 (4): 761–99.

Kucik, Jeffrey. 2012. 'The Domestic Politics of Institutional Design: Producer Preferences over Trade Agreement Rules.' *Economics & Politics* 24 (2): 95–118.

Kucik, Jeffrey, and Reinhardt, Eric. 2008. 'Does Flexibility Promote Cooperation? An Application to the Global Trade Regime.' *International Organization* 62 (3): 477–505.

Maggi, Giovanni, and Staiger, Robert. 2011. 'The Role of Dispute Settlement Procedures in International Trade Agreements.' *Quarterly Journal of Economics* 126 (1): 475–515.

Morgan, David. 2008. 'Dispute Settlement under PTAs: Political or Legal?' Legal Studies Research Paper No. 341. Melbourne University Law School, Carlton, Australia.

Pauwelyn, Joost. 2009. 'Legal Avenues to "Multilateralise Regionalism": Beyond Article XXIV.' In *Multilateralising Regionalism, Challenges for the Global Trading System*, edited by Richard Baldwin and Patrick Low, 368–400. Cambridge: Cambridge University Press.

Pauwelyn, Joost, and Elsig, Manfred. 2013. 'The Politics of Treaty Interpretation: Variations and Explanations across International Tribunals.' In *Interdisciplinary Perspectives on International Law and International Relations*, edited by Jeffrey Dunoff and Mark Pollack, 445–73. Cambridge: Cambridge University Press.

Pelc, Krzysztof J. 2009. 'Seeking Escape: The Use of Escape Clauses in International Trade Agreements.' *International Studies Quarterly* 53 (2): 349–68.

Porges, Amelia. 2011. 'Dispute Settlement.' In *Preferential Trade Agreement Policies for Development: A Handbook*, edited by Jean-Pierre Chauffour and Jean-Christophe Maur, 467–502. Washington, DC: World Bank.

Sattler, Thomas, and Bernauer, Thomas. 2010. 'Gravitation or Discrimination? Determinants of Litigation in the World Trade Organization.' *European Journal of Political Research* 50 (2): 143–67.

Smith, James McCall. 2000. 'The Politics of Dispute Settlement Design: Explaining Legalism in Regional Trade Pacts.' *International Organization* 54 (1): 137–80.

von Stein, Jana. 2013. 'The Engines of Compliance.' In *Interdisciplinary Perspectives on International Law and International Relations*, edited by Jeffrey Dunoff and Mark Pollack, 477–501. New York: Cambridge University Press.

Yarbrough Beth V., and Yarbrough Robert M. 1997. 'Dispute Settlement in International Trade: Regionalism and Procedural Coordination.' In *The Political Economy of Regionalism*, edited by Edward Mansfield and Helen Milner, 134–63. New York: Columbia University Press.

# PART III

## The effects of PTAs

# 14

# Preliminary examination of heterogeneous effects on international trade of economic integration agreements

SCOTT L. BAIER, JEFFREY H. BERGSTRAND
AND MATTHEW W. CLANCE

## A. Introduction

One of the most dramatic changes to the international landscape since 1990 has been the growth in the number of economic integration agreements (EIAs) in the world. Article XXIV of the General Agreement on Tariffs and Trade (GATT) established a means for countries to negotiate bilateral and plurilateral trade agreements outside of the GATT; this article's implications were maintained under the World Trade Organization (WTO). Initially, these agreements were small in number and in scope. However, since 1990 the admissible agreements under Article XXIV have grown in number as well as in scope. Dür and Elsig (Chapter 1 in this volume) report that more than 700 EIAs were signed between the end of World War II and 2013. The WTO website reports that as of July 2013 575 EIAs had been notified to the WTO, of which 379 were in force. Although many agreements in, say, 1965 were free trade agreements and customs unions (the latter with common external tariffs) that lowered tariffs, over time a few common markets (with factor mobility also) and economic unions (with factor mobility, common external tariffs and coordinated

We thank for beneficial comments Andreas Dür, Manfred Elsig, Leonardo Baccini and participants at the conference 'Trade Cooperation: The Purpose, Design and Effects of Preferential Trade Agreements', organised by Dür and Elsig in Bern, Switzerland. We also received helpful comments from seminar participants at the Georgia Institute of Technology, Appalachian State University and the INFER workshop on 'Border and Distance Effects in Economics' at Loughborough, United Kingdom. Finally, we are grateful for excellent research assistance in the construction of the Economic Integration Agreements database from Emma Buckley, Stephen Cray, Christine Hsieh, Mitch Gainer, Ben O'Neill, Clare Robinson, James Schappler and Andrew Weiler.

monetary or fiscal policies) surfaced. The growth in the number of EIAs motivated many scholars in economics and political science to try to better understand the causes and the consequences of increased EIAs.[1] Regarding consequences, much of the initial academic research focused on estimating the *partial* effect of an EIA on the volume of two members' bilateral international trade.[2] Early estimates of these effects of EIAs produced a very wide range of results, including negative (partial) effects; see, for example, Frankel (1997). These early estimates were likely biased because important variables were omitted. For example, most studies did not control for multilateral price (or 'resistance') terms as raised in Anderson (1979), Bergstrand (1985) and Anderson and van Wincoop (2003). Additionally, most studies did not control for the potential endogeneity of the EIAs; see Baier and Bergstrand (2002) and Baier and Bergstrand (2007). However, recent developments in the theoretical economic foundations of gravity equations and econometric evaluation of EIAs has led to more precise and unbiased estimates; see Baier and Bergstrand (2007) and Head and Mayer (2013). In fact, Baier and Bergstrand (2007) provide evidence that, on average over the period 1960–2000, the typical EIA increased two members' trade by about 100 per cent over 10–15 years (partial effect only). In correcting for the omitted variables and potential endogeneity biases, researchers commonly treat all trade agreements' effects as the same, sharing a common average 'treatment effect'. Although most scholars probably believe that there is a great deal of heterogeneity across agreements and their trade effects, previous analyses have focused on measuring an average partial trade effect for all EIAs and assuming the heterogeneity was uncorrelated with other variables in the analysis.

In this chapter, we show that more can be learned about the trade-creating effects of EIAs by moving away from a 'one-size-fits-all' model and by addressing directly the heterogeneous nature of EIAs.[3] In particular, we provide preliminary empirical evidence of several of the factors

---

[1] Formally, we define an EIA in our empirical analysis to be either a free trade agreement, customs union, common market or economic union; we exclude in this chapter one-way and two-way preferential trade agreements, such as Generalized System of Preferences (GSP) agreements.

[2] We are concerned in this study only with estimating partial (or direct) effects, not general equilibrium effects as in Anderson and van Wincoop (2003), Baier and Bergstrand (2009) and Bergstrand, Egger and Larch (2013).

[3] Such concerns have been raised also in Kohl (2012) and Kohl, Brakman and Garretsen (2013).

that can explain the heterogeneity in *ex post* estimates of EIAs' (partial) trade-creating effects.

## B. Methodological issues

At the same time that the modern theory of international trade due to comparative advantage and relative factor endowments developed in the post–World War II era to explain the patterns of international trade using $2 \times 2 \times 2$ general equilibrium models, a small and separate line of empirical research in international trade emerged to provide a statistical explanation for actual aggregate bilateral trade flows among large numbers of pairs of countries. Drawing an analogy with Isaac Newton's Law of Gravitation, these international trade economists noted that observed bilateral aggregate trade flows between any pair of countries $i$ and $j$ could be explained very well using statistical methods by the product of the two countries' gross domestic products ($GDP_i$ $GDP_j$) divided by the distance between the country pair's major economic centres ($DIST_{ij}$). Specifically, these researchers conjectured that

$$TF_{ijt} = \beta_0 (GDP_{it})^{\beta_1} (GDP_{jt})^{\beta_2} (DIST_{ij})^{\beta_3} \varepsilon_{ijt} \qquad (14.1)$$

or

$$\ln TF_{ijt} = \beta_0 + \beta_1 (\ln GDP_{it}) + \beta_2 (\ln GDP_{jt})$$
$$+ \beta_3 (\ln DIST_{ij}) + \ln \varepsilon_{ijt} \qquad (14.2)$$

where $TF_{ijt}$ is the value of the aggregate trade flow from country $i$ to country $j$ in year $t$ and $\varepsilon_{ijt}$ is a log-normally distributed error term.[4] For more than 50 years, this 'gravity equation' has been the workhorse for empirical analyses of international trade flows and quantifying the (partial) effects of EIAs, as well as other trade enhancements or costs, on trade flows. Tinbergen (1962) published the first cross-sectional empirical study of trade flows using the gravity framework to quantify the trade-creating effects of membership in the British Commonwealth or in the BENELUX (Belgium–Netherlands–Luxembourg) agreement. Including dummy variables in Eq. (14.2) for the two agreements, Tinbergen found that membership in the British Commonwealth (BENELUX) increased bilateral trade flows by 5 (4) per cent. Subsequent cross-sectional empirical investigations provided mixed support for the trade-creating effects

---

[4] Equation (14.2) can be estimated only using positive trade flows; Eq. (14.1) can include zeros for $TF_{ijt}$.

of EIAs. For example, Aitken (1973), Abrams (1980), Bergstrand (1985) and Brada and Mendez (1985) found that EIAs tended to increase trade. However, Frankel, Stein and Wie (1995) and Frankel (1997) found that, although some EIAs raised trade, others had no economically or statistically significant effect, and some EIAs apparently lowered trade. Frankel (1997) found that membership in the European Union (EU) is often associated with *lower* bilateral trade. This is surprising since the European Union is one of the oldest agreements that has also grown in membership and depth of integration over time.

However, with time, theoretical economic foundations for the gravity equation of trade have developed. One of the notable shortcomings of many of the empirical estimates of EIA effects on trade in earlier (atheoretical) studies was the omission of prices and failure to account properly for their endogeneity. Anderson (1979) was the first to show in a formal general equilibrium model that trade flows were related multiplicatively to a country pair's GDPs, an inverse function of bilateral distance and an index of the (GDP-weighted) remoteness of exporter *i* from all of its destination markets. But he set all countries' prices to unity. Bergstrand (1985) allowed prices to vary endogenously and showed that a gravity equation such as Eq. (14.1) or Eq. (14.2) could be derived to also include the price of exporter *i*'s product in importer *j* relative to a constant elasticity of substitution (CES) price index of importer *j*'s prices from all exporters. As shown in Arkolakis, Costinot and Rodriguez-Clare (2012), there is now a set of 'quantitative trade models' that yield isomorphic gravity equations including relative price terms based on Armington, Ricardian, Krugman and Melitz type models; see Anderson and van Wincoop (2003) for the Armington model, Eaton and Kortum (2002) for the Ricardian model, Baier and Bergstrand (2001) for the Krugman model and Chaney (2008) for the Melitz model.

Arkolakis, Costinot and Rodriguez-Clare (2012) show, for instance, that the seminal Melitz (2003) model yields a theoretical gravity equation of the form

$$TF_{ijt}^m = N_{it}^m Y_{jt}^m \left( \frac{(a_{Lit}^m)^{-\gamma^m} w_{it}^{-\gamma^m} \tau_{ijt}^{-\gamma^m} f_{ijt}^{-[\gamma^m/(\sigma^m-1)-1]}}{\sum_{k=1}^K N_{kt}^m (a_{Lkt}^m)^{-\gamma^m} w_{kt}^{-\gamma^m} \tau_{kjt}^{-\gamma^m} f_{kjt}^{-[\gamma^m/(\sigma^m-1)-1]}} \right),$$

$$(14.3)$$

where $TF_{ijt}^m$ is the trade flow from exporter *i* to importer *j* in year *t* in 'good' (industry) *m*, $N_{it}$ is the number of firms in *i* (exporting and nonexporting) that produce (differentiated) products in good *m*, $Y_{it}^m$ is the expenditure in $j$ on good $m_t$, $a_{Lit}^m$ is the lower bound of the Pareto distribution of productivities in $m$ in $i$, $\gamma^m$ is an index of productivity heterogeneity among firms in good $m$, $\omega_{it}$ is the wage rate in $i$, $\tau_{ijt}$ is variable trade costs of country $i$'s products into $j$, $f_{ijt}$ is fixed export costs from $i$ to $j$, $\sigma^m$ is the elasticity of substitution in consumption and $\gamma^m > \sigma^m - 1$.[5] Note that the term in large parentheses is a standard representation of relative prices in the gravity equation but now also reflects productivity heterogeneity (through $\gamma^m$) and fixed exporting costs ($f_{ijt}$). In the context of these models, variable trade costs $\tau_{ij,t}$ affect $X_{ij,t}^m$ via both the intensive and extensive margins, but fixed export costs $f_{ij,t}$ affect trade via the extensive margin. As Chaney (2008) demonstrates in one Melitz-type model, $\gamma^m = (\sigma^m - 1) + [\gamma^m - (\sigma^m - 1)]$, where $\sigma^m - 1$ represents the intensive-margin elasticity of variable trade costs, whereas $\gamma^m - (\sigma^m - 1)$ is the extensive-margin elasticity of variable trade costs. For the purposes of this chapter, the variables of interest are $\tau_{ijt}$ and $f_{ijt}$. Typically, researchers have assumed that the formation of an EIA (such as a free trade agreement) between $i$ and $j$ lowers $\tau_{ijt}$. However, EIAs are broad agreements reaching beyond elimination of tariff rates and variable trade costs; they are also likely to lower fixed export costs $f_{ijt}$.

Although many of the variables in Eq. (14.3) are difficult to measure, to isolate the partial effects of changes in $\tau_{ijt}$ and $f_{ijt}$ on $TF_{ijt}$ researchers have employed exporter-year and importer-year fixed effects to account for several of the time-varying exporter $i$ and importer $j$ multilateral (or country-specific) variables, suggesting in log-linear form

$$\ln TF_{ijt} = \beta_0 + \eta_{it} + \theta_{jt} + \beta_1(\ln \tau_{ijt}) + \beta_2(\ln f_{ijt}) + \ln \varepsilon_{ijt} \quad (14.4)$$

where $\eta_{it}$ is an exporter-year fixed effect and $\theta_{jt}$ is an importer-year fixed effect. In principle, an EIA's effect on the trade flow would be through declines in $\tau_{ijt}$ or $f_{ijt}$ or both. One could potentially estimate the effect on $TF_{ijt}$ of the formation of an EIA by introducing a dummy variable, $EIA_{ijt}$, that takes the value 1 (0) if an EIA exists (does not exist) between $i$ and $j$ in year $t$ as a proxy for $\tau_{ijt}$ and $f_{ijt}$. However, two important shortcomings of this approach come to mind.

First, many bilateral factors that influence bilateral trade flows are time invariant but vary across country pairs, such as bilateral distance, adjacency and historical colonial ties. A useful modification of Eq. (14.4)

---

[5] For finite means in the theory, $\gamma^m/(\sigma^m - 1)$ must exceed 1. We assume the case in which fixed export costs are paid by importers, that is, the case of $\mu = 0$ in Arkolakis, Costinot and Rodriguez-Clare (2012), Eq. (23).

is the additional inclusion of a time-invariant pair fixed effect ($\psi_{ij}$) or this fixed effect interacted with a time trend ($\psi_{ij} \times$ *Trend*). Since the EIA dummy would only change from 0 to 1 in the year an EIA went into effect, the partial effect of an EIA on the trade between two countries would be captured by the time-series variation in both variables. Moreover, one could also allow for lagged effects of EIAs on trade using lagged values of $EIA_{ijt}$ in the regression. For now (ignoring lagged EIA effects) this suggests the specification

$$\ln TF_{ijt} = \beta + \eta_{it} + \theta_{jt} + \psi_{ij} + \alpha(EIA_{ijt}) + \nu_{ijt} \qquad (14.5)$$

where $\nu_{ijt} = \ln \varepsilon_{ijt}$. It turns out that specification (14.5), emphasised in Baier and Bergstrand (2007), addresses another issue that researchers have found to be of concern because it can potentially bias estimates of the partial effects of EIAs on trade flows. It accounts for endogeneity of EIAs, that is, the potential feedback effect of trade on selection into EIAs. Since annual trade flows change rapidly over time but decisions by pairs of governments to form EIAs are slow-moving events (and most of the determination of selection into EIAs can be explained by cross-sectional factors), specification (14.5) with $ij$ fixed effects (or alternatively a first-difference version of (14.5)) suffers from little EIA endogeneity bias. By contrast, previous cross-sectional estimates of partial EIA effects using gravity models suffer from endogeneity bias. Alternatively, one could use instrumental variables in a cross-section; however, it is difficult to find identification, since most cross-sectional variables that explain bilateral trade flows also explain the probability of a bilateral EIA.[6]

Second, whereas correcting for endogeneity of EIAs using panel techniques results in consistent estimates of the average treatment effect, it seems unlikely that the treatment effect is the *same* for all types of agreements and country pairs. To assess the impact of different trade agreements on bilateral trade flows, the normal course methodologically has been to include separate dummy variables for each agreement. Many

---

[6] Another issue is whether $EIA_{ijt}$ is the only *time-varying bilateral* variable that can influence $TF_{ijt}$. In other words, is it not possible that bilateral variable and fixed *trade* costs – $\tau_{ijt}$ and $f_{ijt}$ – may decline over time owing, say, to technological factors, such as falling international relative to intranational costs of communication and information? For our purposes here, using ordinary least squares (OLS) estimation, it turns out that EIAs' partial effects estimates are not biased by such concerns. Using OLS, Baier, Bergstrand and Feng (2014) established this using $ij$ fixed effects interacted with time trends. This was also established recently by Bergstrand, Larch and Yotov (2014) using OLS and a panel of international and intranational trade flows and incorporating appropriate dummy variables to capture changing costs of international relative to intranational trade.

past studies have done this – starting with the first analysis by Tinbergen (1962) noted previously as well as other early cross-sectional studies by Aitken (1973) and Frankel (1997). More recently using specification (14.5) from Baier and Bergstrand (2007), Kohl (2012) used individual agreements' dummy variables. Similarly to the early cross-sectional analyses, the problem with this approach is that estimates of the (partial) trade-creating impacts of agreements are quite fragile and often economically implausible. The main reason is that each of the dummy variables for various agreements has little variation over time; little variation in a right-hand-side (RHS) variable leads to weak estimated effects, especially when the agreement has few members or is short in duration.[7]

Taking a different approach, Baier, Bergstrand and Feng (forthcoming) used a set of dummy variables that categorises the depth of the EIA. Fewer dummy variables led to greater variation in the RHS variables. In their paper, 'deeper' integration agreements tend to create more trade than 'shallower' agreements do; that is, the average treatment effect tends to be higher if the bilateral pair is in a customs union (CU), common market (CM) or economic union (ECU) rather than in a free trade agreement (FTA).

In this chapter, we also allow for heterogeneity in EIAs' effects that are related to economic, institutional and cultural fundamentals that may influence the nature of the agreement and its effect. We show that, by using economic, institutional and cultural factors that are associated with the decision to enter an EIA, we can explain some of the heterogeneity of the trade-creating effects among trade agreements.

Following Cameron and Trivedi (2005: 774), we augment the model in Baier and Bergstrand (2007) to allow for heterogeneous effects of EIAs on trade flows. The methodology can then be applied empirically to all EIAs but also separately to FTAs, CUs, CMs and ECUs. We augment the fixed-effects model in Baier and Bergstrand (2007) to allow for heterogeneity in the effects of EIAs on the trade flows of the respective pairs of countries using

$$\ln TF_{ijt} = \beta + \eta_{it} + \theta_{jt} + \psi_{ij} + \alpha_{ij}(EIA_{ijt}) + v_{ijt}. \qquad (14.6)$$

The sole distinguishing feature between Eq. (14.5) and Eq. (14.6) is that the (partial) effect of changes in $EIA_{ijt}$ on $TF_{ijt}$ is allowed to be *pair specific*.

---

[7] The bulk of agreements have occurred since 1990, with most studies ending in 2005 as a result of data constraints.

In particular, we are using a 'random coefficients' model to estimate Eq. (14.6), allowing

$$\alpha_{ij} = \alpha + a_{ij} \qquad (14.7)$$

where $\alpha_{ij}$ is treated as a 'random parameter'.

## C. Data

Nominal trade flows are from the United Nations' COMTRADE database for the years 1965, 1970, 1975, 1980, 1985, 1990, 1995, 2000 and 2005. Bilateral distances, language, adjacency, religion and common legal origin are from the BACI data set. The data set for EIAs comes from Baier and Bergstrand's data set for 2013.[8] There are 189 countries included in the data set. We consider a bilateral pair in an EIA if the bilateral pair is in an FTA, a CU, a CM or an ECU.[9]

## D. Empirical results

### I. Main results for EIAs

We first estimated the model for EIAs without distinguishing among FTAs, CUs, CMs and ECUs. Figure 14.1 shows a plot of the estimate of $\alpha$ (horizontal line) and estimates of the $\alpha_{ij}$ for the year 2005. We note several distinguishing features of the results. First, the average partial effect of an EIA on ln $TF_{ijt}$ is 0.375 (with a standard error of 0.032). This is right in the middle of estimates that have been reported in the literature recently; see Baier and Bergstrand (2007), Baier, Bergstrand and Feng (forthcoming) and Head and Mayer (2013). Baier and Bergstrand found an estimate for the partial effect of 0.46 for a sample with half the number of countries used here (only 96) for a similar time period, ignoring heterogeneity in the estimate of $\alpha$. We note that this effect excludes lagged values of the EIA dummies, which both Baier and Bergstrand and Baier *et al.* recognised. In this particular study, we are not concerned with time dimensions of the effects; here we are focusing on the cross-sectional heterogeneity of the effects.

Second, there is considerable heterogeneity in the effects of EIAs on trade flows. As Figure 14.1 reveals, and ignoring a few visible outliers,

---

[8] See http://www3.nd.edu/~jbergstr/.
[9] The list of the EIAs and the countries included can be found at http://www3.nd.edu/~jbergstr/.

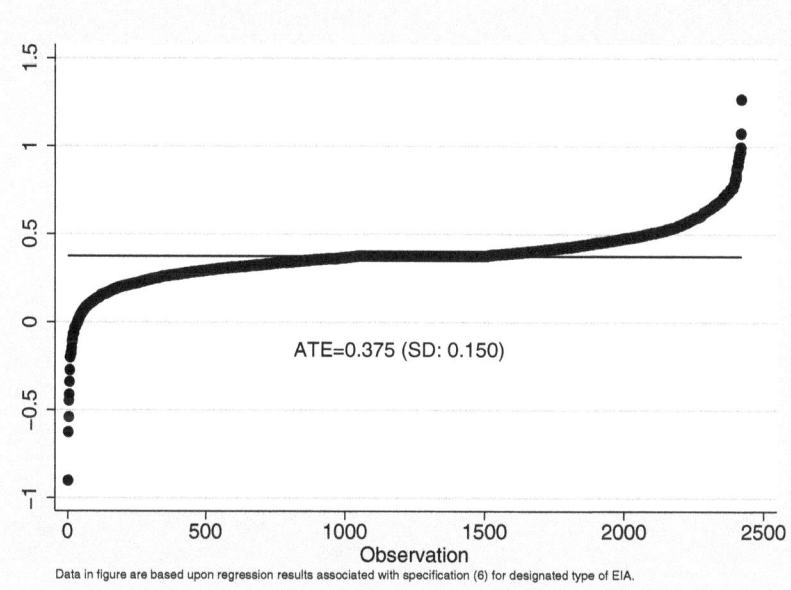

**Figure 14.1**  Treatment effect for all agreements

estimates range from $-0.2$ to $1.0$. In particular, the standard deviation of estimates of $\alpha_{ij}$ is $0.150$. Now, it is important to note, of course, that the $\alpha_{ij}$ estimates span *all* types of EIAs: FTAs, CUs, CMs and ECUs. So, the variation in $\alpha_{ij}$ estimates may reflect fundamental differences in the depth of the agreements. However, we will show in the subsequent section that the heterogeneity in EIA trade effects is not due entirely to heterogeneity in the depth of the agreement.

### II. Heterogeneity in EIA effects due to depth of agreement

Every EIA is unique because each treaty is unique. Thus, the trade effect of every EIA on members' trade is likely to differ. Unfortunately, using a separate dummy variable for every different EIA in existence yields *weak* estimated results, owing to absence of sufficient variation in the RHS dummy variables in a panel. Evidence of this volatility is shown in Baier, Bergstrand and Vidal (2007) and Kohl (2012).

However, one of the obvious factors that is likely to explain the heterogeneity in EIA effects is the 'depth' of an EIA. Even though every EIA is unique, EIAs can be categorised according to their relative depth. Notably,

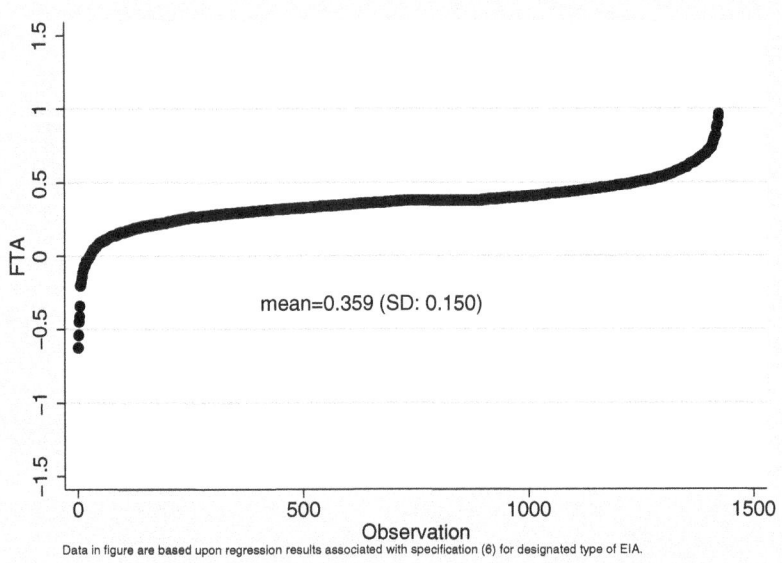

mean=0.359 (SD: 0.150)

Data in figure are based upon regression results associated with specification (6) for designated type of EIA.

**Figure 14.2**   Treatment effect for all free trade agreements

the literature has come to consider FTAs and CUs as the lowest levels of economic integration. CMs, allowing factor as well as goods and services mobility, are considered to be a higher level of economic integration. Finally, ECUs are considered the highest level of economic integration, with goods, services and factor mobility alongside coordinated monetary policies, fiscal policies, or both.

Accordingly, we categorised the estimates of the $\alpha_{ij}s$ according to whether they were FTAs, CUs, CMs or ECUs. Figures 14.2–14.5 present the distributions of partial effects for FTAs, CUs, CMs and ECUs, respectively. As expected, FTAs have the lowest average partial effect at 0.359. Yet this partial effect is not much different from that for all EIAs, shown in Figure 14.1. The average partial effect for a customs union is 0.400 and that for a common market is 0.406. We see then that the 'type' of an agreement does not have an economically significant effect on explaining the dispersion in average partial effects. Finally, Figure 14.5 reveals that for the 'deepest' type of EIA – ECUs – the average partial effect is slightly lower than that for CUs and for CMs. However, the subsample of ECUs does not include just the eurozone economies; it also includes two economic unions in Africa that may not be as effective as eurozone

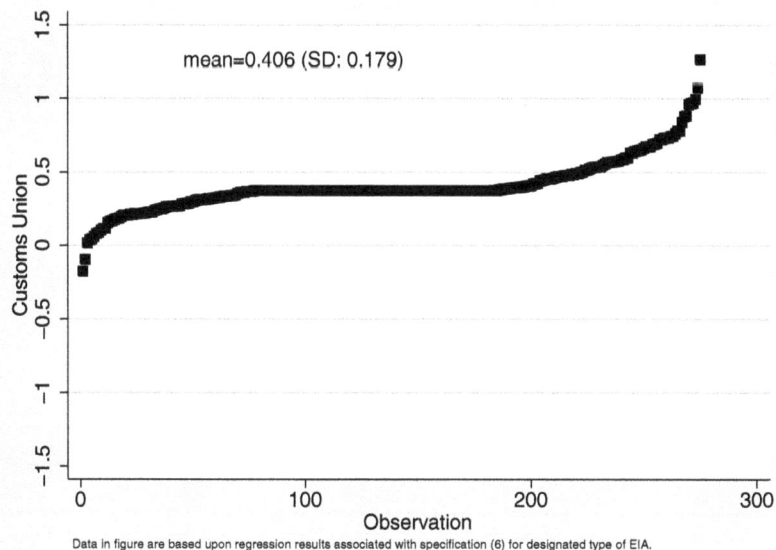

mean=0.406 (SD: 0.179)

Data in figure are based upon regression results associated with specification (6) for designated type of EIA.

**Figure 14.3** Treatment effect for all customs union agreements

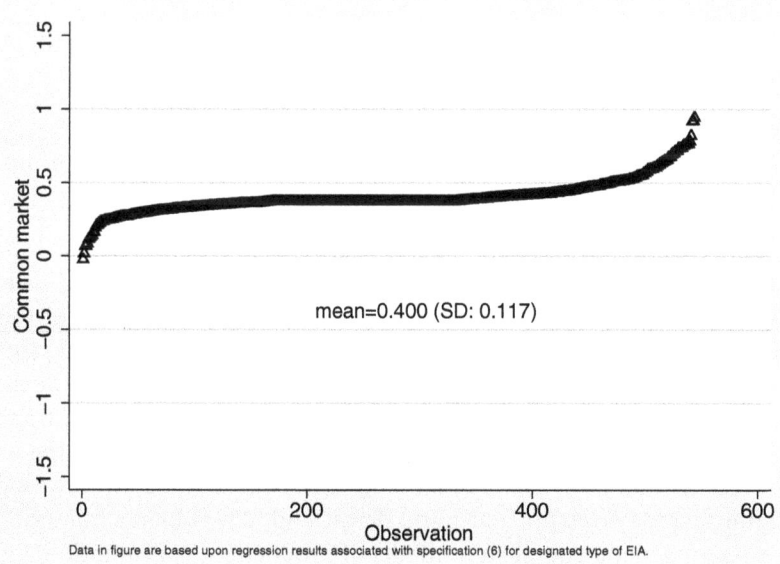

mean=0.400 (SD: 0.117)

Data in figure are based upon regression results associated with specification (6) for designated type of EIA.

**Figure 14.4** Treatment effect for all common market agreements

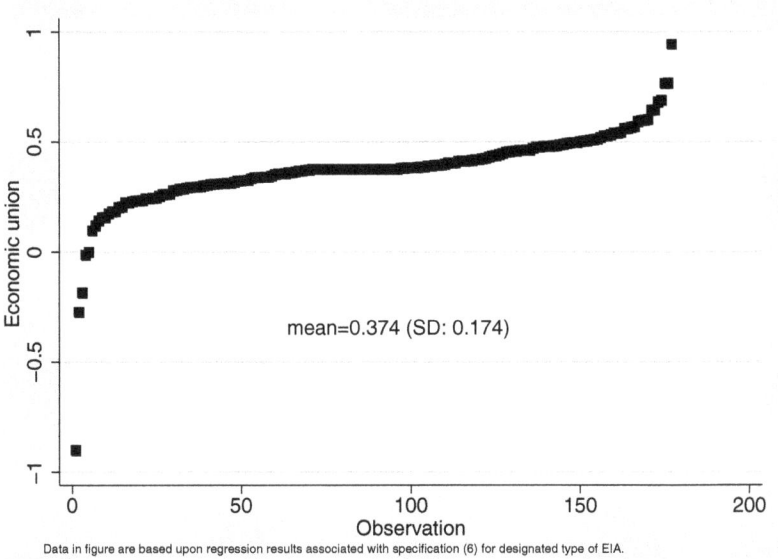

Data in figure are based upon regression results associated with specification (6) for designated type of EIA.

**Figure 14.5**   Treatment effect for all economic union agreements

membership (West African Economic and Monetary Union, or UEMOA, and Economic and Monetary Community of Central Africa, or CEMAC).

### III. Economic, institutional and cultural determinants of heterogeneous EIA partial effects

As just established, some of the heterogeneity in trade effects of EIAs can be explained by differences in the depth of the EIA. However, there remains much of the heterogeneity in partial effects to explain. In this section, we argue that much of the heterogeneity in EIAs' bilateral trade flow partial effects reflects the potential trade creation, which may be the reason why pairs of governments select into EIAs. Baier and Bergstrand (2004) argued that the likelihood of a pair of governments forming an EIA reflects economic factors that tend to maximise trade creation and minimise trade diversion. Baier and Bergstrand (2004) used a numerical two-sector general equilibrium model of production, consumption and international trade to show that the (net) welfare of the consumers of two partner countries gained more from an EIA: (1) the lower the bilateral trade costs of the country pair, (2) the more 'economically remote' the pair, (3) the larger the pair economically, (4) the more similar the pair in economic size, (5) the wider the pair's relative factor endowment differences and (6) the smaller the difference of the pair's average relative factor endowment relative to that of the rest of the world (*ROW*).

Baier and Bergstrand (2004) found that proxies for these economic factors could explain well for a particular year the likelihood of country pairs having an EIA. In the context of the theoretical model, this implied that country pairs that have agreements *tend* to share the economic characteristics that suggest such agreements are welfare improving. However, welfare improvement reflects gains from trade creation net of losses from trade diversion. Yet, it is likely that the factors that explained the likelihood of an EIA between a pair *also* tend to explain the bilateral trade creation of two countries from the EIA. Consequently, the most likely candidate variables to explain the heterogeneity in the bilateral trade-creating effects of an EIA include such measures.

In this preliminary examination of the sources of heterogeneous EIA effects – that is, in the $\alpha_{ij}s$ – we first examine bilateral factors that tend to explain trade creation from an EIA. Of course, the candidates that come to mind are the well-established time-invariant bilateral economic determinants of trade flows: bilateral distance (*DIST*), adjacency (*ADJ*) and common language (*LANG*). However, in recent analyses researchers have moved on to include historical, cultural and political variables. In this spirit, we include three more common gravity variables: common (official or predominant) religion (*RELIG*), common colonial history (*COL*) and common legal origins (*LEGAL*). Consequently, the next step of the analysis is to explain the cross-sectional variation in the $\alpha_{ij}s$ in terms of these six time-invariant bilateral variables.

Before reviewing the results, we first discuss expected relationships between these bilateral variables and the partial effect of an EIA on two members' trade. First, consider the role of bilateral distance. One of the most prominent relationships examined in the past 20 years is that between distance between a pair of countries and the likely net welfare gains from the pair forming an EIA. It is well documented that much of the growth in numbers of EIAs has been between pairs of countries in the same region. For this reason, many EIAs are called *regional* trade agreements. In the spirit of Frankel (1997), who showed that a pair of countries benefit more from an FTA the more 'natural' they are as trading partners, Baier and Bergstrand (2004) showed the net welfare gains for a pair of countries tended to rise – and the probability that the pair had an EIA was higher – the smaller the distance between the two countries. It follows that if two countries that are closer tend to benefit more from an EIA, the two countries' EIA is likely to have deeper liberalisation (in terms of depth of tariff reductions and scope of liberalisation). Consequently, we would expect a negative relationship between bilateral distance and the partial effect estimate ($\alpha_{ij}$).

Second, consider the role of adjacency of two countries (*ADJ*). Two countries tend to be natural trading partners if they share a common land border; sharing a common land border reduces trade costs, just like shorter distance does. For analogous reasons to those applying to distance, we would expect that two countries with a common land border should have a larger welfare gain from an EIA, a higher probability of an EIA and deeper liberalisation. Consequently, we would expect a positive relationship between a dummy indicating a common land border and the partial effect estimate ($\alpha_{ij}$).

Third, consider the role of common language of two countries (*LANG*). Two countries tend to be natural trading partners if they share a common language; sharing a common language reduces trade costs, just like shorter distance does. For analogous reasons to those applying to distance, we would expect that two countries with a common (official or predominant) language should have a larger welfare gain from an EIA, a higher probability of an EIA and deeper liberalisation. Consequently, we would expect a positive relationship between a dummy indicating a common language and the partial effect estimate ($\alpha_{ij}$).

Fourth, consider the role of common religion shared by two countries (*RELIG*). Two countries tend to be more natural trading partners if they share a common religion because of the role of networking and trust embedded in this sharing. Having a common religion reduces trade costs, just like shorter distance does. For analogous reasons to those applying to distance, we would expect that two countries with a common (official or predominant) religion should have a larger welfare gain from an EIA, a higher probability of an EIA and deeper liberalisation. Consequently, we would expect a positive relationship between a dummy indicating a common religion and the partial effect estimate ($\alpha_{ij}$).

The final two factors have potentially more ambiguous relationships with trade, welfare gains from EIAs and likely depth of liberalisation. The following two variables differ from the previous four because they are related not only to trade costs but also to the costs of forming EIAs. The two variables are dummy variables for having a common colonial history (*COL*) and having a common legal origin (*LEGAL*). Whereas

Table 14.1 *Determinants of EIA partial effects*

|  | Year – 1965 | Year – 1985 | Year – 2005 | All years |
|---|---|---|---|---|
| Constant | 0.299** | 0.395** | 0.350** | 0.359** |
|  | (0.057) | (0.014) | (0.005) | (0.004) |
| DIST | −0.032 | 0.018* | −0.020** | −0.015** |
| (Log of) | (0.031) | (0.009) | (0.004) | (0.002) |
| ADJ | 0.025 | 0.015 | 0.008 | −0.006 |
|  | (0.040) | (0.020) | (0.010) | (0.006) |
| LANG | −0.122** | 0.063** | 0.011 | 0.019** |
| (Common) | (0.044) | (0.016) | (0.008) | (0.005) |
| RELIG | −0.005 | 0.064** | 0.045** | 0.047** |
| (Common) | (0.067) | (0.019) | (0.009) | (0.005) |
| COL | (Omitted) | −0.056 | −0.027 | −0.012 |
|  |  | (0.041) | (0.016) | (0.010) |
| LEGAL | −0.018 | −0.050** | −0.036** | −0.040** |
| (Common) | (0.050) | (0.015) | (0.007) | (0.004) |
| $R^2$ | 0.126 | 0.090 | 0.036 | 0.035 |

* Statistical significance at the 5 per cent level in a two-tailed $t$-test.
** Statistical significance at the 1 per cent level in a two-tailed $t$-test.

positive values for *COL* and *LEGAL* can be considered to reduce trade costs, which may increase both the likelihood of forming an EIA and the degree of liberalisation, a pair of countries with a common legal origin, a common colonial history or both may face *smaller gains* from a treaty. The purpose of a treaty is to promote harmonisation of laws. If the countries have a common legal origin, colonial history or both, they may already have harmonised laws. Hence, country pairs with common legal origins, common colonial histories or both may be associated with *lower* partial effect estimates ($\alpha_{ij}$).

Table 14.1 presents the results of regressing the $\alpha_{ij}$s on the six time-invariant bilateral variables. We estimate the model for three individual cross sections (years 1965, 1985 and 2005) as well as for all nine years of the sample (1965, 1970, . . . , 2005). We note several striking results. First, bilateral distance (*DIST*) has a negative and statistically significant effect on an EIA's effect on bilateral trade in 1965 and 2005 and in the specification for all years, as expected. Why are most EIAs regional? The gains from trade, the likelihood of an EIA and the likelihood of deeper liberalisation are larger for countries that are close.

The second variable is adjacency (*ADJ*). In all three individual years, the partial effect is positive, but it is statistically insignificant. For the specification with all years, the partial effect is only slightly different from zero and is statistically insignificant.

The third variable examined is common language (*LANG*). Table 14.1's far right-hand column for all years suggests that country pairs with a common language tend to have greater trade-creation effects than do those with dissimilar languages. This result is consistent with our expectation. The result is statistically significant. Moreover, for the years 1985 and 2005, the partial effect is positive and also statistically significant for 1985. One notable and interesting result regarding language in Table 14.1 is the plausible result that – in 1965 – dissimilar languages tend to increase the effect of an EIA. Of course, the prominent EIAs of 1965 were the European Economic Community, or EEC (starting in 1958), and the European Free Trade Association, or EFTA (starting in 1960). There is still considerable debate among researchers as to the original motivation for the EEC. Many argue that political motivation – to preclude further European wars on the heels of the end of World War II – was the key driver; others believe economic gains via linking countries through trade creation was the main motivation. Table 14.1's results for 1965 suggest that countries with different languages had the largest effects. It is important to note that the largest members of the original EEC – France, Germany and Italy – all had different languages, and most of the members of EFTA had different languages.

The fourth variable is the common religion dummy (*RELIG*). For 1985, for 2005 and for all years, if two countries that formed an EIA had a common religion, the trade-creating effect of an EIA was larger. Common religion may well have had a trade-cost-reducing effect because of greater trust, lower information costs and cultural similarity of two countries with a shared religious orientation.

Finally, we find that sharing a common legal origin (*LEGAL*) and sharing a common colonial history (*COL*) tend to have *negative* effects on EIAs' partial effects, as discussed previously. In particular, sharing a common legal origin had both an economically and statistically significant negative effect on the partial effect. This result is consistent with the perspective that sharing a common legal history is likely to have reduced the gains from harmonisation through an EIA (since harmonisation had already occurred via their common legal origins), reducing the EIA's effect.

## E. Conclusion

The purpose of this study was to provide a preliminary examination of the determinants of 'heterogeneity' of the effects of economic integration agreements on trade flows. As most EIAs are unique, measuring the *ex post* (partial) effects of EIAs on trade flows is challenging. The researcher is typically faced with two poor alternatives: use a separate dummy variable to capture the effect of each separate agreement or use one dummy variable to capture all agreements. The former method is compromised by too little variation in the RHS variable to generate a robust partial effect of particular agreements. The latter method is compromised by treating all EIAs as the same 'treaty' even though researchers know that is not true.

This chapter has examined estimates of EIAs' partial effects using a random coefficients econometric model, which allows different country pairs' agreements to have different effects. Several major conclusions can be drawn from our empirical analysis. First, although there is a wide range of these partial effects using state-of-the-art gravity-equation methodology, there is much less variation than suggested by earlier studies that did not control adequately for multilateral price variables or self-selection of country pairs into such agreements. Second, and somewhat surprisingly, there was much less variation in average partial effects by type of EIA than perhaps anticipated; FTAs had average effects not that much smaller than EIAs with deeper degrees of integration. Third, we showed that the heterogeneity in agreements' partial effects could be explained by several economic, political and institutional variables, such as bilateral distance, common language, common religion and common legal origins. These results suggest that future research should examine further, theoretically and empirically, the interactions of EIAs' effects with economic, political and institutional heterogeneity.

## References

Abrams, Richard K. 1980. 'International Trade Flows under Flexible Exchange Rates.' *Federal Reserve Bank of Kansas City Economic Review*, March, 3–10.
Aitken, Norman D. 1973. 'The Effect of the EEC and EFTA on European Trade: A Temporal Cross-Section Analysis.' *American Economic Review* 63 (5): 881–92.

Anderson, James. 1979. 'A Theoretical Foundation for the Gravity Equation.' *American Economic Review* 69 (1): 106–16.

Anderson, James, and van Wincoop, Eric. 2003. 'Gravity with Gravitas: A Solution to the Border Puzzle.' *American Economic Review* 93 (1): 170–92.

Arkolakis, Costas, Costinot, Arnaud, and Rodriguez-Clare, Andrés. 2012. 'New Trade Models, Same Old Gains?' *American Economic Review* 102 (1): 94–130.

Baier, Scott, and Bergstrand, Jeffrey. 2001. 'The Growth of World Trade: Tariffs, Transport Costs, and Income Similarity.' *Journal of International Economics* 53 (1): 1–27.

2002. 'On the Endogeneity of International Trade Flows and Free Trade Agreements.' Unpublished manuscript, University of Notre Dame, Notre Dame, IN.

2004. 'The Economic Determinants of Free Trade Agreements.' *Journal of International Economics* 64 (1): 29–63.

2007. 'Do Free Trade Agreements Actually Increase Members' International Trade?' *Journal of International Economics* 71 (1): 72–95.

2009. 'Bonus Vetus OLS: A Simple Method for Approximating International Trade-Cost Effects Using the Gravity Equation.' *Journal of International Economics* 77 (1): 77–85.

Baier, Scott, Bergstrand, Jeffrey, and Feng, Michael. Forthcoming. 'Economic Integration Agreements and the Margins of International Trade.' *Journal of International Economics.*

Baier, Scott, Bergstrand, Jeffrey, and Vidal, Erika. 2007. 'Free Trade Agreements in the Americas: Are the Trade Effects Larger than Anticipated?' *World Economy* 30 (9): 1347–77.

Bergstrand, Jeffrey. 1985. 'The Gravity Equation in International Trade: Some Microeconomic Foundations and Empirical Evidence.' *Review of Economics and Statistics* 67 (3): 474–81.

Bergstrand, Jeffrey, Egger, Peter, and Larch, Mario. 2013. 'Gravity Redux: Estimation of Gravity-Equation Coefficients, Elasticities of Substitution and General Equilibrium Comparative Statics under Asymmetric Bilateral Trade Costs.' *Journal of International Economics* 89 (1): 110–21.

Bergstrand, Jeffrey, Larch, Mario, and Yotov, Yoto. 2014. 'Economic Integration Agreements, Border Effects, and Distance Elasticities in the Gravity Equation.' CESifo Working Paper Series No. 4502. CESifo, Munich.

Brada, Josef C., and Mendez, José A. 1985. 'Economic Integration among Developed, Developing, and Centrally Planned Economies: A Comparative Study.' *Review of Economics and Statistics* 67 (4): 549–56.

Cameron, Colin A., and Trivedi, Pravin. 2005. *Microeconometrics – Methods and Applications.* Cambridge: Cambridge University Press.

Chaney, Thomas. 2008. 'Distorted Gravity: The Intensive and Extensive Margins of International Trade.' *American Economic Review* 98 (4): 1707–21.

Eaton, Jonathan, and Kortum, Samuel. 2002. 'Technology, Geography and Trade.' *Econometrica* 70 (5): 1741–79.

Frankel, Jeffrey. 1997. *Regional Trading Blocs*. Washington, DC: Institute for International Economics.

Frankel, Jeffrey, Stein, Ernesto, and Wie, Shang-jin. 1995. 'Trading Blocs and the Americas: The Natural, the Unnatural, and the Super-Natural.' *Journal of Development Economics* 47:61–95.

Head, Keith, and Mayer, Thierry. 2013. 'Gravity Equations: Workhorse, Toolkit, and Cookbook.' CEPR Working Paper No. 9322. Centre for Economic Policy Research, London.

Kohl, Tristan. 2012. 'Trade Agreements Galore.' Unpublished manuscript, University of Groningen, Groningen, the Netherlands.

Kohl, Tristan, Brakman, Steven, and Garretsen, Harry. 2013. 'Do Trade Agreements Stimulate International Trade Differently?' Unpublished manuscript, University of Groningen, Groningen, the Netherlands.

Melitz, Marc J. 2003. 'The Impact of Trade on Intra-Industry Reallocations and Aggregate Industry Productivity.' *Econometrica* 71 (6): 1695–1725.

Tinbergen, Jan. 1962. *Shaping the World Economy: Suggestions for an International Economic Policy*. New York: Twentieth Century Fund.

# 15

# Effects of deep versus shallow trade agreements in general equilibrium

PETER EGGER AND SERGEY NIGAI

## A. Introduction

There is heterogeneity across different types of preferential trade agreements (PTAs). Whereas some agreements exclusively liberalise goods and services trade, others extend multilateral cooperation beyond import tariffs and cover such issues as international policy alignment in competition, anti-dumping policies and environmental laws. We account for such heterogeneity by classifying PTAs according to the number of issues that they cover (shallow-medium-deep) and find that – at the same tariff – deeper PTAs have a substantially bigger effect on trade and welfare.

Even though it is often treated as homogeneous, trade preferentialism differs substantially across PTAs. Unless they are part of a customs union with a common outside tariff, even members of the World Trade Organization (WTO) differ to a great extent in terms of the most-favoured-nation (MFN) outside tariff they charge. Many of the developed countries have substantially lowered their tariffs on most tariff lines since the inception of the General Agreement on Tariffs and Trade (GATT). In fact, many developed countries have bound many of their most-favoured-nation tariffs at zero. This is much less common for developing economies. Hence, by design, PTAs among the developed countries will be able to apply a much smaller preference margin than PTAs among developing countries would be able to do. Moreover, the number of tariff lines on which a preference margin could be offered is smaller among developed than among

The authors would like to thank Scott L. Baier for a very useful discussion of an earlier version of the paper presented at the World Trade Forum on 'Trade Cooperation: The Purpose, Design and Effects of Preferential Trade Agreements' organized by the World Trade Institute on 28–29 September 2013. Moreover, the authors have benefited from useful comments made by Andreas Dür, Simon Evenett, Helen Milner, Marcelo Olarreaga and others on that occasion.

developing economies. Clearly, that was not the case half a century ago, when the first PTAs covered by GATT were put into force in Europe. Then, the tariff lines covered and the preferences extended were substantial. Moreover, PTAs not only are heterogeneous regarding the scope and preferences in terms of tariffs but also differ in other domains. A categorisation of the WTO distinguishes 52 different issues that are covered in at least some PTAs. Some of these issues fall under the WTO mandate, but others do not. For instance, the issues covered range from investment protection over product and factor market regulation to the application of environmental standards.[1]

Though it is well established that PTAs generally increase international trade flows (see, e.g., Baier and Bergstrand 2007, 2009; Egger *et al.* 2011), the heterogeneity of PTAs raises the following two questions for the international economist. First, what is the impact of PTAs on trade beyond tariff liberalisation, and, second, is it desirable to have PTAs which reach further out beyond tariff liberalisation? This chapter aims at providing an answer to these two questions on the basis of structural quantitative analysis. We set up an Eaton and Kortum (2002) type gravity model of bilateral aggregate goods trade for 124 economies in the year 2008. We estimate this model subject to general equilibrium constraints and calibrate it to the data. The estimation suggests that the direct semielasticity (through the parameters on scope-range-specific binary indicator variables) rises with the scope of issues covered by PTAs beyond their impact through tariff reduction. However, this finding provides limited insights into the effects, since countries and country pairs differ in terms of geography, size and multilateral as well as preferential trade liberalisation. To gain insights into the impact of the depth of PTAs, we conduct a counterfactual experiment, which obeys general equilibrium constraints. In that experiment, we counterfactually turn all PTAs which existed in 2008 into deep ones, no matter whether they were shallow, medium or deep at the outset. This experiment suggests that the response to this counterfactual change is positive on average across all country pairs, but it varies largely (depending on country-pair characteristics). Overall, we would conclude that gaining depth in PTAs would be beneficial in terms of real

---

[1] For instance, issues *under the mandate of the WTO*: tariff liberalisation, provision of information, elimination of export taxes, harmonization of standards, anti-dumping measures, countervailing measures, local content and foreign direct investment regulations. Issues *outside the mandate of the WTO* are following: anticorruption legislation, competition policy, environmental laws, labour market regulation, movement of capital, product market regulation (consumer protection) and taxation.

consumption, no matter whether PTAs deepen within or outside the boundaries of the WTO mandate.

The remainder of the chapter is organised in the following way. The next section briefly discusses the empirical framework. Section C describes the data, Section D summarises the parameter estimation and calibration and Section E reports on the comparative static analysis. The last section provides a brief conclusion.

## B. Empirical framework

### I. General set-up

We utilise a Ricardian multicountry model in the spirit of Eaton and Kortum (2002) and Alvarez and Lucas (2007).[2] We index exporting and importing countries by $n$ and $i$, respectively, and consider a world with $N = 124$ economies. Economies are populated by representative households, and those households are assumed to have uniform preferences across all countries. Economy $n$ is endowed with $L_n$ units of primary production factors (*equipped labour*) that are owned by the representative households. Households in $n$ earn a factor price of $w_n$ per unit of equipped labour. We assume that consumers exhibit constant-elasticity-of-substitution preferences. Firms are heterogeneous in terms of their productivity, and they produce under constant returns to scale. Firms in $n$ draw their total factor productivity $z$ from a Fréchet distribution with country-specific location parameter $\lambda_n$ and common dispersion parameter $\Theta$, where a bigger value of $\Theta > 1$ indicates less dispersion of productivity. Firms produce intermediate goods that are used in bundles to produce intermediates as well as final goods. Formally, intermediate goods output $y_n$ is generated by the technology

$$y_n(z) = z^{-\Theta}\ell_n^{\beta}q_n^{1-\beta} \text{ such that } \beta \in (0, 1), \tag{15.1}$$

where $\ell_n$ is primary factor (equipped labour) input, $q_n$ is the composite intermediate goods input and $\beta$ is the cost share for equipped labour. The quantity $q_n$ is composed of domestic as well as foreign inputs. Since factor costs are different across countries and firms charge marginal cost prices, country-specific producer prices of intermediate goods differ. Moreover, there are ad valorem barriers to exports of intermediate goods from $n$

---

[2] In principle, the effect of PTAs on trade and welfare would be similar in other new trade models (see Arkolakis, Costinot and Rodriguez-Clare, 2012).

to $i$ in the amount of $\tau_{in} \geq 1$. We follow Eaton and Kortum (2002) in assuming a constant-elasticity-of-substitution technology about the bundling of inputs in $q_n$, which establishes a price of the bundle $q_n$ of

$$p_n = (\Psi \Sigma_j \lambda_j (w_j^\beta p_j^{1-\beta})^{-\Theta} \tau_{nj}^{-\Theta})^{-1/\Theta}, \tag{15.2}$$

where $\Psi$ is a common normalising constant that is of no relevance since it cancels out in the analysis. In the model, nominal aggregate (intermediate goods) exports from $n$ to $i$ can be expressed as

$$X_{in} = \Psi \lambda_n (w_n^\beta p_n^{1-\beta})^{-\Theta} \tau_{in}^{-\Theta} / \Sigma_j \lambda_j (w_j^\beta p_j^{1-\beta})^{-\Theta} \tau_{ij}^{-\Theta} (L_i w_i + T_i), \tag{15.3}$$

where $T_i$ is aggregate tariff income in country $i$ and $D_i$ is country $i$'s trade deficit. With goods being used as both intermediates and final goods, the two being sold at the same price, welfare of a representative consumer in $i$ is represented by her real consumption:

$$u_i = (L_i w_i + T_i)/p_i. \tag{15.4}$$

In general equilibrium, payments have to be balanced up to a country-specific constant, at least. Following Dekle, Eaton and Kortum (2007), we assume that total purchases of a country, $(\Sigma_{j=1}^N X_{nj})$, have to equal that country's total exports, $(\Sigma_{n=1}^N X_{ni})$, plus the imbalance parameter $Dn$:

$$(\Sigma_{j=1}^N X_{nj}) = (\Sigma_{n=1}^N X_{ni}) + D_n. \tag{15.5}$$

Replacing $X_{nj}$ and $X_{ni}$ in Eq. (15.5) by the proper expressions according to Eq. (15.3) results in a system of $N$ equations (or constraints).

## II. Stochastics and implementation

For empirical implementation, we assume that the stochastic counterpart to $X_{in}$ in Eq. (15.3) includes a multiplicative error term $\exp(\varepsilon_{in})$. Moreover, we parameterise

$$-\Theta \log(\tau_{in}) = -\Theta \log(1 + t_{in}) + \Sigma_{h=1}^H \alpha_h d_{h,in} + \xi_n + \Sigma_{k=1}^K \gamma_k PTA_{k,in}, \tag{15.6}$$

where $\log(1 + t_{in})$ is the log of the (one-plus) ad valorem tariff rate imposed by $i$ on imports from $n$; $\{d_{1,in}, d_{2,in}, d_{3,in}, d_{4,in}\}$ are binary indicator variables measuring adjacency, colonial ties, common legal origin, common language; $d_{5,in}$ is the log of distance; $\xi_n$ is an exporter-specific asymmetric component of trade costs; and $PTA_{k,in}$ is a binary indicator variable measuring PTAs of different depth. Specifically, $\{1,2,3\}$ measures agreements of the $\{shallow, medium, deep\}$ type, which are defined to cover $[1,7]$, $[8,41]$ and $[42,45]$ issues (cooperation areas), respectively. The choice of definition was on the relative frequency of such agreements. Following Cameron and Trivedi (2005) and Santos Silva and Tenreyro (2006), the model in Eq. (15.3) can be estimated by the Poisson pseudomaximum likelihood (PPML) as:

$$X_{in} = \mu_n \tau_{in}^{-\Theta} m_i \exp(\varepsilon_{in}), \qquad (15.7)$$

$$\mu_n = \lambda_n (w_n^\beta p_n^{1-\beta})^{-\Theta} \qquad (15.8)$$

$$m_j = (L_i w_i + T_i)/\Sigma_j \mu_j \tau_{ij}^{-\Theta} \qquad (15.9)$$

subject to the constraint in Eq. (15.5), when measuring $D_i$ as the total trade deficit (observed in the data).

In counterfactual equilibrium, we will set $PTA_{3,in} = 1$ whenever $\Sigma_{k=1}^{3} PTA_{k,in} = 1$ (hence, if any PTA was in place in 2008). Clearly, $PTA_{1,in} = 0$ and $PTA_{2,in} = 0$ have to be set. We will compare the model predictions of this counterfactual situation with the one for the benchmark case in which $PTA_{k,in}$ is set as observed in 2008. In both the benchmark and the counterfactual situation, we set $w_{USA} = 1$ without loss of generality, we keep $D_i$ constant relative to world GDP and we then solve for $w_i$ from Eq. (15.5). Then, we can straightforwardly solve the system of equations for all other endogenous variables such as $p_n$ and $X_{in}$.

## C. Data

### I. Exports, tariffs and PTAs

All data entering the estimation are based on 124 countries' bilateral sales in the year 2008, that is, $124^2 = 15\,376$ observations when including domestic sales. The dependent variable of interest in this chapter is bilateral export flows from country $n$ to country $i$, $X_{in}$. These data are taken from the United Nations' UNSD Commodity Trade (Comtrade) database (wits.worldbank.org). The four most important explanatory variables are bilateral (trade-weighted) applied tariffs, $t_{in}$, which are measured as a fraction of unity and based on the information on ad valorem tariffs in manufacturing trade available in the UNCTAD Trade Analysis Information System (TRAINS) database (wits.worldbank.org), and three mutually exclusive indicator variables that are based on information on PTAs as provided by the WTO Regional Trade Agreements Information System (rtais.wto.org), namely, $PTA_{1,in}$, which is one for all PTAs with up to 7 provisions made in the agreement and zero otherwise, $PTA_{2,in}$, which is one for all PTAs with between 8 and 41 provisions made in the agreement, and $PTA_{3,in}$, which is one for all PTAs with at least 42 provisions made in the agreement. In Table 15.1, we report average exports and average number of provisions by each of the exporters in the sample.

Table 15.1 suggests that relatively rich countries on average tend to adopt a larger number of provisions. This tendency is also captured in Figure 15.1, where we plot the average number of provisions adopted by each exporter against its average exports. The correlation between the two variables is strong and significant and amounts to 0.40. This is indirect evidence in favour of the hypothesis that the heterogeneity of PTAs in terms of the provisions that they cover should matter for trade flows.

In Table 15.2 we provide some useful information about bilateral exports (in thousands of US dollars) and the three PTA indicators across 52 different provisions. In particular, Table 15.2 summarises average bilateral export flows for each of the 52 provisions considered and the probability of each provision being included in each type of PTA.

For example, two categories (*tariff liberalisation on industrial goods, tariff liberalisation on agricultural goods*) always fall in all three types of PTAs. This suggests that in terms of timing, countries tend to sign these two provisions before committing to deeper cooperation. It is worth emphasising that provisions that are usually thought of as demonstrating a higher degree of economic integration such as cooperation in anti-dumping measures have lower probability of being included in shallow PTAs. Note that shallow PTAs do not cover provisions that require deep integration of legislative systems or specific bilateral treaties such as provisions that cover cooperation in *labour market regulations* or *capital movement* or both. Medium PTAs may include most of the 52 provisions as the respective probabilities are positive. However, the probability of inclusion in medium PTAs is higher for provisions that are either directly or indirectly linked to tariff liberalisations. For example, these provisions include *export taxes, countervailing measures* and others. Finally, deep PTAs cover the vast majority of possible provisions, by design. Hence, though classifying the provisions according to a strict timing hierarchy is difficult in this context, our design captures the fact that shallow

Table 15.1 *Average exports and the average number of adopted provisions in trade agreements*

| ISO | Avg. export | Avg. no. provisions | ISO | Avg. export | Avg. no. provisions | ISO | Avg. export | Avg. no. provisions |
|---|---|---|---|---|---|---|---|---|
| ALB | 7 196.87 | 8.18 | GHA | 3 161.33 | 1.45 | NIC | 6 093.15 | 0.61 |
| ARE | 250 256.6 | 0.55 | GMB | 22.73 | 1.45 | NLD | 1 984 022 | 12.16 |
| ARG | 176 069.8 | 1.23 | GRC | 113 940.4 | 12.15 | NOR | 264 169.1 | 1.3 |
| ARM | 4 610.6 | 0.51 | GRD | 65.31 | 5.01 | NZL | 64 231 | 0.25 |
| AUS | 266 454.4 | 0.44 | GUY | 293.29 | 6.07 | OMN | 23 891.74 | 0.64 |
| AUT | 1 031 006 | 12.15 | HRV | 71 708.53 | 12.35 | PAK | 104 402.9 | 0.22 |
| AZE | 4 956.47 | 0.51 | HUN | 643 304.9 | 12.15 | PER | 65 733.86 | 1.32 |
| BDI | 45.12 | 2.81 | IDN | 353 389.7 | 0.82 | PHL | 266 695.2 | 0.82 |
| BEN | 468.75 | 1.45 | IND | 766 146.5 | 0.13 | POL | 1 046 972 | 12.15 |
| BFA | 253.62 | 1.45 | IRL | 689 905.4 | 12.15 | PRT | 279 568.3 | 12.15 |
| BGR | 101 178.9 | 12.16 | ISL | 24 724.86 | 1.3 | PRY | 3 241.52 | 1.14 |
| BHR | 25 959.88 | 0.59 | ISR | 343 070 | 6.02 | QAT | 8 501.85 | 0.37 |
| BIH | 27 336.89 | 2.43 | ITA | 3 344 991 | 12.16 | ROM | 290 103.3 | 12.16 |
| BLR | 131 812.7 | 0.57 | JAM | 11 879.74 | 5.01 | RUS | 690 217.8 | 0.64 |
| BOL | 5 094.54 | 1.21 | JPN | 4 467 472 | 1.27 | RWA | 115.08 | 2.81 |
| BRA | 682 743.1 | 1.16 | KAZ | 107 069.7 | 0.57 | SAU | 0 | 0.37 |
| BTN | 22.15 | 0.13 | KEN | 13 647.37 | 2.81 | SDN | 429.51 | 2.98 |
| CAF | 38.66 | 0 | KGZ | 2 542.13 | 0.51 | SEN | 5 748.65 | 1.45 |
| CAN | 1 771 761 | 0.52 | KHM | 25 116.3 | 0.82 | SLV | 19 727.29 | 0.61 |
| CHE | 1 347 596 | 1.46 | KNA | 362.52 | 0 | SRB | 53 270.2 | 0.52 |
| CHL | 241 260.5 | 8.88 | KOR | 2 261 536 | 1.88 | SUR | 292.35 | 6.07 |
| CHN | 7 954 516 | 0.6 | KWT | 28 965.52 | 0.46 | SVN | 1 955 51.5 | 12.15 |
| CIV | 7 794.93 | 3.68 | LBN | 13 086.87 | 2.23 | SWE | 957 025.7 | 12.15 |
| CMR | 4 431.38 | 0 | LCA | 487.8 | 5.01 | SYC | 75.94 | 2.88 |
| COL | 87 027.5 | 1.19 | LKA | 39 538.75 | 0.13 | SYR | 28 642.27 | 1.68 |
| CRI | 39 383.42 | 0.61 | LSO | 1 461.43 | 0.85 | TGO | 2 357.08 | 1.45 |
| CYP | 6 467.14 | 12.16 | LTU | 97 019.25 | 12.15 | THA | 813 221.5 | 1 |
| CZE | 882 451.3 | 12.15 | LVA | 39 603.7 | 12.15 | TON | 3.14 | 0 |
| DEU | 8 673 715 | 12.16 | MAR | 97 266.74 | 5.55 | TTO | 35 835.02 | 5.01 |
| DNK | 512 561.4 | 12.15 | MDA | 6 994.54 | 1.02 | TUN | 96 141.16 | 5.94 |
| DOM | 26 128.04 | 5.62 | MDG | 8 727.2 | 2.81 | TUR | 734 572.7 | 2.6 |
| DZA | 9 813.37 | 6.68 | MDV | 0.12 | 0.13 | TZA | 4 700.49 | 0.87 |
| ECU | 12 373.44 | 1.09 | MEX | 1 633 769 | 7.57 | UGA | 3 928.57 | 2.81 |
| EGY | 72 867.73 | 9.26 | MLI | 727.81 | 1.45 | UKR | 346 094.9 | 0.52 |
| ESP | 1 559 236 | 12.15 | MOZ | 12 594.24 | 0.87 | URY | 12 529.74 | 1.19 |
| ETH | 956.36 | 2.81 | MRT | 0.88 | 0 | USA | 6 912 956 | 1.69 |
| FIN | 547 902.5 | 12.15 | MUS | 10 284.45 | 2.88 | VEN | 33 555.66 | 1.06 |
| FJI | 1 039.07 | 0 | MWI | 654.96 | 3.15 | YEM | 3 383.33 | 0.19 |
| FRAU | 3 244 607 | 12.16 | MYS | 671 628.1 | 0.82 | ZAF | 368 600.4 | 7.55 |
| GAB | 1 804.13 | 0 | NAM | 17 264.78 | 0.86 | ZMB | 29 650.68 | 3.02 |
| GBR | 2 358 568 | 12.15 | NER | 180.09 | 1.45 | ZWE | 4 802.67 | 3.15 |
| GEO | 6 053.92 | 0 | NGA | 19 775.16 | 1.45 | | | |

*Note:* ISO stands for the country code defined by the International Organization for Standardization. Average exports are measured in thousands of US dollars.

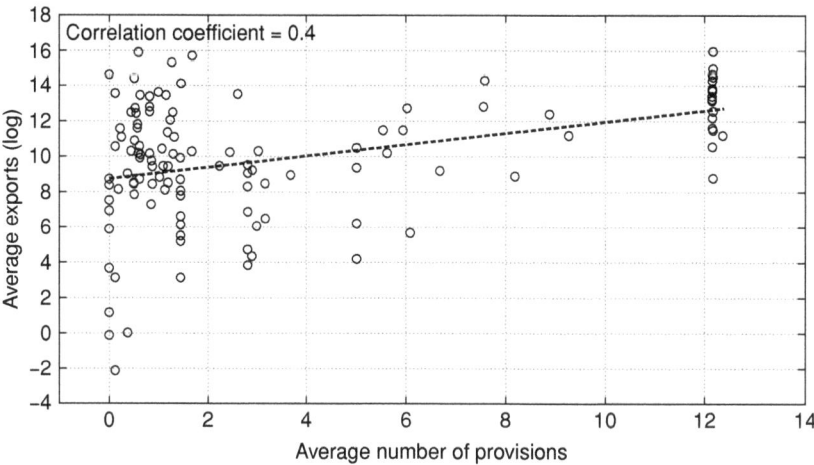

**Figure 15.1**    Correlation between average exports and the number of provisions adopted

PTAs almost exclusively include tariff liberalisation, that deep PTAs are characterised by the deepest form of integration when all provisions are in force and that medium PTAs are between the two categories.[3]

## II. Tariffs and other variables

We need two classes of other variables. First, a set of gravity variables is taken from the geographical database of the Centre d'Etudes Prospectives et d'Informations Internationales (www.cepii.fr/CEPII/en). These variables are the (log of) one plus ad valorem tariff rate, (log of) bilateral distance and four binary indicator variables: adjacency (1 if there is a common land border and 0 otherwise), colonial ties (1 if one country was formerly a colony of the other and 0 otherwise), common legal origin (1 if two countries' judicial codex has the same origin and 0 else), common language (1 if two countries share at least one common official language and 0 otherwise). Moreover, we use information on manufacturing output from the United Nations' UNIDO database and the

---

[3] Egger and Wamser (2013) discuss strategic motives in adoption of bilateral provisions.

Table 15.2 *Types of trade agreements*

| No. | Type of provision | Avg. export | $PTA_{1,in}$ | $PTA_{2,in}$ | $PTA_{3,in}$ |
|---|---|---|---|---|---|
| 1 | Tariff liberalisation on industrial goods | 1 776 700 | 1 | 1 | 1 |
| 2 | Tariff liberalisation on agriculture goods | 1 776 700 | 1 | 1 | 1 |
| 3 | Customs | 1 749 161 | 0.519 5 | 0.998 7 | 1 |
| 4 | Export taxes | 1 863 164 | 0.454 5 | 0.823 8 | 1 |
| 5 | SPS (harmonization of SPS measures) | 1 162 129 | 0 | 0.547 3 | 0 |
| 6 | TBT (WTO Agreement on TBT) | 2 049 469 | 0.064 9 | 0.724 1 | 1 |
| 7 | STE (affirm. of XVII GATT provision) | 2 323 715 | 0 | 0.573 4 | 1 |
| 8 | AD (anti-dumping rights and obligations) | 1 911 788 | 0.490 3 | 0.974 5 | 1 |
| 9 | CVM (countervailing measures rights) | 2 129 575 | 0.042 2 | 0.815 5 | 1 |
| 10 | State aid | 2 230 889 | 0.448 1 | 0.627 7 | 1 |
| 11 | Public procurement | 2 388 289 | 0 | 0.590 7 | 1 |
| 12 | TRIMs (local, export performance of FDI) | 3 937 505 | 0.039 0 | 0.204 3 | 0 |
| 13 | GATS (liberalisation of trade in services) | 1 323 855 | 0.039 0 | 0.671 8 | 0 |
| 14 | TRIP (harmonisation of standards) | 2 217 187 | 0 | 0.672 4 | 1 |
| 15 | Anticorruption | 1 359 558 | 0 | 0.049 2 | 0 |
| 16 | Competition policy | 1 976 544 | 0.454 5 | 0.819 9 | 1 |
| 17 | Environmental laws | 2 116 933 | 0 | 0.664 1 | 1 |
| 18 | IPR (accessing treaties beyond TRIPS) | 2 252 336 | 0 | 0.667 9 | 1 |
| 19 | Investment | 2 232 960 | 0.039 0 | 0.697 3 | 1 |
| 20 | Labour market regulation | 1 442 491 | 0 | 0.337 2 | 0 |
| 21 | Movement of capital | 2 033 997 | 0 | 0.726 1 | 1 |
| 22 | Consumer protection | 3 083 110 | 0 | 0.169 9 | 1 |
| 23 | Data protection | 2 301 677 | 0 | 0.325 7 | 1 |
| 24 | Agriculture | 2 092 733 | 0 | 0.489 1 | 1 |
| 25 | Approximation of legislation | 2 893 415 | 0 | 0.221 6 | 1 |
| 26 | Audio visual | 3 069 650 | 0 | 0.164 8 | 1 |
| 27 | Civil protection | 0 | 0 | 0.000 0 | 0 |
| 28 | Innovation policies | 12 385 | 0 | 0.205 6 | 0 |

Table 15.2 (cont.)

| No. | Type of provision | Avg. export | $PTA_{1,in}$ | $PTA_{2,in}$ | $PTA_{3,in}$ |
|-----|-------------------|-------------|--------------|--------------|--------------|
| 29 | Cultural cooperation | 2 072 328 | 0 | 0.427 2 | 1 |
| 30 | Economic policy dialogue | 2 898 176 | 0 | 0.185 8 | 1 |
| 31 | Education and training | 2 244 922 | 0 | 0.373 6 | 1 |
| 32 | Energy | 2 111 651 | 0 | 0.641 1 | 1 |
| 33 | Financial assistance | 1 759 622 | 0 | 0.546 0 | 1 |
| 34 | Health | 303 396 | 0 | 0.151 3 | 0 |
| 35 | Human rights | 2 551 988 | 0 | 0.282 2 | 1 |
| 36 | Illegal immigration | 3 221 847 | 0 | 0.136 0 | 1 |
| 37 | Illicit drugs | 2 395 087 | 0 | 0.316 1 | 1 |
| 38 | Industrial cooperation | 1 986 508 | 0 | 0.470 6 | 1 |
| 39 | Information society | 1 753 473 | 0 | 0.568 3 | 1 |
| 40 | Mining | 610 941 | 0 | 0.118 1 | 0 |
| 41 | Money laundering | 2 799 880 | 0 | 0.223 5 | 1 |
| 42 | Nuclear safety | 20 000 000 | 0 | 0.021 7 | 0 |
| 43 | Political dialogue | 2 442 453 | 0 | 0.311 6 | 1 |
| 44 | Public administration | 3 547 561 | 0 | 0.088 1 | 1 |
| 45 | Regional cooperation | 1 649 554 | 0 | 0.681 4 | 1 |
| 46 | Research and technology | 1 637 188 | 0 | 0.646 2 | 1 |
| 47 | SME (technical assistance, access to finance) | 3 286 921 | 0 | 0.149 4 | 1 |
| 48 | Social matters | 1 647 458 | 0 | 0.632 8 | 1 |
| 49 | Statistics | 2 393 285 | 0 | 0.316 1 | 1 |
| 50 | Taxation | 4 121 473 | 0 | 0.019 2 | 1 |
| 51 | Terrorism | 3 493 341 | 0 | 0.088 1 | 1 |
| 52 | Visa and asylum | 3 920 305 | 0 | 0.056 2 | 1 |

Note: Average exports are measured in thousands of US dollars.
FDI, foreign direct investment; IPR, intellectual property rights; SME, small and medium-sized enterprise; SPS, sanitary and phytosanitary; STE, state trading enterprise; TBT, technical barriers to trade; TRIMs, trade-related investment measures.

World Bank's World Development Indicators (data.worldbank.org/datacatalog/world-development-indicators).[4]

Table 15.3 summarises the 1st, 5th, 25th, 50th, 75th, 95th and 99th percentiles along with the average and the standard deviation for each

---

[4] Consistent with the literature, we imputed manufacturing output from the value added data from the World Bank's World Development Indicators database.

Table 15.3 *Trade cost variables*

| Percentile | Trade | ln (1 + *tariff*) | Adjacency | Colonial relationship | Common legal origin | Common language | ln (*distance*) |
|---|---|---|---|---|---|---|---|
| 1 | 0 | 0 | 0 | 0 | 0 | 0 | 5.514 8 |
| 5 | 0 | 0 | 0 | 0 | 0 | 0 | 7.028 9 |
| 10 | 0 | 0 | 0 | 0 | 0 | 0 | 7.511 1 |
| 25 | 0 | 0.016 4 | 0 | 0 | 0 | 0 | 8.288 3 |
| 50 | 345 | 0.066 8 | 0 | 0 | 0 | 1 | 8.840 3 |
| 75 | 26 198 | 0.115 2 | 0 | 0 | 1 | 1 | 9.231 7 |
| 90 | 422 168 | 0.15 85 | 0 | 0 | 1 | 1 | 9.506 1 |
| 95 | 1 612 251 | 0.180 4 | 0 | 0 | 1 | 1 | 9.651 5 |
| 99 | 15 100 000 | 1 | 1 | 1 | 1 | 1 | 9.801 7 |
| Mean | 1 915 353 | 0.073 0 | 0.02 15 | 0.016 3 | 0.312 1 | 0.682 2 | 8.606 6 |
| SD | 59 700 000 | 0.062 1 | 0.144 9 | 0.126 7 | 0.463 4 | 0.465 6 | 1.094 0 |

of the variables used in this and in the previous subsection. As the table suggests, about a quarter of our sample is characterised by zero trade flows.[5] The tariff data indicate that ad valorem tariffs were relatively low in 2008. At the 25th percentile level the (log) tariff rate was only 0.0164, while at the 95th percentile the respective rate was 0.1804. In general, developing countries face and impose higher tariff rates in manufacturing.

### D. Parameter estimation and model calibration

In order to obtain the necessary parameters to estimate $\tau_{in}^{-\Theta}$, we estimate the model in Eq. (15.3) with exporter and importer fixed effects (capturing $\mu_n$ and $m_i$, respectively) and parameterise $\tau_{in}^{-\Theta}$ as in Eq. (15.6), using tariffs and PTA variables as introduced in Section B.I and nontariff trade cost variables as described in Section B.II. We estimate the model by Poisson pseudomaximum likelihood because of its robustness against heteroscedasticity (see Santos Silva and Tenreyro 2006). The corresponding estimates and standard errors are summarised in Table 15.4.

---

[5] For a discussion of zeros in international trade, see Helpman, Melitz and Rubinstein (2008), Chor (2010), Baldwin and Harrigan (2011) and Egger *et al.* (2011).

Table 15.4 *Estimation results*

| Variable | Coef. | SE |
|---|---|---|
| Log one-plus-tariff | −6.2522 | 1.4257 |
| Adjacency | 0.6197 | 0.0737 |
| Colonial relationship | 0.1573 | 0.0806 |
| Common legal origin | 0.2351 | 0.0507 |
| Common language | 0.4860 | 0.0898 |
| Log of distance | −0.4186 | 0.0171 |
| (Shallow) $PTA_1$ | 0.3717 | 0.1027 |
| (Medium) $PTA_2$ | 0.5466 | 0.0810 |
| (Deep) $PTA_3$ | 0.9007 | 0.0949 |
| $Pseudo\text{-}R^2$ | 0.9931 | |

Notice that all parameters have the expected sign. First of all, $^\wedge\Theta \approx 6.2522$ is very consistent with earlier findings (see Egger and Nigai 2013). Second, trade costs decline (trade rises) with adjacency, colonial ties, common legal origin and common language, and trade costs rise (trade declines) with greater geographical distance. The magnitude of the parameters is consistent with that reported in earlier research. Third, and most importantly for the present purpose, trade costs decline (trade rises) with the depth of PTAs measured by the number of issues covered. Moreover, the direct impact of greater depth on trade is not linear. To see this, let us linearly interpolate the change in coefficients between $PTA_{1,in}$, where the average number of issues covered is 4, and $PTA_{2,in}$, where the average number of issues covered is 23.5. From this, we estimate a linear coefficient increase of about 0.0183 per issue covered. Extrapolating this from $PTA_{2,in}$ (with 23.5 issues covered on average) to $PTA_{3,in}$ (with 42.5 covered issues on average) would yield a coefficient of 1.1067. However, the estimated coefficient on $PTA_{3,in}$ is 0.9007, which is smaller. We could do the same exercise, assuming that the direct impact rises log-linearly with the number of issues. Then, we would project the ascent of the coefficient from $PTA_{2,in}$ to $PTA_{3,in}$ on the basis of the change from $PTA_{1,in}$ to $PTA_{2,in}$, assuming a log-linear (rather than a linear) relationship between the change in coefficients with depth and the number of issues covered. This procedure would lead to a predicted coefficient on $PTA_{3,in}$ of 0.7521, which is much smaller than the estimated

0.9007 on $PTA_{3,in}$. Hence, the relationship is more concave (convex) than predicted by a linear (log-linear) function of the number of issues covered.[6]

## E. Comparative static analysis

In models of the kind analyzed here, $-\Theta$ measures the effect of a decline in $-\Theta \log(\tau_{in})$ due to a marginal increase in $(1 + t_{in})$. This is different from the marginal response of $X_{in}$ for various reasons. First, tariff income changes with $(1 + t_{in})$, which is not captured by $-\Theta$. Second, the denominator of $X_{in}$ changes in accordance with Eq. (15.7)/(15.9). Third, $w_n$ changes in response to a change in $(1 + t_{in})$, according to Eq. (15.5). Clearly, the same is true for discrete changes as induced by entering PTAs of the shallow, medium or deep kind: their parameters do not reflect total responses of bilateral trade, $X_{in}$, to such agreements. With inherently asymmetric countries (in terms of the number and type of PTAs signed, of other trade costs, of factor endowments and of productivity), the same change in PTA policy (e.g. entering a deep PTA, or changing a shallow PTA into a deep PTA) will have different effects across country pairs and countries.

What we have to do to gauge the total effects on trade flows $X_{in}$ and, eventually, on utility, $u_i = (w_i L_i + T_i)/(\Psi \Sigma_j \lambda_j (w_j^\beta p_j^{1-\beta})^{-\Theta} \tau_{ij}^{-\Theta})^{-1/\Theta}$ (which, from a utilitarian perspective, corresponds to welfare), is to solve for benchmark $\{(w_i), (p_i), (X_{in})\}$ and counterfactual $\{(w_i'), (p_i'), (X_{in}')\}$ as a function of benchmark $\tau_{in}$ and counterfactual $\tau_{in}'$. In this section, we focus on such an exercise, keeping all parameters constant, except for the estimated counterparts to $\gamma_1$ (on $PTA_{1,in}$) and $\gamma_2$ (on $PTA_{2,in}$) in Eq. (15.6). Hence, the change from benchmark $\tau_{in}$ to counterfactual $\tau_{in}'$ considered here is entirely due to making existing shallow and medium PTAs deep, *keeping non-PTA members outside PTAs and keeping deep PTAs deep as well as keeping tariffs constant*. Hence, we focus entirely on the costs and benefits of deepening PTAs due to institutional, nontariff factors – to insiders as well as outsiders of PTAs.

In the counterfactual experiments we use $\Delta$ to denote counterfactual change in percentage for an arbitrary variable, $a$, such that if $a'$ is its

---

[6] The results are robust to including more bilateral observable variables such as a currency union dummy. However, many of such variables are covered either directly or indirectly in the 52 provisions considered.

Table 15.5 *Results of the counterfactual experiment*

| ISO | Δ net exp. | Δ welfare | $\Delta\tau_{ij}$ | $PTA_{1,in}$ | $PTA_{2,in}$ | $PTA_{3,in}$ |
|-----|-----------|-----------|-------------------|--------------|--------------|--------------|
| ALB | −3.9162 | 0.9922 | −0.1332 | 0 | 3 | 23 |
| ARE | 4.9344 | 1.2843 | −0.7197 | 11 | 0 | 0 |
| ARG | 14.9803 | 0.9115 | −0.4885 | 0 | 11 | 0 |
| ARM | 4.7686 | 1.6728 | −0.3109 | 0 | 7 | 0 |
| AUS | 20.2444 | 1.6214 | −0.1332 | 0 | 3 | 0 |
| AUT | 2.0343 | 1.3748 | −1.0845 | 3 | 20 | 23 |
| AZE | 12.2097 | 1.1954 | −0.3109 | 0 | 7 | 0 |
| BDI | −6.0612 | 1.0221 | −0.5329 | 0 | 12 | 0 |
| BEN | −2.8172 | 1.1335 | −0.3997 | 0 | 9 | 0 |
| BFA | −5.5357 | 0.8507 | −0.3997 | 0 | 9 | 0 |
| BGR | 2.7445 | 1.017 | −1.0845 | 3 | 20 | 23 |
| BHR | 25.439 | 2.888 | −0.7642 | 11 | 1 | 0 |
| BIH | 25.6803 | 7.715 | −1.1547 | 0 | 26 | 0 |
| BLR | 6.5394 | 1.349 | −0.3319 | 1 | 6 | 0 |
| BOL | 20.569 | 1.6745 | −0.4885 | 0 | 11 | 0 |
| BRA | 6.1335 | 0.5187 | −0.4885 | 0 | 11 | 0 |
| BTN | 1.378 | 1.5536 | −0.2617 | 4 | 0 | 0 |
| CAF | −8.8174 | 0.9682 | 0 | 0 | 0 | 0 |
| CAN | 26.6032 | 9.1377 | −0.1332 | 0 | 3 | 0 |
| CHE | 35.5239 | 16.4062 | −1.5937 | 23 | 2 | 0 |
| CHL | 28.2475 | 5.2207 | −1.5988 | 0 | 36 | 0 |
| CHN | 9.3477 | 1.4026 | −0.4814 | 6 | 2 | 0 |
| CIV | 23.4969 | 1.9676 | −1.4211 | 0 | 32 | 0 |
| CMR | −5.4603 | 0.4908 | 0 | 0 | 0 | 0 |
| COL | 11.7235 | 1.2443 | −0.4885 | 0 | 11 | 0 |
| CRI | 16.7577 | 3.1499 | −0.1776 | 0 | 4 | 0 |
| CYP | 6.576 | 1.1292 | −1.0845 | 3 | 20 | 23 |
| CZE | 0.7201 | 0.8387 | −1.0845 | 3 | 20 | 23 |
| DEU | 3.0366 | 1.3091 | −1.0845 | 3 | 20 | 23 |
| DNK | 1.1628 | 0.6941 | −1.0845 | 3 | 20 | 23 |
| DOM | 37.9599 | 2.502 | −1.1991 | 0 | 27 | 0 |
| DZA | 37.718 | 2.7308 | −1.0214 | 0 | 23 | 0 |
| ECU | 11.6904 | 0.7823 | −0.4885 | 0 | 11 | 0 |
| EGY | 35.8624 | 2.4742 | −2.2297 | 11 | 34 | 0 |
| ESP | 2.1207 | 0.5371 | −1.0845 | 3 | 20 | 23 |
| ETH | −3.5597 | 1.0674 | −0.5329 | 0 | 12 | 0 |
| FIN | 2.064 | 0.7824 | −1.0845 | 3 | 20 | 23 |

(*cont.*)

Table 15.5 (cont.)

| ISO | Δ net exp. | Δ welfare | Δτij | PTA1,in | PTA2,in | PTA3,in |
|-----|-----------|-----------|------|---------|---------|---------|
| FJI | −7.1778 | 1.0459 | 0 | 0 | 0 | 0 |
| FRA | 2.8708 | 0.8959 | −1.0845 | 3 | 20 | 23 |
| GAB | −5.9721 | 0.8615 | 0 | 0 | 0 | 0 |
| GBR | 1.7788 | 0.827 | −1.0845 | 3 | 20 | 23 |
| GEO | −4.8594 | 0.9168 | 0 | 0 | 0 | 0 |
| GHA | −2.6538 | 0.534 | −0.3997 | 0 | 9 | 0 |
| GMB | −5.0928 | 1.5576 | −0.3997 | 0 | 9 | 0 |
| GRC | 5.4472 | 0.7796 | −1.0845 | 3 | 20 | 23 |
| GRD | 17.8396 | 3.7767 | −1.0214 | 0 | 23 | 0 |
| GUY | 25.0121 | 3.8494 | −1.5099 | 0 | 34 | 0 |
| HRV | 1.9761 | 0.6762 | −1.1733 | 3 | 22 | 23 |
| HUN | 1.1269 | 1.1944 | −1.0845 | 3 | 20 | 23 |
| IDN | 23.2442 | 4.5792 | −0.3319 | 1 | 6 | 0 |
| IND | 1.5229 | 0.2751 | −0.3061 | 4 | 1 | 0 |
| IRL | 0.9311 | 0.8052 | −1.0845 | 3 | 20 | 23 |
| ISL | 30.0376 | 9.379 | −1.5493 | 23 | 1 | 0 |
| ISR | 20.3107 | 9.4485 | −1.0658 | 0 | 24 | 0 |
| ITA | 2.5504 | 0.628 | −1.0845 | 3 | 20 | 23 |
| JAM | 13.7779 | 3.6867 | −1.0214 | 0 | 23 | 0 |
| JPN | 17.6785 | 1.8238 | −0.4651 | 1 | 9 | 0 |
| KAZ | 11.0907 | 1.7598 | −0.3319 | 1 | 6 | 0 |
| KEN | −1.3432 | 0.443 | −0.5329 | 0 | 12 | 0 |
| KGZ | 9.1672 | 1.7417 | −0.3109 | 0 | 7 | 0 |
| KHM | 25.5333 | 12.358 | −0.3319 | 1 | 6 | 0 |

Note: ISO stands for the country code defined by the International Organization for Standardization.

counterfactual value:

$$\Delta a = 100 \times (a'/a - 1).$$   (15.10)

We are mainly interested in two outcomes in our experiment: the associated changes in bilateral trade flows and welfare. We measure these two variables using percentage changes in net trade flows (by exporter) and changes in welfare (by exporter), which we name {Δ net exp.} and {Δ welfare}, respectively. We report them along with percentage changes in trade costs and the number of total PTAs in the benchmark equilibrium in Table 15.5 for each exporter.

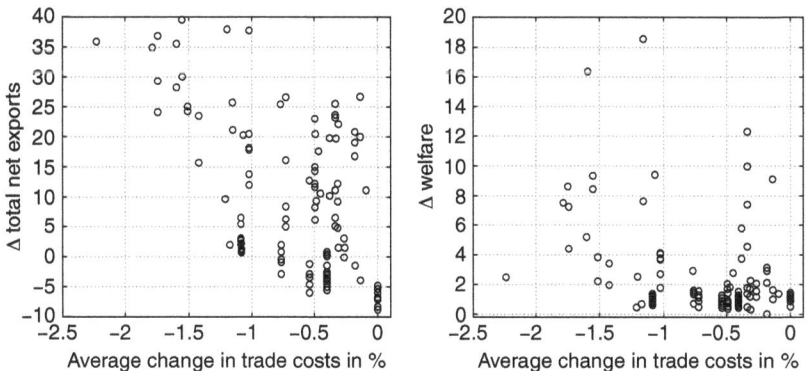

**Figure 15.2**   Counterfactual experiments

On average, the counterfactual experiment reduces the average level of trade costs by 0.7 per cent. Naturally, the reductions in $\tau_{ij}$ are highly heterogeneous and depend on how many PTAs (shallow and medium) each country pair had in the benchmark equilibrium. As Table 15.5 suggests, this reduction in trade costs on average increases (net) exports by 9.2 per cent and welfare by 2.4 per cent.

In the counterfactual experiment we reduce trade costs in a heterogeneous manner, which leads to highly heterogeneous changes in net exports. We see in the left panel of Figure 15.2 that, even though all trade costs decrease, countries with a relatively sharper decline in trade costs experience an increase in net exports. As only relative trade costs matter, countries in which the decline in $\tau_{ij}$ is less drastic experience a decline in their net exports. Lower trade costs generally lead to lower prices everywhere. Hence, the vast majority of countries in our sample benefits from deeper PTAs. This is depicted in the right panel of Figure 15.2, where most countries experience welfare gains up to 10 per cent, and a few enjoy even higher increases in welfare. In general, the effects on the welfare are not negligible, and there appears to be considerable scope for deeper, welfare-improving bilateral economic integration, even at unchanged tariffs.

## F. Conclusion

This work shows that there is considerable heterogeneity in bilateral and multilateral trade agreements. Depending on the degree of economic integration, measured by the number of provisions covered in trade agreements, we classify PTAs into three broad types: shallow, medium and deep. We estimate a structural gravity equation and find that the effect of PTAs on international trade depends greatly on the degree of economic integration. We use these estimates in a Ricardian general equilibrium model of trade to quantitatively assess the effect of shifting from shallow and medium to deep trade agreements. We find that there is scope for improving overall welfare through establishing deeper trade agreements. On average, extending shallow and medium PTAs to deep ones would lead to a 2.4 per cent increase in real welfare with some countries experiencing as much as 16–18 per cent in terms of welfare without changing their bilateral tariffs.

## References

Alvarez, Fernando, and Lucas, Robert E., Jr. 2007. 'General Equilibrium Analysis of the Eaton-Kortum Model of International Trade.' *Journal of Monetary Economics* 54 (6): 1726–68.

Arkolakis, Costas, Costinot, Arnaud, and Rodríguez-Clare, Andrés. 2012. 'New Trade Models, Same Old Gains?' *American Economic Review* 102 (1): 94–130.

Baier, Scott L., and Bergstrand, Jeffrey H. 2007. 'Do Free Trade Agreements Actually Increase Members' International Trade?' *Journal of International Economics* 71 (1): 72–95.

2009. 'Estimating the Effects of Free Trade Agreements on International Trade Flows Using Matching Econometrics.' *Journal of International Economics* 77 (1): 63–76.

Baldwin, Richard, and Harrigan, James. 2011. 'Zeros, Quality, and Space: Trade Theory and Trade Evidence.' *American Economic Journal: Microeconomics* 3 (2): 60–88.

Cameron, A. Colin, and Trivedi, Pravin K. 2005. *Microeconometrics: Methods and Applications.* Cambridge: Cambridge University Press.

Chor, Davin. 2010. 'Unpacking Sources of Comparative Advantage: A Quantitative Approach.' *Journal of International Economics* 82 (2): 152–67.

Dekle, Robert, Eaton, Jonathan, and Kortum, Samuel S. 2007. 'Unbalanced Trade.' *American Economic Review* 97 (2): 351–55.

Eaton, Jonathan, and Kortum, Samuel S. 2002. 'Technology, Geography, and Trade.' *Econometrica* 70 (5): 1741–79.

Egger, Peter H., Larch, Mario, Staub, Kevin, and Winkelmann, Rainer. 2011. 'The Trade Effects of Endogenous Preferential Trade Agreements.' *American Economic Journal: Economic Policy* 3 (3): 113–43.

Egger, Peter H., and Nigai, Sergey. 2013. 'Asymmetric Trade Costs, Trade Imbalances and the World Income Distribution.' Unpublished manuscript, ETH Zurich.

Egger, Peter H., and Wamser, Georg. 2013. 'Effects of the Endogenous Scope of Preferentialism on International Goods Trade.' *B.E. Journal of Economic Analysis and Policy* 13 (2): 709–31.

Helpman, Elhanan, Melitz, Marc, and Rubinstein, Yona. 2008. 'Estimating Trade Flows: Trading Partners and Trading Volumes.' *Quarterly Journal of Economics* 123 (2): 441–87.

Santos Silva, J. M. C., and Tenreyro, Silvana. 2006. 'The Log of Gravity.' *Review of Economics and Statistics* 88 (4): 641–58.

# 16

# Revisiting the trade effects of services agreements

## A. Introduction

One of the striking features of trade diplomacy since 1995 has been the pace of preferential goods trade liberalisation and rule making. More recently, a similar trend is observed regarding services trade. Of the 83 preferential trade agreements (PTAs) notified to the World Trade Organization (WTO) and in force prior to the year 2000, 73 (87.9 per cent) featured provisions dealing exclusively with trade in goods. Since then and until August 2013, another 176 PTAs went into force of which 105 (59.7 per cent) also include provisions on services trade.[1] This development indicates the rising importance of services trade in general, the growing need felt by countries to place such trade on a firmer institutional and rule-making footing and the attractiveness of doing so on an expedited basis via preferential negotiating platforms (Sauvé and Shingal 2011).

Economic literature is replete with theoretical models and empirical analyses documenting the impact of PTAs on trade between partner countries. Most of this work, however, traditionally looked at trade in merchandise goods only. An important reason for this was the lack of available data on bilateral services trade. This lacuna was, however, filled with the publication of the Organisation for Economic Co-operation and Development (OECD)'s database on bilateral services trade;[2] since its

I would like to thank the NCCR Trade Regulation (www.nccr-trade.org) for financial support and Sébastien Miroudot for generous use of the updated OECD database used in this chapter.
[1] As of 15 August 2013, the total number of services trade agreements (STAs) in force was 118. These included three alliances (Mercado Común del Sur (MERCOSUR), European Free Trade Association (EFTA) and Caribbean Community and Common Market (CARICOM)) in which an STA was negotiated after 2000 in addition to a preexisting trade agreement in goods.
[2] In 2002, the OECD Secretariat presented data on total trade in services, broken down by partner country, for 26 OECD member countries from 1999 to 2002. This has now been

publication Grünfeld and Moxnes (2003), Mirza and Nicoletti (2004), Ceglowski (2006), Kimura and Lee (2006), Kox and Lejour (2006), Walsh (2006), Lennon (2008), Shingal (2009), Marchetti (2011) and Egger, Larch and Staub (2012) have used this data set to examine the trade effect of services accords on aggregate and disaggregated services trade flows.

The earlier papers in this literature were constrained by limited coverage both in terms of the country sample and time period. However, Marchetti (2011) was able to exploit a larger data set comprising 30 OECD exporters and 55 OECD and non-OECD importers over 1999–2006. Egger, Larch and Staub (2012), on the other hand, focused on bilateral services trade among 16 European OECD countries over 1999–2006. This literature is also diverse in terms of the model specifications, estimation methodologies and the magnitudes of the estimated trade effects.[3] Shingal (2009) was the first paper in the services literature to endogenise services trade agreement (STA) membership and account for its lagged effects on trade empirically, whereas none of the other cited papers have addressed these issues.

In this chapter, we revisit the trade effects of services agreements using the OECD's updated database on bilateral services trade flows with greater country (35 exporters and 238 importers) and time coverage (1999–2010). We also base our empirical analyses on recent developments in the estimation of structural gravity models (for instance, see Head and Mayer 2013). In addition to accounting for the phasing in of STAs empirically and the treatment of STA membership as endogenous, we also examine trade effects of STA membership allowing for zero trade flows.

Our results suggest a (weakly significant) trade effect of 16.1 per cent from having a services accord (13.7 per cent at the intensive margin). This effect rises to 26.1 per cent for the intra–European union (EU) trading partners in our sample, with the intensive margin results much higher at 53.4 per cent. The services trade effect is also found to become significantly accentuated once anticipation effects of accession are included in the analysis, but only at the intensive margin. These results also suggest that the maximum impact of a services accord is felt the farthest in time

extended to cover 35 reporting countries from the OECD, 238 OECD and non-OECD partner countries and 12 years (1999–2010).
3  For instance, Grünfeld and Moxnes (2003) and Walsh (2006) found the trade effects to be statistically insignificant, whereas Lennon (2008), Shingal (2009) and Marchetti (2011) reported estimates of around 15 per cent. The trade effects were higher in Ceglowski (2006) (38–68 per cent), Kimura and Lee (2006) (24.5 per cent) and Kox and Lejour (2006) (30–62 per cent) though the last studied only the EU15.

from actual accession; thus services agreements seem to have a significant 'announcement effect' for firms already engaged in services trade.

The rest of the chapter is structured as follows. In the next section, we present the theoretical framework underlying our empirical strategy. Section C looks at the data, and Section D discusses estimation issues. Section E discusses the results, and Section F concludes.

## B. Estimating the impact of services accords

Much like bilateral trade in goods, bilateral services exports ($X_{ijt}$, from country $i$ to country $j$ at time $t$) are governed by the same forces of 'gravity', such as the gross domestic products (GDPs) of the exporter and importer, prices and bilateral trade costs (for instance, see Anderson, Milot and Yotov 2011). The last are typically proxied by bilateral distance between capitals of the two countries, incidence of and heterogeneity between (restrictive) services regulation and indicators for common international borders, language, colonial origins, legal systems and membership of PTAs (in the context of this chapter, services trade agreements or $STA_{ijt}$).

Empirically, we have the following model:

$$\ln X_{ijt} = \mu_{ij} + \alpha_{it} + \gamma_{it} + \rho_t + \delta STA_{ijt} + \varepsilon_{ijt} \qquad (16.1)$$

where all the bilateral trade costs are captured in the pairwise fixed effects $\mu_{ij}$ and the exporter-time ($\alpha_{it}$) and importer-time ($\gamma_{jt}$) fixed effects in Eq. (16.1) control for the effect of the respective GDPs and, following Baier and Bergstrand (2007), also account for the time-varying terms in a panel data setting. $\varepsilon_{ijt}$ is the error term.

However, Eq. (16.1) does not account for a significant characteristic of most bilateral trade data – the existence of 'export zeros'.[4] This is even more true of bilateral services trade data, which also tend to report a significant number of missing observations.

Finally, it assumes that STA membership is exogenous. However, in a significant departure from earlier work, researchers (Magee 2004; Baier and Bergstrand 2002, 2004, 2007; Egger, Egger and Greenaway 2008) have begun to treat PTA membership as endogenous based on the intuition that if there is a tendency for countries to 'self-select'[5] themselves into an

---

[4] For instance, see Helpman, Melitz and Rubinstein (2008) and Baldwin and Harrigan (2011).

[5] That is, countries that enter into an agreement are those that already trade significantly with each other and vice versa.

accord, then treating PTA membership as exogenous would underestimate the magnitude of the trade effect .[6]

Egger *et al.* (2011) have provided a reduced form estimation of a theory-consistent gravity model that endogenises the impact of PTA membership and also accounts for trade at both margins. Significantly, the inclusion of pairwise, importer-time and exporter-time fixed effects in Eq. (1) also enables an endogenous treatment of the STA variable (Baier and Bergstrand 2007).

Baier and Bergstrand (2007) also accounted for the phasing in of PTAs by introducing the lagged effects of PTA on trade. Given that every PTA has a phase-in period, typically longer than 10 years,[7] the entire treatment effect on trade cannot be captured in the concurrent year. Following Baier and Bergstrand (2007), we augment Eq. (16.2) to include STA anticipation effects for up to 10 years preceding the coming into effect of the agreement.

## C. Data

Data on $X_{ijt}$ are taken from the OECD's Bilateral Trade in Services database. These include 6095 trading partner pairs between 35 exporting and 238 importing countries from 1999 to 2010 (the list of countries is provided in Table A16.1). Of these, 203 trading partners reported negative services exports, and, assuming reporting errors, these values were taken as zero.[8] In addition, data on services exports were found unreported for 7147 out of 44 322 observations, which, following this literature, were also assumed to be zero.[9] This brought the total number of export zeros in the sample to 19 700 (44.4 per cent of the full sample).

Data on trade agreements are taken from the WTO's Regional Trade Agreements Information System (RTA-IS) database, where $STA = 1$ for agreements notified under Article V of the General Agreement on Trade in Services (GATS) during 1958–2010 and 0 otherwise. Since our data cover the period 1999–2010, if a services agreement was reached

---

[6] For instance, Baier and Bergstrand (2007) find the trade effect from goods agreements to quintuple once PTA membership is endogenised econometrically.

[7] For instance, both the original European Economic Community (EEC) agreement of 1958 and the North American Free Trade Agreement (NAFTA) had a 10-year phase-in provision.

[8] In our sensitivity analyses, we also ran our regressions without these observations but found the results to be qualitatively similar.

[9] Low thresholds for reporting and measurement errors can be responsible for both unreported flows and for export zeros.

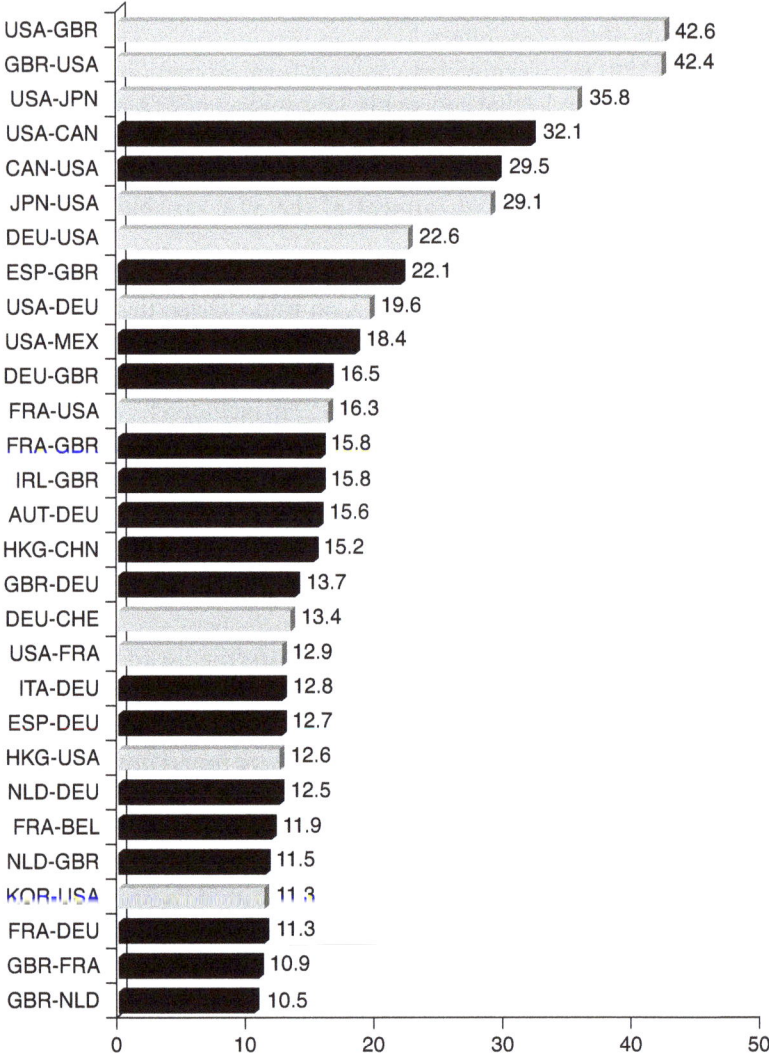

**Figure 16.1**   Top services export flows (US$ billion, average 1999–2010)
*Source:* OECD; author's own calculations
*Note:* Dyads shaded darker had a services trade agreement in force in 2013; those shaded lighter did not.

before 1999, the STA variable takes a value 1 over 1999–2010. On the other hand, if the agreement came into effect after 1999, then the variable takes a value 1 in the year the STA entered into force and every year after that and the value 0 otherwise.

Table 16.1 *Decile distribution of bilateral services exports (avg. 1999–2010)*

| Deciles ($n = 3\,850$) | Avg. $X_{ij}$ (US$million) | STA |
|---|---|---|
| D1 | 3 776.8 | 0.49 |
| D2 | 395 | 0.35 |
| D3 | 133.1 | 0.32 |
| D4 | 53.7 | 0.26 |
| D5 | 24.8 | 0.27 |
| D6 | 11.5 | 0.17 |
| D7 | 5.3 | 0.2 |
| D8 | 2.2 | 0.16 |
| D9 | 0.7 | 0.15 |
| D10 | 0.1 | 0.07 |
| D1/D10 | 28 072.4 | 7.3 |

*Source:* OECD; author's own calculations.

Table A16.2 shows the mean value for both variables, along with the minimum, maximum and the standard deviation.

Figure 16.1 shows trading partner dyads in our sample that had bilateral services exports exceeding US$10 billion over 1999–2010. Looking at these export averages over 1999–2010, we find that 29 trading pairs (0.5 per cent of the 6095 dyads) had bilateral services exports in excess of US$10 billion, and, interestingly, more than half of these (18) had a services trade agreement in force in 2010.

Table 16.1 shows the decile distribution of (positive) bilateral services exports averaged over 1999–2010 and the existence of STAs. The top decile ($n = 385$, accounting for 6.3 per cent of all trading pairs in the sample) had an average services export value of US$3.7 billion; nearly half of these dyads had a services trade agreement in force in 2010. Table 16.1 also suggests that the distribution of bilateral services exports over 1999–2010 was highly skewed with the average for the top decile being more than 28 000 times greater than that of the last decile!

Significantly, as one goes down the deciles, the propensity to negotiate a services accord also declines, which highlights the endogenous relationship between these two variables. Bilateral services exports are also found to be 5.7 times greater amongst all dyads in our sample in the presence of a services accord than otherwise.

## D. Estimation issues

Our equations can be estimated log-linearly using ordinary least squares (OLS). However, this excludes the treatment of export zeros (as the log of zero is not defined), and the incidence of export zeros was fairly high in our data (44.4 per cent). Selection of the appropriate estimator in the presence of zeros is contingent on the process generating the error term. Following Head and Mayer (2013), we found our data to be characterised by a constant variance to mean ratio that suggested the use of the Poisson pseudomaximum likelihood (PPML) for inference. Importantly, PPML[10] estimates remain consistent in the presence of overdispersion, which was also true of our data (see Colin and Trivedi 2005, Santos Silva and Tenreyro 2006).

Unfortunately, PPML estimation with several high-dimensional fixed effects led to nonconvergence. This did not change even with the application of different workaround strategies suggested by Santos Silva and Tenreyro (2010).

Given the need for at least two-high dimensional fixed effects in estimating these equations, another possibility was to use the '2WFE' approach developed by Guimaraes and Portugal (2010). This allows for estimating linear regressions model with two high-dimensional fixed effects with minimal memory requirements. Head and Mayer (2013) find the 2WFE estimator to provide identical estimates to the least squares dummy variable (Harrigan, 1996) without being subject to arbitrary limits. They also recommend the 2WFE over other estimation strategies such as double-demeaning, Bonus Vetus OLS (Baier and Bergstrand 2009) and tetrads (Head, Mayer and Ries 2010). Thus, we estimated our equations log-linearly using the 2WFE estimator.

However, this strategy would work only at the intensive margin. To include export zeros in the 2WFE estimation, we followed the approach of Eaton and Kortum (2001) and assumed that there was a minimum level of services exports $\varepsilon$ such that when gravity-predicted $X_{ijt} < \varepsilon$, the observed value of services exports was zero. Although $\varepsilon$ is unknown, it

---

[10] The PPML advocates the use of a simple Poisson pseudomaximum likelihood because in the presence of heteroscedasticity in the data, the standard log-linearised gravity model yields inconsistent estimates (Santos Silva and Tenreyro 2006). 'An additional problem of log-linearisation is that it is incompatible with the existence of zeroes in trade data, which led to several unsatisfactory solutions, including truncation of the sample and further non-linear transformations of the dependent variable' (Santos Silva and Tenreyro 2006: 653).

Table 16.2 *Results (2WFE) from estimating Eq. (16.1) on positive exports*

| Dep var: ln $X_{ijt}$ | (1) All | (2) Only EU | (3) Only non-EU | (4) One EU |
|---|---|---|---|---|
| $STA_{ijt}$ | 0.128** | 0.428*** | −0.157* | 0.288*** |
|  | (0.041) | (0.046) | (0.077) | (0.050) |
| ATE | 13.7% | 53.4% | −14.5% | 33.4% |
| $N$ | 24 622 | 4 790 | 3 003 | 21 619 |
| df_m | 5 981 | 909 | 1 760 | 5 378 |
| $r^2$ | 0.968 | 0.978 | 0.996 | 0.963 |
| Fixed effects: |  |  |  |  |
| Year | Yes | Yes | Yes | Yes |
| Bilateral | Yes | Yes | Yes | Yes |
| Country-and-time | Yes | Yes | Yes | Yes |

*Note:* Robust standard errors reported in parentheses. ATE, average treatment effect.
# $p < 0.1$
* $p < 0.05$
** $p < 0.01$
*** $p < 0.001$

can be approximated by the minimum observed services exports for each destination market ($minX_j$).

Unlike the practice of adding an arbitrary constant to the export zeros, this approach is more intuitive as the minimum trade flow for a specific importer would tend to reflect differences in market size, competition and trade barriers, as well as reporting and measurement issues. The approach is also consistent with theory and does not require exclusion restrictions. Thus, the equations were also estimated log-linearly by replacing $X_{ijt}$ with ($X_{ijt} + minX_j$) to incorporate the export zeros in the analyses.

## E. Results

The intensive margin results are reported in Table 16.2. In this table, columns I–IV report results for four different samples: all, only-EU, only non-EU, at least one EU. The (services) trade effects range from 13.7 per cent[11] for the full sample to 53.4 per cent among the EU Member States. As in Shingal (2009), services accords did not seem to enhance bilateral services trade among the non-EU trading partners in the sample. On the other hand, even with only one of the partners being from the EU, the

---

[11] This is calculated as $\{\exp(\delta) - 1\}^* 100$, where $\delta$ is the coefficient on the STA variable.

Table 16.3 *Results (2WFE) from estimating Eq. (16.1) on all exports*

| Dep var:<br>ln $(X_{jt} + minX_j)$ | (1)<br>All | (2)<br>Only EU | (3)<br>Only non-EU | (4)<br>One EU |
|---|---|---|---|---|
| STA$_{ijt}$ | 0.149[#]<br>(0.089) | 0.232**<br>(0.086) | −0.035<br>(0.118) | 0.237*<br>(0.119) |
| ATE | 16.1% | 26.1% | −3.4% | 26.7% |
| N | 44 310 | 5 211 | 4 880 | 39 430 |
| df_m | 8 662 | 950 | 2 425 | 7 664 |
| $r^2$ | 0.946 | 0.939 | 0.990 | 0.942 |
| Fixed effects: | | | | |
| Year | Yes | Yes | Yes | Yes |
| Bilateral | Yes | Yes | Yes | Yes |
| Country-and-time | Yes | Yes | Yes | Yes |

*Note:* Robust standard errors reported in parentheses. ATE, average treatment effect.
[#] $p < 0.1$
* $p < 0.05$
** $p < 0.01$
*** $p < 0.001$

(services) trade effect again became positive and economically significant (33.4 per cent). Our intensive margin results are somewhat consistent with those found in the earlier services literature, but the trade effects are smaller than those of goods agreements (for instance, see Baier and Bergstrand 2007).

Table 16.3 reports the results from estimating Eq. (16.5) after incorporating the export zeros in the sample. One would expect these coefficients to have lower magnitudes compared to the baseline results as the regressions now incorporate zero export flows. However, the (services) trade effect for the complete sample seems to be enhanced now, though it is weakly significant. The effects for the EU are reduced, while those for the non-EU partners are statistically indifferent from zero.

The lagged effects of *STA* on trade for all sample countries are reported in Table 16.4. Like Baier and Bergstrand (2007), we too found the average treatment effect (ATE) to be accentuated by including such anticipation effects. These results show that the total ATE increases the further back in time one travels from the year of accession to the *STA*. This suggests that the maximum impact of a services accord may be felt the farthest in time from actual accession and that services agreements seem to have

Table 16.4 *Lagged effects of STAs for positive exports*

| Dep var: ln $X_{ijt}$ | (1) All | (2) All | (3) All | (4) All | (5) All | (6) All | (7) All | (8) All | (9) All | (10) All |
|---|---|---|---|---|---|---|---|---|---|---|
| $STA_{ijt}$ | 0.138** | 0.140** | 0.156*** | 0.169*** | 0.184*** | 0.194*** | 0.199*** | 0.206*** | 0.203*** | 0.206*** |
| | (0.042) | (0.043) | (0.044) | (0.044) | (0.045) | (0.045) | (0.046) | (0.046) | (0.046) | (0.047) |
| $STA_{ijt-1}$ | 0.101 | 0.105 | 0.137 | 0.161[#] | 0.197* | 0.218* | 0.229* | 0.246** | 0.240* | 0.246** |
| | (0.085) | (0.086) | (0.088) | (0.089) | (0.090) | (0.091) | (0.092) | (0.093) | (0.094) | (0.095) |
| $STA_{ijt-2}$ | | 0.018 | 0.055 | 0.081 | 0.117 | 0.143[#] | 0.157[#] | 0.177* | 0.169* | 0.177* |
| | | (0.074) | (0.076) | (0.078) | (0.079) | (0.082) | (0.083) | (0.084) | (0.086) | (0.087) |
| $STA_{ijt-3}$ | | | 0.163* | 0.190* | 0.232** | 0.257** | 0.272** | 0.294*** | 0.285** | 0.294** |
| | | | (0.078) | (0.080) | (0.082) | (0.084) | (0.085) | (0.087) | (0.089) | (0.091) |
| $STA_{ijt-4}$ | | | | 0.110 | 0.152* | 0.180* | 0.195* | 0.220** | 0.211* | 0.220** |
| | | | | (0.072) | (0.074) | (0.077) | (0.078) | (0.080) | (0.082) | (0.085) |
| $STA_{ijt-5}$ | | | | | 0.181* | 0.211** | 0.228** | 0.252** | 0.241** | 0.251** |
| | | | | | (0.077) | (0.080) | (0.082) | (0.084) | (0.086) | (0.090) |
| $STA_{ijt-6}$ | | | | | | 0.106 | 0.123 | 0.150[#] | 0.141[#] | 0.152[#] |
| | | | | | | (0.080) | (0.081) | (0.084) | (0.086) | (0.089) |
| $STA_{ijt-7}$ | | | | | | | 0.095 | 0.125 | 0.113 | 0.123 |
| | | | | | | | (0.096) | (0.098) | (0.101) | (0.104) |
| $STA_{ijt-8}$ | | | | | | | | 0.139 | 0.127 | 0.140 |
| | | | | | | | | (0.101) | (0.104) | (0.108) |

(cont.)

Table 16.4 (cont.)

| Dep var: ln $X_{ijt}$ | (1) All | (2) All | (3) All | (4) All | (5) All | (6) All | (7) All | (8) All | (9) All | (10) All |
|---|---|---|---|---|---|---|---|---|---|---|
| $STA_{ijt-9}$ | | | | | | | | | -0.052 (0.107) | -0.039 (0.111) |
| $STA_{ijt-10}$ | | | | | | | | | | 0.050 (0.117) |
| Total ATE | 14.8% | 15.0% | 37.6% | 43.2% | 157.5% | 188.6% | 207.4% | 303.5% | 285.4% | 303.1% |
| $N$ | 24 622 | 24 622 | 24 622 | 24 622 | 24 622 | 24 622 | 24 622 | 24 622 | 24 622 | 24 622 |
| df_m | 5 982 | 5 983 | 5 984 | 5 985 | 5 986 | 5 987 | 5 988 | 5 989 | 5 990 | 5 991 |
| $r^2$ | 0.968 | 0.968 | 0.968 | 0.968 | 0.968 | 0.968 | 0.968 | 0.968 | 0.968 | 0.968 |
| Fixed effects: | | | | | | | | | | |
| Year | Yes | Yes | Yes | Yes | Yes | Yes | Yes | Yes | Yes | Yes |
| Bilateral | Yes | Yes | Yes | Yes | Yes | Yes | Yes | Yes | Yes | Yes |
| Country-and-time | Yes | Yes | Yes | Yes | Yes | Yes | Yes | Yes | Yes | Yes |

*Note:* Robust standard errors reported in parentheses. Total ATE, sum of the STA coefficient estimates statistically significant at 5 per cent.

# $p < 0.1$
* $p < 0.05$
** $p < 0.01$
*** $p < 0.001$

a significant 'announcement effect'. This said, the respective coefficients retain statistical significance only up to five years preceding the year of accession. Thus, the estimates of the total ATE are arguably more meaningful until $t$ minus 5 and suggest a cumulative trade effect of 157.5 per cent. We also find the coefficients to be more economically significant three to five years preceding accession. Significantly, the (services) trade effect in the actual year of accession also increases monotonically with time with the inclusion of anticipation effects. Notably these effects are larger both compared to the results for services reported by Shingal (2009) and those for goods (Baier and Bergstrand 2007).

We also for the full sample include the export zeros. These (unreported) results lacked statistical significance in most cases.

## F. Conclusion

This chapter revisits the trade effect of services accords using an updated OECD database on bilateral services trade flows and following recent advancements in the literature on the estimation of structural gravity models. Countries are increasingly resorting to preferentialism and going beyond the WTO in making commitments in their PTAs. As mentioned in the introduction to this chapter, this trend has carried on to services as well, especially in the past decade. Given this surge in negotiating STAs, it is important to examine whether these agreements are actually resulting in greater services trade. Moreover, any positive trade effects are also expected to have knock-on effects in the economy leading to greater output and more trade. A neat treatment of such general equilibrium effects is provided by Egger and Nigai (Chapter 15 in this volume).

Unfortunately, the OECD data used in this chapter cover only two ways in which services are supplied: cross-border (mode 1) and consumption abroad (mode 2). Trade via commercial presence (mode 3), which accounts for more than a third of global services trade flows, is not covered in the OECD database. Given this limitation and the fact that much reciprocal services liberalization is aimed at facilitating commercial presence, it would also be useful to examine the results in this chapter by including bilateral data on foreign direct investment (FDI) in services.

The analysis undertaken in this chapter also treats the STA variables as homogeneous, which does not take into account the varying extents of liberalization in different agreements. Baier, Bergstrand and Clance (Chapter 14 in this volume) suggest one useful way of heterogenising the PTA variable.

## Table A16.1 *Sample countries*

**Exporters:** Australia, Austria, Belgium, Canada, Chile, Czech Republic, Germany, Denmark, Spain, Estonia, Finland, France, United Kingdom, Greece, Hong Kong, Hungary, Ireland, Iceland, Israel, Italy, Japan, South Korea, Luxembourg, Mexico, the Netherlands, Norway, New Zealand, Poland, Portugal, Russia, Slovakia, Slovenia, Sweden, Turkey, United States

**Importers:** Aruba, Afghanistan, Angola, Anguilla, Albania Andorra, Netherlands Antilles, United Arab Emirates, Argentina, Armenia, American Samoa, Antarctica, French Southern Territories, Antigua and Barbuda, Australia, Austria, Azerbaijan, Burundi, Belgium, Benin, Burkina Faso, Bangladesh, Bulgaria, Bahrain, Bahamas, Bosnia and Herzegovina, Belarus, Belize, Bermuda, Bolivia, Brazil, Barbados, Brunei Darussalam, Bhutan, Bouvet Island, Botswana, Central African Republic, Canada, Cocos (Keeling) Islands, Switzerland, Chile, China, Côte d'Ivoire, Cameroon, Democratic Republic of Congo, Congo, Cook Islands, Colombia, Comoros, Cape Verde, Costa Rica, Cuba, Christmas Island, Cayman Islands, Cyprus, Czech Republic, Germany, Djibouti, Dominica, Denmark, Dominican Republic, Algeria, Ecuador, Egypt, Eritrea, Spain, Estonia, Ethiopia, Finland, Fiji, Falkland Islands, France, Faroe Islands, Federated States of Micronesia, Gabon, United Kingdom, Georgia, Guernsey, Ghana, Gibraltar, Guinea, Gambia, Guinea-Bissau, Equatorial Guinea, Greece, Grenada, Greenland, Guatemala, French Guiana, Guam, Guyana, Hong Kong, Heard and McDonald Islands, Honduras, Croatia, Haiti, Hungary, Indonesia, Isle of Mann, India, British Indian Ocean Territory, Ireland, Iran, Iraq, Iceland, Israel, Italy, Jamaica, JEY Jordan, Japan, Kazakhstan, Kenya, Kyrgyzstan, Cambodia, Kiribati, St. Kitts and Nevis, South Korea, Kuwait, Lao PDR, Lebanon, Liberia, Libya, St. Lucia, Liechtenstein, Sri Lanka, Lesotho, Lithuania, Luxembourg, Latvia, Macau, Morocco, Moldova, Madagascar, Maldives, Mexico, Marshall Islands, Macedonia, Mali, Malta, Myanmar, Montenegro, Mongolia, Northern Mariana Islands, Mozambique, Mauritania, Montserrat, Mauritius, Malawi, Malaysia, Mayotte, Namibia, New Caledonia, Niger, Norfolk Island, Nigeria, Nicaragua, Niue, the Netherlands, Norway, Nepal, Nauru, New Zealand, Oman, Pakistan, Panama, Pitcairn, Peru, Philippines, Palau, Papua New Guinea, Poland, Puerto Rico, North Korea, Portugal, Paraguay, Palestine, French Polynesia, Qatar, Romania, Russia, Rwanda, Saudi Arabia, Serbia and Montenegro, Sudan, Senegal, Singapore, South Georgia and South S.S., St. Helena, Solomon Islands, Sierra Leone, El Salvador, San Marino, Somalia, Serbia, Sao Tome and Principe, Surinam, Slovakia, Slovenia, Sweden, Swaziland, Seychelles, Syria, Turks and Caicos Islands, Chad, Togo, Thailand, Tajikistan, Tokelau, Turkmenistan, Timor-Leste, Tonga, Trinidad and Tobago, Tunisia, Turkey, Tuvalu, Taiwan, Tanzania, Uganda, Ukraine, U.S. Minor Islands, Uruguay, United States, Uzbekistan, Holy See (Vatican), St. Vincent and the Grenadines, Venezuela Virgin Islands (British), Virgin Islands (U.S.), Vietnam, Vanuatu, Wallis & Futuna Islands, Samoa, Yemen, Yugoslavia, South Africa, Zambia, Zimbabwe

Table A16.2 *Summary statistics*

| Variable | Observations | Mean | SD | Min. | Max. |
|---|---|---|---|---|---|
| $STA_{ijt}$ | 44 322 | 0.13 | 0.34 | 0 | 1 |
| $STA_{ijt-1}$ | 44 322 | 0.01 | 0.10 | 0 | 1 |
| $STA_{ijt-2}$ | 44 322 | 0.01 | 0.10 | 0 | 1 |
| $STA_{ijt-3}$ | 44 322 | 0.01 | 0.10 | 0 | 1 |
| $STA_{ijt-4}$ | 44 322 | 0.01 | 0.11 | 0 | 1 |
| $STA_{ijt-5}$ | 44 322 | 0.01 | 0.11 | 0 | 1 |
| $STA_{ijt-6}$ | 44 322 | 0.01 | 0.10 | 0 | 1 |
| $STA_{ijt-7}$ | 44 322 | 0.01 | 0.09 | 0 | 1 |
| $STA_{ijt-8}$ | 44 322 | 0.004 | 0.07 | 0 | 1 |
| $STA_{ijt-9}$ | 44 322 | 0.004 | 0.06 | 0 | 1 |
| $STA_{ijt-10}$ | 44 322 | 0.003 | 0.05 | 0 | 1 |
| $STA_{ijt+1}$ | 44 322 | 0.002 | 0.05 | 0 | 1 |
| $STA_{ijt+2}$ | 44 322 | 0.002 | 0.04 | 0 | 1 |
| $STA_{ijt+3}$ | 44 322 | 0.002 | 0.05 | 0 | 1 |
| $STA_{ijt+4}$ | 44 322 | 0.002 | 0.05 | 0 | 1 |
| $STA_{ijt+5}$ | 44 322 | 0.002 | 0.05 | 0 | 1 |
|  | 44 322 | 385.1 | 2 068.7 | 0 | 63 564.5 |
| $\ln X_{ijt}$ | 24 622 | 3.8 | 2.6 | −13.8 | 11.1 |
| $X_{ijt} + minX_j$ | 44 322 | 385.5 | 2 068.6 | 0 | 63 564.5 |
| $\ln (X_{ijt} + minX_j)$ | 44 310 | 0.07 | 5.2 | −13.8 | 11.1 |

## References

Anderson, James, Milot, Catherine, and Yotov, Yoto. 2011. 'The Incidence of Geography on Canada's Services Trade.' NBER Working Paper No. 17630. National Bureau of Economic Research, Cambridge, MA.

Baier, Scott, and Bergstrand, Jeffrey. 2002. 'On the Endogeneity of International Trade Flows and Free Trade Agreements.' Unpublished manuscript, University of Notre Dame.

2004. 'Economic Determinants of Free Trade Agreements.' *Journal of International Economics* 64 (1): 29–63.

2007. 'Do Free Trade Agreements Actually Increase Members' International Trade?' *Journal of international Economics* 71 (1): 72–95.

2009. 'Bonus vetus OLS: A Simple Method for Approximating International Trade-Cost Effects Using the Gravity Equation.' *Journal of International Economics* 77 (1): 77–85.

Baldwin, Richard, and Harrigan, James. 2011. 'Zeros, Quality, and Space: Trade Theory and Trade Evidence.' *American Economic Journal: Microeconomics* 3 (2): 60–88.

Cameron, Colin, and Trivedi, Pravin. 2005. *Microeconometrics: Methods and Applications*. New York: Cambridge University Press.

Ceglowski, Janet. 2006. 'Does Gravity Matter in a Service Economy?' *Review of World Economics* 142 (2): 307–29.

Eaton, Jonathan, and Kortum, Samuel. 2001. 'Trade in Capital Goods.' *European Economic Review* 45 (7): 1195–235.

Egger, Hartmut, Egger, Peter, and Greenaway, David. 2008. 'The Trade Structure Effects of Endogenous Regional Trade Agreements.' *Journal of International Economics* 74 (2): 278–98.

Egger, Peter, and Larch, Mario, and Staub, Kevin. 2012. 'Trade Preferences and Bilateral Trade in Goods and Services: A Structural Approach.' CEPR Discussion Paper No. 9051. Centre for Economic Policy Research, London.

Egger, Peter, Larch, Mario, Staub, Kevin, and Winkelmann, Rainer. 2011. 'The Trade Effects of Endogenous Preferential Trade Agreements.' *American Economic Journal: Economic Policy* 3 (3): 113–43.

Grünfeld, Leo, and Moxnes, Andreas. 2003. 'The Intangible Globalization: Explaining the Patterns of International Trade in Services.' Working Paper No. 657. Norwegian Institute of International Affairs, Oslo.

Guimaraes, Paulo, and Portugal, Pedro. 2010. 'A Simple Feasible Procedure to Fit Models with High-Dimensional Fixed Effects.' *Stata Journal* 10 (4): 628–49.

Harrigan, James. 1996. 'Openness to Trade in Manufactures in the OECD.' *Journal of International Economics* 40 (1): 23–39.

Head, Keith, and Mayer, Thierry. 2013. 'Gravity Equations: Toolkit, Cookbook, Workhorse.' CEPII Working Paper No. 27. Centre d'Etudes Prospectives et d'Informations Internationales, Paris.

Head, Keith, Mayer, Thierry, and Ries, John. 2010. 'The Erosion of Colonial Trade Linkages After Independence.' *Journal of International Economics* 81 (1): 1–14.

Helpman, Elhanan, Melitz, Marc, and Rubinstein, Yona. 2008. 'Estimating Trade Flows: Trading Partners and Trading Volumes.' *Quarterly Journal of Economics* 123 (2): 441–87.

Kimura, Fukunari, and Lee, Hyun-Hoon. 2006. 'The Gravity Equation in International Trade in Services.' *Review of World Economics* 142 (1): 92–121.

Kox, Henk, and Lejour, Arjan. 2006. 'The Effects of the Services Directive on Intra-EU Trade and FDI.' *Revue Economique* 57 (4): 747–69.

Lennon, Carolina. 2008. 'Trade in Services and Trade in Goods: Differences and Complementarities.' WIIW Working Papers No. 53. Vienna Institute for International Economic Studies, Vienna.

Magee, Christopher. 2004. 'Endogenous Preferential Trade Agreements: An Empirical Analysis.' *Contributions in Economic Analysis and Policy* 2 (1): 1–17.

Marchetti, Juan. 2011. 'Do Economic Integration Agreements Lead to Deeper Integration of Services Markets?' In *International Handbook on the Economics of*

*Integration, Volume III: Factor, Mobility, Agriculture, Environment and Quantitative Studies*, edited by Miroslav Jovanovic, 435–54. Cheltenham, UK: Edward Elgar.

Mirza, Daniel, and Nicoletti, Giuseppe. 2004. 'What Is So Special about Trade in Services.' Research Paper No. 2. University of Nottingham, Nottingham.

Santos Silva, Joao, and Tenreyro, Silvana. 2006. 'The Log of Gravity.' *Review of Economics and Statistics* 88 (4): 641–58.

———. 2010. 'On the Existence of the Maximum Likelihood Estimates in Poisson Regression.' *Economics Letters* 107 (2): 310–12.

Sauvé, Pierre, and Shingal, Anirudh. 2011. 'Reflections on the Preferential Liberalization of Services Trade.' *Journal of World Trade* 45 (5): 953–63.

Shingal, Anirudh. 2009. 'How Much Do Agreements Matter for Services Trade?' Munich Personal RePEc Archive Paper 32815. http://mpra.ub.uni-muenchen.de/39436/1/MPRA_paper_39436.pdf.

Walsh, Keith. 2006. 'Trade in Services: Does Gravity Hold? A Gravity Model Approach to Estimating Barriers to Services Trade.' Institute for International Integration Studies Discussion Paper No. 183. Institute for International Integration Studies, Dublin.

# 17

---

# Trade agreements as protection from risk

JEFFREY KUCIK

## A. Introduction

How do governments protect themselves from global market risk? The costs and benefits of globalisation cannot be measured solely in terms of predictable changes in trade. Rather, *un*predictable changes – or volatility – in trade flows are also associated with high costs. As with any form of risk in the marketplace, volatility significantly dampens economic activity and reduces welfare. The adverse effects are felt at all levels of the market. In the aggregate, volatility destabilises exchange rates, inflates budget deficits and leads to more frequent and more extreme business cycles (Aizenman and Riera-Crichton 2008; Combes and Saadi-Sedik 2006). For individuals, it leads to decreases in wages and reduced job security (Scheve and Slaughter 2004). In general, domestic economies exposed to high levels of risk suffer many of the adverse welfare effects commonly linked to liberalisation (Blattman, IIwang and Williamson 2007).

In light of these costs, governments have strong incentives to insulate their markets from global economic risk. Recent research shows that preferential trade agreements (PTAs)[1] provide one form of insurance to states (Mansfield and Reinhardt 2008a). The core insight of this literature is that, by promoting the rule of international trade law, PTAs significantly reduce uncertainty in trade *policy*, which is a key source of market volatility. In the context of a more stable policy environment, members of trade agreements experience significantly less risk than nonmembers do.

The new attention being paid to PTAs represents an important departure from the existing literature on risk management. Previously, scholars focused on how governments combat volatility through compensation – that is, providing social insurance to offset the costs of market openness

---

[1] PTAs are defined as formal trade commitments in which the members grant reciprocal market access to one another. These include free trade areas as well as customs unions and partial scope accords.

(Katzenstein 1985; Rodrik 1997). Social insurance is designed (in part) to offset the deleterious effects of risk. The benefit of trade agreements, however, is that they provide states an opportunity to be proactive in combating risk. Unlike the literature on compensation, risk is not viewed as purely exogenous. Instead, states can use formal trade commitments to actively shape the amount of volatility they are likely to face.

This chapter refines our understanding of the conditions under which PTAs effectively insulate members from volatility. It does so by endogenising the role of institutional design. Existing work reveals a broad and robust relationship between PTAs and reduced volatility. However, that work does not test how this relationship depends crucially on specific features of the PTA contract. In practice, PTAs exhibit tremendous variation in the specific legal rules to which members commit (e.g. Johns, forthcoming). This variation is particularly noticeable in the design of dispute settlement systems (Smith 2000) and in the amounts of flexibility that PTAs afford members (Kucik 2012). I argue that this variation has important implications for whether PTAs reduce risk.

There are at least two ways PTAs may reduce volatility. First, simply by setting the 'rules of the game' PTAs prevent ad hoc policy shifts by trade partners. Under a PTA, it is less likely that governments will generate unpredictable changes in trade patterns by erecting unilateral, opportunistic entry barriers. Second, PTAs almost always provide members with some form of flexibility. Flexibility provisions allow members to protect their markets during 'hard times' by sealing off the portion of the domestic economy exposed to threatening foreign competition. Both of these mechanisms highlight the importance of the legal contract signed by states. However, they also implicate *different* features of those contracts. The first mechanism – tying the hands of the members – requires that an agreement has teeth. To prevent unilateral policy shifts, a PTA must have rules that enforce the rule of law, such as a system for dispute settlement. Alternatively, the second mechanism requires that the agreement provides some form of policy leeway to the members via the inclusion of flexibility. Thus, the two proposed channels through which PTAs reduce volatility ought to depend on the design of two different (though not mutually exclusive) features of the contract.

I test the relative strengths of these two mechanisms using original data on the design of 330 PTAs from 1970 to 2009. I find strong support for the importance of flexibility as a determinant of exposure to volatility. Allowing members to temporarily shirk their contractual obligations means that states are better able to insulate their markets from risk, measured as volatility in trade volumes. Conversely, tight constraints on the flexibility system limit members' abilities to utilise escape clauses and *increase* the volatility to which they are exposed. I further explore whether there is an interactive effect and find that the importance of dispute settlement is conditioned by the presence of flexibility provisions.

Note that this chapter does not test behavioural claims directly. I do not provide an analysis of whether specific design features shape the policy decisions of member states. Thus, the results cannot speak to whether particular design outcomes deter (or encourage) certain types of behaviours, such as safeguards or anti-dumping use. However, the results do identify the kinds of contracts that provide better insulation from market risk, all else equal.

## B. Background and theory

The dominant theories of trade preferences focus on how liberalisation exposes at least some portion of the marketplace to costly competition from foreign producers. This competition causes reductions in wages, raises unemployment and leads to eventual closure of firms in the industries that lose from free trade.[2] However, the politics of globalisation are not shaped solely by the predictable consequences of market liberalisation. Unforeseen shocks in the global economy have independent, and equally deleterious, effects on domestic markets.

Volatility in the volume (and in the price) of traded good is the subject of lengthy investigations by economists. Its adverse welfare effects – on states as well as on individuals – are myriad. Exposure to volatility places pressure on governments to spend more, thereby inflating budget deficits (Combes and Saadi-Sedik 2006). It also leads to more frequent, more severe booms and busts in the business cycle. Destabilised exchange rates are similarly linked to volatility (although exchange rate policy may itself be an additional way to hedge against risk) (Aizenman and Riera-Crichton 2008; Frieden 2002). Importantly, these market-wide effects have severe consequences for individuals. Uncertainty in the marketplace can lead to reductions in wages and job losses (Scheve and Slaughter 2004; Traca 2005).

---

[2] Predictions about the precise winners and losers from free trade vary depending on assumptions about the underlying structure of the domestic economy. The costs of trade liberalisation may be concentrated in specific industries or among specific factors of production. In either case, however, the dominant theories of trade preferences recognise that liberalization has adverse welfare consequences for at least some portion of the market.

More detailed descriptions of volatility can be found elsewhere.[3] Suffice it to say, governments ought to have strong incentives to protect their market from risk and its harmful consequences. One possible caveat is that some volatility in the marketplace may benefit certain economic actors. For example, depending on how it is measured, volatility may signal a sharp increase in exports, not just a spike in imports. Similarly, upward shocks in a country's terms of trade – the relative price of exports to imports – may benefit export-oriented firms, whereas downward movements disproportionately harm import-competing firms. As a result, the precise form (and direction) of volatility has targeted consequences.[4] However, in either case, uncertainty in the marketplace makes economic planning more difficult for all traded segments of the economy. Even if firms accrue temporary benefits from volatility, these will not be sustainable. In addition, those short-term gains have to be balanced against the adverse effects of risk, which are felt acutely by those who lose from it. Thus, I assume that, in the aggregate, volatility is welfare reducing.

It is important to point out that the work on PTAs and risk represents a break with the existing literature. Scholars previously focused exclusively on domestic policy strategies for combating volatility. Specifically, social insurance was thought to provide a viable way to insulate domestic markets from volatility (Cameron 1978; Katzenstein 1985; Rodrik 1997). However, recent literature casts doubt on this 'compensation hypothesis', especially in the developing world (Garen and Trask 2005; Rudra 2002, 2004). Developing countries are often handcuffed by acute shortages of the bureaucratic and material resources required to construct (and maintain) comprehensive social safety nets. By way of an alternative, the new research on PTAs shows that the global economy provides built-in mechanisms for risk reduction in the form of trade agreements.[5]

## I. How PTAs reduce risk

Fluctuations in trade levels may come from anything that affects the prices of traded goods or the volumes of trade conducted. Importantly, volatility can result from deliberate policy changes by trade partners. In practice,

---

[3] Useful discussions can be found in Kim (2007) and Mansfield and Reinhardt (2008b), among other places.

[4] See Kucik (2012) for a discussion of the specific sources of risk facing the different traded sectors of the domestic economy.

[5] That is not to say that PTAs are a perfect substitute for social insurance. They serve very different purposes and, not coincidentally, combat risk in unique ways.

one of the primary sources of volatility in trade levels is volatility in trade *policy*. Unilateral, ad hoc policy shifts directly influence the prices of goods and, by extension, demand for those goods. For example, introducing new trade barriers – whether in the form of a tariff or a nontariff barrier – shifts demand away from imported goods[6] and adversely affects exporters in partner countries. In addition, trade barriers deflect goods to other markets, which creates spikes in imports as these goods 'seek a new home'.

Note that we typically assume most states in the global economy are price takers rather than price makers. By implication, small markets may erect trade barriers without having much of an effect (if any) on either the prices or volumes of trade. This assumption is certainly true when looking at the global economy as a whole, where only a few states enjoy market power. However, when talking about trade between specific PTA members, relative market power is always at play (Bagwell and Staiger 2006). In practice, PTA partners are likely to have market power over one another in at least some goods, hence the formation of the agreement in the first place. As a result, the entry barriers that PTA partners introduce are likely to generate the costs associated with volatility, even between small states.

The corollary is that limits on the policy autonomy of trading states can significantly reduce the frequency and severity of trade shocks. This is precisely the logic underlying the idea that trade institutions reduce risk. By imposing the rule of law on member states, institutions prevent volatility-generating policy shifts. The implication is that, perhaps counterintuitively, deeper market liberalisation through the formation of PTAs leads to *less* risk.

Previous work proposes at least two channels through which PTAs reduce members' uncertainty over one another's trade policies, both relating to promoting the rule of international trade law.[7] The first of these is directly related to placing constraints on members' policy. Simply put, PTAs tie members' hands to their liberalising commitments. PTAs, by virtue of the fact that they represent a contract between trade partners, help specify the legally permissible boundaries of trade policy (Finlayson and Zacher 1981). In contrast to a scenario without an agreement, having

---

[6] This assumes that demand is elastic.
[7] Work by Mansfield and Reinhardt (2008a) highlights an additional mechanism, which is the transparency built into the agreement (and the extent to which agreements lead to harmonisation in member-state policy). However, it is not clear how to measure transparency as an independent dimension of agreement design. Having well-specified systems of dispute settlement and flexibility – the focus of this chapter – ought itself to be a transparency-enhancing feature of the contract.

an institution, even if it is a comparatively shallow commitment, ought to make members at least marginally more confident in their trade partners' policies. Thus, specifying the rules of the game provides a measuring stick against which the behaviour of members can be judged. This feature of institutions – setting the rules and thereby making it easier to identify defection – should reduce states' incentives to enact costly policy changes (Abbott *et al.* 2000).

Importantly, PTAs do not need to liberalise trade much in order for them to tie members' hands. Indeed, while economists find that PTAs have significant trade-liberalising effects (Baier and Bergstrand 2007), work in political science notes that foreign policy, as distinct from incentives to trade, often drives agreement formation (Mansfield and Bronson 1997). In particular, some PTAs are formed to advance a national security agenda rather than a purely economic one. In these cases, the agreement may be less concerned with trade liberalisation. Yet, regardless of whether trade agreements generate new trade, they ought to deter fluctuations in trade policy. The ulterior motives of members do not necessarily imply poor implementation or low compliance; the PTA is still important to the member states, be it for economic or foreign policy reasons.

Of course, there is an assumption embedded in this logic that members do not simply flout the agreements into which they enter. There are a variety of reasons to think that PTAs may not actually be able to enforce the rules they establish. For example, time inconsistency problems are known to threaten compliance with any international treaty commitment or organisation (Koremenos 2005). Moreover, even well-intentioned PTAs may be poorly implemented as a result of capacity shortages among the members (or lack of political will) (Gray 2014). In either case, the mere presence of a PTA may be insufficient to constrain states' policy autonomy.

However, there is neither theoretical nor empirical support for these challenges. To begin with, it is important to point out that PTAs are voluntary, not mandatory. It is not obvious why states would form agreements that they intend to wholly ignore. Indeed, nonrandom selection into PTAs is an argument *in favour* of their efficacy – states should be joining only agreements with which they intend to comply. As a result, the contract ought to exert some nonzero influence on the policy decisions of the membership.[8] Evidence on the use of entry barriers supports this claim.

---

[8] I later highlight that these concerns with the 'strength' of PTAs bias against finding any support for the hypotheses. Thus, the possibility that PTAs do very little to tie members' hands results in a more conservative test.

Partners in trade agreements are significantly less likely to impose new barriers against one another (Busch, Raciborski and Reinhardt 2008).

The second channel through which PTAs reduce risk is flexibility. Agreement designers cannot hope to contract around all the possible contingencies that may occur over the life span of an agreement. Instead, flexibility provisions are built into agreements to permit escape when the costs of liberalisation are prohibitively high (Koremenos 2005; Rosendorff 2005). Flexibility provides members the opportunity to erect temporary entry barriers during 'hard times' – that is, when the domestic market is exposed to shocks in trade prices or volumes. The most prominent and widely used example of flexibility is anti-dumping. When states are exposed to abnormally low-priced imports, they may enforce an anti-dumping action by temporarily restricting trade in the affected goods.

The use of anti-dumping in particular is a source of debate among trade economists who disagree about the welfare effects of this 'new protectionism' (Bown 2011; Zanardi 2004). However, flexibility provisions are, in theory, an effective way to reduce risk by essentially allowing member states to retreat from their contractual obligations to liberalise. By (partially) sealing off specific trade flows, flexibility insulates the domestic market from shocks in the global economy. Moreover, a crucial aspect of flexibility provisions is their legal nature. Escape clauses are conceptually distinct from the kinds of entry barriers one could cite as defection. Instead, they are legally permissible avenues through which members can shirk their obligations *without violating the agreement* (Rosendorff and Milner 2001). This implies that flexibility provisions, when invoked within the context of an agreement, should be more predictable and acceptable to the membership. By extension, flexibility use ought not to lead to retaliation among trade partners in the wake of escape.

Of course, flexibility itself has targeted costs and benefits. For example, using safeguards or anti-dumping can be effective in reducing the risks to which import-competing firms are exposed, such as surges in import volumes (or declines in foreign prices). Conversely, given that flexibility effectively reduces market access between states, it is a suboptimal policy for the export-dependent sector. I do not test the sector-specific effects of design in this chapter. Rather, I am chiefly concerned with variation in agreements and the net impact that variation has on aggregate volatility.

Thus, there are two main channels through which PTAs reduce risk: tying members' hands and permitting flexibility. In existing research, both of these mechanisms are grouped under one core feature of trade agreements: strengthening the rule of law (Mansfield and Reinhardt 2008b). Tying the hands of the membership requires that agreements impose a system of rules and regulations. Moreover, permitting escape is effective precisely because flexibility provisions are officially recognised, mutually agreed upon, legalised ways to shirk one's obligations. Note that although the law itself matters in both cases, these two mechanisms highlight two very different features of the law.

## II. The importance of design

A growing literature shows that PTAs exhibit tremendous variation in the design of their rules (e.g. Dür, Baccini and Elsig 2014; Jo 2008). This variation is distinct from the 'depth' of the agreement – that is, the different levels of liberalisation to which members commit (Johns, forthcoming). Agreements also differ in the precise rules included in the contract. For example, some agreements include provisions for the protection of labour, human, intellectual property rights or a combination of these, whereas others do not. Drawing on the arguments laid out in the previous section, I theorise that this variation in the rules has crucial implications for whether PTAs reduce risk.

As mentioned previously, the first mechanism proposed in the literature suggests that agreements can effectively tie the hands of their members, reducing the likelihood that states change their trade policies in an unpredictable manner. I argue that in order for an agreement to deter this form of unilateralism it must be able to generate some nonzero cost for defection. One way in which PTAs can do this is by formalising the settlement of trade disputes.

Enforcement problems are endemic in international institutions. There is persistent debate over the extent to which 'institutions matter', defined as whether they can compel members to pursue policy choices they would not have selected otherwise. Enforcement problems are common to all areas of global governance, but they are arguably less problematic in the context of trade, where formal systems of dispute settlement help deter defection. This is because dispute settlement mechanisms generate costs for the defector (Reinhardt 2002). To begin with, litigation itself consumes time as well as legal and bureaucratic resources. States wishing to avoid these expenditures ought to be more likely to comply. In addition, even if states can easily absorb the costs of litigation, there are reputational costs associated with losing a case. Being sued in an international court, particularly if the respondent loses, sends signals to international and domestic audiences that a government has been noncompliant. Recent work shows that these costs can be significant and that states have incentives to avoid them (Chaudoin, forthcoming). Indeed, these costs are an important driving force behind the high frequency of early (out-of-court) settlements in the World Trade Organization (WTO). Thus, agreements with dispute settlement mechanisms ought to foster greater stability in members' policies. The costs of being sued ought to deter defection in the first place.

However, it is not sufficient to have a dispute settlement mechanism of any type. These mechanisms vary tremendously in the specificity of their rules (Jo 2008; Smith 2000), and this variation matters for risk. Some agreements only specify a process for consultations, whereas others create standing courts with binding authority. I argue that, on average, the efficacy of the dispute settlement mechanism ought to increase in the legalisation of the mechanism. In the following analysis, I expand on Smith (2000) by coding agreements for specific features related to how costly dispute settlement is likely to be. These include, for exam-ple, whether the rules are binding, whether retaliation is authorised and whether there is a formal process for judging implementation of rul-ings (see later discussion). These traits all help give dispute settlement mechanisms 'teeth'. Rather than just specifying a process for consultation or arbitration, having rules relating to the implementation of decisions makes dispute settlement (and its costs) more tangible for states.

Taken together, this logic leads to the prediction that:

> *Hypothesis 1: Members are exposed to less volatility when their agreements include highly legalised systems of dispute settlement.*

The second mechanism – permitting escape – is equally contingent on agreement design. Not all agreements explicitly regulate the use of flexi-bility provisions. For example, 24 per cent of all agreements in the sample either do not mention anti-dumping or do not place any constraints on its use. Those that do place constraints on escape vary significantly. The kinds of rules relating to flexibility are numerous, but the most common ones include limits on the size of the entry barrier a state may put in place as well as the permitted duration. Other common rules relate to manner in which a state demonstrates that dumping has occurred[9] and whether anti-dumping enforcements are eligible for dispute settlement. Similar rules exist relating to safeguards and countervailing duties, which are the other two most commonly invoked escape clauses.

---

[9] Indeed, calculating harm (or the threat thereof) is tremendously controversial and has itself been the subject of several disputes under the World Trade Organization – namely, the disputes relating to the US practice of 'zeroing'.

The presence or absence of these constraints ought to matter. Agreements that include more highly legalised systems of flexibility, by definition, place more burdensome constraints on the membership (Kucik 2012). In short, having more rules implies that the flexibility system is 'harder' to use. This is because requiring, for example, that members demonstrate material injury from dumped goods generates a nonzero cost for the state wishing to escape. In the same way, limiting the severity of temporary entry barriers reduces states' abilities to use flexibility as a substitute for traditional tariff barriers. As a result, states ought to have a more difficult time insulating themselves from risk if the process for invoking a flexibility provision is lengthier, costlier and more legally burdensome.

*Hypothesis 2: Members are exposed to more volatility when their agreements include highly legalised flexibility provisions.*

This second hypothesis raises an important question: why do we observe flexible contracts if they are associated with greater volatility? Existing work shows that a large number of factors are relevant to the formation of PTAs, including political competition between domestic interest groups with conflicting views over agreement design. This chapter does not offer an analysis of formation (other than to correct for nonrandom selection). Instead, it considers the net effects of different design outcomes on aggregate volatility levels. However, it is certainly true that designers are aware of the distributional effects of their decisions when forming contracts. In practice, agreements are not shaped solely by negotiations between prospective members but also by negotiations within each state. These political compromises have important implications for design; states may be able to justify a new agreement to domestic interest groups only if, for example, they build flexibility into the contract as a promise for future protection during hard times. Whether these compromises are good or bad in terms of exposure to volatility is precisely the question of this analysis.

In sum, the existing literature identifies two channels through which PTAs insulate member markets: tying hands and permitting escape. I argue that the effectiveness of these two mechanisms depends crucially on the design of the agreement. While they are not necessarily mutually exclusive, tying hands requires a more legalised agreement, whereas flexibility requires a less legalised one. I test the relative strengths of these two features of PTAs in the remainder of the chapter.

In the following analysis, I also explore whether there is a multiplicative effect. The different elements of PTA design are not chosen in a vacuum.

Instead, we can view dispute settlement and flexibility as two pieces of a larger system of checks and balances within the agreement. For example, states might be willing to concede to greater levels of contractual flexibility if there is also a highly legalised system of dispute settlement to prevent abuse. As a result, these design decisions go hand in hand and are likely to have consequential effects on volatility levels, since they will shape states' underlying incentives to abide by the contract. I explore this relationship in the analysis.

Before moving on to that analysis, it is important to recognise the competing perspectives. According to one view, dispute settlement and flexibility are not two independent dimensions of design but, rather, two elements of the same dimension. Important work in this area, most notably Rosendorff (2005), discusses the World Trade Organization's dispute settlement mechanism as a key feature of flexibility within the regime. In theory, it may be a valid interpretation of dispute settlement to consider it a feature of the broader 'rigidity' of an international trade agreement. However, in the context of risk reduction, there are strong reasons to expect that dispute settlement and flexibility provisions have very different implications for volatility. For those reasons, which I have attempted to clarify, I argue that these two features of agreement design are best measured independently. I describe that process in the following section.

## C. Data and variables

I construct a dyadic data set that includes one observation for each country $i$ with trade partner $j$ for every year $t$ from 1970 to 2010. The data include bilateral trade flows in order to measure volatility as well as data on PTA design taken from Kucik (2012).

### I. Dependent variables

Mansfield and Reinhardt (2008a) published the foundational work in this area, and they provide a lengthy discussion of the various ways in which volatility in trade flows can be measured. Like that paper, this analysis focuses on volatility in exports for the reasons specified earlier. I report tests using the main measure from that paper, which is the simple year-to-year change in exports calculated as follows:

$$Volatility_{i,j,t} = \ln(Exports_{i,j,t}) - \ln(Exports_{i,j,t-1}) \qquad (17.1)$$

where exports from state $i$ to $j$ are logged to account for the highly skewed nature of bilateral trade flows. All economic indicators in this analysis are measured in constant year 2000 US dollars. The measure is an absolute value of the yearly difference because the theory is chiefly concerned with unpredictability in trade flows, not with the direction of that volatility per se.

This measure captures changes in export levels over time. I describe the results when using an alternative measure of volatility, which is the change in state $i$'s share of state $j$'s market. However, this alternative does not correct for exogenous changes in the size of state $j$'s market. The measure of market share may therefore change in a way that does not indicate any real shift in the trade among dyads. Given this ambiguity, volatility in levels is the principal measure used in the analysis.

## II. Explanatory variables

The analysis begins by using a simple dichotomous indicator of where countries $i$ and $j$ share a PTA in year $t$. That indicator, $PTA_{i,j,t}$, ought to be negatively associated with $Volatility_{i,j,t}$. The purpose of including this preliminary variable is to provide a rough replication of Mansfield and Reinhardt (2008a) from which to extend the analysis of design that follows.

Of course, the dichotomous indicator of PTA membership masks any underlying variation in the design of the agreement. To test my hypotheses directly, I construct two measures of PTA design. The first captures the level of legalisation of the dispute settlement mechanism. It extends the coding first put forward by Smith (2000) through all the agreements in this sample. Smith's coding is a widely cited and theoretically sound basis for measuring the sophistication of an agreement's dispute settlement system. Its main strength is the inclusion of indicators of the kinds of parties that have access to the system and, importantly, whether any decisions made under the system are binding on the membership.

I take this coding slightly further by adding two more components to Smith's (2000) list. These are (1) whether there is a formal process for the implementation of any rulings and (2) whether retaliation can be authorised by the dispute settlement body. These two components help indicate whether the dispute settlement process has the potential to sanction respondents that lose cases. One can imagine that states might ignore rulings even if the dispute settlement understanding claims to have binding effect. In the event that members do not abide by rulings, a formal system of implementation provides an additional process of oversight by

Table 17.1 *Components of design measures*

| |
|---|
| Dispute settlement score |
| 1. Third-party review (whether there is a right to an appeal) |
| 2. Third-party rulings (whether the ruling is binding) |
| 3. Judges (whether there is a standing tribunal) |
| 4. Standing (access by states, treaty organs and individuals) |
| 5. Remedy (whether there is direct effect in domestic law) |
| 6. Implementation (whether there is a formal process for implementation) |
| 7. Retaliation (whether the body can authorise material sanction) |
| Rigidity score[a] |
| 1. Investigation is required for authorisation |
| 2. Action is eligible for dispute settlement |
| 3. State must demonstrate injury |
| 4. Limit on size of the measure |
| 5. Limit on duration of the measure |

*Note: Dispute Settlement$_{i,j,t}$* is an extension of Smith (2000). *Rigidity$_{i,j,t}$* is described in greater detail in Kucik (2012).
[a] All five are coded for anti-dumping, safeguards and countervailing duties.

which states can judge whether respondents change offending policies. Similarly, establishing that arbitrators can officially sanction retaliation adds real material consequences to losing a dispute. Thus, I argue that both of these components of the dispute settlement system are valuable additions to any consideration of agreement design.

The second measure gauges the constraints placed on each PTA's flexibility system. This variable is taken from Kucik (2012), where its construction is discussed at length. In short, the data code five individual traits of the three most commonly invoked flexibility provisions – anti-dumping, safeguards and countervailing duties. As mentioned previously, the most frequent and most important constraints on escape clause use include such aspects as clearly defined limits on the size and duration of any new entry barriers.

The specific features of both measures are listed in Table 17.1. All PTAs in the sample are assigned either a 0 or a 1 for the absence or presence of the individual design features listed. I then create an index measure via a simple sum across all of the indicators. The range of *Dispute Settlement$_{i,j,t}$* is from 0 to 7 with a mean of 2.72. The range of *Flexibility$_{i,j,t}$* is from 0 to 15 with a mean of 7.33. There is rich variation across both measures, as illustrated in Figure 17.1. Note in Figure 17.1 that there are

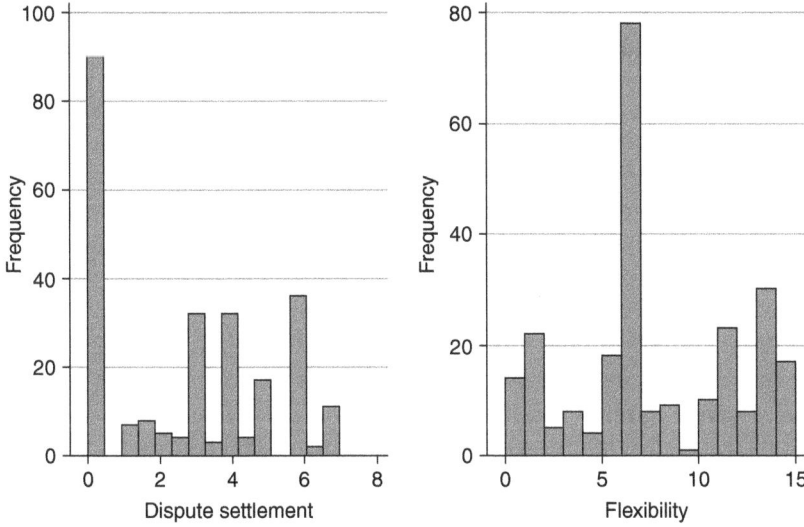

**Figure 17.1**    Distribution of design scores

two peaks in both histograms. It turns out that, in spite of significant differences across the sample of agreements, many PTAs share similar features for a variety of reasons. One of these reasons is the growing trend towards adoption of the rules as they are laid out in the World Trade Organization. A large of number of agreements formed in the past decade adopt wholesale at least some features of the WTO's rules relating to flexibility. Second, there are strong similarities in the agreements signed by clusters of countries. Former Soviet countries as well as European Union (EU) Member States tend to have PTAs that include very similar rules. As a result, we see some clustering around particular design scores in the sample.

Before moving on, note that based on these constructions the dispute settlement indicator ought to be negatively associated with volatility. The escape clause indicator, since it measures *constraints* on flexibility, ought to be positively associated with volatility.

### III. Control variables

The models include a variety of controls designed to capture traits of the individual state or dyad that may confound the relationship between PTA design and volatility. First, I include the per capita incomes of both states in the dyad measured as logged annual gross domestic product (GDP) divided by population ($Income_{i,t}$ and $Income_{j,t}$). Wealthier countries may have more diverse markets or trade more high-end goods that are less susceptible (or prone) to uncertainty in the marketplace. I include an indicator of whether both countries in the dyad are democracies. This variable, $Democratic\ Dyad_{i,j,t}$, is coded as 1 in years in which both members of the dyad have Polity IV scores of 6 or higher. Democratic countries are known to trade more, and the sheer volume of trade may affect volatility. I also include an indicator of state $i$'s overall trade openness ($Openness_{i,t}$) to directly capture how vulnerable a market might be to volatility. This is measured as the sum of exports and imports over GDP.

Also, alternative policy mechanisms might affect the amount of volatility to which a state is exposed. One of these is the exchange rate regime that a given country has in place. More fixed exchange rate commitments ought to help insulate the market against risk. I control for state $i$'s exchange rate regime based on the International Monetary Fund (IMF)'s official classification scheme ($Fixed\ Rate_{i,t}$). Finally, I include a lagged dependent variable since there is likely to be a significant amount of correlation in volatility over time.

## D. Analysis and results

I now test the validity of my hypotheses. To preview the results, there is strong evidence that flexibility has the predicted effect on volatility. When agreements place constraints on the use of escape clauses such as anti-dumping, it is significantly harder for states to protect their markets from risk. We therefore see a robust negative relationship between flexibility and volatility. Dispute settlement mechanisms, on the contrary, do not exert a significant independent effect. However, the interaction of the two reveals an interesting conditional relationship, suggesting that enforcement via dispute settlement *is important* for highly flexible agreements. These results are robust to a variety of specifications and estimation techniques.

### I. Models 1–5: does design affect volatility?

The first set of tests identifies a broad relationship between design and volatility. Before considering the estimates, it is important to note that there is likely to be a great deal of unobserved heterogeneity across dyads in the sample. Failing to account for this variation leads to less demanding tests and a higher likelihood of finding artificially significant estimates.

The data also exhibit traits common to pooled panel data. Specifically, a Breusch–Pagan test confirms the presence of heteroscedasticity, and a Wooldridge test rejects the null hypothesis of no first-order error correlation. To help account for the unobserved heterogeneity, all the models include dyad fixed effects.[10] To tackle the additional problems with the data, I cluster the standard errors by dyad ID. These modifications have the added benefit of helping ensure that the large number of observations in the sample is not driving the results. The general form of the baseline model is as follows:

$$Volatility_{i,j,t} = \beta_0 + \beta_1 PTADesign_{i,j,t} + \beta_2 Z_{i,j,t} + \alpha_{i,j} + \mu_{i,j} \quad (17.2)$$

where $Z_{i,j,t}$ represents a vector of controls, $\alpha_{i,j}$ represents dyad fixed effects and $\mu_{i,j}$ is the clustered error term.

Model 1 confirms the finding in the existing literature that PTAs (of all types) reduce risk (Table 17.2). First, note that the control variables behave largely as expected. For example, countries with fixed exchange rate regimes are exposed to less volatility. Moreover, wealthier nations face less risk, which may be a result of underlying traits of their markets, as mentioned previously. Turning to the main explanatory variable, the difference between being a PTA member and being a nonmember represents an 8 per cent reduction in volatility from 0.797 [0.792, 0.800] to 0.748 [0.728, 0.768].[11] States that are members of PTAs enjoy significantly more stable bilateral trade relationships.

Model 1 provides a firm empirical foundation for looking more closely at design. Models 2 and 3 show the independent effects of dispute settlement design and the rigidity of the escape clause system, respectively (Table 17.2). They reveal that these two features of design are associated with very different levels of risk reduction. In model 2, the sign on *Dispute Settlement*$_{i,j,t}$ is positive, as predicted, but it does not achieve conventional levels of statistical significance. Unsurprisingly, the substantive effect is modest. An increase in dispute settlement legalisation from the 10th to the 90th percentile of the range causes a 3 per cent drop in volatility from 0.744 [0.691, 0.798] to 0.730 [0.694, 0.765]. Contrast this finding with the substantive effect of a comparable move in *Flexibility*$_{i,j,t}$. According to the model 3 estimates, an increase in the constraints on escape clause

---

[10] The estimates remain the same when including year dummies as well. However, I omit those variables from the baseline models.

[11] The figures given in square brackets are the 95 per cent confidence intervals around the point prediction.

Table 17.2 *Baseline results*

| Model variables | (1) | (2) | (3) | (4) | (5) |
|---|---|---|---|---|---|
| $PTA_{i,j,t}$ | −0.048** | | | | |
| | (0.021) | | | | |
| Dispute Settlement$_{i,j,t}$ | | −0.015 | | −0.032** | −0.049** |
| | | (0.009) | | (0.010) | (0.012) |
| Flexibility$_{i,j,t}$ | | | 0.022** | 0.028** | −0.004 |
| | | | (0.006) | (0.006) | (0.008) |
| Interaction$_{i,j,t}$ | | | | | 0.007** |
| | | | | | (0.002) |
| Democratic Dyad$_{i,j,t}$ | −0.037** | −0.051** | −0.058** | −0.054** | −0.054** |
| | (0.007) | (0.016) | (0.017) | (0.017) | (0.017) |
| Income$_{i,t}$ | −0.182** | −0.211** | −0.211* | −0.205** | −0.203** |
| | (0.016) | (0.035) | (0.036) | (0.036) | (0.037) |
| Income$_{j,t}$ | −0.093** | −0.136** | −0.145** | −0.137** | −0.136 |
| | (0.003) | (0.036) | (0.037) | (0.038) | (0.038) |
| Openness$_{i,t-1}$ | −0.003 | 0.007 | 0.005 | 0.005 | 0.005 |
| | (0.003) | (0.006) | (0.005) | (0.005) | (0.005) |
| Fixed Rate$_{i,t-1}$ | −0.010** | −0.007 | −0.008 | −0.006 | −0.006 |
| | (0.002) | (0.006) | (0.006) | (0.006) | (0.006) |
| Volatility$_{i,j,t-1}$ | 0.175** | 0.151** | 0.150** | 0.151** | 0.150** |
| | (0.004) | (0.012) | (0.015) | (0.012) | (0.012) |
| Constant | 2.833** | 3.277** | 3.248 | 3.212** | 3.252** |
| | (0.102) | (0.244) | (0.249) | (0.251) | (0.250) |
| Observations | 242 486 | 40 630 | 41 594 | 39 872 | 39 872 |
| $R^2$ | 0.19 | 0.20 | 0.19 | 0.20 | 0.20 |

*Note:* Robust standard errors in parentheses.
* $p < 0.050$
** $p < 0.001$

use results in a 21 per cent increase from 0.642 [0.608, 0.674] to 0.773 [0.735, 0.811]. Thus, the design of the flexibility system is associated with a much more substantial drop in volatility. Agreements that permit freer invocation of the flexibility systems appear to better insulate the domestic economy.

Models 2 and 3 estimate the effects of dispute settlement and flexibility separately. Model 4 includes both measures in an effort to compare their relative strengths. When included in the same model, both retain the predicted signs and both are highly significant. Note that the two measures

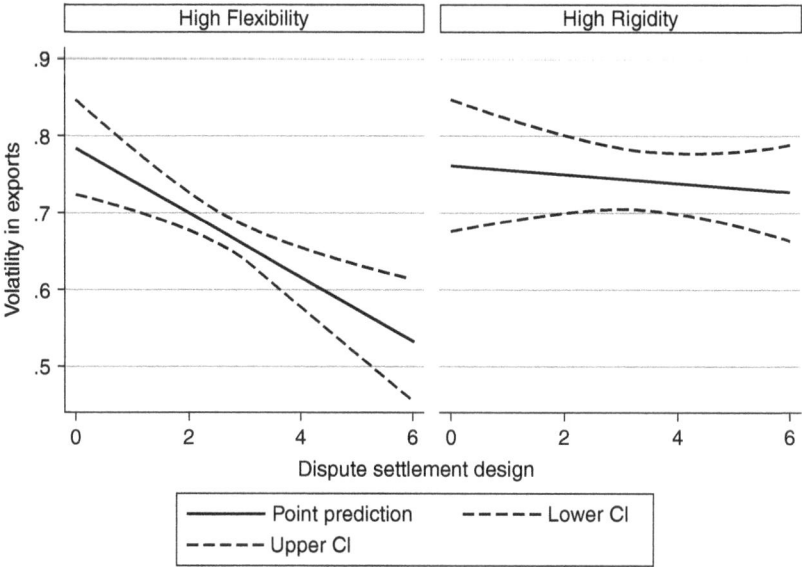

**Figure 17.2**   Substantive effects for model 5

do not appear to be collinear as the correlation between them is a modest 0.28. Moreover, recall the strong theoretical reasons to differentiate these two elements of design. It is therefore unlikely that they capture the same underlying theoretical dimension.

Turning to the estimates, the substantive effects are comparable to the previous models. The same move in dispute settlement legalisation results in a decrease from 0.804 [0.744, 0.864] to 0.771 [0.731, 0.811], or a 3.5 per cent reduction. A similar shift in flexibility results in an increase from 0.630 [0.595, 0.664] to 0.801 [0.759, 0.842]. In spite of the change in significance level of the dispute settlement indicator, these estimates are broadly consistent with models 2 and 3. Flexible agreements benefit members by providing a viable strategy for protecting the market.

Since both features of design show up as significant in model 4 but point in opposite directions, I explore whether there is a multiplicative effect by including the interaction of *Dispute Settlement$_{i,j,t}$* and *Flexibility$_{i,j,t}$* in model 5. This interaction term will help specify the conditions under which different permutations of design outcomes affect volatility. The estimates are reported in Table 17.2. A close look at the multiplicative term reveals an interesting conditional relationship (Figure 17.2 illustrates this finding). The presence of a highly legalised dispute settlement system seems to matter much more in flexible agreements. When states are in highly flexible agreements (low values of the measure), an increasingly legalised dispute settlement system reduces volatility by 32 per cent from 0.784 [0.724, 0.845] to 0.535 [0.456, 0.614]. When agreements are more rigid, however, and states are limited in their abilities to invoke flexibility provisions, the effect of the dispute settlement mechanism is a more modest 11.5 per cent drop from 0.766 [0.693, 0.840] to 0.688 [0.629, 0.749].

This is potentially an intuitive but nevertheless important finding. Having well-specified limits on flexibility use may effectively deter use (and abuse) of escape clauses. For example, an agreement that stipulates the size of an anti-dumping measure that can be enforced ought to result in less disruptive flexibility use than an agreement containing no such restrictions. These more restrictive agreements, therefore, may have less use for a highly legalised system of dispute settlement. Conversely, when states commit to more flexible agreements, having a strong(er) enforcement mechanism becomes increasingly important. In the case of more flexibility arrangements, dispute settlement is relied on to ensure that escape does not occur unchecked.

## II. Model 6: selection bias

The existing work in this area does not find evidence of selection bias. However, it is clearly true that agreements are formed nonrandomly. The same factors that influence the design of a PTA may very well shape exposure to risk. Model 6 estimates a Heckman selection model to correct for any bias resulting from nonrandom selection.

To identify the system of equations, determinants of PTA formation unrelated to volatility have to exist. Selecting instruments is notoriously difficult, but the task is slightly easier in this case. A variety of factors can influence the strength of a dyad's political and economic ties without affecting risk directly. One of these is security alliances. Whether a state is 'friend or foe' is a strong predictor of the likelihood that countries form a PTA together (Gowa 1995). The close link between economic and foreign policy helps explain why a country such as the United States, to name one example, has PTAs with Oman and Jordan. I include $Alliance_{i,j,t}$, which is a dichotomous indicator of whether a dyad shares an alliance in year $t$. I also include a measure of the logged total trade within the dyad. This measure is different from trade openness, which may very well be related to the amount of risk facing a state. The total volume of *Bilateral Trade*$_{i,t-1}$ simply indicates the strength of the bilateral economic ties between countries. The outcome equation reads as follows:

$$Volatility_{i,j,t} = \beta_0 + \beta_1 \, PTA \, Design_{i,j,t} + \beta_2 Z_{i,j,t} + \mu_{i,j}, \quad (17.3)$$

and the selection equation reads as

$$PTA_{i,j,t} = \beta_0 + \beta_1 \, Alliance_{i,j,t} + \beta_2 \, BilateralTrade_{i,j,t} + \beta_3 Z_{i,j,t} + \varepsilon_{i,j}.$$
$$(17.4)$$

The model 6 estimates (Table 17.3) are consistent with those found in model 5. The rules relating to dispute settlement exert a strong influence in those agreements that include very few constraints on flexibility use. As a result, it does not appear that selection bias is contaminating the estimates. Instead, it appears as though there is a durable relationship between flexibility and volatility and in the prediction direction. Moreover, the relationship between dispute settlement and volatility is revealed when looking at the conditional relationship between these two distinct features of design.

### III. Additional robustness checks

Although the baseline model includes a measure of regime type, I conducted a split sample analysis to ensure that the results were not limited to democracies. Regime type is associated with market traits, such as greater trade openness, that are likely to shape risk. Moreover, democratic governments may be more interested in combating risk given its widespread welfare consequences. Nevertheless, the results of models 1–5 remain consistent when the sample is split. The results are similarly consistent when controls are added for Organisation for Economic Co-operation and Development (OECD) and EU membership, a dichotomous indicator for the pre-WTO era and year fixed effects.

The results are not fully consistent, however, when using one of the literature's alternative measures of volatility – change in state *i*'s share of state *j*'s market. When relying on this indicator, rigidity remains positive and significant when included alone (as in model 3) or with dispute settlement (as in model 4). However, all explanatory variables fall just short of conventional levels of statistical significance when including the interaction. As pointed out earlier, however, market share contains more

Table 17.3 *Heckman selection estimation*

| Model variables | (6) Selection $PTA_{i,j,t}$ | (6) Outcome volatility$_{i,j,t}$ |
|---|---|---|
| Dispute Settlement$_{i,j,t}$ | | −0.07*** |
| | | (0.002) |
| Flexibility$_{i,j,t}$ | | −0.004** |
| | | (0.002) |
| Interaction$_{i,j,t}$ | | 0.001*** |
| | | (0.000) |
| Democratic Dyad$_{i,j,t}$ | 0.270*** | 0.342*** |
| | (0.006) | (0.010) |
| Income$_{i,t}$ | −0.117*** | −0.126*** |
| | (0.002) | (0.003) |
| Income$_{j,t}$ | −0.118*** | −0.103*** |
| | (0.002) | (0.003) |
| Openness$_{i,t-1}$ | | −0.001 |
| | | (0.001) |
| Fixed Rate$_{i,t-1}$ | | −0.005** |
| | | (0.002) |
| Volatility$_{i,j,t-1}$ | | 0.093*** |
| | | (0.003) |
| Alliance$_{i,t-1}$ | 0.230*** | |
| | (0.006) | |
| Bilateral Trade$_{i,t-1}$ | 0.082*** | |
| | (0.001) | |
| Constant | 0.890*** | 0.093 |
| | (0.022) | (0.003) |
| Observations | 422 593 | |
| LR test | 7 640.1, 0.000 | |

*Note:* Robust standard errors in parentheses.
* $p < 0.050$
** $p < 0.001$

theoretical ambiguity than trade levels do. A state's share of a trade partner's market can change without dramatic shifts in exports. Therefore, levels are a more direct indicator of whether the bilateral trade relationship has changed for the worse.

## E. Conclusion

Overall, the results are broadly consistent across the various tests. They show that the risk-reducing benefits of PTA membership are, in practice, contingent on the design of the agreement. When PTAs place constraints on flexibility use, it is more difficult for states to protect their domestic interests, and, in turn, members experience significantly greater exposure to volatility. As stressed, the design of the dispute settlement mechanism does not exert a strong independent effect. Yet, there is an interesting conditional relationship. When exploring the interaction of these two design features, it becomes clear that a system of enforcement is highly important in the presence of flexibility. This implies that dispute settlement and flexibility are rationally designed as a system of complementary checks and balances.

These results have a number of interesting implications. First, the strong evidence that flexibility reduces risk helps clarify the kinds of agreements that are more or less efficacious. According to the evidence presented here, agreements that allow members to shirk their contractual obligations are significantly more likely to reduce volatility. This highlights the importance of contractual design. It also points to an additional benefit of flexibility use that must be considered when weighing the relative costs and benefits. Flexibility use is heavily criticised by a variety of trade economists. However, those discussions rarely include an account of risk.

Second, the findings seem to suggest that permitting defection is more beneficial to the membership. If so, that has implications for scholars interested in the extent to which international institutions foster cooperation. It must be reiterated that flexibility provisions are themselves legal instruments, and, as such, their use is distinct from defection through the unilateral imposition of entry barriers. The legally sanctioned nature of escape suggests that trade law is working to protect members' interests. This finding is not trivial. As we know from existing work, this ought to lower the costs of compliance and increase the likelihood of long-lasting cooperation (Kucik and Reinhardt, 2008).

Third, the negative association between *rigidity* and volatility teaches us something about the likely behavioural implications of design. Tighter constraints on flexibility use increase exposure to risk. This implies that states in more rigid agreements are, in practice, using flexibility less frequently to insulate their markets. We can hypothesise, as a result, that PTAs are effectively limiting the policy autonomy of their members. Of course, this claim remains to be tested in future research. Indeed, there are two important things that this chapter does not do. It does not provide direct tests of how design affects behaviour. There is a dearth of evidence on whether design outcomes actually shape states' policy choices in practice. The evidence provided here and elsewhere is only suggestive of that effect. Moreover, this chapter does not measure risk for economies *outside* the PTA. When a state introduces new entry barriers, those imports do not simply evaporate. Trade is deflected to other markets. As a result, flexibility use may benefit state *i* at the cost of *increasing* risk for others. Future work ought to consider these issues, as well as how forms of risk vary. A deeper account of how risk varies, and how its consequences are targeted to specific segments of the domestic market, will clarify the conditions under which PTAs benefit their members.

## References

Abbott, Kenneth W., Keohane, Robert O., Moravcsik, Andrew, Slaughter, Anne-Marie, and Snidal, Duncan. 2000. 'The Concept of Legalization.' *International Organization* 54:401–19.

Aizenman, Joshua, and Riera-Crichton, Daniel. 2008. 'Real Exchange Rate and International Reserves in an Era of Growing Financial and Trade Integration.' *Review of Economics and Statistics* 90:812–15.

Bagwell, Kyle, and Staiger, Robert W. 2006. 'Will International Rules on Subsidies Disrupt the World Trading System?' *American Economic Review* 96: 877–95.

Baier, Scott L., and Bergstrand, Jeffrey H. 2007. 'Do Free Trade Agreements Actually Increase Members' International Trade?' *Journal of International Economics* 71:72–95.

Blattman, Christopher, Hwang, Jason, and Williamson, Jeffrey G. 2007. 'Winners and Losers in the Commodity Lottery: The Impact of Terms of Trade Growth and Volatility in the Periphery 1870–1939.' *Journal of Development Economics* 82:156–79.

Bown, Chad P. 2011. 'Taking Stock of Antidumping, Safeguards and Countervailing Duties, 1990–2009.' *World Economy* 34:1955–98.

Busch, Marc L., Raciborski, Rafal, and Reinhardt, Eric. 2008. 'Does the Rule of Law Matter? The WTO and US Antidumping Investigations.' Emory University Working Paper. Emory University, Atlanta.

Cameron, David. 1978. 'The Expansion of the Public Economy: A Comparative Analysis.' *American Political Science Review* 72:1243–61.

Chaudoin, Stephen. Forthcoming. 'Audience Features and the Strategic Timing of Trade Disputes.' *International Organization*.

Combes, Jean-Louis, and Saadi-Sedik, Tahsin. 2006. 'How Does Trade Openness Influence Budget Deficits in Developing Countries?' *Journal of Development Studies* 42:1401–16.

Dür, Andreas, Baccini, Leonardo, and Elsig, Manfred. 2014. 'The Design of International Trade Agreements: Introducing a New Dataset.' *Review of International Organizations* 9 (3): 353–75.

Finlayson, Jock A., and Zacher, Mark W. 1981. 'The GATT and the Regulation of Trade Barriers: Regime Dynamics and Functions.' *International Organization* 35:561–602.

Frieden, Jeffry A. 2002. 'Real Sources of European Currency Policy: Sectoral Interests and European Monetary Integration.' *International Organization* 56:831–60.

Garen, John, and Trask, Kathleen. 2005. 'Do More Open Economies Have Bigger Governments? Another Look.' *Journal of Development Economics* 77: 533–51.

Gowa, Joanne. 1995. *Allies, Adversaries and International Trade.* Princeton, NJ: Princeton University Press.

Gray, Julia. 2014. 'Life, Death, or Zombies? The Endurance of Inefficient Regional Economic Organizations.' Princeton University Working Paper. Princeton University, Princeton, NJ.

Jo, Hyeran. 2008. *Monitoring Compliance: The Design of Monitoring Institutions in International Cooperation.* PhD thesis, University of Michigan, Ann Arbor.

Johns, Leslie. Forthcoming. 'Depth versus Rigidity in the Design of International Agreements.' *Journal of Theoretical Politics.*

Katzenstein, Peter J. 1985. *Small States in World Markets: Industrial Policy in Europe.* Ithaca, NY: Cornell University Press.

Kim, So Young. 2007. 'Openness, External Risk, and Volatility: Implications for the Compensation Hypothesis.' *International Organization* 61:181–216.

Koremenos, Barbara. 2005. 'Contracting Around International Uncertainty.' *American Political Science Review* 99:549–65.

Kucik, Jeffrey. 2012. 'The Domestic Politics of Institutional Design: Producer Preferences over Trade Agreement Rules.' *Economics and Politics* 24:95–118.

Kucik, Jeffrey, and Reinhardt, Eric. 2008. 'Does Flexibility Promote Cooperation? An Application to the Global Trade Regime.' *International Organization* 62:477–505.

Mansfield, Edward D., and Bronson, Rachel. 1997. 'Alliances, Preferential Trading Arrangements, and International Trade.' *American Political Science Review* 91:94–107.

Mansfield, Edward D., and Reinhardt, Eric. 2008a. 'International Institutions and Terms of Trade Volatility.' Emory University Working Paper. Emory University, Atlanta.

2008b. 'International Institutions and the Volatility of International Trade.' *International Organization* 62:621–52.

Reinhardt, Eric. 2002. 'Tying Hands without a Rope: Rational Domestic Response to International Institutional Constraints.' In *Locating the Proper Authorities: The Interaction of Domestic and International Institutions*, edited by Daniel Drezner, 77–104. Ann Arbor: University of Michigan Press.

Rodrik, Dani. 1997. *Has Globalization Gone Too Far?* Washington, DC: Peterson Institute.

Rosendorff, B. Peter. 2005. 'Stability and Rigidity: Politics and the Design of the WTO's Dispute Resolution Procedure.' *American Political Science Review* 99:389–400.

Rosendorff, B. Peter, and Milner, Helen V. 2001. 'The Optimal Design of International Institutions: Uncertainty and Escape.' *International Organization* 55:829–57.

Rudra, Nita. 2002. 'Globalization and the Decline of the Welfare State in Less-Developed Countries.' *International Organization* 56:411–45.

2004. 'Openness, Welfare Spending, and Inequality in the Developing World.' *International Studies Quarterly* 48:683–709.

Scheve, Kenneth, and Slaughter, Matthew J. 2004. 'Economic Insecurity and the Globalization of Production.' *American Journal of Political Science* 48:662–74.

Smith, James McCall. 2000. 'The Politics of Dispute Settlement Design: Explaining Legalism in Regional Trade Pacts.' *International Organization* 54:137–80.

Traca, Daniel A. 2005. 'Trade Exposure, Export Intensity, and Wage Volatility: Theory and Evidence.' *Review of Economics and Statistics* 87:336–47.

Zanardi, Maurizio. 2004. 'Antidumping Law as a Collusive Device.' *Canadian Journal of Economics/Revue Canadienne d'Economique* 37:95–122.

# 18

## What do we know about preferential trade agreements and temporary trade barriers?

CHAD P. BOWN, BAYBARS KARACAOVALI AND
PATRICIA TOVAR

### A. Introduction

Two of the most important trade policy developments to take place since the 1980s are the proliferation of preferential trade agreements (PTAs) and the ebb and flow of national use of temporary trade barriers such as anti-dumping, safeguards and countervailing duties.[1] Nearly 600 PTAs have now been notified to the World Trade Organization (WTO), with nearly 400 of these in force as of 2013 (World Trade Organization 2013). With respect to temporary trade barrier (TTB) policies, major economies such as Brazil, China, India, Mexico and Turkey went from being TTB nonusers in the late 1980s to the situation whereby a substantial share of their import product lines at some point over the subsequent 20 years became covered by these additional forms of nontariff protection (Bown 2011, 2013a). Furthermore, some of these countries, as well as a number of other major TTB users such as Argentina, Australia, Canada, the European Union

Thanks to Mark Wu and Petros Mavroidis for useful discussions, and thanks for comments on an earlier draft go to Todd Allee, Andreas Dür, Manfred Elsig, Simon Evenett, James Flett, Yoram Haftel, Bernard Hoekman, Soo Yeon Kim, Marcelo Olarreaga, Joost Pauwelyn and participants at the 2013 World Trade Forum in Berne. Aksel Erbahar and Carys Golesworthy provided outstanding research assistance. The World Bank's MDTF-II Trust Fund provided financial support. Any opinions expressed in this chapter are the authors' and should not be attributed to the World Bank. All remaining errors are our own.
[1] The European tradition is to refer to these trade policies collectively as 'trade defence instruments', and the American tradition is to refer to them as 'trade remedies'. The research literature sometimes also refers to them as instruments of 'administered protection' or 'contingent protection'. We choose to refer to them as 'temporary trade barriers' so as to reflect the fact that they impede trade flows and they are legally defined so as to be imposed only temporarily.

(EU), Peru and the United States, also became involved in significant *new* PTAs during this period.[2]

Despite the empirical importance of PTAs and TTBs and the common feature that each can independently have quite discriminatory elements, relatively little is known about the nature of any relationships between PTAs and TTBs. For example, do PTAs lead to more or less use of TTBs overall? Does the composition of the group of trading partners targeted by TTBs change after the implementation of a PTA? That is, after PTAs are implemented, do countries tend to impose TTBs on PTA nonpartners, further reinforcing the preferences already inherent in the PTA? Or do forces conspire to shift TTB use towards PTA partners, in an implicit attempt to restore more nondiscriminatory, most-favoured-nation (MFN)-like treatment that the implementation of the PTA would have disrupted? Does the use of TTBs depend on the existence and type of PTA rules concerning such use, and does this differ for free trade agreements versus customs unions? Furthermore, do PTA partners tend to coordinate TTB activity against third countries in response to common shocks? Finally, what are the political-economic channels that would explain any patterns in the data that emerge?

This chapter analyses a number of political-economic issues that arise as research sheds further light on the intersection of the discriminatory policies of TTBs and PTAs. Our approach is not to attempt to fully address these important questions; instead, we review prior research and we use the legal-political-economic details from four case studies to reveal some of the challenges facing any research that seeks to provide insight into these relationships.

Section B provides a brief introduction to the legal and institutional aspects linking PTAs and TTBs when viewed from the perspective of the multilateral trading system's rules under the General Agreement on Tariffs and Trade/World Trade Organization (GATT/WTO). The WTO system in particular has established some important implications that shape how WTO Members use TTBs against PTA partners and nonpartners, both through the text of its original agreements and through the evolving case law and dispute settlement jurisprudence that may increasingly affect how Members are to interpret certain elements of the agreements.

Section C reviews the existing literature and recent empirical evidence on dynamic aspects of the political economy of trade policy, including the

---

[2] We refer to the European Union (EU) for reasons of consistency, even though in some periods or in certain instances (e.g. WTO dispute settlement) the correct legal entity was technically the European Communities.

general set of factors that determine trade policy formation after countries have signed and implemented a PTA. Section D then reviews the formal empirical work done to date on the relationships between PTAs and country-specific TTBs such as anti-dumping. We conclude that a body of nascent – though promising – work provides suggestive evidence that merits substantial additional scholarly attention.

Section E contains the main analytical contribution of the chapter, which is to provide a contributing explanation as to why, as yet, so little is known about the relationships between the implementation of a PTA, the political-economic shocks that result from the PTA, the subsequent evolution of industry-level demands for TTBs and a government's decision on how to structure its applied TTBs. We use four case studies to illustrate the divergent forces that arise at the intersection of PTAs and TTBs and the range of discriminatory ways that PTA member countries apply TTB measures. The case studies derive from how countries use the WTO's global safeguards policy instrument; our four examples include recent policies applied by a variety of different countries involved in distinct regional trade agreements, including Argentina (MERCOSUR), United States (NAFTA), Turkey (customs union with the EU) and the Dominican Republic (CAFTA-DR).

Although the expectation may be that global safeguards are to be applied on a nondiscriminatory – or MFN – basis, we show that WTO Members actually apply this policy in ways that lead to a range of discriminatory outcomes. Sometimes governments seek to simply reinforce a pro-PTA bias through the way in which they subsequently apply their TTB policies. In other instances, they impose TTBs with an anti-PTA bias as if seeking to restore the MFN-like treatment that had been disrupted as a result of implementation of the PTA.

One implication of our detailed case-study analysis is that there are important measurement and identification challenges for research that seeks to find clear evidence of systematic relationships among PTA formation, the political-economic implications of PTA implementation and subsequent TTB use. We conclude that future research is more likely to bear fruit if it examines not only the full range of TTB policy instruments that are being applied but also many of the subtle details regarding *how* these TTBs are being applied.

## B. Legal and institutional aspects of the GATT/WTO, PTAs and TTBs

Article XXIV of the GATT 1947 allowed PTAs to arise between Contracting Parties in the form of both free trade areas and customs unions.

However, one crucial caveat to Article XXIV is that countries involved in the PTA are not permitted to increase levels of protection on imports from third (nonpartner) countries above their pre-PTA levels. Specifically, Article XXIV: 5(b) states for the case of free trade areas:

> The duties and other regulations of commerce maintained in each of the constituent territories and applicable at the formation of such free-trade area...shall not be higher or more restrictive than the corresponding duties and other regulations of commerce existing in the same constituent territories prior to the formation of the free-trade area.

The GATT 1947 also set out broad conditions under which countries could implement TTBs under Article VI (anti-dumping and countervailing duties) and Article XIX (safeguards). In their simplest form, these provisions permit governments to implement temporary new (higher) trade restrictions after the conduct of an investigation in which the government determines that imports are causing injury to a domestic industry and that those imports are priced too low (anti-dumping), are subsidised (countervailing duties) or are simply growing too quickly (safeguards). Article VI is frequently referred to as containing the 'unfair trade' provisions; thus, any TTB imposed under its auspices is supposed to be trading-partner-specific and is a permitted exception to the GATT's general MFN treatment provisions in Article I. On the other hand, because there is no allegation of 'unfairness' when countries resort to safeguards under Article XIX, any TTB imposed under its auspices is supposed to continue to provide MFN treatment, even if that treatment is a higher level of import protection for all trading partners.

The Uruguay Round agreements establishing the WTO provided additional elaboration on the conditions and procedures by which countries are permitted to use such TTBs via the WTO Agreement on Antidumping, Subsidies and Countervailing Measures, and Safeguards.[3] Nevertheless, the GATT and WTO agreements provide little additional explicit guidance on how governments are to treat imports from PTA partners relative to nonpartners in their conduct of TTB investigations. As we

---

[3] China's 2001 Accession Protocol also permitted existing WTO Members to implement a bilateral, China-specific transitional safeguard that could be used until 2014 (Bown 2010). Although our analysis lumps the four policies together, we do not claim that the four TTBs are completely substitutable, as there are important legal distinctions between when and how they can be used; see, for example, Mavroidis, Messerlin and Wauters (2008). On the GATT/WTO more generally, see Hoekman and Kostecki (2009).

describe in Section E, there have been WTO dispute settlement challenges to specific TTB investigations and applied measures that have led to some additional guidance through the resulting case law and jurisprudence. Nevertheless, some of the main economic questions and concerns that arise when contemplating the coexistence of permissible TTBs and GATT Article XXIV: 5 have gone unaddressed, like most areas of potential conflict between the GATT/WTO and PTAs.

Many PTAs contain specific provisions that articulate ways in which a PTA member's use of TTBs is to be influenced by PTA implementation. Our discussion here draws from a series of research efforts spearheaded by Thomas Prusa, Robert Teh and coauthors that provides a mapping of the text of PTA provisions to the TTB policies of anti-dumping, countervailing duties and safeguards.[4] Their research suggests that PTAs include provisions on TTBs that fall into three categories. PTA provisions may: (1) affect how members use existing TTB policies against each other; (2) introduce new TTB policies that are PTA-partner specific, such as bilateral safeguards; or (3) coordinate use of existing TTB policies across more than one PTA member for those TTB investigations and TTB applications affecting third (PTA nonpartner) countries.

We focus primarily on the first category of PTA provisions that affect how members use existing TTBs against each other, as that is most relevant for our subsequent analysis. A few PTAs eliminate the application of all TTBs between members – the most high-profile example is the EU, where Member States cannot use anti-dumping, countervailing duties or safeguards against imports from another Member State. Many agreements contain provisions spelling out different criteria for the imposition of a particular TTB against partners relative to nonpartners; this, of course, can result in the discouragement of one particular TTB policy instrument from being imposed on members (e.g. global safeguards) relative to another TTB instrument (e.g. anti-dumping). A common provision covering global safeguards is that imports from PTA partners can be excluded from the safeguard application if they do not constitute a 'substantial share' of total imports and if they are not a contributor to the injury to the domestic industry.[5]

Examples from PTA provisions on anti-dumping include higher de minimus dumping margins or import volumes for partners relative to

---

[4] See in particular Teh, Prusa and Budetta (2009), Prusa and Teh (2011) and Prusa (2011).
[5] Nevertheless, for the most part the meaning of 'substantial share' and what defines a contributor to injury are frequently not well specified in PTA texts.

nonpartners, introduction of a 'lesser duty rule' for partners or a differential duration rule for the time that an imposed measure is in effect. Examples from provisions covering countervailing duties and anti-dumping include regional bodies or committees that may be able to influence, modify or even overturn measures to be imposed on PTA partners.

One important implication of the Prusa and Teh line of research is that, to the extent that PTA provisions affect how members use existing TTB provisions against other PTA partners, the provisions appear mostly designed to raise the cost of imposing TTBs against partners relative to nonpartners. Put differently, there are few (if any) provisions in PTAs that would establish more stringent conditions for imposition of a TTB against a nonpartner relative to a PTA partner. Thus, the provisions would appear generally consistent with attempts to discourage TTBs on intra-PTA trade.

The main concern is that the PTAs that contain provisions that explicitly (or implicitly) discourage TTB use against PTA partners do not typically also discourage the *overall* use of TTBs, and thus they do not discourage TTB use against nonpartners. Given the evidence that political-economic shocks spur industry demands for the imposition of a new TTB, any binding PTA provision that discourages use against partners may end up partially pushing TTB demands for additional protection onto imports from PTA nonpartners, ceteris paribus. If left unchecked, a country's overall use of TTBs may end up both being somewhat dubiously motivated and resulting in a pattern of TTB protection arising after PTA implementation that disproportionately targets PTA nonpartners. From this perspective, the country may be seen as violating the spirit of GATT Article XXIV: 5(b), even if it is not necessarily violating the law itself.

## C. How do countries change their trade policies after PTA implementation?

An extensive body of research examines the political-economic forces that shape how countries change their trade policies after they have implemented a PTA. Before turning to the more specific and directed question of any relationships between PTAs and temporary trade barriers, we begin with a review of more general insights stemming from this literature.

Economic theorists have constructed a range of models to examine the impact of preferential liberalisation on subsequent trade policy choices of PTA member countries. Such contributions explore the implications of different assumptions on, inter alia, country sizes; endowments; underlying market structures and conditions of competition; whether governments are politically and/or economically motivated; the timing of policy decisions; and the depth of the PTA in terms of whether it is a free trade agreement versus a customs union (Panagariya 2000). This research has led to the 'building blocks' versus 'stumbling blocks' debate regarding the long-run impact of PTAs on multilateral efforts towards liberalising trade – for example, preferential liberalisation could spur subsequent multilateral liberalisation and MFN tariff cutting, or it could make it more difficult for governments to further cut MFN tariffs or to sustain relatively low applied MFN tariffs. A reasonable conclusion from this body of theoretical economic research is that it could go either way.

Perhaps not surprisingly, then, the empirical evidence on the relationship between preferential liberalisation and subsequent determination of *multilateral*, or *nondiscriminatory*, trade policy is also somewhat mixed. Evidence from the United States (Limão 2006), EU (Karacaovali and Limão 2008), the Dominican Republic–Central America FTA (CAFTA-DR) members (Tovar 2012) and Colombia (Karacaovali 2013) shows that countries raise MFN tariffs or face downward rigidities to further lowering their MFN tariffs after they have cut their tariffs preferentially. On the other hand, evidence from countries in Latin America (Estevadeordal, Freund and Ornelas 2008) and Association of Southeast Asian Nations (ASEAN) members (Calvo-Pardo, Freund and Ornelas 2011) suggests that preferential tariff cuts can lead to further multilateral tariff cuts.

Freund and Ornelas (2010) have posited one intuitively appealing potential explanation for the seemingly conflicting results. Preferential tariff cuts in Latin America would have otherwise resulted in substantial 'preference margins' – defined as the difference between a product's applied MFN tariff (facing PTA nonpartners) and a product's applied preferential tariff (facing PTA partners). Because this could have led to costly trade diversion in the form of increased imports from relatively inefficient industries in PTA partners at the expense of those in more efficient PTA nonpartners (Viner 1950), policymakers may have felt economic pressure to also lower their MFN tariffs. On the other hand, because preference margins resulting from the US and EU PTAs were not as large, trade diversion may have been of insufficient concern to put pressure on policymakers with respect to their MFN tariffs relative to other (noneconomic) considerations highlighted by Limão (2007) in particular.

A potential complementary explanation for the divergent results that has yet to be explored rigorously is whether the relatively short-run analysis and examination of a limited set of policy instruments (preferential tariffs and multilateral tariffs) does not tell the whole story. For instance, there may be additional policy instruments – such as TTBs or other non-tariff forms of protection – that arise to either complement or substitute for the changes in preferential and multilateral tariffs. Furthermore, it may take additional time for preferential or multilateral tariff changes to induce political-economic shocks, and thus take more time for the long-run (total) impact on trade policy – through consideration of all policy instruments – to be fully revealed. Finally, future research may also benefit from consideration of recent innovations in the more general economic literature on the determinants of trade policy formation in light of countries' trade agreement commitments under the WTO that may impose constraints on the various trade policy instruments at their disposal.[6]

## D. Anti-dumping and country-specific TTB use by PTA member countries

The results of recent empirical research described in the last section suggest that in some circumstances PTAs may lead members to offer MFN tariff reductions, whereas in others they may lead members to face upward pressure, downward rigidities or both on their MFN tariffs. Furthermore, the work by Prusa and Teh described in Section B identifies a number of institutional aspects of PTAs that could affect how TTBs are used against partners versus nonpartners. This section examines trends in the data and existing research that has begun to improve understanding of the relationships among preferential tariffs, multilateral tariffs and use of TTBs such as anti-dumping, countervailing duties, global safeguards and the China-specific transitional safeguard introduced as part of China's WTO accession in 2001.

---

[6] Important recent empirical contributions to this literature include those of Broda, Limão and Weinstein (2008), Bagwell and Staiger (2011), Limão and Tovar (2011) and Ludema and Mayda (forthcoming). Bown and Crowley (2013b) is perhaps most relevant to the context described here as it examines the incentives for the United States to apply TTBs in the context of self-enforcing trade agreements such as the WTO; however, even this analysis does not take into consideration the impact of or constraints related to PTAs.

Table 18.1 summarises the prevalence of TTB instruments of protection in effect as of 2011, in terms of their import coverage across policy-imposing economies (Bown 2011, 2013a). Column 1 presents information on the import coverage of the anti-dumping policy alone, the most 'popular' TTB policy instrument in use as of 2011. Economies such as Argentina, Brazil, China, the EU, India, Turkey and the United States were each estimated to have anti-dumping measures in effect in 2011 that covered more than 1.7 per cent of their imports. For each of these economies, there has also been at least one period over the previous 15 years in which their imposed anti-dumping measures covered at least 2 per cent of their imports in any given year, peaking as high as 3.2 per cent for China in 2011, 3.7 per cent for the EU in 1997, 5.5 per cent for the United States in 1998 and 5.8 per cent for India in 2011 (Bown 2013a: Fig. 1a).

Interestingly, Table 18.1 also indicates that many of the significant users of TTBs by 2011 had been nonusers of these particular policy instruments in the late 1980s. For many emerging economies in particular, only since they underwent periods of unilateral, preferential or multilateral liberalisation in the 1990s has there been a significant increase in the use of the TTB instruments. One important question, of course, is the nature of the relationship between these forms of liberalisation – not only with respect to each other (as highlighted by research described in the previous section) but also through changes to other time-varying protection policies, and in particular through nontariff instruments such as TTBs.

An additional way to motivate the importance of understanding how applied TTBs relate to PTAs is to consider case studies of individual countries. Turkey, for example, went from being a nonuser of TTBs in the late 1980s to becoming, by some measures, the trading system's second-most active user of TTBs by 2011, trailing only India – for example, see Table 18.1, columns 2 and 6. Furthermore, during this same period, Turkey went from having control over its entire set of trade policy instruments to an outcome whereby many of its trade policy instruments were constrained via a voluntary PTA (Karacaovali 2011). In particular, Turkey formed a customs union with the EU in the mid-1990s; as such, Turkey then implemented bilateral free trade with EU Member States over most goods imports (applied preferential tariffs of zero towards imports from EU members), and it adopted and implemented the EU's applied MFN tariff towards most goods that it imported from third countries. The TTB policies of anti-dumping, safeguards and countervailing duties became the few remaining trade policy instruments at the Turkish government's disposal and discretion.

Table 18.1 *TTB policy-imposing economies and affected imports in 2011*

| Economy (year of economy's first AD initiation) | 2011 trade-weighted share of imports... | | | | | Product line share of imports... | |
|---|---|---|---|---|---|---|---|
| | ...subject to AD only (1) | ...subject to all TTBs (2) | ...from China subject to all TTBs (3) | ...from other emerging economies subject to all TTBs (4) | ...from high-income economies subject to all TTBs (5) | ...subject to all TTBs in 2011 (6) | ...subject to all TTBs in 2001 (7) |
| **G-20 emerging economies** | 3.0[a] | 3.3[a] | 10.8[b] | 2.3[b] | 1.7[b] | 3.2[a] | 1.5[a] |
| 1. India (1992) | 5.8 | 6.3 | 21.9 | 3.0 | 2.7 | 6.9 | 2.8 |
| 2. Turkey (1989) | 2.6 | 4.3 | 16.0 | 4.2 | 2.1 | 6.9 | 1.5 |
| 3. China (1997) | 3.2 | 3.2 | – | 1.1 | 3.9 | 1.4 | 0.3 |
| 4. Argentina (NA) | 2.5 | 2.5 | 6.8 | 1.9 | 1.2 | 3.3 | 2.4 |
| 5. Brazil (1988) | 1.7 | 1.7 | 4.4 | 1.0 | 1.2 | 1.9 | 1.2 |
| 6. Indonesia (1996) | 0.8 | 1.2 | 2.4 | 1.5 | 0.8 | 1.8 | 0.9 |
| 7. South Africa (NA) | 0.3 | 0.3 | 0.4 | 0.3 | 0.3 | 0.6 | 1.3 |
| 8. Mexico (1987) | 0.3 | 0.3 | 0.5 | 0.7 | 0.2 | 1.1 | 23.4 |
| **Other emerging economies** | | | | | | | |
| 1. Pakistan (2002) | 1.4 | 1.4 | 2.5 | 2.0 | 0.7 | 0.3 | – |
| 2. Peru (1992) | 1.3 | 1.3 | 3.6 | 1.3 | 0.3 | 2.5 | 0.8 |
| 3. Thailand (1994) | 1.2 | 1.2 | 1.2 | 0.8 | 1.3 | 0.6 | <0.1 |
| 4. Colombia (1991) | 0.5 | 0.5 | 3.4 | 0.1 | <0.1 | 0.9 | 0.4 |
| 5. Malaysia (NA) | 0.2 | 0.2 | <0.1 | 0.4 | 0.1 | <0.1 | <0.1 |

| Economy | | | | | |
|---|---|---|---|---|---|
| 6. Philippines (1994) | <0.1 | <0.1 | <0.1 | 0.1 | 0.1 | 0.3 |
| 7. Chile (1994) | <0.1 | <0.1 | <0.1 | 0.0 | <0.1 | 0.8 |
| **G-20 high-income economies** | 2.1 | 2.2 | 1.9 | 4.7 | 1.9 | 1.8 |
| 1. United States (1922) | 3.9 | 4.0 | 3.6 | 8.3 | 5.8 | 4.6 |
| 2. European Union (1968) | 1.7 | 1.8 | 1.2 | 4.2 | 3.1 | 2.3 |
| 3. Canada (NA) | 0.7 | 0.7 | 0.5 | 2.1 | 1.1 | 2.2 |
| 4. Australia (1950s) | 0.4 | 0.5 | 0.1 | 1.2 | 0.7 | 0.6 |
| 5. South Korea (NA) | 0.4 | 0.4 | 0.9 | 0.6 | 0.6 | 0.6 |
| 6. Japan (1982) | <0.1 | <0.1 | <0.1 | <0.1 | <0.1 | 0.1 |
| **Other high-income economies** | | | | | | |
| 1. New Zealand (NA) | 1.1 | 1.1 | 0.3 | 0.4 | 0.4 | 0.1 |
| 2. Israel (1991) | 0.3 | 0.3 | 0.1 | 1.7 | 0.3 | 0.1 |
| 3. Taiwan, China (1984) | 0.2 | 0.2 | <0.1 | 0.8 | 0.4 | 0.1 |

*Source:* derived from Bown (2013a: Table 1), Bown (2013c) and Vandenbussche and Zanardi (2008).

*Note:* Shares of nonoil imports. Ranked by column 2 within each category of policy-imposing economy. NA, not available; TTB, temporary trade barrier and includes anti-dumping (AD), countervailing duties, global safeguards and China-specific transitional safeguards.

[a] Aggregation does not include Mexico as policy-imposing economy.

[b] Aggregation does not include China or Mexico as policy-imposing economies.

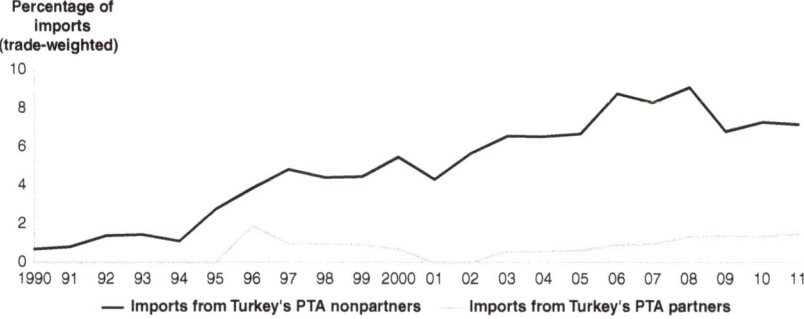

**Figure 18.1** Turkey's imports subject to imposed temporary trade barriers by PTA partner status
*Source:* Derived from Bown (forthcoming, Figure 4). Temporary Trade Barriers include antidumping, global safeguards, countervailing duties, and the China-specific transitional safeguard. PTA = preferential trade agreement.

Figure 18.1 provides information on the share of Turkey's imports each year that is subject to some imposed TTB, split into whether the imports derive from its PTA partners or from PTA nonpartners, for Turkey's PTAs in effect that year. Turkey's PTA partners include members of the EU, of course, a set of countries that make up the source of more than 50 per cent of its goods imports in some years. The figure reveals that by 2011, more than 6 per cent of Turkey's imports from PTA nonpartners was subject to a Turkish TTB, whereas less than 1 per cent of Turkey's imports from PTA partners was subject to a TTB. Although the differential predates the implementation of the customs union, the fact that this differential has grown since PTA implementation raises the concern that Turkey's TTBs may be being used to deepen the already existing preferences found within its PTAs.

Given the increased prevalence of both PTAs and country-specific TTB use through instruments such as anti-dumping in particular, what does existing empirical research suggest is the relationship between the two? Prusa and Teh (2010) provide a cross-country study using data since the 1980s; this study contains the most systematic empirical work to date. Their first compelling piece of evidence comes from the raw data, which are aggregated and normalised across all PTAs. They reveal that in the 10 years prior to implementation of PTAs, the aggregate count of anti-dumping filings between (eventual) PTA partners is nearly six cases higher per year than in the years after PTA implementation; that is, anti-dumping activity between (eventual PTA) partners falls substantially after PTA implementation. In subsequent econometric analysis they esti-mate a negative binomial regression model of determinants of the counts of bilateral anti-dumping filings, paying particular attention to potential differential treatment between PTA partners and nonpartners, both before and after the implementation of the PTA. Their research is conducted at the relatively aggregate level, and thus it also includes a number of macroeconomic control variables (domestic and foreign real gross domestic product (GDP) growth, real exchange rates, bilateral trade flows) that the associated literature examining the impact of business cycles on import protection has found to affect the filing of anti-dumping initiations.

Prusa and Teh (2010) find that the overall (net) effect of PTA implementation on anti-dumping activity is small. Nevertheless, they also present strong evidence of a compositional impact across the trading partners that are targeted by anti-dumping activity as a result of PTAs being implemented. They report that PTAs decrease the incidence of bilateral anti-dumping filings between members by 33–55 per cent, and PTAs increase the incidence of bilateral anti-dumping filings against nonmembers by 10–30 per cent. The results show more sizeable changes for PTAs that also contain specific anti-dumping provisions.

These results are somewhat different from an earlier and more narrowly defined empirical analysis by Blonigen (2005) that was designed to examine whether NAFTA was reining in US anti-dumping and countervailing duty activity against Canada and Mexico. That research examined data from 1980 to 2000 and found little evidence that NAFTA increased import volumes or that the new provisions in the PTA – that is, NAFTA's Chapter 19, in which partners could use a special dispute settlement process to challenge each other's use of anti-dumping and countervailing duties – affected the frequency of US anti-dumping initiations or US government decisions in cases against Canada and Mexico.

Despite empirical progress in this line of research, there are still a number of unsettled issues regarding the potential role of other non-PTA factors, which may be confounded with the rise of PTAs. One example can be inferred from the results described earlier; Estevadeordal, Freund and Ornelas (2008) remind us that much of the liberalisation taking place during the 1990s was not only through the implementation of PTAs but also through cuts to applied MFN tariffs. Distinguishing the impact on TTBs arising from PTA liberalisation from the impact arising from multilateral liberalisation is likely to be an important, albeit difficult task for future informative research.

A second and related example from the last 20 years, which has also undoubtedly given rise to a substantial amount of TTB use, has been

China's export growth and increasing competitiveness in global markets. Even before its WTO accession in 2001, China had become the top foreign target of many high-income and emerging economy TTB users (Bown 2010; Messerlin 2004). Indeed, a comparison of column 3 with column 2 of Table 18.1 for 2011 indicates that, for most policy-imposing economies, a much larger share of their imports from China has been targeted with TTBs than their overall share of imports. Yet, because China is not a member of most countries' PTAs, simple correlations would attribute the fact that countries are increasing their TTB use against China to the trend that countries increasingly use TTBs against PTA nonpartners relative to partners. An open question is whether this is more of a China-specific effect than it is a PTA-specific effect.

Finally, one additional limiting concern with the rigorous empirical work conducted to date is that much of it is focused on only the anti-dumping policy instrument. Although anti-dumping is the most prevalent of the TTBs in use across the trading system, a number of countries have used policies with quite similar attributes – for example, global safeguards – to respond to certain political-economic shocks. Thus, a focus on anti-dumping alone, especially when considering more recent data on TTB policy application since 1995, could be incomplete.[7] The difference between columns 2 and 1 in Table 18.1 reveals that policies other than anti-dumping made up an important share of overall TTB use for countries such as India and Turkey in 2011. Policies such as global safeguards have also experienced episodes of importance for economies such as Argentina, Brazil, the EU and the United States since the mid-1990s (Bown 2011, 2013a). Furthermore, Bown and Crowley (2013a, 2013b) and Bown and Tovar (2011) find *stronger* evidence for the relationships between a variety of political-economic shocks and implementation of TTBs when the measures of TTBs are defined to include safeguards and anti-dumping than when the measures of TTBs are limited to anti-dumping.

Nevertheless, although safeguards are supposed to be applied on a nondiscriminatory basis, the next section reveals that the reality of how countries apply safeguards is much more complex. For example, many countries impose safeguards in a way that frequently replicates the outcomes of anti-dumping application in that such measures discriminate

---

[7] There is also the possibility that PTA member countries are using special PTA-specific TTBs – such as the PTA safeguard that a number of PTAs have introduced, as discussed in Section B. Much less is known about the actual use of such PTA provisions in practice as data on their systematic use are as yet unavailable.

substantially across different types of export sources. The next set of questions includes whether this discrimination occurs across export sources depending on PTA partner and nonpartner status, and if so, the political-economic channels that give rise to such patterns.

### E. Safeguards application: insights from four case studies

The WTO's Agreement on Safeguards sets out expectations that Members that impose an import-restricting safeguard are supposed to apply it on a relatively nondiscriminatory (MFN) basis. Nevertheless, countries have discretion as to how they apply their global safeguards, and thus how they ultimately treat imports deriving from PTA partners. We use four examples of actual safeguard applications to reveal that WTO Members that are also members of PTAs apply their safeguards towards PTA partners and nonpartners in quite different ways.

Table 18.2 summarises the range of discriminatory uses of safeguards found in the four case studies: Argentina's 1997 safeguard on footwear, the United States' 2002 safeguard on steel, Turkey's 2006 safeguard on footwear and the Dominican Republic's 2009 safeguard on polypropylene bags and tubular fabric. The categorisation addresses a number of different questions for each safeguard. For example, did the safeguard investigation consider the differential foreign sources that caused the potential injury to the domestic industry and how might those sources have been influenced by PTA implementation? Did the application of that particular safeguard contain discriminatory elements regarding PTA partners versus nonpartners? Finally, was there a likely discriminatory effect of the applied safeguard on the resulting trade flows? The last row of Table 18.2 provides an overall summary assessment of whether the safeguard reinforced the existing discrimination already inherent in the PTA ('pro-PTA' discrimination) or pushed against the existing discrimination in the PTA in order to make the outcome more MFN-like ('anti-PTA' discrimination).

These case studies have been chosen in order to draw specific attention to the relationship between discriminatory elements of PTAs and TTBs. We examine details of the policies derived from the World Bank's Temporary Trade Barriers Database (Bown 2013c) and data matched to trade flows at the six-digit Harmonized System (HS) level from UN Comtrade. Because even use of the *same* policy instrument can result in a whole range of discriminatory motivations and outcomes, these case studies reveal that policy details matter.

Table 18.2 *The discriminatory nature of safeguards in the four case studies*

| Question | Argentina – footwear in 1997 | US – steel in 2002 | Turkey – footwear in 2006 | Dominican Republic – tubular fabrics and polypropylene bags in 2009 |
|---|---|---|---|---|
| How discriminatory was the safeguard investigation, in terms of considering the foreign cause of injury? | • Disregarded that injury likely caused by increase in imports from PTA partner alone, these imports stemming from PTA implementation | • Injury likely caused by increase in imports from PTA nonpartners, unrelated to PTA implementation | • Injury likely caused by increase in imports from PTA nonpartners and PTA partners | • Injury likely caused by increase in imports from PTA nonpartners and PTA partners |
| How discriminatory was the applied safeguard? | • Safeguard applied only on PTA nonpartners | • Safeguard applied only on PTA nonpartners | • Safeguard applied on both PTA nonpartners and PTA partners<br>• However, safeguard applied as specific duties; this resulted in de facto higher ad valorem equivalent tariff imposed on PTA nonpartners than on PTA partners | • Safeguard applied on both PTA nonpartners and PTA partners<br>• However, safeguard applied by denoting final overall rate of protection; this resulted in de facto higher safeguard tariff imposed on imports from PTA partners than from PTA nonpartners |
| How discriminatory was the trade flow impact of the applied safeguard? | • Substantial additional imports from PTA partners and sharp decline in imports from PTA nonpartners | • Additional imports from PTA partners and sharp decline in imports from PTA nonpartners | • Slowed import growth from both PTA partners and nonpartners | • Drastic reduction in import levels from both PTA partners and nonpartners |
| Overall conclusion? | Additional *pro-PTA* discrimination | ← | → | Additional *anti-PTA* discrimination |

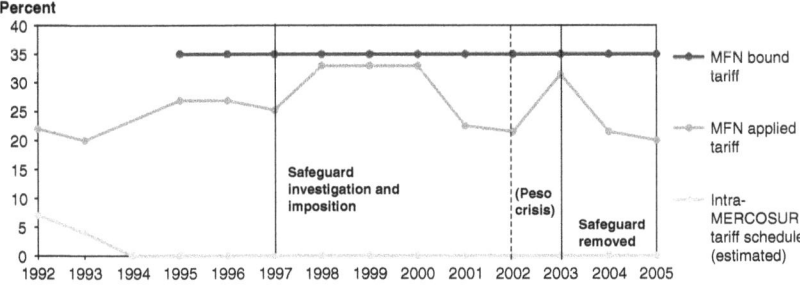

**Figure 18.2** Argentina's average tariffs on imports of footwear in categories subject to the 1997 safeguard

*Source:* Constructed by the authors with 6-digit HS import data from UN Comtrade via WITS and Bown (2013).

## *I. Argentina's safeguard on footwear in 1997*

One extreme possibility resulting from PTA formation is that the PTA leads to an import surge from PTA partners that triggers demands for initiation of a TTB investigation, resulting in the policy-imposing country creating additional preference margins by imposing an additional import-restricting TTB on PTA *nonpartners* only. Argentina's application of a safeguard on footwear products in 1997 arguably illustrates such an example.

In 1992, Argentina started implementing scheduled MERCOSUR tariff cuts towards PTA partners such as Brazil. For imported products such as footwear, Figure 18.2 illustrates that the expectation under MERCOSUR was that Argentina would apply a zero tariff against imports from MERCOSUR partners by 31 December 1994. Meanwhile, Argentina's MFN import tariff applied towards footwear imports supplied by MERCOSUR nonpartners was 22 per cent in 1992. The average MFN applied tariff was reduced to 20 per cent in 1993 before increasing to nearly 27 per cent in 1995 and then to 33 per cent in 1998.[8] At the end of the Uruguay Round, Argentina had committed to a 35 per cent WTO legal binding tariff rate for imported footwear products over which it promised not to raise its MFN applied tariffs.

---

[8] Argentina had also imposed a policy of minimum specific duties on imports of footwear (in addition to textiles and apparel) in 1993; these remained in place until 1997. The specific duties were subject to a separate WTO dispute brought by the United States – one concern was that the ad valorem equivalent of the minimum specific duties applied during certain periods could end up being higher than the 35 per cent rate that was Argentina's legal binding commitment for these products made at the end of the Uruguay Round.

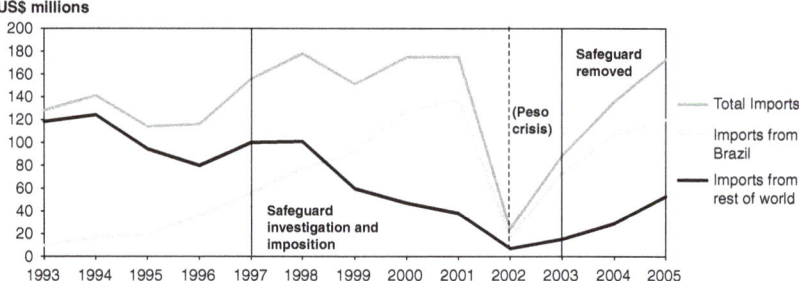

**Figure 18.3**   Argentina's imports of footwear in categories subject to the 1997 safeguard
*Source:* Constructed by the authors with 6-digit HS import data from UN Comtrade via WITS and Bown (2013).

Prior to 1997, Argentina's total imports of footwear had increased considerably – Figure 18.3 reveals an almost 25 per cent increase in the value of total imports between 1993 and 1997. Major foreign suppliers of these products at the time included MERCOSUR partner countries such as Brazil as well as MERCOSUR nonpartners such as China, Indonesia, South Korea and to a lesser extent Thailand, Vietnam and the EU. While Argentina's total imports of footwear were increasing during this period, Figure 18.3 also reveals that there was a substantial compositional change in the foreign sources of those imports. Between 1993 and 1997, Argentina's imports of footwear from Brazil increased by roughly 500 per cent – from less than US$10 million to nearly US$56 million. On the other hand, Argentina's footwear imports from the rest of the world actually declined by 15 per cent – from US$118 million in 1993 to US$100 million in 1997.

The compositional change to Argentina's footwear imports is suggestive evidence that a major source of any injury in Argentina taking place because of a surge in footwear imports was most likely due to increased trade from Brazil rather than increased imports from some other (MERCOSUR nonpartner) country. Moreover, the timing of the MERCOSUR scheduled tariff reductions, and even the slight increases in the MFN applied rates against MERCOSUR nonpartners, also suggests that the increase in imports from Brazil was at least partially related to the new preferential tariff treatment that the MERCOSUR agreement afforded to imports from Brazil.

In 1997, Argentina initiated a safeguard investigation covering footwear product categories in which total imports were worth more than US$150 million. Argentina ended up imposing the safeguard import restriction in 1997 in the form of a specific duty that ranged from US$0.84 to US$16.90 per pair of shoes, depending on the particular HS product code.

However, Argentina's application of the safeguard in 1997 included the controversial decision to exempt from the application the imports that arrived from MERCOSUR partners such as Brazil. This implied that during the period that the safeguard would be in effect, Argentina's imports from foreign suppliers such as China, Indonesia, Vietnam and the EU would face the specific duties of the applied safeguard in addition to the MFN applied tariff rate, whereas imports from Brazil and other MERCOSUR countries would continue to enjoy the lower PTA tariff rate and would not face the additional specific duties spelled out in the applied safeguard measure.

Not surprisingly, Argentina's footwear imports from Brazil continued to increase after application of the safeguard in 1997. Indeed, Brazil more than doubled its import market share in Argentina between 1997 and 2001 from 36 per cent to 78 per cent, in response to this additional preference margin, as Argentina's imports from non-MERCOSUR partners continued to decline under the applied safeguard. (Argentina's 'peso crisis' in 2001–2 and the devaluation of the currency led to a collapse in imports across the board in 2002; thus, the reduction in footwear imports in 2002 shown in Figure 18.3 is due to this separate phenomenon distinct from the impact of the applied safeguard.)

Argentina's decision to apply a safeguard in this manner was also highly controversial under the rules of the WTO. In 1998, the EU initiated a WTO dispute (*Argentina – Footwear*) which resulted in panel and Appellate Body rulings that established precedent-setting case law on the issue of 'parallelism'; that is, the WTO decision that a policy-imposing economy must apply a safeguard against imports from the *same* set of countries as those that it had considered in the safeguard investigation.[9] In this instance, Argentina had considered imports from Brazil in the investigation determining the cause of injury to Argentina's domestic footwear industry, but it had exempted imports from Brazil in the application of the safeguard. In response to the WTO's ruling, in 2000 Argentina terminated the safeguard and initiated a new safeguard investigation, at the end of which it applied a tariff rate quota on imports of a subset of the products considered under the original investigation.

---

[9] Pauwelyn (2004) provides a discussion of this and subsequent WTO legal decisions and jurisprudence on the issue of parallelism.

This particular case study identifies the sort of outcome that economists, ever mindful of the inefficient allocation of resources, worry would become prevalent after countries implemented their PTAs. That is, the formation of the PTA leads to a surge in imports from PTA partners, and although this leads to injury in one country and triggers a TTB investigation, the TTB ends up being applied only against PTA nonpartners, thus further increasing the preference margin and the economic efficiency concerns associated with trade diversion. And though such outcomes may be even more prevalent for country-specific TTB policies, such as antidumping, it is important to identify that similar discriminatory outcomes can also arise under application of the global safeguard policy.

## II. United States' safeguard on steel in 2002

The next two examples illustrate how WTO Members have (and have not) responded to the WTO's parallelism mandate, as well as some of the continuing concerns left unsolved by the parallelism ruling.

In 2001, the United States initiated a safeguard investigation on imports of steel products. The United States ended up exempting its PTA partner countries from application of the safeguard when it imposed import-restricting duties in early 2002 of up to 30 per cent. In a later WTO dispute settlement challenge to the US safeguard that followed the *Argentina – Footwear* dispute, the United States argued that its safeguard investigation had attempted to follow the 'parallelism' principle by not including imports from NAFTA partner countries Mexico and Canada, as well as other PTA partners, in the injury analysis and determination. Nevertheless, the complainants in the case – including the EU, Japan, Brazil, China, South Korea, Switzerland and New Zealand – disagreed that the United States had implemented the parallelism mandate properly in the conduct of its investigation (World Trade Organization 2003).

Bown (2013b) provides evidence that US PTA partners responded to the additional preference provided by the exemption to the applied safeguard on other exporters by significantly increasing their exports of steel products relative to those other countries. Indeed, US imports from PTA partners in affected product categories increased by more than 50 per cent in the 12 months following the imposition of the safeguard, while imports of products from suppliers that were not exempted faced a decline of 30 per cent. Nevertheless, unlike the *Argentina – Footwear* case described earlier, Bown (2013b: Table 3) reports that US imports of the steel products from these PTA partners were relatively small both before (less than 0.5 per cent of imports of steel products ultimately subject to the safeguard) and after (less than 1.0 per cent) the application of the safeguard.

One lesson learned from examination of these data on the US safeguard application on steel is that even countries that follow the guidance of the parallelism mandate do not insulate themselves from the economic concerns associated with trade diversion. Thus, even if imports from PTA partners were not the cause of injury, the granting of additional preferences to PTA partners by exempting them from a safeguard that has been applied against imports from PTA nonpartners will not prevent subsequent import surges from relatively less efficient export industries in PTA partners.

### III. Turkey's safeguard on footwear in 2006

Next consider Turkey, which has become one of the most frequent users of safeguards in the WTO system. Although Turkey's applied safeguards are interesting for a number of reasons (Bown, forthcoming), here we focus on how its safeguard applications treat imports from the EU. Turkey and the EU have a free trade agreement governing bilateral trade, and they also share a common external MFN applied tariff through a customs union arrangement. Nevertheless, despite the customs union that coordinates MFN applied tariffs, each economy administers separately and independently its TTB policies, such as safeguards.

Turkey has attempted to adhere to the WTO's parallelism principle in its safeguard cases in a manner quite different from the approach chosen by the United States in the steel safeguard case. Thus, Turkey typically *includes* imports from the EU in the injury determination in the safeguard investigation and then subsequently also applies any resulting safeguard measure to imports from the EU. On its face, this approach appears less likely to result in additional preferences and discrimination in favour of the trading partners that already receive one layer of preferences and benefits from discrimination through the PTA.

Nevertheless, although Turkey applies its safeguards to imports deriving from the EU, in a number of instances it has chosen to structure the applied policy so as to minimise the incidence of the imposed trade restriction on EU exporters. Turkey typically does not apply its safeguards as an ad valorem duty, which is relatively nondiscriminatory across trading partners. Instead, Turkey structures its applied safeguards as either *specific duties* or *price undertakings* (based on minimum price thresholds,

US$ millions

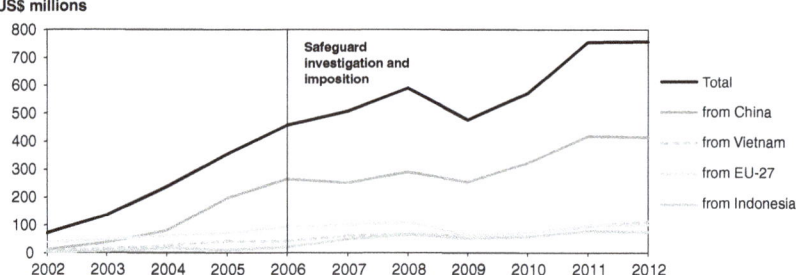

**Figure 18.4**   Turkey's imports of footwear from selected source countries
*Source:* Constructed by the authors with 6-digit HS import data from UN Comtrade
via WITS and Bown (2013).

US$ millions

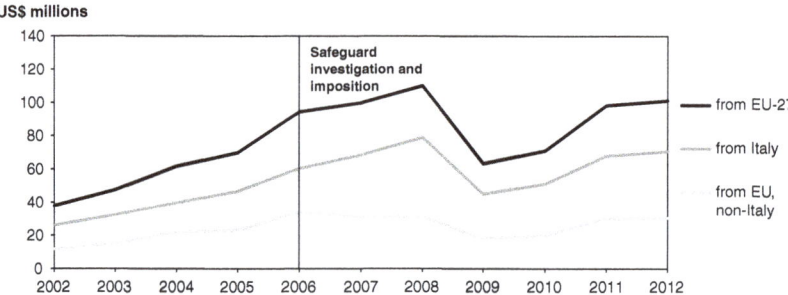

**Figure 18.5**   Turkey's imports of footwear from selected EU source countries
*Source:* Constructed by the authors with 6-digit HS import data from UN Comtrade
via WITS and Bown (2013).

above which no additional duties are imposed); these policies can have
much more discriminatory effects across foreign sources.[10]

One telling example began in 2006 when Turkey initiated a safe-
guard investigation on imports of almost US$500 million in footwear.
Figure 18.4 reveals that more than half of these imports derived from
China, though other major foreign suppliers included the EU (nearly
US$100 million), Vietnam (US$42 million) and Indonesia (US$20 mil-
lion). Figure 18.4 and Figure 18.5 indicate that imports of footwear from

[10] Turkey has recently applied safeguards as price undertakings on vacuum cleaners, motor-
cycles, electrical appliances and matches; in these cases it has established price cutoffs
(under which duties would be applied) that were well below the average price of imports
from the EU of the goods under investigation. Turkey has also recently applied safeguards
as specific duties on steam irons, spectacle frames and travel goods and handbags. Data
on average Turkish import prices across foreign sources frequently suggest that significant
imports from the EU in these particular products derived from countries such as Italy
and France and may have been higher-end varieties for which a safeguard applied as a
specific duty would be expected to have less of an impact.

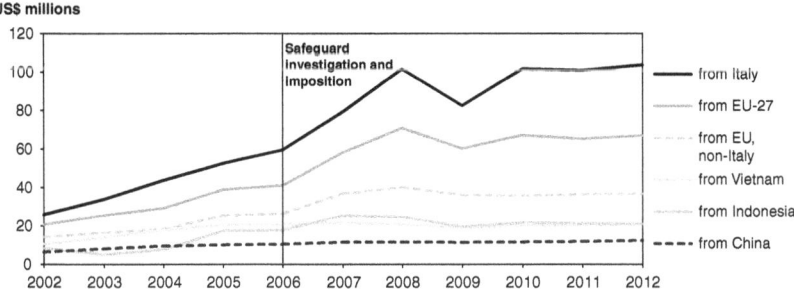

US$ millions

- from Italy
- from EU-27
- from EU, non-Italy
- from Vietnam
- from Indonesia
- from China

Safeguard investigation and imposition

**Figure 18.6**   Turkey's import prices of footwear from selected source countries
*Source:* Constructed by the authors with 6-digit HS import data from UN Comtrade via WITS and Bown (2013).

both China and the EU had been increasing in the years leading up to the initiation of Turkey's safeguard investigation. Finally, of the nearly US$100 million in Turkey's annual footwear imports deriving from the EU, roughly 70 per cent was from Italy, with much smaller shares of the Turkish import market being held by Spain, Portugal and Romania (Figure 18.5).

Turkey applied a safeguard in the form of a specific duty per pair of footwear of US$2–3, depending on the category of investigated product. However, the applied specific duty did not depend on the trading partner; that is, Turkey also applied the duties to imports from customs union partner countries in the EU. Figure 18.6 provides additional information on Turkish import prices for footwear across different foreign sources. The unit value data on Turkish import prices revealed by Figure 18.6 suggest that the specific duty of US$2–3 would have had much less of an effect on imports of European-produced footwear than on imports from other foreign sources. The average imported price of footwear in 2006 was US$41 per pair from EU countries, whereas it was US$11 per pair from China, US$18 per pair from Indonesia and US$21 per pair from Vietnam. Thus, to the extent that footwear imports from some EU members were higher quality/higher price models, the application in the form of a specific duty, in terms of its ad valorem equivalent based on those average unit values, was less onerous for the EU exporters (5–7 per cent) relative to China (15–21 per cent), Indonesia (10–14 per cent) or Vietnam (9–13 per cent) than it would have been had Turkey applied a safeguard as an ad valorem duty that was common to all sources of imports.

Furthermore, this example points out that the application of a safeguard as a specific duty may also have important differential effects even within the PTA partner economy. Figure 18.6 shows that the average price, measured as the unit value, on footwear imports from Italy in 2006 was US$60 per pair, whereas from all other EU Member States (mainly Spain, Portugal and Romania) the average unit value on footwear imports was only US$26 per pair. Thus the applied safeguard of US$2–3 per pair was likely to have the least impact on the high-end Italian footwear (ad valorem equivalent of an additional 3–5 per cent tariff) and the greatest impact on EU-produced footwear imported from Spain, Portugal and Romania (an additional 7–10 per cent).

## IV. Dominican Republic's safeguard on polypropylene bags and tubular fabric in 2009

A final example of how countries apply safeguards so as to impact PTA partners is taken from the other extreme and involves a policy-imposing country that has arguably used the safeguard to *restore* MFN treatment between PTA partners and nonpartners that had been disrupted because of the PTA.

Consider the Dominican Republic's 2009 safeguard on imports of polypropylene bags and tubular fabric. This safeguard was at least partially structured to address an increase in imports from PTA partners arising around the time of implementation of the CAFTA-DR, which entered into force for the United States, El Salvador, Guatemala, Honduras and Nicaragua in 2006 and for the Dominican Republic in 2007.[11]

Before the CAFTA-DR was implemented in 2007, the Dominican Republic applied an MFN tariff of 14 per cent on all foreign imports of tubular fabric and 20 per cent on all imports of polypropylene bags. The tariff on tubular fabric was cut to zero for CAFTA-DR trading partners in 2007. For polypropylene bags, the Dominican Republic was required to cut this tariff rate preferentially as of 2007 by 2 percentage points annually on a 10-year harmonised schedule. The MFN applied tariff would remain at 14 per cent for tubular fabric and 20 per cent for polypropylene bags for all other (CAFTA-DR nonpartner) countries. The Dominican Republic's WTO tariff binding commitment was 40 per cent for both products.

Figure 18.7 illustrates the Dominican Republic's import market for polypropylene bags and tubular fabric in the years prior to and following

---

[11] This section draws heavily on the analysis in Bown and Wu (2014), which provides a legal-economic analysis of the formal WTO dispute in which CAFTA-DR partners Costa Rica, Guatemala, Honduras and El Salvador challenged how the Dominican Republic applied this safeguard.

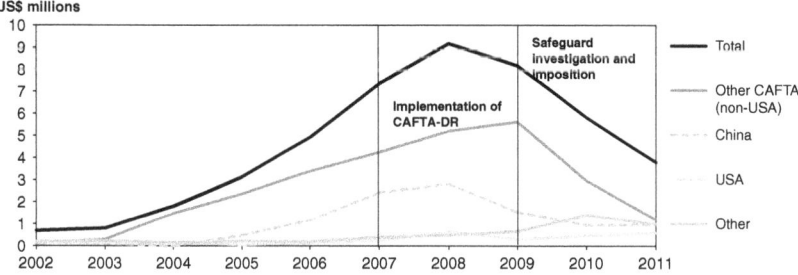

**Figure 18.7** Dominican Republic's imports of polypropylene bags and tubular fabrics
*Source:* Derived from Bown and Wu (forthcoming, Figure 3).

the implementation of CAFTA-DR. The value of Dominican Republic imports of these two products from all sources had nearly doubled from US$4.9 million to US$9.1 million between 2006 (the year prior to CAFTA-DR's entry into force) and 2008 (the first full year following the reduction of tariffs as required by CAFTA-DR).

In 2009, the Dominican Republic initiated a safeguard investigation on imports of these two products. In late 2010, the Dominican Republic applied a safeguard measure on polypropylene bags and tubular fabric from all (non–de minimis) countries – both CAFTA-DR partners and nonpartners alike. Similarly to the case of Turkey described previously, the Dominican Republic followed the parallelism principle by including its CAFTA-DR partners in the investigation and subjecting CAFTA-DR partners to the applied safeguard.

However, the distinctive economic element to this particular safeguard application is how the Dominican Republic treated its CAFTA-DR partners. In this case, the Dominican Republic imposed a safeguard that resulted in an *overall* level of ad valorem import duty protection of 38 per cent for tubular fabrics and polypropylene bags. That is, the Dominican Republic did not differentiate this new level of total protection based on either the foreign source or the (nonsafeguard) tariff rate that it would have otherwise applied to these products in the absence of an applied safeguard measure.

Note the distinction here relative to how WTO Members traditionally apply a safeguard measure, which is most typically applied as an *additional* duty that is imposed 'on top of' the current duty that foreign exporters already faced. In this particular case, exporters from CAFTA–DR partners would otherwise have paid a 0 per cent tariff on tubular fabric as a result of the PTA, whereas CAFTA-DR nonpartners such as China would have

US$ millions

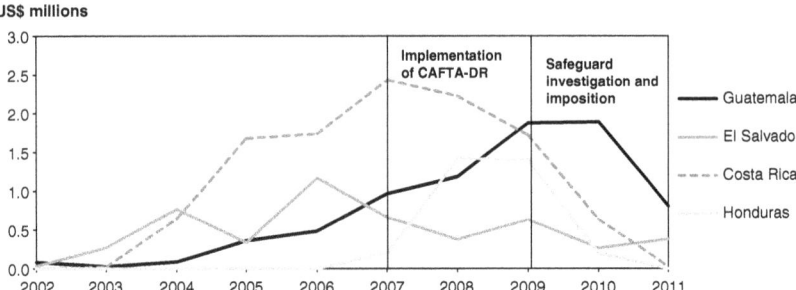

**Figure 18.8**    Dominican Republic's imports of polypropylene bags and tubular fabrics from selected CAFTA source countries
*Source:* Derived from Bown and Wu (forthcoming, Figure 3).

paid a 14 per cent applied MFN tariff on tubular fabric. Put differently, in this instance the Dominican Republic was attempting to implement a safeguard measure that would impose a higher *additional* ad valorem tariff on tubular fabric imports from CAFTA-DR partners (38 per cent, since the initial rate was 0 per cent as a result of the PTA) than it was imposing on tubular fabric imports from CAFTA-DR nonpartners, such as China (24 per cent, since the initial rate was the MFN applied rate of 14 per cent).

Are there apparent trends in the data that would explain the Dominican Republic's attempt, in this instance, to structure an applied safeguard so as to restore the MFN treatment that otherwise had been dismantled following implementation of the CAFTA-DR PTA? Figure 18.7 indicates that imports of polypropylene bags and tubular fabric did increase from CAFTA partners following CAFTA-DR implementation; however, imports from these countries were also increasing before the implementation of the PTA. (Figure 18.8 suggests that the increase of imports stemming from CAFTA-DR was also the result of an increase in imports from a number of different partners *within* the CAFTA-DR.)

Nevertheless, Figure 18.7 reveals that imports also increased substantially (coincidentally) after CAFTA-DR implementation from CAFTA-DR *nonpartners*, especially imports from China. Recall that China continued to face the Dominican Republic's MFN applied tariff rate until the application of the safeguard, at which point imports from China fell precipitously.

Thus one final curiosity from this case is the Dominican Republic's differential treatment towards China, which was the Dominican Republic's largest single foreign source of these imports by 2008, and from which a substantial share of the import growth and new competition for

Dominican Republic producers had arisen. Given how safeguards have been applied historically, the attempt by the Dominican Republic to apply an overall import restriction of 38 per cent can be interpreted as actually applying a more favourable rate towards imports from China (since it was starting at a 14 per cent tariff) than was applied to its CAFTA-DR partners (since they were starting at a 0 per cent tariff rate). This is somewhat surprising, especially in light of the data described in Table 18.1, column 3, on TTB use across countries, which otherwise disproportionately tends to target imports from China with more protection.

## F. Conclusion

Two of the most important trade policy phenomena of the past three decades are the proliferation of PTAs and increased national use of TTBs such as anti-dumping, safeguards and countervailing duties. This chapter analyses some of the interactions and relationships between PTAs and TTBs by reviewing recent data on the increased import coverage of TTBs and the research literature on how countries conduct their trade policy after the implementation of PTAs.

Our main analytical contribution is to use four case studies of how PTA members have applied the global safeguard policy to provide a clearer systemic understanding of the intersection between these potentially discriminatory trade policies. The case studies reveal that sometimes governments seek to reinforce a pro-PTA bias in their applied TTB policies, whereas at other times governments may seek to reverse the incentives created by PTA implementation and to restore more MFN-like treatment by imposing policies with an anti-PTA bias. Sometimes more protection gets imposed on PTA nonpartners, even when the import surge leading to the injury to the domestic industry came primarily from PTA partners (Argentina's safeguard on footwear). In other instances, more protection gets imposed on PTA partners, even when the import surge leading to the injury to the domestic industry also derived from PTA nonpartners (Dominican Republic's safeguard on polypropylene bags and tubular fabric). Discerning the nature of the discrimination requires careful examination of both the form of the applied measures – for example, specific duties or price undertakings in lieu of ad valorem duties – and the potential differences in the additional level of protection imposed across PTA partners versus nonpartners.

To conclude, it is worth describing some of the political-economic channels that may explain why governments seek to differentiate between

PTA partners and nonpartners in how they apply TTBs after implementation of a PTA. In some instances, perhaps the economic efficiency concerns of trade diversion resulting from the PTA coupled with the inability to further cut applied MFN tariffs (à la Freund and Ornelas 2010) create the incentive for countries to restore more MFN-like treatment by imposing TTBs on PTA partners. Or it could be that because of political-economy influences, industries may switch from lobbying for protection from applied tariffs to TTBs. On the other hand, political-economic shocks may arise after implementation of a PTA based on a new-found coalescence of shared political-economic interests across PTA partners that trigger more TTB use against nonpartners. An economic motive could be the larger economic bloc resulting from the PTA seeks to take advantage of new opportunities to exercise market power vis-à-vis third countries. A political or redistributive motive could be made possible if the PTA changes lobbying incentives by firms or even unions whose influence may be newly able to cross national borders. There is a substantial need for additional research clarifying both the trends in the underlying data on PTAs and TTBs and these potential underlying political-economic channels through which such relationships may arise.

## References

Bagwell, Kyle, and Staiger, Robert W. 2011. 'What Do Trade Negotiators Negotiate About? Empirical Evidence from the World Trade Organization.' *American Economic Review* 101 (4): 1238–73.

Blonigen, Bruce A. 2005. 'The Effects of NAFTA on Antidumping and Countervailing Duty Activity.' *World Bank Economic Review* 19 (3): 407–24.

Bown, Chad P. 2010. 'China's WTO Entry: Antidumping, Safeguards, and Dispute Settlement.' In *China's Growing Role in World Trade*, edited by Robert C. Feenstra and Shang-Jin Wei, 281–337. Chicago: University of Chicago Press.

2011. 'Taking Stock of Antidumping, Safeguards and Countervailing Duties, 1990–2009.' *World Economy* 34 (12): 1955–98.

2013a. 'Emerging Economies and the Emergence of South–South Protectionism.' *Journal of World Trade* 47 (1): 1–44.

2013b. 'How Different Are Safeguards from Antidumping? Evidence from U.S. Trade Policies Toward Steel.' *Review of Industrial Organization* 42 (4): 449–81.

2013c. 'Temporary Trade Barriers Database.' World Bank. http://econ. worldbank.org/ttbd/. Accessed 15 June 2013.

Forthcoming. 'Trade Policy Flexibilities and Turkey: Tariffs, Antidumping, Safeguards, and WTO Dispute Settlement.' *World Economy*.

Bown, Chad P., and Crowley, Meredith A. 2013a. 'Import Protection, Business Cycles, and Exchange Rates: Evidence from the Great Recession.' *Journal of International Economics* 90 (1): 50–64.

2013b. 'Self-Enforcing Trade Agreements: Evidence from Time-Varying Trade Policy.' *American Economic Review* 103 (2): 1071–90.

Bown, Chad P., and Tovar, Patricia. 2011. 'Trade Liberalization, Antidumping, and Safeguards: Evidence from India's Tariff Reform.' *Journal of Development Economics* 96 (1): 115–25.

Bown, Chad P., and Wu, Mark. Forthcoming. 'Safeguards and the Perils of Preferential Trade Agreements: Dominican Republic – Safeguard Measures.' *World Trade Review.*

Broda, Christian, Limão, Nuno, and Weinstein, David E. 2008. 'Optimal Tariffs and Market Power: The Evidence.' *American Economic Review* 98 (5): 2032–65.

Calvo-Pardo, Hector, Freund, Caroline, and Ornelas, Emanuel. 2011. 'The ASEAN Free Trade Agreement: Impact on Trade Flows and External Trade Barriers.' In *Costs and Benefits of Economic Integration in Asia*, edited by Robert J. Barro and Jong-Wha Lee, 157–86. Oxford, England: Oxford University Press.

Estevadeordal, Antoni, Freund, Caroline, and Ornelas, Emanuel. 2008. 'Does Regionalism Affect Trade Liberalization toward Non-Members?' *Quarterly Journal of Economics* 123 (4): 1531–75.

Freund, Caroline, and Ornelas, Emanuel. 2010. 'Regional Trade Agreements.' *Annual Review of Economics* 2 (1): 139–66.

Hoekman, Bernard M., and Kostecki, Michael. 2009. *The Political Economy of the World Trading System: The WTO and Beyond.* 3rd edn. New York: Oxford University Press.

Karacaovali, Baybars. 2011. 'Turkey: Temporary Trade Barriers as Resistance to Trade Liberalisation with the European Union?' In *The Great Recession and Import Protection: The Role of Temporary Trade Barriers*, edited by Chad P. Bown, 367–410. London: CEPR and World Bank.

2013. 'Trade Policy Determinants and Trade Reform in a Developing Country: The Case of Colombia.' University of Hawaii at Manoa Working Paper. University of Hawaii, Manoa.

Karacaovali, Baybars, and Limão, Nuno. 2008. 'The Clash of Liberalizations: Preferential vs. Multilateral Trade Liberalization in the European Union.' *Journal of International Economics* 74 (2): 299–327.

Limão, Nuno. 2006. 'Preferential Trade Agreements as Stumbling Blocks for Multilateral Trade Liberalization: Evidence for the U.S.' *American Economic Review* 96 (3): 896–914.

2007. 'Are Preferential Trade Agreements with Non-Trade Objectives a Stumbling Block for Multilateral Liberalization?' *Review of Economic Studies* 74 (3): 821–55.

Limão, Nuno, and Tovar, Patricia. 2011. 'Policy Choice: Theory and Evidence from Commitment via International Trade Agreements.' *Journal of International Economics* 85 (2): 186–205.

Ludema, Rodney, and Mayda, Anna Maria. Forthcoming. 'Do Terms-of-Trade Effects Matter for Trade Agreements? Theory and Evidence from WTO Countries.' *Quarterly Journal of Economics.*

Mavroidis, Petros C., Messerlin, Patrick A., and Wauters, Jasper M. 2008. *The Law and Economics of Contingent Protection in the WTO.* Cheltenham, UK: Edward Elgar.

Messerlin, Patrick A. 2004. 'China in the World Trade Organization: Antidumping and Safeguards.' *World Bank Economic Review* 18 (1): 105–30.

Panagariya, Arvind. 2000. 'Preferential Trade Liberalization: The Traditional Theory and New Developments.' *Journal of Economic Literature* 38 (2): 287–331.

Pauwelyn, Joost. 2004. 'The Puzzle of WTO Safeguards and Regional Trade Agreements,' *Journal of International Economic Law* 7 (1): 109–42.

Prusa, Thomas J. 2011. 'Trade Remedy Provisions.' In *Preferential Trade Agreement Policies for Development,* edited by Jean-Pierre Chauffour and Jean-Christophe Maur, 179–96. Washington, DC: World Bank.

Prusa, Thomas J., and Teh, Robert. 2010. 'Protection Reduction and Diversion: PTAs and the Incidence of Antidumping Disputes.' NBER Working Paper No. 16276. National Bureau of Economic Research, Cambridge, MA.

———. 2011. 'Contingent Protection Rules in Regional Trade Agreements.' In *Preferential Trade Agreements,* edited by Kyle Bagwell and Petros C. Mavroidis, 60–114. Cambridge: Cambridge University Press.

Teh, Robert, Prusa, Thomas J., and Budetta, Michele. 2009. 'Trade Remedy Provisions in Regional Trade Agreements.' In *Regional Rules in the Global Trading System,* edited by Antoni Estevadeordal, Kati Suominen and Robert Teh, 166–249. Cambridge: Cambridge University Press.

Tovar, Patricia. 2012. 'Preferential Trade Agreements and Unilateral Liberalization: Evidence from CAFTA.' *World Trade Review* 11 (4): 591–619.

Vandenbussche, Hylke, and Zanardi, Maurizio. 2008. 'What Explains the Proliferation of Antidumping Laws?' *Economic Policy* 23 (1): 98–103.

Viner, Jacob. 1950. *The Customs Union Issue.* New York: Carnegie Endowment for International Peace.

World Trade Organization. 2003. *United States – Definitive Safeguard Measures on Imports of Certain Steel Products: Final Reports of the Panel.* WT/DS248/R. www.wto.org/english/tratop_e/dispu_e/cases_e/ds248_e.htm.

World Trade Organization. 2013. 'Regional Trade Agreements.' http://wto.org/english/tratop_e/region_e/region_e.htm. Accessed 19 September 2013.

# PART IV

PTAs and the multilateral trading system

# The dialectical relationship of preferential and multilateral trade agreements

THOMAS COTTIER, CHARLOTTE SIEBER-GASSER AND
GABRIELA WERMELINGER

## A. Introduction

Multilateralism and preferentialism are often perceived and depicted as distinct and alternative avenues for the pursuit of trade policies of market access, nondiscrimination and market integration. Comparing the two, it is generally accepted that the multilateral avenue under most-favoured-nation (MFN) treatment is preferable for the purpose of avoiding trade diversions. Governments turn to preferential trade only for want of a better alternative in the pursuit of reciprocal and balanced trade relations where multilateralism is not available or has failed. We are currently witnessing the heyday of preferentialism and a proliferation of bilateral or plurilateral agreements for a number of well-known reasons:

1. the stalling of the 2001 World Trade Organization (WTO) Doha Development Agenda on core issues after more than a decade of negotiations under the new conditions of a multipolar world no longer controlled by transatlantic relations;
2. the 2001 accession of China to the WTO, its ascent to the world's manufacturing centre and the need of many countries to protect their industries from Chinese competition (in particular in textiles) while remaining willing to form free trade zones suitable to attract investment to smaller countries;
3. the current negotiations on the plurilateral Transpacific Partnership (TPP) and on the Transatlantic Trade and Investment Partnership (TTIP), both covering nearly a third of world exports (Deutsch 2013: 3; Kotschwar and Schott 2013), which represent a culmination of contemporary efforts to stimulate trade and job creation by recourse to what amounts to a new plurilateralism among nations.

Contemporary preferences for bilateral and plurilateral avenues, however, cannot ignore that these avenues are, and remain, closely related to multilateralism and global trading rules. Preferentialism and multilateralism are not two independent and distinct avenues for the pursuit of market access and regulatory policies. Historically, they build on each other in a dialectical process, closely related and linked through regulatory bridges and references. They influence and direct each other in various ways. We argue that both are integral parts of the same process moving towards regulatory convergence as a side effect of economic integration. Different regulatory aspects of multilateralism and preferentialism underline how strongly these practices are intertwined: much of the body of existing and emerging preferential agreements builds on the common law of the multilateral systems, often simply restating existing rules without going much beyond them, and sometimes even falling short of them.

At the same time, new multilateral rules are often derived from models developed earlier in preferential trade agreements (PTAs). The principle of MFN ensures that multilateralism and preferentialism do not evolve independently of each other. It produces significant spillovers of preferential agreements. Standards developed and agreed in a preferential agreement have effects beyond the parties involved and provide the basis for general regulation applicable to third parties, too. This is of key importance for regulatory convergence and is one of the main factors in putting pressure on members to eventually reconvene multilateral trade negotiations.

Such effects and the need to develop uniform and coherent regulatory standards have led in parallel to a number of preferential, plurilateral and multilateral regulatory initiatives. We submit that the process will eventually encourage the return to multilateralism and negotiations in international fora, in particular the WTO, while traditional market access may remain subject to preferential relations among nations. Such burden sharing between different regulatory fora should be reflected in future WTO rules providing the overall backbone of the system. Enhanced transparency on the realities of global value chains will further promote this process.

With a view to analysing their interaction, we summarise the history of the dialectical relationship between preferentialism and multilateralism. This chapter mainly focuses on the evolution of international protection of intellectual property rights and of services. The multilateral regulation of the Agreement on Trade-Related Aspects of Intellectual Property Rights (TRIPS Agreement) and others derives from years of regulatory experience and the numerous preferential agreements around the globe. The General Agreement on Trade in Services (GATS) and others, on the other hand, entered the pluri- or multilateral stage early on. We observe two main avenues for the regulatory dialogue between the preferential and the multilateral level: (1) multilateral regulation derived from experiences of preferential regulation, and (2) multilateral regulation as a starting point for any regulation at all.

## B. A brief historical account

History shows that trade liberalisation and trade regulation essentially follow two different paths: trade regulation may at its inception move from preferential relations to plurilateral and multilateral frameworks. Conversely, the impetus may be provided at the outset by multilateralism, eventually moving towards preferential relations building upon the multilateral edifice. Whereas the former corresponds to normal relations of sovereign states in the Westphalian system, the latter often stems from fundamental paradigm shifts, in particular after periods of war and struggle. The post–World War II order thus was framed multilaterally with the Bretton Woods Institutions and the General Agreement on Tariffs and Trade (GATT), which largely replaced traditional peace treaties. Both traditions of regulatory evolution can be observed in the history of different areas of trade regulation in international economic law. History even shows movement occurring in waves, for example, moving from preferentialism towards multilateralism and then back again to preferentialism only to approach multilateralism over again. This shifting movement between multilateralism and preferentialism is what we call a dialectical relationship.

We illustrate the dialectical relationship of preferential and multilateral trade regulation mainly by means of two case studies on the history of intellectual property (IP) and the history of services trade; the regulation of IP protection constituted the first multilateral regulatory framework in international trade regulation. Protection of IP was established in 1883 and 1886 with the Paris Convention on the Protection of Industrial Property and the Berne Convention on the Protection of Literary and Artistic Works. The conventions grew out of a number of PTAs. Subsequent areas of trade regulation have done so, too, for example, most prominently, the GATT. The conventions on IP protection eventually also provided the framework to negotiate the TRIPS Agreement. This agreement represents the epitome of multilateralism and the emergence of global law on a very detailed level. IP protection thus serves as an example of how preferential rules spread to multilateral agreements.

The 1995 GATS, on the other hand, was the first agreement worldwide to introduce a comprehensive and sophisticated structure, definition and language for the regulation of trade in services. Instead of being influenced by years of experience of preferential trade regulation, the multilateral GATS had considerable influence on the design and structure of subsequent PTAs. Thus it serves as an example of how multilateral provisions spread to preferential agreements.

The following paragraphs describe the history of the dialectical relationship of preferential and multilateral trade regulation in detail, depicting parallels and differences between the different areas of regulation.

### I. The case of IP protection: from preferential to multilateral agreements

An enquiry into the historical relationship may start with the observation that PTAs – if they existed at all – constituted the main form, next to unilateral measures, in the early days of international trade. This is true both for bilateral agreements liberalising trade following the Cobden–Chevalier Treaty in 1860 and the web of bilateral Friendship, Commerce and Navigation treaties protecting investment and establishment (see, e.g., Lampe 2011; Sachs 1984:195ff. and Alschner 2013).

The history of a multilateral agreement usually tells us that the subject of regulation was first regulated on a bilateral and preferential basis. The proliferation of such agreements eventually forms a critical mass that provides the basis for consolidation and further plurilateral and multilateral developments. Once either it was generally agreed that the subject of regulation was of relevance for a larger number of states or the web of different preferential commitments had become so complex that the system was at risk of failure, the ground for multilateral efforts was prepared. Governments agreed that multilateral regulation of the subject was timely and necessary. The process took into account the experience gained on the preferential level. The advent of the GATT in 1947 is a prominent example. The trade rules embodied in GATT mainly stem from the experience of the generation of bilateral PTAs concluded by the United States between 1934 and 1945 under the US Reciprocal Trade Agreement Act 1934 (see, e.g., Rhodes 1993: 53ff.). Article 23 of GATT, establishing the concepts of nullification and impairment and the concepts of violation and nonviolation complaints, was copied verbatim from such trade agreements (see, e.g., Tuthill *et al.* 1985: 6). They still inform jurisprudence today and remind us where we come from.

The first multilateral agreements on trade-related issues were, however, the Paris Convention on the Protection of Industrial Property (1883) and the Berne Convention on the Protection of Literary and Artistic Works (1886). They derived from a series of PTAs that provided the critical mass for harmonisation under the roof of a multilateral treaty. Their history is rooted in the invention of the printing press in Europe in the late fifteenth century and is marked by the desire to strike a balance between privileges, later on individual rights, and the public domain and open access to the commercial use of information. Although trade in printed books quickly took off, the emergence of cross-border protection of authors' rights was lagging behind, leaving imported copies unprotected. Authors were left with little recourse since legal protection was granted only nationally (Löhr 2010: 37ff.). It was not until the late eighteenth century that the concept of IP protection began to be recognised internationally.

While the number of national acts and case law on copyright and on industrial property (patents and trademarks) increased in the nineteenth century, rules varied in their scope of application, in the rights granted and in the duration of the rights granted (Ricketson and Ginsburg 2006: 22ff.). Since national law proved to be ineffective for cross-border protection within the expanding international market in Europe, obtaining legal security in the form of largely uniform levels of protection became more and more pressing.[1] Subsequently, a series of preferential agreements with the inclusion of the principles of MFN and national treatment (NT) were adopted to ensure a better harmonised legal environment for IP. They had a minimising impact on the imbalance between countries with high protection and countries with low protection. A bilateral system emerged with France (and its copyrights interests) at the heart of it (Ricketson and Ginsburg 2006: 29–39). (See Figure 19.1.)

These early PTAs were commonly signed among states originating from the same geographical and linguistic region. As Figure 19.1 illustrates, the number of PTAs had reached a critical mass by the second part of the nineteenth century. Coherent regulation became increasingly

---

[1] Famous authors and composers such as Victor Hugo, Emile Zola and Giuseppe Verdi fought for the recognition of authors' rights and the prolongation of the period of protection to secure economic rights and income opportunities. Opponents argued that culture is in the public domain and should be open to everyone. They feared that exclusive rights for authors would raise prices and make works, arts and knowledge inaccessible.

BILATERAL CONVENTIONS IN FORCE IN 1886
(The numeral after each country is the total number of conventions to which that country is party.)

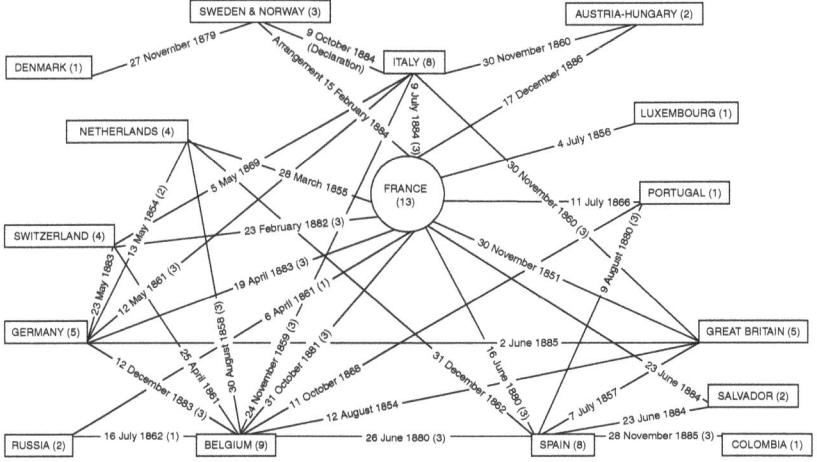

*Note:* The following numerals refer to those in parentheses next to the date of signature.
(1) Both denounced by Russia in 1885 to have effect from 14 July 1887 re France & 14 January 1887 re Belgium.
(2) Not ratified by the Netherlands.
(3) Treaties with most favoured nation clauses.

**Figure 19.1** Bilateral conventions in force in 1886
*Source:* Reproduced from Ricketson and Ginsburg (2006) by permission of Oxford University Press.

problematic and triggered discussions. The period of industrialisation was also an age of increasing international meetings on the subject (World Intellectual Property Organization 2004: 241–2). These platforms were used to demonstrate the need for cross-border recognition of intellectual property rights (IPRs). Exemplary of this trend was the planned International Exhibition of Industrial Property Inventions in Vienna in 1873. It failed to take place since foreign exhibitors refused to attend: they were afraid that their ideas would be stolen and pirated for commercial use in other countries (World Intellectual Property Organization 2004: 241). The need for a harmonised international framework governing IPRs, thus, became more and more evident.

This desire to coordinate patent and trademark protection marked the birth of the first pluri- or multilateral convention on industrial property – the Paris Convention for the Protection of Industrial Property[2] –

---

[2] It was initially signed by 14 members. Until World War II, the membership stagnated at 19 members and later increased to 172 members.

in 1883 (Abbott, Cottier and Gurry 2011: 3). More or less in parallel, multilateralisation in IP protection culminated in the first multilateral convention on copyright, the Berne Convention for the Protection of Literary and Artistic Works in 1886 (Ricketson 2011: 430–1). Both conventions ever since have established the basis for IP protection in their respective member states. Both conventions established an international bureau for administering the treaties in Berne, which later merged into the World Intellectual Property Organization (WIPO), established in 1967 in Geneva.

The Berne Convention established a higher level of substantive harmonisation than did the Paris Convention; its rules still provide much of the basis for international copyright protection today (see Abbott, Cottier and Gurry 2011: 3).[3] However, protection of industrial property, in particular of patents, remained deficient. WIPO's efforts to further develop the international system failed as a result of resistance from the newly independent and developing countries (Abbott, Cottier and Gurry 2011: 3–5; Drahos 2001).

At the end of the Tokyo Negotiation Round of the GATT, negotiations were launched on a draft Anti-Counterfeit Code by the United States and the European Community (EC). Up until then, the GATT had not dealt with IP protection except as a matter of regulation within GATT Article III and of lawful trade restrictions within the general exceptions of GATT Article XX.[4] The effort to conclude an Anti-Counterfeit Code failed but eventually led to the negotiating mandate of Punta Del Este in 1986, taking up negotiations with a view to removing the trade distortions mainly caused by the lack of protection of IPRs (Cottier 1991). With these efforts ongoing, no return to PTAs can be observed, except for including the protection of IPRs in bilateral investment agreements as a standard against arbitrary expropriation and regulatory taking (see United Nations Conference on Trade and Development 2007; see also Drahos 2001 and United Nations Conference on Trade and Development 2012:16, 133; Nadakavukaren Schefer 2013; Dolzer and Schreuer 2012). The efforts of all industrialised countries clearly focused on the emerging negotiations under the umbrella of the Uruguay Round of the GATT.

---

[3] Although the Paris and Berne Conventions were widely adopted (with the United States joining the latter convention only in 1986), other international agreements that were concurrently concluded achieved considerably less acceptance.

[4] See United States – Section 337 of the Tariff Act of 1930, Report by the Panel, adopted on 7 November 1989 (L/6439 – 36S/345).

Although developing countries strongly resisted at first, the effort initially led by the United States obtained strong support from developed
countries, in particular the European Union (EU) Member States, Japan
and Switzerland (Mercurio 2006: 217ff.). Coinciding with the end of
the Cold War and the fall of the Berlin Wall, negotiations culminated
in the conclusion of the multilateral TRIPS Agreement, which entered
into force in 1995. This multilateral agreement established extensive standards and fully incorporated the substantive provisions of the Berne
Convention and the Paris Convention. It forms part of the WTO and is
fully subject to multilateral dispute settlement under the dispute settlement mechanism of the WTO. It amounts to the most advanced regulatory agreement, heralding a new age of international trade regulation in
IPRs (Abbott, Cottier and Gurry 2011: 4). At the same time, the TRIPS
Agreement was designed as a minimal standard, thus allowing countries to adopt stronger protection of IPRs both unilaterally or in future
PTAs.

The success of the TRIPS Agreement and the Uruguay Round in general
provided the impetus for subsequent multilateral efforts within WIPO.
In 1996 WIPO entered into a cooperation agreement with the WTO and
expanded its role by addressing evolving issues related to new technology
and the Internet that were not covered by the Berne Convention and
that were not yet included in WTO law. The WIPO Copyright Treaty
(WCT) and the WIPO Performances and Phonograms Treaty (WPPT)
were adopted in 1996, reinforcing protection against piracy. Another
objective of these new treaties was to create consistency between WTO
and WIPO rules (Abbott, Cottier and Gurry 2011: 429ff.).

At the same time, developing countries increasingly opposed integration, and efforts in multilateral fora declined. In particular, attempts to
strengthen criteria on patenting inventions failed, and a draft patent law
treaty has remained unadopted. Countries increasingly turned to bilateral and plurilateral efforts. The forum shifted. Apart from an amendment
of the TRIPS Agreement negotiated for the implementation of the Doha
Declaration on Public Health (Doha Declaration on the TRIPS Agreement
and Public Health adopted on 14 November 2001, WT/MIN(01)/DEC/2,
adopted on 20 November 2001), all efforts within the WTO failed. Negotiations became protracted, and progress in treaty-making was limited to
the adoption of a treaty in copyright law defining fair use for people with
disabilities (Marrakesh Treaty to Facilitate Access to Published Works for
Persons Who Are Blind, Visually Impaired, or Otherwise Print Disabled,
VIP/DC/8 Rev., adopted on 31 July 2013).

Based on the TRIPS Agreement, IP protection became a standard item in PTAs, introducing so-called TRIPS-plus standards of additional protection. Partly these rules filled lacunae in the TRIPS Agreement (such as test data protection),[5] and partly they curtailed rights existing under the agreement (such as parallel imports or flexibilities in plant variety protection).[6]

With respect to the enforcement of IPRs, industrialised countries negotiated the Anti-Counterfeiting Trade Agreement (ACTA) with a view to creating a new plurilateral benchmark that could eventually be used as a reference in bilateral negotiations, in particular with emerging countries (Yu 2011: 1). The draft of ACTA was negotiated by a group of developed countries outside the context of existing institutions (Drahos 2001; Kaminski 2011: 1–5). ACTA was designed as a plurilateral agreement on IPRs, aiming at a higher level of international standards of protection and at better enforcement. ACTA builds on the language of TRIPS but introduces its own institution. As a plurilateral agreement it was meant to lie outside the context of the institutional checks and balances built into the WTO (Kaminski 2009). Thus, just like the shift from WIPO to WTO, which was exacted by powerful countries, the agenda for the shift from WTO to ACTA was pushed by the same group of countries. ACTA eventually failed, mainly as a result of resistance in the European Parliament. Negotiations were not sufficiently inclusive, and an emerging community of Internet users were afraid of having their liberties impaired (e.g. Bridy 2012).

In conclusion, the evolution of international IP protection clearly demonstrates how a dialectical relationship of preferential, bilateral, plurilateral and multilateral fora has existed for decades. The cycle of alternating preferentialism and multilateralism creates opportunities for additional gains through shifting the forum of regulation: it allows for faster and facilitated negotiations and for the consolidation of gains. Developed countries seek to fragment developing country coalitions and take advantage of the bargaining asymmetries in bilateral negotiations. The strategy of developed countries lies in forcing developing countries to make compromises in favour of developed countries' interests (Drahos 2003). One of the reasons why developing countries negotiate PTAs, and enter into

---

[5] For example, US–Chile (2004) establishes a patent-registration linkage and exclusive rights to pharmaceutical test data.

[6] See, for example, Agreement between the United States of America and the Hashemite Kingdom of Jordan on the Establishment of a Free Trade Area, signed by both parties in October 2000.

bilateral compromises in Iprs, is that they seek advantages in other areas but also have to react to the pressure resulting from unilateralism of other countries (Abbott, Cottier and Gurry 2011: 34ff.). This is referred to as the 'global ratchet' by Drahos (2003: 7; also Mercurio 2006: 222–3).

Multilateral and preferential rules are closely knit by the principle of MFN. The clause in TRIPS Article 4 does not include an exception for PTAs. As a consequence, any PTA negotiated outside the multilateral context that contains higher IP standards assists in the resetting of international standards and is crucial for negotiations with developing countries. Developing countries will have to grant the protection that developed countries agreed on in a compromise to all other nations. Once a critical mass of PTAs is reached, TRIPS-plus standards will in turn become new minimum standards that will benefit the countries in negotiating stronger multilateral IP protection in another round of WTO negotiations (Abbott, Cottier and Gurry 2011: 5; Mercurio 2006: 223).[7] Preferential standards on IP protection, both on substantive protection and in terms of enforcement, thus entail significant spillover effects.

Thus, we conclude that the policies of international IPRs are embedded in a cycle of alternation between preferential and multilateral standard setting: a higher level of standards of protection in preferentialism, and harmonisation of regulation through multilateral consolidation of minimum standards. Such processes can take place concurrently as has been seen with the evolution of the Berne Convention and the TRIPS Agreement (Drahos 2001: 7; Mercurio 2006: 235; also Helfer 2004). The challenges for the future, however, raise the question whether the dialectical process inevitably leads to ever increasing standards of protection, ignoring equally legitimate concerns of competition and open access to information. The regulatory dynamics led to a general debate on necessary ceilings for IPRs (Ruse-Khan 2009; Ruse-Kahn and Kur 2008). Such ceilings inherently need to be introduced by a future generation of multilateral rules in a revised TRIPS, forming part of an overall approach reflecting the dialectical relationship of multilateral and bilateral rules.[8]

---

[7]  The effects of the evolution of TRIPS-plus standards are mainly detrimental to developing countries as they will be challenged with a reduction of flexibilities and will thus face difficulties in particular with regard to public health. The only way for developing countries to counteract the increasing influence of developed countries' coalitions is to form coalitions of their own. The consolidation of stronger IP protection on a multilateral level under the auspices of the WTO thus remains unrealistic at present.

[8]  See below Chapter IV(C).

## II. The case of liberalising trade in services: from multilateral to preferential trade agreements

The first PTAs to mention services trade all involved the EC,[9] starting with the EC Treaty of Rome in 1957 and continuing, aside from association agreements, with the economic partnership agreements between the EC and African countries. The Caribbean countries followed suit,[10] and in 1985, the United States concluded its first PTA in services.[11] Generally, however, services trade regulation is a relatively young discipline. It mainly developed within the case law of the European Court of Justice on freedom of services but lags behind other areas, in particular trade in goods and free movement of persons, in terms of legislative measures and levels of market access within the EU.[12] Similarly, the field was of minor importance in PTAs. The main impetus in this field came from multilateralism.

In parallel to the first preferential attempts to regulate trade in services, research developed in academia. Hugh Corbet, who had established the Trade Policy Research Centre in London in 1968, commissioned Brian Griffiths from the London School of Economics to undertake a study of international flows of services and restriction on transactions in the services sector. The resulting book, *Invisible Barriers to Invisible Trade* (published in 1975), became the starting point for much of the subsequent work in the field of services trade liberalisation. More or less concomitantly, the Organisation for Economic Co-operation and Development (OECD) countries identified the need for action in light of the increasing importance of the services sector to ensure liberalisation and nondiscrimination, and the United States adopted the strategy of including services in international trade negotiations. Consequently, the Tokyo Round resulted in a few references to services, but only insofar as they affected trade in goods (see Feketekuty 1988: 296–304).

---

[9] EC Treaty of Rome (1957), EC Greece Association Agreement (1961), Yaoundé I (196), Arusha Agreement II (1969) and Yaoundé II (1996).

[10] CARICOM (1973) and Organisation of Eastern Caribbean States (1981).

[11] Israel–US (1985).

[12] See the debate on the so-called Bolkestein Directive, Proposal for a Directive of the European Parliament and of the Council on Services in the Internal Market, Brussels, 5 March 2004: the directive was aiming at establishing a single market for services within the EU and was seen as providing an important kick-start to the Lisbon Agenda. Before the directive was adopted as the Directive 2006/123/EC on 27 December 2006, it was subject to substantial modifications, which finally did not establish a single market for services, but strengthened the principle of free movement and transparency in the EU services market.

The main aim during the following years was to provide background information on services trade. In the 1980s, the United States conducted bilateral consultations and negotiations on services trade liberalisation with both Canada and Israel. These negotiations also served as 'dress rehearsals' for the multilateral negotiations (Feketekuty 1988: 313). During the process of collecting information on trade liberalisation in services, all the industrialised countries came to the conclusion that services trade is in their interest. Thus, they aimed at putting services trade on the agenda of the GATT for new multilateral trade negotiations.

However, in 1984, this attempt failed because no consensus could be reached between developed and developing countries. Only after many meetings with developing country representatives was the agenda for the Uruguay Round of multilateral trade negotiations, including negotiations on services trade liberalisation, approved in 1986 in Punta Del Este. This subsequently led to the establishment – separate from the GATT – of the multilateral treaty for trade in services, the GATS (Feketekuty 1988: 321).

To date, little substantial trade liberalisation has been achieved through the GATS because country schedules by and large codify existing domestic legislation. True trade liberalisation in services has mainly been achieved through the negotiating process of WTO accession and through PTAs. Despite the comparative advantages of the GATS vis-à-vis PTAs (dispute settlement process, policy coordination between ministries and securing of domestic policy reforms) (Adlung 2007), it is primarily viewed as an exercise in binding the status quo (Stephenson 2002: 192). Thus, as multilateral negotiations on trade liberalisation in services have not yet produced the desired outcome, and as services trade regulation is still a relatively young discipline in international economic law, countries have increasingly focused on pushing trade liberalisation in services forward through PTAs.

Yet it is important to stress that GATS initially developed and defined the conceptual terms and notions of trade liberalisation and regulation. Ever since its adoption, the agreement and its disciplines have formed and shaped subsequent efforts at liberalisation. PTAs build upon the conceptual framework developed during the multilateral talks of the Uruguay Round and use either positive or negative listings for scheduling commitments.

In parallel with the increasing preferentialism in services trade regulation, the plurilateral initiative behind the Trade in Services Agreement

(TiSA) seeks to bind GATS-plus levels while exerting pressure on the multilateral level to take up the negotiations again. Since TiSA is expected to go substantially beyond the scope of GATS regulation, it has the potential to introduce innovative and new regulation. It, thus, fits perfectly into the dialectical relationship described here between preferentialism and multilateralism.

While industrialised countries such as the United States and the members of the EC initiated multilateral negotiations on the liberalisation of trade in services, they were also among the first nations to conclude PTAs in services. In South America, with its tradition of regional integration, the trend is more towards consolidation and deepening of the existing frameworks – for example, by adding services to an existing PTA in goods – than towards negotiating new agreements. In the Asia-Pacific region, on the other hand, a large number of mostly bilateral – new – PTAs in goods and services are being negotiated or have recently come into force (Crawford and Fiorentino 2005: 10–13). In South Asia, India has been the main focus of PTA activities, shifting only relatively slowly from a focus on goods and agriculture to services (Chanda 2011). Finally, PTA dynamics in Africa and in the Middle East show signs of following the global trends, namely, those of consolidation of existing agreements and expanding around the globe (Crawford and Fiorentino 2005: 13). However, services remain generally underrepresented in economic integration efforts on the African continent and in Arab countries.

Figure 19.2 illustrates that before the Uruguay Round, little was happening internationally with respect to the regulation of cross-border trade in services. Around 1990, only 10 PTAs with binding commitments in trade liberalisation in services existed, and only 8 PTAs listed liberalisation of trade in services as a goal for the future. Additionally, 7 of those 10 agreements with commitments to liberalise trade in services involve the EC. In parallel to the final phase of the Uruguay Round, between 1990 and 1995, preferential trade liberalisation in services took off: during this period, 23 new agreements listed liberalisation of trade in services as a future goal, and 17 PTAs with substantial commitments on liberalisation of trade in services were concluded. Among these 17 agreements were the early cornerstones of international regulation of services trade, the EC Maastricht Treaty (1992), the European Economic Area (1992) and the North American Free Trade Agreement (NAFTA) (1992).

The EC Treaty of Rome, which was apparently the first trade agreement with a separate chapter on services trade, already provided a relatively

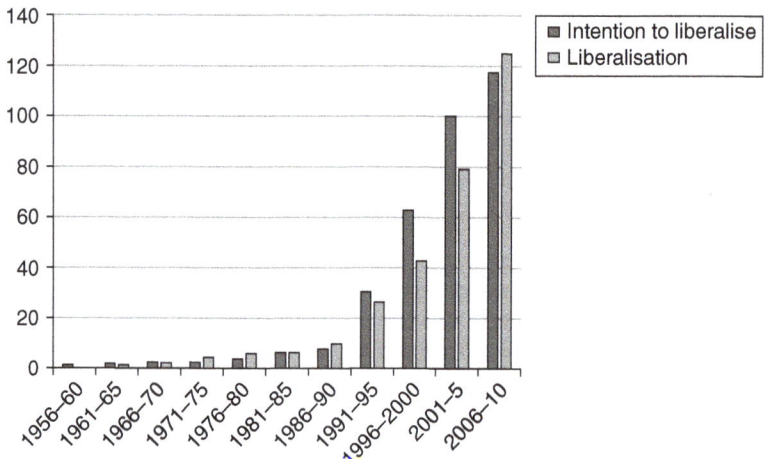

**Figure 19.2** PTAs with commitments to liberalise, or an intention to liberalise, trade in services (1956–2010)
*Source:* Derived from DESTA data set (Dür, Baccini and Elsig 2014) and WTO.[13]

comprehensive definition of services trade, even indicating that services can be delivered in different ways:[14]

> Services within the meaning of this Treaty shall be deemed to be services normally supplied for remuneration, to the extent that they are not governed by the provisions relating to the free movement of goods, capital and persons. Services shall include in particular: (a) activities of an industrial character; (b) activities of a commercial character; (c) artisan activities; and (d) activities of the liberal professions. Without prejudice to the provisions of the Chapter relating to the right of establishment, a person supplying a service may, in order to carry out that service, temporarily exercise his activity in the State where the service is supplied, under the same conditions as are imposed by that State on its own nationals.

It is interesting to note that, at least in Europe, from the very beginning of regulation of trade in services, mode 4 supply of services (temporary movement of natural persons) was considered so essential that it was explicitly mentioned.

The initial structure and language of the regulation of services trade were later introduced by the EC in its economic partnership agreements

---

[13] Notified RTAs (online). Available at: http://rtais.wto.org/UI/PublicMaintainRTAHome. aspx. Accessed 16 March 2014.

[14] EC Treaty of Rome (1957), Article 60.

(EPAs) around the globe. The chapter on services in Yaoundé I, for example, introduces MFN[15] and establishes a binding commitment[16] to liberalising the provision of services:[17]

> Services within the meaning of this Convention shall be deemed to be services normally provided against remuneration, in so far as they are not governed by the provisions relating to trade, the right of establishment and movements of capital. Services shall include in particular activities of an industrial character, activities of a commercial character, artisan activities and activities of the liberal professions, excluding wage-earning activities.

More or less the same language and structure appear in the Arusha Agreement II, with some clarifications, such as use of the term *employed persons* (instead of 'wage-earning activities').[18] Yaoundé II furthermore strengthens MFN by stating that both de facto and de jure discrimination are to be abandoned.[19] However, Yaoundé II still uses the same definition of services as did Yaoundé I. Also, Lomé I and Lomé II follow more or less the language and structure of Yaoundé I and Yaoundé II.

In Lomé III and Lomé IV, services are given special attention with a separate chapter referring to the importance of services for economic development and by an outlining of the most development-effective services sectors. Interestingly, in Lomé III and Lomé IV, commitments in liberalisation of trade in services have again disappeared from the agreement. It remains striking that the parties to Lomé did not consider it necessary to include a definition of the term *services* in the agreement.

Whereas a definition of services is entirely missing from the agreement, EC–Turkey introduced the first standstill obligation on services trade:[20]

> The Contracting Parties shall refrain from introducing as between themselves new restrictions on the freedom of establishment and the free supply of services.

The Caribbean Community (CARICOM) is apparently the first agreement in the world to which the EC is not a party that includes regulation of trade in services and establishes its own language for preferential treatment while building on the European definition of services:[21]

1. Each Member State agrees as far as practicable to extend to persons belonging to other Member States preferential treatment over persons

---

[15] Yaoundé I (1964), Article 30.   [16] Yaoundé I (1964), Article 29.
[17] Yaoundé I (1964), Article 32.   [18] Arusha Agreement II (1969), Article 19.
[19] Yaoundé II (1969), Article 31.   [20] EC–Turkey (1970), Additional Protocol, Article 41.
[21] CARICOM (1973), Article 36.

belonging to States outside the Common Market with regard to the provision of services.

2. For the purposes of this Article the term 'services' shall be considered as services for remuneration provided that they are not governed by provisions relating to trade, the right of establishment or movement of capital and includes, in particular, activities of an industrial or commercial character, artisan activities and activities of the professions, excluding activities of employed persons.

Whereas the Organisation of East Caribbean States introduces 'the abolition, as between Member States, of the obstacles to the free movement of persons, services and capital'[22] as a principle of the common market, it refers later in the treaty specifically only to the free movement of persons[23] and to transportation.[24] Thus, as an exception to the rule, partial liberalisation of trade in services is established, with a specific focus on one sector and one aspect of services trade.

Israel–US, then, is the first agreement establishing a comprehensive and encompassing structure for the regulation of liberalisation of trade in services. Given the novelty of the rules, it was first added as a separate – not legally binding – declaration to the main treaty between Israel and the United States. The declaration provided in general for NT,[25] provided a detailed definition of services and services sectors,[26] included transparency provisions[27] and set a date for the review of the effectiveness of the measures in the declaration.[28] Through the transparency provision, the first form of a negative-list approach is introduced: the parties to the agreement are required to notify the other party about nonconforming

---

[22] Organisation of Eastern Caribbean States (1981), Agreement Establishing the East Caribbean Common Market, Article 3(c).

[23] Organisation of Eastern Caribbean States (1981), Agreement Establishing the East Caribbean Common Market, Article 12.

[24] Organisation of Eastern Caribbean States (1981), Agreement Establishing the East Caribbean Common Market, Article 16.

[25] Israel–US (1985), Declaration on Trade in Services, Article 3: 'Each Party will endeavor to assure that trade in services with the other nation is governed by the principle of national treatment.'

[26] Israel–US (1985), Declaration on Trade in Services, Article 1.

[27] Israel–US (1985), Declaration on Trade in Services, Article 7: 'Each Party will make public its domestic laws and regulations affecting trade in services and notify the other Party of laws and regulations which discriminate against a service exported from the other nation.'

[28] Israel–US (1985), Declaration on Trade in Services, Article 9: 'The parties will review the effectiveness of this Declaration not later than eighteen months from the date that this Declaration is signed.'

measures that will be upheld even after signing the declaration.[29] Furthermore, the definition and list of services are interesting:[30]

> Definition: Trade in services takes place when a service is exported from the supplier nation and is imported into the other nation. Services encompass, but are not limited to, transportation; travel and tourism services; communications; banking services, insurance; other financial activities; professional services, such as consulting in construction, engineering, accounting, medicine, education, and law, and the providing of other professional services such as management consulting; computer services; motion pictures; advertising.

The different modes of supply, however, are completely absent from the agreement. Furthermore, there is no general definition of the term *service*; rather, services are defined via sectors and subsectors, and the parties to the declaration supposedly attribute the same meaning to the term *service*.

The protocol on trade in services of the Australia New Zealand Closer Economic Relations Agreement (ANZCERTA) adopted in 1988 finally establishes legally binding, far-reaching, detailed liberalisation of trade in services, based on a negative-list approach. It defines the provision of services as follows:[31]

> Provision of services includes: (a) the production, distribution, marketing, sale and delivery of a service; and (b) for the purpose of the activities referred to in the previous sub-paragraph of this paragraph: (i) access to and use of domestic distribution systems; and (ii) rights of establishment.

It basically opens the entire services market for liberalisation, providing for nonrestricted market access, NT and MFN.[32] The few exemptions to this general rule are listed in a separate annex to the protocol, and it is fairly safe to say that the ANZCERTA liberalises services trade to an extent that up until 1988 was absolutely unique.

In the same year, the Canada–US agreement was concluded. It uses similar language to the ANZCERTA, while at the same time not providing for full market access and being based on a positive-list approach. Regulation is sophisticated, and, aside from a positive listing, some services sectors are also listed with a separate annex in the agreement. On its scope and coverage, the Canada–US agreement says:[33]

---

[29]  Israel–US (1985), Declaration on Trade in Services, Article 7.
[30]  Israel–US (1985), Declaration on Trade in Services, Article 1.
[31]  ANZCERTA (1988), Protocol on Trade in Services, Article 3.
[32]  ANZCERTA (1988), Protocol on Trade in Services, Articles 4–6.
[33]  Canada–US (1988), Article 1401.

1. This Chapter shall apply to any measure of a Party related to the provision of a covered service by or on behalf of a person of the other Party within or into the territory of the Party.
2. In this Chapter, provision of a covered service includes:
   a. the production, distribution, sale, marketing and delivery of a covered service and the purchase or use thereof;
   b. access to, and use of, domestic distribution systems;
   c. the establishment of a commercial presence (other than an investment) for the purpose of distributing, marketing, delivering, or facilitating a covered service; and
   d. subject to Chapter Sixteen (Investment), any investment for the provision of a covered service and any activity associated with the provision of a covered service.

Thus, the Canada–US agreement generally covers all modes of supply, although it still lists them in a rather indirect manner. NT is generally provided;[34] however, no distinction between market access regulation and NT regulation is made. As a result of the positive-list approach, liberalisation is applied only to the services sectors that are listed by either party to the agreement. Thus, in general, Canada–US is less liberal than is ANZCERTA.

Finally, while the EC Maastricht Treaty and the European Economic Area (EEA) were more or less aligned with the European agreements that preceded them, the NAFTA treaty introduced a number of new aspects of regulation of trade in services. Arguably, NAFTA served to a considerable extent as a role model for the GATS. For instance, NAFTA is the first agreement to introduce a more or less identical definition of the modes of supply to that used in the GATS:[35]

cross-border provision of a service or cross border trade in services means the provision of a service: (a) from the territory of a Party into the territory of another Party, (b) in the territory of a Party by a person of that Party to a person of another Party, or (c) by a national of a Party in the territory of another Party, but does not include the provision of a service in the territory of a Party by an investment, as defined in Article 1139 (Investment Definitions), in that territory.

Unlike the Canada–US agreement, NAFTA reintroduced the negative-list approach, together with the separate annexes to the services chapter for specific sectors of services trade. It establishes NT[36] and MFN,[37] and

---

[34] Canada–US (1988), Article 1402.   [35] NAFTA (1992), Article 1213.
[36] NAFTA (1992), Article 1202.   [37] NAFTA (1992), Article 1203.

it addresses the challenges of behind-the-border barriers to trade with an extensive provision on licensing and certification.[38]

From this overview of the first provisions regulating services trade, it becomes obvious that no single PTA served as a blueprint for the GATS. Furthermore, although a couple of preferential attempts to regulate services trade preceded the GATS, experiences with services trade regulation must have been limited, to say the least, at the time that services were added to the Uruguay Round. Thus, the GATS is not only the first multilateral agreement regulating services trade but also the first agreement worldwide establishing coherent and specific regulation of services trade. Although the GATS was inspired by previous agreements on the bilateral and regional levels, it nevertheless introduced a unique structure and a unique set of general rules.

With the exception of IP protection, the willingness to negotiate a multilateral agreement on trade in services was not fostered by the simple need for multilateral rules to bring coherence to a confusing web of different provisions stemming from a large number of PTAs. Rather it stems from the conviction that services trade had become important for the world economy and that regulation was in everyone's best interest.

Therefore, the GATS serves as a prime example of the potential of a multilateral forum to take up new areas of regulation and to establish basic rules and commitments for everyone from the very beginning. It is, however, generally agreed that as a result of the Doha Round later getting stuck, the initial momentum of the GATS has diminished. The agreement was meant to provide the basic stepping stone for a global regulatory framework of services trade regulation. The world is still waiting for the next building brick to follow the initial agreement; preferentialism has taken the lead in regulation of services trade and presumably will influence the next stage of multilateral regulation of services trade in much the same way as preferentialism influenced the TRIPS.

## C. Emerging patterns of the dialectical relationship

Following the establishment of the WTO, PTAs often focused on so-called WTO-plus elements, strongly building on the body of WTO law. It was a matter of filling lacunae, or securing particular interests, in particular

---

[38] NAFTA (1992), Article 1210.

in the field of IP, that could be achieved bilaterally, but not in a multi-lateral context. Many of these agreements are concluded among major markets and noncontiguous countries. The idea of regional integration was expanded to transcontinental preferential trade. Thereafter, it became appropriate to speak of PTAs and to look at regional trade agreements (RTAs) as a subcategory.

PTAs were partly introduced for political reasons. Partly, they responded to the needs of globalisation, which no longer primarily seeks more integrated markets with adjacent neighbouring countries. This became particularly true for Latin America and Africa, where ties with distant markets are often closer than the ties with neighbouring countries operating under different political rule. A new generation of bilateral PTAs emerged during the Doha Development Round that was initiated in 2001 but that has been stalled since 2006. The accession of China to the WTO in 2001 fundamentally changed the basic equation of the multilateral system and reduced the willingness of WTO Members to negotiate multilaterally. As a consequence, countries continued their policies of preferentialism.

Recently, a new dimension in the form of new plurilateral agreements has been added. In 2010, negotiations on the TPP commenced. These negotiations are being conducted by 12 countries in North America, Latin America and Asia and include the United States and Japan.[39] In July 2013, the EC and the United States commenced negotiations on the TTIP, technically a preferential agreement, yet encompassing 50 US states and 28 EU Member States. These countries account for 50 per cent of world trade and 30 per cent of world gross domestic product (GDP). (For more on TTIP, see Hansen-Kuhn and Suppan 2013, and for more on TPP, see Voon 2013.)

These emerging patterns differ from those of previous periods in a number of respects. First, the TPP and the TTIP are being negotiated among countries that in the past represented the backbone of the multi-lateral system. No longer are preferential agreements typically concluded between a large market and smaller ones, the latter adjusting to the templates and regulations of the larger one. Second, these negotiations are neither multilateral nor bilateral in the traditional sense. They form a new generation of plurilateralism, taking into account the interest of

---

[39] Negotiations were commenced by Chile, New Zealand, Singapore, Brunei, United States, Australia, Vietnam and Peru and were eventually expanded to include Malaysia, Canada, Mexico and Japan.

a considerable number of countries in necessarily complex negotiations. Measured against universalism at the WTO, they appear to be exponents of what may be called minilateralism or, more exactly, mini-multilateralism (Drache 2011; Herman 2011; Naim 2009; Powell and Low 2011). Third, the architecture of these future agreements inherently includes a sophisticated institutional architecture that goes beyond traditional patterns of bilateral agreements. In TTIP, regulatory convergence is considered to be a horizontal and ongoing task, which may only begin with the conclusion of treaty negotiations (BusinessEurope 2013). Innovative channels for exchanging information, mutual dialogue on planned and suggested legislation and regulation, joint initiatives in international standard-setting bodies and enquiry points – all under the umbrella of a joint Regulatory Cooperation Council – are new ideas in the field. None of them are supposed to reduce constitutional rule-making powers in legislation and regulation on either side of the Atlantic. Yet an ongoing and informed dialogue may lay the foundation for common solutions and global leadership where it seems feasible, be it technical barriers to trade, services, IP or investment protection. The framework could evolve into a transatlantic forum for regular and continued interaction. It stresses the idea that ongoing processes and dialogue – rather than fixed rules – increasingly shape modern agreements.

Although these future agreements legally amount to PTAs, in essence, they amount to a new type of global regionalism that cannot be compared to prior states of preferential trade – except for the foundation of GATT in 1947, when 23 countries mutually pledged MFN treatment. If they remain within the boundaries set by existing trade and investment law, and if they remain reluctant to allow other countries to join, they may – instead of replacing the WTO – eventually provide enough incentive, resulting from not only regulatory pressure but also economic interests, once again to take up trade negotiations on the universal multilateral level. This assessment derives from the nature of the regulatory tasks ahead.

Historically, parallel negotiations by the world's leading economies in multiple regulatory fora – within the multilateral WTO, the plurilateral TiSA, ACTA, TPP or TTIP, and the preferential level – have never before been seen to this extent. Interestingly, this development was sparked by the establishment of the WTO with all its multilateral agreements in the mid-1990s. Ever since, countries have shown an increasing interest in the regulation of trade relations, be it on a preferential, a plurilateral or a multilateral basis. Given that a possible parallel evolution of regulation in multiple fora creates new challenges for the preservation of regulatory coherence, the regulatory dialogue between multilateralism and preferentialism today is different from how it used to be. Generally, trade regulation today is facing a new challenge, that of regulatory burden sharing between the different levels of regulation that currently apply to trade relations.

## D. Regulatory burden sharing

### I. The impact of regulating behind-the-border issues

Many of the topics addressed by modern bilateral and plurilateral trade and investment agreements today relate to what we call behind-the-border issues (Cottier 2014). Whereas tariffs remain important in selected areas and in agriculture, the main trade barriers today result from nontariff measures, differences in regulation and the absence of harmonised standards. This is true for trade both in goods and in services. Increasingly, processes and production methods (PPMs) are moving towards centre stage and define market access for products in light of policy concerns such as labour standards, the protection of the environment and climate change mitigation. The structure of regulatory challenges will change patterns of negotiations essentially for the three following reasons.

First, countries negotiating behind-the-border issues within PTAs are likely to adjust to the rules and standards of larger markets. The United States, the EC and other large markets thus offer their distinct templates, based on which agreements are formed. Smaller countries and markets regularly adjust to these templates. A country negotiating with two or more large markets may therefore find itself in a position of having to adopt different templates to address the same behind-the-border issue. The general nature of regulation of the matter, however, does not allow the adoption of two different standards in domestic legislation. It is, for example, not possible to adopt a system protecting geographical indications with one entity and a system of collective marks with another, where both are responding to different criteria. Domestic legislation is bound to be uniform and to apply in the same manner to all addressees from home and abroad. The regulation of nontariff barriers thus has significant spillover effects. Bilaterally negotiated settlements will be equally implemented to the benefit of third parties, yet will fall short of reciprocal treatment. The need to operate on a single and uniform legal standard in domestic law for practical reasons thus implies a significant de facto MFN effect. This effect may even be legally mandatory, as the example of

IP showed. Enhanced standards of protection in PTAs are to be extended to all members of the WTO alike.[40]

Second, as the proliferation of PTAs continues, more and more countries will face the problem of accepting divergent templates. They will conclude that by far the best solution is to negotiate on the basis of a template that is multilaterally defined and alike for all different partners (see also Relaño 2006: 99). We therefore submit that, in the long run, members of the WTO will return to Geneva and will take up negotiations on behind-the-border issues multilaterally. In a dialectical relationship, the tide will turn and return to the WTO. We need to take into account the regulatory shift and the legal nature of future regulatory issues. It may well be that classical issues of market access, in particular tariffs and quantitative restrictions, will remain a matter of preferentialism under WTO law and will mainly be left to PTAs. The foundations of standard setting and norms and standards having the effect of harmonisation or mutual recognition may, however, increasingly shift to WTO and multilateral negotiations.

Third, the world economy of the twenty-first century may no longer require foremost the establishment of regional or transcontinental preferential markets, but rather it needs a regulatory framework that fosters and enables global value chains. Increasing insights into the structure of division of labour as well as the increasingly blurred distinctions between trade in goods and trade in services will call for a coherent regulatory framework allowing optimal allocation of resources and economies of scale in the production and distribution of both goods and services. Existing fragmentation by means of rules of origin, trade remedies that depend on the particular origin of a good, will become increasingly difficult to apply.

Insights in the interest of returning to the universal multilateralism of the WTO will change attitudes to negotiations. Members will no longer block and veto negotiations but will carefully balance the pros and cons of preferential negotiations, which often leave them in a less advantageous position than can be expected from a balanced multilateral process. We are likely to see a different attitude to norm making and a more flexible approach towards bringing about compromise and thus avoiding stalemate. The present Doha Development Agenda is largely influenced by new blocking powers that governments are able to operate. The insight into the downside, the price to be paid for PTAs, and the problem of

---

[40] See Chapter II(A).

responding to divergent templates are likely to bring about changes of attitude in a learning process.

Trade negotiations in the WTO will change accordingly. No longer will it be a matter of formal trade rounds primarily seeking market access. Rather, it will be a matter of norm making comparable to the process of legislation in fields that are not inherently connected. The WTO is likely to see an ongoing legislative process with results, successes and failures, varying on a project-by-project basis. Negotiating on different services sectors; combining negotiations on trade and energy; no longer treating goods, services, IPRs and investment separately from each other; linking trade and production standards in labour relations, environmental protection and climate change; and the emergence of disciplines on antitrust and unfair competition will shape the day-to-day business of norm making in the WTO.

WTO negotiations are likely to be strongly influenced by existing bilateral and plurilateral agreements. Modern universalism in the WTO may increasingly serve as a mechanism for binding and extending the status quo to other parties in order to simplify global trade relations and ensure a minimum level of regulatory coherence. In this respect, the contents of the TTIP and the TTP are of particular interest: once these two mega-regionals have agreed to a certain regulatory structure, it will be hard for the rest of the world to maintain different regulations. It is thus likely that the TTIP and the TTP will influence multilateral regulation strongly in the future. Although this is a natural consequence of the dialectical relationship of multilateralism and preferentialism, the regulatory consequences of the TTIP and the TTP for the rest of the world are unlikely to take into account the interests of other countries, in particular small developing and least-developed countries. If negotiations on these regulatory issues had taken place in the WTO, developing countries would have had a way to influence the outcome. The way it looks right now, the stalling of the Doha Round has deprived the group of economically less powerful countries of their chance to actively participate in rule making.

## II. Identifying areas of legitimate preferential market access

Not all areas are equally suited to a return to universal trade regulation. Paradoxically, classic nonregulatory market issues, in particular the reduction of tariff protection and of quantitative restrictions on goods and services, are likely to stay with PTAs. For instance, in the area of services trade, researchers around the world agree that certain services sectors are more suitable than others for both multilateral regulation and multilateral liberalisation to the benefit of all WTO Members (e.g. Sauvé and Shingal 2011; Van der Marel and Shepherd 2013). The potential exists to use the flexibilities already present in the current regulatory framework of the WTO to do justice to the levels of suitability of the different areas of trade regulation. These flexibilities can be found, for instance, in Article V of the GATS. The provision allows for sectoral liberalisation of trade in services in a PTA on condition that a number of requirements are met (Sieber-Gasser, forthcoming). Or they can be found in GATS Article VII, which deals with the recognition of diplomas. Such recognition involves a high level of mutual trust and thus is primarily suitable for preferential avenues. The same holds true for mutual recognition agreements that reciprocally recognise product standards and modes of testing. Generally, the recognition of standards and diplomas is unlikely to be suitable for multilateral application in the near future.

Another area of legitimate preferential market access may be seen in PTAs involving least-developed countries and developing countries: depending on the level of economic development and on the structure of the economy, preferentialism may justifiably, for a limited period, be a more appropriate forum for trade regulation and economic integration than multilateralism. The legal basis for preferentialism driven by development policies can be found in the special and differential treatment in WTO law or in specific provisions explicitly addressing least-developed and developing countries (see, e.g., Slaughter 2004; Feichtner 2012; Cullet 2003; Low 2007; Cottier 2006).

There might also be an area of trade regulation in which de facto preferential market access is embedded in the subject of regulation, for instance, government procurement or IP protection. There are areas of trade regulation that today assume a certain level of development that has not yet been reached by all Members of the WTO. In these cases, nontariff barriers to trade create de facto preferential market access for those countries that can afford to meet certain standards. Thus, different levels of specialisation and technological capacity naturally lead to increasing preferentialism in the sectors that are most affected by technological change (e.g. Egger and Shingal 2013).

Thus, multilateralism will generally be increasingly busy with questions of regulatory coherence in the future, while market access commitments will increasingly be found in PTAs. In parallel to this development, certain areas of trade regulation may move entirely to the most appropriate forum of regulation: for some areas this is the multilateral forum, whereas for other areas it is preferentialism.

## III. Constitutionalising WTO rules

From the beginning, the multilateral system was meant to evolve in tandem with MFN and preferential relations within regions. Regional developments have served as major incentives for trade liberalisation on the multilateral level, such as the creation of the EC Common Market in 1957. PTAs are more than an exception to the rule. They should be regulated and governed in a way that allows them to serve as laboratories for future WTO disciplines, rendering them stepping stones to multilateralism (Cottier 2005: 597).

Seeking a proper balance between trade creation and trade diversion by PTAs, WTO law expounds basic and well-known requirements in order to justify departures from MFN under GATT Article XXIV and GATS Article V. The multilateral trading system essentially channels preferential trade into two lawful avenues: customs unions and free trade agreements. The law seeks to avoid ad hoc and selective privileges and requires agreements to be comprehensive, entailing substantially all the trade and substantial sectorial coverage. It requires the gradual abolition of all tariffs and quantitative restrictions and does not allow compensation by burdening third parties (Cottier and Oesch 2004; Islam and Alam 2009).

More flexible rules exist for agreements among developing countries. Yet the rules essentially provide a framework with which PTAs should comply. The framework inherently entails that WTO rules override subsequent PTAs and render their application and operation dependent upon compliance. Yet, in reality and in contemporary law, no such hierarchy exists.

Today, PTAs are on a par with WTO law. They are often later in time than corresponding WTO law and prevail under the doctrine of *lex specialis*. Violations of WTO law do not impair the validity and application of these agreements. Among parties to a PTA, the disciplines of WTO law are thus without impact, as none of the parties to the PTA is inclined to challenge the agreement under WTO law. Third parties claiming MFN may do so. Yet, case law shows considerable reluctance to engage in litigation. There is what may be called a silent conspiracy to leave WTO disciplines without precision (Cottier and Oesch 2004: 370ff.).[41] Today,

---

[41] The most prominent cases include *EC – Bananas*, WT/DS27, which established that no measure was a priori excluded from the scope of application of the GATS (see also Mattoo 2000: 53ff.); *Turkey – Textiles*, WT/DS34/AB/R, para. 48, in which the Appellate Body said that 'substantially all the trade' is not the same as all the trade but is also considerably

virtually all Members of the WTO are involved in PTAs and do not wish to limit policy space. Efforts have been made by WTO Members to increase the scrutiny of PTAs upon notification. The Secretariat today is mandated to assess compatibility. Yet the law stops short of attaching any strings to such review, and, at the most, Members can deny approval of conformity, however, without this having legal or practical consequences. Consequently, approval has been granted to almost all PTAs notified so far with a single exception (e.g. Abass 2004; Stevens and Kennan 2001).

The current framework and the way it is handled contribute significantly to the entanglement of trade policy with a great number of agreements that are not compatible with WTO law. To some extent, it is possible to read WTO law as being superior under the Vienna Convention on the Law of Treaties (Cottier and Foltea 2006). Greater coherence, however, would suggest introducing a clause into the WTO agreement comparable to Article 103 of the United Nations Charter. The provision establishes the primacy of obligations under the UN Charter, preempting rules laid down in other international agreements. A comparable provision in the WTO agreement would state that all PTAs concluded are subject to the disciplines of WTO law. Another idea in this context is to extend jurisdiction of the WTO to encompass PTAs, thus developing the WTO dispute settlement system into an equivalent of a World Trade Court.[42]

Currently, we are far from a consensus on that point. Yet, as evidence of trade diversion induced by noncompatible PTAs may increase over time, showing the costs of preferentialism, the international community may learn that a proper and dialectical balance of multilateral and preferential trade agreements provides long-term benefits to all. Again, it is a matter of tearing down Chinese walls and moving towards greater coherence.

## E.  Conclusion

We conclude by calling for a rather more relaxed and confident attitude towards the future of multilateralism in trade regulation based on the evidence of a long-lasting, stable, dialectical relationship between preferentialism and universal multilateralism. Historically, the two avenues

---

more than merely some of the trade; and *Canada – Autos*, WT/DS139/R, WT/DS142/R, para. 10.271, which ruled that a PTA based on GATS Article V had to establish higher levels of liberalisation among its members than the GATS did.

[42]  See the contribution by James Flett (Chapter 22 in this volume).

are closely linked and their relationship – although characterised by regulatory waves in one or direction or the other – proves to be a stable and consistent one. Although the usual direction of development is from bilateralism to multilateralism, the opposite can equally be observed in choosing appropriate fora for rule making. Both avenues are essentially part of the same process: the convergence of the global market. MFN, which is spread throughout the vast majority of multilateral and preferential trade agreements, automatically leads towards de jure and de facto multilateralisation. It exerts considerable spillover effects on preferential trade regulation.

We suggest a shift in the focus of multilateral trade negotiations to regulatory issues, as opposed to increasing liberalisation, and to measures conducive to global value-added production. A number of factors speak in favour of enhancing recourse to multilateral fora. The shift to nontariff barriers induces the need to adopt uniform templates and nondiscriminatory regulations among different countries. Lessons will be learnt that nontariff barriers and regulatory convergence are best addressed multilaterally as countries face difficulties in adapting their own legislation and regulations to fit with often diverging templates emanating from different international agreements with different partners. Incoherent preferential regulation at some point becomes unmanageable (spaghetti bowl effect) and ties the two avenues closely together. Successful conclusions of plurilateral agreements encompassing large shares of world trade will foster convergence and recourse to WTO negotiations. At the same time, we outline how flexibilities in WTO law can be used where close relations and mutual trust form the basis of relations. There are distinct areas that will remain more suitable for preferential trade. They include market access issues and areas where mutual trust is critical, such as access to labour markets or mutual recognition of product standards. On this basis, the relationship of multilateral and preferential rules calls for further clarification and a more constitutional understanding of the relationship that subjects PTAs to the multilateral disciplines of WTO rules.

## References

Abass, Abou. 2004. 'The Cotonou Trade Regime and WTO Law.' *European Law Journal* 10 (4): 439–62.

Abbott, Frederick, Cottier, Thomas, and Gurry, Francis. 2011. *International Intellectual Property in an Integrated World Economy*. 2nd edn. New York: Wolters Kluwer.

Adlung, Rudolf. 2007. *The Contribution of Services Liberalisation to Poverty Reduction: What Role for the GATS?* Geneva: World Trade Organization, Economic Research and Statistics Division.

Alschner, Wolfgang. 2013. 'Americanization of the Bit Universe: The Influence of Friendship, Commerce and Navigation (FCN) Treaties on Modern Investment Treaty Law.' *Goettingen Journal of International Law* 5(2). http://papers. ssrn.com/sol3/papers.cfm?abstract_id=2309467. Accessed 16 March 2014.

Bridy, Annemarie. 2012. 'Copyright Policymaking as Procedural Democratic Process: A Discourse-Theoretic Perspective on ACTA, SOPA, and PIPA.' *Cardozo Arts and Entertainment* 30:153–64.

BusinessEurope. 2013. 'Advancing Regulatory Cooperation in the Transatlantic Trade and Investment Partnership.' Position Paper. Business Europe, Brussels.

Chanda, Rupa. 2011. 'Mapping the Universe of Services Disciplines in Asian PTAs.' NCCR Trade Regulation Working Paper No. 33. National Centre of Competence in Research, Bern.

Cottier, Thomas. 1991. 'The Prospects for Intellectual Property in GATT.' *Common Market Law Review* 28 (2): 383–414.

2005. 'The Erosion of Non-Discrimination: Stern Warning without True Remedies.' *Journal of International Economic Law* 8 (3): 595–601.

2006. 'From Progressive Liberalisation to Progressive Regulation in WTO Law.' *Journal of International Economic Law* 9 (4): 779–821.

2014. 'International Economic Law in Transition from Trade Liberalization to Trade Regulation.' *Journal of International Economic Law*. doi:10.1093/jiel/jgu029.

Cottier, Thomas, and Foltea, Marina. 2006. 'Constitutional Functions of the WTO and Regional Trade Agreements.' In *Regional Trade Agreements and the WTO Legal System*, edited by Lorand Bartels and Federico Ortino, 43–76. Oxford, England: Oxford University Press.

Cottier, Thomas, and Oesch, Matthias. 2004. *International Trade Regulation: Law and Policy in the WTO, the European Union and Switzerland.* Bern/London: Staempfli/Cameron May.

Crawford, Jo-Ann, and Fiorentino, Roberto V. 2005. 'The Changing Landscape of Regional Trade Agreements.' WTO Discussion Paper No. 8. World Trade Organization, Geneva.

Cullet, Philippe. 2003. *Differential Treatment in International Environmental Law.* Aldershot, England: Ashgate.

Deutsch, Klaus Günter. 2013. *Atlantic Unity in Global Competition: T-TIP in Perspective.* Frankfurt: Deutsche Bank AG DB Research. http://www.dbresearch. com/PROD/DBR_INTERNET_EN-PROD/PROD0000000000318466/ Atlantic+unity+in+global+competition%3A+T-TIP+in+perspective.PDF.

Dolzer, Rudolf, and Schreuer, Christoph. 2012. *Principles of International Invest-ment Law.* 2nd edn. Oxford, England: Oxford University Press.

Drache, Daniel. 2011. 'Reform at the Top: What's Next for the WTO? A Second Life? A Socio-Political Analysis.' *Onati Socio-Legal Series* 1 (4).

Drahos, Peter. 2001. 'BITs and BIPs: Bilateralism in Intellectual Property.' *Journal of World Intellectual Property* 4 (6): 792–807.

2003. *Expanding Intellectual Property's Empire: The Role of FTAs.* Barcelona: GRAIN. http://www.eldis.org/go/home&id=17906&type=Document#.U9 LbOWP1ooE. Accessed 23 September 2013.

Dür, Andreas, Baccini, Leonardo, and Elsig, Manfred. 2014. 'The Design of Interna-tional Trade Agreements: Introducing a New Dataset.' *Review of International Organizations* 9 (3): 353–75.

Egger, Peter, and Shingal, Anirudh. 2013. 'Determinants of Services Trade Agree-ments: Regulatory Incidence and Convergence.' Working Paper. Forum for Research in Empirical International Trade, San Rafael, CA.

Feichtner, Isabel. 2012. *The Law and Politics of WTO Waivers: Stability and Flexibility in International Law.* Cambridge: Cambridge University Press.

Feketekuty, Geza. 1988. *International Trade in Services: An Overview and Blueprint for Negotiations.* Cambridge, MA: Ballinger.

Hansen-Kuhn, Karen, and Suppan, Steve. 2013. *Promises and Perils of the TTIP: Negotiating a Transatlantic Agricultural Market, Institute for Agriculture and Trade Policy IATP.* Washington, DC: Heinrich Böll Foundation.

Helfer, Laurence R. 2004. 'Regime Shifting: The TRIPS Agreement and the New Dynamics of International Intellectual Property Lawmaking.' *Yale Journal of International Law* 29 (1): 1–83.

Herman, Dan. 2011. 'From Multi- to Mini-lateralism: Globalization's Next Stage?' http://www.cigionline.org/publications/2011/6/multi-mini-lateralism-globalization's-next-stage. Accessed 16 March 2014.

Islam, Md Rizwanul, and Alam, Shawkat. 2009. 'Preferential Trade Agreements and the Scope of GATT Article XXIV, GATS Article V and the Enabling Clause: An Appraisal of GATT/WTO Jurisprudence.' *Netherlands International Law Review* 56 (1): 1–34.

Kaminski, Margot E. 2009. 'The Origins and Potential Impact of the Anti-Counterfeiting Trade Agreement (ACTA).' *Yale Journal of International Law* 34 (2): 247–56.

2011. 'An Overview and the Evolution of the Anti-Counterfeiting Trade Agree-ment (ACTA).' PIJIP Research Paper no. 17. American University Washing-ton College of Law, Washington, DC.

Kotschwar, Barbara, and Schott, Jeffrey J. 2013. 'The Next Big Thing? The Trans-Pacific Partnership and Latin America.' *Americas Quarterly*, Spring.

Lampe, Markus. 2011. 'Explaining Nineteenth-Century Bilateralism: Economic and Political Determinants of the Cobden–Chevalier Network.' *Economic History Review* 64 (2): 644–68.

Löhr, Isabella. 2010. *Die Globalisierung geistiger Eigentumsrechte. Neue Strukturen der internationalen Zusammenarbeit 1886–1952.* Göttingen: Verlag Vandenhoeck & Ruprecht, Kritische Studien zur Geschichtswissenschaft, Band 195.

Low, Patrick. 2007. 'Is the WTO Doing Enough for Developing Countries?' In *WTO Law and Developing Countries*, edited by George A. Bermann and Petros C. Mavroidis, 324–57. Cambridge: Cambridge University Press.

Mattoo, Aaditya. 2000. 'MFN and the GATS.' In *Regulatory Barriers and the Principle of Non-Discrimination in World Trade Law*, edited by Thomas Cottier, Petros C. Mavroidis and P. Blatter, 51–100. Ann Arbor: University of Michigan Press.

Mercurio, Bryan. 2006. 'TRIPS-plus Provisions in FTAs: Recent Trends.' In *Regional Trade Agreements and the WTO Legal System*, edited by Lorand Bartels and Federico Ortino, 215–38. New York: Oxford University Press.

Nadakavukaren Schefer, Krista. 2013. *International Investment Law: Text, Cases and Materials.* Cheltenham, England: Edward Elgar.

Naim, Moses. 2009. 'Minilateralism: The Magic Number to Get Real International Action.' *Foreign Policy*, July/August.

Powell, Stephen Joseph, and Low, Trisha. 2011. 'Is the WTO Quietly Fading Away? The New Regionalism and Global Trade Rules.' *Georgetown Journal of Law and Public Policy* 9 (2): 261–82.

Relaño, Francesc. 2006. 'Global Governance by Means of Regional Integrations: Problems, Opportunities and Prospects.' In *Global Society: Conflict or Cooperation?* edited by Nina Slanevskaya, 96–101. St. Petersburg: NESTOR.

Rhodes, Carolyn 1993. *Reciprocity, U.S. Trade Policy, and the GATT Regime.* Ithaca, NY: Cornell University Press.

Ricketson, Sam. 2011. 'The Birth of the Berne Union.' In *International Intellectual Property in an Integrated World Economy*, 2nd edn., edited by Frederick M. Abbott, Thomas Cottier and Francis Gurry, 430–35. New York: Wolters Kluwer.

Ricketson, Sam, and Ginsburg, Jane C. 2006. *International Copyright and Neighbouring Rights: The Berne Convention and Beyond.* Oxford, England: Oxford University Press.

Ruse-Khan, Henning G. 2009. 'Time for a Paradigm Shift? Exploring Maximum Standards in International Intellectual Property Protection.' *Trade, Law and Development* 1 (1): 56–102.

Ruse-Khan, Henning G., and Kur, Annette. 2008. 'Enough Is Enough – The Notion of Binding Ceilings in International Intellectual Property Protection.' Research Paper Series No. 09-01. Max Planck Institute for Intellectual Property, Competition and Tax Law, Munich. http://ssrn.com/abstract=1326429. Accessed 16 March 2014.

Sachs, Wayne. 1984. 'The New U.S. Bilateral Investment Treaties.' *Berkeley Journal of International Law* 2 (1): 192–224.

Sauvé, Pierre, and Shingal, Anirudh. 2011. 'Reflections on the Preferential Liberalization of Services Trade.' NCCR Trade Regulation Working Paper
No. 2011/05. National Centre of Competence in Research, Bern.

Sieber-Gasser, Charlotte. Forthcoming. 'South–South Preferential Trade Agreements in Services: Exploring the Boundaries of International Economic Law.'
PhD dissertation, University of Bern, Bern.

Slaughter, Matthew J. 2004. 'Infant-Industry Protection and Trade Liberalisation
in Developing Countries.' Research Report. USAID, Washington, DC.

Stephenson, Sherry M. 2002. 'Regional versus Multilateral Liberalisation of Services.' *World Trade Review* 1 (2): 187–209.

Stevens, Christopher, and Kennan, Jane. 2001. 'Post Lomé WTO-Compatible Trading Arrangements.' Commonwealth Economic Paper Series. Commonwealth
Secretariat, London.

Tuthill, L. Lee, Guth, Joanne E., Skidmore, Kim A., and Gibson, Paul. 1985. Review
of the Effectiveness of Trade Dispute Settlement under the GATT and the
Tokyo Round Agreements. Report to the Committee on Finance. Washington, DC: United States International Trade Commission.

United Nations Conference on Trade and Development. 2007. 'Intellectual Property
Provisions in International Investment Arrangements.' *IIA Monitor*, no. 1.
http://unctad.org/en/docs/webiteiia20071_en.pdf.

2012. *Expropriations: A Sequel: UNCTAD Series on Issues in International Investment Agreements II*. New York: UNCTAD.

Van der Marel, Erik, and Shepherd, Ben. 2013. 'Services Trade, Regulation and
Regional Integration: Evidence from Sectoral Data.' *World Economy* 36 (11):
1393–1405.

Voon, Tania. 2013. *Trade Liberalisation and International Co-operation: A Legal
Analysis of the Trans-Pacific Partnership Agreement*. Cheltenham, England:
Edward Elgar.

World Intellectual Property Organization. 2004. *WIPO Intellectual Property Handbook: Policy, Law and Use*, 2nd edn. Geneva: World Intellectual Property
Organization.

Yu, Peter. 2011. 'ACTA and Its Complex Politics.' *WIPO Journal* 3 (1): 1–16.

# 20

## Forget about the WTO

### The network of relations between PTAs and double PTAs

JOOST PAUWELYN AND WOLFGANG ALSCHNER

### A. Introduction

The very definition of *preferential trade agreements* (PTAs) channels our attention almost exclusively to the relationship between PTAs and the World Trade Organization (WTO): PTAs are 'preferential' as compared to the WTO benchmark. Although this relationship is an important one, the lasting proliferation of PTAs compels us to also look in a different direction. This contribution addresses an often overlooked question: what is the relationship *between* PTAs? More specifically, we inquire into what happens if two countries conclude not one but two (or more) PTAs with each other ('double PTAs')? Think of Canada and the United States concluding, first, the US–Canada Free Trade Agreement (FTA) and, second, the North American Free Trade Agreement (NAFTA) or, more recently, the United States and Mexico negotiating NAFTA and then the Trans-Pacific Partnership (TPP) or Trade in Services Agreement (TiSA)?

To the extent that interactions between PTAs received legal attention, it concerned the relationship between PTAs concluded by *different* countries sets. Naumann (2006), for example, compared rules of origin between PTAs concluded by the European Union (EU) with several third countries. Successive PTAs between the *same* countries, however, have largely escaped legal scrutiny. This is understandable in so far as, historically, double PTAs were of little practical significance. They occurred as by-products of shifting regional integration projects: as one forum fell in disuse without being formally terminated (e.g. the Latin American Integration Association), a new one was established (e.g. MERCOSUR) (see Kaltenthaler and Mora 2002). This changed only relatively recently with states purposely concluding double PTAs. Of particular significance is the move from what we call (somewhat inaccurately)[1] 'regional' to 'mega-regional' trade agreements: two (or more) countries conclude a PTA and, subsequently, a second PTA is negotiated between a larger group of countries. Examples of this trend are current efforts to conclude the Common Market for Eastern and Southern Africa–East African Community–Southern African Development Community (COMESA-EAC-SADC) Tripartite in Africa and the TPP.[2] Yet, as will be discussed, this move from regional to mega-regional is just one subset of a growing universe of double PTAs.

Section B offers four reasons why the limits imposed by WTO rules on PTAs (as well as plurilateral trade agreements) must not be overrated. This should redirect attention away from the WTO–PTA relationship towards relations between PTAs. Section C describes the current network of PTAs in force, its structure and centrality features – using basic methods of network analysis – and also assesses the frequency of double PTAs. Section D analyses the possible reasons for concluding double PTAs. Section E assesses ways in which successive PTAs involving the same countries can interrelate in legal terms.

## B. Forget about the WTO: does the WTO really restrict the conclusion of preferential and plurilateral trade agreements?

The vertical, top-down WTO–PTA relationship is, at least in legal terms, much overrated. The restrictions that WTO rules impose in respect of a subset of WTO Members concluding PTAs or, for that matter, plurilateral trade agreements (PAs)[3] have at least four serious limitations.

---

[1] The terminology is inaccurate to the extent a first 'regional' trade agreement must not necessarily be between countries in the same geographical region (it could be the US–Australia FTA, followed by the TPP). It may further be inaccurate to the extent that 'mega-regional' covers any subsequent trade agreement that includes at least the two parties to the first trade agreement (but not all WTO Members); in other words, a 'mega-regional' trade agreement could have dozens of parties but could also have just three parties (the NAFTA is a good example, as the NAFTA followed after the US–Canada FTA).

[2] See www.comesa-eac-sadc-tripartite.org/ and www.ustr.gov/tpp for more information.

[3] By 'plurilateral trade agreements' (PAs), we understand all trade-related agreements concluded between a subset of WTO Members that are not notified under GATT Article XXIV, the Enabling Clause or GATS Article V. In most cases, PAs, rather than liberalising substantially all trade between partners, are sector- or topic-specific, such as the Agreement on Government Procurement (GPA) or the Information Technology Agreement (ITA). On this definition, PAs can exchange concessions on a discriminatory basis (as the GPA does, limiting benefits to GPA parties) or on an MFN basis (as the ITA does, extending benefits to all WTO Members).

First, WTO Members – be it in committee or dispute settlement – do not really check or challenge whether PTAs actually comply with General Agreement on Tariffs and Trade (GATT) Article XXIV, the Enabling Clause (pursuant to which PTAs exclusively between developing countries can be concluded) or General Agreement on Trade in Services (GATS) Article V.[4] Moreover, GATT Article XXIV and, even more so, GATS Article V and, certainly, the Enabling Clause offer a great deal of wiggle room for WTO Members to conclude PTAs of all sorts. This is a widely known reality (Pauwelyn 2009).

Second, and often overlooked, WTO provisions on PTAs and PAs never prohibit such agreements. They only control when these agreements can be discriminatory, that is, reserve benefits to the parties to the PTA or PA, excluding other WTO Members.

If, for example, NAFTA were not to meet GATT Article XXIV conditions, NAFTA would not terminate or become invalid. GATT Article XXIV would simply not be available to justify, for example, US preferences granted to Canada, but not to the EU. GATT Article I (most-favoured-nation (MFN) treatment) would then oblige the United States to give NAFTA preferences also to the EU (or to get rid of NAFTA preferences in the first place)[5]. Put in legal terms, GATT Article XXIV is not a *prohibition*, but an *exception*. This follows the spirit of trade liberalisation that underlies the WTO: WTO Members are quite content when a country agrees to further liberalise trade; such further liberalisation must, however, be extended to all WTO Members unless the conditions in GATT Article XXIV are met. Not meeting these conditions does not invalidate the agreement; it only invalidates the Article XXIV exception to MFN. In the Agreement on Trade-Related Aspects of Intellectual Property Rights (TRIPS Agreement), there is no Article XXIV-type exception to MFN to begin with. This means that TRIPS-plus (provisions in) PTAs – such as the Anti-Counterfeiting Trade Agreement (ACTA) – must be extended to all

---

[4] Since 2006 the WTO's ambition has been lowered to that of transparency (see Hoekman, Chapter 21 in this volume): 'With the advent of the Transparency Mechanism in 2006, there is no longer any effort by WTO Members to approve new PTAs'). With few exceptions, WTO Members have also refrained from challenging or even referring to PTAs in WTO dispute settlement.

[5] Another way for the United States to keep NAFTA concessions preferential in this scenario would be to obtain a waiver under Article IX:3 of the WTO agreement or a two-thirds majority decision under GATT Article XXIV:10. Following an adverse dispute settlement ruling, the United States could also maintain its MFN violation but negotiate compensation or agree to suffer retaliation.

WTO Members. This automatic extension is the baseline for TRIPS-plus PTAs. A trade in goods PTA that does not meet Article XXIV conditions would only lead to the same default result: MFN extension (not invalidation of the PTA).

A similar confusion may arise around Article X:9 of the WTO agreement concerning so-called plurilateral trade agreements (PAs). Article X:9 states that WTO Members can add a PA to Annex 4 'exclusively by consensus'. This does not, however, prohibit WTO Members from concluding a PA unless all WTO Members agree. Outside Annex 4 (think of the Information Technology Agreement (ITA)) or outside the WTO altogether (think of ACTA), a subgroup of WTO Members can agree to whatever plurilateral agreement they like. However, when such plurilateral agreement confers benefits subject to MFN, WTO rules mandate that these benefits be granted to all WTO Members. The consensus referred to under Article X:9 is not a precondition for concluding a plurilateral agreement; it is a precondition for concluding a *discriminatory* plurilateral agreement that becomes *part of the WTO treaty* (i.e. part of Annex 4, but not extending its benefits to all WTO Members).[6] The core legal effect of adding a plurilateral agreement to Annex 4 is, indeed, that it allows (but does not require) the plurilateral to deviate from MFN (another legal consequence is that, as part of the WTO treaty, the Dispute Settlement Understanding (DSU) becomes available to enforce the Annex 4 plurilateral agreement).[7] Article II:3 of the Agreement Establishing the WTO

---

[6] Another way to conclude a discriminatory or preferential PA, without violating MFN, would be to obtain an explicit waiver under Article IX:3 of the WTO agreement or for the PA to become a PTA, that is, to meet GATT Article XXIV/GATS Article V, as is the intention for the TISA currently under negotiation (but often referred to as a PA).

[7] Appendix 1 to the DSU lists as 'agreements covered by the understanding' plurilateral trade agreements in Annex 4 to the WTO agreement. However, the appendix explicitly lists the four PAs that were part of Annex 4 in 1994 (when the DSU was concluded; since then, two of these PAs have been terminated). This seems to indicate that for a new PA, part of Annex 4, to become a 'covered agreement' subject to the DSU, the DSU would need to be amended to include in Appendix 1 the new PA. Amending the DSU requires the consensus of all WTO Members (including those not party to the PA) but takes effect upon approval by the WTO Ministerial Conference. Unlike, for example, TRIPS amendments, DSU amendments do not require ratification by individual WTO Members. See Article X:8 of the WTO agreement. Such an amendment of the DSU could be made at the same time as the PA is included in Annex 4, both decisions requiring a consensus of all WTO Members. In addition, for each PA listed in Appendix 1 to the DSU to be subject to the DSU requires a decision by the parties to the PA in question 'setting out the terms for the application of the Understanding [DSU] to the individual agreement, including any special or additional rules or procedures for inclusion in Appendix 2, as notified to the DSB' (DSU Appendix 1, in fine). As a result, for a new PA part of Annex 4 to be subject to

explicitly provides that 'the Plurilateral Trade Agreements [in Annex 4] do not create either obligations or rights for Members that have not accepted them'. Article XVI of the same agreement further states that the provisions in this agreement (including Article II:3) 'prevail' over the provisions of any of the multilateral trade agreements, including MFN provisions in, for example, GATT, the Agreement on Technical Barriers to Trade (TBT), GATS or TRIPS.

Third, where a PTA/PA addresses matters not covered by the WTO (so-called WTO-extra) and not subject to one of the WTO's limited MFN provisions – for example, questions of competition, labour, the environment or certain aspects of foreign investment – the PTA/PA is not even subject to MFN. It can then be preferential even though, as a PTA, it does not meet the conditions in GATT Article XXIV (or GATS Article V) or, as a PA, it was never approved by consensus under Article X:9 nor part of Annex 4. Not all WTO agreements include an MFN clause (not, for example, the Agreement on Subsidies and Countervailing Measures (SCM) or the Agreement on Trade-Related Investment Measures (TRIMs)). Moreover, where they are found, MFN clauses cover matters falling only within the scope of the agreement (principle of *ejusdem generis*).[8] GATT Article I:1 MFN, for example, covers concessions only in respect of (1) customs duties and charges and related rules and formalities, and (2) internal taxes and regulations covered by GATT Articles III:2 and 4. As a result, since GATT Article III:8 excludes government procurement (and domestic production subsidies) from the scope of Article III, government procurement is not subject to GATT MFN in the first place. Hence, the WTO Agreement on Government Procurement (GPA) is preferential (its benefits can be reserved to GPA parties and must not be extended to all WTO Members) for two reasons: (1) GATT Article I MFN does not apply to government procurement; (2) in any event, as an Annex 4 agreement, the GPA does not 'create either obligations or rights for Members that have not accepted' the GPA, pursuant to Article II:3 of the Agreement Establishing the WTO.[9]

---

the DSU: (1) Appendix 1 to the DSU would need to be amended by consensus, and (2) an explicit decision to that effect must be taken by the PA parties themselves (*not* including other WTO Members) detailing the DSU's application to the PA.

[8] See 1978 ILC Draft Articles on MFN Clauses, Article 9: 'Under a [MFN] clause the beneficiary State acquires... *only those rights which fall within the limits of the subject matter of the clause*' (emphasis added).

[9] GATS Article II MFN has a broader scope of application than GATT Article I MFN, extending to concessions in respect of 'any measure covered by this Agreement [GATS]', elsewhere defined as all 'measures affecting trade in services' (but excluding, for example,

Fourth, the fact that PTA/PA provisions in the WTO – be it GATT Article XXIV or WTO Article X:9 – are not *prohibitions* but (MFN) *exceptions* also has crucial consequences for so-called WTO-minus provisions in PTAs/PAs, that is, those where PTA/PA parties condone, among themselves, trade-related measures that would otherwise violate WTO rules (e.g. certain trade sanctions following human rights violations that would violate GATT Article XI and that cannot be justified under GATT Article XX): WTO-minus provisions are valid/legal as between PTA/PA parties;[10] since such provisions do not confer benefits (quite the opposite, they allow for more restrictions), WTO rules on MFN are not even violated; consequently, there is no need to invoke (let alone meet all the conditions in) the exception of GATT Article XXIV or to seek WTO consensus to add the plurilateral agreement to Annex 4.[11]

The four preceding caveats seriously temper the importance of the WTO–PTA/PA relationship and, more specifically, the constraints that WTO provisions impose on PTAs/PAs. This makes the relation *between* PTAs all the more interesting and important. This is the question we examine next.

## C. A network analysis of PTAs

To better understand the global system of PTAs, we turn to network analysis. Network analysis investigates the structure of a system based on the relationships (or *ties*) that connect its individual, constituent elements (or *nodes*). In our context, PTAs are the ties that connect countries as nodes, together forming the PTA network.

services supplied in the exercise of governmental authority and government procurement of services, carved out from GATS, and thus GATS MFN, in Article I:3(b) and Article XIII). TRIPS Article 4 MFN applies 'with regard to the protection of intellectual property', which is, however, more restrictively defined in footnote 4 as 'matters affecting the availability, acquisition, scope, maintenance and enforcement of intellectual property rights as well as those matters affecting the use of intellectual property rights specifically addressed in this Agreement'.

[10]  But see Flett (Chapter 22 in this volume): 'There should not normally be any WTO minus provisions in the FTA, and any doubtful provisions could be dealt with by interpreting them in conformity with WTO law.'

[11]  The question remains, however, what the WTO Appellate Body (AB) would do with such a WTO-minus provision in a PTA in a case where one of the PTA parties turns its back on its PTA commitments and challenges the trade restriction it consented to under the PTA as a violation of WTO rules. More specifically, would the AB be willing to refer to the PTA provision as a defence or legal impediment to finding a WTO violation? See Pauwelyn (2003b).

Although the theoretical roots of network analysis date back to the eighteenth century, only very recently did scientists begin to realise its full potential and versatility. Since the late 1990s, network analysis has been increasingly used by scholars in the social, natural and computer sciences to study systems of varying complexity, ranging from patterns of friendship among members of a karate club (Zachary 1977) to the functioning of the brain or the Internet (Newman 2010: 3). Recently, network analysis has also been employed in the study of law, including the network of the American federal judiciary (Katz and Stafford 2010), the authority of US Supreme Court decisions (Fowler and Sangick 2008) and, in the realm of international law, the network of international investment arbitrators (Puig 2014).

Network analysis comes with an elaborate toolkit that comprises both visualisations and computational measurements of network, node or tie properties. Together, they allow, among others, (1) the identification of nodes that are particularly important (or central) in a system, (2) categorisation of the different relationships between nodes, (3) delineation of subgroups (or clusters) in a system and description of its overall density and (4) determination of the robustness or vulnerability of systems to change. Network analysis can thus reveal novel insights into the current structure and historical evolution of a given system (Pauwelyn 2014).

The system of PTAs has, to our knowledge, not yet been subject to a network analysis. Although we do not seek, in this chapter, to exhaust the network analysis toolbox, our investigation is a first step to employ network analytical instruments in order to confirm, challenge and add to the current state of knowledge of the PTA universe.

## I. Our data set

To investigate the PTA network we rely on a simplified version of the WTO database on RTAs.[12] The WTO RTA data set lists 260 PTAs that are in force.[13] From the list we eliminated 12 entries because of the particular nature of the agreements, for example, EU enlargement

---

[12] The RTA database is available at rtais.wto.org/UI/PublicMaintainRTAHome.aspx. The terminology used by the WTO is somewhat confusing and different from that in this volume: what we call PTAs are referred to by the WTO as RTAs. The WTO uses the term *PTAs* for 'preferential trade arrangements', which are *unilateral* trade preferences granted by a country to other countries such as under the Generalized System of Preferences (GSP).

[13] As of 15 October 2013.

treaties.[14] We disaggregated the remaining 248 PTAs according to their underlying bilateral ties or dyads (e.g. NAFTA represents three bilateral ties connecting the United States–Canada, United States–Mexico and Canada–Mexico).[15] To simplify our analysis further, we consider the EU-28 as one single WTO Member so that we are left with 131 WTO Members.

Our data set involves 187 states or customs unions. The most active countries in today's PTA network are the EU (34 agreements), the European Free Trade Association (EFTA) states (Switzerland: 27, Iceland: 26, Norway: 26, Liechtenstein: 25), closely followed by Chile (22), Turkey (19) and Singapore (19). The United States ranks 12th with 14 PTAs in force. Two WTO Members in the data set have no PTAs in force: Mongolia and Mauritania.

## II. The PTA network

Although it is common knowledge that most WTO Members are also party to a PTA, little is known about how tightly or loosely knit the PTA network is. In network analysis this idea is expressed by a network's density, which describes what percentage of possible node relations is actually covered by a tie. Of a maximum number of 8515 bilateral relations between the 131 WTO Members that could be covered by a PTA, 10.4 per cent, or 889 ties, of intra-WTO bilateral relations are covered by at least one PTA. Hence, the PTA network covers about every 10th bilateral intra-WTO relationship. In comparison, the investment treaty network is roughly twice as dense with 20 per cent of bilateral relations (as between all countries, not just WTO Members) being covered by investment treaties (United Nations Conference on Trade and Development 2011: 102).

---

[14] In addition to accession and enlargement treaties, we excluded the Global System of Trade Preferences among Developing Countries (1988) and the Protocol on Trade Negotiations (1971) from our analysis as both agreements with their large and diverse membership are very different from the other treaties in the database and hence cannot usefully be compared to other PTAs.

[15] For multiparty PTAs, we do not rely on a simple list of countries party to such an agreement as this could misrepresent the underlying legal relations. The Association of Southeast Asian Nations (ASEAN)–China FTA, for instance, would be misrepresented as applicable also in intra-ASEAN relations. Instead, we maintain the true constellation of legal relations, by using membership in a regional grouping on one side (e.g. ASEAN members disaggregated) and the other contracting state (e.g. China) on the other side. We assume that all members of that grouping have signed and ratified the agreement in question.

## Distribution of PTAs

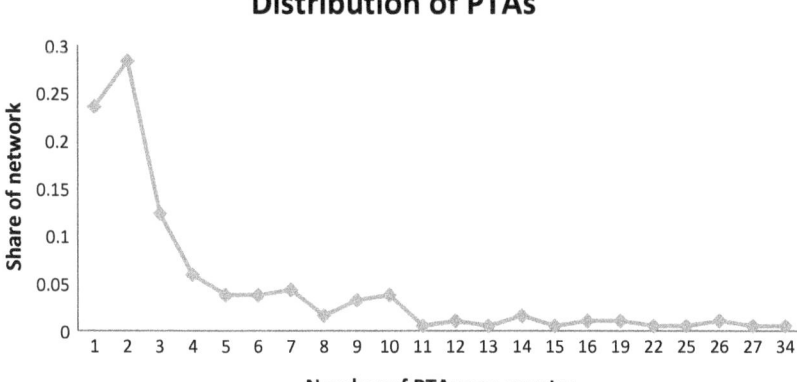

**Figure 20.1**    Few countries have many PTAs, many countries have few PTAs

We next look at how the PTAs are distributed (for all countries not just WTO Members). Were PTA relations to be randomly distributed in the system, then we would expect to find only a small share of countries with very many or with very few PTAs; most states would have a medium number of PTAs – graphically, this distribution is known as the 'bell curve'. This is not what we find, however. The distribution of PTAs rather more closely, albeit not perfectly, resembles a 'power law' curve in which we find that a few countries have many PTAs, whereas many other countries have few PTAs (Figure 20.1). Put differently, rather than a 'democratic' network in which most countries have the same number of PTAs, there are a few 'hub' countries that dominate the PTA network (see Barabási and Bonabeau 2003).

The PTA network shares this (approximate) characteristic of power law distribution with many other complex systems, such as the Internet (Matwyshyn 2003). There are two principal reasons why complex systems have such a structure. First, as these systems grow over time, older nodes have more opportunities to acquire new links than the newcomers that have just joined the system have (Barabási and Bonabeau 2003: 54–5). Second, new connections follow the logic of 'preferential attachment' – those nodes that are already well linked are more likely to attract new ties. Put differently, the 'rich get richer' (Barabási and Bonabeau 2003: 55). Applied to our context, one of the reasons why the EU has so many PTAs is that it began concluding PTAs early on, and another is that other countries wanted to improve their position in the network by seeking a PTA with the well-connected hub EU.

Networks that follow a power law logic also display unique characteristics (Barabási and Bonabeau 2003: 55–8). They are extremely robust in
the face of a random attack on or a withdrawal of nodes. Were a country
like Cuba or Mali to terminate its PTAs, the PTA network would remain
largely intact. In contrast, these networks are extremely vulnerable when
it comes to attacks on or withdrawal of the most central nodes. The structure of the PTA network would be fundamentally altered were the EU to
withdraw from its treaties. Power law distribution also has an effect on
diffusion within the system. New norms that are adopted by hub countries are more likely to spread within the network than is legal innovation
undertaken by peripheral members. Hence, any reform or modification
of the PTA network has to be channelled through the central countries in
order to be effective.

We turn next to what network analysis is perhaps best known for –
its visualisations.[16] For this we prepared a matrix that describes whether
a country dyad is covered by a PTA. Figure 20.2 depicts the resulting
global PTA network using a 'stress minimisation' algorithm visualising
the shortest paths between nodes. We colour-code for WTO membership
and weigh the size of each country's circle by the number of ties it has (the
more ties it has, the larger the circle). The visualisation shows a network
that is characterised by regional clusters that are grouped around the EU
as pivoting point.

This basic visualisation of the PTA network yields a number of interesting insights.

• **Regionalism still dominates PTA structures.** Most clusters of PTAs
correspond to specific regions. This should temper the statement that
there is already a shift taking place from 'regional' to 'inter-' or 'mega-
regional' PTAs. A notable exception is that the countries of South East
and East Asia form a larger cluster with countries from the Americas
(right-hand side of the network).
• **WTO membership has little influence on a country's participation
in regional PTAs notified by WTO Members or the number of ties
covered by PTAs.** Non–WTO Members are not left out of the global
network of PTAs concluded by WTO Members. On the contrary, some
non–WTO Members, such as Libya, as a node between Arab and African
region PTAs, occupy central positions in the network.

---

[16] Today, a range of network analysis software is freely available. Our visualisations are
produced with VISONE.

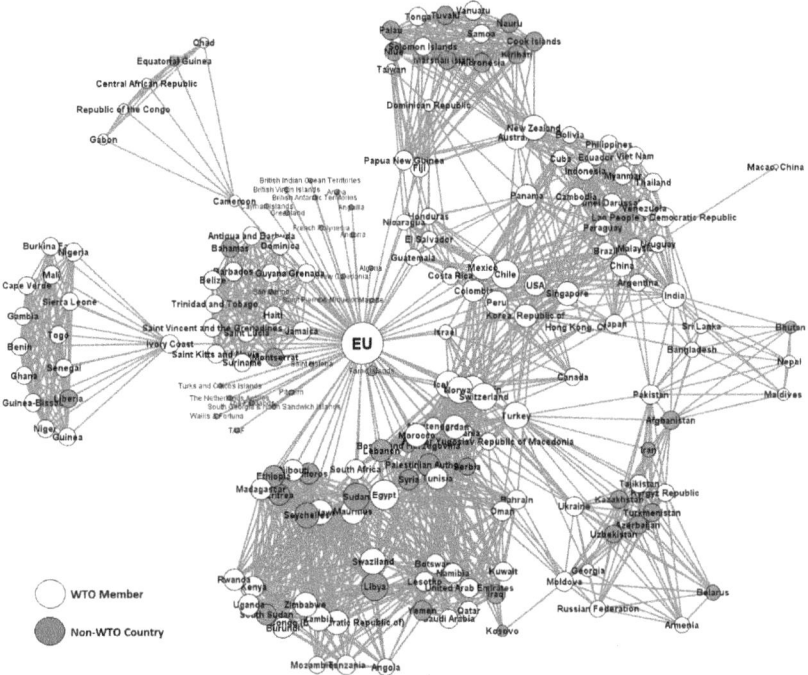

**Figure 20.2**    The global PTA network

- **Europe is the centre of the network.** The most central node and pivoting point in the PTA network is the EU; closely adjacent are the EFTA members; the United States, in contrast, appears sidelined.

These results find further support when we look at some of the network's computed measures. The first measure we consider is *centrality*, which expresses a node's importance in a system. There are a range of different centrality measures – each using different node attributes to assess a node's importance. Table 20.1 summarises three centrality measures of the top 15 countries in the PTA network: (1) degree centrality (the sum of ties that a country has); (2) betweenness centrality (which measures the extent to which a node lies on paths between other nodes) and (3) eigenvector centrality (which does not simply count the number of ties a country has but also looks at the importance of the nodes/countries with which that country has ties, giving each node a score proportional to the sum of the scores of its neighbours). A country may have a large

Table 20.1 *Centrality of countries in the PTA network*

| Top 15 | Centrality | | Betweenness | | Eigenvector | |
|---|---|---|---|---|---|---|
| 1 | EU | 80 | EU | 21 529 | Egypt | 0.239 4 |
| 2 | Egypt | 39 | Ivory Coast | 4 816 | Sudan | 0.214 4 |
| 3 | Chile | 34 | Turkey | 3 555 | Libya | 0.206 1 |
| 4 | Sudan | 34 | Korea, Rep. of | 2 422 | Swaziland | 0.197 3 |
| 5 | Libya | 33 | Chile | 2 299 | EU | 0.196 4 |
| 6 | Switzerland | 32 | Cameroon | 1 810 | Mauritius | 0.188 7 |
| 7 | Iceland | 31 | Fiji | 1 440 | Malawi | 0.184 6 |
| 8 | Norway | 31 | Papua New Guinea | 1 440 | Seychelles | 0.184 6 |
| 9 | Liechtenstein | 30 | Egypt | 1 052 | Congo, Dem. Rep. of | 0.176 3 |
| 10 | Swaziland | 30 | Switzerland | 1 045 | Zambia | 0.176 3 |
| 11 | Turkey | 30 | Iceland | 861 | Zimbabwe | 0.176 3 |
| 12 | Mauritius | 28 | Norway | 861 | Comoros | 0.154 8 |
| 13 | New Zealand | 28 | Liechtenstein | 815 | Djibouti | 0.154 8 |
| 14 | Australia | 27 | Singapore | 810 | Eritrea | 0.154 8 |
| 15 | Malawi | 27 | Australia | 805 | Ethiopia | 0.154 8 |

eigenvector either if it 'has many neighbors or because it has important neighbours (or both)' (Newman 2010: 170).

These measures confirm the importance of the EU in the global PTA network. At the same time, the comparatively low eigenvector score of the EU (rank 4) highlights that many EU PTAs have been concluded with minor trading partners. EU PTAs with major players such as the United States, China, Japan or ASEAN still remain to be concluded. Other somewhat counterintuitive results, such as the high ranking of North African countries such as Egypt, Libya and Sudan, can be explained by the fact that these countries are members of several multiparty (in contrast to bilateral) PTAs, which places them centrally in certain regions without, however, attaining global relevance.

### III. The depth of the PTA network

Up to now we have treated all PTAs as equal. Now we refine our analysis by taking into account the different 'depths' of PTAs. Some agreements go further than others in advancing trade liberalisation and economic integration. As a measurement, we use the depth index proposed by Dür and colleagues ranging from 0 (shallow agreement) to 7 (deep agreement)

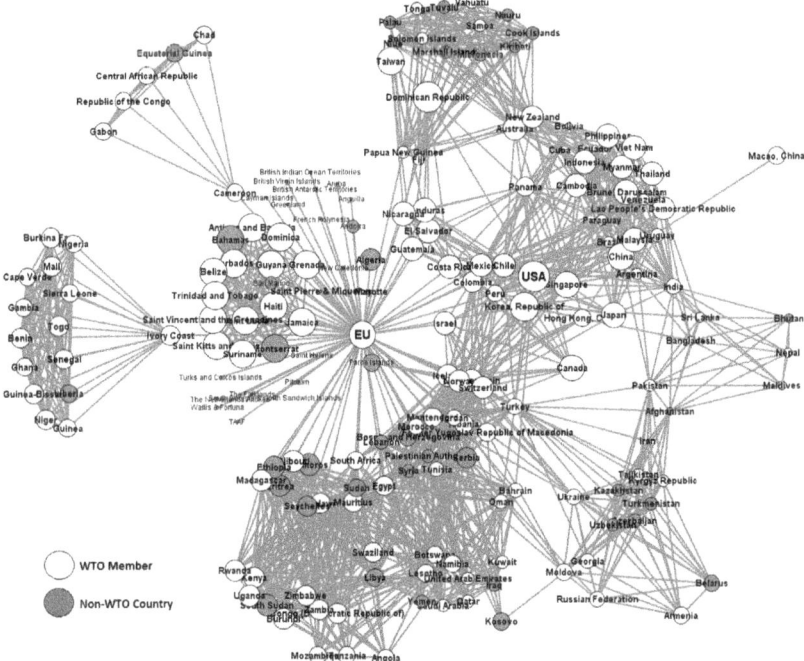

**Figure 20.3**   Who signs the deepest agreements on average?

(Dür, Baccini and Elsig 2014).[17] For 44 of our sample of 248 PTAs in force, the Dür *et al.* data set contains no depth measure, leaving us with 204 entries.

In Figure 20.3, we reproduce the visualisation of the PTA network, but, this time, the size of a country circle is not the degree centrality of a country (as earlier) but the average depth of the PTAs signed by that country.[18] The visualisation of the ties and the colour-coding remain unchanged.

---

[17]   The depth measure is an additive index of seven variables: (1) whether the agreement foresees a reduction of all tariffs to zero and (2) whether it contains substantive provisions in six areas (services, investment, standards, public procurement, competition and intellectual property rights).

[18]   We calculate the average using only the agreements for which we have depth data. There are some drawbacks in using the average depth of PTAs in force, since countries with few, but deep PTAs may be portrayed as having 'deeper' agreements than a country that has multiple PTAs, some being very shallow and others being very deep. Countries that have only signed PTAs for which we have no depth data are coded as 0 depth.

The visualisation provides a more nuanced view of the PTA network.

- **Quality trumps quantity?** The EU, as the most central player, signs more shallow agreements on average than does the United States, Taiwan, Dominican Republic or South Korea. This may be because the EU signed a number of shallow agreements in its early years. Recent EU agreements tend to be deeper. Vice versa: countries such as the United States, Taiwan, Singapore, South Korea, Canada and Japan may be able to compensate for their lack of centrality by offering deeper agreements that liberalise trade further than those of more centrally situated countries.
- **Strong disparities in depth between regions.** In Asia and the Americas, deep PTAs abound. In contrast, PTAs in Africa, the Middle East and Central Asia remain generally shallow.
- **Some disparities in depth within regions.** Even though countries tend to cluster together regionally in the PTA network, they often remain far apart when it comes to treaty depth. China has much deeper agreements than India does. Chile has signed deeper PTAs than Peru has.

Shifting our focus from the network's nodes to the ties, Figure 20.4 displays the average depth of each bilateral relationship. Darker colours indicate greater depth. We again use the average, since some relationships, as explained in further detail later, are governed by more than one PTA.[19]

The visualisation confirms that, especially in the Americas and South East Asia, PTAs tend to be deep. A few countries form hubs from which deep PTAs spread. Figure 20.5 visualises this deep PTA network (depth of 6–7), the size of the country circle indicating degree centrality. The EU, the United States, Chile, Mexico, Singapore, Australia and New Zealand are central players in this network. Also noteworthy is the absence of non–WTO Members (apart from the Bahamas) in this network.

The fact that the deep PTA network is dominated by a few interconnected players and consists almost exclusively of WTO Members may be favourable to multilateralism. Many of the rules enshrined in deep PTAs are what is called 'WTO-extra' commitments covering issues that may become the subject of future rule making at the multilateral level. The fact that these rules are crafted today by a handful of interconnected hub

---

[19] The average is a suitable measure since only 2.6 per cent of our overlapping PTA ties display a difference of depth of more than 3. Depth entries that are not available are coded as 0.

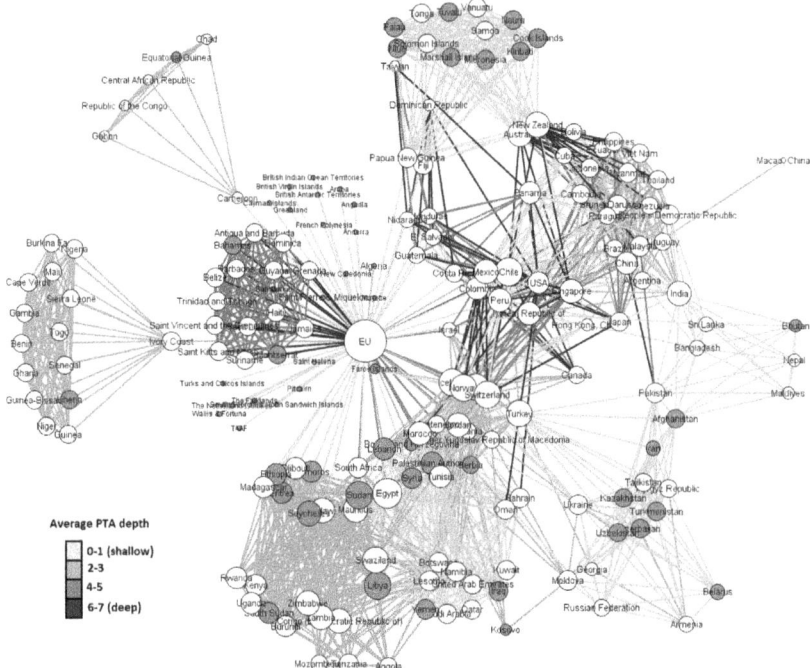

**Figure 20.4**   The depth of PTAs

countries[20] rather than isolated clusters of independent rule makers is likely to facilitate the convergence of views and the emergence of a coherent body of WTO-extra norms. As these deep PTA rule makers are also centrally positioned in the network as a whole, they are more likely to play a significant role in the diffusion of new norms. Hence, having a small club, instead of isolated islands, of rule makers may favour consensus building for multilateral negotiations.

## IV. The turn to mega-regionals

Whereas historically the PTA phenomenon was mainly associated with regionalism, ongoing negotiations are likely to change this dramatically.

---

[20] Figure 20.5 also indicates that, currently, the EU is not fully integrated into the triangle formed by the United States, Chile and Australia. This in turn suggests that different models or clusters of deep PTAs exist. See also Baccini, Dür and Haftel (Chapter 7 in this volume). The conclusion of the EU–US TTIP would change this network constellation.

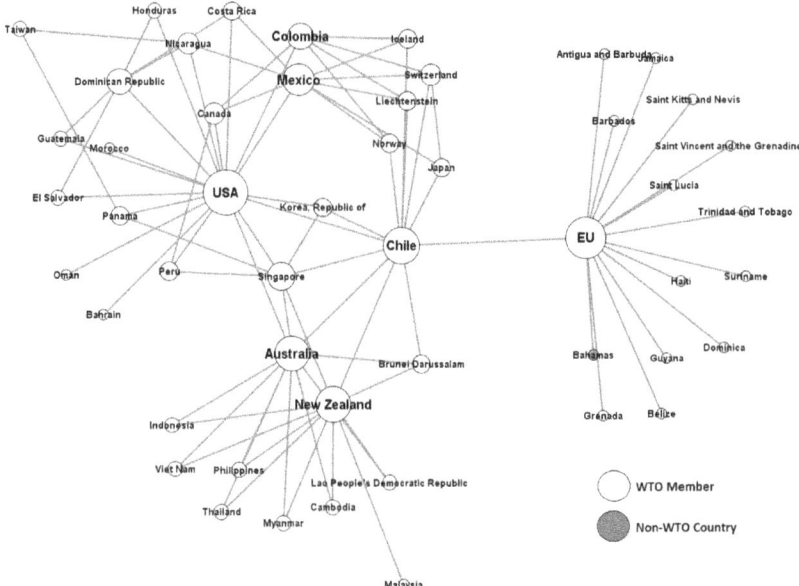

Figure 20.5    The network of deep PTAs

The TPP, the Transatlantic Trade and Investment Partnership (TTIP) and the Regional Comprehensive Economic Partnership (RCEP) are likely to have a major impact on the existing PTA network. These envisaged agreements are often referred to as *mega*-regionals, not only because they aim to connect regions rather than just countries but also because their economic impact is likely to be significant.

To assess their impact on the PTA network, we engage in a thought experiment. What happens to the PTA network if we add the TTIP, TPP and RCEP to our data set?[21] The results are depicted in Figure 20.6, which focuses on the part of the network most affected by this change.

The conclusion of these three agreements will move the United States closer to the network's centre, and the nodes of the Asia-Pacific region will cluster together. The proliferation of mega-regionals will thus lead to a tighter global PTA network. If the trend continues, existing clusters will

---

[21]  We are well aware of the limitations of this thought experiment. Since our database includes only agreements that are in force, the PTA network in force will have changed by the time TTIP, TPP and RCEP are ratified. Moreover, we are merely cherry-picking three regionals among a range of agreements under negotiation. The results of our thought experiment should thus be taken as a mere illustration of a possible future trend.

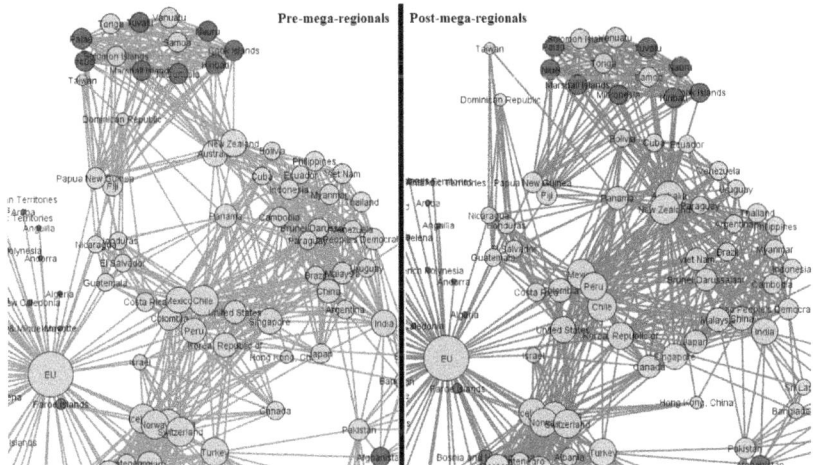

**Figure 20.6**   An Asia–America cluster emerges through mega-regionals

converge, transforming the pivot-cluster network into a 'ball of wool'–like PTA network that will more closely resemble today's network of investment treaties (Figure 20.7).

## D. The phenomenon of double PTAs

A highly underresearched aspect of the PTA universe is the multiple PTAs that govern the same bilateral relationship. For the sake of simplicity we use the shorthand 'double PTAs', although sometimes more than two agreements overlap. The phenomenon of double PTAs is widespread in the PTA network. Every fifth bilateral relationship governed by a PTA tie is subject to more than one PTA (corresponding to 4.3 per cent of all possible intra-WTO bilateral relations). Seventy-eight WTO Members (or three-fifths of the 131 WTO Members) have at least one bilateral relationship covered by multiple PTAs, and 99 out of the 248 PTAs from the WTO database are affected by this overlap (i.e. overlap with at least one other PTA in at least one bilateral relationship). These statistics underscore the relative frequency of double PTAs both in overall numbers and with respect to the number of WTO Members that actually face this overlap.[22]

---

[22] This number still underestimates the prevalence of double PTAs in two ways. First, since not every PTA actually in force is notified to the WTO, we may miss some of the existing overlap. Second, because the WTO database covers only PTAs that have entered into

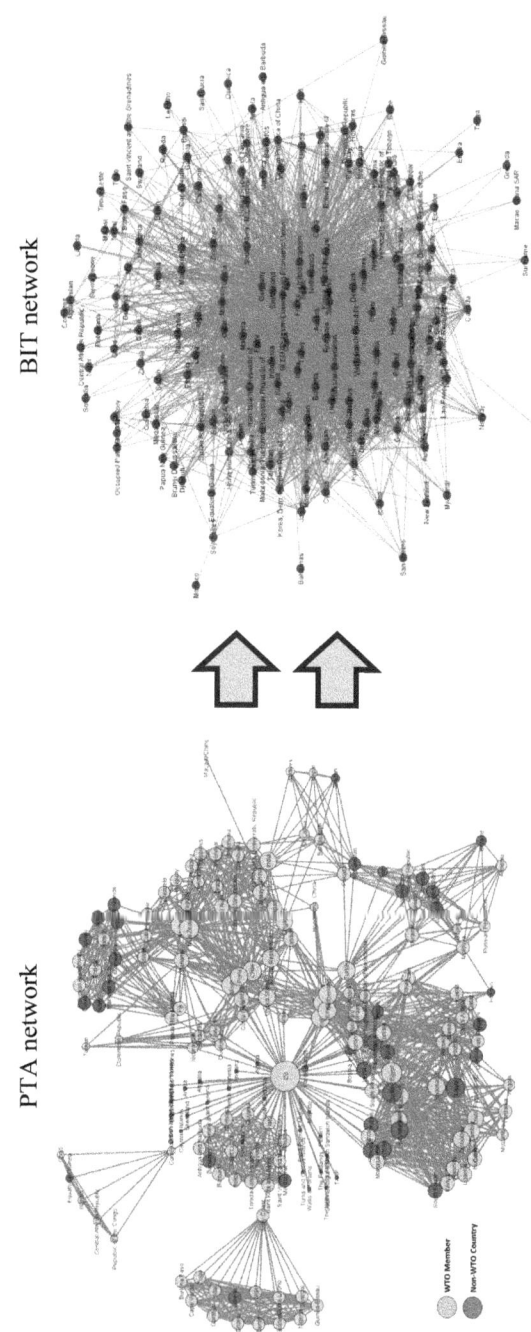

**Figure 20.7** Mega-regionals are likely to transform the PTA network to resemble the appearance of the bilateral investment treaty (BIT) network

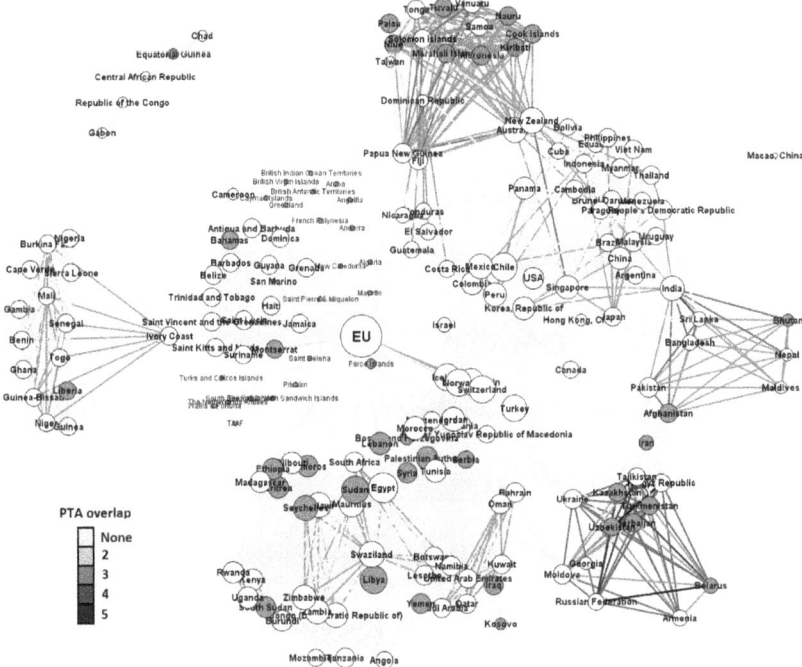

Figure 20.8    Double PTAs in the PTA network

## I. The double PTA network

Figures 20.8, 20.9 and 20.10 depict the network of double PTAs. In each figure, we colour-code for the number of overlapping PTAs (which range from two to five overlapping treaties). The more PTAs overlap, the darker will be the tie. Interestingly, double PTAs concentrate on the regional level and thus far do not exist intraregionally (Figure 20.9). The Asian web of double PTAs is noteworthy as it spans across subregions of the continent. In Figure 20.10, we extend our thought experiment on mega-regionals to the double PTA network. We observe a merger of the Asian and the American double PTA clusters into a greater Pacific area. Also, with the conclusion of the TPP, the United States would, for the first time, become a member of overlapping PTAs. Hence, the turn to mega-regionals is likely to further increase the frequency of overlapping PTAs.

force, the signed but not yet effective agreements are not taken into account. Hence, the phenomenon of double PTAs is likely to be even more widespread.

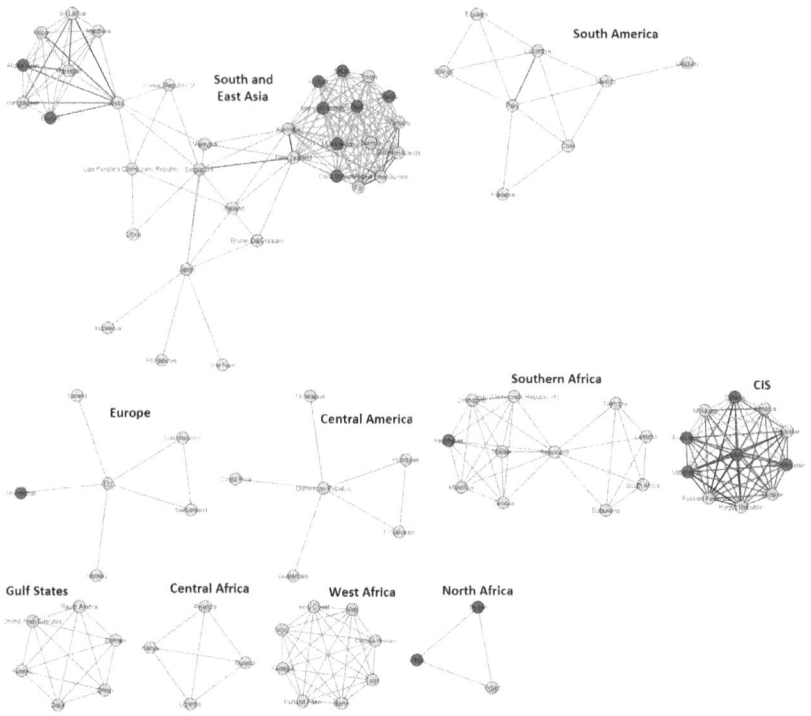

Figure 20.9   The double PTA network

The overlap of PTAs raises a number of intriguing questions. Why do countries enter into overlapping agreements in the first place? Why do some regions seem to have a dense network of overlapping agreements, whereas others do not? Do overlapping PTAs necessarily increase trade liberalisation and economic integration? What are the legal issues arising from overlapping PTAs? We address each of these questions in turn.

## II. Categorising double PTAs

There are both economic and noneconomic factors explaining a country's move to conclude double PTAs. These typically coincide and are empirically difficult to disentangle. To provide one example, the ongoing TPP negotiations are driven in part by the expectation of large economic benefits – the United States alone expects gains from the TPP of

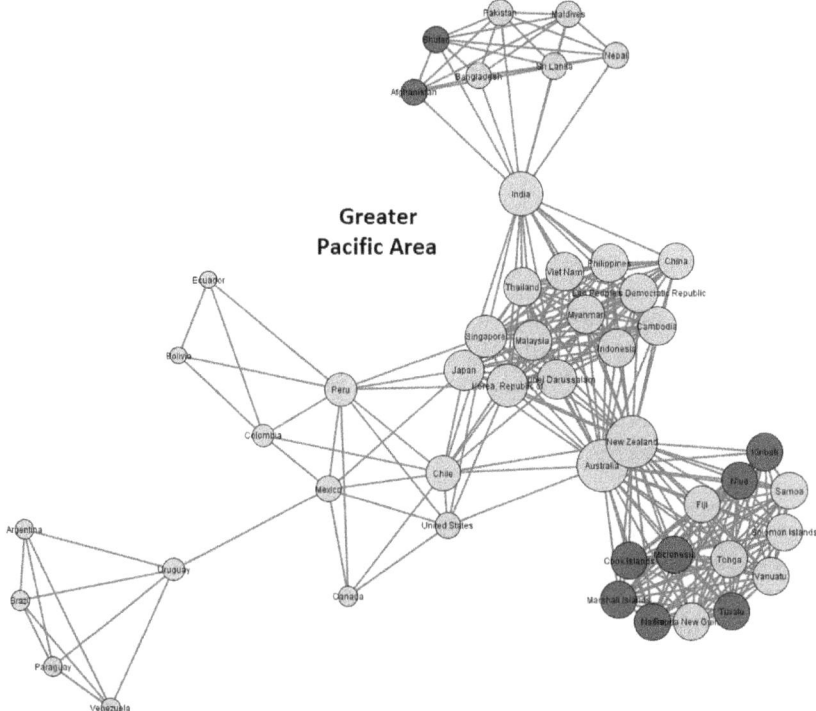

**Greater Pacific Area**

**Figure 20.10**    The double PTA network after the conclusion of mega-regionals (extract)[23]

US$14 billion by 2025.[24] At the same time, the United States is also pursuing political and strategic objectives in shaping the 'Pacific Century'. Similarly, other Pacific countries expect an increase of trade flows arising from TPP; but there is also considerable 'social' pull for countries to join the TPP negotiations regardless of ensuing economic benefits in order to be in the club rather than left out.[25] Nevertheless, a closer look at the

---

[23]   Regions other than South and East Asia and South America remain unchanged as compared to Figure 20.8.

[24]   See Joshua Meltzer, Testimony before the US House Small Business Committee, 'The Significance of the Trans-Pacific Partnership for the United States,' 16 May 2012, available at www.brookings.edu/research/testimony/2012/05/16-us-trade-strategy-meltzer.

[25]   The TPP started off as an FTA negotiation among Brunei, Chile, New Zealand and Singapore in 2005. In 2008, the United States entered into talks with these four countries with a view to joining the grouping. Since then the TPP has developed considerable centrifugal force. Australia, Peru and Vietnam joined the negotiations in 2008, Malaysia in 2010, Mexico and Canada in 2012 and Japan in March 2013. At the time of writing,

universe of existing double PTAs suggests that the mix of political and functional economic considerations differs considerably among agreements, countries and regions. In this section, we propose a tentative categorisation of double PTAs, distinguishing between those driven by mainly (1) historical/political motives and those driven by (2) functional/ economic goals.

## III. Double PTAs as a mainly historical/political phenomenon

Double PTAs not only result from careful economic calculation but also can be the product (and sometimes the by-product) of political considerations. Some double PTAs are the result of historical accidents, others are purposely orchestrated to form new alliances and still others may have been mere photo opportunities.

### 1. Skeletons in the cupboard

Like skeletons in the cupboard, some double PTAs are the remnants of failed, or less successful, regional economic integration efforts primarily dating back to the 1970s and 1980s. For example, in 1975 the Asia Pacific Trade Agreement (APTA) was signed, regrouping six countries, including China, South Korea, Lao People's Democratic Republic (PDR) and India. Although APTA is still used as a framework for regional economic cooperation,[26] the member states have turned to other, more dynamic, venues to advance their regional economic integration agenda. Whereas China, South Korea and India each seek to expand their own PTA network through bilateral treaties, including in the region, Lao PDR joined ASEAN to further regional integration. Similarly, the 1980 Latin American Integration Association (LAIA) is today outstripped by MERCOSUR and the Andean Community.

Skeletons-in-the-cupboard-type double PTAs are recognisable by a wide gap in depth: the early agreement being much more shallow than the later agreement. To take one of the previous examples, LAIA has a coded depth of 0 (very shallow) in the Dür et al. data set. In contrast, MERCOSUR, if one adds its goods and its services components, is much deeper being coded as 5. Albeit displaying less integrative depth than

---

speculations abound as to whether South Korea and China, among others, will join the talks.

[26] Several APTA framework agreements were signed between 2009 and 2011 on investment, services and trade facilitation. See www.unescap.org/tid/apta.asp.

MERCOSUR, the Andean Community also goes considerably further than LAIA and is coded as 2. Where countries abandon (but do not terminate) stifled negotiation fora for more dynamic regional groupings, skeletons in the cupboard continue to give rise to double-PTAs.

## 2. Paper tigers

Some of the double PTAs in place today may also be mere paper tigers. The density of double PTAs in the WTO database is highest among Commonwealth of Independent States (CIS) countries. However, these overlapping PTAs do not translate into deeper economic integration. Of the five PTAs in force between Russia and Belarus,[27] the three treaties that have been coded by Dür et al. display similar levels of depth (either 1 or 2). This finds further support when we look at the Horn et al. data set of coded PTA content (Horn, Mavroidis and Sapir 2010).[28] A comparison of the 1994 CIS Treaty with Ukraine's subsequent PTAs with Belarus, Kazakhstan, Turkmenistan and Russia reveals that the earlier CIS Treaty actually contains deeper WTO-plus commitments than do three of the four subsequent PTAs. Although three of the PTAs also cover competition policy in contrast to the CIS, this is the only WTO-extra area covered in the PTAs. Hence, bilateral PTAs overlapping with the 1994 CIS Treaty add little or nothing to the degree of liberalisation and harmonisation achieved by the 1994 CIS Treaty. Therefore, double PTAs, or in this case even quadruple or quintuple PTAs, do not necessarily translate into deeper levels of integration but are sometimes mere paper tigers.

## 3. Bridge between regions

A final group of double PTAs at the midpoint between political and economic motivations results from countries serving as bridges between regions. Although the PTA network reveals that PTAs in force today are still based on regionalism, these regions are not always neatly separated, but intersect at their edges. Double PTAs then arise between the countries that lie at that intersection. This is particularly common in Africa. Egypt, Libya and Sudan, for instance, are all linked by their membership in both

---

[27] These include the Eurasian Economic Community, the Russian Federation–Belarus FTA, Russian Federation–Belarus–Kazakhstan Customs Union, the Common Economic Zone treaty and the 2011 Commonwealth of Independent States FTA, which entered into force in 2012. Unfortunately, the 2011 treaty has not yet been coded, so we use its 1994 predecessor, which has been coded, for the purpose of this analysis.

[28] The data set is available at www.wto.org/english/res_e/publications_e/wtr11_dataset_e. htm.

the Pan-Arab Free Trade Area (PAFTA) and Common Market for Eastern and Southern Africa (COMESA). Similarly, Swaziland and Mauritius
are both members of the Southern African Development Community
(SADC) and COMESA. Since these countries build bridges between two
multimember PTAs, they are important for regional networks – that is
why these countries tend to have high eigenvector scores (see Table 20.1).

### IV. Double PTAs as a mainly functional/economic phenomenon

The core economic reason for WTO Members to conclude PTAs has been
to further liberalise or to integrate more deeply as between two or a subset
of like-minded WTO Members, especially in the absence of progress at
the multilateral WTO level. Think of the EU or NAFTA as compared
to the WTO. In contrast, multiple economic integration motives may
explain why two countries engage in a second PTA. These reasons for
concluding double PTAs can be classified into at least four broad groups.
Importantly, different provisions in a second PTA may be explained by
different reasons. Moreover, the reasons why some dyads of countries
exist within a mega-regional may be different from those that apply to
other dyads within the same agreement.

### 1. Deeper integration

There are at least three ways in which double PTAs can deepen integration between two countries. First, two countries may simply decide
to conclude a second PTA or a new PTA between themselves to further
liberalise or integrate their trade relations (if this second, overlapping
PTA does not really add anything, it would fall under the 'paper tiger'
type set out earlier).

Second, following an original PTA, countries may decide to join a
broader and deeper mega-regional trade agreement (with more state
parties than the first). In so doing, they deepen their integration with
both existing PTA partners and new countries (with which they had
no prior PTA relationship). For instance, by concluding the ASEAN–
Australia–New Zealand FTA (AANZFTA), Australia and New Zealand
undertook investment commitments that they had not assumed under
their prior bilateral PTA.[29] Also the Japan–ASEAN FTA contains WTO-
plus and WTO-extra commitments, for example, on the environment,

---

[29] In the meantime, both countries have agreed on an Investment Protocol to be part of
the Australia–New Zealand Closer Economic Relations Trade Agreement. However, the
protocol (in contrast to AANZFTA) does not provide for investor–state arbitration.

agriculture or energy, not present in some of the overlapping, earlier PTAs of individual ASEAN members with Japan.[30] A potential future example is the United States and Mexico in the TPP further dropping tariffs, quotas or other trade restrictions still allowed under NAFTA.

Third, and conversely, two countries may be part of a broad regional PTA and subsequently decide to further integrate only between themselves. For example, in 2005 the ASEAN–China FTA was concluded and three years later in 2008 the ASEAN member Singapore signed an additional FTA with China. As compared to the ASEAN–China Agreement, the China–Singapore FTA contains much deeper WTO-plus commitments, for example, in the fields of sanitary and phytosanitary (SPS) measures or technical barriers to trade (TBT), furthering the harmonisation of standards, and more extensive legally enforceable WTO-extra obligations, for example, on industrial cooperation as well as immigration issues.[31] Similar trends may be observed in Africa, where some member states of the Economic Community of West African States (ECOWAS) (integration depth 2) decided in 1994 to integrate further among themselves by signing the West African Economic and Monetary Union (WAEMU) Treaty (integration depth 4).

## 2. Minimum floor expansion

Double PTAs may also result from a mega-regional trade agreement to extend a minimum floor of liberalisation and rule convergence to a larger group of countries. In that scenario, as between the parties to both PTAs, the later (mega-regional) PTA is less (not more) liberalising. For example, as between Canada and the United States, certain NAFTA commitments could continue to go deeper than subsequent TPP obligations. Obviously, as between these parties and third parties that only joined the later mega-regional (e.g. as between the United States and Malaysia), trade is further liberalised through the creation of a minimum floor.

Such arrangements may be particularly frequent where earlier, regional PTAs regroup countries with very different levels of development. Here mega-regionals can set rules based on the lowest common denominator, while allowing countries to go beyond a one-size-fits-all approach in bilateral or subregional PTAs. That may be one of the reasons why we observe a higher frequency of double PTAs involving ASEAN members, which include low-income economies (Cambodia), lower-middle-income economies (Lao PDR, Indonesia, the Philippines, Vietnam),

---

[30]  The WTO-extra commitments, however, are excluded from dispute settlement.
[31]  See Horn *et al.* database, *supra* note 27.

upper-middle-income economies (Malaysia, Thailand) and high-income economies (Brunei, Singapore).

Scenarios where PTAs expand to include new members so as to set common minimum floor rules are a good example of 'multilateralising regionalism'. They represent a broader process of consolidation through PTA creation, as opposed to the conventional story of PTA creation often portraying PTAs as necessarily a further step in the fragmentation of international trade regulation.

### 3. Backsliding

A second PTA between the same two countries may also reintroduce or tolerate the (re)introduction of trade restrictions that were previously outlawed under the first PTA. This could happen, for example, by including broader exceptions in the second PTA or carving out particular measures or sectors from the second PTA that were covered in the first (think of TPP excluding all tobacco measures from its scope of application, whereas such measures are disciplined in NAFTA and earlier PTAs). Here, the later PTA is – between the same two countries – less liberalising than the first.

### 4. Legal innovation

In some situations it is difficult to decide whether one provision is more or less liberalising or leads to deeper integration than another. Sometimes PTAs simply define or address an issue differently. These differences can be accidental or introduced on purpose, with the intention of changing the meaning of a treaty provision as compared to a previous PTA.

This process is particularly apparent in the recent investment chapters of PTAs, where clarifications on the meaning of 'investment', 'fair and equitable treatment' or 'expropriation' are introduced[32] but are absent in earlier bilateral agreements involving the same parties (or a subset thereof). Depending on the form that these clarifications take, they may also be understood as a backsliding on investment protection commitments.

### V. Legal issues arising from double PTAs

The legal relationship between WTO and PTA rules remains relatively simple: they co-exist.[33] First, in the relation between PTA parties and

---

[32] See, for instance, AANZFTA, Chapter 11, which contains numerous clarifying notes, for example, Article 6 (2) and footnotes 1–4, 7–9, 12–13, 15.

[33] For an in-depth discussion of overlapping investment treaties, including PTAs with an investment chapter, see Wolfgang Alschner (2014), 'Regionalism and Overlap in

other WTO Members, as discussed previously, for a PTA to be preferential (i.e. to exclude other WTO Members), the PTA must comply with GATT Article XXIV, the Enabling Clause or GATS Article V. If it fails to do so, the PTA remains valid but, to the extent MFN applies, concessions exchanged in the PTA must be extended to all WTO Members. Second, in terms of conflict or priority rules in the relation *between* PTA parties, a PTA can explicitly provide that it prevails over WTO rules (as NAFTA does) or, in the event there is silence on this matter, can be presumed to be *lex specialis* (the more specific rule) and in most cases also *lex posterior* (the rule later in time) so that PTA rules normally prevail over WTO rules.

In contrast, the relationship between successive PTAs that include the same two parties can take many different forms with varying degrees of complexity. The scenarios are bifurcated into two broad categories. There are scenarios in which successive PTAs are consolidated so that only one PTA is in force at any given time ('one PTA at a time') versus scenarios in which two PTAs co-exist ('two PTAs side by side'). In the 'one PTA at a time' scenario, successive PTAs do not add to the fragmentation or overlap of international trade rules. In contrast, the 'two PTAs side by side' scenario leads to a formal double PTA situation (as visualised earlier) and may, depending on the circumstances, multilateralise regionalism or further fragment the trade system.

## 1. Consolidation: one PTA at a time

i. **Termination**    The later PTA can simply terminate the earlier one. TPP could terminate NAFTA and become the new agreement regulating US–Mexico trade. In this scenario, only the second PTA remains in existence. There is no question of overlap or conflict. Termination has the advantage of clarity and finality. Termination remains, however, relatively rare. One example is the Mexico–Central America FTA, which, in Article 21.7, terminates existing bilateral FTAs between Mexico and El Salvador, Guatemala, Honduras and Nicaragua. It may become a more frequent option in light of the EU's policy to replace bilateral (investment) treaties concluded by EU members with EU-negotiated PTAs.[34] The transition from GATT to WTO also used termination (of GATT and related codes) as the legal solution regulating the interrelationship between GATT and

Investment Treaty Law – Towards Consolidation or Contradiction?' in the *Journal of International Economic Law*, volume 17, issue 2.
34  See EU Regulation No. 1219/2012 of 12 December 2012 establishing transitional arrangements for bilateral investment agreements between Member States and third countries, *Official Journal of the European Union* 20 Dec 2012, L 351/40, recital 5. The EU proposal

WTO.[35] Such termination, however, only makes sense in the context of certain reasons to conclude a second PTA. For some (not all) deeper integration scenarios (in which, assuming that the second PTA goes further than the first, the first may well terminate). In contrast, it would not necessarily make sense, for example, in the minimum floor expansion context (if TPP is broader, but not deeper, than NAFTA, there is no reason to terminate NAFTA). Besides termination that is explicitly provided for in the later treaty, termination can also be implied following the rules of Article 59:1 of the Vienna Convention on the Law of Treaties (VCLT).[36]

in the leaked investment chapter of the Canada–EU Trade Agreement (CETA) Article X.18 reads in this regard:

Relationship with other Agreements

1. This Agreement replaces the agreements between Member States of the European Union and Canada listed in Annex (Y). The provisions of such agreements shall cease to apply from the date of entry into force of this Agreement.

2. In the event of the provisional application of this agreement, the application of the provisions of the agreements mentioned in paragraph 1) shall be suspended as of the date of provisional application of this agreement in accordance with Article X [Final Provisions] and until such agreements are replaced in accordance with the provisions of paragraph 1). The suspension shall be terminated in the event the provisional application is terminated.

3. Notwithstanding paragraphs 1 and 2, claims may be submitted pursuant to the provisions of the agreements listed in Annex (Y), regarding treatment accorded while the said agreements were in force, pursuant to the rules and procedures established in them, and provided that no more than three (3) years have elapsed since the date of suspension of the agreement pursuant to paragraph 2, or if the agreement is not suspended pursuant to paragraph 2, the date of entry into force of this Agreement. Where a claim has been submitted to arbitration under an agreement listed in Annex (Y), the provisions of such agreement shall remain applicable to the extent necessary for the purposes of the arbitration and the execution and enforcement of any award.

The leaked text is available at www.tradejustice.ca/leakeddocs/

35   See Moore (1996) and Marceau (1995). And formally: GATT Contracting Parties, Transitional Co-existence of the GATT 1947 and the WTO Agreement – Decision of 8 December 1994 adopted by the Preparatory Committee for the WTO and the CONTRACTING PARTIES to GATT 1947, L/7583 (13 December 1994); Preparatory Committee for the World Trade Organization Sub-Committee on Institutional, Procedural and Legal Matters, *Transitional Arrangements – Note by the Secretariat* PC/IPL/W/5 (7 September 1994).

36   Article 59:1 VCLT provides: 'A treaty shall be considered as terminated if all the parties to it conclude a later treaty relating to the same subject matter and: (*a*) it appears from the later treaty or is otherwise established that the parties intended that the matter should be governed by that treaty; or (*b*) the provisions of the later treaty are so far incompatible with those of the earlier one that the two treaties are not capable of being applied at the same time.'

**ii. Accession**   Instead of concluding an entirely new PTA among a broader group of countries, an existing PTA could be amended and expanded to include new members. The second (e.g. mega-regional) PTA could then be achieved through accession. Instead of negotiating an entirely new TPP, countries could 'accede' to NAFTA. Although accession provisions in PTAs are quite common and their usage may seem like a natural way to move from regional to mega-regional trade agreements, in practice, accession by new members to an existing PTA is extremely rare (the major exception being the EU). Like termination, accession has the advantage of simplicity: only one PTA is and remains in force. Whereas termination may, in some treaties, trigger so-called survival clauses (e.g. in bilateral investment treaties (BITs)), amendment or accession is not likely to have this effect.

**iii. Suspension**   Another option is for the second PTA (e.g. a mega-regional) to suspend the operation of an earlier PTA (regional) and to do so for as long as the second PTA remains in place. As with termination and accession, following suspension, only one PTA exists at any given time. The advantage of suspension (over termination), however, is that the earlier PTA would revive in the case that the second PTA, for whatever reason, ends. This avoids having to renegotiate (bilateral) PTA relations when a broader, regional PTA fails. Suspension is used primarily in PTA investment chapters with respect to earlier BITs so as to safeguard continuous investment protection in case the PTA fails (in which case the old BIT 'revives').[37]

**iv. Incorporation**   A final option consists in partially consolidating two PTAs by incorporating certain chapters of one PTA in the other PTA. The China–Singapore FTA is a case in point, incorporating, *mutatis mutandis*, the ASEAN–China FTA investment chapter (Article 84(1)) rather than devising new investment disciplines. This still leaves two PTAs in co-existence, but when it comes to the specific disciplines incorporated we have only one set of PTA disciplines (not two). This is why we classify incorporation under the 'one PTA at a time' scenario. Incorporation can be efficient because it directs negotiators' attention to areas where differentiation (e.g. deeper integration or legal innovation) of overlapping

---

[37] Canada–Peru FTA (2008) Article 845 suspending the Canada–Peru BIT (2006). See also Panama–United States FTA (2007) Article 1.3(2) or Morocco–United States FTA (2004) Article 1.2 (3).

treaty layers is warranted. It also helps to streamline a country's legal commitments.

## 2. Coexistence: two PTAs side by side

In formal double PTA scenarios (such as those depicted in Figures 20.8 to 20.10), the earlier PTA remains in place. Here, a number of complications arise. Aside from the costs to traders of finding the relevant rules applicable to their transactions, and costs to states of managing (and complying with) overlapping commitments, the two most worrisome complications concern the overlap and interaction of parallel dispute settlement fora and what to do in case of contradictory norms.

**i. Overlap and interaction of parallel PTA dispute settlement fora**   The existence of parallel adjudication mechanisms is well known in the context of WTO–PTA relations, but how does the issue play out in double PTA cases? In principle, the same tools that govern, for example, the relationship between WTO panels and NAFTA panels could also manage the relationship between a NAFTA and a TPP panel. This is also done in practice. Chapter 17, Article 5 of the ASEAN–Australia FTA, for example, provides the following choice of forum clause:

> Where a dispute concerning any matter arises under *this Agreement and under another international agreement* to which the Parties to the dispute are party, the Complaining Party may select the forum in which to address that matter and that forum shall be used to the exclusion of other possible fora in respect of that matter.

Such a broad choice of forum clause, if recognised by the Panel hearing the case, would bar a complainant from relitigating the same dispute either at the WTO or at a parallel PTA.

Importantly, overlapping trade disputes are not the only possible litigation arising from double PTAs. As many recent PTAs also contain investment chapters that include a state's consent to investor–state arbitration, coordination issues may also arise between (1) investor–state tribunals and trade tribunals under two different treaties between the same parties (Pauwelyn 2006) and (2) investor–state tribunals that are concurrently or subsequently seized by the same investor over the same measure against the same host state yet under two different treaties.

Although parallel investment litigation is not unknown – the famous Central European Media Enterprises Ltd. (CME)/Lauder arbitrations being a notorious example[38] – it has thus far been perceived as a problem of nationality planning where one corporate entity purposely structures its investment using multiple 'home countries' to benefit from several investment treaties. In the case of double-PTAs, however, such sophistication is unnecessary as the same investor with the same nationality can bring a claim to two different fora (there is only one home state, but two applicable PTAs are in force with the same host state). The situation is thus more akin to (although certainly not exactly the same as) the coordination issues arising out of the interaction between domestic courts and international arbitral tribunals. Here too, at least a priori, the same dispute with identical parties could be litigated at two different levels. It follows that the tools to manage interaction between domestic courts and arbitral tribunals may also help to solve conflicts between double PTAs.

The most relevant among these tools are waiver clauses. The ASEAN Comprehensive Investment Agreement, for instance, provides in Article 34(1)c that the notice of arbitration must be

> accompanied by the disputing investor's written waiver of the disputing investor's right to initiate or continue any proceedings before the courts or administrative tribunals of the disputing Member State, *or other dispute settlement procedures, of any proceeding with respect to any measure* alleged to constitute a breach referred to in Article 32 (Claim by an Investor of a Member State).

Hence, the waiver extends to 'other dispute settlement procedures' than those of the host state, preventing an investor from initiating new proceedings under a parallel PTA. The leaked TPP investment chapter is similar but even more explicit. Footnote 21 to Article 12.20 states: 'For greater certainty, this [i.e. other dispute settlement procedures] includes any dispute settlement mechanism under any existing trade or bilateral investment agreement.'

Whether or not a waiver will effectively bar an investor from seizing a parallel arbitral forum under an overlapping treaty depends on the wording of the waiver. The trilateral China–Japan–South Korea investment agreement, for instance, limits its waiver to 'any right to initiate before any competent *court of the disputing Contracting Party* with respect to any measure of the disputing Contracting Party'.[39] This arguably still

---

[38]  *CME Czech Republic B.V.* v. *The Czech Republic,* UNCITRAL, Final Award, 14 March 2003, available at www.italaw.com/cases/281, and *Ronald S. Lauder* v. *The Czech Republic,* UNCITRAL, Final Award, 1 September 2001, available at www.italaw.com/cases/610.
[39]  Article 15 (6), italics added.

permits the submission of a claim to a parallel arbitral tribunal under an overlapping agreement.

**ii. Conflict of PTA norms**   Whereas in the WTO–PTA relationship, as between PTA parties, the logical approach is to assume priority of the (more liberalising, more recent) PTA over WTO rules (with the exception, of course, of the MFN issue discussed earlier, which goes beyond PTA parties and affects third country members of the WTO), in the double PTA case, it is not so clear that the later PTA must always prevail. Depending on the reasons discussed previously for concluding the second PTA, different priority rules could be arrived at.

Where the later PTA is motivated by the minimum floor consolidation scenario, it makes sense to explicitly provide that the earlier (deeper) PTA prevails. To avoid any backsliding, the later PTA may also provide that to the extent a provision in an earlier PTA is more trade liberalising, the earlier PTA prevails. Conversely, in situations of legal innovation and conscious backsliding, it makes sense to explicitly provide that the second PTA prevails. The same is normally true also for the deeper integration scenario. In reality, it is often difficult to discern whether a change in the substantive treaty content is motivated by legal innovation or conscious backsliding rather than the desire to set a minimum standard. What conflict rules are chosen may therefore provide useful insights into the motivation behind the conclusion of double PTAs.

*The earlier/original PTA prevails.* The majority of regional and mega-regional treaties encountered today affirm existing obligations, which according to VCLT Article 30(2) will lead the earlier (usually bilateral) treaty to prevail. The ASEAN–Australia–New Zealand FTA, for example, states in Chapter 18 Article 2:

1. Each Party reaffirms its rights and obligations under the WTO Agreement and other agreements to which the Parties are party.
2. Nothing in this Agreement shall be construed to derogate from any right or obligation of a Party under the WTO Agreement and other agreements to which the Parties are party.[40]

The agreement goes on to affirm the right of member countries to conclude future bilateral agreements. This treaty practice thus suggests that minimum standard setting through (mega) regional treaties combined with deeper integration in bilateral agreements is the main force behind

---

[40]   Similarly, Article 20 ASEAN–China FTA (Trade in goods).

such double PTAs. To that extent, the double PTA phenomenon represents a process of consolidation or gradual multilateralisation of regionalism rather than a further step in the fragmentation of international trade regulation.

*The more favourable PTA prevails.* Rather than adopting a time-based approach, the ASEAN–Japan PTA solves conflicts with a view to promoting deeper integration, stipulating in Article 10 (2):

> Nothing in this Agreement shall be construed to derogate from any obligation of a Party vis-à-vis another Party under agreements to which these Parties are parties, if such an obligation *entitles the latter Party to treatment more favourable than that accorded by this Agreement*. [emphasis added]

*Ad hoc negotiation in case of conflict.* Either self-standing as in the Singapore–Australia FTA[41] or in connection with the reaffirmation of existing obligations,[42] a number of agreements provide for ad hoc consultations among the state parties in case of an inconsistency with a view to finding a mutually agreeable solution.

*Silence.* To be avoided whenever possible, negotiators of the second PTA could also leave the question of conflict or overlap open. This is the case for instance with the PTA concluded between India and Sri Lanka in 1999, which does not mention the overlapping Asia-Pacific Trade Agreement. Such silence would trigger the fallback conflict rules of public international law (Pauwelyn 2003a). There is a presumption against conflict, and interpretation methods can be used to read two PTA provisions harmoniously. Where no ambiguity or room for interpretation exists and a genuine conflict arises (that is not explicitly regulated in either treaty), in normal cases (and as between parties to both PTAs) the more recent PTA prevails (Article 30 VCLT). However, if the provision in the earlier PTA is more specific (or the earlier PTA is between a smaller group of countries), there is scope to apply the *lex specialis* principle to the effect that the earlier (not the later) PTA prevails. To avoid the uncertainty related to this situation, PTA negotiators should explicitly regulate PTA overlaps in the respective treaties, depending on the scenarios or reasons for concluding a second PTA, as discussed previously. Remaining silent shifts the task from negotiators to adjudicators and may lead to surprising

---

[41] Chapter 17, Article 5: 'In the event of any inconsistency between this Agreement and any other agreement to which both Parties are parties, the Parties shall immediately consult with each other with a view to finding a mutually satisfactory solution in accordance with customary rules of public international law.'

[42] For example, ASEAN–Australia–New Zealand, Chapter 18, Article 2(3).

results. That said, also adjudicators should take account of the diverse reasons for concluding double PTAs in their ultimate decision. Conflict rules in public international law can be reduced to the question of what the state parties really intended or what the current expression of state will is. To arrive at this current expression of state will, it is likely to be important to examine the reasons why different PTAs were concluded.

## E. Conclusion

Ever since the creation of the WTO, scholarly research has focused primarily on the relations between the WTO and PTAs. The recent trend of states concluding mega-regional trade agreement now warrants a shift of attention to the relationship between PTAs. One of the new issues that will require further scholarly work is the increasingly widespread phenomenon of double PTAs. In this chapter, we have offered a first insight into the universe of double PTAs and the reasons for their emergence and proliferation. We also highlighted the different strategies that states adopt in consolidating (or not) overlapping PTAs as well as the legal implications that arise if parallel trade agreements involving the same parties co-exist. In that context, negotiators and scholars have to think ahead and decide how the norms and dispute settlement mechanisms of overlapping PTAs are supposed to interact.

Let us be clear, however, that this new research agenda, in spite of our provocative title, is not oblivious to or entirely detached from the debate on the relationship between PTAs and the WTO or between regionalism and multilateralism. Quite to the contrary, a more sophisticated understanding of how PTAs interact will allow us to better assess how regionalism can be a stepping stone or stumbling block for multilateralism. On the one hand, our network analysis revealed that the rules of tomorrow are made in deep PTAs by a limited group of countries that are centrally placed in the network. Hence, we should expect a relatively homogeneous process of WTO-extra norm creation and diffusion. On the other hand, the fact that many of these norms are made and diffused outside of the WTO and without the input of many countries also raises concerns as to their global relevance and legitimacy.

The recent success of the Bali WTO Ministerial Conference gives rise to hope that the WTO's negotiating arm is not as crippled as it was for many years. At the same time, the newly gained momentum is not likely to readily translate into negotiated advances in other areas within and beyond the Doha Agenda. This is why the increasingly complex network of PTAs deserves our full attention both to identify the myriad of challenges it gives rise to and to enhance its potential for multilateralism.

## References

Alschner, Wolfgang. 2014. 'Regionalism and Overlap in Investment Treaty Law – Towards Consolidation or Contradiction?' *Journal of International Economic Law* 17(2).

Barabási, Albert-László, and Bonabeau, Eric. 2003. 'Scale-Free Networks.' *Scientific American,* May. www.scientificamerican.com/article.cfm?id=scale-free-networks. Accessed 10 October 2013.

Dür, Andreas, Baccini, Leonardo, and Elsig, Manfred. 2014. 'The Design of International Trade Agreements: Introducing a New Dataset.' *Review of International Organizations* 9 (3): 353–75.

Fowler, James H., and Sangick, Jeon. 2008. 'The Authority of Supreme Court Precedent.' *Social Networks* 30 (1): 16–30. doi:10.1016/j.socnet.2007.05.001.

Horn, Henrik, Mavroidis, Petros C., and Sapir, André. 2010. 'Beyond the WTO? An Anatomy of EU and US Preferential Trade Agreements.' *World Economy* 33 (11): 1565–88. doi:10.1111/j.1467–9701.2010.01273.x.

Kaltenthaler, Karl, and Mora, Frank O. 2002. 'Explaining Latin American Economic Integration: The Case of Mercosur.' *Review of International Political Economy* 9 (1): 72–97.

Katz, Daniel M., and Stafford, Derek K. 2010. 'Hustle and Flow: A Social Network Analysis of the American Federal Judiciary.' *Ohio State Law Journal* 71:457–509.

Marceau, Gabrielle. 1995. 'Transition from the GATT to WTO – A Most Pragmatic Operation.' *Journal of World Trade* 29 (5): 147–63.

Matwyshyn, Andrea M. 2003. 'Of Nodes and Power Laws: A Network Theory Approach to Internet Jurisdiction through Data Privacy.' *Northwestern University Law Review* 98(2).

Moore, Patrick M. 1996. 'The Decisions Bridging the GATT 1947 and the WTO Agreement.' *American Journal of International Law* 90:317–28.

Naumann, Eckart. 2006. 'Comparing EU Free Trade Agreements – Rules of Origin.' *InBrief 6I.* www.ecdpm.org/inbrief6i. Accessed 10 October 2013.

Newman, Mark E. J. 2010. *Networks: An Introduction.* New York: Oxford University Press.

Pauwelyn, Joost. 2003a. *Conflict of Norms in Public International Law: How WTO Law Relates to Other Rules of International Law.* Cambridge Studies in International and Comparative Law. Cambridge: Cambridge University Press.

    2003b. 'How to Win a WTO Dispute Based on Non-WTO Law: Questions of Jurisdiction and Merits.' *Journal of World Trade* 37 (6): 997–1030.

2006. 'Adding Sweeteners to Softwood Lumber: The WTO-NAFTA "Spaghetti Bowl" Is Cooking.' *Journal of International Economic Law* 9:1–10.

2009. 'Legal Avenues to "Multilateralizing Regionalism": Beyond Article XXIV.' In *Multilateralizing Regionalism*, edited by Richard Baldwin and Patrick Low. Cambridge: Cambridge University Press.

2014. 'At the Edge of Chaos: Foreign Investment Law as a Complex Adaptive System, How It Emerged and How It Can Be Reformed.' *ICSID Review*. http://dx.doi.org/10.2139/ssrn.2271869.

Puig, Sergio 2014. 'Social Capital in the Arbitration Market.' *European Journal of International Law* 25. http://papers.ssrn.com/sol3/papers.cfm?abstract_id=2311418.

United Nations Conference on Trade and Development. 2011. *World Investment Report 2011: Non-Equity Modes of International Production and Development*. Geneva: United Nations.

Zachary, Wayne W. 1977. 'An Information Flow Model for Conflict and Fission in Small Groups.' *Journal of Anthropological Research* 33:452–73.

# 21

# Plurilateral agreements, variable geometry and the WTO

## A. Introduction

The global trade regime embodied in the General Agreement on Tariffs and Trade/World Trade Organization (GATT/WTO) has provided an important framework for countries to agree to trade policy disciplines and commitments, as well as a mechanism through which these can be enforced. Although membership of low-income countries in the GATT in 1948 was limited – 12 of the original 23 signatories were developing economies – in the 1960s a substantial expansion of developing country membership began. After the creation of the WTO, membership continued to expand steadily, standing at 160 currently, up from 124 in 1995. Some 20 countries are in the process of negotiating accession.

The first round of multilateral trade negotiations launched under WTO auspices in Doha, Qatar, in 2001 was called the Doha Development Agenda (DDA). The inclusion of the word *development* reflected the increasing influence of developing countries in the WTO and their perception that more needed to be done to address a perceived 'development deficit'. The key objectives of many developing countries included making special and differential treatment (SDT) provisions more effective and operational, improving preferential (nonreciprocal) access to major markets, recognizing the need to improve trade capacity and address supply constraints and 'rebalancing' the rules and disciplines of the WTO by addressing instances of 'reverse SDT' – existing provisions in the

Earlier versions of this chapter were presented at the KIEP-ECIPE-Seoul National University conference 'Free Trade Agreements: Revisiting the Reality of FTA Competition', Seoul, 23 May 2013, and the World Trade Forum in Bern in September 2013. I am grateful to Chul Chung, Thomas Cottier, Deborah Elms, Manfred Elsig, Moonsung Kang, Patrick Messerlin and participants at both conferences for helpful comments and suggestions.

WTO permitting high-income countries to use policies that distort trade. Examples include tariff escalation, agricultural subsidy policies and barriers to the cross-border movement of natural persons providing services. Progress was made after 2001 on the preferential market access and aid elements of this agenda. Milestones include the launch of the 'duty-free, quota-free' market access initiative for the least developed countries (LDCs) and the Aid for Trade initiative at the 2005 WTO Ministerial meeting in Hong Kong. Further progress was made at the Bali Ministerial in December 2013 with the conclusion of negotiations on the Agreement on Trade Facilitation. But to date no progress has been made in redefining multilateral disciplines[1] or agreeing on a set of new reciprocal market access commitments and policy disciplines affecting trade in agricultural products, manufactures or services, let alone initiating discussions on policy areas that are of increasing concern in terms of generating negative spillovers or where cooperation is needed to address global challenges such as food security or climate change.

There has been much discussion and analysis of the factors that led to the deadlock in the DDA. Among the more compelling arguments are that the cost of nonagreement is low and that the potential upside from agreeing on a deal spanning the issues that are on the table is limited. Wolfe (2013), among others, stresses changes in the structure of the world economy, and in particular the explosive growth of China, as the key factor that made the DDA agenda, as conceived in 2001 and restructured in 2003, increasingly less relevant as time passed. A fundamental reason for the breakdown in the talks was the difference between what Organisation for Economic Co-operation and Development (OECD) countries, in particular the United States, wanted to obtain from the large emerging markets, especially China, Brazil and India, and what these countries were willing to offer and were looking for in return. Subjects that would generate substantial interest and engagement by industry groups – such as the prospect of significant liberalisation of services trade – were never the focus of serious negotiations, which is the main reason services talks are currently being pursued among a subset of countries outside the WTO.

One consequence of the DDA deadlock has been that efforts to negotiate liberalisation and new rules of the game have increasingly shifted

---

[1] An exception with regard to 'rebalancing' the rules is the insistence by India at the Bali Ministerial that it not be bound by the Uruguay Round domestic support limits for agriculture when implementing its domestic programme to provide households with subsidised staple foods.

away from the WTO. Major preferential trade agreements (PTAs) are being negotiated among small groups of countries, including the United States and the European Union (EU). These follow on from a large number of bilateral trade agreements that have already been negotiated by countries that are pursuing aggressive trade liberalisation and integration strategies in Europe, Latin America and East Asia. The shift to PTAs raises numerous questions regarding the possible consequences for the multilateral trading system, for the countries that are driving efforts to negotiate mega-regionals, for the emerging economies that are not participating in the mega-regionals that include the EU and United States and for the large number of developing countries that are either excluded altogether or are only bit players in the mega-regionals. Time will tell to what extent efforts to establish mega-regional trade and investment agreements among small groups of countries will succeed in going significantly beyond what is covered by the WTO. But it is clear that the world has changed as far as trade cooperation is concerned, in that the WTO is not playing the role that was envisaged when it was created in 1995: namely, that it was to be the multilateral forum for the negotiation of new policy disciplines on trade-related policies broadly defined.

The agreement reached at the December WTO Ministerial meeting in Bali was important for the multilateral trading system – showing that progress can be made in developing new rules of the game. The Agreement on Trade Facilitation in particular will help countries around the world improve the operation and governance of national border management systems and reduce uncertainty and trade costs for traders. The big question confronting WTO Members post-Bali is whether it will be possible to devise and implement a work programme that offers better prospects for a multilateral deal to liberalise trade in agricultural products, manufactured goods and services and to begin to address policy spillovers in areas that so far have been kept off the WTO table, such as investment, competition and industrial policies. The instruction by ministers to their negotiators to come up with a road map to conclude the Doha Round negotiations recognises implicitly if not explicitly that a rethink, of both what is on the table and the modalities of cooperation and negotiation of new agreements, is needed.

This chapter discusses possible approaches that could be taken by WTO Members to support greater multilateral cooperation on trade-related policies. Pursuit of one or more of these options could comprise elements of the road map or work programme called for by the 2013 WTO

Ministerial conference in Bali. After a brief overview of the state of play on PTAs (Section B), I discuss three options that could be pursued in the WTO in response to the revealed preference for PTAs: using WTO mechanisms as 'deliberation' devices so as to enhance a common understanding of the (spillover) impacts of policies that are currently not subject to WTO disciplines (Section C), increasing the transparency of what is done in PTAs and identifying 'good practices' that could be pursued multilaterally (Section D) and making greater use of opportunities to conclude critical mass and plurilateral agreements under the umbrella of the WTO so as to accommodate additional variable geometry within the WTO (Section E). Section F offers some concluding remarks.

## B. The shift to PTAs: drivers and implications

Preferential trade agreements (PTAs) have been proliferating for many years. Whereas in the pre-WTO period 'serious' PTAs were mostly between large industrialised nations (i.e. the EU and the United States) and developing countries (so-called North–South agreements) or involved countries that shared common borders,[2] more recently OECD countries have begun to negotiate PTAs between themselves. Examples include the PTAs signed by the Republic of Korea with the EU and the United States, the proposed Trans-Pacific Partnership (TPP), the recently concluded EU–Canada agreement, the launch of talks on a Transatlantic Trade and Investment Partnership (TTIP) between the United States and the EU, the initiation of an effort to negotiate a Trade in Services Agreement (TiSA) and the Regional Comprehensive Economic Partnership (RCEP).[3] TTIP is a bilateral EU–US initiative, although in practice it will be quadrilateral given that Mexico and Canada are part of the North American Free

---

[2] Most notably the agreements negotiated by and between European countries, which account for a significant share of PTAs. Other important regional agreements between OECD member countries are NAFTA and the CER agreement between Australia and New Zealand.

[3] At the time of writing (December 2013), RCEP involves 16 countries: the 10 members of ASEAN (Brunei, Cambodia, Indonesia, Laos, Malaysia, Myanmar, the Philippines, Singapore, Thailand and Vietnam) and 6 countries with which the Association of Southeast Asian Nations (ASEAN) has a free trade agreement (Australia, China, India, Japan, the Republic of Korea and New Zealand). The TiSA includes Australia, Canada, Chile, Chinese Taipei, Colombia, Costa Rica, Hong Kong China, Iceland, Israel, Japan, the Republic of Korea, Mexico, New Zealand, Norway, Panama, Paraguay, Pakistan, Peru, Switzerland, Turkey and the United States. The TPP spans Australia, Brunei, Canada, Chile, Japan, Malaysia, Mexico, New Zealand, Peru, Singapore, the United States and Vietnam.

Trade Agreement (NAFTA) and both countries also have bilateral trade agreements with the EU. Developing countries are participating in the RCEP, TPP and the TiSA talks, but the first two of these are regional arrangements and thus by design exclude the majority of the WTO membership. The TiSA is limited to a group of 'really good friends of services'. It does not include the majority of developing nations, although China has made clear that it wants to be part of the negotiations. A large number of developing countries, including the poorest ones (the LDCs), have remained outside these new initiatives, and many would not want to be involved even if they could (as is the case with TiSA, which in principle is open to any country).[4] Instead, many of these countries emphasise the need for concluding the DDA, continued application of the 'less than full reciprocity' principle and the need to safeguard 'policy space' to be able to intervene in trade.[5]

The many PTAs in force and under negotiation reveal that the difficulty of reaching agreement in the DDA is not due to unwillingness by governments to make binding trade-policy-related commitments or to agree on new trade-policy-related disciplines. Instead, as already noted, the shift towards PTAs is in part a reflection of the fact that the major players in the WTO cannot 'get to yes' in the Doha negotiations (Evenett 2013; Wolfe 2013). There has been extensive speculation about the motivations of the United States in particular in pursuing specific PTAs, especially the TPP. Clearly economic factors play a role (i.e. a desire to increase trade opportunities), as do foreign policy considerations – although the latter are arguably less dominant than is sometimes argued (Schott, Kotschwar and Muir 2013). Another factor may be a desire by the United States and the EU to signal that there is an outside option and to make that threat credible. PTAs have historically been a driver for the conclusion of multilateral trade agreements – examples being the periodic expansion of the European Economic Community, which helped spur the United States to

---

[4]  In practice the ability to participate is conditional in the sense that countries that did not join the talks early on will later find it more difficult to become participants in the ongoing negotiations on the substance of an agreement – once the talks have advanced and the outlines of an agreement have been agreed among participants, new countries are likely to have to wait until the 'original' TiSA countries have finalised an agreement before they can negotiate their accession.

[5]  This negotiating strategy has had some positive results in addressing some of the perceived 'development deficit' that motivated the design of the DDA, including more duty-free, quota-free (DFQF) access, the Aid for Trade (AFT) initiative and the Enhanced Integrated Framework for the LDCs. See Hoekman (2013).

drive the Kennedy and Tokyo Rounds, and the negotiation of the Canada–US FTA followed by NAFTA, which has been argued to have played a role in inducing countries to conclude the Uruguay Round (Hoekman and Kostecki 2009). It may be that the TPP and TTIP will induce similar dynamics and bring countries back to the WTO (Cottier, Sieber-Gasser and Wermelinger, Chapter 19 in this volume; Wolfe 2013). Even if this is the case, there may be an extended period during which the WTO stagnates.

Much will depend on what eventually is negotiated in the mega-regionals – in particular the extent to which they result in economically meaningful outcomes and the degree to which these imply discrimination against products coming from nonparties. Although there are strong economic forces that are likely to keep markets open – for example, the increasing role of global value chains and international production networks – rules of origin, regulatory convergence and mutual recognition among members of mega-regionals may create incentives for companies to locate in a bloc or to source from firms located within a bloc. Traditional types of trade diversion created by the discriminatory abolition of tariffs are unlikely to be significant given the low level of applied tariffs in most of the countries that are involved in the TPP and TTIP.[6] There may nonetheless be de facto trade diversion insofar as the PTAs reduce the market-segmenting effects of differences in regulatory policies. This will depend on whether firms located outside the PTA will be able to demonstrate compliance with the relevant regulatory norms. In practice it could be difficult to exclude third-country firms from benefiting from initiatives that lower the fixed costs associated with demonstrating conformity with product or process regulations that apply in PTA member countries.

A challenge for the many countries that are excluded from most of the mega-regional negotiations is to identify actions that can be taken to reduce potential downsides or to increase benefit from these initiatives. This is an important question not only for all the countries in Africa, the Middle East, Central and South Asia and those parts of Latin America that are not part of the TPP, RCEP or the TiSA but also for the East Asian countries that are not members of the TPP – not just China but also six of the ASEAN member countries, including Indonesia, the Philippines and

---

[6] In part such additional costs will be low because most participants already have free trade agreements with each other.

Thailand. And this applies to some 130 WTO Members when it comes to the TTIP.

One response is to pursue PTAs in turn – which of course is already (and has been) occurring. This can help generate greater trade between a set of countries that are growing more rapidly than the EU and United States and where traditional barriers to trade are substantially higher. If such PTAs result in meaningful preferential liberalisation, the associated trade diversion could become an incentive for a renewed effort to conclude multilateral deals. Given that the coverage and depth of PTAs involving large emerging economies such as India or Brazil are (will be) significantly more limited than the TPP or TTIP, the magnitude of any such incentives is likely to be small.

Another response is to devote greater effort to addressing matters of common concern and interest in the WTO. As has been noted by many observers, a number of the market access and trade policy issues that are central to the DDA will not be addressed in the PTAs – for example, agricultural support policies and subsidies of various kinds (such as investment incentives and brown and green energy subsidies, among others). Nor will the PTAs improve market access or investment conditions in the large emerging economies given that these countries are mostly not participating in the mega-regionals. This suggests that sooner or later there will be a renewed focus on the WTO by the 'majors'. However, it is not at all clear why cooperation in the WTO must extend to all WTO Members. There is an extensive literature in both economics and political science pointing to the efficiency benefits of cooperation that is limited to subsets of agents and entities – be they individuals, communities or nations. That one size does not fit all has become a platitude, but it is important to recognise that global harmonisation of policies is not necessarily first best from a global welfare perspective.

Certain elements of what is on the table in the mega-regionals involve disciplines in areas that may not be seen to be in the national interest of countries that are not participants. Examples may include labour-rights-related policies, stronger intellectual property disciplines and binding investor–state arbitration, among others. Given a desire to include disciplines on such matters in PTAs, whether a reflection of strongly held societal beliefs or simply the result of political economy realities (i.e. a necessary condition for ratification of any trade agreement), many excluded countries may not be willing to consider joining these PTAs even if this was an option. In this case, presumably these countries would also oppose suggestions to address these issues in the WTO. That said, some (perhaps many) WTO Members may be interested in implementing some (perhaps many) of the procedural or substantive provisions that figure in a PTA and thereby improve market access opportunities for their firms, but cannot do so. Moreover, such countries may have interests of their own in specific areas of trade policy that are not covered by the PTAs. The WTO offers a mechanism for countries to table such matters and explore the approaches to address the associated spillover effects.

A premise of what follows is that the strong revealed preference for PTAs suggests a need to devote more effort in the WTO to exploiting opportunities for subsets of WTO Members ('clubs' – Lawrence 2006) to deliberate on policies that are not (yet) subject to the WTO rules or disciplines and to explore the potential for formation of clubs of different types. Several complementary approaches could be pursued to this effect: (1) using the WTO as a venue for 'policy deliberation', (2) expanding the transparency function of the WTO to learn from PTA experiences and (3) preparing the ground for formation of clubs – which may comprise critical mass cooperation or formal plurilateral agreements that apply only to signatories.

## C. WTO as a mechanism for deliberation

Much of the agenda of the new vintage PTAs concerns the trade-impeding effects of regulatory policies – various forms of nontariff measures. Examples are product regulation (to achieve health, safety or security objectives), licensing requirements, certification and conformity assessment procedures, and regulation that determines the degree of competition that prevails on services markets. Such measures cannot simply be abolished as the presumption is that they fulfil a specific social or economic purpose, even if the effect is to restrict trade. Addressing the trade effects of regulation requires first an understanding at the national level of the effects of prevailing policies and the likely impacts of alternative welfare-enhancing reforms. Many such reforms will not require actions by other governments (trading partners), but international agreements on the rules of the game may help both to attract the required attention to an issue and to overcome resistance by those with vested interests. Indeed, international cooperation can help countries identify potentially beneficial reforms. But such cooperation is likely to require not so much reciprocal exchanges of policy commitments – the standard modality of trade negotiations – but more a focus on processes that centre attention on building an understanding of the status quo, possible alternatives and the potential gains from reforms.

Different approaches can be envisaged in pursuing cooperation between states on policies that generate negative externalities. Binding international law – the modus operandi of the WTO – is one option. Others include 'soft law' forms of cooperation that revolve around mechanisms through which agents can raise issues that they perceive as damaging to their interests and the design of processes to assess such claims and identify options for addressing them. Determining which approach is appropriate requires a process of deliberation and mutual learning. The WTO offers a variety of mechanisms to its members through which they can interact, ranging from subcommittees to working groups and informal 'friends of' a particular subject or issue. Nothing precludes a group of countries from discussing trade-related policies and issues that are not subject to WTO disciplines. The main constraint is having access to WTO Secretariat staff to support a particular endeavour, a matter that can be addressed if there is a willingness to do so. Determining whether there is a possible need or basis for an agreement in an area requires deliberation. The same is true regarding the form any cooperation on an issue should take, which will depend among other things on the extent to which national policies create negative spillovers and the magnitude of the costs of free-riding by countries that are unwilling to cooperate.

Hoekman and Mattoo (2013) suggest the formation of 'knowledge platforms' that would act as vehicles through which countries can assess or analyse the impacts of current policy regimes and identify beneficial reforms and what it will take to implement them. Such platforms would connect stakeholders to different sources of expertise – local, regional, global; facilitate knowledge exchange; build on existing networks of regulators and industry associations; and connect with both the donor community for support for implementation of reforms in developing countries and the business community. The latter has a direct stake in pro-competitive reforms and needs to play an active role in monitoring progress in implementing reforms and holding governments accountable for the results. Although the proposed approach is undoubtedly a complex, resource-intensive, time-consuming exercise, shifting the focus of international cooperation in this direction is arguably a necessary condition for 'ownership' and political support for putting in place policies that will enhance competitiveness.

No deliberative mechanism exists in the WTO that performs a 'knowledge platform' function or that is designed to discuss complementary sets

of policies and identify how they interact to affect trade costs and investment location decisions. Given the complexity of today's organisation of
global trade and investment flows this may explain why business appears
to be less engaged in and supportive of the WTO than was the case during
the Uruguay Round. Creating platforms that allow (encourage) examination of the various policy silos that all have an impact on supply chain
trade, that help identify which policy areas should be prioritised and that
recognise whether there are important 'gaps' in the existing coverage of
WTO agreements would at a minimum be informative (Hoekman 2013).
But better knowledge may also support unilateral action by governments
seeking to improve the competitiveness of firms located in their jurisdictions, and, over time, such engagement could prepare the ground for new
agreements or the deepening of existing disciplines.

## D. Engaging with PTAs: transparency and learning

Elements of the types of cooperation discussed in the previous section
are part of the new-vintage PTAs. This may take the form of mechanisms for the exchange of information, of fora for interaction between
business associations, investors and civil society groups and governments
and of various economic and noneconomic forms of cooperation (e.g.
facilitation of cross-border movement of business personnel and of students). PTAs often create a variety of official bodies that are tasked with
implementation of the agreement in specific areas and that can act as
mechanisms through which regulators and other officials from the participating countries establish working relationships.

PTAs provide a learning opportunity – not just for the countries that
are members but also for those that are not. The proliferation of PTAs
offers the WTO membership as a whole an opportunity to learn from the
many experiments and approaches that are being pursued. PTAs are in
some sense laboratories. The results of experiments that are successful in
specific PTAs may be transferable. Over time WTO Members may come
to the view that embedding some of the processes and approaches that
have proved successful in a PTA context into the WTO is desirable. A
precondition for such learning is transparency: WTO Members need to
have information on what is being done in the PTA context. Rather than
this information determined individually, it is much better collated by
the WTO Secretariat. Ideally, signatories to the PTAs would agree to provide information and share their experiences of implementation with the
broader WTO membership. But independent of whatever information

PTA members are willing to provide in this regard, the WTO Secretariat should be mandated to analyse and report on the specific processes or approaches that have been implemented in PTAs and to assess their impacts on economic outcomes.

Whatever the approaches used and the mechanisms put in place in a PTA, WTO Members could use a 'PTA transparency mechanism' as a means of consulting and interacting with stakeholders – especially the business community – that are knowledgeable as regards the operation of specific PTAs. Business will be most aware of what is and what is not working and is a key source of objective information on what is being done in a PTA, its effectiveness and impact and data on the costs and benefits of what has been implemented. Business needs to be an integral part of any transparency and learning process in a way that goes beyond 'consultations' and 'dialogue'. It has a key role to play in helping to understand the effects and effectiveness of PTAs in reducing (regulatory) barriers to trade by providing the data that are needed to assess 'PTA performance'.

An important contribution the WTO could make in this regard is to significantly expand what is done today by the Committee on Regional Trade Agreements (CRTA) and Transparency Review Mechanism. Collecting and analysing information on the factors affecting implementation of PTA disciplines would allow a much better understanding of what actually is being done in the PTA context, not just in terms of policy but also in terms of institutional change and strengthening, specific types of cooperation and interactions between PTA members and the investments that are made as part of the implementation of PTA provisions. Current monitoring of PTAs by the Secretariat focuses primarily on documenting the provisions of PTAs. This is not particularly informative for countries seeking to understand what is entailed in implementing those provisions and the outcomes that are generated. Bringing in and using firm- and industry-level data on variables of interest – such as trade costs and clearance times – would help WTO Members to better understand whether and how PTA procedures and disciplines contribute towards improving economic outcomes and performance. This will require collaboration with the business community, as data on implementation and its impacts are critical inputs into any assessment of progress made in addressing specific barriers and helping WTO Members to better understand why approaches in a PTA are or are not effective. A constraint in this connection is that business may be hesitant to make relevant data publicly available for fear of adverse reactions by government agencies or because of worries about revealing useful information to competitors. Conversely, governments may discount information provided by business because of perceptions that firms will seek to remove any policies that raise their costs even if the underlying measures are implemented efficiently by the administrative bodies responsible for enforcement of policy. The WTO Secretariat could become a trusted intermediary, acting as the depository of data provided by business and ensuring that this is relevant and appropriate in measuring and assessing the impacts of implementation of specific measures agreed by the signatories of a PTA.[7]

## E. Variable geometry beyond PTAs: critical mass and plurilateral agreements[8]

The WTO offers three mechanisms for Members to form 'clubs' that allow them to move forward with an agenda of common interest: negotiating a PTA that is justified under Article XXIV GATT or Article V GATS, negotiating agreements among subsets of WTO Members that apply on a most-favoured-nation (MFN) basis (i.e. all WTO Members benefit from what is agreed among the subset even if they do nothing themselves) – so-called critical mass agreements (CMAs) – and conclusion of a plurilateral agreement (PA) under Article II.3 WTO. The latter provision permits subsets of the WTO Membership to agree to certain disciplines applying to signatories only. In contrast to a PTA, which must cover substantially all trade in goods (Article XXIV GATT) or have substantial sectoral coverage of services (Article V GATS), CMAs and PAs can be issue- or policy-specific. An example of a CMA is the Information Technology Agreement (ITA) that eliminated tariffs on imports of certain IT products for a group of WTO Members. This agreement was implemented on an MFN basis through tariff commitments made by each signatory. Other examples of CMAs that are sectoral in nature are so-called zero-for-zero agreements for certain chemicals, agricultural machinery, medical equipment, scientific equipment and construction equipment and for certain services (e.g. the agreements on basic telecommunications and on financial services) (Hoekman and Kostecki 2009).

---

[7] Such a role is played by other international organisations for other types of data – for example, the International Chamber of Commerce (ICC) for data on trade finance and the World Bank for firm- and household-level data.

[8] What follows draws on Hoekman and Mavroidis (2013), which undertakes a comprehensive comparison and assessment of the PA and PTA approaches to cooperation between subsets of WTO Members.

Four Pas were incorporated into the WTO in 1995 as 'Annex 4 agreements': the International Dairy Agreement, the International Bovine Meat Agreement, the Agreement on Civil Aircraft and the Agreement on Government Procurement (GPA). The first two of these agreements have since been terminated, whereas many of the provisions of the Agreement on Civil Aircraft have been superseded by the WTO Agreement on Subsidies and Countervailing Measures and the GPA (as the latter was expanded to encompass rules on public purchases of civil aircraft). Thus, the GPA is essentially the only extant PA. It has seen periodic renegotiation and expansion of coverage.

Many voices have argued for greater recourse to CMAs and Pas as a way of allowing subsets of countries to move forward on an issue and permitting progress to be made on rule making under the umbrella of the WTO (e.g. Bacchus 2012; Elsig 2010; Gallagher and Stoler 2009; Harbinson 2009; Lawrence 2006; Levy 2006; Mendoza, 2012). There is, however, significant opposition to expanding the number of such agreements in the WTO. This contrasts with the general acceptance of PTAs. All WTO Members are parties to at least one PTA, and some are parties to dozens. Indeed, the WTO website reports that more than 500 PTAs have been notified to the WTO, some 400 of which remain in force.

What PTAs and Pas have in common is that both permit (but do not require) discrimination. All three types of agreements liberalise trade or define rules of the game for a subset of the WTO Membership that shares similar views and wants to go beyond prevailing WTO disciplines. Both CMAs and Pas must by definition go beyond existing WTO rules. As already noted, an important difference is that CMAs are applied on an MFN basis, whereas Pas can be discriminatory. Another major difference is that Article X.9 of the WTO agreement stipulates that the Ministerial Conference of the WTO may decide to add an agreement to the existing set of Pas listed in Annex 4 'exclusively by consensus'. In contrast, CMAs are simply conditional on agreement among a group of WTO Members to go further in a given policy area while accepting free-riding by countries that decide not to participate.

A major difference between PTAs and CMAs and Pas is that PTAs tend to be closed clubs – most PTAs do not include provisions that allow any other country to join should it wish to do so. Those that foresee accession often limit this to countries that are geographically proximate. This helps explain the proliferation of PTAs – a new agreement tends to be negotiated between members of any given PTA and nonmembers. Pas in contrast are 'open' – in principle, no WTO Member can be excluded from a PA once it has been negotiated and accepted as an Annex 4 agreement as long as countries satisfy whatever conditions apply for membership (i.e. conform to the disciplines that constitute the substantive provisions of the PA). The basic premise underlying a PA is to allow variable geometry and differentiation – allowing for countries to join if and when they consider this to be in their interest.

As mentioned, many countries strongly oppose the pursuit of PAs, whereas CMAs have been constrained in practice by the fact that large emerging economies have tended to resist participation, resulting in perceptions that not enough of the benefits of a proposed CMA (sectoral zero-for-zero deal) would accrue to those that were willing to participate. At the same time, the revealed preference of most WTO Members has been to engage in discriminatory PTAs. Given that PAs in principle offer an alternative to PTAs, what explains the lack of interest in using this option? A number of arguments have been put forward.

## I. Backdoor inclusion of controversial issues

One objection to PAs is that they could open the door to agreements among subsets of countries on controversial issues such as labour or environmental standards. However, existing WTO disciplines provide assurances that efforts to incorporate new PAs on controversial issues can be blocked. The high threshold for approval of any new PA guarantees that WTO Members have the ability to block PAs that are deemed to be inconsistent with what they believe should be addressed in the trading system.

## II. Erosion of MFN

PAs differ from PTAs in that the former can be much narrower in scope. A PTA will usually cover many policy areas, ranging from trade in goods and services to investment, intellectual property rights and various forms of (often soft law) cooperation. In contrast to a PTA, a PA may deal with just one issue. The agreements on dairy and bovine meat are examples of very narrow product-specific agreements, and the PA on civil aircraft deals with a specific sector. A sector-specific PA is an example of a deal that the rules in Article XXIV GATT and Article V GATS were designed to preclude. Clearly, a PA that is designed to extend narrowly defined market access concessions only to WTO Members that reciprocate will imply a blatant undercutting of the MFN rule and a shift to a world in which small countries without the ability to affect their terms of trade could end up being excluded from the benefits of (reciprocal) market opening by a group of countries. Such PAs therefore can be expected to be rejected by those that are excluded from (or have simply decided not to participate in) the PA. If the potential club members go ahead and conclude such a PA outside the WTO that undercuts existing WTO commitments, affected WTO Members can – and presumably will – challenge it in the WTO for violation of the MFN rule. An implication is that PAs can be used to deal with new regulatory and other policy disciplines but cannot be used as a way for some countries to move forward on market access liberalisation for products covered by the WTO on a sectoral or other basis – as that would violate MFN. The GPA is a PA because procurement is explicitly excluded from the reach of Article III GATT (national treatment) and the GATS (Article XIII.1; although the GATS calls for negotiations on procurement of services to be launched two years after the entry into force of the agreement, i.e. 1997).[9]

## III. Precedent-setting and first-mover advantages

More generally, PAs define the rules of the game in a specific area that go beyond what is in the WTO at present, and these will be difficult to change subsequently if and when initial nonsignatories decide to participate. Experience with the GPA illustrates that it is difficult to amend (renegotiate) disciplines so that a plurilateral approach may well become analogous to the *Acquis Communautaire* for prospective members of the EU – that is, nonnegotiable. Even if countries initially opt out, over time they may develop an interest in joining but may have different perspectives on the desirable content of the substantive obligations embedded in the PA. This means that there is a first mover's advantage that should not be underestimated – in practice, the incumbents will define the substance of the rules of the club. This may result in a long-term bifurcation in the WTO Membership, splitting 'insiders' from 'outsiders'.

In practice, given the great heterogeneity in levels of development, social preferences, endowments and so forth that prevail, it is inevitable that a PA might address issues that are not seen to be priorities for some (many) WTO Members. This is arguably a good reason to have the PA

---

[9] Such talks have been taking place in the Working Party on GATS Rules since 1995, but no progress has been made on the matter – leaving the GPA as the sole instrument dealing with procurement of services (as well as goods).

option in the first place, as it allows countries to cooperate on a given policy area. But there is also the possibility that a group of countries may seek to negotiate a PA with the strategic objective of excluding others. Clearly, much will depend on what the club ends up agreeing to and what the outside options are for the club if the PA option is rejected by nonparticipating WTO Members. In practice, the outside option will be a PTA – as is revealed by the path that has been taken by both the EU and the United States. PAs will define the rules for nonmembers down the road if and when they want to join, but the precedent-setting effects of the initial negotiation should not be overblown. Large countries will be able to negotiate terms – if incumbents do not demonstrate any flexibility in this regard, the end result will be that the benefits of the PA for signatories are reduced as outsiders will not have an interest in joining. Accession discussions can be a useful trigger for the incumbents to reconsider the utility of specific provisions if this is tabled by prospective new members.

## IV. Capacity constraints and other asymmetries

There are major differences in capacities to engage in discussions on regulatory matters and participate in a fully informed way. In practice LDCs are likely to be among the least able to engage in PA talks that focus on regulatory policies that are not covered by the WTO. Whatever the subject of a PA, consideration could be given to extending whatever is negotiated among a club of WTO Members to all LDCs on a nonreciprocal basis. This would help reduce the extent of any discrimination, would be one way to give meaning to the LDC waiver and would ensure that PAs have a development dimension. Of course, the value of such action will depend on the capacity of the LDCs to benefit from (make use of) whatever is agreed among the PA members. In practice, even if a PA opens up market access opportunities for signatories, LDCs may not have the capacity to benefit, especially if satisfying specific minimum standards is a precondition. This suggests that to be meaningful any PA that extends benefits to LDCs should include an aid for trade component – for example, mechanisms to assist the LDCs to improve their standards and regulation to the level that is required to enable them to benefit from what is agreed in the PA. Such mechanisms will need to be tailored to whatever the associated capacity-building needs are. One possibility would be to develop PA-specific 'platforms' that help LDCs, as well as other developing countries with an interest in acceding to the PA, to undertake diagnostic analysis, identify action plans and implement needed reforms with funding and assistance from high-income PA signatories. Including an operational aid for trade dimension in PAs could enhance the relevance of PAs for low-income countries and give these agreements a development dimension.

## V. Erosion of negotiating coin

Another objection to moving down the PA track is that it may result in cherry-picking issues that matter a lot for certain interest groups or countries. Once these particular issues have been addressed, these groups no longer have an incentive to engage in the domestic political process to push through reforms in other areas that are of interest to trading partners and for which they are willing to 'pay' with concessions in other areas that would benefit the home country. Thus, PAs may result in WTO Members giving up negotiating chips that could have been used to obtain a broader deal in a multilateral negotiation. The fundamental premise underlying large trade rounds is that they permit issue linkage: country A can get something it wants by giving up something that country B wants, and the trade may involve items that have nothing to do with each other. If PAs are negotiated for specific issues, the scope for such linkage may decline. Much depends here on the subject matter of a potential PA and on contracting costs.[10] If it does not offer much in the way of negotiating leverage for the countries that are involved – that is, nobody is inclined to 'pay' much for a deal – the 'linkage downside' will be small. The absence of linkage potential might, under some circumstances, act as an incentive to join the PA in the first place as it reduces the opportunity cost of participation. But there is no presumption that this will be the case. If such opportunity costs are high, the countries concerned will have the option of not participating in the PA.

The salience of many of the objections summarised here depends on the substance and coverage of a PA. If an issue area is already subject to WTO disciplines, any PA will by definition result in greater fragmentation of applicable rules, whether the focus is on policy disciplines or involves signatories granting discriminatory market access to each other in an area

---

[10] See Horn and Mavroidis (2013) for an analysis of the conditions under which separate agreements dominate a broader 'single undertaking' agreement that encompasses a variety of issue linkages. Given uncertainty regarding the overall size of the 'cake' that is defined by an agreement that spans many issue areas, and the costs associated with negotiations, including the opportunity costs of delay, there may be good reasons for governments to pursue separate agreements as opposed to big bang package deals in which everything is conditional on everything else.

that is not covered by the WTO. If the PA is on a new issue that is not covered by the WTO, it may be precedent setting, but there is no issue of fragmentation or undercutting MFN as this rule currently does not apply. This is not the case for agreements that deepen or extend existing rules. Hoekman and Mavroidis (2013) argue that if a PA involves regulatory disciplines – procedural or substantive – for a policy area that is not covered by the WTO, there is a much lower likelihood that it could have negative repercussions for nonsignatories

A major disincentive for the pursuit of additional PAs in the WTO is the requirement that inclusion of any new PA be accepted by all WTO Members, including those that have no interest in participating ('exclusively by consensus'). Arguably, consensus is not needed to ensure that proposed PAs are consistent with the overall objectives of the WTO and will not negatively affect nonparticipants. Shifting to a less stringent criterion such as 'substantial coverage' of world trade or production would remove the ability of nonparticipants to block new PAs (Hufbauer and Schott 2012).[11] An alternative that gives dissenting views greater weight would be to agree that if more than one-third of Members were opposed, the PA could not proceed. This would continue to provide the assurance that proposed PAs on controversial subjects can be rejected while removing the ability of just a few members to block a new PA. In the EU context, so-called Enhanced Cooperation Agreements require participation by 9 out of 27 member states (now 28) in instances in which consensus cannot be obtained on an issue (Hoekman and Mavroidis 2013).

## F. Conclusion

The deadlock in the Doha Round and the shift by the United States, EU and other countries towards mega-regional PTAs reflects an assessment by the countries concerned that what is on the table in the DDA is not of sufficient interest. PTAs appear to have become the revealed preferred route for trade cooperation in the near term for the United States and the EU. Time will tell how much will be achieved in the new-vintage PTAs. Insofar as the PTAs generate new approaches towards dealing with the market-segmenting effects of (differences in) regulatory policies, they can help all countries identify approaches that can usefully be emulated.

---

[11] They suggest a minimum coverage of 40 per cent of world trade as opposed to the norm of 90 per cent that empirically has defined the feasibility of critical mass agreements in the GATT/WTO.

Most of the mega-regionals that are currently being negotiated are effectively closed to the majority of WTO Members as a result of their regional nature; the only exception is the TiSA, which in principle is open to any WTO Member. Although the TiSA, if the talks are successfully concluded, will most likely be structured as a PTA under Article V GATS, in many ways it is an example of a PA. It does not lend itself to being incorporated into the WTO as a PA because it will build on the GATS and encompass national treatment and market access commitments by signatories across all services sectors. It remains to be seen to what extent the commitments that are made by TiSA signatories will discriminate against nonparticipants; that is, to what extent it will end up having the characteristics of a CMA as opposed to a traditional PTA. The TiSA talks illustrate, however, that WTO Members are willing to pursue negotiations (cooperation) on a plurilateral basis.

All WTO Members have a strong interest in understanding what is achieved in modern PTAs that deal with 'behind-the-border' policies. Using the WTO infrastructure to document, analyse and assess the approaches that are implemented by PTAs to reduce regulatory barriers would not just help ensure greater transparency but also support a process of learning about what works and what does not. Bringing the business community into such processes would help ensure that they are sufficiently granular, that the WTO membership develops a more comprehensive understanding of the impact – and the associated costs and benefits – of the various approaches implemented in PTAs and that specific features of PTAs that could be multilateralised are identified. Plurilateral agreements offer one vehicle for such multilateralisation given the likelihood that at any point in time there will be many WTO Members that will not be ready to adopt the disciplines and mechanisms in question.

PAs are just one possible form of club formation under the WTO's auspices. They are not mechanisms that can help overcome the differences regarding market access and agricultural support policies that have blocked a deal in the DDA. These require traditional multilateral negotiations and issue linkage. Most probably this will have to involve an agenda that goes beyond that of the DDA. Determining which additional policy issues should be put on the table requires a process of deliberation. The suggestions that have been put forward in this chapter would help generate a better understanding among WTO Members of what such issues might be and, equally important, differentiate between matters that require agreement among all members and matters in which cooperation is best limited to governments that are like-minded. In the latter case, the benefits of cooperation might need to be restricted to participants – that is, a PA – or extended to all members – that is, a CMA. Many of the issues that are on the table in the new-vintage PTAs are regulatory in nature. In such areas it is understandable that countries are inclined to pursue small numbers of agreements and arrangements – establishing the trust needed for regulatory cooperation and convergence requires time and regularly recurring bilateral interaction. But it seems perverse to insist – as is implied by the explicit rejection of the PA option by some WTO Members – that if countries want to cooperate on regulatory matters that influence trade and investment, they must either negotiate a PTA or cooperate outside the ambit of the WTO.

Given the deadlock that currently prevails between the major traders, movement in the proposed directions will require leadership by some WTO Members. The initiative for discussing new issues in the WTO could come from participants in mega-regionals or from countries that are excluded and have different views and approaches to some of the policy areas that are addressed in such arrangements. Many of the policy areas that generate negative effects on trading partners are not on the table in (mega-)regionals. It is also important that the economic value of whatever is done through (mega-)regionals is highly dependent on the extent to which these agreements result in policy changes and improve market access opportunities. Without the participation of large countries such as China, India and Brazil, the effects of the new PTAs that centre on the United States and the EU can be only limited. As argued by Cottier, Sieber-Gasser and Wermelinger (Chapter 19 in this volume), preferential engagement and multilateral cooperation have always been complementary channels for countries to address trade policy spillovers. At times one is 'ahead' of the other, but the two paths have tended to be closely linked. The chances are that this will continue to be the case in the future, but the process can be helped along by countries that are not, cannot or do not want to be at the forefront of (mega-)regional integration.

There is no reason why such countries should look to China, Brazil or India to agree to move forward on a policy matter that they believe is in their interest to pursue or for them to wait until it becomes clear what will emerge from the TPP, RCEP or TTIP initiatives. At the 2013 WTO Public Forum, the trade minister for Costa Rica suggested launching a dialogue on investment policies among a subset of WTO Members. Such an effort would be an example of what has been argued for in this chapter. Many policy areas generate negative spillovers and should be of interest to groups of countries, independent of the countries' income level or size, to table and discuss in the WTO. Examples are export restrictions, which are detrimental to net importing countries, 'green' subsidies (ranging from minimum feed-in prices for electricity generated from renewable resources to subsidies for the development or use of specific technologies) and digital trade barriers and data protection and privacy policies.[12] Some of these issues may not lend themselves to the negotiation of binding rules on a plurilateral basis; others might. What matters is that discussions on new issues are held under the umbrella of the WTO as opposed to governments coming to the view that new issues can be tackled only in bilateral or (mega-)regional PTA settings.

## References

Bacchus, James. 2012. 'A Way Forward for the WTO.' In *The Future and the WTO: Confronting the Challenges: A Collection of Short Essays*, edited by Ricardo Meléndez-Ortiz, Christophe Bellmann and Miguel Rodriguez Mendoza, 6–9. Geneva: International Centre for Trade and Sustainable Development. http://ictsd.org/i/publications/138578/. Accessed 27 January 2014.

Elsig, Manfred. 2010. 'WTO Decision-Making: Can We Get a Little Help from the Secretariat and the Critical Mass?' In *Redesigning the WTO for the 21st Century*, edited by Debra Steger, 60–79. Ottawa: Wilfred Laurier University Press.

Evenett, Simon. 2013. 'The Doha Round Impasse: A Graphical Account.' CEPR Discussion Paper No. 9780. Centre for Economic Policy Research, London.

Evenett, Simon, and Jara, Alejandro, eds. 2013. *Building on Bali: A Work Programme for the WTO*. CEPR e-book. London: VoxEU.

Gallagher, Peter, and Stoler, Andrew. 2009. 'Critical Mass as an Alternative Framework for Multilateral Trade Negotiations.' *Global Governance* 15 (3): 375–92.

Harbinson, Stuart. 2009. 'The Doha Round: "Death-Defying Agenda" or "Don't Do it Again"?' ECIPE Working Paper. European Centre for International Political Economy, Brussels.

Hoekman, Bernard. 2013. 'Adding Value.' *Finance and Development*, December, 22–4.

Hoekman, Bernard, and Kostecki, Michel. 2009. *The Political Economy of the World Trading System*. 3rd edn. Oxford, England: Oxford University Press.

Hoekman, Bernard, and Mattoo, Aaditya. 2013. 'Liberalizing Trade in Services: Lessons from Regional and WTO Negotiations.' *International Negotiation* 18:131–51.

---

[12] Many papers discuss possible subjects for cooperation and rule making – see, for example, Mattoo and Subramanian (2009) and the contributions to Melendez-Ortiz, Bellmann and Mendoza (2012) or Evenett and Jara (2013).

Hoekman, Bernard, and Mavroidis, Petros Constantinos. 2013. 'WTO à la Carte or WTO "Menu du Jour": Assessing the Case for Plurilateral Agreements.' Working Paper RSCAS No. 58. European University Institute (EUI), Firenze.

Horn, Henrik, and Mavroidis, Petros Constantinos. 2013. 'MEAs in the WTO: Silence Speaks Volumes.' European University Institute (EUI). http://dx.doi.org/10.7916/D8ZC80W6.

Hufbauer, Gary, and Schott, Jeff. 2012. 'Will the World Trade Organization Enjoy a Bright Future?' Policy Brief 12–11. Peterson Institute for International Economics, Washington, DC.

Lawrence, Robert. 2006. 'Rulemaking amidst Growing Diversity: A "Club of Clubs" Approach to WTO Reform and New Issue Selection.' *Journal of International Economic Law* 9 (4): 823–35.

Levy, Philip. 2006. 'Do We Need an Undertaker for the Single Undertaking? Angles of Variable Geometry.' In *Economic Development and Multilateral Trade Cooperation*, edited by Simon Evenett and Bernard Hoekman, 417–38. London: Palgrave Macmillan.

Mattoo, Aaditya, and Subramanian, Arvind. 2009. 'From Doha to the Next Bretton Woods: A New Multilateral Trade Agenda.' *Foreign Affairs*, January/February.

Melendez-Ortiz, Ricardo, Bellmann, Christophe, and Mendoza, Miguel Rodriguez, eds. 2012. *The Future and the WTO: Confronting the Challenges: A Collection of Short Essays.* Geneva: International Centre for Trade and Sustainable Development. http://ictsd.org/i/publications/138578/. Accessed 27 January 2014.

Mendoza, Miguel Rodriguez. 2012. 'Toward Plurilateral Plus Agreements.' In *The Future and the WTO: Confronting the Challenges: A Collection of Short Essays*, edited by Ricardo Meléndez-Ortiz, Christophe Bellmann and Miguel Rodriguez Mendoza, 27–32. Geneva: International Centre for Trade and Sustainable Development. http://ictsd.org/i/publications/138578/. Accessed 27 January 2014.

Schott, Jeffrey, Kotschwar, Barbara, and Muir, Julia. 2013. *Understanding the Trans-Pacific Partnership.* Washington, DC: Peterson Institute for International Economics.

Wolfe, Robert. 2013. 'First Diagnose, Then Treat: What Ails the Doha Round?' Working Paper RSCAS No. 85. European University Institute (EUI), Firenze.

# 22

# Referring PTA disputes to the WTO dispute settlement system

JAMES FLETT

## A. Introduction

Parties to a preferential trade agreement (PTA) generally want mandatory and binding dispute settlement, and they make provision for it. And yet curiously, with some exceptions, such procedures are rarely used. This chapter considers why that is so. It then considers whether standard or special terms of reference could be used to receive PTA disputes into the World Trade Organization (WTO) dispute settlement system, concluding that, once there was consensus on the issues of financing and scheduling in principle, this would be possible, without any modification of the Dispute Settlement Understanding (DSU) and without any significant change to current practice. It goes on to consider the advantages of such an approach both for the PTA parties and other WTO Members. Finally, it comments on other issues: financing, scheduling, third parties, concentration of adjudicative responsibility and WTO consistency of the PTA.[1]

## B. PTA parties want mandatory and binding dispute settlement

It is clear that when WTO Members conclude PTAs they still want effective dispute settlement, which means mandatory jurisdiction and binding adjudications. They have not forgotten 50 years of General Agreement on

---

European Commission, Legal Service, WTO Team. Any views expressed are personal. The author frequently represents the European Union (EU) in WTO litigation.

[1] This chapter does not address the general question of the relationship between WTO and PTA law (World Trade Organization 2011). Nor does it contribute to the debate about which law a WTO adjudicator might apply if a party (or WTO Member) were to object, nor to the discussion about conflicts and how to resolve them (Marceau and Wyatt 2010). Finally, it does not consider how PTAs could be brought into WTO dispute settlement through modification of the DSU (Gao and Lin 2008).

Tariffs and Trade (GATT) frustration. They do not want ambiguity and unilateralism, but security and predictability. One can discuss the details, but these key features of the architecture are uncontroversial. If anything, the deeper you go – as well as having a better mutual understanding to enable you to avoid disputes – at the same time, the more important it is to have an effective dispute settlement system, capable of dealing with the most thorny issues. Furthermore, one formal dispute settlement case can be the basis for settling many similar disputes, and this can considerably facilitate the operation of a PTA. This is why most contemporary PTAs provide for mandatory and binding dispute settlement (Allee and Elsig, Chapter 13 in this volume; Chase *et al.* 2013).

Further evidence for these propositions is in the documents submitted by GATT Members to the Uruguay Round Negotiating Group on Dispute Settlement and in the associated Notes by the Secretariat.[2] Whether or not these may be described as preparatory work or evidence of the circumstances of conclusion, within the meaning of Article 32 of the Vienna Convention, these 85 documents are informative. They run to hundreds of pages, span three years[3] and contain comments from all GATT Members expressing an interest, these being a range of countries from around the globe, actively engaged in the conclusion of PTAs.[4] The message conveyed by these documents of the need for effective dispute settlement is clear, and it is a message that is no less pertinent today.

## C. The low level of use of PTA dispute settlement procedures

Despite this, with one or two specific exceptions, such as certain provisions of the North American Free Trade Agreement (NAFTA), there is a relatively low level of use of PTA dispute settlement procedures. There have been almost 500 WTO disputes, whilst the number of PTA disputes remains very small, despite the proliferation of PTAs (Chase *et al.* 2013; World Trade Organization 2011). The proposition that PTAs are so successful that there has been no need to engage such procedures is implausible. Rather, it seems more plausible that there are other factors inhibiting the use of PTA dispute settlement procedures. The literature

---

[2] WTO document series MTN.GNG/NG13.     [3] 6 April 1987 to 24 October 1990.
[4] Argentina, Austria, Brazil, Australia, Canada, the European Economic Community, Hong Kong, Hungary, Jamaica, Japan, Korea, Mexico, New Zealand, Nicaragua, Norway on behalf of the Nordic countries, Peru, United States, Uruguay, Switzerland.

on this issue is well summarised in Chase *et al.* 2013. There are four main points.

## I. The desire to foster a cooperative relationship and the associated reluctance to litigate

One of these factors is probably a desire to foster a cooperative relationship with a PTA partner and an associated reluctance to have recourse to litigation. The existence of a PTA implies the existence of staff specifically dedicated to the management of the PTA. The people who negotiate PTAs, and who may seek the insertion of dispute settlement provisions based on their own experience of international trade law, are not necessarily the same people who will subsequently manage a particular PTA. Senior staff entrusted with such a task may be more likely to be administrators or economists than lawyers. There is a certain political atmosphere focused on the proposition that cooperation is more fruitful than litigation, in the same way that firms regularly doing business with each other tend not to litigate. This is one of the factors that probably explains why PTA dispute settlement provisions are rarely used.

## II. Overlaps between WTO law and PTA law

Another reason why PTA dispute settlement procedures are rarely used relates to the substantive relationship between WTO and PTA law. This is sometimes referred to as the question of whether PTAs are WTO-plus or WTO-minus (this latter situation would, by definition, be inconsistent with WTO law). Perhaps a better way to reference the issue is simply WTO-different, because in practice it can be difficult to say, in a mechanistic way, whether two different abstract terms are just that: different, or whether one is more constraining than the other. This is an iteration of the so-called mandatory–discretionary problem. It is a philosophical question. It means that it is very difficult to design a dispute settlement system in which the WTO aspects of a PTA issue are referred to the WTO, whilst the so-called WTO-plus aspects are referred to the PTA. Instead, WTO rules tend to be recast or referred to in PTAs, and the more modern approach is to allow the parties to choose in which jurisdiction they will litigate. This is permitted by Article 23(1) of the DSU, because even if the substance of the WTO and PTA obligations is the same or overlaps (such as, for example, a national treatment rule), the PTA obligation is simply not the same obligation as the WTO obligation. Thus, given the choice,

PTA parties are quite likely to prefer to litigate, for example, a question of necessity, in the WTO rather than under the PTA, even when this involves referencing the PTA as a fact or as context pursuant to Article 31(3)(c) of the Vienna Convention.[5]

### III. Appointing and financing adjudicators and clerical staff

Another issue that arises in PTA dispute settlement is the appointing and financing of adjudicators and clerical staff. Arbitrators have to be paid, and the money has to come from somewhere. More importantly, they need qualified secretarial support, appropriately paid. This can be problematic. Bilateral investment treaty (BIT) arbitrations involve firms with a financial interest that are willing to pay, given the prospect of restitution. BIT arbitrators and lawyers, operating with something of a revolving door, have created around themselves a system in which they are all well remunerated (Eberhardt and Olivet 2012). This does not work for PTAs, and even the strongest proponents of PTAs are having doubts about the wisdom of BITs, as these latter instruments are divorced from their historical contexts and increasingly used against the countries that designed them in the first place. There can be very real internal problems about how to finance such litigation, and particularly about which government department is going to be responsible for the financial burden.

These issues are less to the fore in the WTO, which has a Secretariat, the establishment of which is provided for in the DSU. The significance of the issue is understated in the literature because WTO staff are reticent about publicly acknowledging the important role of the Secretariat in dispute settlement. The fact is, however, that the Secretariat plays a central role. Panellists remain underpaid part-timers who usually have substantial day jobs. Furthermore, there appears to be a policy of continuing to appoint diplomats who may not have the time, knowledge, capacity or inclination to engage heavily in the details of a particular dispute. Perhaps this reflects a view that this is an important way of ensuring that these people have an investment in the system. Perhaps it is designed to maintain the weight of the Secretariat in the process. Whatever the reasons, the fact remains that the adjudicators would not be able to function at all without the

---

[5] Appellate Body Report, *EC – Large Civil Aircraft*, paras. 839–55 (with respect to the so-called 1992 Agreement).

support of the Secretariat. The prospect of replicating these structures in the context of a PTA can be very challenging.

### IV. A lack of critical mass and the substantial investment required to catch up with the WTO dispute settlement system

Another problem is lack of familiarity and use, and the associated fragmentation. To properly interpret and apply PTA law on a particular issue, it will be necessary to fix the issue within the broader context of the PTA. Some of these PTAs are substantial documents, and this can be a formidable task. Understanding the system may require a substantial investment of time and resources. By comparison, a great many aspects of the DSU have already been clarified in almost 500 WTO disputes. None of the comparable issues will have been clarified under the PTA. Furthermore, each PTA may be different, so each time a fresh issue is considered a substantial investment of time and resources is necessary. Even WTO Members with substantial resources, and that participate regularly in WTO dispute settlement, have issues with maintaining capacity. It is far from clear that maintaining the capacity necessary to litigate across a whole range of PTAs is a viable proposition.

### D. Standard and special terms of reference as a mechanism for receiving PTA disputes into the WTO dispute settlement system

The issues of the jurisdiction of the WTO dispute settlement system, the applicable law in WTO disputes and the jurisdiction or terms of references of particular WTO adjudicators are usually discussed from the perspective of what one party can impose on another. That is, from the perspective of what is *mandatory*, in the sense that the DSU provides for mandatory dispute settlement (Van Damme 2009). It was in this context, for example, that the Appellate Body stated that it saw no basis in the DSU for adjudication of non-WTO disputes, that is, over the objections of one of the parties.[6] This chapter does not contribute to that discussion.

Rather, this chapter poses a different question: what is *permitted* by the WTO agreement, and particularly the DSU, when the parties to a

---

[6] Appellate Body Report, *Mexico – Soft Drinks*, para. 56; Arbitration Panel Report, *EC – Hormones (US) (Article 22.6 – EC)*, para. 50; Panel Report, *EC – Large Civil Aircraft*, para. 7.89.

particular dispute wish to agree to submit it to the jurisdiction of a WTO panel and other WTO Members do not object.

There are two key related questions: (1) does WTO law allow for the possibility that what would otherwise be nonapplicable law could be applied by a WTO adjudicator? and (2) if so, what provisions and procedures would govern the process, and, specifically, is it enough that the parties to a particular agreement or dispute agree, or must the WTO Members agree by consensus? In thinking about these questions, it is helpful to first recall the position with respect to multilateral and plurilateral WTO law.

## I. WTO multilateral and plurilateral mechanisms for referencing other law

WTO Members could agree to enlarge the scope of multilateral WTO law by amending the WTO agreement. The voting procedures are complex but, in essence, preserve the principle of consensus in practice.[7] The WTO agreement also provides for plurilateral trade agreements. They are part of the WTO agreement, binding Members that have acceded to them, but not others.[8] The WTO is also to provide the framework for the implementation, administration and operation of the plurilateral trade agreements.[9] Agreements may become plurilateral trade agreements only by *consensus*.[10] However, institutional structures, decision making, amendment, accession, nonapplication, acceptance, entry into force, withdrawal and reservation are governed by the terms of the plurilateral trade agreement itself.[11] Existing plurilateral trade agreements are covered agreements, and new PTAs could likewise be added to the list, but the applicability of the DSU to a plurilateral agreement is subject to a *decision by the parties* to the plurilateral agreement.[12] Only the parties to a plurilateral trade agreement may participate in a dispute concerning a plurilateral trade agreement.[13] Other provisions of the DSU are similarly tailored to the special case of plurilateral trade agreements.[14] Consistent

---

[7] WTO Agreement, Article X. In theory, with some exceptions, a three-fourths majority could require other Members to join the new treaty or withdraw from the WTO.
[8] WTO Agreement, Article II:3.     [9] WTO Agreement, Article III:1.
[10] WTO Agreement, Article X:9.
[11] WTO Agreement, Articles IV:8, IX:5, X:10, XII:3, XIII:5, XIV:4, XV:2, XVI:5.
[12] DSU, Appendix 1, final para.     [13] DSU, Article 2.1.
[14] DSU, Articles 3.9 (authoritative interpretation), footnote 4 (joining consultations in case of a substantial trade interest), Article 22.3(g)(i) (retaliation) and Appendix 2 (special or additional rules).

with these provisions, plurilateral trade agreements have been the subject of DSU proceedings.[15]

Thus, WTO law recognises the possibility of WTO law in the form of an agreement among only some WTO Members. There is no minimum required number of parties. Two would be sufficient. Thus, a bilateral agreement could be a plurilateral trade agreement. Furthermore, there is no requirement that a plurilateral trade agreement be open to all WTO Members: as indicated previously, accession is governed by the terms of the plurilateral trade agreement itself. Significantly, as indicated previously, the applicability of the DSU to a plurilateral agreement is subject to a *decision by the parties* to the plurilateral agreement.

## II. How far can one go with standard terms of reference?

Articles 6.2 and 7.3 of the DSU refer to 'standard terms of reference'. This refers to the text in Article 7.1, even though it requires completion in each case of the name or names of the covered agreements, the name of the party or parties referring the matter to the Dispute Settlement Body (DSB) and the document reference (generally of the panel request). Articles 6.2 and 7.3 also refer to 'special terms of reference'.

It is helpful to first consider how far standard terms of reference can go in terms of applicable law, and particularly PTAs. As indicated earlier, the purpose is not to engage in general terms in the theoretical debate on what the limits of applicable WTO law are. Rather, the purpose is to list, in a more pragmatic way, which other documents are actually expressly referred to in the covered agreements or the case law.

Clearly, WTO applicable law includes the covered agreements, as set out in Appendix 1 of the DSU. But the scope of applicable WTO law is broader. Some covered agreements refer to other documents. For example, the Agreement on Trade-Related Aspects of Intellectual Property Rights (TRIPS Agreement) refers to a number of other documents in the field of intellectual property. There are many other examples of permeability between the covered agreements and other documents. For example: Articles 31–3 of the Vienna Convention,[16] in particular,

---

[15] The Agreement on Government Procurement was discussed at length in Panel Report, *Korea – Procurement*. The Agreement on Trade in Civil Aircraft was referenced in the Panel and Appellate Body Reports in *EC – Large Civil Aircraft*.

[16] Article 3.2 of the DSU; Vienna Convention on the Law of the Treaties, adopted 22 May 1969, opened for signature 23 May 1969, entered into force 27 January 1980, United Nations, Treaty Series, Vol. 1155, p. 331.

Article 31(3)(c) of the Vienna Convention;[17] general principles of public international law (Mitchell 2008); other provisions of the Vienna Convention (Flett 2012); the International Law Commission (ILC) Articles on State Responsibility and the ILC Articles on the Responsibility of International Organisations;[18] the United Nations Charter;[19] the Havana Charter;[20] the Codex Alimentarius Commission, the World Organisation for Animal Health (OIE) (formerly International Office of Epizootics), the International Plant Protection Convention (IPPC), and other relevant international organizations open for membership to all WTO Members and identified by the SPS Committee;[21] the International Organization for Standardization/ International Electrotechnical Commission (ISO/IEC) Guide 2 1991 General Terms and their Definitions Concerning Standardization and Related Activities;[22] the relevant international standards referred to in the Agreement on Technical Barriers to Trade (TBT Agreement);[23] the Organisation for Economic Co-operation and Development (OECD) Arrangement on Officially Supported Export Credits;[24] international accounting standards;[25] documents incorporated through the waiver provisions of Article IX:3 of the WTO agreement;[26] the Enabling Clause;[27] documents incorporated through schedules;[28]

---

[17] Appellate Body Report, *EC – Large Civil Aircraft*, paras. 839–55 (with respect to the so-called 1992 Agreement).
[18] Appellate Body Report, *US – Anti-Dumping and Countervailing Duties (China)*, paras. 305–16.
[19] GATT 1994, Article XXI(c).
[20] GATT 1994, Article XXIX, ad Note to Article XXIX:1 and ad Note to Article II:4.
[21] Agreement on the Application of Sanitary and Phytosanitary Measures (SPS Agreement), Annex A, para. 3.
[22] TBT Agreement, Annexes 1 and 3.       [23] Notably, TBT Agreement, Article 2.4.
[24] Item (k) of Annex I to the SCM Agreement; Appellate Body Report, *Brazil – Aircraft*, para. 180.
[25] Anti-Dumping Agreement, Article 2.2.1.1.
[26] See, for example: *EC – Bananas III* with reference to the *Lomé Convention*. See also: the WTO waivers with respect to the Kimberly Process (General Council Waiver Concerning Kimberly Process Certification Scheme for Rough Diamonds, Decision of 15 May 2003, WT/L/518 (27 May 2003)) and the TRIPS waiver (General Council, Implementation of Paragraph 6 of the Doha Declaration on the TRIPS Agreement and Public Health, Decision of 30 August 2003, WT/L/540 (2 September 2003)).
[27] Decision on Differential and More Favourable Treatment, Reciprocity, and Fuller Participation of Developing Countries, GATT Document L/4903, 28 November 1979, BISD 26S/203. See, in particular, Appellate Body Report, *EC – Tariff Preferences*.
[28] *GATT 1994*, Article II:7; Appellate Body Report, *EC – Poultry*, para. 79; Panel Reports, *EC – IT Products* (which concerned the manner in which the EC had implemented in its schedules the Ministerial Declaration on Trade in Information Technology Products (the ITA)). The ITA is not a WTO plurilateral trade agreement within the meaning of

mutually agreed solutions;[29] Article XX(d) of the GATT 1994;[30] inter-governmental commodity agreements pursuant to Article XX(h) of the GATT 1994; case law of the Court of International Justice (Flett 2012); and other secondary WTO law.[31] Domestic and international documents may also be referred to as fact or evidence of fact and possibly also evidence of meaning.[32]

In this context, it should also be recalled that, based on what is usually the current practice, the standard terms of reference are essentially determined by the panel request. However, a panel's terms of reference clearly also extend to provisions cited by the defending Member, usually in its first written submission, even if they are in another covered agreement. This legal fact does not sit comfortably with the way the standard terms of reference in Article 7.1 are commonly understood. This raises the possibility of a slightly different approach, based on the existing text of Article 7.1. According to this approach, on receipt of a *first* panel request, a defending Member could produce its own document referring to the Dispute Settlement Body (DSB) the related matter of its defence. The standard terms of reference would then have to be completed by referring both to the covered agreement or agreements cited by the complaining Member and to the covered agreement or agreements cited by the defending Member; the 'name of party' would have to be completed with a reference to both parties (this plural approach is currently used in any event in cases involving multiple complainants); and the 'document' would likewise have to be completed with a reference to both documents (as is also currently

---

Annex 4 of the WTO Agreement, but an agreement concluded among 49 WTO Members representing about 97 per cent of world trade in the relevant products.

29   Appellate Body Reports, *EC – Bananas III (Article 21.5 – Ecuador II)/EC – Bananas III (Article 21.5 – US)*, paras. 199–229.

30   Appellate Body Report, *Mexico – Soft Drinks*, paras. 66–80.

31   Appellate Body Report, *US – Clove Cigarettes*, paras. 237–297 (with respect to the Doha Ministerial Decision on Implementation-Related Issues and Concerns, as a subsequent agreement between the parties pursuant to Article 31(3)(a) of the Vienna Convention); Appellate Body Report, *US – Tuna II (Mexico)*, paras. 365–99 (with respect to the TBT Committee Decision on Principles for the Development of International Standards, Guides and Recommendations with Relation to Articles 2, 5, and Annex 3 to the Agreement, also as a subsequent agreement between the parties pursuant to Article 31(3)(a) of the Vienna Convention).

32   See, for example, Panel Report, *EC – Biotech*, paras. 7.64–7.96, with respect to information obtained from Codex, the Food and Agriculture Organization of the United Nations (FAO), the IPPC Secretariat, the World Health Organization (WHO), OIE, the Convention on Biological Diversity (CBD) Secretariat and the United Nations Environment Programme (UNEP).

done in any event in cases involving multiple complainants). The 'second DSB' rule in Article 6.1 of the DSU would give the defending Member time (at least 10 days) in which to do this (and this may, in fact, be the function of that rule). The panel's terms of reference would then be properly completed. This 'double document' approach to terms of reference is exactly what is done in the context of Articles 22.2 and 22.6 of the DSU, where the retaliation request and the objection are considered, together, to perform the function of delineating the terms of reference.

This raises the issue of what other documents the defending Member might refer to in its documentary part of the standard terms of reference. For example, the defending Member could argue that the measure at issue was mandated or permitted by some other law. If these questions were to be considered relevant by a panel, then the complaining Member would be entitled to respond that the measure at issue was not mandated or permitted by such other law and in fact was prohibited by other provisions in the same document or indeed in other documents.

Of particular interest in the context of this chapter are the documents, including PTAs, notified to the WTO pursuant to Article XXIV of the GATT 1994. There are already two situations in which such documents could come before a WTO panel on the basis of standard terms of reference.

The first possibility is that a PTA, like any measure attributable to two or more WTO Members, is capable of being a measure at issue in a DSU dispute.[33] This means that, as is the case with domestic law, the *meaning* of PTA provisions is a matter for the WTO dispute settlement system and ultimately a mixed question of law and fact capable of appeal.[34]

The second possibility is that consistency of a PTA with Article XXIV may also be raised as a defence to a claim directed against a measure implementing such PTA.[35] Once again, this may also require an assessment of the *meaning* of certain PTA provisions.

This is precisely what the PTA parties would be seeking in the situation envisaged in this chapter: an adjudication on the interpretation (and

---

[33] Appellate Body Report, *US – Corrosion-Resistant Steel Sunset Review*, para. 81. In DS263 *EC – Measures Affecting Imports of Wine*, Argentina cited several bilateral agreements between the EU and third countries as measures at issue, claiming them to be inconsistent with various provisions of the covered agreements (WT/DS263/1 of 12 September 2002).

[34] Appellate Body Report, *US – Section 211 Appropriations Act*, para. 105; Appellate Body Report, *India – Patents (US)*, paras. 65–6 and 68; Appellate Body Report, *China – Auto Parts*, para. 225.

[35] Appellate Body Report, *Turkey – Textiles*, paras. 42–63.

eventually also the application) of a specific PTA provision. If *any WTO Member* could bring the PTA parties before the WTO dispute settlement system to demand an interpretation of a specific PTA provision, and if a defendant acting alone could bring a PTA before the WTO dispute settlement system to demand an interpretation of a specific PTA provision, then one may wonder why the PTA parties should not be in a position to do the same thing, at least by agreement. Further support for this view may be found in Article 25 of the DSU, which provides for arbitration within the WTO of disputes on issues defined by the parties, subject only to the agreement of the parties (Cottier, Sieber-Gasser and Wermelinger, Chapter 19 in this volume). The reference in Article 25 to Articles 21 and 22 of the DSU would be no bar to such an approach, given that they would only apply *mutatis mutandis* and therefore could be adapted to the particular circumstances of the dispute.

Thus, in considering what might be permissible or impermissible using special terms of reference, it is important to take into account that already with standard terms of reference it is permissible to draw into WTO litigation a wide range of documents, beyond the specific text of the covered agreements themselves, including, in specific circumstances, the text of PTAs.

### III. Procedural aspects of special terms of reference

Articles 6 and 7 of the DSU refer to four actors: the applicant, the parties, the DSB and the DSB Chair. The problem is to unscramble their different roles with respect to special terms of reference, correctly identifying both the *applicable* procedure and the procedure used *as a matter of practice.*

The applicant alone cannot determine special terms of reference. Article 7.1 refers to the agreement of the parties to the dispute. Article 7.1 also refers to a period of 20 days from establishment. In practice, DSB minutes tend to provide for establishment with the standard terms of reference, although, as a matter of law, this is just a clerical record of something that flows automatically from Article 7. Even if DSB minutes were to record standard terms of reference, the parties could still agree otherwise within 20 days. Thus, panels are established with (generally standard) terms of reference that are provisional, in the sense that the parties may agree otherwise within 20 days.

Article 7.3 provides that, in establishing a panel, the DSB may authorise its Chair to draw up the terms of reference in consultation with the parties to the dispute, subject to the provisions of paragraph 1. This does not refer to the standard terms of reference, which do not need to be drawn up (apart from filling in the gaps), being set out in paragraph 1, and which do not require DSB authorisation, other than through establishment by negative consensus. With respect to special terms of reference, the DSB is not obliged to give the authorisation, merely *permitted.* The procedure for the DSB authorisation is not stated. Since Article 7.3 does not provide for the DSB to take a decision (it merely provides that the DSB may authorise), the consensus rule in Article 2.4 of the DSU does not govern. On the other hand, nor could it be said that the DSB authorisation would be by negative consensus or automatic.[36] The question is not therefore governed by the DSU. The DSB Rules of Procedure provide that, where a matter is not governed by the DSU or the DSB Rules of Procedure, the DSB shall follow the Rules of Procedure of the General Council.[37] The matter is also not governed by the DSB Rules of Procedure. The Rules of Procedure of the General Council refer to Article IX of the WTO agreement,[38] which in turn refers to the practice of consensus, failing which, majority voting.

This conclusion is supported by a systematic contextual analysis of the DSU. A number of provisions of the DSU refer expressly to a DSB decision by consensus not to adopt a proposal before it: these are the negative consensus or automatic procedures in the DSU.[39] These are the 'rules and procedures' of the DSU that provide for the DSB to take a decision by consensus, within the meaning of Article 2.4 of the DSU. Footnote 1 clarifies that the DSB is deemed to decide by consensus if no Member present formally objects. This means that the DSB procedures for panel establishment, report adoption, surveillance and retaliation *cannot require a DSB decision,* because that would have to be by consensus, which would block the system. Thus, they proceed automatically and not by way of a decision. Several other DSU provisions refer to decisions by

---

[36] Appellate Body Report, *US – Large Civil Aircraft,* paras. 480–549.
[37] Rules of Procedure for Meetings of the Dispute Settlement Body, WT/DSB/9, Article 1.
[38] Rules of Procedure for Sessions of the Ministerial Conference and Meetings of the General Council, Chapter VII, Rule 33.
[39] DSU, Articles 6.1 (panel establishment), 16.4 (panel adoption), 17.14 (Appellate Body report adoption), 21.6 (surveillance of implementation) and 22.6/22.7 (retaliation). These are also the matters referred to in DSU Article 2.1, second sentence. There is a somewhat academic discussion about whether the referral to arbitration in Article 22.6 results from the objection or involves the DSB. In the latter case, it would in any event be by negative consensus or automatic, given the context.

the Members,[40] or a panel,[41] or the DSB Chair,[42] or one of the parties,[43] but there are no other references to DSB decisions. This leaves open the question of what procedure applies in other situations when the DSB may act.[44] This cannot be consensus because that could lead to a blockage of the system through the nonconvening of DSB meetings.[45]

Article 7.3 is subject to the provisions of paragraph 1. This does not mean that the special terms of reference must comply with the text of the standard terms of reference. However, it does mean that the parties must agree to the special terms of reference, as drawn up by the Chair. It also means that the special terms of reference must be drawn up and circulated to all WTO Members within 20 days. The only question is whether the Chair has any authority not to draw up the special terms of reference agreed by the parties or whether the role is one of clerical activity. Some other provisions of the DSU place obligations or responsibilities on the Chair,[46] as well as on the Director-General,[47] and this fact has been recognised in the case law.[48] Thus, it is submitted that the Chair also has a specific role in this context, which is to protect the interests of any WTO Members that may have been outvoted in circumstances in which the DSB authorises the special terms of reference by majority voting. Those interests could be only financial or with respect to scheduling. Thus, provided that these issues are adequately provided for in general terms, the point should pass by consensus in practice, and the Chair's responsibility would never be engaged.

---

[40] DSU, Articles 3.9, 3.12 and 26.2, and Appendix 1, final para. and Appendix 2.

[41] DSU, Articles 12.1, 21.5 and 22.7 and Appendix 3, para. 6 and Appendix 4, para. 1.

[42] DSU, Article 12.10. Article 1.2 provides for the Chair to make a determination, and Article 7.3 provides for the Chair to draw up special terms of reference. The DSB Chair is also consulted by the Director-General on panel composition and informs the Members about composition (DSU, Article 8.7).

[43] DSU, Articles 16.4, 17.5 and 22.3(e).

[44] DSU Article 2.1, first and final sentences (administer these rules, other than by negative consensus); Article 2.2 (inform the relevant WTO Councils and Committees); Article 2.3 (meet); footnotes 5, 7, 8 and 11 (convene a meeting); Article 7.3 (authorise DSB Chair to draw up special terms of reference); Article 17.2 (appoint and reappoint Members of the Appellate Body); Articles 21.7 and 21.8 (further action if a matter is raised by a developing country).

[45] Consistent with this, the DSU itself is entrenched in the WTO constitution, requiring consensus for amendment (WTO Agreement, Article X:8); at the same time, authoritative interpretations of the DSU may be given by three-fourths majority, as with any other covered agreement (WTO Agreement, Article IX:2).

[46] For example, Article 1.2 of the DSU.     [47] For example, Article 8.7 of the DSU.

[48] Appellate Body Report, *US – Large Civil Aircraft*, paras. 480–549.

Article 7.3 provides for the terms of reference thus drawn up to be circulated to all Members and that, if other than standard terms of reference
are agreed upon, any Member may raise any point relating thereto in the
DSB. The term *agreed* refers to the agreement of the parties as referenced
in paragraph 1 and recalled in paragraph 3. At the same time, it also refers
to the agreement of the DSB (in practice by consensus, but, ultimately, by
majority voting) to authorise the Chair to draw up the special terms of
reference. It is significant that other Members may raise any point relating
to the special terms of reference, but no more than that. This echoes the
rights of Members to express their views on panel and Appellate Body
Reports, but not to block them.[49] This confirms that the procedure for the
DSB authorisation, although in practice consensus, is ultimately majority
voting; otherwise, as a matter of logic, all Members would have the right
to block the special terms of reference as finally drawn up.

Thus, the procedures for special terms of reference may be summarised
as follows. At least by the time of consultations, and ideally in the PTA
itself, the parties to the dispute would have identified their wish for
special terms of reference. They would separate their standard terms of
reference, which would pass by negative consensus, and their special terms
of reference, which would not. At least 10 days before the relevant DSB
meeting, the panel request would be circulated.[50] Also at least 10 days
before the same DSB meeting, and with a separate following agenda item,
the parties would circulate a document setting out their agreed special
terms of reference. At the DSB meeting, the panel would be established
with standard terms of reference pursuant to the first agenda item and
the negative consensus procedure. The DSB would then authorise the
special terms of reference, acting in practice by consensus and ultimately
by majority voting. In this latter case, the Chair would be responsible
for ensuring that the interests of Members opposing the special terms of
reference would be appropriately taken into account, which would be the
case once sufficient provision concerning financing and scheduling had
been made.

This approach is in harmony with the situation regarding plurilateral
trade agreements because it strikes the same balance between Members
with different interests. In the context of plurilateral trade agreements,
all WTO Members must agree if an agreement is to become a plurilateral trade agreement. However, the application of the dispute settlement

---

[49]  DSU, Articles 16.4 and 17.14.
[50]  DSU, footnote 5; DSB Rules of Procedure, Rules 2 and 4.

system to such a plurilateral trade agreement is reserved for a decision by the parties to the plurilateral trade agreement. In principle, a WTO Member could insist that an agreement *exclude* recourse to the DSU before agreeing to it becoming a plurilateral trade agreement. However, at least as a political matter, it would seem very difficult for such a Member to maintain such a position indefinitely, at least once sufficient provision had been made with respect to financing and scheduling. Once the plurilateral trade agreement is in place, access to the DSU would be a matter for the parties to that agreement.

The proposition that this chapter is considering is of far less import. There is no sense in which the PTA in question would become a plurilateral trade agreement. It is merely a question of whether or not the parties to the PTA might make use of the DSU. Once sufficient provision has been made about financing and scheduling, then it is quite appropriate that the centre of gravity of this decision should rest with the parties to the agreement and dispute in question. As outlined, appropriate checks and balances would remain to protect the interests of other WTO Members.

With these observations in mind, it is worth recalling that although the applicable procedure for establishing panels is negative consensus, the DSU provides that the DSB is deemed to have decided by consensus if no Member present formally objects.[51] Although defending Members typically posture during DSB meetings, it is very rare to read in DSB minutes that they formally object, not least, no doubt, because it is pointless to formally object to what you cannot prevent. Thus, even if the applicable procedure is negative consensus, in practice Members always act by consensus, once they have understood it to be in their interests to do so. Consequently, once all Members are satisfied in general terms with respect to the financing and scheduling issues, they will have understood that they would have no interest in objecting to PTA parties borrowing the DSU, and, like all DSU matters, such a request could pass in practice by consensus. In short, no change from current practice would be required.

*IV. Substantive aspects of special terms of reference*

Special terms of reference have been used to deal with procedural issues related to multiple complaints. The DSU contains a provision relating to multiple complaints, which provides either for a single panel or for different panels with the same panellists and a harmonised timetable.[52]

---

[51] DSU, footnote 1.   [52] DSU Article 9.

One possibility is for a single panel to be established to examine multiple *pending* panel requests, which can certainly be done with standard terms of reference that simply refer to more than one panel request. Another situation that sometimes arises is that subsequent panel requests are to be referred to a panel that has already been established, and the standard technique is to modify the existing terms of reference of the existing panel using special terms of reference.[53]

However, the mere fact that this is the primary manner in which special terms of reference have been used recently does not preclude the possibility that they might be used for other purposes. For example, in *Brazil – Desiccated Coconut*, special terms of reference were used to bring into the litigation three documents: a communication from Brazil, which itself referred to a position paper from Brazil, and a record of the discussions at the DSB meeting of 21 February 1996.[54] If this was possible, it should also be possible to refer to a document that contains reciprocal rights and obligations of the parties, at least if the parties were to agree. The DSU is simply silent on this point.[55]

Thus, the question boils down to whether or not there is any impediment in WTO law to the mooted course of action. It is difficult to identify any. One objection might be that as a matter of principle the jurisdiction or terms of reference of a court in a particular case can never be wider than the jurisdiction of the relevant dispute settlement system itself. It is not clear, however, what the source of this proposition might be. In this context, the treaties governing the EU provide an interesting point of reference.

First, Article 273 of the Treaty on the Functioning of the European Union (TFEU) provides that the European Court of Justice (ECJ) shall have jurisdiction in any dispute between EU Member States that relates to the subject matter of the EU treaties if the dispute is submitted to it under a special agreement between the parties. Article 259 TFEU *already provides* for an action between EU Member States in which one considers that another has *failed to fulfil an obligation* under the treaties. Thus, Article 259 TFEU is the analogue to a violation dispute between two WTO Members under the provisions of the DSU. Article 273 TFEU is something else. The requirement is simply that the dispute relates to the

---

[53] See, for example, Panel Report, *EC – Computer Equipment*, paras. 1.4–1.11 and 4.9–4.15
[54] Appellate Body Report, *Brazil – Desiccated Coconut*, p. 22; WT/DS22/3 of 29 January 1996, referring to SCM/193.
[55] Panel Report, *EC – Large Civil Aircraft*, para. 7.324.

subject matter of the EU treaties, which is a rather open condition. As a general rule, the substantive content of PTAs may be said to relate to the subject matter of the WTO agreement, not least because they are required to be notified pursuant to Article XXIV. Thus, EU law provides for the possibility for EU adjudicators to take jurisdiction in a particular case, if requested to do so by two EU Member States, *even if such case takes them outside the realm of EU law obligations*, provided only that the case relates to the subject matter of the EU treaties.

Second, Article 272 TFEU provides for the ECJ to have jurisdiction pursuant to any arbitration clause contained in a contract concluded by or on behalf of the EU, whether that contract be governed by public or private law. Although the contract must have been concluded by or on behalf of the EU (and we are not in this chapter discussing agreements concluded by or on behalf of the WTO), nevertheless it must have also been concluded by another party. It refers to *any* governing law, whether *public* or *private*. This once again appears to confirm that, in principle, there is nothing problematic about an EU adjudicator taking jurisdiction in a particular case, if effectively requested to do so by two parties to a contract, *even if such case takes the adjudicator outside the realm of EU law obligations*.

These provisions support the view that there is no impediment in principle to WTO adjudicators being properly called upon to adjudicate non-WTO law, through the use of special terms of reference, provided that the applicable procedures and appropriate substantive limits are respected. The only remaining objection might be that it is not expressly provided for in the DSU itself (as it is expressly provided for in EU law in the relevant EU treaty). However, if, as discussed in this chapter, all WTO Members were to agree by consensus to the proposed course of action, it is difficult to see that this would continue to be a valid objection.

This conclusion is also supported by the jurisprudence of the Permanent Court of International Justice (PCIJ). In the *Serbian Loans* case, the court was called upon to decide issues solely on the basis of *municipal* law. The case was submitted to the court by *special agreement*, and the court had to consider whether it had jurisdiction. It concluded that it had such jurisdiction by virtue of Article 36(1) of its statute, which provided for cases to be referred by special agreement. The court considered that, where two states had agreed to refer a matter to the court, *even a matter otherwise outside the court's jurisdiction*, it had an inherent duty to exercise jurisdiction, *even in the absence of any specific provision in its statute to that effect.*[56]

What are the limits to what PTA parties could refer to the WTO? The title of the WTO agreement and the preamble to the WTO agreement would tend to suggest that the matter referred should relate to the subject matter of the WTO agreement, and specifically trade. Thus, for example, a pure human rights dispute would not be appropriate. Of course, it may not always be easy to dissociate a nontrade issue from a trade issue, and it may always be possible for parties to present a particular matter as trade related, but that would be a question that would ultimately rest with the WTO dispute settlement system, which would remain free to decline to rule if it considered that the matter was not trade related. This approach is supported by the concept of plurilateral trade agreements, which, as the name suggests, should be trade related. It is further supported by the fact that the PTA in question is likely to have been notified under Article XXIV. Finally, it is also interesting to note that this is precisely the filter applied in Article 273 TFEU. It would therefore appear to provide a reasonable parameter for what it would be feasible for PTA parties to refer to the WTO dispute settlement system. In similar vein, a similar parameter would have to be that the dispute would really have to be an international dispute between the two PTA parties.

In short, the key limits to what PTA parties would be able to refer to the WTO dispute settlement system would be as follows: the matter referred should relate to an obligation contained in an agreement notified pursuant to Article XXIV, it should be a trade-related dispute and it should be a dispute between two WTO Members, not a domestic or other international dispute in disguise.

### E. Advantages for PTA parties in referring a PTA dispute to the WTO dispute settlement system

*I. Accessing skilled adjudicators and clerical staff*

The first advantage is having access to skilled adjudicators and clerical staff, not only with respect to panels but also particularly with respect to the Appellate Body. The Appellate Body, which acts in a collegial fashion

---

[56] (1929), PCIJ, Ser. A, no. 20, pp. 16–20; *Brazilian Loans* case (1929), PCIJ, Ser. A, no. 21, p. 101.

even if appeals are heard by three Members,[57] represents an extraordinary and unique concentration of expertise on international trade-related disputes, and it is unlikely that the PTA parties will find a better or more balanced adjudicator elsewhere. Furthermore, the Secretariat, insofar as it services and supports both panels and the Appellate Body, contains within it the broadest and deepest accumulation of knowledge and experience on international trade matters that is available anywhere in the world. It is difficult to see that these structures would be anything other than highly attractive for PTA parties seeking an efficient and balanced adjudication.

## II. Benefiting from the accumulated wisdom of WTO jurisprudence

In similar vein, PTA parties bringing a dispute to the WTO dispute settlement system would have the opportunity to benefit from the accumulated wisdom of WTO jurisprudence. There have now been almost 500 WTO disputes, resulting in hundreds of reports, clarifying thousands of issues. Whilst PTA law may be different, it may also be sufficiently similar to WTO law that the litigating PTA parties would have a high degree of confidence that similar issues would be settled in a similar way. This is hugely advantageous in terms of the efficiency of the proceedings. It is hard to see why, in general terms, this would not be an attractive proposition for PTA parties.

## III. Tailoring the WTO dispute settlement system to the specific requirements of the PTA litigants

Another advantage for PTA parties would be the opportunity to tailor the WTO dispute settlement system to their requirements. Some PTA parties might not want all features of the DSU. Perhaps, for example, they would not want compliance proceedings or appeals. Or maybe they would only want the chance to appeal following a PTA adjudication. If so, they could simply select from the WTO DSU menu and reflect this in the PTA. They could even improve the DSU, for example, with respect to open hearings, *amicus curiae* and sequencing. The point is that what could be used are the key resources of the WTO knowledge system and the people who come with it, tailored to the requirements of the PTA parties.

---

[57] Working Procedures for Appellate Review, Rule 4(3).

## IV. Controlling costs

Another advantage for PTA parties would be the opportunity to control costs. If a matter is referred to a PTA dispute with autonomous adjudicators and support staff, it is far from clear that it would possible to say in advance exactly how much it would cost. By contrast, based on its experience, and given the structures that it already has in place, the WTO may be much better placed to price the litigation and give the disputing PTA parties certainty on the issue of costs.

### F. Advantages for other WTO Members in agreeing to the resolution of PTA disputes by the WTO dispute settlement system

Why should other WTO Members agree to allow the PTA parties to borrow the DSU? Obviously, WTO Members that are parties to PTAs might have a similar interest, but what about the others, especially given the financial implications? The answer is that such arrangements could be a source of *income* for the WTO. Huge sums of money are involved in BIT arbitrations, and the costs for the PTA parties if they were to conduct autonomous PTA litigation would be significant. At the same time, there is an extraordinary bank of knowledge and experience at the WTO. This is an asset of great value that PTA parties will not find elsewhere. Further, these are in essence, to some extent, fixed costs, in the sense that the system is already there. So, why could a fee structure not be devised that, in terms of costs, would place such PTA litigation, referred to the WTO, somewhere between the fees of WTO litigation (which is free) and those of BIT litigation, and which would make a substantial financial contribution to the WTO budget? The only problem would be to price the service at the right level. But this pricing problem is just a technical issue, which the WTO Secretariat is uniquely well placed to settle, given its experience in dealing with complex economic issues.

### G. How the resolution of PTA disputes by the WTO dispute settlement system could be financed

Turning more specifically to the question of financing, as indicated previously, it is probably fair to say that this is an issue of potential interest to all Members. Therefore, it is probably an issue that would have to be the subject of a consensus decision by all WTO Members addressing the issue in general terms if special terms of reference are to be used. The principle would have to be that PTA disputes heard by the WTO dispute settlement system would have to make a significant contribution to the financing of the WTO dispute settlement system. For example, the costs of dealing with such a dispute could be estimated, then doubled, so that, in principle, any PTA dispute heard would finance one other WTO dispute. The details of the pricing should be left to the Secretariat, acting under the authority of the Director-General. Provision would have to be made for ensuring that any fee schedule would keep pace with inflation. It could also be possible to make provision for special and differential treatment so that developing countries could bring their PTA disputes to the WTO without charge.

Some thought would have to be given to whether to fix a fee schedule as a function of particular cases, such as by reference to the claims, pages of briefing and pages of exhibits involved, or whether it would rather be feasible to fix one price for all disputes. Probably neither model would be entirely satisfactory, so it might be preferable to have some flexibility on the issue. One approach would be to have one price in principle for all PTA disputes. However, at the time of the panel request identifying the PTA dispute, the Director-General could have the possibility, at the request of the PTA parties, to fix a lower amount. This could be appropriate if, for example, the dispute is straightforward. Alternatively, in the case of a very large PTA dispute, the Director-General could have the authority to indicate to the PTA parties that the WTO dispute settlement system could deal with the dispute only on the basis of a fee that would be some multiple of the basic fee. The PTA parties could then consider whether they wish to go ahead on that basis. This approach would provide the PTA parties with reasonable certainty about costs in advance and at the same time provide flexibility to fix a price appropriate to the circumstances of a particular case.

In terms of the basic price itself, it would be important for the WTO to take into consideration not only what it would cost to adjudicate such a case in the WTO but also what it would cost the PTA parties to adjudicate the dispute themselves. Logically, the price should at least lie between these two amounts. The WTO is itself uniquely well placed to ascertain the first of these. As to the second, it could draw guidance from what information is available regarding BIT arbitrations. Where the price would actually be set between these two extremes would depend on demand.

## H. How scheduling conflicts between WTO disputes and PTA disputes could be resolved by the WTO dispute settlement system

The other issue of legitimate concern to all WTO Members could be scheduling. On this issue, the principle established by consensus could be that no PTA case is ever to cause delay to any WTO case.

At the level of panels, this should not normally be an issue as regards the adjudicators themselves, since they are appointed on an ad hoc basis. As regards the Secretariat, it would be a matter for the WTO to judge whether it would be necessary to employ support staff on an ad hoc basis or whether it would be possible to have recourse to the existing WTO staff.

At the level of the Appellate Body, some issues have recently arisen concerning scheduling. In practice, the approach in principle appears to be that appeals should be heard and completed in the order in which they arise or could arise. The preference appears to be, when necessary, to extend the 60-day rule in Article 16.4 of the DSU, by DSB decision by consensus, rather than have a situation in which the Appellate Body is not able to meet the 90-day rule in Article 17.5 of the DSU. An alternative to this queue system could permit smaller appeals to be decided faster than, and effectively overtake, larger appeals. With this in mind, the scheduling issue could easily be dealt with by PTA parties acknowledging that the Appellate Body is not in any event bound by the rule in Article 17.5 of the DSU. This would give the Appellate Body the flexibility necessary to adjust the scheduling of a pending PTA dispute in order to give priority to a WTO dispute that would subsequently come on appeal.

## I. Third parties

Some thought would have to be given to the role of third parties. In a mixed WTO–PTA case, they would have the third-party rights afforded to them by the WTO. In a pure PTA dispute, it would be for the PTA parties to determine the role of third parties. If a would-be third party were to have a particular interest, for example, because it has a specific trade interest or is party to a PTA with a similar provision, then it would always have the opportunity to file an *amicus curiae* brief (at least on the basis of the panel request), which the PTA adjudicator would have the discretion to take into account.

## J. Concentration of responsibility for international dispute settlement

Some might worry about a concentration of responsibility for dispute settlement. This should not be an issue of particular concern. In practice, as a matter of fact, the same individuals often already sit in multiple jurisdictions. In any event, all WTO Members have cases about which some domestic constituents have expressed strong opinions. The point is that once the need for binding dispute settlement is accepted, that is the important point, and not the outcomes in particular cases. All civilised nations recognise that the rule of law is fundamental both internally and in their relations with others. In any event, this issue could also be tackled in the PTA or possibly also in the panel request. For example, parties could agree that, at the outset of panel proceedings, they must agree in one sense or another whether a particular issue will be susceptible to appeal.

## K. How the WTO dispute settlement system would process PTA disputes, given the obligation on WTO Members to ensure that their PTAs are consistent with the WTO agreement

Finally, some thought would have to be given to the interface between WTO law and WTO-plus or WTO-minus provisions in the PTAs, including consistency with Article XXIV of the GATT 1994. This issue has already been touched on. There would not appear to be any insurmountable obstacles. There should not normally be any WTO-minus provisions in the PTA, and any doubtful provisions could be dealt with by interpreting them in conformity with WTO law, to the extent necessary. Also, the PTA should be consistent with Article XXIV, although there does remain a theoretical possibility that this might not be the case. However, this issue should not normally be the issue placed before the WTO adjudicator by the PTA parties. In any event, perhaps it would not be so terrible to have a WTO-appointed adjudicator nevertheless enforcing such a provision, wearing as they would be another hat.

## L. Conclusion

PTA parties generally need and want mandatory and binding dispute settlement and make provision for it. Despite this, PTA dispute settlement is rarely used because of a desire to foster a cooperative relationship, the difficulty of distinguishing so-called WTO-plus provisions, serious logistical obstacles and the lack of an established jurisprudence. Without modification of the DSU, standard or special terms of reference could be used to receive PTA disputes into the WTO dispute settlement system. At least once there was consensus on the issues of financing and scheduling in principle, this would be possible, without any significant change to current practice. There would be substantial advantages for the PTA parties: they would have access to a substantial resource for the settlement of their dispute, could tailor the system to their own requirements and could control costs. There would also be advantages for other WTO Members. In particular, an appropriate scale of fees could ensure that PTA disputes could cross-finance WTO disputes. Such an approach could make a substantial long-term contribution to systemic integration in international trade law.

## References

Chase, Claude, Yanovich, Alan, Crawford, Jo-Ann, and Ugaz, Pamela. 2013. 'Mapping of Dispute Settlement Mechanisms in Regional Trade Agreements – Innovative or Variations on a Theme?' Staff Working Paper ERSD-2013-07. World Trade Organization, Economic Research and Statistics Division, Geneva.

Eberhardt, Pia, and Olivet, Cecilia. 2012. *Profiting from Injustice: How Law Firms, Arbitrators and Financiers Are Fuelling an Investment Arbitration Boom*. Brussels: Corporate Europe Observatory and the Transnational Institute.

Flett, James. 2012. 'Importing Other International Regimes into World Trade Organization Litigation.' In *Regime Interaction in International Law – Facing Fragmentation*, edited by Margaret Young, 261–304. Cambridge: Cambridge University Press.

Gao, Henry, and Lin, L. C. 2008. 'Saving the WTO from the Risk of Irrelevance: The WTO Dispute Settlement Mechanism as a "Common Good" for RTA Disputes.' *Journal of International Economic Law* 11 (4): 899–925.

Marceau, Gabrielle, and Wyatt, Julian. 2010. 'Dispute Settlement Regimes Intermingled: Regional Trade Agreements and the WTO.' *Journal of International Dispute Settlement* 1 (1): 67–95.

Mitchell, Andrew D. 2008. *Legal Principles in WTO Disputes*. Cambridge: Cambridge University Press.

Van Damme, Isabelle. 2009. 'Jurisdiction, Applicable Law, and Interpretation.' In *The Oxford Handbook of International Trade Law*, edited by Daniel Bethlehem,

Donald McRae, Rodney Neufeld and Isabelle Van Damme, 298–343. Oxford, England: Oxford University Press.

World Trade Organization. 2011. 'The Relationship between PTAs and the WTO.' In *World Trade Report 2011. The WTO and Preferential Trade Agreements: From Co-Existence to Coherence*, 187–91. Geneva: World Trade Organization.

# INDEX

AANZFTA. *See* ASEAN-Australia-New Zealand FTA (AANZFTA)

Acharya, Amitav, 134

ACTA. *See* Anti-Counterfeiting Trade Agreement (ACTA)

ad hoc arbitration, 330

ADB. *See* Asian Development Bank (ADB)

Adidas, 138

Affinity of Nations Index, 107

Afghanistan, 170

Africa, 520

African countries, 127

Agreement on Civil Aircraft, 545

Agreement on Government Procurement (GPA), 275–6, 501, 545

Agreement on Subsidies and Countervailing Measures (SCM), 501, 545

Agreement on Technical Barriers to Trade (TBT Agreement), 246, 500–1, 562. *See also* technical barriers to trade (TBT)

Agreement on Trade Facilitation, 534, 535

Agreement on Trade-Related Aspects of Intellectual Property Rights. *See* TRIPS Agreement

Agreement on Trade-Related Investment Measures (TRIMs), 501

Aid for Trade, 534

air transportation, 38

Al Qaeda, 48

Algeria, 313

Alliance Treaty Obligations and Provisions (ATOP), 67

alliances, military/security, 121

Amazon Cooperation Treaty, 122–6

Amazon Mechanical Turk (MTurk), 123

American National Election Study (ANES), 115

AMU. *See* Arab Maghreb Union (AMU)

Andean Community, 170, 518

Andorra, 42

ANES. *See* American National Election Study (ANES)

Anglo-French commercial treaty of 1860, 3

Anti-Counterfeit Code, 471

Anti-Counterfeiting Trade Agreement (ACTA), 2, 473, 499

anti-dumping, 414–15, 437, 440–7

ANZCERTA. *See* Australia New Zealand Closer Economic Relations Agreement (ANZCERTA)

APEC. *See* Asia Pacific Economic Cooperation (APEC)

Appellate Body, 572, 576

Apple Inc., 47

APTA. *See* Asia-Pacific Trade Agreement (APTA)

Arab Maghreb Union (AMU), 41, 302, 313

arbitration, 327

Argentina, 433, 441

safeguard on footwear, 449–52

ARIC. *See* Asian Regional Integration Center (ARIC)

armed conflicts, 296–301
Arusha agreements, 479
ASEAN. *See* Association of Southeast
    Asian Nations (ASEAN)
ASEAN Comprehensive Investment
    Agreement, 527
ASEAN Free Trade Area, 136, 139,
    148–9
ASEAN Way, 134
ASEAN-Australia-New Zealand FTA
    (AANZFTA), 520, 526, 528
ASEAN-China FTA, 521, 525
ASEAN-Japan FTA, 520–1, 529
Asia, 134–52
    audiovisual services commitments
        to PTAs in, 240
    deep integration PTAs in, 138–40,
        143–5
    free trade agreements in, 134–6,
        140–3
    multinational firms in, 137
    production networks, 137–8
    Trans-Pacific Partnership
        agreement, 140
Asia-Pacific Economic Cooperation
    (APEC), 49
Asia-Pacific Trade Agreement (APTA),
    135, 518, 529
Asian Development Bank (ADB), 135
Asian Regional Integration Center
    (ARIC), 135
Association of Southeast Asian Nations
    (ASEAN), 49, 137, 295, 302,
    305, 312, 439, 521, 538
ATOP. *See* Alliance Treaty Obligations
    and Provisions (ATOP)
audiovisual goods and services,
    218–43
    audiovisual service sectors, 227–8
    goods-only agreements, 222
    good-service agreements, 222
    overview, 218–20
    services commitments to PTAs,
        225–34
        coding, 228–30
        cultural factors in, 238–9
        cultural proximity and, 239–42
        economic size and, 236–8

negative-list format, 226, 230
negotiating leverages and, 236
net exporters of services and,
    236–8
net importers of services and,
    235–6
positive-list format, 225–6, 230
variation in, 234–42
treatment in preferential trade
    agreements, 220–34
world trade in, 220
World Trade Organization and,
    242–3
Australia, 1, 76, 96, 129, 141, 171, 218,
    239, 289–90, 433, 510
Australia New Zealand Closer
    Economic Relations Agreement
    (ANZCERTA), 481–2
Australia–Chile Free Trade, 287

Bahrain–Jordan agreement, 297
Baldwin, Richard, 137
Bali Ministerial Conference, 16, 534,
    535
Bangkok Declaration, 295
Bangladesh, 96, 104, 129, 142
barriers to trade, 246
behind-the-border integration, 138
Belarus, 519
Benelux Economic Union, 328, 357
Berne Convention on the Protection of
    Literary and Artistic World,
    467, 471
bilateral distance, 367–8, 369
bilateral investment treaties (BITs), 46,
    319
bilateral trade agreements, 45. *See also*
    multilateral trade agreements;
    plurilateral trade agreements
    credibility-driven PTAs and, 98–9,
        101
    export zeroes, 394
    reasons in proliferation of, 465
bilateralism, 33–5
BITs. *See* bilateral investment treaties
    (BITs)
Bolivia, 105
Bombardier, 288

borders
common, 368
multilateral trade agreements and, 486–8
Brazil, 56, 288–9, 433, 441, 450, 452
Bretton Woods Institutions, 467, 469
Breusch-Pagan test, 423
BRIC countries, 56
British Commonwealth, 357
Brunei, 1, 76, 129, 522
Buy American provisions, 277
buy national policies, 277, 287

CACM. See Central American Common Market (CACM)
CAFTA. See Central American Free Trade Agreement (CAFTA)
Cambodia, 138
Canada, 3, 6, 76, 114, 129, 434, 445, 476, 482
cultural industries, 218, 222–3
PTAs with United States, 497
trade in audiovisual goods and services, 221
Canada–Chile FTA, 185
Canada–US Automotive Products Trade Agreement, 175
Canada–US Free Trade Agreement (CUSFTA), 114
capital allocation, inefficiencies in, 83
Caribbean Community (CARICOM), 48, 170, 231, 305, 479–80
Caribbean Court of Justice, 328
Caribbean Forum (CARIFORUM), 176, 224, 227
CARICOM. See Caribbean Community (CARICOM)
CARIFORUM. See Caribbean Forum (CARIFORUM)
Central American Common Market (CACM), 7, 170, 297, 312
Central American Free Trade Agreement (CAFTA), 282
Central American Integration System (SICA), 295
Central European Media Enterprises Ltd., 526

Central Product Classification (CPC), 227–8
CEPGL. See Economic Community of Great Lakes Countries (CEPGL)
chair, selection of, 332–4
Chile, 1, 76, 129, 171, 176, 279, 504, 510
Chile–China PTA, 224
China, 5, 56, 113, 433, 441, 446, 450, 454, 455, 465, 510, 518, 538
China–Japan–South Korea investment agreement, 527
China–Singapore FTA, 521, 525
CIS. See Commonwealth of Independent States (CIS)
CMAs. See critical mass agreements (CMAs)
Cobden Chevalier Agreement (1860), 468
Codex Alimentarius Commission, 562
Cold War, 4, 40, 42
Colombia, 129, 313, 439
colonial history, 368–9, 370–1
colonial relationship, 69
Columbia, 138
COMESA. See Common Market for Eastern and Southern Africa (COMESA)
commercial agreements
demand for/supply of, 30–1
peace promotion and, 297
Committee on Regional Trade Agreements (CRTA), 543, 544–6
common land border, 368
common market, 361
Common Market for Eastern and Southern Africa (COMESA), 174, 224, 305, 313, 498, 520
Common Security and Defence Policy, 307
Commonwealth of Independent States (CIS), 313, 519
compensation hypothesis, 411
competition policy, 246–70
free trade and, 262–3
overview, 247–8

in preferential trade agreements
  (PTAs), 251–6
  form of, 253–6
  over time, 256
  prior studies of, 249–51
  as protectionism, 260–2
COMTRADE database, 362
conflicts, 30
Congress of Vienna (1815), 33
constant elasticity if substitution
  (CES), 358
consultations, 325–6
consumption, 28
containerized shipping, 38
contiguity, 68
Convention on the Diversity of
  Cultural Expressions, 224
Corbet, Hugh, 475
Corn Laws (1846), 33
Corruption Index, 110
Corruption Perception Index, 94, 110
Costa Rica, 114, 129
Court of International Justice, 563
CPC. See Central Product
  Classification (CPC)
credibility-driven PTAs, 86–91
  in agreements with relatively large
    partners, 90–1, 99
  as commitment device, 89–90, 99
  credibility motivations in, 92–8
  impact on bilateral trade flows,
    98–9, 101
  value of, 101–5
critical mass agreements (CMAs), 543,
  544–6
cross-sector retaliation, 339
CRTA. See Committee on Regional
  Trade Agreements
cultural distance, 238–9
cultural industries, 218, 222–3
currency blocs, 37
CUSFTA. See Canada–US Free Trade
  Agreement (CUSFTA)
customs union, 361

deep integration PTAs, 138–40,
  374–90
  case study, 148–51

cross-sectional analysis of, 146–8
data, 378–84
definition of, 117
empirical framework, 376–8
exports, 378–81
features of, 139
general set-up, 376–7
implementation, 377–8
investment provisions in, 148–51
public procurement rules and, 280
vs. shallow trade agreements,
  374–90
tariffs, 378–84
Trans-Pacific Partnership
  agreement, 140
deep trade agreements. See deep
  integration PTAs
delegation, in dispute settlement,
  341–2
democracy, 58–9
Design of Trade Agreements (DESTA)
  Database, 11, 105, 183, 248,
  477
dictatorships, 60
differentiated goods, 199–201
dispute, statistical model, 67
dispute settlement, 319–50, 555–78
  advantages for other WTO
    Members, 574
  advantages for PTA parties, 572–4
    cost control, 574
    tailoring to specific requirements
      of litigants, 573
    WTO jurisprudence, 573
  binding, 555–6
  concentration of responsibility in,
    577
  conceptualization of, 340–7
    delegation, 341–2
    enforcement, 343–5
    flexibility, 345, 346–7
    information provision, 342–3
    settlement promotion, 345–6
  in double PTAs, 526–8
  exceptions/exemptions, 339–40,
    347
  financing of, 574–5
  forum choice in, 331, 344

dispute settlement (*cont.*)
  implementation of, 336–9
  legal, 330–1
  low level of use, 556–9
    adjudicators and clerical staff,
      558–9
    cooperative relationship in, 557
    lack of critical mass, 559
    need of substantial investment,
      559
    overlaps between WTO and PTA
      laws, 557–8
    reluctance to litigate in, 557
  mandatory, 555–6
  overview, 319–20, 555
  in preferential trade agreements,
    323–40
  previous research on, 320–3
  proceedings, 331–6
    chair selection, 332–4
    enforcement process, 335–6
    interim report, 334
    joint committee action, 332
    mutually agreeable solution,
      335–6
    separate opinions, 334–5
    time limits, 335
  protection from risk and, 416–17
  provisions, 324–5
  sanctions in, 344
    forms of, 339
    provision, 337–8
    selection of, 338
  scheduling conflicts, 576
  terms of references, 559–72
    multilateral/plurilateral
      mechanisms, 560–1
    special, procedural aspects of,
      565–9
    special, substantive aspects of,
      569–72
    standard, 561–5
  third parties in, 576
  types of, 325–31
    arbitration, 327
    consultations, 325–6
    legal dispute settlement, 330–1
    mediation, 326–7

  overlap, 329–30
  reference to external body, 328–9
  standing body, 328
  WTO agreement and, 577
Dispute Settlement Body (DSB),
  563–4, 565–9
dispute settlement mechanism (DSM),
  300, 342–3, 345
distance
  bilateral, 367–8, 369
  capital-to-capital, 68
  cultural, 238–9
  psychic, 118–20, 128
Doha Declaration on Public Health,
  472
Doha Development Agenda. *See* Doha
  Round
Doha Round, 16, 17, 48, 231, 465, 484,
  533–4
domestic politics, 57–61
  democracy, 58–9
  public officials, 58
  statistical model, 66–7
  veto players, 60–1
Dominican Republic, 456–9
Dominican Republic–Central America
  FTA (CAFTA-DR), 114, 439,
  456–9
domino theory, 64
double preferential trade agreements,
  497–531. *See also* preferential
  trade agreements (PTAs)
  categorising, 516–18
  coexistence of PTAs, 526–30
    ad hoc negotiation, 529
    conflict of PTA norms, 528–30
    earlier/original PTA, 528–9
    favourable PTA, 529
    overlap/interaction of dispute
      settlement fora, 526–8
    silence, 529–30
  as functional/economic
    phenomenon, 520–2
    backsliding, 522
    deeper integration, 520, 521
    legal innovation, 522
    minimum floor expansion,
      521–2

as historical/political phenomenon,
518–20
bridge between regions, 519–20
paper tigers, 519
remnants of failed regional
economic integration, 518–19
legal issues, 522–30
accession, 525
coexistence, 526–30
consolidation, 523–6
incorporation, 525–6
suspension, 525
termination, 523–4
network, 515–16
overview, 497–8
plurilateral trade agreements,
498–502
statistics, 513
WTO restrictions, 498–502
DSB. See Dispute Settlement Body
(DSB)
DSM. See dispute settlement
mechanism (DSM)
dyads, 68, 74–5

EAC. See East African Community
(EAC)
ease of adjustment, 198–9
East African Community (EAC), 231,
295, 312, 498
East African Court of Justice, 328
economic agreements
bilateral regulatory competition,
44–6
competition for bilateralism, 33–5
political/economic blocs, 36–7
post–Cold War (1991–2000), 44–6
post–Industrial Revolution
(1840–1914), 33–5
post–information revolution
(2001–13), 48–9
post–World War I (1920s and
1930s), 36–7
post–World War II (1947–90), 41–2
supply and demand, 30–1
Economic and Monetary Community
of Central Africa, 170, 224,
366

Economic Community of Central
African States, 312
Economic Community of Great Lakes
Countries (CEPGL), 41
Economic Community of West African
States (ECOWAS), 224, 296,
302, 313, 521
economic exchanges, 25–50
evolution of infrastructures and
agreements, 31–49
post–Cold War (1991–2000),
42–6
post–Industrial Revolution
(1840–1914), 31–5
post–information revolution
(2001–13), 46–9
post–World War I (1920s and
1930s), 34, 35–7
post–World War II (1947–90),
38–42
infrastructure for, 26–31
commercial agreements, 30–1
political, 29–30
technological, 27–9
economic integration agreements
(EIAs), 355–71
data set for, 362
growth in number of, 355–6
heterogeneous effects on trade flows,
361, 362–3
cultural factors, 366–71
due to depth of agreement,
363–6
economic factors, 366–71
institutional factors, 366–71
models, 357–62
economic partnership agreements
(EPAs), 139, 478
economic size, 118, 127, 128–9
economic union, 361
ECOWAS. See Economic Community
of West African States
(ECOWAS)
Ecuador, 313
EEA. See European Economic Area
(EEA)
EFTA. See European Free Trade
Association (EFTA)

Egypt, 520
EIAs. *See* economic integration
    agreements (EIAs)
*ejusdem generis* principle, 501
Enabling Clause, 142, 562
endogenous tariff formation, 196
enforcement process, in dispute
    settlement, 343–5
Enhanced Cooperation Agreements,
    550
equipped labour, 376
Ethiopia, 94, 96, 105
EU. *See* European Union (EU)
European Coal and Steel Community,
    9
European Commission, 170, 285
European Community
    bilateral agreements, 42
    emulation of, 41–2
European Community–Jordan PTA,
    253
European Community–Montenegro
    agreement, 277
European Court of Justice, 170, 328
European Economic Area (EEA), 282,
    477
European Economic Community
    (EEC), 7, 9, 170, 370, 537
European Free Trade Association
    (EFTA), 42, 176, 227, 282, 370,
    504
European Union (EU), 1, 313, 434,
    450, 472
    anti-dumping measures, 441
    audiovisual goods and services, 223
    bilateral agreements, 45
    Common Security and Defence
        Policy, 307
    footwear exports, 452, 454
    procurement practices, 283
    PTA model, 170–1, 174–5
    Stabilization and Association
        Agreements, 223
    trade agreements with former
        colonies, 113
EU–Singapore PTA, 224
exchange control bloc, 37
executive branch, 60

export zeros, 394
exports, 210, 378–81

Factory Asia, 137
family trees, 239
FDIs. *See* foreign direct investments
    (FDIs)
FedEx, 47
financial aid, 179
first-mover advantages, 547–8
flags of convenience, 38
flexibility, 414–15, 417–18
footwear, safeguard on, 449–52, 453–6
foreign direct investments (FDIs), 46,
    144, 147
    deep integration PTAs and, 148–51
former colonies, 69
France, 96
free trade agreements, 361
    ASEAN–Australia–New Zealand
        FTA, 520, 526, 528
    ASEAN–China FTA, 521, 525
    ASEAN–Japan FTA, 520–1, 529
    in Asia, 134–6, 140–3
    Canada–Chile FTA, 185
    Canada–US Free Trade Agreement,
        114
    Central American Free Trade
        Agreement, 282
    Central American Free Trade
        Agreement–Dominican
        Republic, 114, 439, 456–9
    China–Singapore FTA, 521, 525
    competition policy and, 246–63,
        270
    full, 7
    India–Bhutan FTA, 136
    Japan–ASEAN FTA, 520–1, 529
    Japan–Peru FTA, 142
    Korea–USA FTA, 136, 143
    Mexico–Central America FTA, 523
    partial, 6
    Singapore–Australia FTA, 529
    South Asian Free Trade Agreement,
        4, 167
    Turkey–Korea FTA, 142
free trade areas, 436
FTAs. *See* free trade agreements

fuzzy-set qualitative comparative
analysis (fsQCA), 309

Gap, 138
garments industry, 138
GATS. *See* General Agreement on
Trade in Services (GATS)
GATT. *See* General Agreement on
Tariffs and Trade (GATT)
GDP. *See* gross domestic product
(GDP)
General Agreement on Tariffs and
Trade (GATT), 3, 56, 467
Article III, 221, 501, 547
Article V, 142
Article VI, 436
Article XIX, 436
Article XX, 225, 471, 563
Article XXIV, 4, 116, 142, 197, 355,
436, 490, 499–500, 544, 546,
564
contracting parties, 198
deep integration PTAs and, 138
deep vs. shallow PTAs and, 374–5
enabling clause, 4
membership, 74, 533
multilateral trade agreements and,
468
nondiscrimination clauses in, 255
in post–World War II period, 38, 40
prevalence of PTA and, 64–5
PTA design and, 189
PTA formation and, 68
termination of, 523
General Agreement on Trade in
Services (GATS), 17, 467, 468,
476–7, 483
Article III.1, 547
Article V, 116, 395, 489, 490, 499,
544, 546
Article VII, 489
Article XVI, 228
Article XVII, 228
audiovisual services commitments,
230–1, 232
electronic media, 221
supply modes in, 228
General Electric, 137

geographical proximity, 118, 128
Germany, 283
global value chains (GVCs), 47
gold bloc, 37
gold standard, 35
Government Herfindahl index, 96
governments
bargaining weight of, 94–6
definition of, 84
lobbying rent, 84
PTA as commitment device, 89–90,
99
in agreements with large partners,
90–1, 99
social welfare and, 88–9
tariff bounds, 85
welfare mindedness of, 93–4
GPA. *See* Agreement on Government
Procurement (GPA)
gravitation models, 118–20, 357–60
gravity model, 118
Greater Arab Free Trade Area, 303
Griffiths, Brian, 475
gross domestic product (GDP),
144–5
coefficient estimates of, 73
PTA formation and, 69
public procurement and, 275
ratio, 67–8
Grossman–Helpman model, 93,
196–7, 198
Grubel–Lloyd index, 209
Gulf Cooperation Council (GCC), 227
GVCs. *See* global value chains (GVCs)

H&M, 138
Harmonized System of the World
Customs Organization (1992),
208
Havana Charters, 562
heads of state, 60
hegemony, 61–2, 68, 74, 307
Herfindahl index, 96
HIIT. *See* horizontal intra-industry
trade (HIIT)
Hong Kong, 231, 240
horizontal intra-industry trade (HIIT),
203, 209, 211–13

Iceland, 42, 504
ICSID. *See* International Centre for
    Settlement of Investment
    Disputes (ICSID)
IGOs. *See* intergovernmental
    organizations (IGOs)
IIPTAs. *See* investment-inclusive PTAs
    (IIPTAs)
ILC. *See* International Law
    Commission (ILC)
IMF. *See* International Monetary Fund
    (IMF)
Imperial Preference System (IPS), 37
import-penetration ratio, 94
India, 56, 96, 129, 170, 224, 433, 441,
    510, 518, 529
India–Bhutan FTA, 136
India–Singapore PTA, 224
Indonesia, 129, 137, 138, 210, 231,
    450, 454, 455, 521
information provision, 342–3
Information Technology Agreement
    (ITA), 16, 500, 544
institutions-based integration, 170–1
intellectual property, 468–74
intergovernmental organizations
    (IGOs), 179–80, 188–9
interim report, 334
intermediate goods, 376–7
International Centre for Settlement of
    Investment Disputes (ICSID),
    46
International Court of Justice, 328
International Dairy Agreement, 545
International Exhibition of Industrial
    Property Inventions (1873),
    470
international governance, 167–91
International Law Commission (ILC),
    562
International Monetary Fund (IMF),
    181, 235, 288
International Organization for
    Standardization/International
    Electrotechnical Commission
    (ISO/IEC), 562
International Plant Protection
    Convention, 562

international politics
    asymmetric power relationships in,
        62–3
    hegemony, 61–2
    political-military cooperation in, 63
    of preferential trade agreements,
        61–71
    statistical model, 67–8
    strategic interdependence in, 63–4
International Standard Industrial
    Classification (ISIC), 209
International Trade Commission
    (ITC), 200
International Trade Organization
    (ITO), 39
intra-industry trade, 198–9
    exports, 210
    horizontal, 203, 209, 211–13
    import-competing industries,
        209–10
    most-favoured-nation tariff and,
        207–8
    operationalisation and data, 207–11
    tariff liberalisation and, 201–7
    tariffs and, 207
    trade type, 208–9
    vertical, 203–6, 209, 211–13
intra-regional trade, 188
investment-inclusive PTAs (IIPTAs),
    46, 48
*Invisible Barriers to Invisible Trade*
    (Griffiths), 475
IPS. *See* Imperial Preference System
    (IPS)
Ireland, 286
Islamic countries, 127
Israel, 476, 480–1
Israel–US agreement, 175
ITA. *See* Information Technology
    Agreement (ITA)
ITC. *See* International Trade
    Commission (ITC)
ITO. *See* International Trade
    Organization (ITO)

Jaccard coefficient, 172
Japan, 1, 5, 76, 94, 113, 171, 207, 210,
    231, 240, 282, 452, 472

Japan–ASEAN FTA, 520–1, 529
Japan–Peru FTA, 142
joint committee action, 332

Kantian peace framework, 297
knowledge platforms, 541–2
Korea–USA FTA, 136, 143
Kuwait, 231

LAIA. See Latin American Integration
    Association (LAIA)
language
    pairs, 239
    of partner countries, 127, 368, 370
    phylogenies, 239
    psychic distance and, 120
    PTA models and, 183
Lao PDR–Thailand PTA, 142
Lao People's Democratic Republic, 518
Lao People's Revolutionary Party
    (LPRP), 521
Laos, 129
Latin America, 3, 4
    preferential trade agreements, 251
Latin American Integration
    Association (LAIA), 4, 497, 518
Lawrence, Robert Z., 138
LDCs. See least developed countries
    (LDCs)
League of Arab States, 303
League of Nations, 36
least developed countries (LDCs), 534
legal origin, 368–9, 370–1
Libya, 520
Liechtenstein, 504
Lisbon Treaty, 174, 180–1
Lithuania, 283
LL Bean, 138
lobbying rent, 84
Lomé Conventions, 173, 479
London School of Economics, 475

Maastricht Treaty, 170, 477, 482
Malaysia, 1, 76, 129, 137, 210, 522
Mano River Union (MRU), 296, 302
markets
    access to, 29
    preferential access to, 488–9

structure, 29
Marks and Spencer, 138
Mauritania, 504
mediation, 326–7
mega-agreements, 129
mega-regionals, 7, 511–13, 538
Melitz model, 358, 359
MERCOSUR. See Southern Common
    Market (MERCOSUR)
Mexico, 76, 83, 129, 171, 231, 433,
    445, 510
Mexico–Central America FTA, 523
MFN. See most-favoured-nation
    (MFN)
Microsoft, 289
military alliance, 121
minilateralism, 485
mini-multilateralism, 485
minimum floor expansion, 521–2
monetary sanctions, 339
Mongolia, 135, 504
Montevideo Treaty (1980), 170
Morocco, 313
Most Economically Advantageous
    Tender (MEAT), 283
most-favoured-nation (MFN), 36, 93,
    207–8, 479, 485
    deep vs. shallow PTAs and, 374
    plurilateral trade agreements and,
    546–7
    in post–Industrial Revolution, 34,
    35–7
    preferential trade agreements and,
    466
    PTA implementation and, 439
    temporary trade barriers and, 435
MRU. See Mano River Union (MRU)
MTurk (Amazon Mechanical Turk),
    123, 127
Multilateral Agreement on Investment,
    2
multilateral trade agreements, 16–19.
    See also bilateral trade
    agreements; plurilateral trade
    agreements; trade agreements
    border issues, 486–8
    dialectical relationships, 487–8
    dispute settlement and, 560–1

multilateral trade agreements (*cont.*)
   historical background, 467–83
   intellectual property protection and,
      468–74
   liberalisation in services trade and,
      475–83
   nondiscrimination principle, 116
   preferential trade agreements and,
      465–92
   reasons in proliferation of, 465
   regulatory burden sharing in,
      486–91
   WTO rules, 490–1
multilateralising regionalism, 522
multinational corporations, 137–8
mutually agreeable solution (MAS),
   335–6

NAFTA. *See* North American Free
   Trade Agreement (NAFTA)
Napoleonic Wars, 33
natural trading partners, 113–29
   adjacency of, 368, 370
   common colonial history of, 368–9,
      370–1
   common language of, 368, 370
   common legal origin of, 368–9,
      370–1
   common religion of, 368, 370
   conjoint analysis of, 122–6
   distance between, 367–8, 369
   economic size of, 118, 127, 128–9
   geographical proximity of, 118, 128
   military or security alliance, 121
   political system, 120–1
   postmaterialism, 121–2
   preferential trade agreements and,
      116–17
   psychic distance of, 118–20, 128
   theoretical arguments for, 117–22
negative integration, 138
negative-list agreement, 226, 230
nested security institutions, 301–13
   analysis of necessary conditions,
      309–13
   explanations for, 305–9
   hegemony and, 307–8
   within regional economic
      organisations, 302–5

new regionalism, 4, 113, 116
new trade theory, 198
New Zealand, 1, 76, 129, 141, 225, 239,
   452, 510
New Zealand–Taiwan PTA, 224
Nike, 138
nondiscrimination principle, 116
North American Free Trade Agreement
   (NAFTA), 4, 8, 41, 64, 113
   anti-dumping/countervailing duty
      activities and, 445
   deep integration PTAs and, 139
   negative-list approach, 482
   preferential trade agreements and, 83
   PTA model, 171, 175–6, 177
North Atlantic Treaty Organization
   (NATO), 303
North–South agreements, 536
Norway, 231, 276, 504

OAS. *See* Organisation of American
   States (OAS)
ocean shipping, 38–9
OECD. *See* Organisation for Economic
   Co-operation and
   Development (OECD)
offshoring, 43
Oman, 285
Organisation for Economic
   Co-operation and
   Development (OECD), 247,
   392–3, 395, 534, 562
Organisation of American States
   (OAS), 251, 303
Organisation of East Caribbean States,
   480
Ottawa agreements, 3
outsourcing, 43
outward processing trade, 137
Oxford Archaeology, 290

Pacific Basin Economic Council
   (PBEC), 134
Pacific Economic Cooperation Council
   (PECC), 134
Pacific Islands Forum (PIF), 305, 312
PAFTA. *See* Pan-Arabian Free Trade
   Area (PAFTA)
Pakistan, 231

Pan-Arabian Free Trade Area (PAFTA), 520
Papua New Guinea, 141, 142
Paraguay, 232
parallelism, 452–3
Paris Convention on the Protection of Industrial Property, 467, 469, 470
PBEC. See Pacific Basin Economic Council (PBEC)
Peace Research Institute Oslo (PRIO), 67
PECC. See Pacific Economic Cooperation Council (PECC)
Peru, 1, 76, 129, 224, 313, 434, 510
Petrobras, 288–9
Philippines, 129, 137, 210, 231, 521, 538
PIF. See Pacific Islands Forum (PIF)
plurilateral trade agreements, 498–502, 533–53. See also bilateral trade agreements; multilateral trade agreements; trade agreements
    backdoor inclusion of controversial issues in, 546
    capacity constraints and, 548–9
    critical mass agreements and, 543, 544–6
    dispute settlement and, 560–1
    first-mover advantages, 547–8
    most-favoured-nation rule and, 546–7
    negotiations in, 549–50
    precedent-setting and, 547–8
    reasons in proliferation of, 465
    shift to PTAs, 536–40
    WTO provisions on, 498 502
Poisson pseudomaximum likelihood (PPML), 378
Political Constraint index, 145
political infrastructure, 29–30
    evolution of
        post–Cold War (1991–2000), 43–4
        post–Industrial Revolution (1840–1914), 33
        post–information revolution (2001–13), 47–8

post–World War I (1920s and 1930s), 35–6
post–World War II (1947–90), 39–41
    factors in
        international distribution of power, 29–30
        international institutions, 30
        political economic ideologies, 29
        wars and violent conflicts, 30
    scope, 29
    stability, 29
political leaders, and trade agreements, 58–9
political system, 120–1
political-military cooperation, 63
polypropylene bags, 456–9
Portugal, 283, 455
positive integration, 138
positive-list agreement, 226, 230
post–Cold War (1991–2000), 42–6
    bilateral regulatory competition, 44–6
    economic agreements, 44–6
    estimated coefficients of, 74
    political infrastructure, 43–4
    technological infrastructure, 42–3
post–Industrial Revolution (1840–1914), 31–5
    economic agreements, 33–5
    political infrastructure, 33
    technological infrastructure, 31–5
post–information revolution (2001–13), 46–9
    economic agreements, 48–9
    political infrastructure, 47–8
    technological infrastructure, 47
postmaterialism, 121–2
post–World War I (1920s and 1930s), 34, 35–7
    economic agreements, 36–7
    political and economic blocs, 36–7
    political infrastructure, 35–6
    technological infrastructure, 35
post–World War II (1947–90), 38–42
    economic agreements, 41–2
    political infrastructure, 39–41
    technological infrastructure, 38–9

power
  asymmetric relationship, 62–3
  international distribution of, 29–30
  political-military, 63
preference margins, 439
preferential tariffs, 85
preferential trade agreements (PTAs),
    1–20, 374–90
  anti-dumping and, 440–7
  antitrust provisions in, 238–9
  audiovisual media in, 220–34
  classification, 116
  cluster analysis of, 172–6, 183–90
  coexistence of, 526–30
    ad hoc negotiation, 529
    conflict of PTA norms, 528–30
    earlier/original PTA, 528–9
    favourable PTA, 529
    overlap/interaction of dispute
      settlement fora, 526–8
    silence, 529–30
  competition policy provisions in,
    251–6
    in 1945–2010, 264–9
    articles, 257–9
    chapters, 257–9
    form of, 253–6
    over time, 256
    presence and specific content on,
      259–60
    prior studies of, 249–51
  credibility-driven, 86–91
  deep agreements, 117
  deep integration, 138–40
  deep vs. shallow, 374–90
    comparative static analysis,
      386–9
    data, 378–84
    empirical framework, 376–8
    exports, 378–81
    general set-up, 376–7
    implementation, 377–8
    model calibration, 384–6
    parameter estimation, 384–6
    tariffs, 378–84
  definition of, 1–3
  design of, 11–13
    clusters in, 169

    models, 168
    variation in, 167–8
  dispute settlement provisions in,
    319–50
    conceptualization of, 340–7
    exceptions/exemptions, 339–40,
      347
    forum choice in, 331, 344
    implementation of, 336–9
    previous research on, 320–3
    proceedings, 331–6
    sanctions in, 344
    types of, 325–31
  domestic politics in formation of,
    57–61
    democracy, 58–9
    public officials, 58
    veto players, 60–1
  double. See double preferential trade
    agreements
  effects of, 14–16
  external influences on design of,
    168–9, 176–80
    common membership in IGOs,
      179–80
    financial aid, 179
    number of members, 177–8, 188
    number of models, 177
    trade dependence, 178–9
  historical background, 467–83
  institutions-based integration,
    170–1
  intellectual property protection and,
    468–74
  international politics of, 61–71
    asymmetric power relationships
      in, 62–3
    hegemony, 61–2
    political-military cooperation in,
      63
    strategic interdependence in,
      63–4
  intra-industry trade and, 195–214
  investment-inclusive, 46, 48
  models, 169–76
    EU model, 170–1, 174–5, 183–90
    NAFTA model, 171, 175–6,
      183–90

Southern model, 170, 172–3
multilateral trade agreements and,
 465–92
dialectical relationships, 483–6
intellectual property protection,
 468–74
legitimate preferential market
 access, 488–9
liberalisation in services trade,
 475–83
regulatory burden sharing,
 486–91
WTO rules, 490–1
multilateral trading system and,
 16–19
natural trading partners and,
 116–17
network, 504
depth of, 508–11
Europe as centre of, 507
mega-regionals, 511–13
regionalism, 506
visualisation of, 509–10
WTO membership, 506
network analysis of, 502–13
data sets, 503–4
overlaps with WTO laws, 557–8
overview, 1–3
past and present, 3–8
peace promotion and, 297–8
political economy of, 56–78
proliferation of, 25, 56–7, 113, 167,
 433
as protection from risk, 408–30
background and theory, 410–18
control variables, 421–2
dependent variables, 418–19
design of rules, 415–18
design's effect on volatility, 422–6
explanatory variables, 419–21
flexibility provisions, 417–18
legalised systems of dispute
 settlement, 415–18
mechanisms, 409
risk reduction, 411–15
selection bias, 426–7
PTA implementation and, 438–40
public procurement and, 275

reasons for signing, 8–11
reasons in proliferation of, 465
research design, 180–3
control variables, 182–3
dependent variables, 180–1
explanatory variables, 181–2
rules-based integration, 171
selection and endogeneity issues in,
 145–6
shallow agreements, 117
signed between 1957 and 2009, 171
statistical model of ratification,
 65–6
domestic politics, 66–7
independent variables, 68–71
international politics, 67–8
tariff liberalisation in, 201–7
tariffs and, 195–214
temporary trade barriers and,
 433–60
transparency and learning, 542–4
value of, 101–5
weak governments and, 82–105
WTO provisions on, 498–502
PRIO. See Peace Research Institute
 Oslo (PRIO)
private protection, 262
Procter & Gamble, 137
production
technological infrastructure and, 28
vertical specialisation of, 39
production networks, 47
in Asia, 137–8
deep integration PTAs and, 143–5
endogeneity of, 146
protectionism, 260–2
Protocol of Guatemala (1993), 170
Protocol on Cultural Cooperation, 224
Prusa, Thomas, 437
psychic distance, 118–20, 128
PTAs. See preferential trade agreements
 (PTAs)
public procurement, 275
cross-border, 277
definition of, 275
discrimination in, 276–7, 285–6
domestic suppliers, 289
foreign suppliers, 288–9

public procurement (*cont.*)
  GDP and, 275
  government incentives in, 286
  in multilateral trade negotiations,
    275
  rules, 280–3
    deep integration PTAs and, 280
    ineffectiveness of, 283–6
    in preferential trade agreements,
      277–80
    in PTA templates, 280
    taxpayers and, 289
public spheres, 167–91
Punta Del Este, 471, 476

Qatar, 231
quantitative trade models, 358

random coefficients model, 361
ratification
  dyads, 68
  statistical model, 65–6
  veto players in, 60–1
RCEP. *See* Regional Comprehensive
    Economic Partnership (RCEP)
Reciprocal Trade Agreements Act
    (RTAA), 3, 37, 468
regime type, 66, 72
Regional Comprehensive Economic
    Partnership (RCEP), 49,
    511–13, 536
Regional Cooperation Council,
    485
regional economic organisations
    (REOs), 41–2, 296
  bilateral agreements, 45
  security institutions within, 302–5
regional trade agreements, 367, 484
Regional Trade Agreements
    Information System (RTA-IS),
    395
regionalism, 6, 506
Reichsmark (RM) bloc, 37
religion, 119–20, 183, 368, 370
REOs. *See* regional economic
    organisations (REOs)
retaliation, 339
Ricardo–Viner model, 197

risks, 408–30
  control variables, 421–2
  dependent variables, 418–19
  explanatory variables, 419–21
  flexibility provisions, 414–15,
    417–18
  legalised systems of dispute
    settlement and, 416–17
  PTA design and, 415–18
  reduction of, 411–15
  selection bias, 426–7
  volatility, 409, 410–11, 422–6
Romania, 285–6, 455
Rome Treaty (1957), 7, 170, 174,
    180–1, 185, 475, 477–8
RTAA. *See* Reciprocal Trade
    Agreements Act (RTAA)
rules-based integration, 171
Russia, 56, 519

SAARC. *See* South Asian Association
    for Regional Cooperation
    (SAARC)
SACU. *See* South African Customs
    Union (SACU)
SADC. *See* Southern African
    Development Community
    (SADC)
safeguards, 447–59
  Argentina, 449–52
  Dominican Republic, 456–9
  footwear, 449–52, 453–6
  polypropylene bags, 456–9
  steel, 452–3
  tubular fabric, 456–9
  Turkey, 453–6
  United States, 452–3
same-sector retaliation, 339
sanctions
  cross-sector retaliation, 339
  forms of, 339
  monetary sanctions, 339
  provision, 337–8, 344
  retaliation, 339
  same-sector retaliation, 339
  selection of, 338
  suspension of benefits of equivalent
    effect, 339

sanitary and phytosanitary (SPS) rules, 45
SCM. *See* Agreement on Subsidies and Countervailing Measures (SCM)
Seattle WTO Ministerial Conference (1999), 48
second unbundling, 137
security alliance, 121
security institutions, 301–13
  analysis of necessary conditions, 309–13
  categories of security cooperation, 302–3
  explanations for nesting of, 305–9
  hegemony and, 307–8
  within regional economic organisations, 302–5
selection bias, 426–7
separate opinions, 334–5
September 11 attacks, 47
*Serbian Loans* case, 571–2
services PTAs. *See also* audiovisual goods and services
  cultural factors in, 238–9
  economic size and, 236–8
  negotiating leverages and, 236
  net exporters of services and, 236–8
  net importers of services and, 235–6
  trade effects of, 392–403
    data, 395–7
    estimation issues, 398–9
    estimation of, 394–5
  trade liberalisation and, 475–83
  variation in, 234–42
  World Trade Organization and, 242–3
shallow trade agreements, 138, 374–90
  data, 378–84
  vs. deep trade agreements, 374–90
  definition of, 117
  empirical framework, 376–8
  exports, 378–81
  general set-up, 376–7
  implementation, 377–8
  stochastics, 377–8
  tariffs, 378–84

shipping, 38–9
Siemens, 287
simple matching coefficient, 172
Singapore, 1, 76, 94, 96, 129, 137, 210, 224, 231, 240, 504, 510, 522
Singapore–Australia FTA, 529
Single European Act (1986), 114, 170
Single Market Programme, 4
Smoot–Hawley tariffs, 36
social welfare, 88–9
South African Customs Union (SACU), 295
South Asian Association for Regional Cooperation (SAARC), 295
South Asian Free Trade Agreement, 4, 167
South Korea, 207, 210, 218, 224, 450, 452, 510, 518
South Korea–ASEAN PTA, 211
South Pacific Regional Trade and Economic Cooperation Agreement (SPARTECA), 42
Southern African Development Community (SADC), 179, 296, 302, 312, 313, 498, 520
Southern Common Market (MERCOSUR), 175, 227, 231, 296, 302, 449–51, 497, 518
Southern model, 170, 172–3
Spain, 455
Sri Lanka, 529
Stabilization and Association Agreement with Macedonia (2001), 171
Stabilization and Association Agreements, 223
standing body, 328, 330
steel products, safeguard on, 452–3
sterling bloc, 37
Sudan, 520
supply chains, 43
suspension of benefits of equivalent effect, 339
Sweden, 96
Switzerland, 5, 114, 231, 282, 452, 472, 504
Syria, 42

Taiwan,  142, 231, 240, 510
Tanzania,  232
Target,  138
tariff bounds,  85
tariffs,  196–8, 378–84
    intra-industry trade and,  207
    liberalisation,  201–7
technical barriers to trade (TBT),  45,
        116, 521. *See also* Agreement on
        Technical Barriers to Trade
        (TBT)
technological infrastructure
    consumption and,  28
    costs of making exchanges and,  27
    evolution of
        post–Cold War (1991–2000),
            42–3
        post–Industrial Revolution
            (1840–1914),  32
        post–information revolution
            (2001–13),  47
        post–World War I (1920s and
            1930s),  35
        post–World War II (1947–1990),
            38–9
    production and,  28
    trade structure and,  27–8, 29
    value-to-weight ratio and,  27
Tegucigalpa Protocol (1991),  295
Teh, Robert,  437
temporary trade barriers (TTBs),  437
    anti-dumping and,  433–47, 460
    country-specific,  440–7
    GATT and,  435–8
    PTA provisions on,  437, 438
    safeguards,  447–59
        Argentina's safeguard on
            footwear,  449–52
        Dominican Republic's safeguard
            on polypropylene bags/tubular
            fabric,  456–9
        Turkey's safeguard on footwear,
            453–6
        United States' safeguard on steel,
            452–3
        World Trade Organization and,
            435–8
terrorists,  47
textiles industry,  138

Thailand,  96, 137, 210, 450, 522, 538
time limits,  335
Tokyo Round,  471, 475
Tokyo Round Government
        Procurement Code,  275
Toyota,  137
TPP. *See* Trans-Pacific Partnership
        (TPP)
trade
    estimated coefficients of,  73
    total value of,  68
trade agreements,  295–314
    armed conflicts and,  296–301
    bilateral. *See* bilateral trade
        agreements
    free. *See* free trade agreements
    multilateral. *See* multilateral trade
        agreements
    nested security institutions and,
        301–13
        explanations for,  305–9
        hegemony,  307–8
        within regional economic
            organisations,  302–5
    plurilateral. *See* plurilateral trade
        agreements
    preferential. *See* preferential trade
        agreements (PTAs)
    as protection from risk,  408–30
    standard theory of,  82
trade barriers,  412
trade blocs,  37
Trade in Services Agreement (TiSA),
        476, 536–7
Trade Policy Research Centre,  475
trade structure,  196–8
trading partners, natural,  113–29
    adjacency of,  368, 370
    common colonial history of,  368–9,
        370–1
    common language of,  368, 370
    common legal origin of,  368–9,
        370–1
    common religion of,  368, 370
    conjoint analysis of,  122–6
    distance between,  367–8, 369
    economic size of,  118, 127, 128–9
    geographical proximity of,  118, 128
    military or security alliance,  121

political system, 120–1
postmaterialism, 121–2
preferential trade agreements and,
 116–17
psychic distance of, 118–20, 128
theoretical arguments for, 117–22
Transatlantic Trade and Investment
 Partnership (TTIP), 1, 76, 113,
 465, 484–5, 488, 511–13, 536,
 539
Trans-Pacific Partnership (TPP), 1, 49,
 76, 113, 139, 140, 465, 484, 488,
 536, 538
Transparency International, 110
Transparency Review Mechanism,
 543, 544–6
transportation services, post–World
 War II (1947–90), 38–9
Treaty of Lisbon, 174, 180–1
Treaty of Montevideo (1980), 170
Treaty of Rome (1957), 170, 174,
 180–1, 185, 475, 477–8
Treaty on the European Union, 114
Treaty on the Functioning of the
 European Union (TFEU),
 570–1
TRIMs. See Agreement on
 Trade-Related Investment
 Measures (TRIMs)
Trinidad and Tobago, 96, 104
TRIPS Agreement, 17, 466, 467, 472,
 474, 499
TTBs. See temporary trade barriers
 (TTBs)
TTIP. See Transatlantic Trade and
 Investment Partnership (TTIP)
tubular fabric, 456–9
Turkey, 441–4, 453–6, 504
Turkey–Korea FTA, 142

Ukraine, 6
United Arab Emirates, 231
United Kingdom, 3, 283, 287–8
United Nations Charter, 491
United Nations Commodity Trade
 Statistics Database, 110
United Nations Conference on Trade
 and Development (UNCTAD),
 46, 235

United Nations Economic and Social
 Commission for Asia and the
 Pacific (UNESCAP), 140–1
United Nations Economic, Scientific,
 and Cultural Organization
 (UNESCO), 224
United Nations Industrial
 Development Organization
 (UNIDO), 209
United Nations Registry of Broad
 Economic Categories, 144
United Parcel Service (UPS), 43, 47
United States, 129, 434, 510
 anti-dumping measures, 441,
 445
 audiovisual services commitments
 to PTAs, 231
 commitment to liberal international
 economy, 39–41
 cultural proximity to, 239–42
 preferential trade agreements, 113
 PTAs with Canada, 497
 Reciprocal Trade Agreements Act
 (1934), 3
 safeguard on steel, 452–3
 trade in audiovisual goods and
 services, 221
 Trans-Pacific Partnership, 1, 76
Uppsala Conflict Data Program, 307
upstream firms, 206
Uruguay, 232
Uruguay Round, 17, 44, 223, 436, 449,
 476, 477, 538, 542

Venezuela, 96, 313
vertical intra-industry trade (VIIT),
 203–6, 209, 211–13
vertical specialisation trade, 137
veto players, 60–1, 66–7, 72–3
Vienna Convention on the Law of
 Treaties, 491, 524, 561
Vietnam, 1, 76, 129, 137, 138, 450,
 454, 455, 521
VIIT. See vertical intra-industry trade
 (VIIT)
Villiers, Theresa, 288
volatility, 410–11, 417–18
 design and, 422–6
voters, and trade agreements, 58–9

WAEMU. *See* West African Economic
    and Monetary Union
    (WAEMU)
Walmart, 138
wars, 30
Warsaw Pact, 4
WDI. *See* World Development
    Indicators (WDI)
weak governments
    bargaining weight of, 94–6
    definition of, 84
    lobbying rent, 84
    PTA as commitment device, 89–90,
        99
    in agreements with large partners,
        90–1, 99
    social welfare and, 88–9
    tariff bounds, 85
    welfare mindedness of, 93–4
West African Economic and Monetary
    Union (WAEMU), 167, 366,
    521
Wilmar, 137
WIPO Copyright Treaty (WCT), 472
WIPP Performances and Phonograms
    Treaty (WPPT), 472
Wooldridge test, 423
World Bank Governance Indicators, 94
World Development Indicators (WDI),
    110, 144, 182
World Integrated Trade Solution
    (WITS), 211
World Intellectual Property
    Organization (WIPO), 471,
    472
World Organisation for Animal Health,
    562
World Trade Organization (WTO), 2
    Agreement on Government
        Procurement, 275–6
    Agreement on Safeguards, 447–59
    Agreement on Technical Barriers to
        Trade, 246
    Annex 4 agreements, 545

Article IX:3, 562
Article X:9, 500–1, 545
audiovisual goods and services in,
    242–3
audiovisual media and, 218
border issues and, 487–8
Committee on Government
    Procurement, 275
creation of, 43–4, 56
deep vs. shallow PTAs and, 374–5
dispute settlement system, 577
double preferential trade agreements
    and, 498–502
as mechanism for deliberation,
    540–2
membership in, 74, 533
Ministerial Conference (1999), 48
overlaps with PTA laws, 557–8
plurilateral trade agreements and,
    498–502
preferential trade agreements and,
    16–19, 64–5, 68, 328–9,
    498–502, 539–40, 542–4
PTA design and, 189
Regional Trade Agreements
    Information System, 395
rules, 490–1
services trade, 392
tariff liberalisation and, 197
temporary trade barriers and, 434
WTO+ rules, 45
WTO-extra norms, 510
WTO-minus provisions, 502
WTO-X provisions, 45
Worldwide Governance Indicators
    Database, 110
WPPT. *See* WIPP Performances and
    Phonograms Treaty (WPPT)
WTO. *See* World Trade Organization
    (WTO)

Yaoundé agreements, 173, 479

zero-for-zero agreements, 544

Lightning Source UK Ltd.
Milton Keynes UK
UKHW02f1104230818
327669UK00021B/666/P

9 781107 444676